Available Means

*Pittsburgh Series
in Composition, Literacy,
and Culture*

David Bartholomae
and Jean Ferguson Carr,
Editors

Available Means

An Anthology of Women's Rhetoric(s)

Edited by Joy Ritchie and Kate Ronald

University of Pittsburgh Press

Published by the University of Pittsburgh Press,
Pittsburgh, Pa., 15261

Copyright © 2001, University of Pittsburgh Press

All rights reserved

Manufactured in the United States of America

Printed on acid-free paper

10 9 8 7 6 5 4 3 2 1

Please see the first page of each selection
for copyright and permissions information.

Library of Congress Cataloging-in-Publication Data
Available means : an anthology of women's rhetoric(s) / edited by
Joy Ritchie and Kate Ronald.
    p. cm. — (Pittsburgh series in composition, literacy, and culture)
Includes bibliographical references and index.
    ISBN 0-8229-4152-X (alk. paper) — ISBN 0-8229-5753-1 (pbk. : alk.
paper)
    1. Speeches, addresses, etc.—Women authors. I. Ritchie, Joy S.
II. Ronald, Kate. III. Series.
PN6122 .A85 2001
808.85'0082—dc21   2001002290

For

Barbara DiBernard
and
Ila M. Schneebeck
Laura Ronald Harpring
Suzanne Hamrick Ronald

CHRONOLOGICAL TABLE OF CONTENTS

Acknowledgments   xiii
Introduction   xv

ASPASIA   1
"Pericles' Funeral Oration" from Plato's *Menexenus* (c. 387–367 B.C.E.)   2

DIOTIMA   9
"On Love" from Plato's *Symposium* (c. 360 B.C.E.)   10

HORTENSIA   16
"Speech to the Triumvirs" (42 B.C.E.)   17

HELOÏSE   20
From "Letter 1. Heloise to Abelard" (1132)   21

JULIAN OF NORWICH   25
From *Revelations of Divine Love* (c. 1390s)   26

CATHERINE OF SIENA   29
"Letter 83: To Mona Lapa, her mother, in Siena" (1376)   30

CHRISTINE DE PIZAN   32
From *The Book of the City of Ladies* (1404)   33

MARGERY KEMPE   43
From *The Book of Margery Kempe* (1436)   44

QUEEN ELIZABETH I   48
"To the Troops at Tilbury" (1588)   49

JANE ANGER   50
From *Jane Anger Her Protection for Women . . .* (1589)   51

RACHEL SPEGHT   61
From *A Mouzzel for Melastomus* (1617)   62

MARGARET FELL   66
From *Womens Speaking Justified, Proved and Allowed by the Scriptures*
(1666)   67

SOR JUANA INÉS DE LA CRUZ   71
From "La Respuesta" (1691)   72

MARY ASTELL   79
From *A Serious Proposal to the Ladies* (1694)   80

LADY MARY WORTLEY MONTAGU   84
"Letter to Lady Bute" (1753)   85

BELINDA   89
"Petition of an African Slave" (1782)   90

MARY WOLLSTONECRAFT   92
From *A Vindication of the Rights of Woman* (1792)   93

CHEROKEE WOMEN   106
"Cherokee Women Address Their Nation" (1817)   107

MARIA W. STEWART   109
"Lecture Delivered at the Franklin Hall" (1832)   110

SARAH GRIMKÉ   114
"Letter to Theodore Weld" (1837)   115

ANGELINA GRIMKÉ WELD   119
"Address at Pennsylvania Hall" (1838)   120

MARGARET FULLER   125
From *Woman in the Nineteenth Century* (1845)   126

SENECA FALLS CONVENTION   138
"Declaration of Sentiments and Resolutions" (1848)   139

SOJOURNER TRUTH   143
"Speech at the Woman's Rights Convention, Akron, Ohio" (1851)   144

FRANCES ELLEN WATKINS HARPER   147
"We Are All Bound Up Together" (1866)   148

SUSAN B. ANTHONY   151
From *The United States of America v. Susan B. Anthony* (1873)   152

SARAH WINNEMUCCA   157
From *Life Among the Piutes* (1883)   158

ANNA JULIA COOPER   163
"The Higher Education of Women" (1892)   164

ELIZABETH CADY STANTON   171
From "The Solitude of Self" (1892)   172

FANNIE BARRIER WILLIAMS   179
From "The Intellectual Progress of the Colored Women of the United
States since the Emancipation Proclamation" (1893)   180

IDA B. WELLS   188
"Lynch Law in All its Phases" (1893)   189

CHARLOTTE PERKINS GILMAN   204
From *Women and Economics* (1898)   205

GERTRUDE BUCK   211
"The Present Status of Rhetorical Theory" (1900)   212

MARY AUGUSTA JORDAN   218
From *Correct Writing and Speaking* (1904)   219

MARGARET SANGER   223
"Letter to the Readers of *The Woman Rebel*" (1914)   224

EMMA GOLDMAN   226
From "Marriage and Love" (1914)   227

ALICE DUNBAR NELSON   233
"Facing Life Squarely" (1927)   234

DOROTHY DAY   237
"Memorial Day in Chicago" (1937)   238

VIRGINIA WOOLF   241
"Professions for Women" (1942)   242

ZORA NEALE HURSTON   247
"Crazy for This Democracy" (1945)   248

SIMONE DE BEAUVOIR   252
From the Introduction to *The Second Sex* (1952)   253

RACHEL CARSON   259
"A Fable for Tomorrow" (1962)   260

FANNIE LOU HAMER   262
"The Special Plight and the Role of the Black Woman" (1971)   263

ADRIENNE RICH   267
"When We Dead Awaken: Writing as Re-Vision" (1971)   268

HÉLÈNE CIXOUS   283
From "Sorties" (1975)   284

COMBAHEE RIVER COLLECTIVE   291
"The Combahee River Collective Statement" (1977)   292

AUDRE LORDE   301
"The Transformation of Silence into Language and Action" (1977)   302

MERLE WOO   306
"Letter to Ma" (1980)   307

ALICE WALKER   314
"In Search of Our Mothers' Gardens" (1983)   315

EVELYN FOX KELLER   323
From *A Feeling for the Organism* (1983)   324

ANDREA DWORKIN   330
"I Want A Twenty-Four Hour Truce During Which There Is No Rape"
(1983)   331

PAULA GUNN ALLEN   340
"Grandmother of the Sun: Ritual Gynocracy in Native America"
(1986)   341

GLORIA ANZALDÚA   356
"How to Tame a Wild Tongue" (1987)   357

JUNE JORDAN 366
"Don't You Talk About My Momma!" (1987) 367

TRINH T. MINH-HA 377
From *Woman, Native, Other* (1989) 378

BELL HOOKS 382
"Homeplace (a site of resistance)" (1990) 383

NANCY MAIRS 391
"Carnal Acts" (1990) 392

TERRY TEMPEST WILLIAMS 401
"The Clan of One-Breasted Women" (1991) 402

PATRICIA WILLIAMS 409
"The Death of the Profane" (1991) 410

TONI MORRISON 416
"The Nobel Lecture in Literature" and "The Acceptance Speech"
(1993) 417

MINNIE BRUCE PRATT 424
"Gender Quiz" (1995) 425

DOROTHY ALLISON 435
From *Two or Three Things I Know for Sure* (1995) 436

NOMY LAMM 454
"It's a Big Fat Revolution" (1995) 455

LESLIE MARMON SILKO 462
"Yellow Woman and a Beauty of the Spirit" (1996) 463

RUTH BADER GINSBURG 471
From *United States v. Virginia et al.* (1996) 472

RUTH BEHAR 478
"Anthropology That Breaks Your Heart" (1996) 479

GLORIA STEINEM 489
"Supremacy Crimes" (1999) 491

APPENDIX A: Alternative/Rhetorical Table of Contents   495

A Select Bibliography of Works on Women's Rhetorics   510

Index   517

ACKNOWLEDGMENTS

As with most feminist projects, *Available Means* is a collaborative work. We thank our colleagues whose research and scholarship in women's rhetorics has inspired us to create this anthology: Cheryl Glenn, Susan Jarratt, Shirley Wilson Logan, Andrea Lunsford, Krista Ratcliffe, Jackie Jones Royster, and Lynn Worsham. We are indebted to members of the Coalition of Women Scholars in the History of Rhetoric for their support and their suggestions. Other friends gave us suggestions and pointed us toward many women rhetors who appear here: Kathy Boardman, Dottie Broaddus, Amy Goodburn, Daniel Justice, Debbie Minter, Cindy Moore, Malea Powell, Hilda Raz, Hephzibah Roskelly, and Sharon Harris. Our students inspired us with their enthusiasm as they studied many of these texts and challenged us with their insights about women's rhetorical practices.

The work of putting this anthology together also involved many people: Lisa Mahle-Grisez, Tom Pace, and Kay Siebler at Miami University researched and drafted headnotes; Stephanie Gustafson, Donna Epler, Laura Ellen, Andrea Skiles, and Mary Trauthen, students at the University of Nebraska, Lincoln, scanned and proofread texts; Laura Harpring graciously edited the headnotes and introduction; and Dennis Alcorn and George Ritchie encouraged us along the way. We especially thank Cindy DeRyke for her skill in putting this unwieldy manuscript together and Carol Sickman-Garner for her careful copyediting.

We appreciate the support of the Department of English and the Humanities Center at the University of Nebraska, Lincoln, and of the Department of English and the Office for the Advancement of Scholarship and Teaching at Miami University.

> I say that even later someone will remember us.
> —Sappho

Sappho's prediction came true; fragments of work by the earliest woman writer in Western literate history have in fact survived into the twenty-first century, but not without peril. Sappho's writing remains only in fragments, partly due to the passage of time, but mostly as a result of systematic efforts to silence women's voices and prevent women's speaking and writing. Although Sappho does not appear in this anthology, her hopeful boast captures the impetus behind our efforts here: gathering women's rhetorics together in order to remember that the rhetorical tradition indeed includes women. Yet, making that simple statement was not so easy even five years ago. Teaching courses in the history of rhetoric since the 1980s, we had learned to anticipate our students' question: "Where are the women?" But until very recently, including women in historical overviews of the rhetorical tradition required making what often seemed like arbitrary and isolated choices. Should we read Aspasia alongside Plato? Virginia Woolf with I. A. Richards? Could Toni Morrison replace Bakhtin? Mary Wollstonecraft supersede George Campbell? When we began teaching courses in women's rhetoric six years ago, making even some of the primary texts of women's rhetorics accessible to students required a great deal of effort, and we still worried that our selections were haphazard, our choices arbitrary. In other words, we wished for a collection of rhetorics by women, gathered together in one place.

Inspired by groundbreaking recovery of and commentary on women's rhetorics from Andrea Lunsford, Shirley Wilson Logan, Cheryl Glenn, Jacqueline Jones Royster, and Krista Ratcliffe, we realized that we needed this anthology, especially in teaching rhetoric. Instead of scrambling to copy parts of Margaret Fuller or snippets of Ida B. Wells for our students, or preparing bibliographies so that students could read these excerpts in the context of other women rhetoricians, we conceived of a collection that would put the spiritual rhetorics of Julian of Norwich and Paula Gunn Allen between the same covers, that would put the political rhetoric of Hortensia in the same volume as the "Declaration of Sentiments" and the "Combahee River Collective Statement." Therefore, our main impulse in gathering this material together is to make a diverse collection available to scholars and students. We are inspired and indebted to other collections of women's rhetorics, particularly Shirley Wilson Logan's *With Pen and Voice: A Critical Anthology of Nineteenth Century African American Women*, Karlyn Kohrs Campbell's *Man Cannot Speak for Her*, and Miriam Schneir's two-volume anthology of feminist writing. A few of the texts from those collections appear here, but *Available Means* aims for a larger, longer view of women's rhetorics, not limited to a particular moment in history or a particular political/rhetorical purpose. Although many of the texts here may be familiar to readers, these pieces have not been gathered together before under the name of rhetoric. More importantly, we believe this anthology documents and demonstrates an emerging tradition of women's rhetorics—a long-standing tradition, yet one so "new" that its primary texts have not until now been collected; a tradition that has existed only in the shadows for centuries because women's writing and speaking have not been gathered together as "rhetoric." Without this gathering, women's rhetorical means, what Shirley Wilson Logan calls "recurrences" (xiv) or Jacqueline Jones Royster calls "traces of a stream," have not been available for study. We realize that gathering these primary texts in one place raises important questions. For example, how does the collection define women's rhetorics? What principles of selection led to including some writers and not others? We attempt to answer those questions below. But we begin first by offering seventy women rhetoricians in a room of their own, not out of our desire to name or fix a women's canon of rhetoric but in order to gather a richer, more available means for remembering and studying women's rhetorics and for changing rhetorical theories and practices.

Of course this gathering participates in multiple communities of women rhetors, and we would like to explore for a moment the metaphors that have led us to think of our work as a "gathering." In the last five years, "Rhetorica" has been "reclaimed." In putting together the first collection of scholarly commentary on women in the rhetorical tradition, Andrea Lunsford says that the essays there:

> do not attempt to redefine a "new" rhetoric, but rather to interrupt the seamless narrative usually told about the rhetorical tradition and to open up possibilities for multiple rhetorics, rhetorics that would not name and valorize one, traditional, competitive, agonistic and linear mode of rhetorical discourse but would rather incorporate other, often dangerous moves: breaking the silence, naming in personal terms, employing dialogics, recognizing and using the power of conversation, moving centripetally toward connections and valuing— indeed insisting upon—collaboration. (6)

Part of our desire in compiling this anthology was to document the interruptions to the rhetorical tradition that women's rhetorics offer, but Lunsford's provisional language here—"interrupt," "open up," "multiple"—helped us to keep our readings of women's rhetorics fluid rather than fixed.

Another metaphor we kept firmly in our minds was that rhetoric has also been "retold" and "regendered." Cheryl Glenn's study of women rhetors from antiquity through the Renaissance demonstrates that "women's rhetorical lives have always existed, among the innumerable, interminable, clear examples of public, political, agonistic, masculine discourse" (175). She argues that "a regendered, retold tradition opens up—not closes down—investigation into rhetorical practices" (173). This anthology continues this work by gathering—always a woman's metaphor—primary works that both illustrate and, we hope, extend the work of reclamation, recovery, and reconceptualization.

Our decision to title this collection with Aristotle's famous definition of rhetoric as the "discovery of the available means of persuasion" reflects our desire to locate women squarely within rhetoric but also to acknowledge that their presence demands that rhetoric be reconceived. The discovery of the available means was for Aristotle an act of invention that always assumed the right to speak in the first place and, even prior to that, assumed the right to personhood and self-representation, rights that have not long been available to women. For centuries, even the means of basic literacy were denied to women. Rhetorical education was designed by and for upper-class males well into the twentieth century. Throughout the years covered in this anthology (the fifth century B.C.E.–1999), women must repeatedly argue for the right to speak in public at all. Over and over again, they must claim the right to name themselves rather than to be named. Many of these texts, from the fourteenth to the twentieth century, read as if a particular woman is writing or claiming the right to speak for the first time, without a history of writing behind her; too often it feels eerily as if she is writing alone. The act of invention for women, then, begins in a different place from Aristotle's conception of invention: women must first invent a way to speak in the context of being silenced and rendered invisible as persons. This is doubly true for poor women and women of color. We think this realization is fundamental, particularly for many students who may not know that women were historically prohibited from public speech, denied access to literacy, education, and the power of language. This anthology, we hope, documents the means women used to claim their rights as rhetors and seeks to ensure that those means will, indeed, remain available and visible for women.

We want to reclaim Aristotle's words, then, to mark the ways in which women have discovered various means by which to make their voices heard. But we also intend by our title to point to the ways that women have discovered different means of persuasion, often based in contexts other than those Aristotle might have imagined: the kitchen, parlor, and nursery; the garden; the church; the body. Further, women have redefined and subverted traditional means and ends of argument and in the process have reinvented rhetoric based in epistemologies more varied than Aristotle's. Sor Juana Inés de la Cruz, for example, suggests in writing about the philosophies of the kitchen that "had Aristotle prepared victuals he would have written more." So we use the term "available means" both to connect with and depart from the rhetorical tradition. Some women writers were well schooled in the traditional methods of persuasion of their day: appeals to logic and emotion, evidence from historical or religious authority, or conventions of style or structure. Margaret Fell's

Womens Speaking Justified is one clear example of a woman using the available means for unexpected ends—citing scripture to prove women's equality. Ida B. Wells's use of statistical evidence and her restrained use of logic to argue against lynching in the Jim Crow South provide another.

But we also include in this anthology women's writing that may not meet and that may even defy traditional rhetorical criteria and categories—especially concerning *ethos*, or the appeal of the speaker's "character." Some of the selections here may seem less than eloquent. Others may seem to fail to take into account the sensibilities of an audience or readership because they blur traditional gender boundaries or raise issues of women's sexuality, or because the speaker is confrontational, angry, and resistant to decorum, institutions, and hegemonic discourses. Here we think of Heloise's subversive comments about marriage, Zora Neale Hurston's ironic parody of democracy, and Dorothy Allison's risky discussion of sexual power and violence. Although we use the simple plural "rhetorics" in this introduction for ease of reading, we title this collection with the parenthetical plural "rhetoric(s)" to highlight not only these tensions between accommodation and resistance but also to point to differences within an emerging rhetorical tradition.

We hope that the diversity of texts in this anthology will not only highlight these tensions but will also resist the almost inevitable fixing or solidifying tendencies that any gathering of work into an anthology suggests. *Women's Rhetorics* should not suggest an absolute internal coherence to any tradition, even, as Shirley Wilson Logan points out, in the rather homogeneous examples of African American women's public discourse that she gathers in her anthology *With Pen and Voice*, or, we should add, the clearly masculinist tradition of rhetoric with a capital *R*. Nor do we want to diminish the importance or erase the uniqueness of the "traces of a stream" that Royster and Logan have recovered. We know that the very act of gathering and using any category—gender, race, class—can limit one's perception. But we also recognize that just as literary criticism has sometimes arbitrarily created a separate feminine tradition of literature, we may seem to be following a similar pattern. On the other hand, we think the risk is worth the rewards; any group that has been absent or silent must first demarcate and identify its own terrain to establish a presence where one has not existed.

After all, there has been little sense of a tradition of women using or creating rhetorical means for themselves and their causes, except in the tradition of late-nineteenth-century African American women that Shirley Wilson Logan and Jacqueline Jones Royster have recently delineated or in the strategies used by turn-of-the-century African American and European American club women that Anne Ruggles Gere describes. In the absence of any sense of "recurrences"—common practices, themes, and *topoi* in women's rhetoric—students and scholars need to posit a tentative tradition if only to begin to have a fruitful and generative conversation about it. Otherwise we have no collective memory of our rhetorical past, and that absence only reproduces invisibility, silence, and misrepresentation. As Paula Gunn Allen says: "the roots of oppression are to be found in the loss of memory" (210).

Gerda Lerner reminds us that the "absence of a tradition" has historically kept women from developing what she calls "group consciousness": "Women had no history—so they were told; so they believed. Thus, ultimately, it was men's hegemony over the symbol system which most decisively disadvantaged women" (219). Histories of rhetoric follow the pattern of women's absence that Lerner describes; when a woman does appear, she is often described in heroic terms, alone and rising above her natural capabilities. Much recent work in women's rhetorics tends to valorize exceptional women writers. Glenn, for example, describes Aspasia as an "exceptional hero in a new rhetorical narrative" (44), and she casts Julian of Norwich and Margery Kempe's rhetoric as an "extraordinary kind of transcendent inclusiveness, theological and linguistic inclusiveness" (116). Certainly these descriptions accurately describe the accomplishments of these women, and Glenn's bringing them into the canon of rhetoric, analyzing their influence on rereading that canon, has been invaluable work, work that has made this anthology possible. However, we worry that the method of "recovering" women's rhetoric by describing isolated incidents of one or two brilliant, brave (and often white and privileged) women somehow gaining a platform through sheer will or inspiration keeps the "recurrences" or the "traces" of the emerging tradition invisible. This recovery practice also isolates various communities of women from each other and prevents us from asking such questions as: What rhetorical means have white women borrowed from women of color? What rhetorical strategies does the public rhetoric of late-nineteenth-century African American women have in common with white women's public discourse? This form of recovery also isolates women's rhetorics from the masculinist rhetorical tradition, distorting our understanding of women's use of the various means on which they called to speak and write.

For example, when Patricia Bizzell and Bruce Herzberg include Margaret Fell in *The Rhetorical Tradition,* theirs is most certainly an act of recovering and reclaiming women's rhetorics. But Fell's words read very differently between Francis Bacon and John Locke in *The Rhetorical Tradition* than they do between Rachel Speght and Sor Juana Inés de la Cruz, where Fell appears in *Available Means.* One way of recovering Fell is to read her in terms of Enlightenment values of reason, appeals to authority, and logical argument, as Bizzell and Herzberg seem to do. We argue that another method of recovery, one that makes Fell's tract more powerful and gives it much more historical weight, is to read her before and after other women writers who are also attempting to justify women's speaking. Alongside Rachel Speght, Sor Juana Inés de la Cruz, Sojourner Truth, Virginia Woolf, and June Jordan, Fell is no longer an oddity. Instead, her writing highlights one of the fundamental goals of women rhetors: discovering the means to speak or write in the first place. So although we realize that this anthology runs the risk of "canonizing" the writers we have chosen to include, we also hope that in conversation and context the study of women's rhetorical practice across differences of race, class, sexual orientation, and historical and physical locations will unsettle homogenizing tendencies that recreate traditional, exclusive rhetorical frameworks.

Principles of Gathering

We realize that we must to try to answer the questions: Why these works? Why not others? Our overall goal in selecting texts for inclusion here has been twofold. We do want to make available the texts that have been the subject of so much exciting recovery and retelling of women's rhetorical history. But we also want to continue to unsettle this emerging canon with other works that have surprised us as readers and that have caused us to examine our assumptions about women's rhetorics. First, then, we include the primary works that seem to be emerging as central to scholarship in women's rhetoric: Aspasia, Margery Kempe, Margaret Fuller, and Ida B. Wells, for example. We also chose many of the "famous" works by women writers on what it means to write as a woman: Virginia Woolf (but not "A Room of One's Own"), Adrienne Rich, Nancy Mairs, Alice Walker, and Hélène Cixous. It is important, we think, to expand definitions of women's rhetorics to include some of the arguments about how women's writing might constitute its own genre, what women need in order to write, what women's writing can accomplish. We also picked some of the writers who have advanced the cause of women's rights to public participation, to education, and to civil and human rights: Hortensia, Mary Astell, Maria Stewart, Sarah and Angelina Grimké, Anna Julia Cooper, Margaret Sanger, and Audre Lorde. Many of the works gathered here could be titled "manifestos," and we believe that women's public arguments must be part of any emerging canon of rhetoric by women. Finally, we chose works that have inspired us and our students; that stretch our understanding of rhetoric; that challenge and redefine traditional notions of invention, arrangement, style, memory, and delivery. For example, women have often written in unprivileged or devalued forms such as letters, journals, and speeches to other women. Saint Catherine of Siena's and Sarah Grimké's *letters;* Alice Dunbar Nelson's *newspaper columns;* Patricia Williams's critical legal essays, which are pointedly labeled as "the *diary* of a law professor"; Dorothy Day's *meditations* on public events; and Rachel Carson's *fable* that introduces her argument about chemical degradation of the environment provide some of the examples of an expanded definition of rhetorical form.

Not only have women rhetors used transgressive forms, but the subjects about which they have written have also often transgressed or, sometimes more problematically, blurred the boundaries between public and private discourse. Because for most of Western history women were excluded from political, ecclesiastical, or intellectual forums, women writers and speakers often draw on the exigencies that surround them. They write of the necessity of an education, the perils of marriage, the catastrophe of abuse, the conditions of women's poverty, or the pleasures of women's sexualities. Besides their unruly form or content, many of the works here appear because of the context/location of the writer. In other words, we also wanted to gather writers who have not been heard in any tradition. We emphasize in our selections that discussions of women's rhetorics often overlook the specific influences of women's embodiment, physicality, and location. Audre Lorde's rhetoric arises from her experience of breast cancer; Nancy Mairs connects voice, style, and her physical disability; Sarah Winnemucca's location as "translator" of the white man's governmental mandates shapes her rhetoric. This anthology, then, extends the study of women's rhetoric to include writing that has emerged from contexts other than those normally sanctioned as rhetoric.

Sappho is not here because she wrote poetry, and excluding any form of "literary" text was our conscious choice. There are many excellent collections of women's literary writing, most notably *The Norton Anthology of Women's Literature,* and we did not want to reproduce that work here. We do not mean to suggest that we can draw a clear line between literature and rhetoric; in fact, we think that many of the selections here could easily appear in a collection of literary writing. Some do. But our focus remains the gathering of rhetorics, and we rather arbitrarily define rhetoric by form, excluding poetry and story and concentrating on nonfiction prose. Our tentative definition of rhetorics here also involves the writer's purpose—most often to persuade or inform—although many works blur the boundaries between "teaching" and "delighting." We also tried to make selections according to the writer's sense of audience—often of a live group of listeners or a real reader but always of an urgent need to communicate. Finally, and perhaps most importantly, *Available Means* is intended for use in the classroom, as an anthology for students, and our selections are guided always by that awareness. We also want to use this collection as a site to help us and our students discover more available means, either as models for practice or tenets from which to construct our own practices of speaking and writing.

We are no doubt making the selection process sound much easier than it actually was. Sometimes we were unable to obtain permission to reprint texts that we would have liked to include. We were also constrained by length, yet we attempted to include selections that colleagues and students recommended. We relied on other people, particularly in areas outside our own expertise, which is the Western male rhetorical tradition and European/American women writers. We sometimes deliberately excluded pieces that are widely available elsewhere. We also tried to avoid narrowly professional work in composition. We are still nervous about the selections here, concerned that this table of contents might not represent a broad enough range of women's perspectives, that we have overlooked women writers because of our own disciplinary and histor-

ical blinders. We also have attempted to consider how the texts we have selected and our readings of them may reflect our whiteness, the extent to which
we are "playing in the dark," to use Toni Morrison's term, using the experience
of women of color to figure our own experience as we read these texts.

We realize also that some of the selections might seem to essentialize wom-
en's rhetoric or conflate women's rhetoric with feminism. As Campbell points
out, there is an inevitable link between any rhetorical effort and the struggle for
women's rights because before women could argue any other issues, they often
had to claim the right to speak in the first place (19). It is difficult to separate
the history of women's rhetorics from the history of the struggle for women's
rights because the desire/demand for rights so often becomes the impetus for
writing. Finally, we worry that in our introductions to these women, we have
constructed resemblances that may overlook crucial distinctions or, on the
other hand, that we have failed to see connections across time and space.

At first, we constructed a grand scheme of organization that in many ways
drove our selection process; for example, we had sections on "writing the
body," on "women writing to women," on "women's manifestos," and on "private writing." In fact we had twelve such categories. But the more we gathered
material, the more sense it made to get out of these women's way and just let
them speak to each other across centuries. So although we provide an alternative, thematic table of contents to help subvert the linear thinking that may follow from chronology, we present these women rhetors first in simple chrono-
logical order.

A Gathering of Means

Despite our concerns about "fixing" or "essentializing" a definition of women's
rhetorics, we nevertheless do see emerging in this gathering of women rhetors
a recurring set of rhetorical strategies and exigencies that speak to one another
across continents and generations. Some writers, like Mary Wollstonecraft and
Anna Julia Cooper, used traditional forms and methods of proof to challenge
and resist the ways in which the rhetorical tradition kept women from participating in public debate. Other women writers consciously developed alternative means of persuasion. Virginia Woolf, Margaret Fuller, Leslie Marmon
Silko, and Sojourner Truth rely less on traditional logical and ethical appeals
than on appeals to experience, to irony, and on the constant assertion of their
own *ethos*, since ethical appeal, by definition, has been historically denied to
women. Still other women writers find alternative means of persuasion in the
creation of a "women's language." Toni Morrison, Minnie Bruce Pratt, and Patricia Williams, for example, consciously create new styles and generic forms in
order to break out of the confines of a rhetorical tradition that they believe re-
inscribes women in powerless and silent positions.

But these are obvious examples. It is easy enough to show how Angelina
Grimké Weld uses traditional arguments from the Bible and turns them on

their head or to credit Cixous with naming the body as a new rhetorical *topoi*. But we have found ourselves looking for rhetorical theory in less obvious places and wanting our students to have more means available to them, more possibilities for inspiration, imitation, and their own rhetorical action. We are expecting that studying women's rhetorics should make a difference, that it should change practice—our own and our students'—and that it seeks to change the practices that govern our lives in more tangible ways. Isn't this, then, another mark of women's rhetoric? That it works toward, inspires, calls for change? And moreover that it engages in changed practice and offers strategies to readers for enacting change themselves? We believe that readers will see, for example, how women writers have added to the canon of rhetoric new *topoi*, new topics/places from which arguments can be made. We have already suggested that different *topoi*—the kitchen, the garden, the conversation between women —offer new strategies for inventing arguments, mounting evidence, and persuading audiences. In other words, women's rhetorics expand the locus of rhetoric for all speakers and writers. Further, we hope readers will see that what Lunsford calls the "often dangerous moves" (6) by women rhetors can be read as the "available means" of writing for the women's rhetorics in this book. Some of these strategies, moves, and means are worth pointing to in the beginning of this collection. We explore the following means, or *topoi*, as suggestive rather than exhaustive.

One of the poignant and telling arguments for this anthology in the first place is the recurring theme across two millennia of women's yearning and determination to acquire the right to literacy and education. One of the first women rhetors in this emerging canon, Margery Kempe, did not write at all. She was illiterate, and we only have her story as narrated to a male scribe, yet the irrepressible impulse to write and to be heard still comes across in her book. Even highly educated women sometimes speak to us only through male translations. Aspasia, the centerpiece of much current historiography, comes to us ventriloquized through the pens of men authorized to write history and philosophy. There has been much recent discussion about how to treat rhetors like Aspasia or Hortensia, since their works survive only in the context of Plato and Plutarch. However, we are less interested in arguments about historiography than we are in pointing out the obvious: women have been silenced throughout history, and time and again women have had to argue for the right to speak and the right to an education. This theme does not end with mass literacy or permission to speak in public. From Mary Astell in 1694 through Anna Julia Cooper in 1892, Virginia Woolf in 1942, and Ruth Bader Ginsburg in 1996, readers will hear the same argument for basic rights to education and participation in the public sphere. Each context demands different appeals, form, evidence, and rhetorical *ethos*, but this central argument becomes one of the major *topoi* of women's rhetorics.

Susan Jarratt suggests that women have understood that their rhetoric has a double role as "both figurative and political act" (9). One of the touchstones of women's rhetorics has been this political and figurative act: asserting the right to speak, an act that challenges established power relations. And this act challenges the very definition of women's subjectivity. For men, the right to speak, traditionally assumed, is located in the power of personhood. When women make this assertion, they are not simply asserting the right to be heard in public; they are claiming to be full persons in opposition to accepted defective identities. In making this claim they threaten to destabilize the social order. We can hear the momentous world-shaking claims in women's writing from Christine de Pizan and Sojourner Truth to Gloria Anzaldúa and Dorothy Allison, even when these writers use conventional rhetorical strategies. Many women rhetors appropriated whatever rhetorical means they knew in order to argue for the right to speak, and they also subverted conventional rhetoric by using traditional means to argue for radical goals. One of the basic *topoi* of women's rhetorics, then, might be said to include accommodation and subversion working together in very important ways.

Because of the complex political and figurative function of women's writing and speaking, we think it is important to recognize that women's rhetorical situations demand different means or new means for using traditional strategies. From Aristotle to contemporary rhetoricians like Lloyd Bitzer, definitions of rhetorical context have been posed as complex but nonetheless "universal." The selections here should assist in the work of expanding and complicating definitions of rhetorical context because they address one of the glaring omissions from traditional analyses: the exigency of gender in any given discourse. Since male rhetorical contexts have come to stand for Rhetoric itself, it is especially necessary now to consider the multiple, varied contexts and identities of women writers and the gendered nature of rhetorical contexts, communicative strategies, and epistemology. But the selections here also highlight differences in contexts and exigencies among women. White women's arguments for education and for the franchise are marked by the social class and white privilege of their writers. Likewise, while women like Virginia Woolf argued that women must be free to write about their bodies and their sexuality to throw off the constraints of purity and nineteenth-century womanhood, African American women like Fannie Barrier Williams were attempting to reclaim their bodies from the sexualized stigma that slavery had placed on their bodies.

One of the most basic tools of rhetorical analysis is to ask of any discourse the question, "Who is speaking?" Denied the right to speak, women have had to redefine traditional notions of speaker and writer. Women have taken great risks to assert an "I" that disrupts the accepted identity of woman writer and that in doing so counters the limited identities—"virgin," "true woman," "whore," or "martyr"—in which women have typically been defined. As Jarratt suggests, women's attempts to write and speak publicly have a "figurative" function; they work as a means of taking hold of and controlling the tools of representation. So another overarching strategy evident in this collection is women finding the means to represent themselves rather than to be represented by others. Rachel Speght and Jane Anger re-present women in opposition to the popular tracts of their time denigrating women. Fannie Barrier Williams attempts to reconstruct the debased representation of African American women in postslavery nineteenth-century America. Audre Lorde, some eighty years later, also recognized that "if we do not define ourselves for ourselves, we will be defined by others—for their use and to our detriment" (45). And Nomy Lamm attempts to overturn representations of women that focus on fat and body image. One of the most important exigencies for women has been to refute, correct, and revise depictions of womanhood that have placed women in inferior, vilified, stigmatized positions.

Beyond redefinition and reconstruction of representations of women, another common *topoi* among many of the selections here is that the term "woman" becomes a problematized, expanded, and diversified category, multiple rather than unified and ennobled rather than debased. As they claim the means of representing themselves, many women rhetors construct an alternative subjectivity for women and in the process claim what minority women writers have helped us identify as oppositional identities, providing a new set of discourses, making available a new set of "means" on which women can draw in order to continue to define women's subjectivity. Sojourner Truth's pointing to her own body to expand the definition of "woman," Emma Goldman's radical redefinition of "woman" outside of marriage, and Paula Gunn Allen's reclaiming the ancient epistemology of the grandmothers are some examples of these new means. These rhetorical means, then, become a form of rhetorical action, seeking to change the underlying cultural ideologies that shape women's place in the society but also providing an alternative discourse to confront the deficient internalized views of women perpetuated by the culture.

Susan Jarratt argues that women's rhetorics also address what is unspecified in much rhetorical theory: "the specificity and materiality of difference." She goes on to point out how feminists have staged "a double session of rhetoric" (a term she attributes to Gayatri Spivak), "simultaneously naming and reconstructing difference . . . [giving] names to language that articulates difference while exposing the power relations at work in acts of naming" (9). As so many feminist theorists point out, "woman" is a multiple location, and the emerging tradition of women's rhetorics represented here asserts the differences among women, the differential privileges those differences entail, as well as the dangers of erasing or ignoring those differences. Thus, we hope that reading the variety of women's rhetorics here will help readers explore the ethical dimensions of women's relationships with "others," including other women. Some of the most important assertions of difference come as nonwhite and postcolonial women attempt to unsettle and disrupt the thinking of white Western women to show how dominant definitions of womanhood, including those held by white feminists, often erase the experience of other women. For example, while we are drawn to the writing of white women reformers included here, we recognize that they do not often challenge the use of the term "women," which may exclude women of color or minimize vast differences in privilege between women. As bell hooks says,

> For them it served two purposes. First, it allowed them to proclaim white men the oppressors while making it appear linguistically that no alliances existed between white women and white men based on shared racial imperialism. Second, it made possible for white women to act as if alliances did exist between themselves and non-white women in our society, and by doing so they could deflect attention away from their classism and racism. (140)

Sojourner Truth, Fannie Barrier Williams, Alice Dunbar Nelson, and the writers of the "Combahee River Collective Statement" make such demands of white women and white feminists. Other assertions of difference, like that of Minnie Bruce Pratt, occur as women attempt to demonstrate the cultural construction of gender itself and to break up the male/female binary and assert the existence of multiple gender positions. Therefore, another recurring strategy, or *topoi*, in this anthology is finding the means to enact and "compose" the fluid, fragmented subjectivity of women. Many times those means include innovative nonlinear style, the use of women's experience as evidence, and a mixture of genres and languages. In their rhetorical practices, many writers also acknowledge that gender identities are not "natural" or "given" but that women's subjectivities are socially constructed within the ideologies of cultural, racial, and economic situations, as Frances Watkins Harper, Charlotte Perkins Gilman, and Simone de Beauvoir argue. In making this assertion, women rhetors break down the monolithic assertion of white, male (or female), "universal" experience and foreground especially the identities of women of color, poor women, women with disabilities, colonized women and/or those dislocated in a postcolonial world, lesbian women, and transsexuals.

Finally, we would like to point to the fact that many of the writers gathered here use physicality as a *topoi* from which to write. Virginia Woolf argued in 1942 that women writers must "tell the truth about their own experiences as a body," and many selections here, from both before and after her challenge, include women exploring not only their relationship to their own physical embodiment but also their integral connection to the wider bodies and spaces of the natural and public world in which women reside. Margery Kempe may be one of the first women to do so in her use of bodily expressions of groaning and sobbing to express her controversial religious experiences. Some women rhetors in this collection cross boundaries of propriety by exposing and exploring the subterranean parts of women's lives. In the process the traditional notion of rhetorical propriety is stood on its head. "Writing the body" allows women to circumvent the linguistic, rhetorical, and epistemological constraints that would deny women a location from which to speak. Embodied rhetoric, as Hélène Cixous, Nancy Mairs, and Gloria Anzaldúa pointedly remind us in selections here, defines another alternative space from which women claim authority and evidence.

These means, "recurrences," and *topoi* we highlight here—claiming the right to speak; asserting new locations from which to write and speak; re-representing and validating the diversity of women speakers/writers; redefining what counts as evidence—emerge from our own reading and collaborative work with these texts. We want readers to find their own connections, to see what means become available, to gather these rhetorics together in their own view and use them to create and to reimagine rhetorical history and their own rhetorical practices.

Gathering Practice and Theory Together

In the absence of a body of rhetorical theory by women, we also believe these essays, speeches, and letters have important implications for rhetorical theory and the teaching of writing. We have gathered here a number of pieces that are overtly theoretical, offering advice to women on how to persuade and how to communicate effectively, such as those by Gertrude Buck, Mary Augusta Jordan, Virginia Woolf, and Hélène Cixous. But most of the selections in this anthology are acts of rhetoric, not rhetorical theory. Perhaps that is one of the reasons why a tradition of women's rhetoric has not been written—or seen. Women's rhetorical acts cannot be neatly separated from women's rhetorical theory despite the existence of these categories in the masculinist rhetorical tradition, where rhetorical theory arises from practices within specific contexts and communities—traditionally the male contexts of law, politics, and the church. Rhetorical theory begins as a description of practice, then becomes a prescription for practice, often separated from the context out of which it grew in the first place. The very exigency of women's rhetorical situations has left little room for leisurely or abstract theorizing, unconnected to practical action. But more to the point, women have purposefully sought to keep the context, the immediacy of experience, attached to theorizing rather than creating an abstract set of prescriptions disconnected from the contexts or stripped of the exigencies of everyday life. We believe many of the texts here substantiate Minnie Bruce Pratt's claim that "we can not move theory into action unless we can find it in the eccentric and wandering ways of our daily life. I have written the stories that follow to give theory flesh and breath."

We hope that this anthology invites its readers to reconceptualize definitions of rhetorical theory to include women's writing practice and to read women's rhetorics *as theory*. In other words, our work with this range of women's rhetorics suggests to us that praxis—the intersection of theory and practice—is a central feature of women's rhetorical stances. Many writers here demonstrate the immediate connection between theory and action, between reflection on practice and practice itself. We think this connection between theory and practice is the ground for the very newest and perhaps most important work in women's rhetorics. Some of this work has already begun. Krista Ratcliffe, in *Anglo American Feminist Challenges to the Rhetorical Traditions*, overtly seeks to "extrapolate" theories of rhetoric from "women's and/or feminist critiques of language as well as from the textual strategies of such critiques" (4). Ratcliffe reads Virginia Woolf, Mary Daly, and Adrienne Rich in order to "contribute to the continuing conversation about feminisms and the rhetorical tradition by inviting teachers not only to question how Woman, women, and feminists have been located as part of, and apart from, these [canonical, rhetorical] traditions but also to explore the implication of such locations for rhetorical history, theory, and pedagogy" (6). Reading these three twentieth-century women writers both within and against such categories as location, material conditions, invention, style, arrangement, memory, and audience, Ratcliffe also offers models for some of the principles of selection and arrangement in *Available Means*. This anthology surely partakes of Ratcliffe's goal—"not only to locate gender gaps but also to imagine new texts of rhetorical history, theory and pedagogy" (28)—and extends that goal by gathering together texts by women situated much farther from the center of that history and theory than the three Anglo American feminists Ratcliffe reads in her book.

Andrea Lunsford reminds us that we have to "listen hard" in order to see rhetorical theory "because the tradition has never recognized the forms, strategies, and goals used by many women as 'rhetorical'" (6). As we have put this anthology together, we have tried to be the kind of readers who listen hard for theory within texts that often seem largely personal, practical, or occasional. For example, we include here Minnie Bruce Pratt writing about her history as a lesbian and about the inadequacy of binary categories of male and female, the heterosexism they represent and their inability to accurately name human experience. We believe that in so writing she "theorizes"—she explicates the entanglements of identity and language, the power of naming as it constructs human identities, and also the inadequacy of language to represent the multiplicity and fluidity of potential identities available beyond the male/female binary. Through her discussion of transgendered experience, Pratt presents a theory about the relationships of power embedded in the discourses of gender and sexuality and about the way in which rhetoric can control difference, can keep it within bounds or allow resistance. We also include selections from Dorothy Allison's *Two or Three Things I Know for Sure*, a narrative that began as a performance piece and that we believe presents an alternative rhetorical theory, as Allison tells the story of reclaiming her life from its abusive beginnings. In this "story," she is exploring epistemology—always a foundation for rhetorical theory—arguing that truth is constructed in language, invented and arranged in order to survive. In doing so she suggests the provisionality of reality but also the necessity of rhetorical action to change one's reality.

As we have attempted to "listen hard" to women writers and speakers in order to hear rhetorical theory enacted, we have recognized that many of the writers who collapse theory and practice are women of color: bell hooks, Toni Morrison, Leslie Marmon Silko, Gloria Anzaldúa. We believe this is because they—more than white, privileged women—have had to theorize a way first of getting heard; they have had to create the rhetorical means to re-present themselves as persons who can speak, who are not invisible. Those on the unequal side of power must always be more theoretical, more rhetorically analytical. The homeplace, as bell hooks conceives of it, is a site of refuge, but it is also a site of theory. The borderland and the margin, as Anzaldúa demonstrates, are places that demand theorizing if one is to survive. Storytelling becomes theory as Toni Morrison uses an old folktale to articulate a theory of responsible language use, and bell hooks shows us that rhetorical theory often arises from the material reality of women's lives. With her stories of Yellow Woman, Silko highlights the differences between white culture and the aesthetic, moral, and rhetorical values of her Laguna Pueblo people. Although white European American women are also often disenfranchised and alienated from power, for them the rhetorical situation is sometimes more naturalized, invisible, and thus not as available for reflection, problematizing, or analysis. For this reason we can see in the texts gathered here, particularly in those from the twentieth century, the ways in which white women learned from African American, Native American, Asian American, and Latina/Chicana women and lesbians of color to question and to place in an economic, historical, and political perspective issues of gender, race, class, and sexuality.

Gathering Rhetorics for the Future

We see *Available Means* as a next step in what Louise Phelps and Janet Emig call "a uniquely transitional moment when everything is yet to be decided" (408). We are at an important but ironic moment as feminists, as rhetoricians, and as teachers. Women have long been outside the canon of rhetoric; now, we are at the beginning of a moment of canon and theory formation, as Lunsford's, Logan's, Royster's, and Ratcliffe's work clearly shows. And as these scholars continually insist, questions remain at the heart of this work: What is women's rhetoric? What is the difference between reading women's writing rhetorically (analyzing their rhetorical methods, the use of their available means) and claiming that a given work by a woman *is* rhetorical theory? Who belongs in the emerging canon of women's/feminist rhetoric? And how can this recovery work and this reconfiguring of rhetorical theory be useful to students of writing and rhetoric and women's studies? Rhetoric and composition, argue Phelps and Emig, have a "heritage of an indigenous though subterranean feminism that awaits critical articulation and elaboration" (418). In *Available Means* we hope to provide some of that elaboration by gathering for students and teachers a body of women's writing that can be usefully investigated in order to subvert and enlarge conceptions of both rhetorical theory and practice.

In this moment of defining women's rhetorics we hope that this anthology will spark questions like these: What do we have available to us in the body of women's writing that we might consider as rhetorical theory? What qualities might a work of women's writing need to possess in order for us to consider it as rhetorical theory? And finally, what blinders are preventing us from reading more of women's rhetoric as theory? We strongly believe that these questions are even more important than their answers. We can't wait for the answers, however, because it is important, too, for students to begin to study a body of women's writing as rhetorical theory in order for them to move towards changed rhetorical practice in their own lives.

FOR FURTHER READING

Allen, Paula Gunn. "Who Is Your Mother? Red Roots of White Feminism." In *The Sacred Hoop: Recovering the Feminine in American Indian Traditions*, 209–21. Boston: Beacon Press, 1992.

Anzaldúa, Gloria. "La Conciencia de la Mestiza: Toward a New Consciousness." In *Borderland/La Frontera: The New Mestiza*, 77–101. San Francisco: Aunt Lute, 1987.

Bitzer, Lloyd. "Rhetorical Situation." *The Philosophy of Rhetoric.* 1 (1968): 1–14.

Bizzell, Patricia, and Bruce Herzberg, eds. *The Rhetorical Tradition: Readings from Classical Times to the Present.* Boston: Bedford Books of St. Martin's Press, 1990.

Campbell, Karlyn Kohrs. *Man Cannot Speak for Her.* 2 vols. New York: Praeger, 1989.

Gere, Anne Ruggles. *Intimate Practices: Literacy and Cultural Work in U.S. Women's Clubs, 1880–1920.* Urbana: University of Illinois Press, 1997.

Glenn, Cheryl. *Rhetoric Retold: Regendering the Tradition from Antiquity through the Renaissance.* Carbondale: Southern Illinois University Press, 1997.

hooks, bell. "Race and Feminism: The Issue of Accountability." In *Ain't I a Woman: Black Women and Feminism*, 119–58. Boston: South End Press, 1981.

Jarratt, Susan. "As We Were Saying." In *Feminism and Composition Studies: In Other Words*, edited by Susan Jarratt and Lynn Worsham, 1–18. New York: Modern Language Association, 1998.

Lerner, Gerda. *The Creation of Patriarchy.* New York: Oxford University Press, 1986.

Logan, Shirley Wilson. *"We Are Coming": The Persuasive Discourse of Nineteenth-Century Black Women.* Carbondale: Southern Illinois University Press, 1999.

———, ed. *With Pen and Voice: A Critical Anthology of Nineteenth-Century African-American Women.* Carbondale: Southern Illinois University Press, 1995.

Lorde, Audre. "Scratching the Surface: Some Notes on Barriers to Women and Loving." In *Sister Outsider: Essays and Speeches*, 45–52. Freedom, Calif.: The Crossing Press, 1984.

Lunsford, Andrea, ed. *Reclaiming Rhetorica: Women in the Rhetorical Tradition.* Pittsburgh: University of Pittsburgh Press, 1995.

Morrison, Toni. *Playing in the Dark: Whiteness and the Literary Imagination.* Cambridge: Harvard University Press, 1992.

Phelps, Louise Weatherbee, and Janet Emig, eds. *Feminine Principles and Women's Experience in American Composition and Rhetoric.* Pittsburgh: University of Pittsburgh Press, 1995.

Pratt, Minnie Bruce. "Gender Quiz." In *S/HE*, 11–24. Ithaca: Firebrand Books, 1995.

Ratcliffe, Krista. *Anglo-American Feminist Challenges to the Rhetorical Traditions: Virginia Woolf, Mary Daly, Adrienne Rich.* Carbondale: Southern Illinois University Press, 1996.

Royster, Jacqueline Jones. *Traces of a Stream: Literacy and Social Change Among African American Women.* Pittsburgh: University of Pittsburgh Press, 2000.

Schneir, Miriam, ed. *Feminism: The Essential Historical Writings.* New York: Random House, 1972.

———, ed. *Feminism in Our Time: The Essential Writings, World War II to the Present.* New York: Random House, 1994.

Available Means

Aspasia

C. 410 B.C.E.

The selection below was written by a man, reporting the words of another man, who is reporting yet another man's words but claiming that the words were written by a woman—Aspasia of Miletus. Although filtered through the mouths of three male rhetors, Aspasia belongs in this collection of women's rhetorics because hers is one of the first—if not the very first—woman's voice in the history of the Western rhetorical tradition. We do not have any of Aspasia's writing firsthand, but Plato names her as his "excellent mistress in the art of rhetoric" (*Menexenus* 235e). Cheryl Glenn describes Aspasia as "an exceptional hero in a new rhetorical narrative" (*Rhetoric Retold* 44).

Born in Miletus (now Turkey) in the fifth century B.C.E., Aspasia was well educated, politically astute, and outspoken at a time when Athenian women were confined almost exclusively to the home and rarely permitted a public voice or education. Almost everything about her life and her rhetoric is remarkable, starting with the fact that we know of her at all. The accomplishments of Aspasia are recorded by Plato, Cicero, and Plutarch, who all praised her as both rhetorician and political philosopher. Described most fully in Plato's *Menexenus* (excerpted below) and in Plutarch's *Lives of the Noble Grecians and Romans*, the Aspasia these men depict is a powerful woman indeed at a time when almost all of the references to women relate only to their roles as wives, mothers, or daughters. Plutarch reports that many Athenians, including Pericles, consulted Aspasia for "instruction in the art of speaking" (201).

In the following excerpt from Plato's dialogue *Menexenus*, Plato suggests that Aspasia herself, not Pericles, wrote the famous funeral oration for those killed in the Peloponnesian Wars in 431 B.C.E. Pericles ruled Athens for over thirty years as a distinguished soldier, statesman, and orator ostensibly without equal. Yet in this dialogue, Plato puts Pericles' famous oration into the mouth of Aspasia, claiming that while "Pericles spoke . . .she composed." Pericles and Aspasia were lovers; and although she was at the center of the political and rhetorical debates of her day, Aspasia herself could not have delivered any oration, much less the public ritual of healing and celebration that a funeral oration accomplished. Yet Socrates attributes its ideas of public good and of the connection of place and people, as well as the oration's rhetorical effect of creating a community among all who heard it and mourned the dead, to Aspasia, equating her skill with what he would later call a true art of rhetoric. Aspasia's speech follows the conventions of a classical funeral oration, drawing on rhetorical "topics" familiar to her audience, such as the heroic deeds of ancestors and the source of all goodness in Athenian soil. Some scholars read Aspasia's oration as Plato's ironic parody of the excesses of rhetoric in Athens, particularly as practiced and taught by non-Athenians. But as part of the history of women's rhetoric, it may be more important to note that Socrates describes Aspasia's rhetorical genius as having "made" many other good speakers; in other words, Socrates treats her as a teacher of men in Athens. Despite the fact that we cannot read her rhetoric directly but only through the words of men, we can remember Aspasia as the only woman we know of who dared to compose and teach among men in Athens, the place where our rhetorical tradition began, a tradition that has since excluded so many women.

"Pericles' Funeral Oration" from Plato's *Menexenus*

C. 387–367 B.C.E.

Socrates: But why, my friend, should he not have plenty to say? Every rhetorician has speeches ready-made, nor is there any difficulty in improvising that sort of stuff. Had the orator to praise Athenians among Peloponnesians, or Peloponnesians among Athenians, he must be a good rhetorician who could succeed and gain credit. But there is no difficulty in a man's winning applause when he is contending for fame among the persons whom he is praising.

Menexenus: Do you think not, Socrates?

Socrates: Certainly not.

Menexenus: Do you think that you could speak yourself if there should be a necessity, and if the Council were to choose you?

Socrates: That I should be able to speak is no great wonder, Menexenus, considering that I have an excellent mistress in the art of rhetoric—she who has made so many good speakers, and one who was the best among all the Hellenes, Pericles, the son of Xanthippus.

Menexenus: And who is she? I suppose that you mean Aspasia.

Socrates: Yes, I do, and besides her I had Connus, the son of Metrobius, as a master, and he was my master in music, as she was in rhetoric. No wonder that a man who has received such an education should be a finished speaker. Even the pupil of very inferior masters—say, for example, one who had learned music of Lamprus and rhetoric of Antiphon the Rhamnusian— might make a figure if he were to praise the Athenians among the Athenians.

Menexenus: And what would you be able to say if you had to speak?

Reprinted from Plato. *Menexenus.* In *The Dialogues of Plato*, vol. 2, translated by Benjamin Jowett, 516–33. London: Oxford University Press, 1892.

Socrates: Of my own wit, most likely nothing, but yesterday I heard Aspasia composing a funeral oration about these very dead. For she had been told, as you were saying, that the Athenians were going to choose a speaker, and she repeated to me the sort of speech which he should deliver—partly improvising and partly from previous thought, putting together fragments of the funeral oration which Pericles spoke, but which, as I believe, she composed.

Menexenus: And can you remember what Aspasia said?

Socrates: I ought to be able, for she taught me, and she was ready to strike me because I was always forgetting.

Menexenus: Then why will you not rehearse what she said?

Socrates: Because I am afraid that my mistress may be angry with me if I publish her speech.

Menexenus: Nay, Socrates, let us have the speech, whether Aspasia's or anyone else's, no matter. I hope that you will oblige me.

Socrates: But I am afraid that you will laugh at me if I continue the games of youth in old age.

Menexenus: Far otherwise, Socrates. Let us by all means have the speech.

Socrates: Truly I have such a disposition to oblige you that if you bid me dance naked I should not like to refuse, since we are alone. Listen then. If I remember rightly, she began as follows, with the mention of the dead.

There is a tribute of deeds and of words. The departed have already had the first, when going forth on their destined journey they were attended on their way by the state and by their friends; the tribute of words remains to be given to them, as is meet and by law ordained. For noble words are a memorial and a crown of noble actions, which are given to the doers of them by the hearers. A word is needed which will duly praise the dead and gently admonish the living, exhorting the brethren and descendants of the departed to imitate their virtue, and consoling their fathers and mothers and the survivors, if any, who may chance to be alive of the previous generation. What sort of a word will this be, and how shall we rightly begin the praises of these brave men? In their life they rejoiced their own friends with their valor, and their death they gave in exchange for the salvation of the living. And I think that we should praise them in the order in which nature made them good, for they were good because they were sprung from good fathers. Wherefore let us first of all praise the goodness of their birth, secondly, their nurture and education, and then let us set forth how noble their actions were, and how worthy of the education which they had received.

And first as to their birth. Their ancestors were not strangers, nor are these their descendants sojourners only, whose fathers have come from another country, but they are the children of the soil, dwelling and living in their own land. And the country which brought them up is not like other countries, a stepmother to her children, but their own true mother; she bore them and nourished them and received them, and in her bosom they now repose. It is meet and right, therefore, that we should begin by praising the land which is their mother, and that will be a way of praising their noble birth.

The country is worthy to be praised, not only by us, but by all mankind—first, and above all, as being dear to the gods. This is proved by the strife and contention of the gods respecting her. And ought not the country which the gods praise to be praised by all mankind? The second praise which may be fairly claimed by her is that at the time when the whole earth was sending forth and creating diverse animals, tame and wild, she our mother was free and pure from savage monsters, and out of all animals selected and brought forth man, who is superior to the rest in understanding, and alone has justice and religion. And a great proof that she brought forth the common ancestors of us and of the departed is that she provided the means of support for her offspring. For as a woman proves her motherhood by giving milk to her young ones—and she who has no fountain of milk is not a mother—so did this our land prove that she was the mother of men, for in those days she alone and first of all brought forth wheat and barley for human food, which is the best and noblest sustenance for man, whom she regarded as her true offspring. And these are truer proofs of motherhood in a country than in a woman, for the woman in her conception and generation is but the imitation of the earth, and not the earth of the woman. And of the fruit of the earth she gave a plenteous supply, not only to her own, but to others also, and afterward she made the olive to spring up to be a boon to her children, and to help them in their toils. And when she had herself nursed them and brought them up to manhood, she gave them gods to be their rulers and teachers, whose names are well known, and need not now be repeated. They are the gods who ordered our lives, and instructed us, first of all men, in the arts for the supply of our daily needs, and taught us the acquisition and use of arms for the defense of the country.

Thus born into the world and thus educated, the ancestors of the departed lived and made themselves a government, which I ought briefly to commemorate. For government is the nurture of man, and the government of good men is good, and of bad men bad. And I must show that our ancestors were trained under a good government, and for this reason they were good, and our contemporaries are also good, among whom our departed friends are to be reckoned. Then as now, and indeed always, from that time to this, speaking generally, our government was an aristocracy—a form of government which receives various names, according to the fancies of men, and is sometimes called democracy, but is really an aristocracy or government of the best which has the approval of the many. For kings we have always had, first hereditary and then elected, and authority is mostly in the hands of the people, who dispense offices and power to those who appear to be most deserving of them. Neither is a man rejected from weakness or poverty or obscurity of origin, nor honored by reason of the opposite, as in other states, but there is one principle—he who appears to be wise and good is a governor and ruler. The basis of this our government is equality of birth, for other states are made up of all sorts and unequal conditions of men, and therefore their governments are unequal—there are tyrannies and there are oligarchies, in which the one party are slaves and the others masters. But we and our citizens are brethren, the children all of one mother, and we do not think it right to be one another's masters or servants, but the natural equality of birth compels us to seek for legal equality, and to recognize no superiority except in the reputation of virtue and wisdom.

And so their and our fathers, and these, too, our brethren, being nobly born and having been brought up in all freedom, did both in their public and private capacity many noble deeds famous over the whole world. They were the deeds of men who thought that they ought to fight both against Hellenes for the sake of Hellenes on behalf of freedom, and against barbarians in the common interest of Hellas. Time would fail me to tell of their defense of their country against the invasion of Eumolpus and the Amazons, or of their defense of the Argives against the Cadmeans, or of the Heraclidae against the Argives. Besides, the poets have already declared in song to all mankind their glory, and therefore any commemoration of their deeds in prose which we might attempt would hold a second place. They already have their reward, and I say no more of them, but there are other worthy deeds of which no poet has worthily sung, and which are still wooing the poet's Muse. Of these I am bound to make honorable mention, and shall invoke others to sing of them also in lyric and other strains, in a manner becoming the actors. . . .

Such were the actions of the men who are here interred, and of others who have died on behalf of their country; many and glorious things I have spoken of them, and there are yet many more, and more glorious, things remaining to be told—many days and nights would not suffice to tell of them. Let them not be forgotten, and let every man remind their descendants that they also are soldiers who must not desert the ranks of their ancestors, or from cowardice fall behind. Even so I exhort you this day, and in all future time, whenever I meet with any of you, shall continue to remind and exhort you, O ye sons of heroes, that you strive to be the bravest of men. And I think that I ought now to repeat what your fathers desired to have said to you who are their survivors, when they went out to battle, in case anything happened to them. I will tell you what I heard them say, and what, if they had only speech, they would fain be saying, judging from what they then said. And you must imagine that you hear them saying what I now repeat to you.

Sons, the event proves that your fathers were brave men, for we might have lived dishonorably, but have preferred to die honorably rather than bring you and your children into disgrace, and rather than dishonor our own fathers and forefathers—considering that life is not life to one who is a dishonor to his race, and that to such a one neither men nor gods are friendly, either while he is on the earth or after death in the world below. Remember our words, then, and whatever is your aim let virtue be the condition of the attainment of your aim, and know that without this all possessions and pursuits are dishonorable and evil. For neither does wealth bring honor to the owner, if he be a coward; of such a one the wealth belongs to another, and not to himself. Nor do beauty and strength of body, when dwelling in a base and cowardly man, appear comely, but the reverse of comely, making the possessor more conspicuous, and manifesting forth his cowardice. And all knowledge, when separated from justice and virtue, is seen to be cunning and not wisdom; wherefore make this your first and last and constant and all-absorbing aim—to exceed, if possible, not only us but all your ancestors in virtue, and know that to excel you in virtue only brings us shame, but that to be excelled by you is a source of happiness to us. And we shall most likely be defeated, and you will most likely be victors in the contest, if you learn so to order your lives as not to abuse or waste the reputation of your ancestors, knowing that to a man who has any self-respect, nothing is more dishonorable than to be honored, not for his own sake, but on account of the reputation of his ancestors. The honor of parents is a fair and noble treasure to their posterity, but to have the use of a treasure of wealth and honor, and to leave none to your successors, because you have neither money nor reputation of your own, is alike base and dishonorable. And if you follow our precepts you will be received by us as friends, when the hour of destiny brings you hither, but if you neglect our words and are disgraced in your lives, no one will welcome or receive you. This is the message which is to be delivered to our children.

Some of us have fathers and mothers still living, and we would urge them, if, as is likely, we shall die, to bear the calamity as lightly as possible, and not to condole with one another, for they have sorrows enough, and will not need anyone to stir them up. While we gently heal their wounds, let us remind them that the gods have heard the chief part of their prayers, for they prayed, not that their children might live forever, but that they might be brave and renowned. And this, which is the greatest good, they have attained. A mortal man cannot expect to have everything in his own life turning out according to his will, and they, if they bear their misfortunes bravely, will be truly deemed brave fathers of the brave. But if they give way to their sorrows, either they will be suspected of not being our parents, or we of not being such as our panegyrists declare. Let not either of the two alternatives happen, but rather let them be our chief and true panegyrists, who show in their lives that they are true men, and had men for their sons. Of old the saying, 'Nothing too much,' appeared to be, and really was, well said. For he whose happiness rests with himself, if possible, wholly, and if not, as far as possible, who is not hanging in suspense on other men, or changing with the vicissitude of their fortune, has his life ordered for the best. He is the temperate and valiant and wise, and when his riches come and go, when his children are given and taken away, he will remember the proverb, 'Neither rejoicing overmuch nor grieving overmuch,' for he relies upon himself. And such we would have our parents to be—that is our word and wish, and as such we now offer ourselves, neither lamenting overmuch, nor fearing overmuch, if we are to die at this time. And we entreat our fathers and mothers to retain these feelings throughout their future life, and to be assured that they will not please us by sorrowing and lamenting over us. But, if the dead have any knowledge of the living, they will displease us most by making themselves miserable and by taking their misfortunes too much to heart, and they will please us best if they bear their loss lightly and temperately. For our life will have the noblest end which is vouchsafed to man, and should be glorified rather than lamented. And if they will direct their minds to the care and nurture of our wives and children, they will soonest forget their misfortunes, and live in a better and nobler way, and be dearer to us.

This is all that we have to say to our families, and to the state we would say, Take care of our parents and of our sons—let her worthily cherish the old age of our parents, and bring up our sons in the right way. But we know that she will of her own accord take care of them, and does not need any exhortation of ours.

This, O ye children and parents of the dead, is the message which they bid us deliver to you, and which I do deliver with the utmost seriousness. And in their name I beseech you, the children, to imitate your fathers, and you, parents, to be of good cheer about yourselves, for we will nourish your age, and take care of you both publicly and privately in any place in which one of us may meet one of you who are the parents of the dead. And the care of you which the city shows, you know yourselves, for she has made provision by law concerning the parents and children of those who die in war; the highest authority is specially entrusted with the duty of watching over them above all other citizens, and they will see that the fathers and mothers have no wrong done to them. The city herself shares in the education of the children, desiring as far as it is possible that their orphanhood may not be felt by them. While they are children she is a parent to them, and when they have arrived at man's estate she sends them to their several duties, in full armor clad; and bringing freshly to their minds the ways of their fathers, she places in their hands the instruments of their fathers' virtues. For the sake of the omen, she would have them from the first begin to rule over their own houses arrayed in the strength and arms of their fathers. And as for the dead, she never ceases honoring them, celebrating, in common for all, rites which become the property of each, and in addition to this, holding gymnastic and equestrian contests, and musical festivals of every sort. She is to the dead in the place of a son and heir, and to their sons in the place of a father, and to their parents and elder kindred in the place of a guardian—ever and always caring for them. Considering this, you ought to bear your calamity the more gently, for thus you will be most endeared to the dead and to the living, and your sorrows will heal and be healed. And now do you and all, having lamented the dead in common according to the law, go your ways.

You have heard, Menexenus, the oration of Aspasia the Milesian.

Menexenus: Truly, Socrates, I marvel that Aspasia, who is only a woman, should be able to compose such a speech—she must be a rare one.

Socrates: Well, if you are incredulous, you may come with me and hear her.

Menexenus: I have often met Aspasia, Socrates, and know what she is like.

Socrates: Well, and do you not admire her, and are you not grateful for her speech?

Menexenus: Yes, Socrates, I am very grateful to her or to him who told you, and still more to you who have told me.

Socrates: Very good. But you must take care not to tell of me, and then at some future time I will repeat to you many other excellent political speeches of hers.

Menexenus: Fear not. Only let me hear them, and I will keep the secret.

Socrates: Then I will keep my promise.

FOR FURTHER READING

Glenn, Cheryl. *Rhetoric Retold: Regendering the Tradition from Antiquity through the Renaissance.* Carbondale: Southern Illinois University Press, 1997.

———. "Sex, Lies, and Manuscript: Refiguring Aspasia in the History of Rhetoric." *College Composition and Communication* 45.2 (1994): 180–99.

Jarratt, Susan, and Rory Ong. "Aspasia: Rhetoric, Gender, and Colonial Ideology." In *Reclaiming Rhetorica: Women in the Rhetorical Tradition,* edited by Andrea Lunsford, 9–24. Pittsburgh: University of Pittsburgh Press, 1995.

Plutarch. *Lives of the Noble Grecians and Romans.* Translated by John Dryden. Introduction by Rev. Arthur Hugh Clough. New York: Modern Library, 1932.

Diotima

FOURTH CENTURY B.C.E.

Like the rhetoric of Aspasia, what we know of Diotima of Mantinea's rhetoric is reported through the words of her male contemporaries—in this case, through the words of Socrates as written by Plato in the *Symposium*. Diotima has been a site of conflict for historians who question her existence at all, since her only speech on record is reproduced by Plato. Nevertheless, feminist historiographers such as Cheryl Glenn and C. Jan Swearingen read Plato's representation of Diotima as a move to preserve the rhetoric of women even as he appropriates it.

Although she acknowledges that Diotima may be "an unlikely candidate for inclusion in any rhetorical tradition," C. Jan Swearingen argues that Diotima "merits close study, as the trace of women teachers, speakers, and religious celebrants" in classical history (25–26). Plato describes Diotima as a priestess, philosopher, and teacher, whose rhetorical skills remind him of "one of our best Sophists" (*Symposium* 208c). The only woman to contribute to the speeches on love in this dialogue, Diotima argues that Love is a spirit that moves between the gods and humans, connecting them through discourse and desire. In fact, as Swearingen suggests, Diotima insists that "desire, trust, love, and pity . . . are the very animating essence of discourse" (48).

Diotima's speech, then, links rhetoric to "intersubjectivity" and provides early evidence that women both practiced and theorized rhetoric (Swearingen 48). As Cheryl Glenn describes the place of Diotima in the *Symposium*, her feminine presence—including her references to the body, the family, and the private realm—"enhances—rather than detracts from—the powerful homoeroticism" of this dialogue (45). Diotima teaches Socrates how to transcend a base physical desire and move toward a philosophy of "perfect love and intellectual intercourse that reproduces the form of immutable beauty" (Glenn 45). Once again, we see Socrates claiming that one of his greatest teachers is a woman.

"On Love" from Plato's *Symposium*

C. 360 B.C.E.

And now I'm going to leave you in peace, because I want to talk about some lessons I was given, once upon a time, by a Mantinean woman called Diotima— a woman who was deeply versed in this and many other fields of knowledge. It was she who brought about a ten years' postponement of the great plague of Athens on the occasion of a certain sacrifice, and it was she who taught me the philosophy of Love. And now I am going to try to connect her teaching—as well as I can without her help—with the conclusions that Agathon and I have just arrived at. Like him, I shall begin by stating who and what Love is, and go on to describe his functions, and I think the easiest way will be to adopt Diotima's own method of inquiry by question and answer. . . .

. . . There are many spirits, and many kinds of spirits, too, and Love is one of them.

Then who were his parents? I asked.

I'll tell you, she said, though it's rather a long story. On the day of Aphrodite's birth the gods were making merry, and among them was Resource, the son of Craft. And when they had supped, Need came begging at the door because there was good cheer inside. Now, it happened that Resource, having drunk deeply of the heavenly nectar—for this was before the days of wine— wandered out into the garden of Zeus and sank into a heavy sleep, and Need, thinking that to get a child by Resource would mitigate her penury, lay down beside him and in time was brought to bed of Love. So Love became the follower and servant of Aphrodite because he was begotten on the same day that she was born, and further, he was born to love the beautiful since Aphrodite is beautiful herself.

Then again, as the son of Resource and Need, it has been his fate to be always needy; nor is he delicate and lovely as most of us believe, but harsh and arid, barefoot and homeless, sleeping on the naked earth, in doorways, or in the very streets beneath the stars of heaven, and always partaking of his mother's poverty. But, secondly, he brings his father's resourcefulness to his designs upon the beautiful and the good, for he is gallant, impetuous, and energetic, a mighty hunter, and a master of device and artifice—at once desirous and full of wisdom, a lifelong seeker after truth, an adept in sorcery, enchantment, and seduction. . . .

Very well, then. And that being so, what course will Love's followers pursue,

Plato. *Symposium.* In *The Collected Dialogues of Plato.* Edited by Edith Hamilton and Huntington Cairns. Translated by Michael Joyce. Copyright ©1961 by Princeton University Press. Reprinted by permission of Princeton University Press.

and in what particular field will eagerness and exertion be known as Love? In fact, what *is* this activity? Can you tell me that, Socrates?

If I could, my dear Diotima, I retorted, I shouldn't be so much amazed at *your* grasp of the subject, and I shouldn't be coming to you to learn the answer to that very question.

Well, I'll tell you, then, she said. To love is to bring forth upon the beautiful, both in body and in soul.

I'm afraid that's too deep, I said, for my poor wits to fathom.

I'll try to speak more plainly, then. We are all of us prolific, Socrates, in body and in soul, and when we reach a certain age our nature urges us to procreation. Nor can we be quickened by ugliness, but only by the beautiful. Conception, we know, takes place when man and woman come together, but there's a divinity in human propagation, an immortal something in the midst of man's mortality which is incompatible with any kind of discord. And ugliness is at odds with the divine, while beauty is in perfect harmony. In propagation, then, Beauty is the Goddess of both fate and travail, and so when procreancy draws near the beautiful it grows genial and blithe, and birth follows swiftly on conception. But when it meets with ugliness it is overcome with heaviness and gloom, and turning away it shrinks into itself and is not brought to bed, but still labors under its painful burden. And so, when the procreant is big with child, he is strangely stirred by the beautiful, because he knows that beauty's tenant will bring his travail to an end. So you see, Socrates, that Love is not exactly a longing for the beautiful, as you suggested.

Well, what is it, then?

A longing not for the beautiful itself, but for the conception and generation that the beautiful effects.

Yes, no doubt you're right.

Of course I'm right, she said. And why all this longing for propagation? Because this is the one deathless and eternal element in our mortality. And since we have agreed that the lover longs for the good to be his own forever, it follows that we are bound to long for immortality as well as for the good—which is to say that Love is a longing for immortality.

So much I gathered, gentlemen, at one time and another from Diotima's dissertations upon Love.

And then one day she asked me, Well, Socrates, and what do you suppose is the cause of all this longing and all this love? Haven't you noticed what an extraordinary effect the breeding instinct has upon both animals and birds, and how obsessed they are with the desire, first to mate, then to rear their litters and their broods, and how the weakest of them are ready to stand up to the strongest in defense of their young, and even die for them, and how they are content to bear the pinch of hunger and every kind of hardship, so long as they can rear their offspring?

With men, she went on, you might put it down to the power of reason, but how can you account for Love's having such remarkable effects upon the brutes? What do you say to that, Socrates?

Again I have to confess my ignorance.

Well, she said, I don't know how you can hope to master the philosophy of Love, if *that's* too much for you to understand.

But, my dear Diotima, I protested, as I said before, that's just why I'm asking you to teach me—because I realize how ignorant I am. And I'd be more than grateful if you'd enlighten me as to the cause not only of this, but of all the various effects of Love.

Well, she said, it's simple enough, so long as you bear in mind what we agreed was the object of Love. For here, too, the principle holds good that the mortal does all it can to put on immortality. And how can it do that except by breeding, and thus ensuring that there will always be a younger generation to take the place of the old?

Now, although we speak of an individual as being the same so long as he continues to exist in the same form, and therefore assume that a man is the same person in his dotage as in his infancy, yet, for all we call him the same, every bit of him is different, and every day he is becoming a new man, while the old man is ceasing to exist, as you can see from his hair, his flesh, his bones, his blood, and the rest of his body. And not only his body, for the same thing happens to his soul. And neither his manners, nor his disposition, nor his thoughts, nor his desires, nor his pleasures, nor his sufferings, nor his fears are the same throughout his life, for some of them grow, while others disappear.

And the application of this principle to human knowledge is even more remarkable, for not only do some of the things we know increase, while some of them are lost, so that even in our knowledge we are not always the same, but the principle applies as well to every single branch of knowledge. When we say we are studying, we really mean that our knowledge is ebbing away. We forget, because our knowledge disappears, and we have to study so as to replace what we are losing, so that the state of our knowledge may seem, at any rate to be the same as it was before.

This is how every mortal creature perpetuates itself. It cannot, like the divine, be still the same throughout eternity; it can only leave behind new life to fill the vacancy that is left in its species by obsolescence. This, my dear Socrates, is how the body and all else that is temporal partakes of the eternal; there is no other way. And so it is no wonder that every creature prizes its own issue, since the whole creation is inspired by this love, this passion for immortality.

Well, Diotima, I said, when she had done, that's a most impressive argument. I wonder if you're right.

Of course I am, she said with an air of authority that was almost professorial. . . .

Well then, she went on, those whose procreancy is of the body turn to woman as the object of their love, and raise a family, in the blessed hope that by doing so they will keep their memory green, 'through time and through eternity.' But those whose procreancy is of the spirit rather than of the flesh—and they are not unknown, Socrates—conceive and bear the things of the spirit. And what are they? you ask. Wisdom and all her sister virtues; it is the office of every poet to beget them, and of every artist whom we may call creative.

Now, by far the most important kind of wisdom, she went on, is that which governs the ordering of society, and which goes by the names of justice and moderation. And if any man is so closely allied to the divine as to be teeming with these virtues even in his youth, and if, when he comes to manhood, his first ambition is to be begetting, he too, you may be sure, will go about in search of the loveliness—and never of the ugliness—on which he may beget. And hence his procreant nature is attracted by a comely body rather than an ill-favored one, and if, besides, he happens on a soul which is at once beautiful, distinguished, and agreeable, he is charmed to find so welcome an alliance. It will be easy for him to talk of virtue to such a listener, and to discuss what human goodness is and how the virtuous should live—in short, to undertake the other's education.

And, as I believe, by constant association with so much beauty, and by thinking of his friend when he is present and when he is away, he will be delivered of the burden he has labored under all these years. And what is more, he and his friend will help each other rear the issue of their friendship—and so the bond between them will be more binding, and their communion even more complete, than that which comes of bringing children up, because they have created something lovelier and less mortal than human seed.

And I ask you, who would not prefer such fatherhood to merely human propagation, if he stopped to think of Homer, and Hesiod, and all the greatest of our poets? Who would not envy them their immortal progeny, their claim upon the admiration of posterity?

Or think of Lycurgus, she went on, and what offspring he left behind him in his laws, which proved to be the saviors of Sparta and, perhaps, the whole of Hellas. Or think of the fame of Solon, the father of Athenian law, and think of all the other names that are remembered in Grecian cities and in lands beyond the sea for the noble deeds they did before the eyes of all the world, and for all the diverse virtues that they fathered. And think of all the shrines that have been dedicated to them in memory of their immortal issue, and tell me if you can of *anyone* whose mortal children have brought him so much fame.

Well now, my dear Socrates, I have no doubt that even you might be initiated into these, the more elementary mysteries of Love. But I don't know whether you could apprehend the final revelation, for so far, you know, we are only at the bottom of the true scale of perfection.

Never mind, she went on, I will do all I can to help you understand, and you must strain every nerve to follow what I'm saying.

Well then, she began, the candidate for this initiation cannot, if his efforts are to be rewarded, begin too early to devote himself to the beauties of the body. First of all, if his preceptor instructs him as he should, he will fall in love with the beauty of one individual body, so that his passion may give life to noble discourse. Next he must consider how nearly related the beauty of any one body is to the beauty of any other, when he will see that if he is to devote himself to loveliness of form it will be absurd to deny that the beauty of each and every body is the same. Having reached this point, he must set himself to be the lover of every lovely body, and bring his passion for the one into due proportion by deeming it of little or of no importance.

Next he must grasp that the beauties of the body are as nothing to the beauties of the soul, so that wherever he meets with spiritual loveliness, even in the husk of an unlovely body, he will find it beautiful enough to fall in love with and to cherish—and beautiful enough to quicken in his heart a longing for such discourse as tends toward the building of a noble nature. And from this he will be led to contemplate the beauty of laws and institutions. And when he discovers how nearly every kind of beauty is akin to every other he will conclude that the beauty of the body is not, after all, of so great moment.

And next, his attention should be diverted from institutions to the sciences, so that he may know the beauty of every kind of knowledge. And thus, by scanning beauty's wide horizon, he will be saved from a slavish and illiberal devotion to the individual loveliness of a single boy, a single man, or a single institution. And, turning his eyes toward the open sea of beauty, he will find in such contemplation the seed of the most fruitful discourse and the loftiest thought, and reap a golden harvest of philosophy, until, confirmed and strengthened, he will come upon one single form of knowledge, the knowledge of the beauty I am about to speak of.

And here, she said, you must follow me as closely as you can.

Whoever has been initiated so far in the mysteries of Love and has viewed all these aspects of the beautiful in due succession, is at last drawing near the final revelation. And now, Socrates, there bursts upon him that wondrous vision which is the very soul of the beauty he has toiled so long for. It is an everlasting loveliness which neither comes nor goes, which neither flowers nor fades, for such beauty is the same on every hand, the same then as now, here as there, this way as that way, the same to every worshiper as it is to every other.

Nor will his vision of the beautiful take the form of a face, or of hands, or of anything that is of flesh. It will be neither words, nor knowledge, nor a something that exists in something else, such as a living creature, or the earth, or the heavens, or anything that is—but subsisting of itself and by itself in an eternal oneness, while every lovely thing partakes of it in such sort that, however much the parts may wax and wane, it will be neither more nor less, but still the same inviolable whole.

And so, when his prescribed devotion to boyish beauties has carried our candidate so far that the universal beauty dawns upon his inward sight, he is almost within reach of the final revelation. And this is the way, the only way, he must approach, or be led toward, the sanctuary of Love. Starting from individual beauties, the quest for the universal beauty must find him ever mounting the heavenly ladder, stepping from rung to rung—that is, from one to two, and from two to *every* lovely body, from bodily beauty to the beauty of institutions, from institutions to learning, and from learning in general to the special lore that pertains to nothing but the beautiful itself—until at last he comes to know what beauty is.

And if, my dear Socrates, Diotima went on, man's life is ever worth the living, it is when he has attained this vision of the very soul of beauty. And once you have seen it, you will never be seduced again by the charm of gold, of dress, of comely boys, or lads just ripened to manhood; you will care nothing for the beauties that used to take your breath away and kindle such a longing in you, and many others like you, Socrates, to be always at the side of the beloved and feasting your eyes upon him, so that you would be content, if it were possible, to deny yourself the grosser necessities of meat and drink, so long as you were with him.

But if it were given to man to gaze on beauty's very self—unsullied, unalloyed, and freed from the mortal taint that haunts the frailer loveliness of flesh and blood—if, I say, it were given to man to see the heavenly beauty face to face, would you call *his*, she asked me, an unenviable life, whose eyes had been opened to the vision, and who had gazed upon it in true contemplation until it had become his own forever?

And remember, she said, that it is only when he discerns beauty itself through what makes it visible that a man will be quickened with the true, and not the seeming, virtue—for it is virtue's self that quickens him, not virtue's semblance. And when he has brought forth and reared this perfect virtue, he shall be called the friend of god, and if ever it is given to man to put on immortality, it shall be given to him.

This, Phaedrus—this, gentlemen—was the doctrine of Diotima.

FOR FURTHER READING

Glenn, Cheryl. *Rhetoric Retold: Regendering the Tradition from Antiquity through the Renaissance.* Carbondale: Southern Illinois University Press, 1997.

Halperin, David M, John Winkler, and Froma Zeitlin, eds. *Before Sexuality: The Construction of Erotic Experience in the Ancient World.* Princeton: Princeton University Press, 1990.

Swearingen, C. Jan. "A Lover's Discourse: Diotima, Logos, and Desire." In *Reclaiming Rhetorica: Women in the Rhetorical Tradition,* edited by Andrea Lunsford, 25–52. Pittsburgh: University of Pittsburgh Press.

Hortensia

1 B.C.E.

Hortensia is the only classical woman rhetor whose words, in her own words, are recorded by history. Cheryl Glenn tells us that Hortensia "stands alone in her oratorical achievement" and that "only Hortensia is recognized as successfully entering the domain of persuasive public oratory, or rhetoric" (70). In 42 B.C.E., the triumvirate of Mark Antony, Octavian, and Lepidus proposed to raise money for the war against the assassins of Julius Caesar. They ordered fourteen hundred of the richest Roman women to report the values of their properties so that the Roman state could tax these women to pay for the civil war. A group of women opposed to the prospect of a civil war that had already cost many lives marched into the Roman Forum, demanding to be heard. Hortensia spoke for the group, and her famous speech was later praised by Quintilian and recorded by Appian when he wrote his history of Rome in 200 A.C.E. It must have made quite an impression, for the triumvirs reduced the number of women subject to the tax to four hundred, and they agreed to tax the richest men as well.

We know little about Hortensia's life, except that she was the daughter of Quintus Hortensius, an orator himself. Some historians describe his daughter's speech as containing "the image of her Father's eloquence" (Valerius Maximus 8.3.3). But as Glenn says, Hortensia spoke her own words in her own right, fueled by anger at the request to support a war she had no part in initiating or approving. This speech, indeed, could be considered one of the first instances of the now classic "no taxation without representation" argument. Speaking in the Forum at all was an amazing feat; turning the rhetorical strategies taught by Cicero and Quintilian solely for male use into weapons for women's rights makes Hortensia one of the first recorded adapters of the available means of persuasion, even though those means were not supposed to be at her disposal. We honor her courage and her skill by reprinting her words, as Appian did, for a wider public in this collection.

"Speech to the Triumvirs"

42 B.C.E.

While these events were taking place, Lepidus enjoyed a triumph for his exploits in Spain, and an edict was displayed in the following terms: "May fortune favour us. Let it be proclaimed to all men and women that they celebrate this day with sacrifices and feasting. Whoever shall fail to do so shall be put on the list of the proscribed." Lepidus led the triumphal procession to the Capitol, accompanied by all the citizens, who showed the external appearance of joy, but were sad at heart. The houses of the proscribed were looted, but there were not many buyers of their lands, since some were ashamed to add to the burden of the unfortunate. Others thought that such property would bring them bad luck, or that it would not be at all safe for them to be seen with gold and silver in their possession, or that, as they were not free from danger with their present holdings, it would be an additional risk to increase them. Only the boldest spirits came forward and purchased at the lowest prices, because they were the only buyers. Thus it came to pass that the triumvirs, who had hoped to realize a sufficient sum for their preparations for the war, were still short by 200,000,000 drachmas.

The triumvirs addressed the people on this subject and published an edict requiring 1400 of the richest women to make a valuation of their property, and to furnish for the service of the war such portion as the triumvirs should require from each. It was provided further that if any should conceal their property or make a false valuation they should be fined, and that rewards should be given to informers, whether free persons or slaves. The women resolved to beseech the women-folk of the triumvirs. With the sister of Octavian and the mother of Antony they did not fail, but they were repulsed from the doors of Fulvia, the wife of Antony, whose rudeness they could scarce endure. They then forced their way to the tribunal of the triumvirs in the forum, the people and the guards dividing to let them pass. There, through the mouth of Hortensia, whom they had selected to speak, they spoke as follows: "As befitted women of our rank addressing a petition to you, we had recourse to the ladies of your households; but having been treated as did not befit us, at the hands of Fulvia, we have been driven by her to the forum. You have already deprived us of our fathers, our sons, our husbands, and our brothers, whom you accused of having wronged you; if you take away our property also, you reduce us to a condition unbecoming our birth, our manners, our sex. If we have done you wrong, as you

Reprinted from Appian. "Speech to the Triumvirs." In *Appian's Roman History: The Civil Wars*, vol. 4, edited by T. E. Page, E. Capps, W. H. D. Rouse, L. A. Post, and E. H. Warmington, and translated by Horace White, 191–99. Cambridge: Harvard University Press, 1913.

say our husbands have, proscribe us as you do them. But if we women have not voted any of you public enemies, have not torn down your houses, destroyed your army, or led another one against you; if we have not hindered you in obtaining offices and honours, why do we share the penalty when we did not share the guilt?"

"Why should we pay taxes when we have no part in the honours, the commands, the state-craft, for which you contend against each other with such harmful results? 'Because this is a time of war,' do you say? When have there not been wars, and when have taxes ever been imposed on women, who are exempted by their sex among all mankind? Our mothers did once rise superior to their sex and made contributions when you were in danger of losing the whole empire and the city itself through the conflict with the Carthaginians. But then they contributed voluntarily, not from their landed property, their fields, their dowries, or their houses, without which life is not possible to free women, but only from their own jewellery, and even these not according to fixed valuation, not under fear of informers or accusers, not by force and violence, but what they themselves were willing to give. What alarm is there now for the empire or the country? Let war with the Gauls or the Parthians come, and we shall not be inferior to our mothers in zeal for the common safety; but for civil wars may we never contribute, nor ever assist you against each other! We did not contribute to Caesar or to Pompey. Neither Marius nor Cinna imposed taxes upon us. Nor did Sulla, who held despotic power in the state, do so, whereas you say that you are reestablishing the commonwealth."

While Hortensia thus spoke the triumvirs were angry that women should dare to hold a public meeting when the men were silent; that they should demand from magistrates the reasons for their acts, and themselves not so much as furnish money while the men were serving in the army. They ordered the lictors to drive them away from the tribunal, which they proceeded to do until cries were raised by the multitude outside, when the lictors desisted and the triumvirs said they would postpone till the next day the consideration of the matter. On the following day they reduced the number of women, who were to present a valuation of their property, from 1400 to 400, and decreed that all men who possessed more than 100,000 drachmas, both citizens and strangers, freedmen and priests, and men of all nationalities without a single exception, should (under the same dread of penalty and also of informers) lend them at interest a fiftieth part of their property and contribute one year's income to the war expenses.

FOR FURTHER READING

Glenn, Cheryl. *Rhetoric Retold: Regendering the Tradition from Antiquity through the Renaissance.* Carbondale: Southern Illinois University Press, 1997.

Lefkowitz, Mary R., and Maureen B. Fant. *Women's Life in Greece and Rome: A Sourcebook in Translation.* Baltimore: Johns Hopkins University Press, 1992.

Valerius Maximus, Quintus. *His Collection of the Memorable Acts and Sayings of Orators, Philosophers, Statesmen, and Other Illustrious Persons of the Ancient Romans, and Other Foreign Nations, Upon Various Subjects, Together with the Life of That Famous Historian.* London: 1684.

Heloise

c. 1100–c. 1163

Heloise demonstrated a mastery of philosophy and rhetoric rare for a woman of the twelfth century, and her argument about women and marriage is revolutionary even today. Heloise received her early education through her uncle, Fulbert, a canon of Notre Dame in Paris, and also from Benedictine nuns in the monastery where she spent her childhood. As her intellectual ability became apparent, Fulbert hired the renowned teacher and philosopher Peter Abelard to tutor her. Their relationship became one of the most famous love stories in history, although according to Abelard's own account, his pedagogy and seduction were often coercive and violent. After the birth of their son, they married secretly but, at Abelard's insistence, took up their separate monastic lives. Fulbert, furious with Abelard for dishonoring his family and betraying his trust, arranged for his servants to castrate Abelard—an event, Abelard wrote later, both cruel and redemptive. Both members of the couple became prominent religious authorities, and Abelard is often credited with beginning modern academic philosophical methods. Heloise has often been viewed as the lesser thinker, whose views were merely derivative of other philosophers and whose rhetoric was too emotional to function in the disciplined binary logic that Abelard espoused. But a number of contemporary scholars have reread Heloise's thought and rhetoric as revolutionary and disruptive of her teacher's ideas.

The excerpt here is from one of the letters that Heloise wrote to Abelard as part of their famous exchange. In it she responds personally and passionately after reading his confessional autobiography. But Heloise's letter is more than an emotional outburst from a castoff lover. It also disputes the very foundations of Abelard's teachings on the meaning of religious life, love, and ethics. Heloise's letter joins passionate, assertive, and logical rhetorics to argue against Abelard's view of marriage, his view of the sexuality of women and their roles in marriage. Heloise asserts a woman's personhood beyond the role of wife who exists only with and through her husband when she claims, "The name of wife may seem more sacred or more binding, but sweeter for me will always be the word mistress . . . or whore." Marriage, she argues, carries too much worldly association with wealth, property, and title rather than emulating the elevated friendships, or *gratia*, to which philosophers ought to aspire. In her argument, she demonstrates her knowledge of classical texts such as Cicero's *De amicitia* and she cites the authority of an earlier woman philosopher and rhetorician, Aspasia, on the classical ideals of the philosopher. But in addition to this erudite display, Heloise refuses the fixed oppositional categories that Abelard espouses and instead articulates a nondualistic, wholistic view of soul and body, of passion and reason, and of ethical responsibility and the care involved in human relationships. Philosopher Andrea Nye points to the groundbreaking qualities of Heloise's writing when she asserts that if were they followed, Heloise's thought and rhetoric might lead to an intellectual community that

> would have to accommodate passionate speech that comes from the problematic experience of women and of men. It would be motivated by a concern for mutual understanding that can stabilize and repair relations between persons. Its discussions would be critical and, at the same time, constructive of new forms of understanding . . .informed by Heloise's and Aspasia's wisdom, their subtle, sensitive, mobile, flexible women's tongues. (41)

Using her philosophical wisdom and rhetorical skill, Heloise not only recasts her own position from that of subordinate, seduced student to that of scholar and rhetorician but also asserts an epistemology that resonates with feminist scholars today.

From "Letter I. Heloise to Abelard"

1132

To her master, or rather her father, husband, or rather brother, his handmaid, or rather his daughter, wife, or rather sister; to Abelard, Heloise.

Not long ago, my beloved, by chance someone brought me the letter of consolation you had sent to a friend. I saw at once from the superscription that it was yours, and was all the more eager to read it since the writer is so dear to my heart. I hoped for renewal of strength, at least from the writer's words which would picture for me the reality I have lost. But nearly every line of this letter was filled, I remember, with gall and wormwood, as it told the pitiful story of our entry into religion and the cross of unending suffering which you, my only love, continue to bear.

In that letter you did indeed carry out the promise you made your friend at the beginning, that he would think his own troubles insignificant or nothing, in comparison with your own. First you revealed the persecution you suffered from your teachers, then the supreme treachery of the mutilation of your person, and then described the abominable jealousy and violent attacks of your fellow-students, Alberic of Rheims and Lotulf of Lombardy. You did not gloss over what at their instigation was done to your distinguished theological work or what

Reprinted from *The Letters of Abelard and Heloise,* translated by Betty Radice, 109, 113–15, 117–18. London: Penguin Classics, 1974. Copyright © Betty Radice, 1974. Reproduced by permission of Penguin Books Ltd.

amounted to a prison sentence passed on yourself. Then you went on to the plotting against you by your abbot and false brethren, the serious slanders from those two pseudo-apostles, spread against you by the same rivals, and the scandal stirred up among many people because you had acted contrary to custom in naming your oratory after the Paraclete. You went on to the incessant, intolerable persecutions which you still endure at the hands of that cruel tyrant and the evil monks you call your sons, and so brought your sad story to an end. . . .

You know, beloved, as the whole world knows, how much I have lost in you, how at one wretched stroke of fortune that supreme act of flagrant treachery robbed me of my very self in robbing me of you; and how my sorrow for my loss is nothing compared with what I feel for the manner in which I lost you. Surely the greater the cause for grief the greater the need for the help of consolation, and this no one can bring but you; you are the sole cause of my sorrow, and you alone can grant me the grace of consolation. You alone have the power to make me sad, to bring me happiness or comfort; you alone have so great a debt to repay me, particularly now when I have carried out all your orders so implicitly that when I was powerless to oppose you in anything, I found strength at your command to destroy myself. I did more, strange to say—my love rose to such heights of madness that it robbed itself of what it most desired beyond hope of recovery, when immediately at your bidding I changed my clothing along with my mind, in order to prove you the sole possessor of my body and my will alike. God knows I never sought anything in you except yourself; I wanted simply you, nothing of yours. I looked for no marriage-bond, no marriage portion, and it was not my own pleasures and wishes I sought to gratify, as you well know, but yours. The name of wife may seem more sacred or more binding, but sweeter for me will always be the word mistress, or, if you will permit me, that of concubine or whore. I believed that the more I humbled myself on your account, the more gratitude I should win from you, and also the less damage I should do to the brightness of your reputation.

You yourself on your own account did not altogether forget this in the letter of consolation I have spoken of which you wrote to a friend; there you thought fit to set out some of the reasons I gave in trying to dissuade you from binding us together in an ill-starred marriage. But you kept silent about most of my arguments for preferring love to wedlock and freedom to chains. God is my witness that if Augustus, Emperor of the whole world, thought fit to honour me with marriage and conferred all the earth on me to possess for ever, it would be dearer and more honourable to me to be called not his Empress but your whore.

For a man's worth does not rest on his wealth or power; these depend on fortune, but worth on his merits. And a woman should realize that if she marries a rich man more readily than a poor one, and desires her husband more for his possessions than for himself, she is offering herself for sale. Certainly any woman who comes to marry through desires of this kind deserves wages, not gratitude, for clearly her mind is on the man's property, not himself, and she would be ready to prostitute herself to a richer man, if she could. This is evident from the argument put forward in the dialogue of Aeschines Socraticus by the learned Aspasia to Xenophon and his wife. When she had expounded it in an effort to bring about a reconciliation between them, she ended with these words: "Unless you come to believe that there is no better man nor worthier woman on earth you will always still be looking for what you judge the best thing of all—to be the husband of the best of wives and the wife of the best of husbands."

These are saintly words which are more than philosophic; indeed, they deserve the name of wisdom, not philosophy. It is a holy error and a blessed delusion between man and wife, when perfect love can keep the ties of marriage unbroken not so much through bodily continence as chastity of spirit. But what error permitted other women, plain truth permitted me, and what they thought of their husbands, the world in general believed, or rather, knew to be true of yourself; so that my love for you was the more genuine for being further removed from error. What king or philosopher could match your fame? What district, town or village did not long to see you? When you appeared in public, who did not hurry to catch a glimpse of you, or crane his neck and strain his eyes to follow your departure? Every wife, every young girl desired you in absence and was on fire in your presence; queens and great ladies envied me my joys and my bed. . . .

Remember, I implore you, what I have done, and think how much you owe me. While I enjoyed with you the pleasures of the flesh, many were uncertain whether I was prompted by love or lust; but now the end is proof of the beginning. I have finally denied myself every pleasure in obedience to your will, kept nothing for myself except to prove that now, even more, I am yours. Consider then your injustice, if when I deserve more you give me less, or rather, nothing at all, especially when it is a small thing I ask of you and one you could so easily grant. And so, in the name of God to whom you have dedicated yourself, I beg you to restore your presence to me in the way you can—by writing me some word of comfort, so that in this at least I may find increased strength and readiness to serve God. When in the past you sought me out for sinful pleasures your letters came to me thick and fast, and your many songs put your Heloise on everyone's lips, so that every street and house echoed with my name. Is it not far better now to summon me to God than it was then to satisfy our lust? I beg you, think what you owe me, give ear to my pleas and I will finish a long letter with a brief ending: farewell, my only love.

FOR FURTHER READING

Desmond, Marilynn. "Dominus/Ancilla, Rhetorical Subjectivity and Sexual Violence in the Letters of Heloise." In *The Tongue of the Fathers: Gender and Ideology in Twelfth Cen-*

tury Latin, edited by David Townsend and Andrew Taylor, 35–54. Philadelphia: University of Pennsylvania Press, 1997.

Kamuf, Peggy. *Fictions of Feminine Desire.* Lincoln: University of Nebraska Press, 1982.

Nye, Andrea. "A Woman's Thought or a Man's Discipline?" In *Hypatia's Daughters: Fifteen Hundred Years of Women Philosophers,* edited by Linda Lopez McAlister, 25–47. Bloomington: Indiana University Press, 1996.

Radice, Betty. "Heloise: the French Scholar-Lover." In *Medieval Women Writers,* edited by Katharina M. Wilson, 90–108. Athens: University of Georgia Press, 1984.

Julian of Norwich

1343–1415

Throughout the Middle Ages, Christian theology was written, preached, and interpreted by men who saw God as the father who judged and punished his children. Consequently, this medieval Christian doctrine also created the culture's views of women. Women were held responsible, via Eve, for the fall of humankind, and their natural state was viewed as that of temptress and deceiver. Subsequently, privileged white women were expected to be pure, virginal, and above all, silent. Julian of Norwich challenged the last of these ideas by writing *Revelations of Divine Love*, the earliest extant writing in English by a woman.

Scholars know little of Julian's background. It is believed that she was born about the same time as Chaucer (1343) and that she lived as an anchorite in the English city of Norwich. In 1373, Julian fell seriously ill. During this illness, she received a series of sixteen "showings," or revelations, from God. After her recovery, she spent many years reflecting on these events, and they provide the content of her book. These revelations center on the physical sufferings of Christ and his silent, grieving mother, Mary, as well as on Julian's responses to those visions. Writing in English, using the first-person "I," Julian challenged the teaching of the medieval church, which held that women could not and should not interpret Scripture, much less teach and write seriously—if at all. In her commentary on women in the history of rhetoric, Cheryl Glenn notes that the *Revelations* subvert traditional medieval Christianity by enacting a dialectical relationship with God.

In the excerpts included here, Julian figures God as both mother and father, attributing to Christ the attributes of both woman and man and achieving what Glenn calls a rhetoric of "inclusion" (99). Julian's shocking rendering of Christ as a woman expands Christian doctrine in radical ways and asserts, by extension, the rightful place of women not only as worshipers but also as interpreters and preachers of scripture.

From *Revelations of Divine Love*

C. 1390S

In the chosen, wickedness is turned into blessedness through mercy and grace, for the nature of God is to do good for evil, through Jesus, our mother in kind grace; and the soul which is highest in virtue is the meekest, that being the ground from which we gain other virtues.

And we have all this blessedness through mercy and grace; a kind of blessedness which we might never have known if the quality of goodness which is God had not been opposed. It is by this means that we gain this blessedness; for wickedness has been allowed to rise and oppose goodness, and the goodness of mercy and grace has opposed wickedness and turned it all to goodness and glory for all those who shall be saved; for it is the nature of God to do good for evil.

Thus Jesus Christ who does good for evil is our true mother; we have our being from him where the ground of motherhood begins, with all the sweet protection of love which follows eternally. God is our mother as truly as he is our father; and he showed this in everything, and especially in the sweet words where he says, 'It is I', that is to say, 'It is I: the power and goodness of fatherhood. It is I: the wisdom of motherhood. It is I: the light and the grace which is all blessed love. It is I: the Trinity. It is I: the unity. I am the sovereign goodness of all manner of things. It is I that make you love. It is I that make you long. It is I: the eternal: fulfilment of all true desires.'

For the soul is highest, noblest and worthiest when it is lowest, humblest and gentlest; and from this essential ground we all have our virtues and our sensory being by gift of nature and with the help and assistance of grace, without which we could gain nothing. Our great father, God almighty, who is Being, knew and loved us from before the beginning of time. And from his knowledge, in his marvellously deep love and through the eternal foreseeing counsel of the whole blessed Trinity, he wanted the second Person to become our mother, our brother, our savior. From this it follows that God is our mother as truly as God is our father. Our Father wills, our Mother works, our good lord the Holy Ghost confirms. And therefore it behoves us to love our God in whom we have our being, reverently thanking and praising him for our creation, praying hard to our Mother for mercy and pity, and to our lord the Holy Ghost for help and grace; for our whole life is in these three—nature, mercy and grace; from them we have humility, gentleness, patience and pity, and hatred of sin and wickedness;

for it is a natural attribute of virtues to hate sin and wickedness. And so Jesus is our true mother by nature, at our first creation, and he is our true mother in grace by taking on our created nature. All the fair work and all the sweet, kind service of beloved motherhood is made proper to the second Person; for in him this godly will is kept safe and whole everlasting, both in nature and in grace, out of his very own goodness.

I understood three ways of seeing motherhood in God: the first is that he is the ground of our natural creation, the second is the taking on of our nature (and there the motherhood of grace begins), the third is the motherhood of works, and in this there is, by the same grace, an enlargement of length and breadth and height and deepness without end, and all is his own love.

How we are redeemed and enlarged by the mercy and grace of our sweet, kind and ever-loving mother Jesus; and of the properties of motherhood; but Jesus is our true mother, feeding us not with milk, but with himself, opening his side for us and claiming all our love.

But now it is necessary to say a little more about this enlargement, as I understand it our Lord's meaning, how we are redeemed by the motherhood of mercy and grace and brought back into it our natural dwelling where we were made by the motherhood of natural love; a natural love which never leaves us. Our natural Mother, our gracious Mother (for he wanted to become our mother completely in every way), undertook to begin his work very humbly and very gently in the Virgin's womb. And he showed this in the first revelation, where he brought that humble maiden before my mind's eye in the girlish form she had when she conceived; that is to say, our great God, the most sovereign wisdom of all, was raised in this humble place and dressed himself in our poor flesh to do the service and duties of motherhood in every way. The mother's service is the closest, the most helpful and the most sure, for it is the most faithful. No one ever might, nor could, nor has performed this service fully but he alone. We know that our mothers only bring us into the world to suffer and die, but our true mother, Jesus, he who is all love, bears us into joy and eternal life; blessed may he be! So he sustains us within himself in love and was in labour for the full time until he suffered the sharpest pangs and the most grievous sufferings that ever were or shall be, and at the last he died. And when it was finished and he had born us to bliss, even this could not fully satisfy his marvellous love; and that he showed in these high surpassing words of love, 'If I could suffer more, I would suffer more.'

He could not die any more, but he would not stop working. So next he had to feed us, for a mother's dear love has made him our debtor. The mother can give her child her milk to suck, but our dear mother Jesus can feed us with himself, and he does so most generously and most tenderly with the holy sacrament which is the precious food of life itself. And with all the sweet sacraments he sustains us most mercifully and most graciously. And this is what he meant in those blessed words when he said, 'It is I that Holy Church preaches and teaches to you'; that is to say, 'All the health and life of the sacraments, all the power and grace of my word, all the goodness which is ordained in Holy Church for you, it is I.'

The mother can lay the child tenderly to her breast, but our tender mother Jesus, he can familiarly lead us into his blessed breast through his sweet open side, and show us within part of the Godhead and the joys of heaven, which spiritual certainty of endless bliss; and that was shown in the tenth revelation, giving the same understanding in the sweet words where he says, 'Look how I love you', looking into his side and rejoicing. This fair, lovely word 'mother', it is so sweet and so tender in itself that it cannot truly be said of any but of him, and of her who is the true mother of him and of everyone. To the nature of motherhood belong tender love, wisdom and knowledge, and it is good, for although the birth of our body is only low, humble and modest compared with the birth of our soul, yet it is he who does it in the beings by whom it is done. The kind, loving mother who knows and recognizes the need of her child, she watches over it most tenderly, as the nature and condition of motherhood demands. And as it grows in age her actions change, although her love does not. And as it grows older still, she allows it to be beaten to break down vices so that the child may gain in virtue and grace. These actions, with all that is fair and good, our Lord performs them through those by whom they are done. Thus he is our natural mother through the work of grace in the lower part, for love of the higher part. And he wants us to know it; for he wants all our love to be bound to him. And in this I saw that all the debt we owe, at God's bidding, for his fatherhood and motherhood, is fulfilled by loving God truly; a blessed love which Christ arouses in us. And this was shown in everything, and especially in the great, generous words where he says, 'It is I that you love.'

FOR FURTHER READING

Glenn, Cheryl. *Rhetoric Retold: Regendering the Tradition from Antiquity through the Renaissance.* Carbondale: Southern Illinois University Press, 1997.

Jacoff, Rachel. "God as Mother: Julian of Norwich's Theology of Love." *University of Denver Quarterly* 18 (1983–84): 134–39.

McNamer, Sarah. "The Exploratory Image: God as Mother in Julian of Norwich's Revelations of Divine Love." *Mystics Quarterly* 15 (1989): 21–28.

Ward, Benedicta. "Lady Julian and Her Audience: 'Mine Even-Christian.'" In *The English Religious Tradition and the Genius of Anglicanism*, edited by Geoffrey Rowell, 47–63. London: Oxford University Press, 1992.

Catherine of Siena

Saint Catherine of Siena always wanted to be a preacher. Although Catholic doctrine during the Middle Ages forbade women from mounting the pulpit, Catherine nonetheless prevailed in her own way—by caring for the poor and the sick as a Dominican laywoman; by traveling throughout Italy passionately defending the papacy in the face of the Great Schism of 1378; and, most significantly of all, by dictating nearly four hundred letters to a wide-ranging audience of public figures and private correspondents. She counseled popes and royalty as well as friends and strangers, always insisting on the unity of the Church and the moral integrity of its teachings. Her efforts and accomplishments led the Catholic church in 1970 to grant her the title of Doctor of the Roman Catholic Church—a title she and Teresa of Ávila were simultaneously the first women to bear.

Saint Catherine was born in Siena in 1347. The twenty-fourth of twenty-five children, uneducated, Catherine received a vision of Christ at the age of six and resolved to dedicate her life to God. Subsequently she took a vow of chastity and solitude. In 1364, she was admitted to the Mantellate, a group of Dominican laywomen. Here, Catherine learned to read and, like the English mystic Julian of Norwich, lived in almost total silence and solitude. In 1368, she experienced what she called "a mystical espousal of God" that led her to a realization that love for God also entailed a love and care for others (*Letters* 2). Consequently, she emerged from the Mantellate and began helping the poor and the sick. Shortly afterwards, in 1370, Catherine began dictating letters to various scribes. Her letters were intended to reach across the entire political and religious arena of her time; moreover, they are the first example of writing in Italian by a woman at a time when Latin was considered the only language suitable for politics or religion. In the introduction to the collected edition of Catherine's letters, Suzanne Noffke says that "her letters show a woman moving with a powerful freedom within a culture that ordinarily held women in quiet subservience unless they happened to be born or married into positions of power" (7). Catherine eventually moved to Rome in 1379, where a group of her disciples lived with her in a community. She died there in 1380 at the age of 33.

Noffke also notes the sermon-like style of Catherine's letters. "Though laced with marvelously effective and largely original imagery," Noffke writes, "it is a style not poetic but oratorical—the style, really, of the preacher she had wanted even from childhood to be" (8). Catherine's letter to her mother, Mona Lapa, is an apt example of this form. In the letter, Catherine explains to her mother why she left her home in Siena to become a Dominican. She tells her it was God's will, and she notes that while her mother gave birth to her body, God gave birth to her spirit. Also, she reminds her mother that Mona was glad for Catherine's brother when he left home "for the sake of material gain . . . to win temporal wealth. But now when it is a question of winning eternal life it seems to be so hard that you say you are going to go to pieces." This moralizing and accusatory tone, pronounced with the conviction of a preacher, resonates with the style of many medieval sermons. In other words, even though Catherine was unable to preach from an institutionally sanctioned position, she was able, through her letters, to make her voice heard.

"Letter 83: To Mona Lapa, her mother, in Siena"

1376

In the name of Jesus Christ crucified and of gentle Mary.

Dearest mother in Christ gentle Jesus,

Your poor unworthy daughter Caterina wants to comfort you in the precious blood of God's Son. How I have longed to see you truly the mother of my soul as well as of my body! For I know that if you love my soul more than you love my body, any excessive attachment you may have will die, and my physical absence won't be so wearing on you. No, it will even bring you consolation, and you will be ready to bear any burden for God's honor, knowing that I am being used for that same honor. So long as I am working for God's honor, my soul can't fail to grow in grace and in virtue; so really, dearest mother, if you do love my soul more than my body, you'll not be dejected, but consoled.

I want you to learn from that sweet mother Mary, who for God's honor and our salvation gave us her Son, dead on the wood of the most holy cross. When Mary was left alone after Christ had ascended into heaven, she stayed with the holy disciples; and then she willingly agreed to *their* leaving, for her Son's glory and praise and for the good of the whole world, even though it was wrenching, since they had been a great consolation to each other. She chose the pain of their departure over the consolation of their staying, and this only because of her love for God's honor and our salvation. Now it is from her I want you to learn, dearest mother. You know that I must follow God's will, and I know that you want me to follow it. It was God's will that I go away—and my going was not without mystery, nor without worthwhile results. It was also God's will

Reprinted with permission from *The Letters of St. Catherine of Siena*, translated by Suzanne Noffke, O.P., 252–53. Binghamton: Medieval and Renaissance Texts and Studies, State University of New York, 1988.

that I remain away; it was no mere human decision, and whoever says anything else is lying. And so I must go in the future, following in his footsteps however and whenever it shall please his boundless goodness.

You, my good sweet mother, ought to be happy rather than dejected over having to bear any burden for God's honor and for your salvation and mine. You were glad, I remember, for the sake of material gain when your sons left home to win temporal wealth. But now when it is a question of winning eternal life it seems to be so hard that you say you are going to go to pieces if I don't answer you soon. All this because you love the part of me that I got from you (I mean your flesh, in which you clothed me) more than you love the part of me that I got from God. Lift, lift up your heart and affection a bit to that dear most holy cross, where every burden becomes light. Be willing to put up with a little finite suffering to escape the infinite suffering we deserve for our sins. Take heart now, for love of Christ crucified! And don't imagine that God has forsaken you, or I either. You will in fact be consoled, and that completely. However great the pain may have been, the joy will certainly be greater.

With God's grace, we will be coming home soon. We would be there already had we not been held up by Neri's being very ill. Maestro Giovanni and Frate Bartolomeo have also been ill. . . .

I'll say no more. Give our greetings. . . . Keep living in God's holy and tender love. Gentle Jesus! Jesus love!

FOR FURTHER READING

Fatula, Mary Ann. *Catherine of Siena's Way.* Wilmington, Del.: M. Glazier, 1987.
Petroff, Elizabeth. *Body and Soul: Essays on Medieval Women and Mysticism.* New York: Oxford University Press, 1994.

Christine de Pizan

1365–1430

The words "Je, Christine" ("I, Christine"), repeated throughout Christine de Pizan's work and especially in *The Book of the City of Ladies,* are, Maureen Quilligan says, "a signal mark of Christine's authority, a 'signature' in more ways than one" (12). Christine de Pizan's claim to authority marks her use of innovative rhetorical conventions and her position as the first woman to support herself by writing—as one of the pioneers in women's rhetorical history.

Christine began her career as a writer in Paris after the death of King Charles V, whom her father had served as physician and astrologer. When her father and her husband both died, leaving her to support her family, she turned to writing poetry and ballads and soon achieved fame and powerful patrons. With the publication of her critical commentary on *Roman de la Rose* she made a conscious shift from poetry to social commentary, joining the Renaissance debate about the social roles of women. *The Book of the City of Ladies,* modeled on Augustine's *Civitate Dei,* expands her arguments against the anti-woman writing of her time and joins a tradition of women's writing that would continue throughout the Renaissance and into the seventeenth century with Jane Anger, Rachel Speght, and, in the Americas, Sor Juana Inés de la Cruz. Like these women writers, Christine claimed the authority to "talk back" to men and challenged and resisted misogynist representations of women as evil, inferior, defective, and deficient, instead claiming women's rights to respect, to education, and to public speech and writing. She expanded the arguments against women's oppression beyond those based on women's religious virtue. Women's subjugation, she asserted, is also contrary to the goals of an ideal society.

The Book of the City of Ladies is an allegorical conversation set in motion as Christine questions why God would create the vile creature, woman, depicted for centuries by philosophers as "inclined to and full of every vice." In answer to her fervent question, three ladies—personifications of Reason, Rectitude, and Justice—appear, commissioning her to build a city of ladies, to restore women to their rightful position of nobility and dignity so that "from now on, ladies and all valiant women may have a refuge and defense against the various assailants." Structured as a formal conversation with the three ladies, Christine's work reconstructs the history of women, celebrating women's virtue in contrast to the misogynist claims against women that prompted her to question God in the first place. Christine establishes her intellectual authority and the authority of her experience as she creates an alternative history of women by demonstrating their wisdom and nobility and the foolishness of men who attack them.

From *The Book of the City of Ladies*

1404

1. Here begins the book of the city of ladies, whose first chapter tells why and for what purpose this book was written.

1.1.1

One day as I was sitting alone in my study surrounded by books on all kinds of subjects, devoting myself to literary studies, my usual habit, my mind dwelt at length on the weighty opinions of various authors whom I had studied for a long time. I looked up from my book, having decided to leave such subtle questions in peace and to relax by reading some light poetry. With this in mind, I searched for some small book. By chance a strange volume came into my hands, not one of my own, but one which had been given to me along with some others. When I held it open and saw from its title page that it was by Mathéolus, I smiled, for though I had never seen it before, I had often heard that like other books, it discussed respect for women. I thought I would browse through it to amuse myself. I had not been reading for very long when my good mother called me to refresh myself with some supper, for it was evening. Intending to look at it the next day, I put it down. The next morning, again seated in my study as was my habit, I remembered wanting to examine this book by Mathéolus. I started to read it and went on for a little while. Because the subject seemed to me not very pleasant for people who do not enjoy lies, and of no use in developing virtue or manners, given its lack of integrity in diction and theme, and after browsing here and there and reading the end, I put it down in order to turn my attention to more elevated and useful study. But just the sight of this book, even though it was of no authority, made me wonder how it happened that so many different men—and learned men among them—have been and are so inclined to express both in speaking and in their treatises and writings so many wicked insults about women and their behavior. Not only one or two and not even just this Mathéolus (for this book had a bad name anyway and was intended as a satire) but, more generally, judging from the treatises of all philosophers and poets and from all the orators—it would take too long to

Selection by Christine de Pizan from *The Book of the City of Ladies*. Trans. Earl Jeffrey Richards. New York: Persea Press, Copyright 1982, 1998. Sections I.1.1–I.3.3 and I.8.1–I.8.10. Reprinted by permission of Persea Books, Inc. (New York).

mention their names—it seems that they all speak from one and the same mouth. They all concur in one conclusion: that the behavior of women is inclined to and full of every vice. Thinking deeply about these matters, I began to examine my character and conduct as a natural woman and, similarly, I considered other women whose company I frequently kept, princesses, great ladies, women of the middle and lower classes, who had graciously told me of their most private and intimate thoughts, hoping that I could judge impartially and in good conscience whether the testimony of so many notable men could be true. To the best of my knowledge, no matter how long I confronted or dissected the problem, I could not see or realize how their claims could be true when compared to the natural behavior and character of women. Yet I still argued vehemently against women, saying that it would be impossible that so many famous men—such solemn scholars, possessed of such deep and great understanding, so clear-sighted in all things, as it seemed—could have spoken falsely on so many occasions that I could hardly find a book on morals where, even before I had read it in its entirety, I did not find several chapters or certain sections attacking women, no matter who the author was. This reason alone, in short, made me conclude that, although my intellect did not perceive my own great faults and, likewise, those of other women because of its simpleness and ignorance, it was however truly fitting that such was the case. And so I relied more on the judgment of others than on what I myself felt and knew. I was so transfixed in this line of thinking for such a long time that it seemed as if I were in a stupor. Like a gushing fountain, a series of authorities, whom I recalled one after another, came to mind, along with their opinions on this topic. And I finally decided that God formed a vile creature when He made woman, and I wondered how such a worthy artisan could have deigned to make such an abominable work which, from what they say, is the vessel as well as the refuge and abode of every evil and vice. As I was thinking this, a great unhappiness and sadness welled up in my heart, for I detested myself and the entire feminine sex, as though we were monstrosities in nature. And in my lament I spoke these words:

I.1.2

"Oh, God, how can this be? For unless I stray from my faith, I must never doubt that Your infinite wisdom and most perfect goodness ever created anything which was not good. Did You yourself not create woman in a very special way and since that time did You not give her all those inclinations which it pleased You for her to have? And how could it be that You could go wrong in anything? Yet look at all these accusations which have been judged, decided, and concluded against women, I do not know how to understand this repugnance. If it is so, fair Lord God, that in fact so many abominations abound in the female sex, for You Yourself say that the testimony of two or three witnesses lends credence, why shall I not doubt that this is true? Alas, God, why did You not let me be born in the world as a man, so that all my inclinations would be to serve You better, and so that I would not stray in anything and would be as perfect as a man is said to be? But since Your kindness has not been extended to me, then forgive my negligence in Your service, most fair Lord God, and may it not displease You, for the servant who receives fewer gifts from his lord is less obliged in his service." I spoke these words to God in my lament and a great deal more for a very long time in sad reflection, and in my folly I considered myself most unfortunate because God had made me inhabit a female body in this world.

2. Here Christine describes how three ladies appeared to her and how the one who was in front spoke first and comforted her in her pain,

I.2.1

So occupied with these painful thoughts, my head bowed in shame, my eyes filled with tears, leaning on the pommel of my chair's armrest, I suddenly saw a ray of light fall on my lap, as though it were the sun. I shuddered then, as if wakened from sleep, for I was sitting in a shadow where the sun could not have shone at that hour. And as I lifted my head to see where this light was coming from, I saw three crowned ladies standing before me, and the splendor of their bright faces shone on me and throughout the entire room. Now no one would ask whether I was surprised, for my doors were shut and they had still entered. Fearing that some phantom had come to tempt me and filled with great fright, I made the Sign of the Cross on my forehead.

I.2.2

Then she who was the first of the three smiled and began to speak, "Dear daughter, do not be afraid, for we have not come here to harm or trouble you but to console you, for we have taken pity on your distress, and we have come to bring you out of the ignorance which so blinds your own intellect that you shun what you know for a certainty and believe what you do not know or see or recognize except by virtue of many strange opinions. You resemble the fool in the prank who was dressed in women's clothes while he slept; because those who were making fun of him repeatedly told him he was a woman, he believed their false testimony more readily than the certainty of his own identity. Fair daughter, have you lost all sense? Have you forgotten that when fine gold is tested in the furnace, it does not change or vary in strength but becomes purer the more it is hammered and handled in different ways? Do you not know that the best things are the most debated and the most discussed? If you wish to consider the question of the highest form of reality, which consists in ideas or celestial substances, consider whether the greatest philosophers who have lived and whom you support against your own sex ever resolved whether ideas are false and contrary to the truth. Notice how these same philosophers contradict and criticize one another, just as you have seen in the *Metaphysics* where Aristotle takes their opinions to task and speaks similarly of Plato and other philosophers. And note, moreover, how even Saint Augustine and the Doctors of the Church have criticized Aristotle in certain passages, although he is known as the prince of philosophers in whom both natural and moral philosophy attained their highest level. It also seems that you think that all the words of the philosophers are articles of faith, that they could never be wrong. As far as the poets of whom you speak are concerned, do you not know that they spoke on many subjects in a fictional way and that often they mean the contrary of what their words openly say? One can interpret them according to the grammatical figure of *antiphrasis,* which means, as you know, that if you call something bad, in fact, it is good, and also vice versa. Thus I advise you to profit from their works and to interpret them in the manner in which they are intended in those passages where they attack women. Perhaps this man, who called himself Mathéolus in his own book, intended it in such a way, for there are many things which, if taken literally, would be pure heresy. As for the attack against the estate of marriage—which is a holy estate, worthy and ordained by God—made not only by Mathéolus but also by others and even by the *Romance of the Rose* where greater credibility is averred because of the authority of its author, it is evident and proven by experience that the contrary of the evil which they posit and claim to be found in this estate through the obligation and fault of women is true. For where has the husband ever been found who would allow his wife to have authority to abuse and insult him as a matter of course, as these authorities maintain? I believe that, regardless of what you might have read, you will never see such a husband with your own eyes, so badly colored are these lies. Thus, in conclusion, I tell you, dear friend, that simplemindedness has prompted you to hold such an opinion. Come back to yourself, recover your senses, and do not trouble yourself anymore over such absurdities. For you know that any evil spoken of women so generally only hurts those who say it, not women themselves."

3. Here Christine tells how the lady who had said this showed her who she was and what her character and function were and told her how she would construct a city with the help of these same three ladies.

I.3.1

The famous lady spoke these words to me, in whose presence I do not know which one of my senses was more overwhelmed: my hearing from having listened to such worthy words or my sight from having seen her radiant beauty, her attire, her reverent comportment, and her most honored countenance. The same was true of the others, so that I did not know which one to look at, for the three ladies resembled each other so much that they could be told apart only with difficulty, except for the last one, for although she was of no less authority than the others, she had so fierce a visage that whoever, no matter how daring, looked in her eyes would be afraid to commit a crime, for it seemed that she threatened criminals unceasingly. Having stood up out of respect, I looked at them without saying a word, like someone too overwhelmed to utter a syllable. Reflecting on who these beings could be, I felt much admiration in my heart and, if I could have dared, I would have immediately asked their names and identities and what was the meaning of the different scepters which each one carried in her right hand, which were of fabulous richness, and why they had come here. But since I considered myself unworthy to address these questions to such high ladies as they appeared to me, I did not dare to, but continued to keep my gaze fixed on them, half-afraid and half-reassured by the words which I had heard, which had made me reject my first impression. But the most wise lady who had spoken to me and who knew in her mind what I was thinking, as one who has insight into everything, addressed my reflections, saying:

I.3.2

"Dear daughter, know that God's providence, which leaves nothing void or empty, has ordained that we, though celestial beings, remain and circulate among the people of the world here below, in order to bring order and maintain in balance those institutions we created according to the will of God in the ful-fillment of various offices, that God whose daughters we three all are and from whom we were born. Thus it is my duty to straighten out men and women when they go astray and to put them back on the right path. And when they stray, if they have enough understanding to see me, I come to them quietly in spirit and preach to them, showing them their error and how they have failed, I assign them the causes, and then I teach them what to do and what to avoid. Since I serve to demonstrate clearly and to show both in thought and deed to each man and woman his or her own special qualities and faults, you see me holding this shiny mirror which I carry in my right hand in place of a scepter. I would thus have you know truly that no one can look into this mirror, no matter what kind of creature, without achieving clear self-knowledge. My mir-ror has such great dignity that not without reason is it surrounded by rich and precious gems, so that you see, thanks to this mirror, the essences, qualities, proportions, and measures of all things are known, nor can anything be done well without it. And because, similarly, you wish to know what are the offices of my other sisters whom you see here, each will reply in her own person about her name and character, and this way our testimony will be all the more certain to you. But now I myself will declare the reason for our coming. I must assure you, as we do nothing without good cause, that our appearance here is not at all in vain. For, although we are not common to many places and our knowledge does not come to all people, nevertheless you, for your great love of investigat-ing the truth through long and continual study, for which you come here, soli-tary and separated from the world, you have deserved and deserve, our devoted friend, to be visited and consoled by us in your agitation and sadness so that you might also see clearly, in the midst of the darkness of your thoughts, those things which taint and trouble your heart."

I.3.3

"There is another greater and even more special reason for our coming which you will learn from our speeches: in fact we have come to vanquish from the world the same error into which you had fallen, so that from now on, ladies and all valiant women may have a refuge and defense against the various assailants, those ladies who have been abandoned for so long, exposed like a field without a surrounding hedge, without finding a champion to afford them an adequate defense, notwithstanding those noble men who are required by order of law to protect them, who by negligence and apathy have allowed them to be mistreated. It is no wonder then that their jealous enemies, those outrageous villains who have assailed them with various weapons, have been victorious in a war in which women have had no defense. Where is there a city so strong which could not be taken immediately if no resistance were forthcoming, or the law case, no matter how unjust, which was not won through the obstinance of someone pleading without opposition? And the simple, noble ladies, following the example of suffering which God commands, have cheerfully suffered the great attacks which, both in the spoken and the written word, have been wrongfully and sinfully perpetrated against women by men who all the while appealed to God for the right to do so. Now it is time for their just cause to be taken from Pharaoh's hands, and for this reason, we three ladies whom you see here, moved by pity, have come to you to announce a particular edifice built like a city wall, strongly constructed and well founded, which has been predestined and established by our aid and counsel for you to build, where no one will reside except all ladies of fame and women worthy of praise, for the walls of the city will be closed to those women who lack virtue."

8. Here Christine tells how, under reason's command and assistance, she began to excavate the earth and lay the foundation.

I.8.1

Then Lady Reason responded and said, "Get up, daughter! Without waiting any longer, let us go to the Field of Letters. There the City of Ladies will be founded on a flat and fertile plain, where all fruits and freshwater rivers are found and where the earth abounds in all good things. Take the pick of your understanding and dig and clear out a great ditch wherever you see the marks of my ruler, and I will help you carry away the earth on my own shoulders."

I.8.2

I immediately stood up to obey her commands and, thanks to these three ladies, I felt stronger and lighter than before. She went ahead, and I followed behind, and after we had arrived at this field I began to excavate and dig, following her marks with the pick of cross-examination. And this was my first work:

1.8.3

"Lady, I remember well what you told me before, dealing with the subject of how so many men have attacked and continue to attack the behavior of women, that gold becomes more refined the longer it stays in the furnace, which means the more women have been wrongfully attacked, the greater waxes the merit of their glory. But please tell me why and for what reason different authors have spoken against women in their books, since I already know from you that this is wrong; tell me if Nature makes man so inclined or whether they do it out of hatred and where does this behavior come from?"

Then she replied, "Daughter, to give you a way of entering into the question more deeply, I will carry away this first basketful of dirt. This behavior most certainly does not come from Nature, but rather is contrary to Nature, for no connection in the world is as great or as strong as the great love which, through the will of God, Nature places between a man and a woman. The causes which have moved and which still move men to attack women, even those authors in those books, are diverse and varied, just as you have discovered. For some have attacked women with good intentions, that is, in order to draw men who have gone astray away from the company of vicious and dissolute women, with whom they might be infatuated, or in order to keep these men from going mad on account of such women, and also so that every man might avoid an obscene and lustful life. They have attacked all women in general because they believe that women are made up of every abomination."

"My lady," I said then, "excuse me for interrupting you here, but have such authors acted well, since they were prompted by a laudable intention? For intention, the saying goes, judges the man."

"That is a misleading position, my good daughter," she said, "for such sweeping ignorance never provides an excuse. If someone killed you with good intention but out of foolishness, would this then be justified? Rather, those who did this, whoever they might be, would have invoked the wrong law; causing any damage or harm to one party in order to help another party is not justice, and likewise attacking all feminine conduct is contrary to the truth, just as I will show you with a hypothetical case. Let us suppose they did this intending to draw fools away from foolishness. It would be as if I attacked fire—a very good and necessary element nevertheless—because some people burnt themselves, or water because someone drowned. The same can be said of all good things which can be used well or used badly. But one must not attack them if fools abuse them, and you have yourself touched on this point quite well elsewhere in your writings. But those who have spoken like this so abundantly—whatever their intentions might be—have formulated their arguments rather loosely only to make their point. Just like someone who has a long and wide robe cut from a very large piece of cloth when the material costs him nothing and when no one opposes him, they exploit the rights of others. But just as you have said elsewhere, if these writers had only looked for the ways in which men can be led away from foolishness and could have been kept from tiring themselves in attacking the life and behavior of immoral and dissolute women—for to tell the straight truth, there is nothing which should be avoided more than an evil, dissolute, and perverted woman, who is like a monster in nature, a counterfeit estranged from her natural condition, which must be simple, tranquil, and upright—then I would grant you that they would have built a supremely excellent work. But I can assure you that these attacks on all women—when in fact there are so many excellent women—have never originated with me, Reason, and that all who subscribe to them have failed totally and will continue to fail. So now throw aside these black, dirty, and uneven stones from your work, for they will never be fitted into the fair edifice of your City."

1.8.4

"Other men have attacked women for other reasons: such reproach has occurred to some men because of their own vices and others have been moved by the defects of their own bodies, others through pure jealousy, still others by the pleasure they derive in their own personalities from slander. Others, in order to show they have read many authors, base their own writings on what they have found in books and repeat what other writers have said and cite different authors."

1.8.5

"Those who attack women because of their own vices are men who spent their youths in dissolution and enjoyed the love of many different women, used deception in many of their encounters, and have grown old in their sins without repenting, and now regret their past follies and the dissolute life they led. But Nature, which allows the will of the heart to put into effect what the powerful appetite desires, has grown cold in them. Therefore they are pained when they see that their 'good times' have now passed them by, and it seems to them that the young, who are now what they once were, are on top of the world. They do not know how to overcome their sadness except by attacking women, hoping to make women less attractive to other men. Everywhere one sees such old men speak obscenely and dishonestly, just as you can fully see with Mathéolus, who himself confesses that he was an impotent old man filled with desire. You can thereby convincingly prove, with this one example, how what I tell you is true, and you can assuredly believe that it is the same with many others."

1.8.6

"But these corrupt old men, like an incurable leprosy, are not the upstanding men of old whom I made perfect in virtue and wisdom—for not all men share in such corrupt desire, and it would be a real shame if it were so. The mouths of these good men, following their hearts, are all filled with exemplary, honest, and discreet words. These same men detest misdeeds and slander, and neither attack nor defame men and women, and they counsel the avoidance of evil and the pursuit of virtue and the straight path."

I.8.7

"Those men who are moved by the defect of their own bodies have impotent and deformed limbs but sharp and malicious minds. They have found no other way to avenge the pain of their impotence except by attacking women who bring joy to many. Thus they have thought to divert others away from the pleasure which they cannot personally enjoy."

I.8.8

"Those men who have attacked women out of jealousy are those wicked ones who have seen and realized that many women have greater understanding and are more noble in conduct than they themselves, and thus they are pained and disdainful. Because of this, their overweening jealousy has prompted them to attack all women, intending to demean and diminish the glory and praise of such women, just like the man—I cannot remember which one—who tries to prove in his work, *De philosophia*, that it is not fitting that some men have revered women and says that those men who have made so much of women pervert the title of his book: they transform 'philosophy,' the love of wisdom, into 'philofolly,' the love of folly. But I promise and swear to you that he himself, all throughout the lie-filled deductions of his argument, transformed the content of his book into a true philofolly."

I.8.9

"As for those men who are naturally given to slander, it is not surprising that they slander women since they attack everyone anyway. Nevertheless, I assure you that any man who freely slanders does so out of a great wickedness of heart, for he is acting contrary to reason and contrary to Nature: contrary to reason insofar as he is most ungrateful and fails to recognize the good deeds which women have done for him, so great that he could never make up for them, no matter how much he try, and which he continuously needs women to perform for him; and contrary to Nature in that there is no naked beast anywhere, nor bird, which does not naturally love its female counterpart. It is thus quite unnatural when a reasonable man does the contrary."

I.8.10

"And just as there has never been any work so worthy, so skilled is the craftsman who made it, that there were not people who wanted, and want, to counterfeit it, there are many who wish to get involved in writing poetry. They believe they cannot go wrong, since others have written in books what they take the situation to be, or rather, *mis*-take the situation—as I well know! Some of them undertake to express themselves by writing poems of water without salt, such as these, or ballads without feeling, discussing the behavior of women or of princes or of other people, while they themselves do not know how to recognize or to correct their own servile conduct and inclinations. But simple people, as ignorant as they are, declare that such writing is the best in the world."

FOR FURTHER READING

de Pizan, Christine. *The Treasure of the City of Ladies: or The Book of the Three Virtues.* Translated by Sarah Lawson. London: Penguin Books Ltd., 1985.

Green, Karen. "Christine De Pizan and Thomas Hobbes." In *Hypatia's Daughters: Fifteen Hundred Years of Women Philosophers,* edited by Linda Lopez McAlister, 48–67. Bloomington: Indiana University Press, 1996.

Quilligan, Maureen. *The Allegory of Female Authority: Christine de Pizan's Cite des Dames.* Ithaca: Cornell University Press, 1991.

Margery Kempe

1373–c. 1439

The Book of Margery Kempe is significant for a number of reasons. Not only is it the first autobiography in the English language, but it is also the life story of a woman who weaves the intimate details of her personal experience with the details of her spiritual growth and faith. Margery Kempe's life story, then, is one of the first writings by a woman to resist the distinctions between personal and public discourse; Kempe moves between emotional and logical proofs of her status as a mystic who had directly talked to God.

Margery Kempe was born in Lynn in 1373. She married John Kempe, a cloth maker, and she had fourteen children. According to her autobiography, during the birth of her first child, Margery was visited by a vision of Christ, and from then on Margery continued to experience many mystical visions and in the Holy Land received the "gift of tears"—regular bouts of uncontrollable weeping over the sufferings of Jesus. She undertook many pilgrimages to holy places and journeys to ecclesiastical authorities, including Julian of Norwich. But unlike Julian, Margery continued to live in the "real" world; she tried to establish several businesses, and she remained married to her husband, rejecting the cloistered religious life that many women mystics chose and instead trying to live a spiritual life in the domestic world. Thus, her *Book* is full of references to daily life, especially to Margery's choice of clothing to reflect her spiritual growth, as she makes her personal history parallel to sacred scripture.

Like the majority of women in medieval England, Margery was uneducated and could neither read nor write. In her old age, she dictated her life story to several scribes, who had varying degrees of success in writing down her account. The selection included here is the "Proem" to *The Book of Margery Kempe*, in which she explains the difficulty she had in getting her autobiography written down in the first place. She reveals a stubborn and single-minded *ethos* that Cheryl Glenn argues is "her only means of self-preservation, both within the written text and the text of her life"(108). In other words, this woman insists that the details of her life cannot be separated from the story of her faith. Readers must experience multiple parts of Margery Kempe: as mother, wife, mystic, woman, and author. In creating this blend of personal and spiritual discourse, Margery undermines traditional medieval theology by becoming an authority not only on matters of religion but on her own life as well.

From *The Book of Margery Kempe*

1436

Here begins a short account that will offer sinful wretches both consolation and comfort as well as some understanding of the high and inexpressible mercy of our sovereign Savior Jesus Christ. His blessed name be worshiped and made known forever; for even in our own lifetimes he has been so good as to show us his majesty and kindness in spite of our unworthiness. All our Savior's workings are to teach and guide us, and the grace he works in every creature brings benefit to us all providing we are not without his loving charity.

Therefore our merciful Lord, Jesus Christ, has allowed this short account to be written down in order to glory his holy name; for it touches on a few of his wonderful works how by mercy, by his kindness and in his charity, he stirred and moved this sinful creature to return his love. How, at the prompting of the Holy Spirit, I spent many years promising vows of fasting and many other penances. And yet I always turned back at the least temptation. Indeed I was just like a reed bending at every least breath of wind and only standing upright again when it ceases to blow. This went on until our merciful Lord, Jesus Christ, took pity on his creature, the work of his hands. For he turned my health into sickness and my wealth to poverty; my good name into one constantly blamed by others, their love for me into hatred. For many years I had always been unstable and now I was overtaken by all these reverses; yet I still found myself steadily drawn and still stirred to enter the way of higher perfection, of which Christ our Savior in his own person was our supreme example. He trod it in sorrow, that same path of duty long before us.

Through the mercy of that same Jesus, I want to tell in some part the story of my life. Firstly, how I was touched by the hand of our Lord so that I fell seriously ill, indeed for a long period; I lost my mind, until our Lord by his grace restored me once more. But I will give more details of this later. Then too my worldly possessions, which were many and abundant at the time, were suddenly no more, threadbare and barren. Then I had to let go of pomp, and my pride was laid low and finally cast aside. Those same people who had once looked up to me were now the first to find the sharpest criticisms. Even my relatives and especially my closest friends suddenly turned into ruthless enemies.

I began to wonder at this amazing change, and I came seeking shelter under the wings of my spiritual mother, the Holy Church. I went in all humility to my confessor; I accused myself of all my failings and followed this with much cor-

Reprinted from Kempe, Margery. *The Book of Margery Kempe,* translated by John Skinner, 4–9. New York: Random House, 1998. Copyright ©1998 by John Skinner. Used by permission of Doubleday, a division of Random House, Inc.

poral penance. In a very short time, our Lord visited me with many contrite tears. Day after day I continued to weep, so that many declared openly that I could stimulate my tears at will. But they merely belittled the work of God.

Soon, I became used to being slandered and put down in public, shouted at and reviled by everyone in sight, all on account of the grace and virtue brought by the comfort of the Holy Spirit. Then it became a kind of comfort and inner strength when I suffered any pain for the love of God and on account of the new grace he was working in me. It seemed to me that the more I had to put up with in the way of lies and complaints, the more I grew in grace and in consolation when I meditated on holy things and knew a higher contemplation than I had imagined possible. For I now began to make wonderful speeches and have intimate conversations with our Lord; and he would speak to me and tell my soul how I would be despised for his love; but that I must have patience and set all my trust, all my love, and all my affection on him alone.

Sometimes, the Holy Spirit would inspire me and I would know about many things still hidden but about to happen. But more frequently, while I was absorbed in these sacred speeches and conversations, I would weep and sob so much that people grew very alarmed. But how could they know how homely and intimate our Lord was behaving within my soul? Yet it was hard even for me to tell of the grace that I was feeling; it seemed to come from heaven, to be well beyond the reach of my own power of reason. Besides, my body would be sometimes so enfeebled by the experience of such grace that I always failed to put into words exactly what I felt within my soul.

All the time, I went in fear and trembling of being deluded and deceived by my spiritual enemies. The Holy Spirit often prompted me to seek advice from many different priests who had experience in these matters; I went in search of doctors of divinity, bachelors, bishops—I even consulted more than one archbishop. I had conversations with several anchorites as well; I would tell them of my new way of life, about whatever graces the Holy Spirit of his goodness worked in both my mind and my soul. And all these wise and experienced persons to whom I confided my anxieties, agreed in their advice. Because of the grace our Lord undoubtedly showed me, I began to love him greatly; as to my interior promptings and stirrings of soul, I was also obliged to follow them, trusting that they truly came from the Holy Spirit and not from some evil spirit.

Some of these good priests were so convinced that my experiences were genuine that they went so far as to declare that they would wager their souls before God that I was truly inspired by the Holy Spirit. Some wanted me to have a book written that would tell all about my experiences and revelations; some offered to write it themselves, there and then. But I always refused. I knew in my soul that it was too soon to write anything down. And so it was some twenty years since the start of my first experiencing such feelings and revelations that I agreed to have anything written down. It was then that our Lord was pleased to bid me that I ought indeed arrange for them to be written and recorded: that is to say, the way of life I had adopted, my innermost feelings, and some of the revelations that had been shown me—all so that his goodness might be known to the world at large.

At first, I could find no one suitable to become my scribe; there were some who were qualified enough, yet they simply refused to believe what I had to say. Then I made an arrangement with a man who had recently returned from Germany. He was English by birth but had married a German wife and settled there with their young child. But because he knew me very well, and also, I trust, was moved by the Holy Spirit, he came home to England with his wife and all their worldly goods and lived with me until he had finished writing down all that I wanted to tell him. But it was barely completed before he suddenly died. So then I turned to a priest friend of mine; I put the matter to him, and he agreed to read the manuscript. His verdict was that it was so ill-written that he could barely decipher it. Apparently it was written down in neither English nor German, and the letters were inscribed like none he had ever seen, he told me. Finally, he declared that no one would ever be able to read a word of it, unless they had some special grace. Even so, he promised me that if he could possibly decipher it, he would make a fresh and legible copy.

But then so much evil talk began to arise about my weeping that this priest was afraid to be seen talking to me. And, for the same reason, he was reluctant to make a start on the book for about four years, although I continued to ask him to do something about it. After all this time, he then told me that he was unable to read it and therefore would not help me. He added that he did not want to risk his reputation on such work. And so he handed me on to someone who had been a close friend of my original scribe; he felt confident that this man would be just the one to decipher such appalling handwriting, not least because he had received several letters from the original scribe while he had been living in Germany.

And so I approached this man and asked if he would be willing to help me write a new version of my book, but on condition that it was kept secret as long as I lived. I made him an offer of a very large sum for his work. And so this man agreed to make a start. But the project was doomed from the beginning. He had not written half a page before he complained bitterly that he could not continue: The writing was unintelligible, the book itself without rhyme or reason.

It then transpired that the priest who had first promised to help me with this new transcription had a bad conscience. He knew all along that he had given his promise to write it all out again, provided that he could succeed in reading the original. Knowing that he had not yet tried his best, he asked me if it were at all possible for me to retrieve the book for him. I promptly did so and took the parcel back to my priest with a light heart. I told him that if he would give it a good try, I for my part would pray to God for him and win the grace for him not only to read it at last but also to write it all down again in good order.

He trusted in my prayers and began to study it a second time. And now it seemed to him a good deal easier than it had been before. He began to read it word for word as I sat with him; and sometimes, when there was a difficult passage, I was able to help him through. But I should make one thing clear. This book is not written in the order of events so that one thing follows another exactly as really happened. But things are set down simply as and when I remembered them while I was dictating my story. There was such a long delay in committing everything to writing that I had forgotten the exact time and order of when things actually happened. Yet at the same time I made sure that nothing was written down that did not truly take place.

When my priest friend at last began to write my book, his eyes began to trouble him. Indeed, they failed so that he found difficulty in forming his letters, and he could not even see enough to mend his pen. Yet he could see everything else perfectly well enough. He tried spectacles—perched on the end of his nose—but that only made matters worse than before. He complained to me about his problem. I told him his enemy was envious of the good work he had in hand and would try anything to prevent it. I urged him to do as well as God's grace let him and to carry on. And when he returned to the book once more, he found he could see as well, so he declared, as ever he had before. He was as content working in the daytime or by candlelight

And that is why, in the year of our lord 1436, once he had completed a quire and added one more leaf, he agreed to write this introduction anew in order to give a fuller explanation of how this book came about. So that it was written after this short preface which now follows.

FOR FURTHER READING

Atkinson, Christian. *Mystic and Pilgrim: The Book and the World of Margery Kempe.* Ithaca: Cornell University Press, 1983.

Glenn, Cheryl. *Rhetoric Retold: Regendering the Tradition from Antiquity through the Renaissance.* Carbondale: Southern Illinois University Press, 1997.

Staley, Lynn. *Margery Kempe's Dissenting Fictions.* University Park: Pennsylvania State University Press, 1994.

Queen Elizabeth I

1533–1603

Queen Elizabeth I was a remarkable woman, not only for reigning as England's queen for forty-five years—longer than any British monarch until that time—but also for the writing and the speeches she left behind. These documents show a woman strategically redefining her many selves in order to rule as an effective and popular queen, the most popular England has ever known. Her speeches, in particular, reveal an accomplished and polished rhetor.

Elizabeth was born in 1533, the daughter of Henry VIII and his second wife, Anne Boleyn. When her mother was executed by Henry in 1537, Henry declared Elizabeth illegitimate and promptly remarried. When Elizabeth was ten, her father married his sixth wife, Catherine Parr, who proved to be a loving and generous stepmother. Catherine made sure Elizabeth was well educated. A bright student, Elizabeth received a splendid education in Greek, Latin, French, Italian, and history. In 1553, Elizabeth's half-sister, the Catholic Mary Tudor, ascended the throne and had Elizabeth, a Protestant, imprisoned in the Tower of London. In 1558, Mary died and Elizabeth became queen. Elizabeth presided over the rise of the British Empire: English cities became centers of commerce; the navy controlled principal routes of trade; and the English colonized the Americas, Africa, and India. Throughout her reign, Elizabeth never married. Rather she was wed to her people, as she often mentioned. She died in 1603, at the age of seventy.

Throughout her reign, Elizabeth constructed herself in a variety of roles: monarch, nurturer, virgin, mother to England. In the speech included here, Elizabeth takes on the identity of the strong, demanding monarch, blurring the boundaries between queen and king. "To the Troops at Tilbury" was given by Elizabeth on August 9, 1588, the eve of England's defeat of the Spanish Armada. In the speech, Elizabeth takes on the persona of a male military commander who will remain with the soldiers to the bitter end. At the same time, she uses contemporary assumptions about gender roles to her own ends: "I know I have the body but of a weak and feeble woman; but I have the heart and stomach of a king, and of a king of England too," she declares. Thus, Elizabeth constructs multiple identities for her crown and, in the process, shows a shrewd awareness of audience and situation.

"To the Troops at Tilbury"

1588

My loving people,

We have been persuaded by some that are careful of our safety, to take heed how we commit our selves to armed multitudes, for fear of treachery; but I assure you I do not desire to live to distrust my faithful and loving people. Let tyrants fear, I have always so behaved myself that, under God, I have placed my chiefest strength and safeguard in the loyal hearts and good-will of my subjects; and therefore I am come amongst you, as you see, at this time, not for my recreation and disport, but being resolved, in the midst and heat of the battle, to live or die amongst you all; to lay down for my God, and for my kingdom, and my people, my honour and my blood, even in the dust. I know I have the body but of a weak and feeble woman; but I have the heart and stomach of a king, and of a king of England too, and think foul scorn that Parma or Spain, or any prince of Europe, should dare to invade the borders of my realm; to which rather than any dishonour shall grow by me, I myself will take up arms, I myself will be your general, judge, and rewarder of every one of your virtues in the field. I know already, for your forwardness you have deserved rewards and crowns; and We do assure you in the word of a prince, they shall be duly paid you. In the mean time, my lieutenant general shall be in my stead, than whom never prince commanded a more noble or worthy subject; not doubting but by your obedience to my general, by your concord in the camp, and your valour in the field, we shall shortly have a famous victory over those enemies of my God, of my kingdom, and of my people.

FOR FURTHER READING

Bell, Ilona. "Elizabeth I: Always Her Own Free Woman" In *Political Rhetoric, Power, and Renaissance Women,* edited by Carole Levin and Patricia A. Sullivan, 57–82. Albany: State University of New York Press, 1995.

Frye, Susan. *Elizabeth I: The Competition for Representation.* New York: Oxford University Press, 1993.

Levin, Carole. *The Heart and Stomach of a King: Elizabeth I and the Politics of Sex and Power.* Philadelphia: University of Pennsylvania Press, 1994.

Perry, Maria. *The Word of a Prince: The Life of Elizabeth from Contemporary Documents.* London: Folio Society, 1990.

From *The Public Speaking of Queen Elizabeth: Selections from Her Official Addresses,* ed. George P. Rice, Jr. New York. © 1951 Columbia University Press. Reprinted by permission of the publisher.

Jane Anger

Jane Anger is the first woman to publish a full-length defense in English. Consequently, she is also the first Englishwoman to recognize, in print, that language socially constructs cultural categories—specifically gender. In her pamphlet *Her Protection for Women* (1589), Anger responds to the male-authored *Book his Surfeit in Love*, an example of the popular *querelle des femmes*, or the controversy over the natural condition of women. In these debates, male writers typically presented formal arguments praising or denouncing women. Anger's text takes the male-dominated rhetoric of the genre and turns it on its head. The *Protection* moves, for example, from reasoned defense to passionate attack on the male writer's complaint that he is "surfeited," or sick with the sensual indulgence of women. Note, too, that Anger chooses the plain, direct style in claiming that men's "true vein in writing" is to be "carried away with the manner" rather than the matter of rhetoric.

Scholars know virtually nothing of Anger. Some even speculate that "Jane Anger" is the pseudonym of a male writer and that the *Protection* was merely a ploy by the writer of the *Surfeit* to continue the anti-woman debates. Others, however, insist that Jane Anger is a real woman whose work goes beyond the conventional boundaries of the *querelle des femmes* genre. Lynne Magnusson, for example, argues that Anger deliberately reworks her opponent's misogynist ideas to establish a direct feminine perspective that goes beyond the *querelle* framework.

Along with the text of the *Protection*, included here are two introductory epistles: one addressed to the women of England, the other addressed to women in general. These letters are significant for a number of reasons. They assume some degree of literacy among the audience, an audience that was discouraged at every turn from reading or writing. The *Protection's* opening letters move from apologies for a too-heated defense toward a "combative persona" that Randall Martin says "constitutes most of [the *Protection's*] appeal" (80). The epistles also draw on a variety of rhetorical tools, including much play on words, which Anger employs throughout the work. For example, in the second letter Anger announces, "Fie on the falsehood of men, whose minds go oft a-maddening, and whose tongues cannot so soon be wagging but straight they fall a-railing." Male writers often used women's "wagging tongues" as arguments for keeping women silent. By focusing on the "tongues" of men, Anger uses synecdoche to invert traditional gender attributes. This synecdoche, as Magnusson argues, becomes "the omnipresence and power of the male word

[and] Anger turns back against its maker a discursive practice that itself ration-
alizes and preserves [public] discourse as a male prerogative" (273–74). In other
words, Anger takes traditional stereotypes of women, turns them around, and
applies them to men. And in the process, she takes hold of the master's rhetorical tools to show how language socially constructs gender.

From JANE ANGER HER PROTECTION FOR WOMEN TO
DEFEND THEM AGAINST THE SCANDALOUS REPORT OF A
LATE SURFEITING LOVER, AND ALL OTHER LIKE VENERIANS
THAT COMPLAIN SO TO BE OVERCLOYED WITH WOMEN'S
KINDNESS.

1589

To The Gentlewomen Of England, Health:
Gentlewomen, though it is to be feared that your settled wits will advisedly
condemn that which my choleric vein hath rashly set down, and so perchance
Anger shall reap anger for not agreeing with diseased persons, yet, if with indif-
ferency of censure you consider of the head of the quarrel, I hope you will
rather show yourselves defendants of the defender's title than complainants of
the plaintiff's wrong. I doubt judgement before trial, which were injurious to
the law; and I confess that my rashness deserveth no less, which was a fit of my
extremity. I will not urge reasons because your wits are sharp and will soon
conceive my meaning, ne will I be tedious lest I prove too troublesome, nor
over-dark in my writing for fear of the name of a riddler. But in a word, for my
presumption I crave pardon because it was Anger that did write it, committing
your protection and myself to the protection of yourselves, and the judgement
of the cause to the censures of your just minds.

Yours ever at commandment,
Jane Anger.

To All Women in General, and Gentle Reader Whatsoever:
Fie on the falsehood of men, whose minds go oft a-madding and whose tongues
cannot so soon be wagging but straight they fall a-railing. Was there ever any so
abused, so slandered, so railed upon, or so wickedly handled undeservedly, as
are we women? Will the gods permit it, the goddesses stay their punishing
judgements, and we ourselves not pursue their undoings for such devilish practices? O Paul's steeple and Charing Cross! A halter hold all such persons. Let

Reprinted from Anger, Jane. "Jane Anger Her Protection For Women." In *Women Writers in
Renaissance England*, edited by Randall Martin, 82–96. London: Addison Wesley Longman,
1997.

the streams of the channels in London streets run so swiftly as they may be able alone to carry them from that sanctuary. Let the stones be as ice, the soles of their shoes as glass, the ways steep like Etna, and every blast a whirlwind puffed out of Boreas his long throat, that these may hasten their passage to the devil's haven. Shall surfeiters rail on our kindness? You stand still and say naught. And shall not Anger stretch the veins of her brains, the strings of her fingers, and the lists of her modesty, to answer their surfeitings? Yes truly. And herein I conjure all you to aid and assist me in defence of my willingness, which shall make me rest at your commands. Fare you well.

Your friend,
Jane Anger.

A Protection for Women, Etc.

The desire that every man hath to show his true vein in writing is unspeakable, and their minds are so carried away with the manner as no care at all is had of the matter. They run so into rhetoric as oftentimes they overrun the bounds of their own wits and go they know not whither. If they have stretched their invention so hard on a last as it is at a stand, there remains but one help, which is to write of us women. If they may once encroach so far into our presence as they may but see the lining of our outermost garment, they straight think that Apollo honours them in yielding so good a supply to refresh their sore overburdened heads (through studying for matters to indite of). And therefore, that the god may see how thankfully they receive his liberality (their wits whetted and their brains almost broken with botching his bounty), they fall straight to dispraising and slandering our silly sex. But judge what the cause should be of this their so great malice towards simple women: doubtless the weakness of our wits and our honest bashfulness, by reason whereof they suppose that there is not one amongst us who can or dare reprove their slanders and false reproaches. Their slanderous tongues are so short, and the time wherein they have lavished out their words freely hath been so long, that they know we cannot catch hold of them to pull them out, and they think we will not write to reprove their lying lips. Which conceits have already made them cocks and would (should they not be cravened) make themselves among themselves be thought to be of the game. They have been so daintily fed with our good natures that like jades (their stomachs are grown so queasy) they surfeit of our kindness. If we will not suffer them to smell on our smocks, they will snatch at our petticoats; but if our honest natures cannot away with that uncivil kind of jesting, then we are coy. Yet if we bear with their rudeness and be somewhat modestly familiar with them, they will straight make matter of nothing, blazing abroad that they have surfeited with love, and then their wits must be shown in telling the manner how.

Among the innumerable number of books to that purpose of late unlooked for, the new *Surfeit of an Old Lover* (sent abroad to warn those which are of his own kind from catching the like disease) came by chance to my hands; which, because as well women as men are desirous of novelties, I willingly read over. Neither did the ending thereof less please me than the beginning, for I was so carried away with the conceit of the gentleman as that I was quite out of the book before I thought I had been in the midst thereof, so pithy were his sentences, so pure his words, and so pleasing his style. The chief matters therein contained were of two sorts: the one in the dispraise of man's folly, and the other invective against our sex; their folly proceeding of their own flattery joined with fancy, and our faults are through our folly, with which is some faith. . . .

The greatest fault that doth remain in us women is that we are too credulous, for could we flatter as they can dissemble, and use our wits well as they can their tongues ill, then never would any of them complain of surfeiting. But if we women be so perilous cattle as they term us, I marvel that the gods made not Fidelity as well a man as they created her a woman, and all the moral virtues of their masculine sex as of the feminine kind, except their deities knew that there was some sovereignty in us women which could not be in them men. But lest some snatching fellow should catch me before I fall to the ground, and say they will adorn my head with a feather (affirming that I roam beyond reason, seeing it is most manifest that the man is the head of the woman and that therefore we ought to be guided by them), I prevent them with this answer. The gods, knowing that the minds of mankind would be aspiring, and having thoroughly viewed the wonderful virtues wherewith women are enriched, lest they should provoke us to pride and so confound us with Lucifer, they bestowed the supremacy over us to man, that of that coxcomb he might only boast, and therefore for God's sake let them keep it. But we return to the *Surfeit*.

Having made a long discourse of the gods' censure concerning love, he leaves them (and I them with him) and comes to the principal object and general foundation of love, which he affirmeth to be grounded on women. And now beginning to search his scroll wherein are taunts against us, he beginneth and saith that we allure their hearts to us. Wherein he saith more truly than he is aware of; for we woo them with our virtues and they wed us with vanities; and men, being of wit sufficient to consider of the virtues which are in us women, are ravished with the delight of those dainties which allure and draw the senses of them to serve us, whereby they become ravenous hawks who do not only seize upon us but devour us. Our good toward them is the destruction of ourselves; we being well-formed are by them foully deformed. Of our true meaning they make mocks, rewarding our loving follies with disdainful flouts. We are the grief of man, in that we take all the grief from man; we languish when they laugh, we lie sighing when they sit singing, and sit sobbing when they lie slugging and sleeping. *Mulier est hominis confusio,* because her kind heart cannot so sharply reprove their frantic fits as those mad frenzies deserve. *Aut amat aut odit, non est in tertio:* she loveth good things and hateth that which is evil; she loveth justice and hateth iniquity; she loveth truth and true dealing and hateth lies and falsehood; she loveth man for his virtues and hateth him for his vices. To be short, there is no *medium* between good and bad, and therefore she can be *in nullo tertio*. Plato his answer to a vicar of fools which asked the question, being that he knew not whether to place women among those creatures which were reasonable or unreasonable, did as much beautify his divine knowledge as all the books he did write; for knowing that women are the greatest help that men have (without whose aid and assistance it is as possible for them to live as if they wanted meat, drink, clothing, or any other necessary), and knowing also that even then in his age (much more in those ages which should after follow) men were grown to be so unreasonable, as he could not decide whether men or brute beasts were more reasonable. Their eyes are so curious as, be not all women equal with Venus for beauty, they cannot abide the sight of them; their stomachs so queasy as, do they taste but twice of one dish, they straight surfeit and needs must a new diet be provided for them. We are contrary to men because they are contrary to that which is good. Because they are spurblind they cannot see into our natures, and we too well, though we had but half an eye, into their conditions because they are so bad; our behaviours alter daily because men's virtues decay hourly.

If Hesiodus had with equity as well looked into the life of man as he did precisely search out the qualities of us women, he would have said that if a woman trust unto a man it shall fare as well with her as if she had a weight of a thousand pounds tied about her neck and then cast into the bottomless seas. For by men are we confounded, though they by us are sometimes crossed. Our tongues are light because earnest in reproving men's filthy vices, and our good counsel is termed nipping injury in that it accords not with their foolish fancies. Our boldness rash for giving noddies nipping answers, our dispositions naughty for not agreeing with their vile minds, and our fury dangerous because it will not bear with their knavish behaviours. If our frowns be so terrible and our anger so deadly, men are too foolish in offering occasions of hatred, which shunned, a terrible death is prevented. There is a continual deadly hatred between the wild boar and tame hounds; I would there were the like betwixt women and men unless they amend their manners, for so strength should predominate where now flattery and dissimulation hath the upper hand. The lion rageth when he is hungry, but man raileth when he is glutted. The tiger is robbed of her young ones when she is ranging abroad, but men rob women of their honour undeservedly under their noses. The viper stormeth when his tail is trodden on, and may not we fret when all our body is a footstool to their vile lust? Their unreasonable minds which know not what reason is make them nothing better than brute beasts. . . .

Euthydemus made six kind of women, and I will approve that there are so many of men, which be: poor and rich, bad and good, foul and fair. The great patrimonies that wealthy men leave their children after their death make them rich, but dice and other marthrifts, happening into their companies, never leave them till they be at the beggar's bush, where I can assure you they become poor. Great eaters, being kept at a slender diet, never distemper their bodies but remain in good case; but afterwards, once turned forth to liberty's pasture, they graze so greedily as they become surfeiting jades and always after are good for nothing. There are men which are snout-fair whose faces look like a cream-pot, and yet those not the fair men I speak of; but I mean those whose conditions are free from knavery, and I term those foul that have neither civility nor honesty. Of these sorts there are none good, none rich or fair long. But if we do desire to have them good, we must always tie them to the manger and diet their greedy paunches, otherwise they will surfeit. What shall I say? Wealth makes them lavish, wit knavish, beauty effeminate, poverty deceitful, and deformity ugly. Therefore of me take this counsel:

> Esteem of men as of a broken reed,
> Mistrust them still, and then you well shall speed.

I pray you then, if this be true (as it truly cannot be denied) have not they reason who affirm that a goose standing before a ravenous fox is in as good case as the woman that trusteth to a man's fidelity? For as the one is sure to lose his head, so the other is most certain to be bereaved of her good name, if there be any small cause of suspicion. The fellow that took his wife for his cross was an ass, and so we will leave him; for he loved well to swear on an ale-pot, and because his wife, keeping him from his drunken vein, put his nose out of his socket, he thereby was brought into a mad mood in which he did he could not tell what.

> When provender pricks, the jade will winch, but keep him at a slender ordinary
> and he will be mild enough. The dictator's son was crank as long as his cock
> was crowing, but proving a craven he made his master hang down his head.

Thales was so married to shameful lust as he cared not a straw for lawful love, whereby he showed himself to be endued with much vice and no virtue; for a man doth that oftentimes standing of which he repenteth sitting. The Roman could not, as now men cannot, abide to hear women praised and themselves dispraised, and therefore it is best for men to follow Alphonso his rule: let them be deaf and marry wives that are blind, so shall they not grieve to hear their wives commended nor their monstrous misdoing shall offend their wives' eyesight.

Tibullus, setting down a rule for women to follow, might have proportioned this platform for men to rest in and might have said: every honest man ought to shun that which detracteth both health and safety from his own person, and strive to bridle his slanderous tongue. Then must he be modest and show his modesty by his virtuous and civil behaviours, and not display his beastliness through his wicked and filthy words. For lying lips and deceitful tongues are abominable before God. It is an easy matter to entreat a cat to catch a mouse, and more easy to persuade a desperate man to kill himself. What nature hath made, art cannot mar, and (as this surfeiting lover saith) that which is bred in the bone will not be brought out of the flesh. If we clothe ourselves in sackcloth and truss up our hair in dishclouts, Venerians will nevertheless pursue their pastime. If we hide our breasts it must be with leather, for no cloth can keep their long nails out of our bosoms.

We have rolling eyes and they railing tongues; our eyes cause them to look lasciviously, and why? because they are given to lechery. It is an easy matter to find a staff to beat a dog, and a burnt finger giveth sound counsel. If men would as well embrace counsel as they can give it, Socrates's rule would be better followed. But let Socrates, heaven and earth say what they will, 'man's face is worth a glass of dissembling water'. And therefore to conclude with a proverb: 'write ever, and yet never write enough of man's falsehood' (I mean those that use it). I would that ancient writers would as well have busied their heads about deciphering the deceits of their own sex as they have about setting down our own follies; and I would some would call in question that now which hath ever been questionless. But sithence all their wits have been bent to write of the contrary, I leave them to a contrary vein, and the Surfeiting Lover, who returns to his discourse of love.

Now while this greedy grazer is about his entreaty of love (which nothing belongeth to our matter) let us secretly, ourselves with ourselves, consider how and in what they that are our worst enemies are both inferior unto us and most beholden unto our kindness.

The creation of man and woman at the first (he being formed *in principio* of dross and filthy clay) did so remain until God saw that in him his workmanship was good, and therefore, by the transformation of the dust which was loathsome unto flesh, it became purified. Then, lacking a help for him, God making woman of man's flesh (that she might be purer than he) doth evidently show how far we women are more excellent than men. Our bodies are fruitful, whereby the world increaseth, and our care wonderful, by which man is preserved. From woman sprang man's salvation. A woman was the first that believed, and a woman likewise the first that repented of sin. In woman is only true fidelity; except in her there is no constancy, and without her no housewifery. In the time of their sickness we cannot be wanted, and when they are in health we for them are most necessary. They are comforted by our means, they [are] nourished by the meats we dress, their bodies freed from diseases by our cleanliness, which otherwise would surfeit unreasonably through their own noisomeness. Without our care they lie in their beds as dogs in litter, and go like lousy mackerel swimming in the heat of summer. They love to go handsomely in their apparel and rejoice in the pride thereof; yet who is the cause of it, but our carefulness to see that everything about them be curious? Our virginity makes us virtuous, our conditions courteous, and our chastity maketh our trueness of love manifest. They confess we are necessary, but they would have us likewise evil. That they cannot want us I grant; yet evil I deny, except only in the respect of man who, hating all good things, is only desirous of that which is ill (through whose desire, in estimation of conceit, we are made ill).

But lest some should snarl on me, barking out this reason, that none is good but God, and therefore women are ill, I must yield that in that respect we are ill, and affirm that men are no better, seeing we are so necessary unto them. It is most certain that if we be ill they are worse, for *malum malo additum efficit malum peius;* and they that use ill worse than it should be are worse than the ill. And therefore if they will correct *Magnificat,* they must first learn the signification thereof. That we are liberal they will not deny, sithence that many of them have, *ex confessio* received more kindness in one day at our hands than they can repay in a whole year; and some have so glutted themselves with our liberality as they cry 'no more'. But if they shall avow that women are fools, we may safely give them the lie; for myself have heard some of them confess that we have more wisdom than need is, and therefore no fools, and they less than they should have, and therefore fools. It hath been affirmed by some of their sex that to shun a shower of rain and to know the way to our husband's bed is wisdom sufficient for us women; but in this year of '88 men are grown so fantastical that unless we can make them fools we are accounted unwise. . . .

And now, seeing I speak to none but to you which are of mine own sex, give me leave like a scholar to prove our wisdom more excellent than theirs (though I never knew what sophistry meant).

There is no wisdom but it comes by grace; this is a principle, and *contra principium non est disputandum.* But grace was first given to a woman, because to our Lady; which premises conclude that women are wise. Now *primum est optimum,* and therefore women are wiser than men. That we are more witty, which comes by nature, it cannot better be proved than that by our answers men are often driven to a *non plus;* and if their talk be of worldly affairs, with our resolutions they must either rest satisfied or prove themselves fools in the end. . . .

Now sithence that this overcloyed and surfeiting lover leaveth his love and comes with a fresh assault against us women, let us arm ourselves with patience and see the end of his tongue which explaineth his surfeit. But it was so lately printed as that I should do the printer injury should I recite but one of them, and therefore, referring you to *Boke His Surfeit in Love,* I come to my matter. If to enjoy a woman be to catch the devil by the foot, to obtain the favour of a man is to hold fast his dam by the middle, whereby the one may easily break away and the other cannot go without he carries the man with him. The properties of the snake and of the eel are the one to sting and the other not to be held; but men's tongues sting against nature and therefore they are unnatural. Let us bear with them as much as may be, and yield to their wills more than is convenient; yet if we cast our reckoning at the end of the year we shall find that our losses exceed their gains, which are innumerable. The property of the chameleon is to change himself; but man always remaineth at one stay and is never out of the predicaments of dishonesty and unconstancy. The stinging of the scorpion is cured by the scorpion, whereby it seems that there is some good nature in them. But men never leave stinging till they see the death of honesty. The danger of pricks is shunned by gathering roses glove-fisted, and the stinging of bees prevented through a close hood. But naked dishonesty and bare inconstancy are always plagued through their own folly.

If men's folly be so unreasonable as it will strive against nature, it is no matter though she rewards them with crosses contrary to their expectations; for if Tom Fool will presume to ride on Alexander's horse, he is not to be pitied though he get a foul knock for his labour. But it seems the gentleman hath had great experience of Italian courtesans, whereby his wisdom is showed; for *experientia praestantior arte*, and he that hath experience to prove his case is in better case than they that have all unexperienced book cases to defend their titles.

The smooth speeches of men are nothing unlike the vanishing clouds of the air, which glide by degrees from place to place till they have filled themselves with rain, when breaking, they spit forth terrible showers. So men gloze till they have their answers, which are the end of their travail, and then they bid modesty adieu and, entertaining rage, fall a-railing on us which never hurt them. The rankness of grass causeth suspicion of the serpent's lurking, but his lying in the plain path at the time when woodcocks shoot, maketh the patient passionate through his sting because no such ill was suspected. When men protest secrecy most solemnly, believe them least, for then surely there is a trick of knavery to be discarded; for in a friar's habit an old fornicator is always clothed.

It is a wonder to see how men can flatter themselves with their own conceits. For let us look, they will straight affirm that we love, and if then lust pricketh them, they will swear that love stingeth us; which imagination only is sufficient to make them essay the scaling of half a dozen of us in one night, when they will not stick to swear that if they should be denied of their requests, death must needs follow. Is it any marvel though they surfeit, when they are so greedy? But is it not pity that any of them should perish, which will be so soon killed with unkindness? Yes truly. Well, the onset given, if we retire for a vantage they will straight affirm that they have got the victory. Nay, some of them are so carried away with conceit that, shameless, they will blaze abroad among their companions that they have obtained the love of a woman unto whom they never spake above once, if that. Are not these froward fellows? You must bear with them because they dwell far from lying neighbours; they will say *mentiri non est nostrum*, and yet you shall see true tales come from them as wild geese fly under London bridge. Their fawning is but flattery, their faith falsehood, their fair words allurements to destruction, and their large promises tokens of death, or of evils worse than death. Their singing is a bait to catch us, and their playings plagues to torment us; and therefore take heed of them, and take this as an axiom in logic and a maxim in the law: *nulla fides hominibus*. There are three accidents to men which, of all, are most unseparable: lust, deceit, and malice (their glozing tongues the preface to the execution of their vile minds, and their pens the bloody executioners of their barbarous manners). A little gall maketh a great deal of sweet sour, and a slanderous tongue poisoneth all the good parts in man. . . .

At the end of men's fair promises there is a labyrinth, and therefore ever hereafter stop your ears when they protest friendship, lest they come to an end before you are aware, whereby you fall without redemption. The path which leadeth thereunto is man's wit, and the miles-ends are marked with these trees: folly, vice, mischief, lust, deceit, and pride. These to deceive you shall be clothed in the raiments of fancy, virtue, modesty, love, true-meaning, and hand-someness. Folly will bid you welcome on your way and tell you his fancy concerning the profit which may come to you by this journey, and direct you to vice who is more crafty. He, with a company of protestations, will praise the virtues of women, showing how many ways men are beholden unto us; but our backs once turned, he falls a-railing. Then mischief, he pries into every corner of us, seeing if he can espy a cranny that, getting in his finger into it, he may make it wide enough for his tongue to wag in. Now, being come to lust, he will fall a-railing on lascivious looks and will ban lechery, and with the collier will say, 'the devil take him,' though he never means it. Deceit will give you fair words and pick your pockets, nay, he will pluck out your hearts if you be not wary. But when you hear one cry out against lawns, drawn-works, periwigs, against the attire of courtesans, and generally of the pride of all women, then know him for a wolf clothed in sheep's raiment, and be sure you are fast by the lake of destruction. Therefore take heed of it, which you shall do if you shun men's flattery, the forerunner of our undoing. If a jade be galled, will he not winch? And can you find fault with a horse that springeth when he is spurred? The one will stand quietly when his back is healed and the other go well when his smart ceaseth. You must bear with the old *Lover his Surfeit* because he was diseased when he did write it; and peradventure hereafter, when he shall be well amended, he will repent himself of his slanderous speeches against our sex and curse the dead man which was the cause of it and make a public recantation. For the faltering in his speech at the latter end of his book affirmeth that already he half repenteth of his bargain, and why? because his melody is past. But believe him not, though he should out-swear you, for although a jade may be still in a stable when his gall-back is healed, yet he will show himself in his kind when he is travailing; and man's flattery bites secretly, from which I pray God keep you and me too.

Amen.

Finis

FOR FURTHER READING

Ferguson, Moira, ed. *First Feminists.* Bloomington: Indiana University Press, 1985.

Henderson, Katherine Usher, and Barbara F. McManus, eds. *Half Humankind: Contexts and Texts of the Controversy about Women in England, 1540–1640.* Urbana: University of Illinois Press, 1985.

Magnusson, Lynne. "'His Pen With My Hande': Jane Anger's Revisionary Rhetoric." *English Studies in Canada* 17 (1991): 269–81.

Rachel Speght

c. 1597–?

Literary critic Barbara Lewalski has called Rachel Speght "the first self-pro-claimed and positively identified female polemicist in England" (*Polemics and Poems* xi). Speght is one of the first Western women to recognize, in print, that jokes against women are usually more than just harmless banter. In her polemic *A Mouzell for Melastomus* (a "muzzle" for a "black mouth"), Speght denounces Joseph Swetnam's *Arraignment of Women*, a collection of ribald jokes, bawdy ballads, proverbs, and lore pertaining to women's lechery, vanity, shrewish-ness, and inconstancy. Speght interprets Swetnam's book as a serious attack against women. She offers herself as the embodied refutation of Swetnam's charges against women, and in the process, she shows the faulty logic underly-ing misogyny in general.

Not much is known about Rachel Speght. She was probably born sometime around 1597 to a bourgeois London household. Her father, James Speght, was a Calvinist rector. Nothing is known of her mother, who died shortly after Rachel published her polemic in 1617. For a woman of her time, she received a splendid education. She was well trained in both Latin and biblical exegesis, and she ap-pears to have received some training in logic and rhetoric. Education in rheto-ric during the Renaissance usually meant learning various stylistic schemes and tropes and was a subject reserved mainly for men. This knowledge of rhetoric, in particular, serves her very well in *A Mouzell for Melastomus*.

The selections excerpted here are the introductory epistles to *A Mouzell for Melastomus*. The first letter addresses fellow women, and the second is directed to Swetnam himself. Both letters show a remarkable grasp, for a woman of Speght's time, of classical rhetoric, literature, philosophy, and Protestant the-ology. She quotes from such classical figures as Aristotle and Tacitus, and she draws from various Greek and Roman myths. Her understanding of contempo-rary religious debates is equally impressive and significant. In the letter to Swetnam, for example, she indicates that he has misinterpreted the Bible. Le-walski has noted that in doing so, Speght "undertakes to re-interpret biblical texts so as to make the dominant discourse—Protestant biblical exegesis—yield a more expansive and equitable concept of gender" (*Polemics and Poems* xxi). To make these arguments, Speght relies on a host of stylistic devices, including *an-tistrephon*, in which the rhetor counters an argument by using the same ev-idence as the rhetor's opponent. Speght is also particularly fond of metaphors and similes, and she uses them with devastating effectiveness in furthering her argument against Swetnam.

From *A Mouzzel for Melastomus,* the Cynicall Bayter of, and foul
mouthed Barker against Evahs Sex. Or an Apologeticall Answere
to *that Irreligious and Illiterate* Pamphlet made by Io.Sw. and by
him Intituled *The Arraignement of Women.*

1617

To all vertuous Ladies Honour*able or Worshipfull, and to all other of* Hevahs *sex
fearing God, and loving their just reputation, grace and peace through Christ, to eter-
nall glory.*

It was the similie of that wise and learned *Lactantius,* that if fire, though but
with a small sparke kindled, bee not at the first quenched, it may worke great
mischiefe and dammage: So likewise may the scandals and defamations of the
malevolent in time prove pernitious, if they bee not nipt in the head at their
first appearance. The consideration of this (right Honourable and Worshipfull
Ladies) hath incited me (though yong, and the unworthiest of thousands) to
encounter with a furious enemy to our sexe, least if his unjust imputations
should continue without answere, he might insult and account himselfe a vic-
tor; and by such a conceit deale, as Historiographers report the viper to doe,
who in the Winter time doth vomit forth her poyson, and in the spring time
sucketh the same up againe, which becommeth twise as deadly as the former:
And this our pestiferous enemy, by thinking to provide a more deadly poyson
for women, then already he hath foamed forth, may evaporate, by an addition
unto his former illeterate Pamphlet (intituled *The Arraignement of Women*) a
more contagious obtrectation then he hath already done, and indeed hath
threatned to doe. Secondly, if it should have had free passage without any answere at all (seeing that *Tacere* is, *quasi consentire*) the vulgar ignorant might
have beleeved his Diabolicall infamies to be infallible truths, not to bee in-
fringed; whereas now they may plainely perceive them to bee but the scumme
of Heathenish braines, or a building raised without a foundation (at least from
sacred Scripture) which the winde of Gods truth must needs cast downe to the
ground. A third reason why I have adventured to fling this stone at vaunting
Goliah is, to comfort the mindes of all *Hevahs* sex, both rich and poore, learned
and unlearned, with this Antidote, that if the feare of God reside in their hearts,
maugre all adversaries, they are highly esteemed and accounted of in the eies of
their gracious Redeemer, so that they need not feare the darts of envy or ob-
trectators: For shame and disgrace (saith *Aristotle*) is the end of them that
shoote such poysoned shafts. Worthy therefore of imitation is that example of

Reprinted from Speght, Rachel. "A Mouzzel for Melastomus." In *The Polemics and Poems of Rachel Speght,* edited by Barbara Kiefer Lewalski, 3–5, 7–9. New York: Oxford University Press,
1996.

Seneca, who when he was told that a certaine man did exclaime and raile against him, made this milde answere; Some dogs barke more upon custome then curstnesse; and some speake evill of others, not that the defamed deserve it, but because through custome and corruption of their hearts they cannot speake well of any. This I alleage as a paradigmatical patterne for all women, noble and ignoble to follow, that they be not enflamed with choler against this our enraged adversarie, but patiently consider of him according to the portraiture which he hath drawne of himselfe, his Writings being the very embleme of a monster.

This my briefe Apologie (Right Honourable and Worshipfull) did I enterprise, not as thinking my selfe more fit then others to undertake such a taske, but as one, who not perceiving any of our Sex to enter the Lists of encountring with this our grand enemy among men, I being out of all feare, because armed with the truth, which though often blamed, yet can never be shamed, and the Word of Gods Spirit, together with the example of vertues Pupils for a Buckler, did no whit dread to combate with our said malevolent adversarie. And if in so doing I shall bee censured by the judicious to have the victorie, and shall have given content unto the wronged, I have both hit the marke whereat I aymed, and obtained that prize which I desired. But if *Zoilus* shall adjudge me presumptuous in Dedicating this my *Chirograph* unto personages of so high ranke; both because of my insufficiency in literature and tendernesse in yeares: I thus Apologize for my selfe; that seeing the *Bayter of Women* hath opened his mouth against noble as well as ignoble, against the rich as well as the poore; therefore meete it is that they should be joynt spectators of this encounter: And withall in regard of my imperfection both in learning and age, I need so much the more to impetrate patronage from some of power to sheild mee from the biting wrongs of *Momus*, who oftentimes setteth a rankling tooth into the sides of truth. Wherefore I being of *Decius* his mind, who deemed himselfe safe under the shield of *Caesar*, have presumed to shelter my selfe under the wings of you (Honourable personages) against the persecuting heate of this fierie and furious Dragon; desiring that you would be pleased, not to looke so much *ad opus*, as *ad animum*: And so not doubting of the favourable acceptance and censure of all vertuously affected, I rest

> Your Honours and Worships
> Humbly at commandement.
> Rachel Speght

Not unto the veriest Ideot that *ever set Pen to Paper, but to the* Cynicall Bayter of Women, or *metamorphosed Misogunes*, Joseph Swetnam.

From standing water, which soon putrifies, can no good fish be expected; for it produceth no other creatures but those that are venemous or noisome, as snakes, adders, and such like. Semblably, no better streame can we looke, should issue from your idle corrupt braine, then that whereto the ruffe of your fury (to use your owne words) hath moved you to open the sluce. In which excrement of your roaving cogitations you have used such irregularities touching concordance, and observed so disordered a methode, as I doubt not to tel you, that a very Accidence Schollar would have quite put you downe in both. You appeare heerein not unlike that Painter, who seriously indevouring to pourtray *Cupids* Bowe, forgot the String: for you beeing greedie to botch up your mingle mangle invective against Women, have not therein observed, in many places, so much as a Grammer sense. But the emptiest Barrell makes the lowdest sound; and so we wil account of you.

Many propositions have you framed, which (as you thinke) make much against Women, but if one would make a Logicall assumption, the conclusion would be flat against your owne Sex. Your dealing wants so much discretion, that I doubt whether to bestow so good a name as the Dunce upon you: but Minority bids me keepe within my bounds; and therefore I onlie say unto you, that your corrupt Heart and railing Tongue, hath made you a fit scribe for the Divell.

In that you have termed your virulent foame, *the Beare-bayting of Women,* you have plainely displayed your owne disposition to be Cynicall, in that there appeares no other Dogge or Bull, to bayte them, but your selfe. Good had it been for you to have put on that Muzzell, which Saint *James* would have all Christians to weare; *Speake not evill one of another:* and then had you not seemed so like the Serpent *Porphirus,* as now you doe; which, though full of deadly poyson, yet being toothlesse, hurteth none so much as himselfe. For you having gone beyond the limits not of *Humanitie* alone, but of Christianitie, have done greater harme unto your owne soule, then unto women, as may plainely appeare. First, in dishonoring of God by palpable blasphemy, wresting and perverting everie place of Scripture, that you have alleadged; which by the testimony of Saint *Peter,* is to the destruction of them that so doe. Secondly, it appeares by your disparaging of, and opprobrious speeches against that excellent worke of Gods hands, which in his great love he perfected for the comfort of man. Thirdly, and lastly, by this your hodge-podge of heathenish Sentences, Similies, and Examples, you have set forth your selfe in your right colours, unto the view of the world: and I doubt not but the judicious will account of you according to your demerit: As for the Vulgar sort, which have no more learning then you have shewed in your Booke, it is likely they will applaud you for your paines.

As for your *Bugge-beare* or advice unto Women, that whatsoever they doe think of your Worke, they should conceale it, lest in finding fault, they bewray their galled backes to the world; in which you allude to that Proverbe, *Rubbe a galled horse, and he will kicke:* Unto it I answere by way of Apologie, that though everie galled horse, being touched, doth kicke; yet every one that kickes, is not galled: so that you might as well have said, that because burnt folks dread the fire, therfore none feare fire but those that are burnt, as made that illiterate conclusion which you have absurdly inferred.

In your Title Leafe, you arraigne none but lewd, idle, froward and unconstant women, but in the Sequele (through defect of memorie as it seemeth) forgetting that you had made a distinction of good from badde, condemning all in generall, you advise men to beware of, and not to match with any of these sixe sorts of women, *viz. Good* and *Badde, Faire* and *Foule, Rich* and *Poore.* But this doctrine of Divells Saint *Paul* foreseeing would be broached in the latter times, gives warning of.

There also you promise a Commendation of wise, vertuous, and honest women, when as in the subsequent, the worst words, and filthiest Epithites that you can devise, you bestow on them in generall, excepting no sort of Women. Heerein may you be likened unto a man, which upon the doore of a ocurvie house sets this Superscription, *Heere is a very faire house to be Let:* whereas the doore being opened, it is no better then a dogge-hole and darke dungeon.

Further, if your owne words be true, that you wrote with your hand, but not with your heart, then are you an hypocrite in Print: but it is rather to be thought that your Pen was the bewrayer of the abundance of your minde, and that this was but a little morter to dawbe up agayne the wall, which you intended to breake downe.

The revenge of your rayling Worke wee leave to Him, who hath appropriated vengeance unto himselfe, whose Pen-man hath included Raylers in the Catalogue of them, that shall not inherite Gods kingdome, and your selfe unto the mercie of that just judge, who is able to save and to destroy.

Your undeserved friend,
Rachel Speght

FOR FURTHER READING

Jones, Ann Rosalind. "Counter-attacks on 'the Bayter of Women': Three Pamphleteers of the Early Seventeenth Century." In *The Renaissance Englishwoman in Print: Counterbalancing the Canon,* edited by Anne M. Haselkorn and Betty S. Travitsky, 45–62. Amherst: University of Massachusetts Press, 1990.

Jordan, Constance. *Renaissance Feminism: Literary Texts and Political Models.* Ithaca: Cornell University Press, 1990.

Lewalski, Barbara Kiefer. *Writing Women in Jacobean England.* Cambridge: Harvard University Press, 1993.

——— ed. *The Polemics and Poems of Rachel Speght.* New York: Oxford University Press, 1996.

Martin, Randall, ed. *Women Writers in Renaissance England.* London: Addison Wesley Longman, 1997.

Travitsky, Betty. "The Lady Doth Protest: Protest in the Popular Writings of Renaissance Englishwomen." *English Literary Renaissance* 14 (1984): 255–83.

Margaret Fell

1614–1702

When *Womens Speaking Justified* was published in 1666, its author, the Quaker
Margaret Fell, was imprisoned in Lancaster Castle for refusing to take the Oath
of Allegiance to the Church of England. It seems only appropriate, then, that
Fell's famous essay defending women's right to speak in the church would
appear at a time when she was suffering for speaking her mind. And speaking
her mind is something Fell never retreated from during her long life. In fact, a
judge at one of Fell's trials described her as having an "everlasting tongue" (Trevett 55).

Born Margaret Askew in Lancashire, England, in 1614 to middle-class Protestant parents, she married Judge Thomas Fell in 1631. The couple had eight
children, and after Judge Fell died in 1658, Margaret became an active traveler
and preacher on behalf of the Society of Friends, or Quakers, a group Margaret
joined in 1652 after meeting the Society's founder, George Fox. In 1669, Margaret married George Fox, and until her death in 1702, Fell spoke out for and
championed the Quaker religion, often in the face of persecution in the form of
imprisonment and financial hardship. In addition to publishing *Womens Speaking Justified,* an essay that helped establish a doctrine of equality among the
sexes within the Quaker faith, she helped persuade James II to declare tolerance
for religious dissent, and in 1697 she encouraged William II to continue protection of the Quakers. She is also credited with organizational changes within
Quakerism that gave generations of Quaker women important experience with
administrative, business, and organizational tasks. This resulted in many
Quaker women providing important leadership in abolitionist, suffragist, and
peace movements in the United States.

In their introduction to Fell in *The Rhetorical Tradition,* Patricia Bizzell and
Bruce Herzberg note that Fell "characterizes as a prophet the woman speaking
in public on matters of moral concern, an image that many later feminists
would also adopt" (673). This image of woman as moral speaker and prophet
emerges in *Womens Speaking Justified.* In the excerpt included here, Fell reinter-
prets the Bible—specifically Genesis, I Corinthians, and I Timothy—to make
the claim that women should be allowed to speak in public and in the church.
This reinterpretation was in direct contrast to the male-interpreted doctrine
that forbade women to speak. Like Rachel Speght, Fell uses an argumentative
technique known as *antistrephon,* which turns the rhetor's opponents' arguments and proofs to the rhetor's advantage. Fell claims that traditional interpretations are all taken out of historical and cultural context, and she argues

that the male church officials who exclude women from speaking are going against the word of God. In doing so, Fell contextualizes the scriptures and, instead of relying on "universals," points to the local and the particular, an interpretive technique used by many subsequent feminists to make similar arguments. Fell's prose style is clear and straightforward, and she does not rely on many rhetorical flourishes to make her case. This straightforwardness suggests Fell's confidence in both her argument and her cause. And it suggests why her "everlasting tongue" held such significant authority for many Quaker women who followed after her, including Lucretia Mott, Angelia Grimké Weld, and Susan B. Anthony, who often cited Fell in her speeches.

From *Womens Speaking Justified, Proved and Allowed by the Scriptures*

1666

Whereas it hath been an objection in the minds of many, and several times hath been objected by the clergy, or ministers, and others, against womens speaking in the Church; and so consequently may be taken, that they are condemned for meddling in the things of God; the ground of which objection, is taken from the Apostles words, which he writ in his first Epistle to the *Corinthians*, chap. 14. vers. 34, 35. And also what he writ to *Timothy* in the first Epistle, chap. 2, vers. 11, 12. But how far they wrong the Apostles intentions in these Scriptures, we shall shew clearly when we come to them in their course and order. But first let me lay down how God himself hath manifested his Will and Mind concerning women, and unto women.

And first, when *God created Man in his own image; in the image of God created he them, male and female: and God blessed them, and God said unto them, Be fruitful, and multiply: And God said, Behold, I have given you of every herb*, etc., Gen. 1. Here God joins them together in his own image, and makes no such distinctions and differences as men do; for though they be weak, he is strong; and as he said to the Apostle, *His grace is sufficient*, and his *strength is made manifest in weakness*, 2 Cor. 12.9. And such hath the Lord chosen, even *the weak things of the world, to confound the things which are mighty; and things which are despised, hath God chosen, to bring to nought things that are*, 1 Cor. 1. And God hath put no such difference between the male and female as men would make.

It is true, *The serpent that was more subtle than any* other *beast of the field*, came unto the woman, with his temptations, and with a lie; his subtilty discerning her to be more inclinable to hearken to him; when he said, *If ye eat, your eyes*

Reprinted from Fell, Margaret. *Womens Speaking Justified*. Publication number 194. Los Angeles: William Andrews Clark Memorial Library, University of California, 1979.

shall be opened: and the woman saw that *the fruit was good to make one wise,* there the temptation got into her, and *she did eat, and gave to her husband, and he did eat also,* and so they were both tempted into the transgression and disobedience; and therefore God said unto *Adam,* when that he hid himself when he heard his voice, *Hast thou eaten of the tree which I commanded thee that thou shouldest not eat?* And Adam said, *The woman which thou gavest me, she gave me of the tree, and I did eat.* And the Lord said unto the woman, *What is this that thou hast done?* And the woman said, *The serpent beguiled me, and I did eat.* Here the woman spoke the truth unto the Lord. See what the Lord saith, vers. 15, after he had pronounced sentence on the serpent: *I will put enmity between thee and the woman, and between thy seed and her seed; it shall bruise thy head, and thou shalt bruise his heel,* Gen. 3.

Let this word of the Lord, which was from the beginning, stop the mouths of all that oppose womens speaking in the power of the Lord; for he hath put enmity between the woman and the serpent; and if the seed of the woman speak not, the seed of the serpent speaks; for God hath put enmity between the two seeds, and it is manifest, that those that speak against the woman and her seeds speaking, speak out of the enmity of the old serpents seed; and God hath fulfilled his word and his promise, *When the fulness of time was come, he hath sent forth his Son, made of a woman, made under the Law, that we might receive the adoption of sons,* Gal. 4.4, 5. . . .

Thus we see that Jesus owned the love and grace that appeared in women, and did not despise it, and by what is recorded in the Scriptures, he received as much love, kindness, compassion, and tender dealing towards him from women, as he did from any others, both in his life time, and also after they had exercised their cruelty upon him. . . .

Mark this, you that despise and oppose the message of the Lord God that he sends by women, what had become of the redemption of the whole body of mankind, if they had not believed the message that the Lord Jesus sent by these women, of and concerning his resurrection? And if these women had not thus, out of their tenderness and bowels of love, who had received mercy, and grace, and forgiveness of sins, and virtue, and healing from him, which many men also had received the like, if their hearts had not been so united, and knit unto him in love, that they could not depart as the men did, but sat watching, and waiting, and weeping about the sepulchre until the time of his resurrection, and so were ready to carry his message, as is manifested, else how should his Disciples have known, who were not there?

Oh! blessed and glorified be the glorious Lord, for this may all the whole body of mankind say, though the wisdom of man, that never knew God, is always ready to except against the weak; but the weakness of God is stronger than men, and the foolishness of God is wiser than men. . . .

And now to the Apostles words, which is the ground of the great objection against womens speaking. And first, 1 *Cor.* 14. let the reader seriously read that chapter, and see the end and drift of the Apostle in speaking these words: for the Apostle is there exhorting the Corinthians unto charity, and to desire spiritual gifts, and not to speak in an unknown tongue, and not to be children in understanding, but to be children in malice, but in understanding to be men; and that the spirits of the prophets should be subject to the prophets, for God is not the author of confusion, but of peace: And then he saith, *Let your women keep silence in the Church,* etc.

Where it doth plainly appear that the women, as well as others, that were among them, were in confusion, for he saith, *How is it brethren? when ye come together, every one of you hath a psalm, hath a doctrine, hath a tongue, hath a revelation, hath an interpretation? let all things be done to edifying.* Here was no edifying, but all was in confusion speaking together. Therefore he saith, *If any man speak in an unknown tongue, let it be by two, or at most by three, and that by course, and let one interpret, but if there be no interpreter, let him keep silence in the Church.* Here the man is commanded to keep silence as well as the woman, when they are in confusion and out of order.

But the Apostle saith further, *They are commanded to be in obedience,* as also saith the Law; and *if they will learn any thing, let them ask their husbands at home, for it is a shame for a woman to speak in the Church.*

Here the Apostle clearly manifests his intent; for he speaks of women that were under the Law, and in that transgression as *Eve* was, and such as were to learn, and not to speak publicly, but they must first ask their husbands at home, and it was a shame for such to speak in the Church. And it appears clearly, that such women were speaking among the *Corinthians,* by the Apostles exhorting them from malice and strife, and confusion, and he preacheth the Law unto them, and he saith, in the Law it is written, *With men of other tongues, and other lips, will I speak unto this people,* vers. 2. 21.

And what is all this to women speaking? that have the everlasting Gospel to preach, and upon whom the promise of the Lord is fulfilled, and his Spirit poured upon them according to his word, *Acts* 2. 16, 17, 18. And if the Apostle would have stopped such as had the Spirit of the Lord poured upon them, why did he say just before, *If any thing be revealed to another that sitteth by, let the first hold his peace?* and *you may all prophesy one by one.* Here he did not say that such women should not prophesy as had the revelation and Spirit of God poured upon them, but their women that were under the Law, and in the transgression, and were in strife, confusion and malice in their speaking. . . .

And what is all this to such as have the power and spirit of the Lord Jesus poured upon them, and have the message of the Lord Jesus given unto them? Must not they speak the Word of the Lord because of these undecent and unreverent women that the Apostle speaks of, and to, in these two Scriptures? And how are the men of this generation blinded, that bring these Scriptures, and pervert the Apostles words, and corrupt his intent in speaking of them? And by these Scriptures, endeavour to stop the message of the Word of the Lord God in women, by condemning and despising of them. If the Apostle would have had womens speaking stopped, and did not allow of them, why did he entreat his true yokefellow to help those women who laboured with him in the Gospel? *Phil. 4.3.* And why did the Apostles join together in prayer and supplication with the women, and *Mary* the *Mother of Jesus*, and with his bretheren, *Acts* I.14, if they had not allowed, and had union and fellowship with the Spirit of God, wherever it was revealed in women as well as others? But all this opposing and gain-saying of womens speaking, hath risen out of the bottomless pit, and spirit of darkness that hath spoken for these many hundred years together in this night of apostacy, since the revelations have ceased and been hid. . . .

And so let this serve to stop that opposing spirit that would limit the Power and Spirit of the Lord Jesus, whose Spirit is poured upon all flesh, both Sons and Daughters, now in his Resurrection; and since that the Lord god in the Creation, when he made man in his own Image, he made them *male* and *female;* and since that christ Jesus, as the Apostle saith, was made of a Woman, and the power of the Highest overshadowed her, and the holy Ghost came upon her, and the holy thing that was born of her, was called the *Son of god,* and when he was upon the Earth, he manifested his *love,* and his *will,* and his *mind,* both to the Woman of *Samaria,* and *Martha,* and *Mary* her sister, and several others, as hath been shewed; and after his Resurrection also manifested himself unto them first of all even before he ascended unto his Father. *Now when Jesus was risen, the first day of the week, he appeared first unto Mary Magdalene,* Mark 16.9. And thus the Lord Jesus hath manifested himself and his Power, without respect of Persons, and so let all mouths be stopt that would limit him, whose Power and Spirit is infinite, that is pouring it upon all flesh.

And thus much in answer to these two Scriptures, which have been such a stumbling block, that the ministers of Darkness have made such a mountain of; But the Lord is removing all this, and taking it out of the way. M.F.

FOR FURTHER READING

Bizzell, Patricia, and Bruce Herzberg, eds. *The Rhetorical Tradition: Readings from Classical Times to the Present.* Boston: Bedford Books of St. Martin's Press, 1990.

Irvin, Joyce L., ed. *Womanhood and Radical Protestantism, 1525–1675.* New York: E. Mellon Press, 1979.

Kunze, Bonnelyn Young. *Margaret Fell and the Rise of Quakerism.* Stanford: Stanford University Press, 1994.

Luecke, Marilyn Serraino. "'God Hath Made No Difference Such As Men Would': Margaret Fell and the Politics of Speech." *Bunyan Studies: John Bunyan and His Times* 7 (1997): 73–95.

Trevett, Christine. *Women and Quakerism in the 17th Century.* York, U.K.: Sessions Book Trust, Ebon Press, 1991.

Sor Juana Inés de la Cruz

1651–1695

Sor Juana Inés de la Cruz, a Mexican nun and a prolific writer of poetry, plays, essays, and religious treatises, is one of most renowned writers of Latin America. She has been called "the first feminist in the new world and *La Respuesta* the *Magna Carta* of intellectual liberty for women in America" (Beggs 100). She was evidently a child prodigy who begged her mother to dress her as a boy and send her to the university. At age ten she was sent to Mexico City from her family's hacienda; in Mexico City she was eventually presented at court and entered the service of the Vicereine, who became her life-long friend and supporter. According to her own narrative, she lived in constant conflict between the pleasures of the secular life and her desire for study. In order to chastise herself for her slowness in learning Latin, she would cut her hair—a symbol of beauty for a young woman—to a length of "four to six fingers," vowing to have learned a certain body of material before it grew out.

At the age of twenty, Sor Juana abruptly left secular life and entered a convent, claiming a "room of her own" for her writing and scholarship. Her intellectual biography describes her frustrations with the distractions of the court and her belief that the veil was a suitable choice for one unwilling to marry who wanted to devote herself to study. Although she was dedicated to scholarship, she was also at the center of the most elite intellectual conversations of her time, involving scholars and members of the court.

The "Respuesta," to a fictitious Sor Filotea, was actually a reply to the rebuke she received from the Bishop of Puebla, a member of her intellectual circle. Sor Juana had published a critique of a famous sermon. Although she was well known for her polemical writing, the rebuke from the bishop made it clear that Sor Juana was still in a precarious position as a self-taught woman at a time when the expectations for women's literacy and participation in intellectual life were severely limited. In order to establish her authority to reply to the bishop's rebuke, she presents her intellectual autobiography, justifying her pursuit of the scholarly life and providing a vigorous defense of women's right to speak in church. Like other women writers who sought to justify women's speaking and demonstrate their virtue, Sor Juana uses as evidence the lives of notable women. In a rhetorical move foreshadowing later feminists, she also argues that the knowledge acquired in her social role as a woman is not incompatible with or inferior to the knowledge she acquires through scholarly pursuits: "And what shall I tell you, lady, of the natural secrets I have discovered while cooking? . . . And I often say, when observing these details: had Aristotle prepared victuals, he would have written more."

From "La Respuesta"

1691

My most illustrious *señora,* dear lady. It has not been my will, my poor health, or my justifiable apprehension that for so many days delayed my response. How could I write, considering that at my very first step my clumsy pen encountered two obstructions in its path? The first (and, for me, the most uncompromising) is to know how to reply to your most learned, most prudent, most holy, and most loving letter. For I recall that when Saint Thomas, the Angelic Doctor of Scholasticism, was asked about his silence regarding his teacher Albertus Magnus, he replied that he had not spoken because he knew no words worthy of Albertus. With so much greater reason, must not I too be silent? Not, like the Saint, out of humility, but because in reality I know nothing I can say that is worthy of you. The second obstruction is to know how to express my appreciation for a favor as unexpected as extreme, for having my scribblings printed, a gift so immeasurable as to surpass my most ambitious aspiration, my most fervent desire, which even as an entity of reason never entered my thoughts. Yours was a kindness, finally, of such magnitude that words cannot express my gratitude, a kindness exceeding the bounds of appreciation, as great as it was unexpected—which is as Quintilian said: *aspirations engender minor glory; benefices, major.* To such a degree as to impose silence on the receiver.

When the blessedly sterile—that she might miraculously become fecund— Mother of John the Baptist saw in her house such an extraordinary visitor as the Mother of the Word, her reason became clouded and her speech deserted her; and thus, in the place of thanks, she burst out with doubts and questions: *And whence is to me [that the mother of my Lord should come to me?]* And whence cometh such a thing to *me?* And so also it fell to Saul when he found himself the chosen, the annointed, King of Israel: *Am I not a son of Jemini, of the least tribe of Israel, and my kindred the last among all the families of the tribe of Benjamin? Why then hast thou spoken this word to me?* And thus say I, most honorable lady. Why do I receive such favor? By chance, am I other than an humble nun, the lowliest creature of the world, the most unworthy to occupy your attention? "Where-

Margaret Sayers Peden's translation of *La Respuesta a Sor Filotea,* the first translation of the work into the English language, was originally commissioned by a small independent New England press, Lime Rock Press, Inc., Salisbury, CT. It appeared in 1982 in a limited edition entitled *A Woman of Genius: The Intellectual Autobiography of Sor Juana Inés de la Cruz,* with photographs by Gabriel North Seymour. Copyright ©1982 by Lime Rock Press, Inc. Reprinted with permission. (English translation pages 14, 16, 24, 26, 28, 30, 32, 34, 38, 60, 62, 64, 68, 98.)

fore then speakest thou so to me?" "And whence is this to me?" Nor to the first
obstruction do I have any response other than I am little worthy of your eyes;
nor to the second, other than wonder, in the stead of thanks, saying that I am
not capable of thanking you for the smallest part of that which I owe you. . . .
And, in truth, I have written nothing except when compelled and constrained,
and then only to give pleasure to others; not alone without pleasure of my own,
but with absolute repugnance, for I have never deemed myself one who has any
worth in letters or the wit necessity demands of one who would write; and thus
my customary response to those who press me, above all in sacred matters, is,
what capacity of reason have I? what application? what resources? what rudimentary knowledge of such matters beyond that of the most superficial scholarly degrees? Leave these matters to those who understand them; I wish no
quarrel with the Holy Office, for I am ignorant, and I tremble that I may express
some proposition that will cause offense or twist the true meaning of some
scripture. I do not study to write, even less to teach—which in one like myself
were unseemly pride—but only to the end that if I study, I will be ignorant of
less. This is my response, and these are my feelings.

I have never written of my own choice, but at the urging of others, to whom
with reason I might say, *You have compelled me.* But one truth I shall not deny
(first, because it is well-known to all, and second, because although it has not
worked in my favor, God has granted me the mercy of loving truth above all
else), which is that from the moment I was first illuminated by the light of reason, my inclination toward letters has been so vehement, so overpowering, that
not even the admonitions of others—and I have suffered many—nor my own
meditations—and they have not been few—have been sufficient to cause me to
forswear this natural impulse that God placed in me: the Lord God knows why,
and for what purpose. And He knows that I have prayed that He dim the light of
my reason, leaving only that which is needed to keep His Law, for there are
those who would say that all else is unwanted in a woman, and there are even
those who would hold that such knowledge does injury. And my Holy Father
knows too that as I have been unable to achieve this (my prayer has not been
answered), I have sought to veil the light of my reason—along with my name—
and to offer it up only to Him who bestowed it upon me, and He knows that
none other was the cause for my entering into Religion, notwithstanding that
the spiritual exercises and company of a community were repugnant to the
freedom and quiet I desired for my studious endeavors. And later, in that community, the Lord God knows—and, in the world, only the one who must
know—how diligently I sought to obscure my name, and how this was not permitted, saying it was temptation: and so it would have been. If it were in my
power, lady, to repay you in some part what I owe you, it might be done by telling you this thing which has never before passed my lips, except to be spoken to
the one who should hear it. It is my hope that by having opened wide to you the
doors of my heart, by having made patent to you its most deeply-hidden se-

crets, you will deem my confidence not unworthy of the debt I owe to your most august person and to your most uncommon favors.

Continuing the narration of my inclinations, of which I wish to give you a thorough account, I will tell you that I was not yet three years old when my mother determined to send one of my elder sisters to learn to read at a school for girls we call the *Amigas*. Affection, and mischief, caused me to follow her, and when I observed how she was being taught her lessons I was so inflamed with the desire to know how to read, that deceiving—for so I knew it to be—the mistress, I told her that my mother had meant for me to have lessons too. She did not believe it, as it was little to be believed, but, to humor me, she acceded. I continued to go there, and she continued to teach me, but now, as experience had disabused her, with all seriousness; and I learned so quickly that before my mother knew of it I could already read, for my teacher had kept it from her in order to reveal the surprise and reap the reward at one and the same time. And I, you may be sure, kept the secret, fearing that I would be whipped for having acted without permission. The woman who taught me, may God bless and keep her, is still alive and can bear witness to all I say. I also remember that in those days, my tastes being those common to that age, I abstained from eating cheese because I had heard that it made one slow of wits, for in me the desire for learning was stronger than the desire for eating—as powerful as that is in children. When later, being six or seven, and having learned how to read and write, along with all the other skills of needlework and household arts that girls learn, it came to my attention that in Mexico City there were Schools, and a University, in which one studied the sciences. The moment I heard this, I began to plague my mother with insistent and importunate pleas: she should dress me in boy's clothing and send me to Mexico City to live with relatives, to study and be tutored at the University. She would not permit it, and she was wise, but I assuaged my disappointment by reading the many and varied books belonging to my grandfather, and there were not enough punishments, nor reprimands, to prevent me from reading: so that when I came to the city many marveled, not so much at my natural wit, as at my memory, and at the amount of learning I had mastered at an age when many have scarcely learned to speak well.

I began to study Latin grammar—in all, I believe, I had no more than 20 lessons—and so intense was my concern that though among women (especially a woman in the flower of her youth) the natural adornment of one's hair is held in such high esteem, I cut off mine to the breadth of some four to six fingers, measuring the place it had reached, and imposing upon myself the condition that if by the time it had again grown to that length I had not learned such and such a thing I had set for myself to learn while my hair was growing, I would again cut it off as punishment for being so slow-witted. And it did happen that my hair grew out and still I had not learned what I had set for myself—because my hair grew quickly and I learned slowly—and in fact I did cut it in punishment for such stupidity: for there seemed to me no cause for a head to be adorned with hair and naked of learning—which was the more desired embellishment. And so I entered the religious order, knowing that life there entailed certain conditions (I refer to superficial, and not fundamental, regards) most repugnant to my nature; but given the total antipathy I felt for marriage, I deemed convent life the least unsuitable and the most honorable I could elect if I were to insure my salvation. Working against that end, first (as, finally, the most important) was the matter of all the trivial aspects of my nature which nourished my pride, such as wishing to live alone, and wishing to have no obligatory occupation that would inhibit the freedom of my studies, nor the sounds of a community that would intrude upon the peaceful silence of my books. These desires caused me to falter some while in my decision, until certain learned persons enlightened me, explaining that they were temptation, and, with divine favor, I overcame them, and took upon myself the state which now so unworthily I hold. I believed that I was fleeing from myself, but— wretch that I am!—I brought with me my worst enemy, my inclination, which I do not know whether to consider a gift or a punishment from Heaven, for once dimmed and encumbered by the many activities common to Religion, that inclination exploded in me like gunpowder, proving how *privation is the source of appetite*. . . .

And so I continued, as I have said, directing the course of my studies toward the peak of Sacred Theology, it seeming necessary to me, in order to scale those heights, to climb the steps of the human sciences and arts; for how could one undertake the study of the Queen of Sciences if first one had not come to know her servants?

How, without Logic, could I be apprised of the general and specific way in which the Holy Scripture is written? How, without Rhetoric, could I understand its figures, its tropes, its locutions? How, without Physics, so many innate questions concerning the nature of animals, their sacrifices, wherein exist so many symbols, many already declared, many still to be discovered? How should I know whether Saul's being refreshed by the sound of David's harp was due to the virtue and natural power of Music, or to a transcendent power God wished to place in David? How, without Arithmetic, could one understand the computations of the years, days, months, hours, those mysterious weeks communicated by Gabriel to Daniel, and others for whose understanding one must know the nature, concordance, and properties of numbers? How, without Geometry, could one measure the Holy Arc of the Covenant and the Holy City of Jerusalem, whose mysterious measures are foursquare in their dimensions, as well as the miraculous proportions of all their parts? How, without Architecture, could one know the great Temple of Solomon, of which God Himself was the Author who conceived the disposition and the design, and the Wise King but the overseer who executed it, of which temple there was no foundation without mystery, no column without symbolism, no cornice without allusion, no architrave without significance; and similarly others of its parts, of which the least fillet was never intended solely for the service and complement of Art, but as symbol of greater things? How, without great knowledge of the laws and parts of which History is comprised, could one understand historical Books? Or those recapitulations in which many times what happened first is seen in the narrated account to have happened later? How, without great learning in Canon and Civil Law, could one understand Legal Books? How, without great erudition, could one apprehend the secular histories of which the Holy Scripture makes mention, such as the many customs of the Gentiles, their many rites, their many ways of speaking? How without the abundant laws and lessons of the Holy Fathers could one understand the obscure lesson of the Prophets? And without being expert in Music, how could one understand the exquisite precision of the musical proportions that grace so many Scriptures. . . .

How then should I—so lacking in virtue and so poorly read—find courage to write? But as I had acquired the rudiments of learning, I continued to study ceaselessly divers subjects, having for none any particular inclination, but for all in general; and having studied some more than others was not owing to preference, but to the chance that more books on certain subjects had fallen into my hands, causing the election of them through no discretion of my own. . . .

This manner of reflection has always been my habit, and is quite beyond my will to control; on the contrary, I am wont to become vexed that my intellect makes me weary; and I believed that it was so with everyone, as well as making verses, until experience taught me otherwise; and it is so strong in me this nature, or custom, that I look at nothing without giving it further examination. Once in my presence two young girls were spinning a top and scarcely had I seen the motion and the figure described, when I began, out of this madness of mine, to meditate on the effortless *motus* of the spherical form, and how the impulse persisted even when free and independent of its cause—for the top continued to dance even at some distance from the child's hand, which was the causal force. And not content with this, I had flour brought and sprinkled about, so that as the top danced one might learn whether these were perfect circles it described with its movement; and I found that they were not, but, rather, spiral lines that lost their circularity as the impetus declined. Other girls sat playing at spillikins (surely the most frivolous game that children play); I walked closer to observe the figures they formed, and seeing that by chance three lay in a triangle, I set to joining one with another, recalling that this was said to be the form of the mysterious ring of Solomon, in which he was able to see the distant splendor and images of the Holy Trinity, by virtue of which the ring worked such prodigies and marvels. And the same shape was said to form David's harp, and that is why Saul was refreshed at its sound; and harps today largely conserve that shape.

And what shall I tell you, lady, of the natural secrets I have discovered while cooking? I see that an egg holds together and fries in butter or in oil, but, on the contrary, in syrup shrivels into shreds; observe that to keep sugar in a liquid state one need only add a drop or two of water in which a quince or other bitter fruit has been soaked; observe that the yolk and the white of one egg are so dissimilar that each with sugar produces a result not obtainable with both together. I do not wish to weary you with such inconsequential matters, and make mention of them only to give you full notice of my nature, for I believe they will be occasion for laughter. But, lady, as women, what wisdom may be ours if not the philosophies of the kitchen? Lupercio Leonardo spoke well when he said: how well one may philosophize when preparing dinner. And I often say, when observing these trivial details: had Aristotle prepared victuals, he would have written more. And pursuing the manner of my cogitations, I tell you that this process is so continuous in me that I have no need for books. And on one occasion, when because of a grave upset of the stomach the physicians forbade me to study, I passed thus some days, but then I proposed that it would be less harmful if they allowed me books, because so vigorous and vehement were my cogitations that my spirit was consumed more greatly in a quarter of an hour than in four days' studying books. And thus they were persuaded to allow me to read. And moreover, lady, not even have my dreams been excluded from this ceaseless agitation of my imagination; indeed, in dreams it is wont to work more freely and less encumbered, collating with greater clarity and calm the gleanings of the day, arguing and making verses, of which I could offer you an extended catalogue, as well as of some arguments and inventions that I have better achieved sleeping than awake. I relinquish this subject in order not to tire you, for the above is sufficient to allow your discretion and acuity to penetrate perfectly and perceive my nature, as well as the beginnings, the methods, and the present state of my studies.

Even, lady, were these merits (and I see them celebrated as such in men), they would not have been so in me, for I cannot but study. If they are fault, then, for the same reasons, I believe I have none. Nevertheless, I live always with so little confidence in myself that neither in my study, nor in any other thing, do I trust my judgment; and thus I remit the decision to your sovereign genius, submitting myself to whatever sentence you may bestow, without controversy, without reluctance, for I have wished here only to present you with a simple narration of my inclination toward letters.

I confess, too, that though it is true, as I have stated, that I had no need of books, it is nonetheless also true that they have been no little inspiration, in divine as in human letters. Because I find a Debbora administering the law, both military and political, and governing a people among whom there were many learned men. I find a most wise Queen of Saba, so learned that she dares to challenge with hard questions the wisdom of the greatest of all wise men, without being reprimanded for doing so, but, rather, as a consequence, to judge unbelievers. I see many and illustrious women; some blessed with the gift of prophecy, like Abigail, others of persuasion, like Esther; others with pity, like Rehab; others with perserverance, like Anna, the mother of Samuel; and an infinite number of others, with divers gifts and virtues.

If I again turn to the Gentiles, the first I encounter are the Sibyls, those women chosen by God to prophesy the principal mysteries of our Faith, and with learned and elegant verses that surpass admiration. . . . An Aspasia Milesia, who taught philosophy and rhetoric, and who was a teacher of the philosopher Pericles. An Hypatia, who taught astrology, and studied many years in Alexandria. A Leontium, a Greek woman, who questioned the philosopher Theophrastus, and convinced him. A Jucia, a Corinna, a Cornelia; and, finally, a great throng of women deserving to be named, some as Greeks, some as muses, some as seers; for all were nothing more than learned women, held, and celebrated—and venerated as well—as such by antiquity. . . .

If, most venerable lady, the tone of this letter may not have seemed right and proper, I ask forgiveness for its homely familiarity, and the less than seemly respect in which by treating you as a nun, one of my sisters, I have lost sight of the remoteness of your most illustrious person; which, had I seen you without your veil, would never have occurred; but you in all your prudence and mercy will supplement or amend the language, and if you find unsuitable the *Vos* of the address I have employed, believing that for the reverence I owe you, Your Reverence seemed little reverent, modify it in whatever manner seems appropriate to your due, for I have not dared exceed the limits of your custom, nor transgress the boundary of your modesty.

And hold me in your grace, and entreat for me divine grace, of which the Lord God grant you large measure, and keep you, as I pray Him, and am needful. From this convent of our Father Saint Jerome in Mexico City, the first day of the month of March of sixteen hundred and ninety-one. Allow me to kiss your hand, your most favored.

FOR FURTHER READING

Beggs, Donald. "Sor Juana's Feminism." In *Hypatia's Daughters, Fifteen Hundred Years of Women Philosophers,* edited by Linda Lopez McAlister, 108–27. Bloomington: Indiana University Press, 1996.

Inés de la Cruz, Sor Juana. *A Sor Juana Anthology.* Translated by Alan S. Trueblood. Cambridge: Harvard University Press, 1988.

Paz, Octavio. *Sor Juana or The Traps of Faith.* Translated by Margaret Sayers Peden. Cambridge: Harvard University Press, 1988.

Mary Astell

1666–1731

Mary Astell was one of the first polemicists in England arguing against the contemporary representation of women and seeking to improve women's status. Her plan for a religious retreat for women was a response to the numerous attacks on the frivolity and vanity of women to which Christine de Pizan, Jane Anger, Rachel Speght, and others also responded. But Astell went beyond rebuttal, arguing that to deny women their natural right to education was to consign them to the very intellectual poverty of which they had been accused.

Astell herself was the daughter of a Newcastle coal merchant and was fortunate to receive her education from a clergyman uncle. She remained unmarried and had a valued circle of women friends who must have inspired her ideas about the worth of women's friendships. Several of the women acknowledged her influence in poems praising her, although one also noted Astell's "haughty carriage," despite the fact that she had no stable means of support, and noted that she cultivated the friendship of those who did (Ferguson 181). Some of her wealthy women friends, like Lady Mary Wortley Montagu, supported her financially as well as intellectually and, despite their class privilege, assisted Astell in establishing a charity school for girls, further evidence of Astell's belief in the natural right of all people to an education.

Her argument in part 1 of *A Serious Proposal to the Ladies* for a "religious retirement," Anglican rather than Roman Catholic, also asserts the importance of an intellectual community in which women could teach each other and enjoy women's friendship in a "Happy retreat! which will be introducing you into such *Paradise* as your *Mother Eve* forfeited. . . ." This retreat could even allow women an alternative to marriage, although Astell, conservatively, supported the subjugation of wives to husbands in marriage. In the excerpts here Astell delicately positions her argument in order not to offend the women she addresses but to convince them of the benefits of education to their own souls, as well as to the well-being of others whom they would more ably serve.

In part 2 of the *Proposal*, Astell describes the method and substance of the education she proposes for women. The excerpts here set forth her conception of effective rhetorical practice. She draws from an understanding of classical rhetoric but calls for a more moderate, common-sense approach than either the rigid or excessive examples of argument of her day. In particular, she argues for a greater sensitivity to audience, a less bombastic and agonistic style, and a rhetoric that draws writer and reader into a collaborative search for truth.

From *A Serious Proposal to the Ladies*

1694

Ladies,

Since the Profitable Adventures that have gone abroad in the world have met with so great Encouragement, tho' the highest advantage they can propose, is an uncertain Lot for such matters as Opinion, not real worth, gives a value to; things which if obtained are as flitting and fickle as that Chance which is to dispose of them; I therefore persuade my self, you will not be less kind to a Proposition that comes attended with more certain and substantial Gain; whose only design is to improve your Charms and heighten your Value, by suffering you no longer to be cheap and contemptible. Its aim is to fix that Beauty, to make it lasting and permanent, which Nature with all the helps of Art cannot secure, and to place it out of the reach of Sickness and Old Age, by transferring it from a corruptible Body to an immortal Mind. . . .

Pardon me the seeming rudeness of this Proposal, which goes upon a supposition that there's something amiss in you, which it is intended to amend. My design is not to expose, but to rectify your Failures. To be exempt from mistake, is a privilege few can pretend to, the greatest is to be past Conviction and too obstinate to reform. Even the *men,* as exact as they would seem, and as much as they divert themselves with our miscarriages, are very often guilty of greater faults, and such, as considering the advantages they enjoy, are much more inexcusable. . . .

Although it has been said by Men of more Wit than Wisdom, and perhaps of more malice than either, that Women are naturally incapable of acting Prudently, or that they are necessarily determined to folly, I must by no means grant it. . . . Besides, there are Examples in all Ages, which sufficiently confute the Ignorance and Malice of this Assertion.

Now as to the Proposal, it is to erect a *Monastery,* or if you will (to avoid giving offence to the scrupulous and injudicious, by name which though innocent in themselves, have been abused by superstitious Practices), we will call it a *Religious Retirement,* and such as shall have a double aspect, being not only a Retreat from the World for those who desire that advantage, but likewise, an institution and previous discipline, to fit us to do the greatest good in it; such an Institution as this (if I do not mightily deceive my self) would be the most probable method to amend the present, and improve the future age. . . .

Reprinted from Astell, Mary. *A Serious Proposal to the Ladies for the Advancement of their True and Greatest Interest,* parts I and II. 3rd ed. London: R. Wilkin, at the King's Head, 1694. Reproduction of the original in the British Library. Ann Arbor: University Microfilms International. Microfilm.

You are therefore ladies, invited to a place, where you shall suffer no other confinement, but to be kept out of the road of sin. . . . Happy retreat! which will be introducing you into such *Paradise* as your *Mother Eve* forfeited, where you shall feast on Pleasures, that do not, like those of the World, disappoint your expectations, pall your Appetites, and by the disgust they give you put you on the fruitless search after new Delights, which when obtained are as empty as the former; but such as will make you *truly* happy now, and prepare you to be *perfectly* so hereafter. Here are no serpents to deceive you, whilst you entertain your selves in these delicious Gardens. No provocations will be given in this Amicable Society, but to Love and to good Works, which will afford such an entertaining employment, that you'll have as little inclination as leisure to pursue these Follies, which in the time of your ignorance pass'd with you under the name of love, altho' there is not in nature two more different things, than *true love* and that *brutish passion,* which pretends to ape it. Here will be no Rivalling but for the Love of God, no ambition but to procure his Favor, to which nothing will more effectually recommend you, than a great and dear affection to each other. . . .

The SECOND PART Of the PROPOSAL TO THE LADIES
Wherein a Method is offer'd for the Improvement of their Minds.

V. As Nature teaches us Logic, so does it instruct us in Rhetoric much better than Rules of Art, which if they are good ones are nothing else but those Judicious Observations which Men of Sense have drawn from Nature, and which all who reflect on the Operations of their own Minds will find out 'emselves. The common Precepts of Rhetoric may teach us how to reduce Ingenious ways of speaking to a certain Rule, but they do not teach us how to Invent them, this is Natures work and she does it best; there is as much difference between Natural and Artificial Eloquence as there is between Paint and True Beauty. So that as a good Author well observes, all that's useful in this Art, "is the avoiding certain evil ways of Writing and Speaking, and above all an Artificial and Rhetorical Stile compos'd of false Thoughts, Hyperboles and forc'd Figures which is the greatest fault in Rhetoric."

I shall not therefore recommend under the name of Rhetoric and Art of speaking floridly on all Subjects, and of dressing up Error and Impertinence in a quaint and taking garb; any more than I did that Wrangling which goes by the name of Logic, and which teaches to dispute *for* and *against* all Propositions indefinitely whether they are True or False. It is an abuse both of Reason and Address to press 'em into the Service of a Trifle or an Untruth; and a mistake to think that any Argument can be rightly made, or any Discourse truly Eloquent that does not illustrate and inforce Truth. For the Design of Rhetoric is to remove those Prejudices that lie in the way of Truth, to Reduce the Passions to the Government of Reason; to place our Subject in a Right Light, and excite our Hearers to a due consideration of it. And I know not what exactness of Method, pure and proper Language, Figures, insinuating ways of Address and the like signify, any farther than as they contribute to the Service of Truth by rendering our Discourses Intelligible, Agreeable, and Convincing. They are indeed very serviceable to it when they are duly managed, for Good Sense loses much of its efficacy by being ill express'd, and an ill stile is nothing else but the neglect of some of these, or over doing others of 'em.

Obscurity, one of the greatest faults in Writing, does commonly proceed from a want of Meditation, for when we pretend to teach others what we do not understand our selves, no wonder that we do it at a sorry rate. 'Tis true, Obscurity is sometimes design'd, to conceal an erroneous opinion which an Author dares not openly own, or which if it be discover'd he has a mind to evade. And sometimes even an honest and good Writer who studies to avoid may insensibly fall into it, by reason that his Ideas being become familiar to himself by frequent Meditation, a long train of 'em are readily excited in his mind, by a word or two which he's used to annex to them; but it is not so with his Readers who are perhaps strangers to his Meditations, and yet ought to have the very same Idea rais'd in theirs that was in the Authors mind, or else they cannot understand him. If therefore we desire to be intelligible to every body, our Expressions must be more plain and explicit than they needed to be if we writ only for our selves, or for those to whom frequent Discourse has made our Ideas familiar.

Not that it is necesssary to express at length all the Process our Mind goes thro in resolving a Question, this wou'd spin out our Discourse to an unprofitable tediousness, the Operations of the Mind being much more speedy than those of the Tongue or Pen. But we shou'd fold up our Thoughts so closely and neatly, expressing them in such significant tho few words, as that the Readers Mind may easily open and enlarge them. And if this can be done with facility we are Perspicuous as well as Strong, if with difficulty or not at all, we're then perplext and Obscure Writers. . . .

In a word, I know not a more compendious way to good Speaking and Writing, than to chuse out the most excellent in either as a Model on which to form our selves. Or rather to imitate the Perfections of all, and avoid their mistakes. . . . No sort of Style but has its excellency and is liable to defect: If care be not taken the Sublime which subdues us with Nobleness of thought and Grandeur of Expression, will fly out of sight and by being Empty and Bombast become contemptible. The Plain and Simple will grow Dull and Abject; the Sever dry and Rugged, the Florid vain and impertinent. The Strong instead of rousing the Mind will distract and intangle it by being Obscure . . . Good Sense is the principal thing without which all our polishing is of little Worth, and yet if Ornament be wholly neglected very few will regard us. . . .

And perhaps the great secret of Writing is the mixing all these in so just a proportion that every one may taste what he likes without being disgusted by it contrary. And may find at once that by the Solidity of the Reason, the purity and propriety of Expression, and insinuating agreeableness of Address, his

Understanding is Enlightned, his Affections subdued and his Will duly regulated. . . .

And if we do so I believe we shall find, ther's nothing more improper than Pride and Positiveness, nor any thing more prevalent than an innocent compliance with their weakness. . . . And since many wou'd yield to the Clear Light of Truth were't not for the shame of being overcome, we shou'd Convince but not Triumph, and rather Conceal our Conquest than Publish it. . . .

In short, as Thinking conformably to the Nature of Things is True Knowledge, so th' expressing our Thoughts in such a way, as most readily, and with the greatest Clearness and Life, excites in others the very same Ideas that was in us, is the best Eloquence. For if our Idea be conformable to the Nature of the thing it represent, and its Relations duly stated, this is the most effectual way both to Inform and Perswade, since Truth being always amiable, cannot fail of attracting when she's plac'd in a Right Light, and those to whom we offer her, are made Able and Willing to discern her Beauties.

FOR FURTHER READING

Astell, Mary. *The Christian Religion as Profess'd by a Daughter of the Church.* 1705.
———. *Some Reflections upon Marriage.* 1700.
Ferguson, Moira. *First Feminists: British Women Writers 1578–1799.* Bloomington: Indiana University Press. 1985.

Lady Mary Wortley Montagu

1689–1762

Lady Mary Wortley Montagu spent her whole life doing things she was not supposed to do, breaking most gender boundaries of her time. She wrote essays and poetry and translated a play. She traveled the world and wrote about what she saw and learned. She debated politics and literature in salons with Addison, Steele, Pope, and other eighteenth-century luminaries. She introduced the inoculation of smallpox to England. And, in the midst of these accomplishments, she made a reputation for herself as one of the greatest letter writers in an age of great letter writers.

Montagu was born Mary Pierrepont in 1689. The daughter of an earl, she taught herself Latin and immersed herself in the Roman classics. In 1712 she married, against her father's wishes, a Whig member of parliament, Edward Wortley Montagu. Edward was also the ambassador to Turkey, and Mary accompanied her husband on his numerous adventures abroad. She wrote and published her travel accounts, and she also submitted essays to Addison and Steele's *The Spectator*. She and Edward eventually divorced, and although Montague carried on a passionate correspondence with an Italian writer, Francesco Algarotti, even living in Italy for twenty years, she never remarried.

As the letter included here shows, Montagu was no fan of marriage. Written from Italy in 1753 to Montagu's daughter, this letter implores Lady Bute to allow Montagu's young granddaughter a thorough education. Montagu argues the importance of education for women while at the same time bemoaning the dangers inherent in becoming a woman of learning. In a twist on the common assumption that an educated woman makes a good wife, Montagu argues that learning is most important as solace for women—who, she recommends, should never marry. Moreover, her advice that her granddaughter be warned to conceal her education may be an ironic commentary on the standard assumption that ladies well versed in the arts attract the most prosperous husbands. Educating women, she argues, helps them recognize "Fools" and be content with the "smallness" of their lives and provides them comfort in solitude. Montagu displays her erudition in this letter and gives current readers a realistic glimpse of the ways in which an educated women described and valued her own learning.

"Letter to Lady Bute"

28 January 1753

Dear Child,

You have given me a great deal of Satisfaction by your account of your eldest Daughter. I am particularly pleas'd to hear she is a good Arithmetician; it is the best proofe of understanding. The knowledge of Numbers is one of the cheif distinctions between us and Brutes. If there is any thing in Blood, you may reasonably expect your children should be endow'd with an uncommon Share of good Sense. Mr. Wortley's Family and mine have both produce'd some of [the] greatest Men that have been born in England. I mean Admiral Sandwich, and my Great Grandfather who was distinguish'd by the name of Wise William. I have heard Lord Bute's father mention'd as an extroadinary Genius (tho he had not many oppertunitys of shewing it), and his uncle the present Duke of Argyle has one of the best Heads I ever knew.

I will therefore speak to you as supposing Lady Mary not only capable but desirous of Learning. In that case, by all means let her be indulg'd in it. You will tell me, I did not make it a part of your Education. Your prospect was very different from hers, as you had no deffect either in mind or person to hinder, and much in your circumstances to attract, the highest offers. It seem'd your business to learn how to live in the World, as it is hers to know how to be easy out of it. It is the common Error of Builders and Parents to follow some Plan they think beautifull (and perhaps is so) without considering that nothing is beautifull that is misplac'd. Hence we see so many Edifices raise'd that the raisers can never inhabit, being too large for their Fortunes. Vistos are laid open over barren heaths, and apartments contriv'd for a coolness very agreable in Italy but killing in the North of Brittain. Thus every Woman endeavors to breed her Daughter a fine Lady, qualifying her for a station in which she will never appear, and at the same time incapacitateing her for that retirement to which she is destin'd. Learning (if she has a real taste for it) will not only make her contented but happy in it. No Entertainment is so cheap as reading, nor any pleasure so lasting. She will not want new Fashions nor regret the loss of expensive Diversions or variety of company if she can be amus'd with an Author in her closet. To render this amusement extensive, she should be permitted to learn the Languages. I have heard it lamented that Boys lose so many years in meer learning of Words. This is no Objection to a Girl, whose time is not so precious.

She cannot advance her selfe in any proffession, and has therefore more hours to spare; and as you say her memory is good, she will be very agreably employ'd this way.

There are two cautions to be given on this subject: first, not to think her selfe Learned when she can read Latin or even Greek. Languages are more properly to be calld Vehicles of Learning than Learning it selfe, as may be observ'd in many Schoolmasters, who thô perhaps critics in Grammar are the most ignorant fellows upon Earth. True knowledge consists in knowing things, not words. I would wish her no farther a Linguist than to enable her to read Books in their originals, that are often corrupted and allwaies injur'd by Translations. Two hours application every morning will bring this about much sooner than you can imagine, and she will have leisure enough beside to run over the English poetry, which is a more important part of a Woman's Education than it is generally suppos'd. Many a young Damsel has been ruin'd by a fine copy of Verses, which she would have laugh'd at if she had known it had been stoln from Mr. Waller. I remember when I was a Girl I sav'd one of my Companions from Destruction, who communicated to me an epistle she was quite charm'd with. As she had a natural good taste, she observ'd the Lines were not so smooth as Prior's or Pope's, but had more thought and spirit than any of theirs. She was wonderfully delighted with such a demonstration of her Lover's sense and passion, and not a little pleas'd with her own charms, that had force enough to inspire such elegancies. In the midst of this Triumph, I shew'd her they were taken from Randolph's Poems, and the unfortunate Transcriber was dismiss'd with the scorn he deserv'd. To say Truth, the poor Plagiary was very unlucky to fall into my Hands; that Author, being no longer in Fashion, would have escap'd any one of less universal reading than my selfe. You should encourrage your Daughter to talk over with you what she reads, and as you are very capable of distinguishing, take care she does not mistake pert Folly for Wit and humour, or Rhyme for Poetry, which are the common Errors of young People, and have a train of ill Consequences.

The second caution to be given her (and which is most absolutely necessary) is to conceal whatever Learning she attains, with as much solicitude as she would hide crookedness or lameness. The parade of it can only serve to draw on her the envy, and consequently the most inveterate Hatred, of all he and she Fools, which will certainly be at least three parts in four of all her Acquaintance. The use of knowledge in our Sex (beside the amusement of Solitude) is to moderate the passions and learn to be contented with a small expence, which are the certain effects of a studious Life and, it may be, preferable even to that Fame which Men have engross'd to themselves and will not suffer us to share. You will tell me I have not observ'd this rule my selfe, but you are mistaken; it is only inevitable Accident that has given me any Reputation that way. I have allwaies carefully avoided it, and ever thought it a misfortune.

The explanation of this paragraph would occasion a long digression, which I

will not trouble you with, it being my present design only to say what I think
usefull for the Instruction of my Grand daughter, which I have much at Heart.
If she has the same inclination (I should say passion) for Learning that I was
born with, History, Geography, and Philosophy will furnish her with materials
to pass away chearfully a longer Life than is allotted to mortals. I beleive there
are few heads capable of makeing Sir I[saac] Newton's calculations, but the result of them is not difficult to be understood by a moderate capacity. Do not
fear this should make her affect the character of Lady ———, or Lady ———,
or Mrs. ———. Those Women are ridiculous, not because they have Learning
but because they have it not. One thinks herselfe a compleat Historian after
reading Eachard's Roman History, another a profound Philosopher having got
by heart some of Pope's uninteligible essays, and a third an able Divine on the
Strength of Whitfield's Sermons. Thus you hear them screaming Politics and
Controversie. It is a saying of Thucidides, Ignorance is bold, and knowledge re-
serv'd. Indeed it is impossible to be far advance'd in it without being more
humble'd by a conviction of Human ignorance than elated by Learning.

At the same time I recommend Books, I neither exclude Work nor drawing. I
think it as scandalous for a Woman not to know how to use a needle, as for a
Man not to know how to use a sword. I was once extream fond of my pencil,
and it was a great mortification to me when my Father turn'd off my Master,
having made a considerable progress for the short time I learnt. My over eagerness in the persuit of it had brought a weakness on my Eyes that made it necessary to leave it off, and all the advantage I got was the Improvement of my
Hand. I see by hers that practise will make her a ready writer. She may attain it
by serving you for a Secretary when your Health or affairs make it troublesome
to you to write your selfe, and custom will make it an agreable Amusement to
her. She cannot have too many for that station of Life which will probably be
her Fate. The ultimate end of your Education was to make you a good Wife (and
I have the comfort to hear that you are one); hers ought to be, to make her
Happy in a Virgin state. I will not say it is happier, but it is undoubtedly safer
than any Marriage. In a Lottery where there is (at the lowest computation) ten
thousand blanks to a prize, it is the most prudent choice not to venture.

I have allwaies been so thoroughly persuaded of this Truth that notwithstanding the flattering views I had for you, (as I never intended you a sacrifice
to my Vanity) I thought I ow'd you the Justice to lay before you all the hazards
attending Matrimony. You may recollect I did so in the strongest manner. Perhaps you may have more success in the instructing your Daughter. She has so
much company at home she will not need seeking it abroad, and will more
readily take the notions you think fit to give her. As you were alone in my
Family, it would have been thought a great Cruelty to suffer you no Companions of your own Age, especially having so many near Relations, and I do not
wonder their Opinions influence'd yours. I was not sorry to see you not deter-
min'd on a single Life, knowing it was not your Father's Intention, and con-

tented my selfe with endeavoring to make your Home so easy that you might not be in hast to leave it.

I am afraid you will think this a very long and insignificant Letter. I hope the kindness of the Design will excuse it, being willing to give you every proofe in my power that I am your most affectionate Mother,
A. M. Wortley.

FOR FURTHER READING

Campbell, Jill. "Lady Mary Wortley Montagu and the Historical Machinery of Female Identity." In *History, Gender and Eighteenth-Century Literature,* edited by Beth Fowkes Tobin, 64–85. Athens: University of Georgia Press, 1994.

Grundy, Isobel. *Lady Mary Wortley Montagu: Comet of the Enlightenment.* New York: Oxford University Press, 1999.

Lowenthal, Cynthia. *Lady Mary Wortley Montagu and the Eighteenth-Century Familiar Letter.* Athens: University of Georgia Press, 1994.

Montagu, Lady Mary Wortley. *Essays and Poems and Simplicity, a Comedy.* Edited by Robert Halsband and Isobel Grundy. Oxford: Clarendon Press, 1977.

Belinda

In her petition, Belinda "begins the African American women's autobiographical tradition," according to Sharon Harris (12). Belinda boldly asserts the right
to voice and to personhood as she claims a monetary allowance from her
master's estate after his death. No other record of Belinda's life exists, but her
petition, filed when she was approximately seventy years old, represents an important political strategy in the history of women's rhetoric: the use of autobiographical narrative to establish credibility and authority. Belinda uses her
own experience as evidence of the right to the freedom and financial support
she claims. Her poetic and literary style forecasts that of later slave narratives.
With the romantic, nostalgic depiction of her African home and the emotional
descriptions of the pain at being torn from her family and of her years of loyal
service to her master and "the furrows of time, and her frame feebly bending
under the oppression of years," she employs pathos in persuading her readers
of the weight of her claims. In addition, like white women of the time, she
makes use of the discourses of democracy that undoubtedly surrounded her in
the newly independent nation. She, a woman, a slave, claims for herself that
same struggle that recently "convulsed" the world for the preservation of freedom, a right the "Almighty intended for all the human race."

In recovering this text, Harris points out, in *American Women Writers to 1800*,
that it may have been narrated to a third party or that Belinda may have been
literate and may have written her own petition in the third person in order to
add dignity to her appeal.

"Petition of an African Slave"

1782

Petition of an African Slave, to the legislature of Massachusetts.
To the honourable the senate and the house of representatives, in general court
assembled:
The petition of Belinda, an African,
Humbly shews,

That seventy years have rolled away, since she, on the banks of the Rio de
Valta, received her existence. The mountains, covered with spicy forests—the
vallies; loaded with the richest fruits, spontaneously produced—joined to the
happy temperature of air, which excludes excess, would have yielded her the
most complete felicity, had not her mind received early impressions of the
cruelty of men, whose faces were like the moon, and whose bows and arrows
were like the thunder and lightning of the clouds. The idea of these, the most
dreadful of all enemies, filled her infant slumbers with horror, and her noon-
tide moments with cruel apprehensions! But her affrighted imagination, in its
most alarming extension, never represented distress equal to what she has
since experienced: for before she had twelve years enjoyed the fragrance of her
native groves, and ere she realized that Europeans placed their happiness in the
yellow dust, which she carelessly marked with her infant foot-steps—even
when she, in a sacred grove, with each hand in that of a tender parent, was paying her devotion the great Orisa, who made all things, an armed band of white
men, driving many of her countrymen in chains, rushed into the hallowed
shades! Could the tears, the sighs, and supplications, bursted from the tortured
parental affection, have blunted the keen edge of avarice, she might have been
rescued from agony, which many of her country's children have felt, but which
none have ever described. In vain she lifted her supplicating voice to an in-
sulted father, and her guiltless hands to a dishonoured deity! She was ravished
from the bosom of her country, from the arms of her friends, while the advanced age of her parents, rendering them unfit for servitude, cruelly separated
her from them for ever.

Scenes which her imagination had never conceived of, a floating world, the
sporting monsters of the deep, and the familiar meetings of billows and clouds,
strove, but in vain, to divert her attention from three hundred Africans in
chains, suffering the most excruciating torment; and some of them rejoicing
that the pangs of death came like a balm to their wounds.

Reprinted from Belinda. "Petition of an African Slave." *The American Museum* 1 (June 1787):
538–40. Ann Arbor: University Microfilms International. Microfilm.

Once more her eyes were blest with a continent: but alas! How unlike the land where she received her being! How all things appeared unpropitious. She learned to catch the ideas, marked by the sounds of language, only to know that her doom was slavery, from which death alone was to emancipate her. What did it avail her, that the walls of her lord were hung with splendor, and the dust trodden under foot in her native country, crouded his gates with sordid worshippers! The laws rendered her incapable of receiving property: and though she was a free moral agent, accountable for her own actions, yet never had she a moment at her own disposal! Fifty years her faithful hands have been compelled to ignoble servitude for the benefit of an Isaac Royall, until, as if nations must be agitated, and the world convulsed, for the preservation of that freedom, which the Almighty Father intended for all the human race, the present war commenced. The terrors of men, armed in the cause of freedom, compelled her master to fly, and to breathe away his life in a land, where lawless dominion sits enthroned, pouring blood and vengeance on all who dare to be free.

The face of your petitioner is now marked with the furrows of time, and her frame feebly bending under the oppression of years, while she, by the laws of the land, is denied the enjoyment of one morsel of that immense wealth, a part whereof hath been accumulated by her own industry, and the whole augmented by her servitude.

Wherefore, casting herself at the feet of your honours, as to a body of men, formed for the extirpation of vassalage, for the reward of virtue, and the just returns of honest industry—she prays that such allowance may be made her, out of the estate of colonel Royall, as will prevent her, and her more infirm daughter, from misery in the greatest extreme, and scatter comfort over the short and downward path of their lives: and she will ever pray.

BELINDA

Boston, February, 1782

FOR FURTHER READING

Harris, Sharon, ed. *American Women Writers to 1800*. New York: Oxford University Press, 1996.

Mary Wollstonecraft

1759–1797

Virginia Woolf wrote of Mary Wollstonecraft, "She had been in revolt all her life against tyranny, against law, against convention" (269). Wollstonecraft was born in 1759 and spent the first part of her life fighting for, caring for, and protecting the women she loved. She grew up in a home with a tyrannical and abusive father; in attempts to save her mother from brutal beatings, as a child she would thrash around on the landing outside their bedroom door.

When she was old enough to make her own way, she moved from being a companion to elderly women, to nursing her own dying mother, to nursing her sister "deranged" from childbirth (Wollstonecraft believed her sister to have been abused by her husband), to opening a school with her sister and best friend, to nursing and then burying her best friend, who died in childbirth, and finally to her work as a writer. She spent the last part of her life writing about the injustices done to women in a man's world. She fell in love and had a daughter with Robert Imlay, but she was greatly hurt by his affairs with other women. After two suicide attempts, she met and fell in love with William Godwin. When she discovered she was pregnant, they married. Wollstonecraft died in childbirth at the age of thirty-eight. Her daughter, Mary Wollstonecraft Godwin Shelley, wrote *Frankenstein* and carried on her mother's legacy as a writer.

Mary Wollstonecraft's own writing was a success during her short lifetime. Her book *A Vindication of the Rights of Woman,* originally well received despite its radically progressive ideas, has been published, read, and studied by scholars for over two hundred years. *A Vindication of the Rights of Woman,* because of its well-argued position for women's equality, could be considered a contemporary feminist manifesto, so sophisticated are its ideas and arguments. Wollstonecraft was the first published writer to confront the issue of socialized gender roles. In her book she articulates how girls are socialized and educated differently from boys and how destructive those differences are to girls' development as actualized human beings. Wollstonecraft is clever in her argument. She understood that her audience would consist primarily of men. Therefore, she carefully points out the advantages men themselves would have when women and girls were treated as their equals ("help meets") instead of as their "lap dogs."

Wollestonecraft systematically takes on the writers and thinkers of the day who argued for women's/girls' innate inferiority, patiently and slowly deconstructing their arguments. She frequently evokes parallels between the status of women and slavery, using the rhetoric of the abolitionist movements in Europe and the United States to make her point. She proclaims that she will not rely on pretty language to convince her audience: "I shall be employed about things, not words!—and, anxious to render my sex more respectable members of society, I shall try to avoid that flowery diction which has slided from essays into novels, and from novels to familiar letters and conversation."

From *A Vindication of the Rights of Woman*

1792

After considering the historic page, and viewing the living world with anxious solicitude, the most melancholy emotions of sorrowful indignation have depressed my spirits, and I have sighed when obliged to confess, that either nature has made a great difference between man and man, or that the civilization which has hitherto taken place in the world has been very partial. I have turned over various books written on the subject of education, and patiently observed the conduct of parents and the management of schools; but what has been the result?—a profound conviction that the neglected education of my fellow-creatures is the grand source of the misery I deplore; and that women, in particular, are rendered weak and wretched by a variety of concurring causes, originating from one hasty conclusion. The conduct and manners of women, in fact, evidently prove that their minds are not in a healthy state; for, like the flowers which are planted in too rich a soil, strength and usefulness are sacrificed to beauty; and the flaunting leaves, after having pleased a fastidious eye, fade, disregarded on the stalk, long before the season when they ought to have arrived at maturity. One cause of this barren blooming I attribute to a false system of education, gathered from the books written on this subject by men who, considering females rather as women than human creatures, have been more anxious to make them alluring mistresses than affectionate wives and rational mothers; and the understanding of the sex has been so bubbled by this specious homage, that the civilized women of the present century, with a few exceptions, are only anxious to inspire love, when they ought to cherish a nobler ambition, and by their abilities and virtues exact respect.

In a treatise, therefore, on female rights and manners, the works which have been particularly written for their improvement must not be overlooked; especially when it is asserted, in direct terms, that the minds of women are enfeebled by false refinement; that the books of instruction, written by men of genius, have had the same tendency as more frivolous productions; and that, in the true style of Mahometanism, they are treated as a kind of subordinate beings, and not as a part of the human species, when improveable reason is allowed to be the dignified distinction which raises men above the brute creation, and puts a natural sceptre in a feeble hand.

Yet, because I am a woman, I would not lead my readers to suppose that I mean violently to agitate the contested question respecting the equality or inferiority of the sex; but as the subject lies in my way, and I cannot pass it over without subjecting the main tendency of my reasoning to misconstruction, I shall stop a moment to deliver, in a few words, my opinion. In the government of the physical world it is observable that the female in point of strength is, in general, inferior to the male. It is the law of nature; and it does not appear to be suspended or abrogated in favour of woman. A degree of physical superiority cannot, therefore, be denied—and it is a noble prerogative! But not content with this natural pre-eminence, men endeavour to sink us still lower, merely to render us alluring objects for a moment; and women, intoxicated by the adoration which men, under the influence of their senses, pay them, do not seek to obtain a durable interest in their hearts, or to become the friends of the fellow creatures who find amusement in their society.

I am aware of an obvious inference: from every quarter have I heard exclamations against masculine women; but where are they to be found? If by this appellation men mean to inveigh against their ardour in hunting, shooting, and gaming, I shall most cordially join in the cry; but if it be against the imitation of manly virtues, or, more properly speaking, the attainment of those talents and virtues, the exercise of which ennobles the human character, and which raise females in the scale of animal being, when they are comprehensively termed mankind; all those who view them with a philosophic eye must, I should think, wish with me, that they may every day grow more and more masculine.

This discussion naturally divides the subject. I shall first consider women in the grand light of human creatures, who, in common with men, are placed on this earth to unfold their faculties; and afterwards I shall more particularly point out their peculiar designation.

I wish also to steer clear of an error which many respectable writers have fallen into; for the instruction which has hitherto been addressed to women, has rather been applicable to *ladies,* if the little indirect advice, that is scattered through Sandford and Merton, be excepted; but, addressing my sex in a firmer tone, I pay particular attention to those in the middle class, because they appear to be in the most natural state. Perhaps the seeds of false-refinement, immorality, and vanity, have ever been shed by the great. Weak, artificial beings, raised above the common wants and affections of their race, in a premature unnatural manner, undermine the very foundation of virtue, and spread corruption through the whole mass of society! As a class of mankind they have the strongest claim to pity; the education of the rich tends to render them vain and helpless, and the unfolding mind is not strengthened by the practice of those duties which dignify the human character. They only live to amuse themselves, and by the same law which in nature invariably produces certain effects, they soon only afford barren amusement.

But as I purpose taking a separate view of the different ranks of society, and of the moral character of women, in each, this hint is, for the present, sufficient; and I have only alluded to the subject, because it appears to me to be the very essence of an introduction to give a cursory account of the contents of the work it introduces.

My own sex, I hope, will excuse me, if I treat them like rational creatures, instead of flattering their *fascinating* graces, and viewing them as if they were in a state of perpetual childhood, unable to stand alone. I earnestly wish to point out in what true dignity and human happiness consists—I wish to persuade women to endeavour to acquire strength, both of mind and body, and to convince them that the soft phrases, susceptibility of heart, delicacy of sentiment, and refinement of taste, are almost synonymous with epithets of weakness, and that those beings who are only the objects of pity and that kind of love, which has been termed its sister, will soon become objects of contempt.

Dismissing then those pretty feminine phrases, which the men condescendingly use to soften our slavish dependence, and despising that weak elegancy of mind, exquisite sensibility, and sweet docility of manners, supposed to be the sexual characteristics of the weaker vessel, I wish to shew that elegance is inferior to virtue, that the first object of laudable ambition is to obtain a character as a human being, regardless of the distinction of sex; and that secondary views should be brought to this simple touchstone.

This is a rough sketch of my plan; and should I express my conviction with the energetic emotions that I feel whenever I think of the subject, the dictates of experience and reflection will be felt by some of my readers. Animated by this important object, I shall disdain to cull my phrases or polish my style; I aim at being useful, and sincerity will render me unaffected; for, wishing rather to persuade by the force of my arguments, than dazzle by the elegance of my language, I shall not waste my time in rounding periods, or in fabricating the turgid bombast of artificial feelings, which, coming from the head, never reach the heart. I shall be employed about things, not words! and, anxious to render my sex more respectable members of society, I shall try to avoid that flowery diction which has slided from essays into novels, and from novels into familiar letters and conversation.

These pretty superlatives, dropping glibly from the tongue, vitiate the taste, and create a kind of sickly delicacy that turns away from simple unadorned truth; and a deluge of false sentiments and over-stretched feelings, stifling the natural emotions of the heart, render the domestic pleasures insipid, that ought to sweeten the exercise of those severe duties, which educate a rational and immortal being for a nobler field of action.

The education of women has, of late, been more attended to than formerly; yet they are still reckoned a frivolous sex, and ridiculed or pitied by the writers who endeavour by satire or instruction to improve them. It is acknowledged that they spend many of the first years of their lives in acquiring a smattering of accomplishments; meanwhile strength of body and mind are sacrificed to libertine notions of beauty, to the desire of establishing themselves—the only way women can rise in the world—by marriage. And this desire making mere animals of them, when they marry they act as such children may be expected to act: they dress; they paint, and nickname God's creatures. Surely these weak beings are only fit for a seraglio! Can they be expected to govern a family with judgment, or take care of the poor babes whom they bring into the world?

If then it can be fairly deduced from the present conduct of the sex, from the prevalent fondness for pleasure which takes place of ambition and those nobler passions that open and enlarge the soul; that the instruction which women have hitherto received has only tended, with the constitution of civil society, to render them insignificant objects of desire—mere propagators of fools!—if it can be proved that in aiming to accomplish them, without cultivating their understandings, they are taken out of their sphere of duties, and made ridiculous and useless when the short-lived bloom of beauty is over, I presume that *rational* men will excuse me for endeavouring to persuade them to become more masculine and respectable.

Indeed the word masculine is only a bugbear: there is little reason to fear that women will acquire too much courage or fortitude; for their apparent inferiority with respect to bodily strength, must render them, in some degree, dependent on men in the various relations of life; but why should it be increased by prejudices that give a sex to virtue, and confound simple truths with sensual reveries?

Women are, in fact, so much degraded by mistaken notions of female excellence, that I do not mean to add a paradox when I assert, that this artificial weakness produces a propensity to tyrannize, and gives birth to cunning, the natural opponent of strength, which leads them to play off those contemptible infantine airs that undermine esteem even whilst they excite desire. Let men become more chaste and modest, and if women do not grow wiser in the same ratio, it will be clear that they have weaker understandings. It seems scarcely necessary to say, that I now speak of the sex in general. Many individuals have more sense than their male relatives; and, as nothing preponderates where there is a constant struggle for an equilibrium, without it has naturally more gravity, some women govern their husbands without degrading themselves, because intellect will always govern.

From Chapter IV, "Observations on the State of Degradation to Which Woman Is Reduced by Various Causes"

It would be an endless task to trace the variety of meannesses, cares, and sorrows, into which women are plunged by the prevailing opinion, that they were created rather to feel than reason, and that all the power they obtain, must be obtained by their charms and weakness:

'Fine by defect, and amiably weak!'

And, made by this amiable weakness entirely dependent, excepting what they gain by illicit sway, on man, not only for protection, but advice, is it surprising that, neglecting the duties that reason alone points out, and shrinking from trials calculated to strengthen their minds, they only exert themselves to give their defects a graceful covering, which may serve to heighten their charms in the eye of the voluptuary, though it sink them below the scale of moral excellence?

Fragile in every sense of the word, they are obliged to look up to man for every comfort. In the most trifling dangers they cling to their support, with parasitical tenacity, piteously demanding succour; and their *natural* protector extends his arm, or lifts up his voice, to guard the lovely trembler—from what? Perhaps the frown of an old cow, or the jump of a mouse; a rat, would be a serious danger. In the name of reason, and even common sense, what can save such beings from contempt; even though they be soft and fair?

These fears, when not affected, may produce some pretty attitudes; but they shew a degree of imbecility which degrades a rational creature in a way women are not aware of—for love and esteem are very distinct things.

I am fully persuaded that we should hear of none of these infantine airs, if girls were allowed to take sufficient exercise, and not confined in close rooms till their muscles are relaxed, and their powers of digestion destroyed. To carry the remark still further, if fear in girls, instead of being cherished, perhaps, created, were treated in the same manner as cowardice in boys, we should quickly see women with more dignified aspects. It is true, they could not then with equal propriety be termed the sweet flowers that smile in the walk of man; but they would be more respectable members of society, and discharge the important duties of life by the light of their own reason. 'Educate women like men,' says Rousseau, 'and the more they resemble our sex the less power will they have over us.' This is the very point I aim at. I do not wish them to have power over men; but over themselves.

In the same strain have I heard men argue against instructing the poor; for many are the forms that aristocracy assumes. 'Teach them to read and write,' say they, 'and you take them out of the station assigned them by nature.' An eloquent Frenchman has answered them, I will borrow his sentiments. But they know not, when they make man a brute, that they may expect every instant to see him transformed into a ferocious beast. Without knowledge there can be no morality!

Ignorance is a frail base for virtue! Yet, that it is the condition for which woman was organized, has been insisted upon by the writers who have most vehemently argued in favour of the superiority of man; a superiority not in degree, but essence; though, to soften the argument, they have laboured to prove, with chivalrous generosity, that the sexes ought not to be compared; man was made to reason, woman to feel: and that together, flesh and spirit, they make the most perfect whole, by blending happily reason and sensibility into one character.

And what is sensibility? 'Quickness of sensation; quickness of perception; delicacy.' Thus is it defined by Dr. Johnson; and the definition gives me no other idea than of the most exquisitely polished instinct. I discern not a trace of the image of God in either sensation or matter. Refined seventy times seven, they are still material; intellect dwells not there; nor will fire ever make lead gold!

I come round to my old argument; if woman be allowed to have an immortal soul, she must have, as the employment of life, an understanding to improve.

From Chapter IX, "Of the Pernicious Effects Which Arise from the Unnatural Distinctions Established in Society"

From the respect paid to property flow, as from a poisoned fountain, most of the evils and vices which render this world such a dreary scene to the contemplative mind. For it is in the most polished Society that noisome reptiles and venomous serpents lurk under the rank herbage; and there is voluptuousness pampered by the still sultry air, which relaxes every good disposition before it ripens into virtue.

One class presses on another; for all are aiming to procure respect on account of their property: and property, once gained, will procure the respect due only to talents and virtue. Men neglect the duties incumbent on man, yet are treated like demi-gods; religion is also separated from morality by a ceremonial veil, yet men wonder that the world is almost, literally speaking, a den of sharpers or oppressors.

There is a homely proverb, which speaks a shrewd truth, that whoever the devil finds idle he will employ. And what but habitual idleness can hereditary wealth and titles produce? For man is so constituted that he can only attain a proper use of his faculties by exercising them, and will not exercise them unless necessity, of some kind, first set the wheels in motion. Virtue likewise can only be acquired by the discharge of relative duties; but the importance of these sacred duties will scarcely be felt by the being who is cajoled out of his humanity by the flattery of sycophants. There must be more equality established in society, or morality will never gain ground, and this virtuous equality will not rest firmly even when founded on a rock, if one half of mankind be chained to

its bottom by fate, for they will be continually undermining it through ignorance or pride.

It is vain to expect virtue from women till they are, in some degree, independent of men; nay, it is vain to expect that strength of natural affection, which
would make them good wives and mothers. Whilst they are absolutely dependent on their husbands they will be cunning, mean, and selfish. And the men
who can be gratified by the fawning fondness of spaniel-like affection, have not
much delicacy, for love is not bought, in any sense of the words, its silken wings
are instantly shrivelled up when any thing beside a return in kind is sought. Yet
whilst wealth enervates men; and women live, as it were personal charms, how
can we expect them to discharge those ennobling duties which equally require
exertion and self-denial. Hereditary property sophisticates the mind, and the
unfortunate victims to it, if I may so express myself, swathed from their birth,
seldom exert the locomotive faculty of body or mind; and, thus viewing every
thing through one medium, and that a false one, they are unable to discern in
what true merit and happiness consist. False, indeed, must be the light when
the drapery of situation hides the man, and makes him stalk in masquerade,
dragging from one scene of dissipation to another the nerveless limbs that hang
with stupid listlessness, and rolling round the vacant eye which plainly tells us
that there is no mind at home.

I mean, therefore, to infer that the society is not properly organized which
does not compel men and women to discharge their respective duties, by making it the only way to acquire that countenance from their fellow-creatures,
which every human being wishes some way to attain. The respect, consequently, which is paid to wealth and mere personal charms, is a true north-east
blast, that blights the tender blossoms of affection and virtue. Nature has
wisely attached affections to duties, to sweeten toil, and to give that vigour to
the exertions of reason which only the heart can give. But, the affection which
is put on merely because it is the appropriated insignia of a certain character,
when its duties are not fulfilled, is one of the empty compliments which vice
and folly are obliged to pay to virtue and the real nature of things.

To illustrate my opinion, I need only observe, that when a woman is admired for her beauty, and suffers herself to be so far intoxicated by the admiration she receives, as to neglect to discharge the indispensable duty of a mother,
she sins against herself by neglecting to cultivate an affection that would
equally tend to make her useful and happy. True happiness, I mean all the contentment, and virtuous satisfaction, that can be snatched in this imperfect
state, must arise from well regulated affections; and an affection includes a
duty. Men are not aware of the misery they cause, and the vicious weakness
they cherish, by only inciting women to render themselves pleasing; they do
not consider that they thus make natural and artificial duties clash, by sacrificing the comfort and respectability of a woman's life to voluptuous notions of
beauty, when in nature they all harmonize. . . .

It is a melancholy truth; yet such is the blessed effect of civilization! the most respectable women are the most oppressed; and, unless they have understandings far superiour to the common run of understandings, taking in both sexes, they must, from being treated like contemptible beings, become contemptible. How many women thus waste life away the prey of discontent, who might have practised as physicians, regulated a farm, managed a shop, and stood erect, supported by their own industry, instead of hanging their heads surcharged with the dew of sensibility, that consumes the beauty to which it at first gave lustre; nay, I doubt whether pity and love are so near akin as poets feign, for I have seldom seen much compassion excited by the helplessness of females, unless they were fair; then, perhaps, pity was the soft handmaid of love, or the harbinger of lust.

How much more respectable is the woman who earns her own bread by fulfilling any duty, than the most accomplished beauty!—beauty did I say?—so sensible am I of the beauty of moral loveliness, or the harmonious propriety that attunes the passions of a well-regulated mind, that I blush at making the comparison; yet I sigh to think how few women aim at attaining this respectability by withdrawing from the giddy whirl of pleasure, or the indolent calm that stupifies the good sort of women it sucks in.

Proud of their weakness, however, they must always be protected, guarded from care, and all the rough toils that dignify the mind. If this be the fiat of fate, if they will make themselves insignificant and contemptible, sweetly to waste 'life away,' let them not expect to be valued when their beauty fades, for it is the fate of the fairest flowers to be admired and pulled to pieces by the careless hand that plucked them. In how many ways do I wish, from the purest benevolence, to impress this truth on my sex; yet I fear that they will not listen to a truth that dear bought experience has brought home to many an agitated bosom, nor willingly resign the privileges of rank and sex for the privileges of humanity, to which those have no claim who do not discharge its duties.

Those writers are particularly useful, in my opinion, who make man feel for man, independent of the station he fills, or the drapery, of factitious sentiments. I then would fain convince reasonable men of the importance of some of my remarks, and prevail on them to weigh dispassionately the whole tenor of my observations. I appeal to their understandings; and, as a fellow-creature, claim, in the name of my sex, some interest in their hearts. I entreat them to assist to emancipate their companion, to make her a *help meet* for them!

Would men but generously snap our chains, and be content with rational fellowship instead of slavish obedience, they would find us more observant daughters, more affectionate sisters, more faithful wives, more reasonable mothers—in a word, better citizens. We should then love them with true affection, because we should learn to respect ourselves; and the peace of mind of a worthy man would not be interrupted by the idle vanity of his wife, nor the babes sent to nestle in a strange bosom, having never found a home in their mother's.

From Chapter XII, "On National Education"

My observations on national education are obviously hints; but I principally wish to enforce the necessity of educating the sexes together to perfect both, and of making children sleep at home that they may learn to love home; yet to make private support, instead of smothering, public affections, they should be sent to school to mix with a number of equals, for only by the jostlings of equality can we form a just opinion of ourselves.

To render mankind more virtuous, and happier of course, both sexes must act from the same principle; but how can that be expected when only one is allowed to see the reasonableness of it? To render also the social compact truly equitable, and in order to spread those enlightening principles, which alone can meliorate the fate of man, women must be allowed to found their virtue on knowledge, which is scarcely possible unless they be educated by the same pursuits as men. For they are now made so inferiour by ignorance and low desires, as not to deserve to be ranked with them; or, by the serpentine wrigglings of cunning they mount the tree of knowledge, and only acquire sufficient to lead men astray.

It is plain from the history of all nations, that women cannot be confined to merely domestic pursuits, for they will not fulfil family duties, unless their minds take a wider range, and whilst they are kept in ignorance they become in the same proportion the slaves of pleasure as they are the slaves of man. Nor can they be shut out if great enterprises, though the narrowness of their minds often make them mar, what they are unable to comprehend.

The libertinism, and even the virtues of superiour men, will always give women, of some description, great power over them; and these weak women, under the influence of childish passions and selfish vanity, will throw a false light over the objects which the very men view with their eyes, who ought to enlighten their judgment. Men of fancy, and those sanguine characters who mostly hold the helm of human affairs, in general, relax in the society of women; and surely I need not cite to the most superficial reader of history the numerous examples of vice and oppression which the private intrigues of female favourites have produced; not to dwell on the mischief that naturally arises from the blundering interposition of well-meaning folly. For in the transactions of business it is much better to have to deal with a knave than a fool, because a knave adheres to some plan; and any plan of reason may be seen through much sooner than a sudden flight of folly. The power which vile and foolish women have had over wise men, who possessed sensibility, is notorious; I shall only mention one instance.

Who ever drew a more exalted female character than Rousseau? though in the lump he constantly endeavoured to degrade the sex. And why was he thus anxious? Truly to justify to himself the affection which weakness and virtue had made him cherish for that fool Theresa. He could not raise her to the common level of her sex; and therefore he laboured to bring woman down to her's. He found her a convenient humble companion, and pride made him determine to find some superiour virtues in the being whom he chose to live with; but did not her conduct during his life, and after his death, clearly shew how grossly he was mistaken who called her a celestial innocent. Nay, in the bitterness of his heart, he himself laments, that when his bodily infirmities made him no longer treat her like a woman, she ceased to have an affection for him. And it was very natural that she should, for having so few sentiments in common, when the sexual tie was broken, what was to hold her? To hold her affection whose sensibility was confined to one sex, nay, to one man, it requires sense to turn sensibility into the broad channel of humanity; many women have not mind enough to have an affection for a woman, or a friendship for a man. But the sexual weakness that makes woman depend on man for a subsistence, produces a kind of cattish affection which leads a wife to purr about her husband as she would about any man who fed and caressed her.

Men are, however, often gratified by this kind of fondness, which is confined in a beastly manner to themselves; but should they ever become more virtuous, they will wish to converse at their fire-side with a friend, after they cease to play with a mistress.

Besides, understanding is necessary to give variety and interest to sensual enjoyments, for low, indeed, in the intellectual scale, is the mind that can continue to love when neither virtue nor sense give a human appearance to an animal appetite. But sense will always preponderate; and if women be not, in general, brought more on a level with men, some superiour woman, like the Greek courtezans, will assemble the men of abilities around them, and draw from their families many citizens, who would have stayed at home had their wives had more sense, or the graces which result from the exercise of the understanding and fancy, the legitimate parents of taste. A woman of talents, if she be not absolutely ugly, will always obtain great power, raised by the weakness of her sex; and in proportion as men acquire virtue and delicacy, by the exertion of reason, they will look for both in women, but they can only acquire them in the same way that men do.

In France or Italy, have the women confined themselves to domestic life? though they have not hitherto had a political existence, yet, have they not illicitly had great sway? corrupting themselves and the men with whose passions they played. In short, in whatever light I view the subject, reason and experience convince me that the only method of leading women to fulfil their peculiar duties, is to free them from all restraint by allowing them to participate in the inherent rights of mankind.

Make them free, and they will quickly become wise and virtuous, as men become more so; for the improvement must be mutual, or the injustice which one half of the human race are obliged to submit to, retorting on their oppressors, the virtue of men will be worm-eaten by the insect whom he keeps under his feet.

Let men take their choice, man and woman were made for each other, though not to become one being; and if they will not improve women, they will deprave them!

I speak of the improvement and emancipation of the whole sex, for I know that the behaviour of a few women, who, by accident, or following a strong bent of nature, have acquired a portion of knowledge superiour to that of the rest of their sex, has often been over-bearing; but there have been instances of women who, attaining knowledge, have not discarded modesty, nor have they always pedantically appeared to despise the ignorance which they laboured to disperse in their own minds. The exclamations then which any advice respecting female learning, commonly produces, especially from pretty women, often arise from envy. When they chance to see that even the lustre of their eyes, and the flippant sportiveness of refined coquetry will not always secure them attention, during a whole evening, should a woman of a more cultivated understanding endeavour to give a rational turn to the conversation, the common source of consolation is, that such women seldom get husbands. What arts have I not seen silly women use to interrupt by *flirtation*, a very significant word to describe such a manoeuvre, a rational conversation which made the men forget that they were pretty women.

But, allowing what is very natural to man, that the possession of rare abilities is really calculated to excite over-weening pride, disgusting in both men and women—in what a state of inferiority must the female faculties have rusted when such a small portion of knowledge as those women attained, who have sneeringly been termed learned women, could be singular? Sufficiently so to puff up the possessor, and excite envy in her contemporaries, and some of the other sex. Nay, has not a little rationality exposed many women to the severest censure? I advert to well known facts, for I have frequently heard women ridiculed, and every little weakness exposed, only because they adopted the advice of some medical men, and deviated from the beaten track in their mode of treating their infants. I have actually heard this barbarous aversion to innovation carried still further, and a sensible woman stigmatized as an unnatural mother, who has thus been wisely solicitous to preserve the health of her children, when in the midst of her care she has lost one by some of the casualties of infancy, which no prudence can ward off. Her acquaintance have observed, that this was the consequence of new-fangled notions—the new-fangled notions of ease and cleanliness. And those who pretending to experience, though they have long adhered to prejudices that have, according to the opinion of the most sagacious physicians, thinned the human race, almost rejoiced at the disaster that gave a kind of sanction to prescription.

Indeed, if it were only on this account, the national education of women is of the utmost consequence, for what a number of human sacrifices are made to that moloch prejudice! And in how many ways are children destroyed by the lasciviousness of man? The want of natural affection, in many women, who are drawn from their duty by the admiration of men, and the ignorance of others, render the infancy of man a much more perilous state than that of brutes; yet men are unwilling to place women in situations proper to enable them to acquire sufficient understanding to know how even to nurse their babes.

So forcibly does this truth strike me, that I would rest the whole tendency of my reasoning upon it, for whatever tends to incapacitate the maternal character, takes woman out of her sphere.

But it is vain to expect the present race of weak mothers either to take that reasonable care of a child's body, which is necessary to lay the foundation of a good constitution, supposing that it do not suffer for the sins of its fathers; or, to manage its temper so judiciously that the child will not have, as it grows up, to throw off all that its mother, its first instructor, directly or indirectly taught; and unless the mind have uncommon vigour, womanish follies will stick to the character throughout life. The weakness of the mother will be visited on the children! And whilst women are educated to rely on their husbands for judgment, this must ever be the consequence, for there is no improving an understanding by halves, nor can any being act wisely from imitation, because in every circumstance of life there is a kind of individuality, which requires an exertion of judgment to modify general rules. The being who can think justly in one track, will soon extend its intellectual empire; and she who has sufficient judgment to manage her children, will not submit, right or wrong, to her husband, or patiently to the social laws which make a nonentity of a wife.

In public schools women, to guard against the errors of ignorance, should be taught the elements of anatomy and medicine, not only to enable them to take proper care of their own health, but to make them rational nurses of their infants, parents, and husbands; for the bills of mortality are swelled by the blunders of self-willed old women, who give nostrums of their own without knowing anything of the human frame. It is likewise proper only in a domestic view, to make women acquainted with the anatomy of the mind, by allowing the sexes to associate together in every pursuit; and by leading them to observe the progress of the human understanding in the improvement of the sciences and arts; never forgetting the science of morality, or the study of the political history of mankind.

A man has been termed a microcosm; and every family might also be called a state. States, it is true, have mostly been governed by arts that disgrace the character of man; and the want of a just constitution, and equal laws, have so perplexed the notions of the worldly wise, that they more than question the reasonableness of contending for the rights of humanity. Thus morality, polluted in the national reservoir, sends off streams of vice to corrupt the constituent parts of the body politic; but should more noble, or rather, more just principles regulate the laws, which ought to be the government of society, and not those who execute them, duty might become the rule of private conduct.

Besides, by the exercise of their bodies and minds women would acquire that mental activity so necessary in the maternal character, united with the fortitude that distinguishes steadiness of conduct from the obstinate perverseness of weakness. For it is dangerous to advise the indolent to be steady, because they instantly become rigorous, and to save themselves trouble, punish with severity faults that the patient fortitude of reason might have prevented.

But fortitude presupposes strength of mind; and is strength of mind to be acquired by indolent acquiescence? by asking advice instead of exerting the judgment? by obeying through fear, instead of practising the forbearance, which we all stand in need of our-selves? The conclusion which I wish to draw, is obvious; make women rational creatures, and free citizens, and they will quickly become good wives, and mothers; that is if men do not neglect the duties of husbands and fathers.

Discussing the advantages which a public and private education combined, as I have sketched, might rationally be expected to produce, I have dwelt most on such as are particularly relative to the female world, because I think the female world oppressed; yet the gangrene, which the vices engendered by oppression have produced, is not confined to the morbid part, but pervades society at large: so that when I wish to see my sex become more like moral agents, my heart bounds with the anticipation of the general diffusion of that sublime contentment which only morality can diffuse.

FOR FURTHER READING

Barlowe, Jamie. "Daring to Dialogue: Mary Wollstonecraft's Rhetoric of Feminist Dialogics." In *Reclaiming Rhetorica: Women in the Rhetorical Tradition*, edited by Andrea Lunsford, 117–36. Pittsburgh: University of Pittsburgh Press, 1995.

Goldman, Emma. "Mary Wollstonecraft: Her Tragic Life and Her Passionate Struggle for Freedom." In *A Vindication of the Rights of Woman: A Norton Critical Edition*, edited by Carol H. Poston, 249–56. New York: W. W. Norton and Company, 1988.

Godwin, William. *Memoirs of Mary Wollstonecraft*. Edited by Clark Durant. New York: Greenberg, 1927.

Wollstonecraft, Mary. *Collected Letters of Mary Wollstonecraft*. Edited by Ralph M. Wardle. Ithaca: Cornell University Press, 1979.

———. *The Works of Mary Wollstonecraft*. 7 vols. Edited by Marilyn Butler and Janet Todd. Washington Square: New York University Press, 1989.

Woolf, Virginia. "Mary Wollstonecraft." In *A Vindication of the Rights of Woman: A Norton Critical Edition*, edited by Carol H. Poston, 267–72. New York: W. W. Norton and Company, 1988.

Cherokee Women

Cherokee women held such great power in tribal councils that some white historians described the Cherokees as having a "petticoat government." But colonization, removal, and federal Indian policies eroded women's power substantially during the nineteenth century. According to Marilou Awiakta, Cherokee poet and historian, one of the central social roles of Cherokee women had been to provide wise council. The respected place of women—symbols of the life force and source of connection and balance—is indicated by the title "Beloved," used to refer to revered women, who were charged with being advocates of peace. Nanyehi (Nancy Ward), one of the Cherokee Nation's most revered leaders, achieved her status as War Woman through valor in battle, but upon becoming Beloved Woman she fought for peace, even when it meant warning white squatters of pending Cherokee attacks.

Awiakta tells of the meeting in 1765 between Henry Timberlake and Attakullakulla, a Cherokee chief, who had met to negotiate a treaty. Attakullakulla's initial question to the delegation of whites—"Where are your women?"—was incomprehensible to them, since the lack of women in their delegation seemed irrelevant; to the Cherokee the absence of women indicated the whites' lack of respect and their lack of a centering force. Timberlake's memoirs note with amazement that the chief had brought women in his delegation, "as famous in war as powerful in the council" (Awiakta 471).

It was from their long tradition of being heard and respected as clan mothers that the Cherokee women in 1817 petitioned their husbands, sons, and fathers to resist the colonization and expansionism of American settlers and their government. The United States began pressuring the Cherokees to sell their lands, which had once included parts of seven Southern states, soon after the Hopewell Treaty Council of 1785. Forced removal of the Cherokee Nation began with the 1830 Removal Act and culminated in the decimation of the Cherokee people in the Trail of Tears, during which some estimate that half of the population died.

In their petition (now part of the Andrew Jackson papers in the Library of Congress), the Cherokee women invoke the authority of their place as clan mothers to argue that no more of their lands be sold. They remind their audience that the people are inextricably connected to the land and that land is a vital spiritual source of their identity. While making appeals based on long-held cultural traditions, reminding their audience of fundamental values that should be upheld, they employ the formal rhetorical tradition of the dominant culture.

"Cherokee Women Address Their Nation"

1817

Amovey [Tenn.] in Council 2nd May 1817

[A True Copy] The Cherokee ladys now being present at the meeting of the chiefs and warriors in council have thought it their duties as mothers to address their Chiefs and warriors now assembled.

Our beloved children and head men of the Cherokee nation we address you warriors in council we have raised all of you on the land which we now have, which God gave us to inhabit and raise provisions we know that our country has once been extensive but by repeated sales has become circumscribed to a small tract and never thought it our duty to interfere in the disposition of it till now, if a father or mother was to sell all their lands which they had to depend on which their children had to raise their living on which would be indeed bad and to be removed to another country we do not wish to go to an unknown country which we have understood some of our children wish to go over the Mississippi but this act of our children would be like destroying your mothers. You mothers your sisters ask and beg of you not to part with any more of our lands, we say ours you are descendants and take pity on our request, but keep it for our growing children for it was the good will of our creator to place here and you know our father the great president will not allow his white children to take our country away only keep your hands off of paper talks for it is our own country for if it was not they would not ask you to put your hands to paper for it would be impossible to remove us all for as soon as one child is raised we have others in our arms for such is our situation and will consider our circumstance.

Therefore children don't part with any more of our lands but continue on it and enlarge your farms and cultivate and raise corn and cotton and we your mothers and sisters will make clothing for you which our father the president has recommended to us all we don't charge anybody for selling our lands, but we have heard such intentions of our children but your talks become true at last and it was our desire to forewarn you all not to part with our lands.

Nancy Ward to her children Warriors to take pity and listen to the talks of your sisters, although I am very old yet cannot but pity the situation in which you will hear of their minds. I have great many grand children which I wish they to do well on our land

Nancy Ward

From *Root of Bitterness: Document of the Social History of American Women*, 2nd edition. Ed. Nancy F. Cott, Jeanne Boydston, Anne Braude, Lori Ginzberg, and Molly Ladd-Taylor. Copyright 1966 by Nancy F. Cott. Reprinted with permission of Northeastern University Press. 177–78.

Attested
A Mc Coy Clk.}
Thos. Wilson Secty}

Jenny McIntosh	Widow Tarpin
Caty Harlan	Ally Critington
Elizabeth walker	Cun, o, ah
Susanna Fox	Miss Asty walker
Widow Gunrod	Mrs. M. Morgan
Widow Woman Holder	Mrs. Nancy Fields

FOR FURTHER READING

Awiakta, Marilou. "Amazons in Appalachia." In *Reinventing the Enemy's Language: Contemporary Native Women's Writing of North America*, edited by Joy Harjo and Gloria Bird, 469–78. New York: W. W. Norton and Company, 1997.

Mankiller, Wilma, Gwendolyn Mink, Marysa Navarro, Barbara Smith, and Gloria Steinem, eds. *The Reader's Companion to U.S. Women's History.* Boston: Houghton Mifflin Company, 1998.

Maria W. Stewart

1803–1879

Maria Stewart's public speaking career lasted only one year, but in that short time she earned a unique place in the history of women's rhetoric. Stewart was the first American woman to speak to a mixed audience of both male and female, black and white listeners. Born in Hartford, Connecticut, in 1803 and orphaned at the age of five, Stewart lived with a clergyman's family until she was fifteen; after that, she supported herself as a domestic servant. After her husband died in 1829, Stewart was cheated out of his estate; thereafter, she became committed to activist causes, particularly the plight of Northern blacks. Stewart had no formal education, but she apparently read in the libraries of the clergyman in whose home she grew up. Clearly she learned a good deal about effective forms of public address and about how to appeal to a disparate audience.

Stewart delivered "Lecture at the Franklin Hall" in Boston on September 21, 1832; it was one of four speeches she would deliver that year. She had several of these speeches, as well as a treatise titled *Religion and the Pure Principles of Morality, The Sure Foundation on Which We Must Build,* published in William Lloyd Garrison's abolitionist newspaper, *The Liberator.* Yet Stewart faced an entire culture—including reformist abolitionists—that opposed public speaking by women, most particularly by women of color. In later years, when Angelina and Sarah Grimké began to speak in public against slavery and for women's rights, they were credited with being the first women to do so; that no one acknowledged Stewart's accomplishment was a result, Jean Yellin argues, of "either racism or class bias—or both" (48). Stewart soon realized that her efforts at persuasion would not succeed; exactly one year after the Franklin Hall lecture she delivered a farewell address in Boston in which she expressed disappointment with Boston's failure to listen to her message. Soon after, she moved to New York and became a public-school teacher. During the Civil War, Stewart moved to Washington, D.C., where she continued to teach and also became matron of the Freedmen's Hospital. In 1879, she reprinted her speeches and writings under the title *Meditations from the Pen of Mrs. Maria Stewart.*

"Lecture Delivered at the Franklin Hall" demonstrates Stewart's considerable rhetorical skill. She understands the power of drawing on Scripture for her authority to speak in the first place; she uses both emotional and logical appeals in order to show her mixed audience the effects of racism on Northern free people of color. Vivid and poignant descriptions of "drudgery" and "servitude," carefully wrought questions that ask her audience to see from different perspectives, appeals to patriotism and nationhood, as well as Stewart's own very careful creation of a persona at once so angry that it cannot be stilled and so humble that it dares not speak all add up to a remarkable rhetorical moment. Stewart also carefully plays to her full audience, deftly turning from her black to her white listeners, attempting to enact the very arguments she is presenting. She might have failed in her immediate context, but her achievement still stands.

"Lecture Delivered at the Franklin Hall"

1832

Why sit ye here and die? If we say we will go to a foreign land, the famine and the pestilence are there, and there we shall die. If we sit here, we shall die. Come let us plead our cause before the whites: if they save us alive, we shall live—and if they kill us, we shall but die.

Methinks I heard a spiritual interrogation—"Who shall go forward, and take off the reproach that is cast upon the people of color? Shall it be a woman?" And my heart made this reply—"If it is thy will, be it even so, Lord Jesus!"

I have heard much respecting the horrors of slavery; but may Heaven forbid that the generality of my color throughout these United States should experience any more of its horrors than to be a servant of servants, or hewers of wood and drawers of water! Tell us no more of southern slavery; for with few exceptions, although I may be very erroneous in my opinion, yet I consider our condition but little better than that. Yet, after all, methinks there are no chains so galling as the chains of ignorance—no fetters so binding as those that bind the soul, and exclude it from the vast field of useful and scientific knowledge. O, had I received the advantages of an early education, my ideas would, ere now, have expanded far and wide; but alas! I possess nothing but moral capability—no teachings but the teachings of the Holy Spirit.

I have asked several individuals of my sex, who transact business for themselves, if providing our girls were to give them the most satisfactory references, they would not be willing to grant them an equal opportunity with others? Their reply has been—for their own part, they had no objection; but as it was not the custom, were they to take them into their employ, they would be in danger of losing the public patronage.

And such is the powerful force of prejudice. Let our girls possess whatever amiable qualities of soul they may; let their characters be fair and spotless as in-

Reprinted from Stewart, Maria. "Lecture Delivered at the Franklin Hall." In *Productions of Mrs. Maria Stewart, Presented to the First African Baptist Church and Society, in the City of Boston.* Boston: Friends of Freedom and Virtue, 1835. Reprinted in *Spiritual Narratives*, edited by Henry Louis Gates, 51–56. New York: Oxford University Press, 1988.

nocence itself; let their natural taste and ingenuity be what they may; it is impossible for scarce an individual of them to rise above the condition of servants. Ah! why is this cruel and unfeeling distinction? Is it merely because God has made our complexion to vary? If it be, O shame to soft, relenting humanity! "Tell it not in Gath! publish it not in the streets of Askelon!" Yet, after all, methinks were the American free people of color to turn their attention more assiduously to moral worth and intellectual improvement, this would be the result: prejudice would gradually diminish, and the whites would be compelled to say, unloose those fetters!

> Though black their skins as shades of night
> Their hearts are pure, their souls are white.

Few white persons of either sex, who are calculated for anything else, are willing to spend their lives and bury their talents in performing mean, servile labor. And such is the horrible idea that I entertain respecting a life of servitude, that if I conceived of there being no possibility of my rising above the condition of servant, I would gladly hail death as a welcome messenger. O, horrible idea, indeed! to possess noble souls aspiring after high and honorable acquirements, yet confined by the chains of ignorance and poverty to lives of continual drudgery and toil. Neither do I know of any who have enriched themselves by spending their lives as house domestics, washing windows, shaking carpets, brushing boots, or tending upon gentlemen's tables. I can but die for expressing my sentiments: and I am as willing to die by the sword as the pestilence; for I am a true born American; your blood flows in my veins, and your spirit fires my breast.

I observed a piece in the *Liberator* a few months since, stating that the colonizationists had published a work respecting us, asserting that we were lazy and idle. I confute them on that point. Take us generally as a people, we are neither lazy nor idle; and considering how little we have to excite or stimulate us, I am almost astonished that there are so many industrious and ambitious ones to be found; although I acknowledge, with extreme sorrow, that there are some who never were and never will be serviceable to society. And have you not a similar class among yourselves?

Again. It was asserted that we were a "ragged set, crying for liberty." I reply to it, the whites have so long and so loudly proclaimed the theme of equal rights and privileges, that our souls have caught the flame also, ragged as we are. As far as our merit deserves, we feel a common desire to rise above the condition of servants and drudges. I have learnt, by bitter experience, that continual hard labor deadens the energies of the soul, and benumbs the faculties of the mind; ideas become confined, the mind barren, and, like the scorching sands of Arabia, produces nothing; or like the uncultivated brings forth thorns and thistles.

Again, continual and hard labor irritates our tempers and sours our dispositions; the whole system becomes worn out with toil and fatigue; nature herself becomes almost exhausted, and we care little whether we live or die. It is true, that the free people of color throughout these United States are neither bought nor sold, not under the lash of the cruel driver; many obtain a comfortable support; but few, if any, have an opportunity of becoming rich and independent; and the enjoyments we most pursue are as unprofitable to us as the spider's web or the floating bubbles that vanish into air. As servants, we are respected; but let us presume to aspire higher, our employer regards us no longer. And were it not that the King eternal has declared that Ethiopia shall stretch forth her hands unto God, I should indeed despair.

I do not consider it derogatory, my friends, for persons to live out to service. There are many whose inclination leads them to aspire no higher; and I would highly commend the performance of almost anything for an honest livelihood; but where constitutional strength is wanting, labor of this kind, in its mildest form, is painful. And doubtless many are the prayers that have ascended to Heaven from Afric's daughters for strength to perform their work. Oh, many are the tears that have been shed for the want of that strength! Most of our color have dragged out a miserable existence of servitude from the cradle to the grave. And what literary acquirement can be made, or useful knowledge derived, from either maps, books, or charts, by those who continually drudge from Monday morning until Sunday noon? O, ye fairer sisters, whose hands are never soiled, whose nerves and muscles are never strained, go learn by experience! Had we had the opportunity that you have had to improve our moral and mental faculties, what would have hindered our intellects from being as bright, and our manners from being as dignified as yours? Had it been our lot to have been nursed in the lap of affluence and ease, and to have basked beneath the smiles and sunshine of fortune, should we not have naturally supposed that we were never made to toil? And why are not our forms as delicate, and our constitutions as slender, as yours? Is not the workmanship as curious and complete? Have pity upon us, have pity upon us, O ye who have hearts to feel for other's woes; for the hand of God has touched us. Owing to the disadvantages under which we labor, there are many flowers among us that are

. . . born to bloom unseen
And waste their fragrance on the desert air.

My beloved brethren, as Christ has died in vain for those who will not accept his offered mercy, so will it be vain for the advocates of freedom to spend their breath in our behalf, unless with united hearts and souls you make some mighty efforts to raise your sons and daughters from the horrible state of servitude and degradation in which they are placed. It is upon you that woman depends; she can do but little besides using her influence; and it is for her sake and yours that I have come forward and made myself a hissing and a reproach among the people; for I am also one of the wretched and miserable daughters of the descendants of fallen Africa. Do you ask, why are you wretched and miserable? I reply, look at many of the most worthy and most interesting of us doomed to spend our lives in gentlemen's kitchens. Look at our young men, smart, active and energetic, with souls filled with ambitious fire; if they look forward, alas! What are their prospects? They can be nothing but the humblest laborers, on account of their dark complexions; hence many of them lose their ambition and become worthless. Look at our middle-aged men, clad in their rusty plaids and coats; in winter, every cent they earn goes to buy their wood and pay their rents; the poor wives also toil beyond their strength, to help support their families. Look at our aged sires, whose heads are whitened with the frosts of seventy winters, with their old wood-saws on their backs. Alas, what keeps us so? Prejudice, ignorance, and poverty. But ah! methinks our oppression is soon to come to an end; yea, before the Majesty of heaven, our groans and cries have reached the ears of the Lord of Saboath. As the prayers and tears of Christians will avail the finally impenitent nothing; neither will the prayers and tears of the friends of humanity avail us anything, unless we possess a spirit of virtuous emulation within our breasts. Did the pilgrims, when they first landed on these shores, quietly compose themselves and say, "The Britons have all the money and all the power, and we must continue their servants forever?" Did they sluggishly sigh and say, "Our lot is hard, the Indians own the soil, and we cannot cultivate it?" No; they first made powerful efforts to raise themselves, and then God raised up those illustrious patriots, WASHINGTON and LAFAYETTE, to assist and defend them. And, my brethren, have you made a powerful effort? Have you prayed the legislature for mercy's sake to grant you all the rights and privileges of free citizens, that your daughters may rise to that degree of respectability which true merit deserves, and your sons above the servile situations which most of them fill?

FOR FURTHER READING

Logan, Shirley Wilson. "We Are Coming": The Persuasive Discourse of Nineteenth-Century Black Women. Carbondale: Southern Illinois University Press, 1999.
———, ed. With Pen and Voice: A Critical Anthology of Nineteenth-Century African-American Women. Carbondale: Southern Illinois University Press, 1995.
Richardson, Marilyn. Maria W. Stewart: America's First Black Woman Political Writer: Essays and Speeches. Bloomington: Indiana University Press, 1987.
Royster, Jacqueline Jones. Traces of a Stream: Literacy and Social Change Among African American Women. Pittsburgh: University of Pittsburgh Press, 2000.
Yellin, Jean Fagan. Women and Sisters: The Antislavery Feminists in American Culture. New Haven: Yale University Press, 1989.

Sarah Grimké

1792–1873

Sarah Grimké, not content to leave the work of abolition to the male leaders of her time, tirelessly wrote and spoke against slavery. In one of her letters, she admits, "I feel much as if I were speaking to those who would not hear tho' one rose from the dead" (*Letters of Theodore Dwight Weld* 401). Sarah Grimké, along with her younger sister Angelina Grimké Weld, broke most of the contemporary conventions for white ladylike conduct by speaking in public. After leaving Charleston to join the Society of Friends, the two sisters traveled throughout New England fulfilling speaking engagements in both small parlors and large churches. Their speeches and publications about abolition and women's rights reached thousands of people in New England and the Southern states.

After being harshly criticized for addressing women's rights in her antislavery work, Sarah Grimké responded with *Letters on the Equality of the Sexes* (1838), which was the first major publication about women's rights in the United States. In these letters, as in the letter anthologized below, Grimké uses scripture to support her claims. By quoting Bible verses and passages, she persuades her critics, particularly the clergy, to re-examine their belief that pursuing women's rights was a distraction, a lesser cause in comparison to abolition. She writes, "I cannot see why minds may not be exercised on more than one point without injury to any."

Theodore Weld, Angelina's husband, was one of the original organizers of the American Anti-Slavery Society and a member of the Society of Friends. He held considerable influence on the movement and the Grimkés, and he repeatedly asked the sisters to stop speaking of women's rights. In the letter to Weld included here, Sarah Grimké argues her right to address women's issues in her writing and when she speaks in public on abolition. In her opening line, she describes Angelina as "wrathy" over Weld's advice in previous letters that the sisters confine their speeches to the abolition issue alone. In fact, when adding her own section to the bottom of this letter, Angelina crossed out Sarah's adjective "good" in the second line and substituted the word "bad" above it. Sarah Grimké's response to Weld's advice is perhaps more measured and reasoned, but she is nonetheless passionate in her insistence that women's rights must be connected to human rights.

"Letter to Theodore Weld"

1837

Fitchburg [Mass.] 9/20/37

My dear brother,

Angelina is so wrathy that I think it will be unsafe to trust the pen in her hands
to reply to thy two last ~~good~~ bad long letters. As I feel nothing but gratitude for the
kindness which I am sure dictated them, commingled with wonder at the "mar-
vellables" which they contain, I shall endeavor to answer them and as far as
possible allay the uneasiness which thou seems to feel at the course we are pursuing. My astonishment is as great at thy misconceptions as thine can be at
ours. Truly if I did not know brother Theodore as well as I think I do, I should
conclude his mind was beclouded by the fears which seem to have seized some
of the brotherhood least we should usurp dominion over our lords and masters.
But as I think we are fully agreed that dominion is vested in God only, I shall
proceed. The 2d marvellable is "That we magnifyed the power of the N. E.
Clergy." The mtgs. we have had, generally full, if not crowded, have satisfied
our sister that here she was mistaken. I never tho't so. My convictions for several years past have been that the ministry as now organized is utterly at vari-
ance with the ministry Christ established, tends to perpetuate schism and dis-
union, and therefore must be destroyed; and I believe verily that the Ch. so
called is standing right in the way of all reform. I must say a few words about
brother Wright, towards whom I do not feel certain that the law of love pre-
dominated when thou wrote that part of thy letter relative to him. I do not
think he designed to exhibit us as trophies of his conquests, but simply to
throw his views (and ours incidentally) before the public. We feel prepared to
avow the principles set forth in the "domestic scene." To my own mind they
have long been familiar, altho' I acknowledge that coming in contact with
another mind similarly exercised on these points has given additional strength
and clearness to my views. I wonder that thou canst not perceive the simplicity
and beauty and consistency of the doctrine that all government, whether civil
or ecclesiastical, conflicts with the govt. of Jehovah and that by the Christian,
no other govt. can be acknowledged without leaning more or less on an arm of
flesh. Would God all abolitionists put their trust where I believe H. C. W[right]
has placed his, in God alone. Brother Weld, my heart misgives me for the ab-

Reprinted from *Letters of Theodore Dwight Weld, Angelina Grimké Weld, and Sarah Grimké, Vol. 1,
1822–1844*, edited by Gilbert H. Barnes and Dwight L. Dumond, 446–50. New York: D. Appleton-Century Company, Inc., 1934.

olition cause when I see that A. S. men when smitten on one cheek as R. G. Williams was, instead of turning the other cheek as Jesus commands, appeal to the arm of the law for retaliation. And E. P. Lovejoy keeping arms in his office! Truly I fear we have yet to learn the lesson "Trust in the Lord, for in the Lord Jehovah is everlasting strength." Surely posterity will brand us as hypocrites. The slave must not raise his hand against his oppressor, but we are at liberty to revenge our wrongs. Oh consistency where art thou?

Thou sayest the point at issue between us is whether "you, S. M. and A. E. G., should engage in the public discussion of the rights of women as a distinct topic. Here you affirm and I deny." Now, dear brother, I do not think we ever affirmed that we ought to engage in a public discussion on this subject: all either of us had or now have in view was to throw our views before the public. I have not the least idea of spending any time in answering objections to my letters in the N. E. Spectator; I do not feel bound to take up any caviller. There are my opinions on what I regard as a very important branch of human rights, second to no other. Those who read may receive or reject, or find fault. I have nothing to do with all that. I shall let thee enjoy thy opinion about the opening in the N. E. Spectator; I must wait to see the issue before I conclude it was one of Satan's providences. Thy illustration about the building of the wall serves my purpose admirably. Nehemiah disregarded the scoffs of his enemies, and continued his work; but nevertheless he set half the people in the lower places behind the wall, with their swords, their spears and their bows to guard the workmen. This is all we have done. We have kept steadily on with our A. S. work; we have not held one mtg. less, because we gave a little attention to guard the workmen from the thrusts of the enemies. Thou takes it for granted that our heads are so full of *womans rights, womans rights* that our hearts have grown cold in the cause of the slave, that we have started aside like broken bows. Now we think thou hast verily misjudged us. My cough rendered me incapable of speaking in public. Of course I did not require time to prepare lectures and I really cannot see where is the harm of my writing on any other subject that presented to my mind. I am amazed at thy talking of us as Reformers in the A. S. cause; such a tho't never entered my head. We were the followers and aiders of the Reformers, but we bro't no new artillery into the field; we used the weapons others had used before us. Thou seems to overlook the fact that before a word was written on the subject of womans rights, the Pastoral letter had been issued and that in every place that we lectured the subject of our speaking in public was up for discussion. My reason for giving my views with my name was simply because I wished to be answerable for those views. The idea that my name gave any currency to the opinions I advanced never presented itself; so far from it that I regretted that M. W. Chapman had not undertaken it, because I believed her name would give weight to the sentiments. I thank thee for the suggestion of helping a third person to the argument; it really did not occur to me. Nor did I intend to involve myself in any controversy which would take all my time and strength. Truly my brother thou hast called up a host of difficulties, which if they arise, I shall not encounter; and as to absorbing the public mind I do not see much like it. My letters are quietly received and if any of the subjects therein discussed attract attention I cannot see why minds may not be exercised on more than one point without injury to any. I was not aware that the ministers were playing the part of hypocrites when they said women had no right to speak in public. I believed they tho't what they said.

I do not think women being *permitted* to pray and tell their experience in revivals is any proof that Christians do not think it wrong for women to preach. This is the touchstone, to presume to teach the brethren. Let a woman who has prayed in a revival claim to be the appointed minister of Jesus and to exercise that office by teaching regularly on the sabbath, and she will at once be regarded as a fanatic, or a fool. I know the opposition "arises (in part) from habitually regarding women as inferior beings" but chiefly, I believe, from a desire to keep them in unholy subjection to man, and one way of doing this is to deprive us of the means of becoming their equals, by forbidding us the privileges of education to fit us for the performance of duty. I am greatly mistaken if most men have not a desire that women should be silly. Thou says I have summoned the ministers and churches to surrender. Not I truly. I do not believe, if I remember right, that I have said one word yet in my letters on the subject of womens preaching; we have done exactly what thou sayest we ought to have done, gone right among the ministers and lectured just when and where we could. I agree with thee that moral reform is successfully advanced "by uplifting a great self-evident central principle before all eyes". This has been done by proclaiming human rights and thus the way was prepared for the reception of the doctrine of womans rights. I have read the New Tes. my dear brother, I tho't to edification; but I cannot agree with thee in the application of that text, "I have many things to say," etc. I do not suppose Christ had allusion to the truth of the gospel, these he had declared again and again, but to the sufferings which awaited his disciples after his death; these sufferings he left time and circumstances to unfold as they were strengthened to bear them. If Jesus alluded to any great and important truth, why is none such revealed in the scripture after his ascension? I rejoice with thee that the cause of the slave cannot be destroyed by our misconception of duty, if indeed we have misconceived it, but we believe that if women exercised their rights of thinking and acting for themselves, they would labor ten times more efficiently than they now do for the A. S. cause and all other reformations. Do not wrong us by supposing that in our movements the slave is overlooked. The direction to J. E. Fuller may be continued. We received the Eman. and last Re[corder] and Q[uarterl]y. My cough is much better. I lectured last sabbath at Lunenburg and tuesday at Westminster with very little inconvenience. I see nothing about next winter but trust the Lord will direct our steps. At present we have engagements that will keep us till the middle of Nov. If I may choose, I hope my lot will not be cast in the city of N. Y. Could we travel during the winter in N. Y. or Penn.? We did not know D. A. Payne. I have not said half I have to say but this must suffice for the present as Angelina wishes to try her hand at scolding again. Farewell dear brother, may the Lord reward thee ten fold for thy kindness and keep thee in the hollow of his holy hand—thy sister in Jesus

                                                                                                                                        S. M. G.

FOR FURTHER READING

Grimké, Sarah. *An Epistle to the Clergy of the Southern States.* New York: 1836.
———. *Letters on the Equality of the Sexes and the Condition of Woman, Addressed to Mary Parker, President of the Boston Female Anti-Slavery Society.* Boston: Isaac Knapp, 1838.
Weld, Angela Grimké. *The Public Years of Sarah and Angelina Grimké: Selected Writings, 1835–1839.* Edited by Larry Ceplair. New York: Columbia University Press, 1989.

Angelina Grimké Weld

1805–1879

Angelina Grimké Weld was the first woman in the United States to address a legislative body—the Massachusetts State Legislature in 1838. She testified to support the right to petition the government about slavery. Born in Charleston to slave-owning parents, she observed the oppression of slavery firsthand and resolved to take action. She followed her older sister, Sarah Grimké, north to Philadelphia and joined the Society of Friends. By regularly referring to her upbringing in the South, Angelina Grimké Weld created a strong *ethos* in her rhetoric, demanding that Northerners take no less action than she, a Southerner.

Although Angelina delivered more speeches than her sister, they both wrote and spoke to mixed audiences of up to fifteen hundred people in churches and lecture halls all over New England, and they faced harsh criticism for doing so. Angelina was accustomed to such criticism, though. Her *Appeal to the Christian Women of the Southern States* (1836) was so radical that some Southern postmasters destroyed copies of the book. When she began to introduce women's rights into her public rhetoric about abolition, she faced severe criticism not only from the clergy but also from her early supporters, including John Greenleaf Whittier and Theodore Weld, her husband. In response to them, she writes, "If we surrender the right to speak to the public this year, we must surrender the right to petition next year and the right to write the year after and so on. What then can woman do for the slave when she is herself under the feet of man and shamed into silence?" (*Letters of Theodore Dwight Weld* 430)

The "Address at Pennsylvania Hall" was one of several speeches given that night to both the male and female antislavery societies as part of the dedication ceremonies of the hall. The comments in parentheses, written by the contemporary reporter, describe the scene inside and outside the hall. Delivered while a throng of anti-abolitionists gathered outside throwing rocks at the windows and shouting, the speech bravely censures all those complicit in the system of slavery, including the church, political leaders, and Northern and Southern men and women. Instead of being threatened by the mob, Angelina Grimké Weld incorporates the mob into her rhetoric and asks, "What is a mob? What would the breaking of every window be? What would the leveling of this Hall be? Any evidence that we are wrong or that slavery is a good and wholesome institution?" The following night, Pennsylvania Hall would be burned to the ground.

"Address at Pennsylvania Hall"

1838

Men, brethren and fathers—mothers, daughters and sisters, what came ye out for to see? A reed shaken with the wind? Is it curiosity merely, or a deep sympathy with the perishing slave, that has brought this large audience together? *(A yell from the mob without the building.)* Those voices without ought to awaken and call out our warmest sympathies. Deluded beings! "they know not what they do" [Luke 23:34]. They know not that they are undermining their own rights and their own happiness, temporal and eternal. Do you ask, "what has the North to do with slavery?" Hear it—hear it. Those voices without tell us that the spirit of slavery is here, and has been roused to wrath by our abolition speeches and conventions: for surely liberty would not foam and tear herself with rage, because her friends are multiplied daily, and meetings are held in quick succession to set forth her virtues and extend her peaceful kingdom. This opposition shows that slavery has done its deadliest work in the hearts of our citizens. Do you ask, then, "what has the North to do?" I answer, cast out first the spirit of slavery from your own hearts, and then lend your aid to convert the South. Each one present has a work to do, be his or her situation what it may, however limited their means, or insignificant their supposed influence. The great men of this country will not do this work; the church will never do it. A desire to please the world, to keep the favor of all parties and of all conditions, makes them dumb on this and every other unpopular subject. They have become worldly-wise, and therefore God, in his wisdom, employs them not to carry on his plans of reformation and salvation. He hath chosen the foolish things of the world to confound the wise, and the weak to overcome the mighty.

As a Southerner I feel that it is my duty to stand up here to-night and bear testimony against slavery. I have seen it—I have seen it. I know it has horrors that can never be described. I was brought up under its wing: I witnessed for many years its demoralizing influences, and its destructiveness to human happiness. It is admitted by some that the slave is not happy under the *worst* forms of slavery. But I have *never* seen a happy slave. I have seen him dance in his chains, it is true; but he was not happy. There is a wide difference between happiness and mirth. Man cannot enjoy the former while his manhood is destroyed, and that part of the being which is necessary to the making, and to the enjoyment of happiness, is completely blotted out. The slaves, however, may

Reprinted from Weld, Angela Grimké. "Address at Pennsylvania Hall." In *History of Pennsylvania Hall, Which Was Destroyed by a Mob on the 17th of May, 1838*, edited by Samuel Webb, 131–34. Philadelphia: Merrihew and Gunn, 1838.

be, and sometimes are, mirthful. When hope is extinguished, they say, "let us eat and drink, for to-morrow we die" [Isa. 22:13]. *(Just then stones were thrown at the windows,—a great noise without, and commotion within.)*

What is a mob? What would the breaking of every window be? What would the levelling of this Hall be? Any evidence that we are wrong, or that slavery is a good and wholesome institution? What if the mob should now burst in upon us, break up our meeting and commit violence upon our persons—would this be anything compared with what the slaves endure? No, no: and we do not remember them "as bound with them" [Heb. 13:3], if we shrink in the time of peril, or feel unwilling to sacrifice ourselves, if need be, for their sake. *(Great noise.)* I thank the Lord that there is yet life left enough to feel the truth, even though it rages at it—that conscience is not so completely seared as to be unmoved by the truth of the living God.

Many persons go to the South for a season, and are hospitably entertained in the parlor and at the table of the slave-holder. They never enter the huts of the slaves; they know nothing of the dark side of the picture, and they return home with praises on their lips of the generous character of those with whom they had tarried. Or if they have witnessed the cruelties of slavery, by remaining silent spectators they have naturally become callous—an insensibility has ensued which prepares them to apologize even for barbarity. Nothing but the corrupting influence of slavery on the hearts of the Northern people can induce them to apologize for it; and much will have been done for the destruction of Southern slavery when we have so reformed the North that no one here will be willing to risk his reputation by advocating or even excusing the holding of men as property. The South know it, and acknowledge that as fast as our principles prevail, the hold of the master must be relaxed. *(Another outbreak of mobocratic spirit, and some confusion in the house.)*

How wonderfully constituted is the human mind! How it resists, as long as it can, all efforts made to reclaim from error! I feel that all this disturbance is but an evidence that our efforts are the best that could have been adopted, or else the friends of slavery would not care for what we say and do. The South know what we do. I am thankful that they are reached by our efforts. Many times have I wept in the land of my birth, over the system of slavery. I knew of none who sympathized in my feelings—I was unaware that any efforts were made to deliver the oppressed—no voice in the wilderness was heard calling on the people to repent and do works meet for repentance—and my heart sickened within me. Oh, how should I have rejoiced to know that such efforts as these were being made. I only wonder that I had such feelings. I wonder when I reflect under what influence I was brought up, that my heart is not harder than the nether millstone. But in the midst of temptation I was preserved, and my sympathy grew warmer, and my hatred of slavery more inveterate, until at last I have exiled myself from my native land because I could no longer endure to hear the wailing of the slave. I fled to the land of Penn; for here, thought I, sympathy for the slave will surely be found. But I found it not. The people were kind and hospitable, but the slave had no place in their thoughts. Whenever questions were put to me as to his condition, I felt that they were dictated by an idle curiosity, rather than by that deep feeling which would lead to effort for his rescue. I therefore shut up my grief in my own heart. I remembered that I was a Carolinian, from a state which framed this iniquity by law. I knew that throughout her territory was continual suffering, on the one part, and continual brutality and sin on the other. Every Southern breeze wafted to me the discordant tones of weeping and wailing, shrieks and groans, mingled with prayers and blasphemous curses. I thought there was no hope; that the wicked would go on in his wickedness, until he had destroyed both himself and his country. My heart sunk within me at the abominations in the midst of which I had been born and educated. What will it avail, cried I in bitterness of spirit, to expose to the gaze of strangers the horrors and pollutions of slavery, when there is no ear to hear nor heart to feel and pray for the slave. The language of my soul was, "Oh tell it not in Gath, publish it not in the streets of Askelon" [2 Sam 1:20]. But how different do I feel now! Animated with hope, nay, with an assurance of the triumph of liberty and good will to man, I will lift up my voice like a trumpet, and show this people their transgression, their sins of omission toward the slave, and what they can do towards affecting Southern mind, and overthrowing Southern oppression.

We may talk of occupying neutral ground, but on this subject, in its present attitude, there is no such thing as neutral ground. He that is not for us is against us, and he that gathereth not with us, scattereth abroad. If you are on what you suppose to be neutral ground, the South look upon you as on the side of the oppressor. And is there one who loves his country willing to give his influence, even indirectly, in favor of slavery—that curse of nations? God swept Egypt with the besom of destruction and punished Judea also with a sore punishment, because of slavery. And have we any reason to believe that he is less just now?—or that he will be more favorable to us than to his own "peculiar people?" *(Shouting, stones thrown against the windows, &c.)*

There is nothing to be feared from those who would stop our mouths, but they themselves should fear and tremble. The current is even now setting fast against them. If the arm of the North had not caused the Bastille of slavery to totter to its foundation, you would not hear those cries. A few years ago, and the South felt secure, and with a contemptuous sneer asked, "Who are the abolitionists? The abolitionists are nothing?"—Ay, in one sense they were nothing, and they are nothing still. But in this we rejoice, that "God has chosen things that are not to bring to nought things that are" [1 Cor. 1:28]. *(Mob again disturbed the meeting.)*

We often hear the question asked, "What shall we do?" Here is an opportunity for doing something now. Every man and every woman present may do something by showing that we fear not a mob, and, in the midst of threatenings and revilings, by opening our mouths for the dumb and pleading the cause of those who are ready to perish.

To work as we should in this cause, we must know what Slavery is. Let me urge you then to buy the books which have been written on this subject and read them, and then lend them to your neighbors. Give your money no longer for things which pander to pride and lust, but aid in scattering "the living coals of truth" upon the naked heart of this nation,—in circulating appeals to the sympathies of Christians in behalf of the outraged and suffering slave. But, it is said by some, our "books and papers do not speak the truth." Why, then, do they not contradict what we say? They cannot. Moreover the South has entreated, nay commanded us to be silent; and what greater evidence of the truth of our publications could be desired?

Women of Philadelphia! allow me as a Southern woman, with much attachment to the land of my birth, to entreat you to come up to this work. Especially let me urge you to petition. *Men* may settle this and other questions at the ballot-box, but you have no such right; it is only through petitions that you can reach the Legislature. It is therefore peculiarly *your* duty to petition. Do you say, "It does no good?" The South already turns pale at the number sent. They have read the reports of the proceedings of Congress, and there have seen that among other petitions were very many from the women of the North on the subject of slavery. This fact has called the attention of the South to the subject. How could we expect to have done more as yet? Men who hold the rod over slaves, rule in the councils of the nation: and they deny our right to petition and to remonstrate against abuses of our sex and of our kind. We have these rights, however, from our God. Only let us exercise them: and though often turned away unanswered, let us remember the influence of importunity upon the unjust judge, and act accordingly. The fact that the South look with jealousy upon our measures shows that they are effectual. There is, therefore, no cause for doubting or despair, but rather for rejoicing.

It was remarked in England that women did much to abolish Slavery in her colonies. Nor are they now idle. Numerous petitions from them have recently been presented to the Queen, to abolish the apprenticeship with its cruelties nearly equal to those of the system whose place it supplies. One petition two miles and a quarter long has been presented. And do you think these labors will be in vain? Let the history of the past answer. When the women of these States send up to Congress such a petition, our legislators will arise as did those of England, and say, "When all the maids and matrons of the land are knocking at our doors we must legislate." Let the zeal and love, the faith and works of our English sisters quicken ours—that while the slaves continue to suffer, and when they shout deliverance, we may feel the satisfaction of *having done what we could.*

FOR FURTHER READING

Weld, Angela Grimké. *Appeal to Christian Women of the Southern States.* New York: American Anti-Slavery Society, 1836.

————. *The Public Years of Sarah and Angelina Grimké : Selected Writings, 1835–1839.* Edited by Larry Ceplair. New York: Columbia University Press, 1989.

————. *Selected Works of Angelina Weld Grimké.* Edited by Carolivia Herron. New York: Oxford University Press, 1991.

Weld, Theodore Dwight, Angelina Grimké Weld, and Sarah Grimké. *Letters of Theodore Dwight Weld, Angelina Grimké Weld, and Sarah Grimké.* 2 vols. Edited by Gibert H. Barnes and Dwight L. Dumond. New York: D. Appleton-Century Co., 1934.

Margaret Fuller

1810–1850

"Let them be sea captains," said Margaret Fuller of women's infinite capabilities, capturing in one line her belief in the rights of women to full participation in the public world. *Woman in the Nineteenth Century* is one of the landmark manifestos of women's rights, widely read in the nineteenth century and said to have been a catalyst for the Seneca Falls Convention three years after its publication. (See the "Declaration of Sentiments and Resolutions.")

The most famous woman of her day, Fuller was born in 1810 in Cambridge, Massachusetts, and worked as a poet, travel writer, literary critic, editor, reviewer, teacher, and journalist until her death in 1850. Educated at home in the classics and fluent in several languages—in other words, educated in what she called "the masculine style"—Fuller wrote, talked, and worked with the leading male intellectuals of the nineteenth century, especially those in the Transcendentalist movement. In 1839, she began her famous "Conversations" in Boston, gathering women in her home to discuss various topics such as philosophy, politics, and literature.

From 1840 to 1842, she served as the editor of the famous literary publication *The Dial*, which she cofounded with Ralph Waldo Emerson. In 1846, she was invited by the publisher Horace Greeley to join the staff of the *New York Tribune* as a book-review editor. When Greeley offered Fuller the opportunity to become the first female correspondent for the *Tribune*, she left for Europe, sending back dispatches on European culture, literature, and politics. While visiting Rome in 1847 she fell in love with Marchese Giovanni Angelo d'Ossoli, a nobleman involved in revolutionary activities. They had a child a year later, a son named Angelo. When the Italian revolution failed in 1850, the family sailed to America, but off the coast of New York their ship was wrecked in a storm on July 19, 1850. Her friends, among them Henry David Thoreau, initiated searches, but only the body of their two-year-old son was recovered. A plaque at the Margaret Fuller Memorial on Pyrola Path in Cambridge, Massachusetts, says the following: "By birth a child of New England; by adoption a citizen of Rome; by genius belonging to the world. In youth an insatiable student seeking the highest culture; in riper years teacher, writer, critic of literature and art; in maturer age companion and helper of many earnest reformers in America and Europe."

In 1843, *The Dial* published Fuller's essay "The Great Lawsuit: Man versus Men, Woman versus Women," in which she called for women's equality. She expanded that piece into *Woman in the Nineteenth Century* in 1845. In the ex-

cerpts included here, we have tried to represent the variety and flavor of the
longer work, in which Fuller juxtaposes stories with logical argument, dialogue
with literary analysis, mythical and historical references with commentary
about current culture. (In fact, Fuller uses Aspasia as an example of the kind of
independent woman she envisions as the hope of the future. See "Pericles' Funeral Oration.") Some critics accuse Fuller of writing in a disjointed and haphazard style; Annette Kolodny, however, describes Fuller's prose as "an inten-
tional experiment in feminist prose" (163). Fuller was unwilling to structure her
discourse in "the masculine style," and her work, like her teaching, engages the
reader in conversation and refuses closure or authoritarian stances. Instead,
Woman in the Nineteenth Century asserts that a collaborative voice—of conversation rather than combativeness—is the most effective rhetorical strategy for a
new argument: that women could be anything at all.

From *Woman in the Nineteenth Century*

1845

Of all its banners, none has been more steadily upheld, and under none have
more valor and willingness for real sacrifices been shown, than that of the
champions of the enslaved African. And this band it is, which, partly from a
natural following out of principles, partly because many women have been
prominent in that cause, makes, just now, the warmest appeal in behalf of
woman.

Though there has been a growing liberality on this subject, yet society at
large is not so prepared for the demands of this party, but that they are and will
be for some time, coldly regarded as the Jacobins of their day.

"Is it not enough," cries the irritated trader, "that you have done all you
could to break up the national union, and thus destroy the prosperity of our
country, but now you must be trying to break up family union, to take my wife
away from the cradle and the kitchen hearth to vote at polls, and preach from a
pulpit? Of course, if she does such things, she cannot attend to those of her
own sphere. She is happy enough as she is. She has more leisure than I have,
every means of improvement, every indulgence."

"Have you asked her whether she was satisfied with these *indulgences?*"

"No, but I know she is. She is too amiable to wish what would make me unhappy, and too judicious to wish to step beyond the sphere of her sex. I will
never consent to have our peace disturbed by any such discussions."

Reprinted from Fuller, Margaret. *Woman in the Nineteenth Century.* New York: Greeley and
McElreth, 1845. Reprint, facsimile ed., edited by Joel Myerson and introduced by Madeleine
B. Stern, Columbia: University of South Carolina Press, 1980.

"'Consent—you?' it is not consent from you that is in question, it is assent from your wife."

"Am not I the head of my house?"

"You are not the head of your wife. God has given her a mind of her own."

"I am the head and she the heart."

"God grant you play true to one another then. I suppose I am to be grateful that you did not say she was only the hand. If the head represses no natural pulse of the heart, there can be no question as to your giving your consent. Both will be of one accord, and there needs but to present any question to get a full and true answer. There is no need of precaution, of indulgence, or consent. But our doubt is whether the heart does consent with the head, or only obeys its decrees with a passiveness that precludes the exercise of its natural powers, or a repugnance that turns sweet qualities to bitter, or a doubt that lays waste the fair occasions of life. It is to ascertain the truth, that we propose some liberating measures."

Thus vaguely are these questions proposed and discussed at present. But their being proposed at all implies much thought and suggests more. Many women are considering within themselves, what they need that they have not, and what they can have, if they find they need it. Many men are considering whether women are capable of being and having more than they are and have, *and,* whether, if so, it will be best to consent to improvement in their condition. . . .

But to return to the historical progress of this matter. Knowing that there exists in the minds of men a tone of feeling towards women as towards slaves, such as is expressed in the common phrase, "Tell that to women and children," that the infinite soul can only work through them in already ascertained limits; that the gift of reason, man's highest prerogative, is allotted to them in much lower degree; that they must be kept from mischief and melancholy by being constantly engaged in active labor, which is to be furnished and directed by those better able to think, &c. &c.; we need not multiply instances, for who can review the experience of last week without recalling words which imply, whether in jest or earnest, these views or views like these; knowing this, can we wonder that many reformers think that measures are not likely to be taken in behalf of women, unless their wishes could be publicly represented by women?

That can never be necessary, cry the other side. All men are privately influenced by women; each has his wife, sister, or female friends, and is too much biased by these relations to fail of representing their interests, and, if this is not enough, let them propose and enforce their wishes with the pen. The beauty of home would be destroyed, the delicacy of the sex be violated, the dignity of halls of legislation de-graded by an attempt to introduce them there. Such duties are inconsistent with those of a mother; and then we have ludicrous pictures of ladies in hysterics at the polls, and senate chambers filled with cradles.

But if, in reply, we admit as truth that woman seems destined by nature rather for the inner circle, we must add that the arrangements of civilized life have not been, as yet, such as to secure it to her. Her circle, if the duller, is not the quieter. If kept from "excitement," she is not from drudgery. Not only the Indian squaw carries the burdens of the camp, but the favorites of Louis the Fourteenth accompany him in his journeys, and the washerwoman stands at her tub and carries home her work at all seasons, and in all states of health. Those who think the physical circumstances of woman would make a part in the affairs of national government unsuitable, are by no means those who think it impossible for the negresses to endure field work, even during pregnancy, or the sempstresses to go through their killing labors.

As to the use of the pen, there was quite as much opposition to woman's possessing herself of that help to free agency, as there is now to her seizing on the rostrum or the desk; and she is likely to draw, from a permission to plead her cause that way, opposite inferences to what might be wished by those who now grant it.

As to the possibility of her filling with grace and dignity, any such position, we should think those who had seen the great actresses, and heard the Quaker preachers of modern times, would not doubt, that woman can express publicly the fulness of thought and creation, without losing any of the peculiar beauty of her sex. What can pollute and tarnish is to act thus from any motive except that something needs to be said or done. Women could take part in the processions, the songs; the dances of old religion; no one fancied their delicacy was impaired by appearing in public for such a cause.

As to her home, she is not likely to leave it more than she now does for balls, theatres, meetings for promoting missions, revival meetings, and others to which she flies, in hope of an animation for her existence, commensurate with what she sees enjoyed by men. Governors of ladies' fairs are no less engrossed by such a change, than the Governor of the state by his; presidents of Washingtonian societies no less away from home than presidents of conventions. If men look straitly to it, they will find that, unless their lives are domestic, those of the women will not be. A house is no home unless it contain food and fire for the mind as well as for the body. The female Greek, of our day, is as much in the street as the male to cry, What news? We doubt not it was the same in Athens of old. The women, shut out from the market place, made up for it at the religious festivals. For human beings are not so constituted that they can live without expansion. If they do not get it one way, they must another, or perish.

As to men's representing women fairly at present, while we hear from men who owe to their wives not only all that is comfortable or graceful, but all that is wise in the arrangement of their lives, the frequent remark, "You cannot reason with a woman," when from those of delicacy, nobleness, and poetic culture, the contemptuous phrase "women and children," and that in no light sally of the hour, but in works intended to give a permanent statement of the best experiences, when not one man, in the million, shall I say? no, not in the hundred million, can rise above the belief that woman was made *for man,* when such traits as these are daily forced upon the attention, can we feel that man will always do justice to the interests of woman? Can we think that he takes a sufficiently discerning and religious view of her office and destiny, *ever* to do her justice, except when prompted by sentiment, accidentally or transiently, that is, for the sentiment will vary according to the relations in which he is placed. The lover, the poet, the artist, are likely to view her nobly. The father and the philosopher have some chance of liberality; the man of the world, the legislator for expediency, none.

Under these circumstances, without attaching importance, in themselves, to the changes demanded by the champions of woman, we hail them as signs of the times. We would have every arbitrary barrier thrown down. We would have every path laid open to woman as freely as to man. Were this done and a slight temporary fermentation allowed to subside, we should see crystallizations more pure and of more various beauty. We believe the divine energy would pervade nature to a degree unknown in the history of former ages, and that no discordant collision, but a ravishing harmony of the spheres would ensue.

Yet, then and only then, will mankind be ripe for this, when inward and outward freedom for woman as much as for man shall be acknowledged as a right, not yielded as a concession. As the friend of the negro assumes that one man cannot by right, hold another in bondage, so should the friend of woman assume that man cannot, by right, lay even well-meant restrictions on woman. If the negro be a soul, if the woman be a soul, appareled in flesh, to one Master only are they accountable. There is but one law for souls, and if there is to be an interpreter of it, he must come not as man, or son of man, but as son of God.

Were thought and feeling once so far elevated that man should esteem himself the brother and friend, but nowise the lord and tutor of woman, were he really bound with her in equal worship, arrangements as to function and employment would be of no consequence. What woman needs is not as a woman to act or rule, but as a nature to grow, as an intellect to discern, as a soul to live freely and unimpeded, to unfold such powers as were given her when we left our common home. If fewer talents were given her, yet if allowed the free and full employment of these, so that she may render back to the giver his own with usury, she will not complain; nay I dare to say she will bless and rejoice in her earthly birth-place, her earthly lot. Let us consider what obstructions impede this good era, and what signs give reason to hope that it draws near.

I was talking on this subject with Miranda, a woman, who, if any in the world could, might speak without heat and bitterness of the position of her sex. Her father was a man who cherished no sentimental reverence for woman, but a firm belief in the equality of the sexes. She was his eldest child, and came to him at an age when he needed a companion. From the time she could speak and go alone, he addressed her not as a plaything, but as a living mind. Among the few verses he ever wrote was a copy addressed to this child, when the first locks were cut from her head, and the reverence expressed on this occasion for that cherished head, he never belied. It was to him the temple of immortal intellect. He respected his child, however, too much to be an indulgent parent. He called on her for clear judgment, for courage, for honor and fidelity; in short, for such virtues as he knew. In so far as he possessed the keys to the wonders of this universe, he allowed free use of them to her, and by the incentive of a high expectation, he forbade, as far as possible, that she should let the privilege lie idle.

Thus this child was early led to feel herself a child of the spirit. She took her place easily, not only in the world of organized being, but in the world of mind. A dignified sense of self-dependence was given as all her portion, and she found it a sure anchor. Herself securely anchored, her relations with others were established with equal security. She was fortunate in a total absence of those charms which might have drawn to her bewildering flatteries, and in a strong electric nature, which repelled those who did not belong to her; and attracted those who did. With men and women her relations were noble, affectionate without passion, intellectual without coldness. The world was free to her, and she lived freely in it. Outward adversity came, and inward conflict, but that faith and self-respect had early been awakened which must always lead at last, to an outward serenity and an inward peace.

Of Miranda I had always thought as an example, that the restraints upon the sex were insuperable only to those who think them so, or who noisily strive to break them. She had taken a course of her own, and no man stood in her way. Many of her acts had been unusual, but excited no uproar. Few helped, but none checked her, and the many men, who knew her mind and her life, showed to her confidence, as to a brother, gentleness as to a sister. And not only refined, but very coarse men approved and aided one in whom they saw resolution and clearness of design. Her mind was often the leading one, always effective.

When I talked with her upon these matters, and had said very much what I have written, she smilingly replied: "and yet we must admit that I have been fortunate, and this should not be. My good father's early trust gave the first bias, and the rest followed of course. It is true that I have had less outward aid, in after years, than most women, but that is of little consequence. Religion was early awakened in my soul, a sense that what the soul is capable to ask it must attain, and that, though I might be aided and instructed by others, I must depend on myself as the only constant friend. This self dependence, which was honored in me, is deprecated as a fault in most women. They are taught to learn their rule from without, not to unfold it from within.

"This is the fault of man, who is still vain, and wishes to be more important to woman than, by right, he should be."

"Men have not shown this disposition toward you," I said.

"No! because the position I early was enabled to take was one of self-reliance. And were all women as sure of their wants as I was, the result would be the same. But they are so overloaded with precepts by guardians, who think that nothing is so much to be dreaded for a woman as originality of thought or character, that their minds are impeded by doubts till they lose their chance of fair free proportions. The difficulty is to get them to the point from which they shall naturally develope self-respect, and learn self-help.

"Once I thought that men would help to forward this state of things more than I do now. I saw so many of them wretched in the connections they had formed in weakness and vanity. They seemed so glad to esteem women whenever they could.

"The soft arms of affection," said one of the most discerning spirits, "will not suffice for me, unless on them I see the steel bracelets of strength."

But early I perceived that men never, in any extreme of despair, wished to be women. On the contrary they were ever ready to taunt one another at any sign of weakness, with,

Art thou not like the women, who—

The passage ends various ways, according to the occasion and rhetoric of the speaker. When they admired any woman they were inclined to speak of her as "above her sex." Silently I observed this, and fear it argued a rooted scepticism, which for ages had been fastening on the heart, and which only an age of miracles could eradicate. Ever I have been treated with great sincerity; and I look upon it as a signal instance of this, that an intimate friend of the other sex said, in a fervent moment, that I "deserved in some star to be a man." He was much surprised when I disclosed my view of my position and hopes, when I declared my faith that the feminine side, the side of love, of beauty, of holiness, was now to have its full chance, and that, if either were better, it was better now to be a woman, for even the slightest achievement of good was furthering an especial work of our time. He smiled incredulous. "She makes the best she can of it," thought he. "Let Jews believe the pride of Jewry, but I am of the better sort, and know better."

Another used as highest praise, in speaking of a character in literature, the words "a manly woman."

So in the noble passage of Ben Jonson:

I meant the day-star should not brighter ride,
Nor shed like influence from its lucent seat;
I meant she should be courteous, facile, sweet,
Free from that solemn vice of greatness, pride;
I meant each softest virtue there should meet,
Fit in that softer bosom to abide,
Only a learned and a manly soul,
I purposed her, that should with even powers,
The rock, the spindle, and the shears control
Of destiny, and spin her own free hours.

"Methinks," said I, "you are too fastidious in objecting to this. Jonson in using the word 'manly' only meant to heighten the picture of this, the true, the intelligent fate, with one of the deeper colors." "And yet," said she, "so invariable is the use of this word where a heroic quality is to be described, and I feel so sure that persistence and courage are the most womanly no less than the most manly qualities, that I would exchange these words for others of a larger sense at the risk of marring the fine tissue of the verse. Read, 'a heavenward and instructed soul,' and I should be satisfied. Let it not be said, wherever there is energy or creative genius, 'She has a masculine mind.'"

This by no means argues a willing want of generosity toward woman. Man is as generous toward her, as he knows how to be.

Wherever she has herself arisen in national or private history, and nobly shone forth in any form of excellence, men have received her, not only willingly, but with triumph. Their encomiums indeed, are always, in some sense, mortifying; they show too much surprise. Can this be you? he cries to the transfigured Cinderella; well I should never have thought it, but I am very glad. We will tell every one that you have *"surpassed your sex. . . ."*

Another sign of the times is furnished by the triumphs of female authorship. These have been great and constantly increasing. Women have taken possession of so many provinces for which men had pronounced them unfit, that though these still declare there are some inaccessible to them, it is difficult to say just *where* they must stop.

The shining names of famous women have cast light upon the path of the sex, and many obstructions have been removed. When a Montague could learn better than her brother, and use her lore afterward to such purpose, as an observer, it seemed amiss to hinder woman from preparing themselves to see, or from seeing all they could, when prepared. Since Somerville has achieved so much, will any young girl be prevented from seeking a knowledge of the physical sciences, if she wishes it? De Stael's name was not so clear of offence; she could not forget the woman in the thought; while she was instructing you as a mind, she wished to be admired as a woman; sentimental tears often dimmed the eagle glance. Her intellect too, with all its splendor, trained in a drawing-room, fed on flattery, was tainted and flawed; yet its beams make the obscurest school-house in New-England warmer and lighter to the little rugged girls, who are gathered together on its wooden bench. They may never through life hear her name, but she is not the less their benefactress.

The influence has been such, that the aim certainly is, now, in arranging school instruction for girls, to give them as fair a field as boys. As yet, indeed, these arrangements are made with little judgment or reflection; just as the tutors of Lady Jane Grey, and other distinguished women of her time, taught them Latin and Greek, because they knew nothing else themselves, so now the improvement in the education of girls is to be made by giving them young men as teachers, who only teach what has been taught themselves at college, while methods and topics need revision for these new subjects, which could better be made by those who had experienced the same wants. Women are, often, at the head of these institutions, but they have, as yet, seldom been thinking women, capable to organize a new whole for the wants of the time, and choose persons to officiate in the departments. And when some portion of instruction is got of a good sort from the school, the far greater proportion which is infused from the general atmosphere of society contradicts its purport. Yet books and a little elementary instruction are not furnished, in vain. Women are better aware how great and rich the universe is, not so easily blinded by narrowness or partial views of a home circle. "Her mother did so before her," is no longer a sufficient excuse. Indeed, it was never received as an excuse to mitigate the severity of censure, but was adduced as a reason, rather, why there should be no effort made for reformation.

Whether much or little has been done or will be done, whether women will add to the talent of narration, the power of systematizing, whether they will carve marble, as well as draw and paint, is not important. But that it should be acknowledged that they have intellect which needs developing, that they should not be considered complete, if beings of affection and habit alone, is important.

Yet even this acknowledgment, rather conquered by woman than proffered by man, has been sullied by the usual selfishness. So much is said of women being better educated, that they may become better companions and mothers *for men*. They should be fit for such companionship, and we have mentioned, with satisfaction, instances where it has been established. Earth knows no fairer, holier relation than that of a mother. It is one which, rightly understood, must both promote and require the highest attainments. But a being of infinite scope must not be treated with an exclusive view to any one relation. Give the soul free course, let the organization, both of body and mind, be freely developed, and the being will be fit for any and every relation to which it may be called. The intellect, no more than the sense of hearing, is to be cultivated merely that she may be a more valuable companion to man, but because the Power who gave a power, by its mere existence, signifies that it must be brought out towards perfection.

In this regard of self-dependence, and a greater simplicity and fullness of being, we must hail as a preliminary the increase of the class contemptuously designated as old maids. . . .

If any individual live too much in relations, so that he becomes stranger to the resources of his own nature, he falls, after a while, into a distraction, or imbecility, from which he can only be cured by a time of isolation, which gives the renovating fountains time to rise up. With a society it is the same. Many minds, deprived of the traditionary or instinctive means of passing a cheerful existence, must find help in self-impulse, or perish. It is therefore that, while any elevation, in the view of union, is to be hailed with joy, we shall not decline celibacy as the great fact of the time. It is one from which no vow, no arrangement, can at present save a thinking mind. For now the rowers are pausing on their oars; they wait a change before they can pull together. All tends to illustrate the thought of a wise contemporary. Union is only possible to those who are units. To be fit for relations in time, souls, whether of man or woman, must be able to do without them in the spirit.

It is therefore that I would have woman lay aside all thought, such as she habitually cherishes, of being taught and led by men. I would have her, like the Indian girl, dedicate herself to the Sun, the Sun of Truth, and go no where if his beams did not make clear the path. I would have her free from compromise, from complaisance, from helplessness, because I would have her good enough and strong enough to love one and all beings, from the fulness, not the poverty of being. . . .

But men do *not* look at both sides, and women must leave off asking them and being influenced by them, but retire within themselves, and explore the groundwork of life till they find their peculiar secret. Then, when they come forth again, renovated and baptized, they will know how to turn all dross to gold, and will be rich and free though they live in a hut, tranquil, if in a crowd. Then their sweet singing shall not be from passionate impulse, but the lyrical overflow of a divine rapture, and a new music shall be evolved from this many-chorded world.

Grant her, then, for a while, the armor and the javelin. Let her put from her the press of other minds and meditate in virgin loneliness. The same idea shall re-appear in due time as Muse, or Ceres, the all-kindly patient Earth-Spirit. . . .

O men! I speak not to you. It is true that your wickedness (for you must not deny that, at least, nine thousand out of the ten, fall through the vanity you have systematically flattered, or the promises you have treacherously broken;) yes, it is true that your wickedness is its own punishment. Your forms degraded and your eyes clouded by secret sin; natural harmony broken and fineness of perception destroyed in your mental and bodily organization; God and love shut out from your hearts by the foul visitants you have permitted there; incapable of pure marriage; incapable of pure parentage; incapable of worship; oh wretched men, your sin is its own punishment! You have lost the world in losing yourselves. Who ruins another has admitted the worm to the root of his own tree, and the fuller ye fill the cup of evil, the deeper must be your own bitter draught. But I speak not to you—you need to teach and warn one another. And more than one voice rises in earnestness. And all that *women* say to the heart that has once chosen the evil path, is considered prudery, or ignorance, or perhaps, a feebleness of nature which exempts from similar temptations.

But to you, women, American women, a few words may not be addressed in vain. One here and there may listen. . . .

I believe that, at present, women are the best helpers of one another.

Let them think; let them act; till they know what they need.

We only ask of men to remove arbitrary barriers. Some would like to do more. But I believe it needs for woman to show herself in her native dignity, to teach them how to aid her; their minds are so encumbered by tradition. . . .

You ask, what use will she make of liberty, when she has so long been sustained and restrained?

I answer; in the first place, this will not be suddenly given. I read yesterday a debate of this year on the subject of enlarging women's rights over property. It was a leaf from the class book that is preparing for the needed instruction. The men learned visibly as they spoke. The champions of woman saw the fallacy of arguments, on the opposite side, and were startled by their own convictions. With their wives at home, and the readers of the paper, it was the same. And so the stream flows on, thought urging action, and action leading to the evolution of still better thought.

But, were this freedom to come suddenly, I have no fear of the consequences. Individuals might commit excesses, but there is not only in the sex a reverence for decorums and limits inherited and enhanced from generation to generation, which many years of other life could not efface, but a native love, in woman as woman, of proportion, of "the simple art of not too much," a Greek moderation, which would create immediately a restraining party, the natural legislators and instructors of the rest, and would gradually establish such rules as are needed to guard, without impeding, life.

The Graces would lead the choral dance, and teach the rest to regulate their steps to the measure of beauty.

But if you ask me what offices they may fill; I reply—any. I do not care what case you put; let them be sea-captains, if you will. I do not doubt there are women well fitted for such an office, and, if so, I should be glad to see them in it, as to welcome the maid of Saragossa, or the maid of Missolonghi, or the Suliote heroine, or Emily Plater.

I think women need, especially at this juncture, a much greater range of occupation than they have, to rouse their latent powers. A party of travellers lately visited a lonely hut on a mountain. There they found an old woman that told them she and her husband had lived there 40 years. "Why," they said, "did you choose so barren a spot?" She "did not know; *it was the man's notion.*"

And, during forty years, she had been content to act, without knowing why, upon "the man's notion." I would not have it so.

In families that I know, some little girls like to saw wood, others to use carpenters' tools. Where these tastes are indulged, cheerfulness and good humor are promoted. Where they are forbidden, because "such things are not proper for girls," they grow sullen and mischievous.

Fourier had observed these wants of women, as no one can fail to do who watches the desires of little girls, or knows the ennui that haunts grown women, except where they make to themselves a serene little world by art of some kind. He, therefore, in proposing a great variety of employments, in manufactures or the care of plants and animals, allows for one third of woman, as likely to have a taste for masculine pursuits, one third of men for feminine.

Who does not observe the immediate glow and serenity that is diffused over the life of women, before restless or fretful, by engaging in gardening, building, or the lowest department of art. Here is something that is not routine, something that draws forth life toward the infinite.

I have no doubt, however, that a large proportion of women would give themselves to the same employments as now, because there are circumstances that must lead them. Mothers will delight to make the nest soft and warm. Nature would take care of that; no need to clip the wings of any bird that wants to soar and sing, or finds in itself the strength of pinion for a migratory flight unusual to its kind. The difference would be that *all* need not be constrained to employments, for which some are unfit.

I have urged upon the sex self-subsistence in its two forms of self-reliance and self-impulse, because I believe them to be the needed means of the present juncture.

I have urged on woman independence of man, not that I do not think the sexes mutually needed by one another, but because in woman this fact has led to an excessive devotion, which has cooled love, degraded marriage, and prevented either sex from being what it should be to itself or the other.

I wish woman to live, *first* for God's sake. Then she will not make an imperfect man her god, and thus sink to idolatry. Then she will not take what is not fit for her from a sense of weakness and poverty. Then, if she finds what she needs in man embodied, she will know how to love, and be worthy of being loved.

By being more a soul, she will not be less woman, for nature is perfected through spirit.

Now there is no woman, only an overgrown child.

That her hand may be given with dignity, she must be able to stand alone. I wish to see men and women capable of such relations as are depicted by Landor in his Pericles and Aspasia, where grace is the natural garb of strength, and the affections are calm, because deep. The softness is that of a firm tissue, as when

The gods approve
The depth, but not the tumult of the soul,
A fervent, not ungovernable love.

A profound thinker has said, "no married woman can represent the female world, for she belongs to her husband. The idea of woman must be represented by a virgin."

But that is the very fault of marriage, and of the present relation between the sexes, that the woman does belong to the man, instead of forming a whole with him. Were it otherwise, there would be no such limitation to the thought.

Woman, self-centred, would never be absorbed by any relation; it would be only an experience to her as to man. It is a vulgar error that love, *a* love to woman is her whole existence; she also is born for Truth and Love in their universal energy. Would she but assume her inheritance, Mary would not be the only virgin mother. Not Manzoni alone would celebrate in his wife the virgin mind with the maternal wisdom and conjugal affections. The soul is ever young, ever virgin.

And will not she soon appear? The woman who shall vindicate their birthright for all women; who shall teach them what to claim, and how to use what they obtain? Shall not her name be for her era Victoria, for her country and life Virginia? Yet predictions are rash; she herself must teach us to give her the fitting name.

FOR FURTHER READING

Fuller, Margaret. *The Letters of Margaret Fuller.* 6 vols. Edited by Robert N. Hudspeth. Ithaca: Cornell University Press, 1983–95.

———. *Memoirs of Margaret Fuller Ossoli.* 2 vols. Edited by R. W. Emerson, W. H. Channing, and J. F. Clarke. 1852. New York: Burt Franklin, 1972.

———. *Papers on Literature and Art.* 2 vols. New York: Wiley and Putnam, 1846. Reprint, New York: AMS Press, 1972.

———. *The Portable Margaret Fuller.* Edited by Mary Kelley. New York: Penguin Books, 1994.

———. *Summer on the Lakes, in 1843.* Edited by Susan Smith Belasco. Urbana: University of Illinois Press, 1991.

———. *"These Sad but Glorious Days": Dispatches from Europe, 1846–1850.* Edited by Larry J. Reynolds and Susan Belasco Smith. New Haven: Yale University Press, 1992.

Kolodny, Annette. "Inventing a Feminist Discourse: Rhetoric and Resistance in Margaret Fuller's *Woman in the Nineteenth Century.*" In *Reclaiming Rhetorica: Women in the Rhetorical Tradition,* edited by Andrea Lunsford, 137–66. Pittsburgh: University of Pittsburgh Press, 1995.

Seneca Falls Convention

1848

The "Declaration of Sentiments" reads, "We hold these truths to be self-evident: that all men and women are created equal." It is a line that does not seem so radical today, but it shook the foundations of the U.S. government in 1848. Coauthored by Elizabeth Cady Stanton, Lucretia Coffin Mott, Matilda Gage, Martha Coffin Wright, and Mary Ann McClintock, the "Declaration," one of the most important examples of women's collaborative writing, was presented at Seneca Falls, New York, the site of the first convention to address women's rights in the United States. These collaborators described the event as "a convention to discuss the social, civil, and religious condition and rights of women." The outcomes of the convention were even greater than the organizers imagined. The hostile press coverage backfired, serving only to educate and mobilize women across the nation. The Seneca Falls Convention sparked others like it, and its format became a model for other conventions of the women's movement.

Although the authors were all white women, their movement had its origins in the abolitionist cause, which had demonstrated to them the limitations of their rights as women and provided them a trope through which to figure their own oppression. Wilma Mankiller, former chief of the Cherokee Nation, notes also the important influence Native American matrilineal and matriarchal tribal structures had on emerging feminist ideas, especially since Stanton and Gage both lived in the Iroquois country of upstate New York.

In their mimicry of the "Declaration of Independence," the authors of the "Declaration of Sentiments" appealed to their audience's sense of patriotism while illuminating the injustices and inequalities of American citizenship. After outlining the injuries women suffer as citizens, spouses, workers, and humans, the "Declaration" ends with twelve resolutions. The resolutions demand that women have "immediate admission to all the rights and privileges which belong to them as citizens of the United States." The most controversial resolution was number nine, which demanded that women pursue their right to "elective franchise." After Frederick Douglass spoke on behalf of this resolution, the convention adopted it.

The authors anticipated the opposition of the press and public in their "Declaration" and called for "zealous and untiring efforts." Despite their plea, many convention participants removed their names from the document after malicious attacks by the press. However, as a manifesto of the women's movement, the "Declaration of Sentiments" served as the touchstone for the next seventy-one years of women's suffrage efforts.

"Declaration of Sentiments and Resolutions"

1848

When, in the course of human events, it becomes necessary for one portion of the family of man to assume among the people of the earth a position different from that which they have hitherto occupied, but one to which the laws of nature and of nature's God entitle them, a decent respect to the opinions of mankind requires that they should declare the causes that impel them to such a course.

We hold these truths to be self-evident: that all men and women are created equal; that they are endowed by their Creator with certain inalienable rights, that among these are life, liberty, and the pursuit of happiness; that to secure these rights governments are instituted, deriving their just powers from the consent of the governed. Whenever any form of government becomes destructive of these ends, it is the right of those who suffer from it to refuse allegiance to it, and to insist upon the institution of a new government, laying its foundation on such principles, and organizing its powers in such form as to them shall seem most likely to effect their safety and happiness. Prudence, indeed, will dictate that governments long established should not be changed for light and transient causes; and accordingly, all experience hath shown that mankind are more disposed to suffer, while evils are sufferable, than to right themselves by abolishing the forms to which they were accustomed. But when a long train of abuses and usurpations, pursuing invariably the same object, evinces a design to reduce them under absolute despotism, it is their duty to throw off such government and to provide new guards for their future security. Such has been the patient sufferance of the women under this government, and such is now the necessity which constrains them to demand the equal station to which they are entitled.

The history of mankind is a history of repeated injuries and usurpations on the part of man toward woman, having in direct object the establishment of an absolute tyranny over her. To prove this, let facts be submitted to a candid world.

He has never permitted her to exercise her inalienable right to the elective franchise.

Reprinted from *History of Woman Suffrage, Vol. 1 (1848–1861)*, edited by Elizabeth Cady Stanton, Susan B. Anthony, and Matilda Joslyn Gage, 70–73. New York: Fowler and Wells, 1881.

He has compelled her to submit to laws, in the formation of which she had no voice.

He has withheld from her rights which are given to the most ignorant and degraded men—both natives and foreigners.

Having deprived her of this first right of a citizen, the elective franchise, thereby leaving her without representation in the halls of legislation, he has oppressed her on all sides.

He has made her, if married, in the eye of the law, civilly dead.

He has taken from her all right in property, even to the wages she earns.

He has made her, morally, an irresponsible being, as she can commit many crimes with impunity, provided they be done in the presence of her husband. In the covenant of marriage, she is compelled to promise obedience to her husband, he becoming, to all intents and purposes, her master—the law giving him power to deprive her of her liberty, and to administer chastisement.

He has so framed the laws of divorce, as to what shall be the proper causes of divorce; in case of separation, to whom the guardianship of the children shall be given; as to be wholly regardless of the happiness of women—the law, in all cases, going upon a false supposition of the supremacy of man, and giving all power into his hands.

After depriving her of all rights as a married woman, if single and the owner of property, he has taxed her to support a government which recognizes her only when her property can be made profitable to it.

He has monopolized nearly all the profitable employments, and from those she is permitted to follow, she receives but a scanty remuneration.

He closes against her all the avenues to wealth and distinction, which he considers most honorable to himself. As a teacher of theology, medicine, or law, she is not known.

He has denied her the facilities for obtaining a thorough education—all colleges being closed against her.

He allows her in Church, as well as State, but a subordinate position, claiming Apostolic authority for her exclusion from the ministry, and, with some exceptions, from any public participation in the affairs of the Church.

He has created a false public sentiment, by giving to the world a different code of morals for men and women, by which moral delinquencies which exclude women from society, are not only tolerated but deemed of little account in man.

He has usurped the prerogative of Jehovah himself, claiming it as his right to assign for her a sphere of action, when that belongs to her conscience and to her God.

He has endeavored, in every way that he could, to destroy her confidence in her own powers, to lessen her self-respect, and to make her willing to lead a dependent and abject life.

Now, in view of this entire disfranchisement of one-half the people of this country, their social and religious degradation,—in view of the unjust laws above mentioned, and because women do feel themselves aggrieved, oppressed, and fraudulently deprived of their most sacred rights, we insist that they have immediate admission to all the rights and privileges which belong to them as citizens of the United States.

In entering upon the great work before us, we anticipate no small amount of misconception, misrepresentation, and ridicule; but we shall use every instrumentality within our power to effect our object. We shall employ agents, circulate tracts, petition the state and national legislatures, and endeavor to enlist the pulpit and the press in our behalf. We hope this Convention will be followed by a series of Conventions, embracing every part of the country.

Firmly relying upon the final triumph of the Right and True, we do this day affix our signatures to this declaration. *[Names followed.]*

Resolutions

Whereas, The great precept of nature is conceded to be, "that man shall pursue his own true and substantial happiness." Blackstone, in his *Commentaries* remarks, that this law of Nature being coeval with mankind, and dictated by God himself, is of course superior in obligation to any other. It is binding over all the globe, in all countries, and at all times; no human laws are of any validity if contrary to this, and such of them as are valid, derive all their force, and all their validity, and all their authority, mediately and immediately, from this original; therefore,

Resolved, That such laws as conflict, in any way, with the true and substantial happiness of woman, are contrary to the great precept of nature, and of no validity; for this is "superior in obligation to any other."

Resolved, That all laws which prevent woman from occupying such a station in society as her conscience shall dictate, or which place her in a position inferior to that of man, are contrary to the great precept of nature, and therefore of no force or authority.

Resolved, That woman is man's equal—was intended to be so by the Creator, and the highest good of the race demands that she should be recognized as such.

Resolved, That the women of this country ought to be enlightened in regard to the laws under which they live, that they may no longer publish their degradation, by declaring themselves satisfied with their present position, nor their ignorance, by asserting that they have all the rights they want.

Resolved, That inasmuch as man, while claiming for himself intellectual superiority, does not accord to woman moral superiority, it is pre-eminently his duty to encourage her to speak, and teach, as she has an opportunity, in all religious assemblies.

Resolved, That the same amount of virtue, delicacy, and refinement of behavior, that is required of woman in the social state, should also be required of man, and the same transgressions should be visited with equal severity on both man and woman.

Resolved, That the objection of indelicacy and impropriety, which is so often brought against woman when she addresses a public audience, comes with a very ill-grace from those who encourage, by their attendance, her appearance on the stage, in the concert or in feats of the circus.

Resolved, That woman has too long rested satisfied in the circumscribed limits which corrupt customs and a perverted application of the Scriptures have marked out for her, and that it is time she should move in the enlarged sphere which her great Creator has assigned her.

Resolved, That it is the duty of the women of this country to secure to themselves their sacred right to the elective franchise.

Resolved, That the equality of human rights results necessarily from the fact of the identity of the race in capabilities and responsibilities.

Resolved, therefore, That, being invested by the Creator with the same capabilities, and the same consciousness of responsibility for their exercise, it is demonstrably the right and duty of woman, equally with man, to promote every righteous cause, by every righteous means; and especially in regard to the great subjects of morals and religions, it is self-evidently her right to participate with her brother in teaching them, both in private and in public, by writing and by speaking, by any instrumentalities proper to be used, and in any assemblies proper to be held; and this being a self-evident truth, growing out of the divinely implanted principles of human nature, any custom or authority adverse to it, whether modern or wearing the hoary sanction of antiquity, is to be regarded as a self-evident falsehood, and at war with mankind.

Resolved, That the speedy success of our cause depends upon the zealous and untiring efforts of both men and women, for the overthrow of the monopoly of the pulpit, and for the securing to woman an equal participation with men in the various trades, professions, and commerce.

FOR FURTHER READING

Bacon, Margaret Hope. *Valiant Friend: The Life of Lucretia Mott.* New York: Walker and Co., 1980.

Griffith, Elisabeth. *In Her Own Right: The Life of Elizabeth Cady Stanton.* New York: Oxford University Press, 1984.

Mankiller, Wilma, Gwendolyn Mink, Marysa Navarro, Barbara Smith, and Gloria Steinem, eds. *The Reader's Companion to U.S. Women's History.* Boston: Houghton Mifflin Company, 1998.

Stanton, Elizabeth Cady. *Eighty Years and More: Reminiscences, 1815–1897.* 1898; New York: Schocken Books, 1971.

Sojourner Truth

c. 1797–1883

Sojourner Truth embodied the muscle and grit of a woman determined to change the world with the brilliance of a natural orator's tongue. Born into slavery in New York, Truth knew from personal experience the tragic, barbaric existence of a human being owned like chattel. In 1827 New York state law granted Truth, and all other slaves over the age of twenty-eight, her freedom. Truth worked for twenty more years as a domestic servant before she heard the "calling" that led her to travel around the country, speaking on religious inspiration, abolition, and women's rights, telling the truth about slavery and about the racism of the women's movement. Truth changed her slave name "Isabella" to her more symbolic one, and her powerful oration and rapturous singing drew people to her speeches; having captured a wide audience, she challenged her listeners to live up to the ideals they claimed to espouse.

In addition to her powerful and unique style of rhetoric and her blending of political, social, and religious issues, Truth captivated audiences with her commanding physical presence. She was a dark-skinned African American woman, well over six feet tall, with a booming voice, and her left hand was disfigured from a childhood accident. All these physical characteristics added to people's fascination with Truth. Rarely was any account of a Truth speech written without a description of her physical presence in some detail.

Photographs of Truth bear testimony to her physical presence; her power and life force are evident even in old, withered photos. Her words, however, come to us through secondhand sources. Truth never learned to read or write. All the speeches available are transcriptions, usually by white people, which poses specific questions regarding the transcribers' motives and methods. The speech here, commonly called "Aren't *I* a Woman," is the most famous and most widely read of the limited number of Truth's words we have. It is also the most hotly debated. The original version appeared in *Narrative of Sojourner Truth* in 1875. It was transcribed by Frances Gage, a white woman who presided over the Women's Rights Convention of 1851 and gave Truth the opportunity to deliver the speech at the convention against, it is believed, the wishes of some of the participants. The version printed here, which includes Gage's commentary, was edited by contemporary scholar Karlyn Kohrs Campbell to remove all dialect and ungrammatical structures. Some scholars have suggested that the dialect as written by Gage was entirely false—not representative of any true dialect spoken during the time—and was included to portray Truth as a stereotypical slave. These critics argue that Truth, born and raised in New York, would not have had a Southern dialect and that therefore any representation of dialect was likely created by the transcriber. Some scholars question whether Truth ever delivered this speech at all, suggesting that it was invented by Gage to advance white women's causes.

Despite the controversy surrounding the actual text of this speech, "Aren't *I* a Woman?" remains one of the most important documents in both feminist and women's rhetorical history. These few words—historical or fictional—broke open the ideology of the nineteenth century's assumptions about "true womanhood." By asking "aren't *I* a woman?" Truth confronts her white "patrons" in the suffrage and abolitionist movements, disrupting racist assumptions of womanhood and insisting that women's rights must apply to all women, not just to white ladies. The rhetoric here weaves personal story and religious reference, humor and high seriousness to give the message force. Truth also integrates the reality of her body into her argument, a tangible extension of *ethos*. This powerful rhetoric of the body, along with Truth's landmark naming of the racism inherent in social reform movements at the end of the nineteenth century, presages many of the central issues in women's rhetoric to this day.

Speech at the Woman's Rights Convention, Akron, Ohio

1851

I rose and announced "Sojourner Truth," and begged the audience keep silence for a few moments. The tumult subsided at once, and every eye was fixed on this almost Amazon form, which stood nearly six feet high, head erect, and eye piercing the upper air, like one in a dream. At her first word, there was a profound hush. She spoke in deep tones, which, though not loud, reached every ear in the house, and away through the throng at the doors and windows:—

Well, children, where there is so much racket there must be something out o' kilter. I think that 'twixt the Negroes of the South and the women of the North all a-talking about rights, the white men will be in a fix pretty soon.

But what's all this here talking about? That man over there says that women need to be helped into carriages, and lifted over ditches, and to have the best place everywhere. Nobody ever helps me into carriages, or over mud puddles or gives me any best place *(and raising herself to her full height and her voice to a*

Reprinted from Truth, Sojourner. Speech at the Woman's Rights Convention, Akron, Ohio. In *Key Texts of the Early Feminists*, vol. 2 of *Man Cannot Speak for Her*, edited by Karlyn Kohrs Campbell, 99–102. Westport, Conn.: Greenwood, 1989.

pitch like rolling thunder, she asked), and aren't I a woman? Look at me! Look at my arm! *(And she bared her right arm to the shoulder, showing her tremendous muscular power.)* I have plowed, and planted, and gathered into barns, and no man could head me—and aren't I a woman? I could work as much and eat as much as a man (when I could get it), and bear the lash as well—and aren't I a woman? I have borne thirteen children and seen them almost all sold off into slavery, and when I cried out with a mother's grief, none but Jesus heard—and aren't I a woman? Then they talk about this thing in the head—what's this they call it? *("Intellect," whispered someone near.)* That's it honey. What's that got to do with woman's rights or Negroes' rights? If my cup won't hold but a pint and yours holds a quart, wouldn't you be mean not to let me have my little half-measure full? *(And she pointed her significant finger and sent a keen glance at the minister who had made the argument. The cheering was long and loud.)*

Then that little man in black [a clergyman] there, he says women can't have as much rights as man, 'cause Christ wasn't a woman. Where did your Christ come from? *(Rolling thunder could not have stilled that crowd as did those deep, wonderful tones, as she stood there with outstretched arms and eye of fire. Raising her voice still louder, she repeated,)* Where did your Christ come from? From God and a woman. Man had nothing to do with him. *(Oh! what a rebuke she gave the little man.)*

(Turning again to another objector, she took up the defense of mother Eve. I cannot follower her through it all. It was pointed, and witty, and solemn, eliciting at almost every sentence deafening applause; and she ended by asserting that) If the first woman God ever made was strong enough to turn the world upside down, all alone, these together *(and she glanced her eye over us),* ought to be able to turn it back and get it right side up again; and now they are asking to do it, the men better let them. *(Long-continued cheering.)*

'Bliged to you for hearing on me, and now old Sojourner hasn't got anything more to say.

(Amid roars of applause, she turned to her corner, leaving more than one of us with streaming eyes and hearts beating with gratitude. She had taken us up in her strong arms and carried us safely over the slough of difficulty, turning the whole tide in our favor. I have never in my life seen anything like the magical influence that subdued the mobbish spirit of the day and turned the jibes and sneers of an excited crowd into notes of respect and admiration. Hundreds rushed up to shake hands, and congratulate the glorious old mother and bid her God speed on her mission of "testifying again concerning the wickedness of this here people.")

FOR FURTHER READING

Bernard, Jacqueline. *Journey Toward Freedom: The Story of Sojourner Truth.* 1967; New York: The Feminist Press, 1990.

Logan, Shirley Wilson. *"We Are Coming": The Persuasive Discourse of Nineteenth-Century Black Women.* Carbondale: Southern Illinois University Press, 1999.

———. *With Pen and Voice: A Critical Anthology of Nineteenth-Century African-American Women.* Carbondale: Southern Illinois University Press, 1995.

Painter, Nell Irvin. *Sojourner Truth: A Life, a Symbol.* New York: W. W. Norton and Company, 1996.

Royster, Jacqueline Jones. *Traces of a Stream: Literacy and Social Change Among African American Women.* Pittsburgh: University of Pittsburgh Press, 2000.

Stanton, Elizabeth, Susan B. Anthony, and Matilda J. Gage, eds. *History of Woman Suffrage, Vol. 2, 1861–1876.* Rochester: Charles Mann, 1881. Reprint, New York: Source Book Press, 1970.

Truth, Sojourner. *Narrative of Sojourner Truth; A Bondswoman of Olden Time, with a History of Her Labors and Correspondence Drawn from Her "Book of Life."* 1850; New York: Oxford University Press, 1991.

Frances Ellen Watkins Harper

1825–1911

In 1854, when she was twenty-nine years old, Frances Harper wrote to a friend, "Well, I am out lecturing"—an unusual accomplishment for a young African American woman in the middle of the nineteenth century. Without boasting, Harper says, "My lectures have met with success. . . . My voice is not wanting in strength . . . to reach pretty well over the house" (Still 787). In this letter, Harper captures the beginning of a remarkable career as a writer and speaker, one whose strength of voice indeed reached throughout the United States. Until her death in 1911, Harper was one of the most popular African American writers of the nineteenth century, a social reformer whose poetry, speeches, and essays on abolition, temperance, and women's suffrage unflinchingly confronted the injustices she saw around her.

There is little information about Harper's early life. She was born into a free family in a slave state. Her parents apparently died when she was young, and Harper was raised by her aunt and uncle, attending her uncle's William Watkins Academy for Negro Youth. Watkins's curriculum focused on the classics, the Bible, and elocution, or eloquent speaking, and it is clear that Harper learned her lessons well. When the Missouri Compromise of 1850 made the climate in Maryland hostile to free blacks, Harper left for Columbus, Ohio, where she taught at the Union Seminary from 1850 to 1852. Soon thereafter, she became a traveling lecturer for abolition and other reform movements. Her lyrical poetry, which she often recited during her lectures, echoed her reformist ideals. In all her fiction—including her novel, *Iola Leroy*, published in 1892—Harper echoes the themes of her public speeches; she documents the progress of African Americans during Reconstruction and calls for equal justice for all Americans.

"We Are All Bound Up Together" was delivered to the Eleventh National Woman's Rights Convention, held in New York, where Elizabeth Cady Stanton and Susan B. Anthony also spoke. Harper says in her opening line that she is a "novice upon this platform," but Harper's voice was strong and brave enough to challenge her audience in radical new ways. In recounting her own experiences as a woman recently widowed, left with no legal rights, and as an African American woman forbidden to ride streetcars in Philadelphia, she demonstrates the interconnectedness of race, gender, and social class oppression. And although she proclaims the theme of a community of interest among all women, she boldly challenged white women at the convention, first by questioning the long-held suffragist belief that the vote could correct the ills of the world and next by demanding that white women examine their own complicity in racism, an issue that within a few years would cause serious division in the suffragist movement as Stanton and others asserted the rights of white women over those of African American and immigrant men in debates over the Fifteenth Amendment. Harper's challenge to extend human rights to all people echoes a theme that had been sounded by Sojourner Truth's famous "Aren't *I* a Woman?" speech fourteen years earlier. It also foreshadows twentieth-century calls for equal justice within the women's rights movement, like the "Combahee River Collective Statement." This speech marked the beginning of Harper's prominence in the national women's movement, and until her death Harper remained an advocate for human rights extended across lines of class, race, and gender.

"We Are All Bound Up Together"

1866

I feel I am something of a novice upon this platform. Born of a race whose inheritance has been outrage and wrong, most of my life had been spent in battling against those wrongs. But I did not feel as keenly as others, that I had these rights, in common with other women, which are now demanded. About two years ago, I stood within the shadows of my home. A great sorrow had fallen upon my life. My husband had died suddenly, leaving me a widow, with four children, one my own, and the others stepchildren. I tried to keep my children together. But my husband died in debt; and before he had been in his grave three months, the administrator had swept the very milk crocks and wash tubs from my hands. I was a farmer's wife and made butter for the Columbus market; but what could I do, when they had swept all away? They left me one thing—and that was a looking-glass! Had I died instead of my husband, how different would have been the result! By this time he would have had another wife, it is likely; and no administrator would have gone into his house, broken up his home, and sold his bed, and taken away his means of support.

I took my children in my arms, and went out to seek my living. While I was gone, a neighbor to whom I had once lent five dollars, went before a magistrate and swore that he believed I was a non-resident, and laid an attachment on my very bed. And I went back to Ohio with my orphan children in my arms, without a single feather bed in this wide world, that was not in the custody of the law. I say, then, that justice is not fulfilled so long as woman is unequal before the law.

Reprinted from *We Are All Bound Up Together: Proceedings of the Eleventh National Women's Rights Convention, May 1866*, 45–48.

We are all bound up together in one great bundle of humanity, and society cannot trample on the weakest and feeblest of its members without receiving the curse in its own soul. You tried that in the case of the negro. You pressed him down for two centuries; and in so doing you crippled the moral strength and paralyzed the spiritual energies of the white men of the country. When the hands of the black were fettered, white men were deprived of the liberty of speech and the freedom of the press. Society cannot afford to neglect the enlightenment of any class of its members. At the South, the legislation of the country was in behalf of the rich slaveholders, while the poor white man was neglected. What is the consequence today? From that very class of neglected poor white men, comes the man who stands today with his hand upon the helm of the nation. He fails to catch the watchword of the hour, and throws himself, the incarnation of meanness, across the pathway of the nation. My objection to Andrew Johnson is not that he has been a poor white man; my objection is that he keeps "poor whits" all the way through. (Applause.) That is the trouble with him.

This grand and glorious revolution which has commenced, will fail to reach its climax of success, until throughout the length and brea[d]th of the American Republic, the nation shall be so color-blind, as to know no man by the color of his skin or the curl of his hair. It will then have no privileged class, trampling upon and outraging the unprivileged classes, but will be then one great privileged nation, whose privilege will be to produce the loftiest manhood and womanhood that humanity can attain.

I do not believe that giving the woman the ballot is immediately going to cure all the ills of life. I do not believe that white women are dewdrops just exhaled from the skies. I think that like men they may be divided into three classes, the good, the bad, and the indifferent. The good would vote according to their convictions and principles; the bad, as dictated by preju[d]ice or malice; and the indifferent will vote on the strongest side of the question, with the winning party.

You white women speak here of rights. I speak of wrongs. I, as a colored woman, have had in this country an education which has made me feel as if I were in the situation of Ishmael, my hand against every man, and every man's hand against me. Let me go to-morrow morning and take my seat in one of your street cars—I do not know that they will do it in New York, but they will in Philadelphia—and the conductor will put up his hand and stop the car rather than let me ride.

A Lady—They will not do that here.

Mrs. Harper—They do in Philadelphia. Going from Washington to Baltimore this Spring, they put me in the smoking car. (Loud Voices—"Shame.") Aye, in the capital of the nation, where the black man consecrated himself to the nation's defense, faithful when the white man was faithless, they put me in the smoking car! They did it once; but the next time they tried it, they failed; for I would not go in. I felt the fight in me; but I don't want to have to fight all the time. Today I am puzzled where to make my home. I would like to make it in Philadelphia, near my own friends and relations. But if I want to ride in the streets of Philadelphia, they send me to ride on the platform with the driver. (Cries of "Shame.") Have women nothing to do with this? Not long since, a colored woman took her seat in an Eleventh Street car in Philadelphia, and the conductor stopped the car, and told the rest of the passengers to get out, and left the car with her in it alone, when they took it back to the station. One day I took my seat in a car, and the conductor came to me and told me to take another seat. I just screamed "murder." The man said if I was black I ought to behave myself. I knew that if he was white he was not behaving himself. Are there not wrongs to be righted?

FOR FURTHER READING

Harper, Frances Ellen Watkins. *A Brighter Coming Day: A Frances Ellen Watkins Harper Reader.* Edited by Frances Smith Foster. New York: The Feminist Press, 1990.

Logan, Shirley Wilson. *"We Are Coming": The Persuasive Discourse of Nineteenth-Century Black Women.* Carbondale: Southern Illinois University Press, 1999.

———, ed. *With Pen and Voice: An Anthology of Nineteenth-Century African-American Women.* Carbondale: Southern Illinois University Press, 1995.

Royster, Jacqueline Jones. *Traces of a Stream: Literacy and Social Change Among African American Women.* Pittsburgh: University of Pittsburgh Press, 2000.

Still, William. *The Underground Railroad.* Philadelphia: Porters and Coates, 1872. Reprint, New York: Arno Press, 1968.

Susan B. Anthony

1820–1906

On the morning of November 5, 1872, Susan B. Anthony walked to a nearby polling place and voted. About three weeks later she was arrested for voting illegally. For the three weeks following her arrest, Anthony traveled throughout the county where she was to be tried, delivering in every single village a lecture titled, "Is It a Crime for a Citizen of the U.S. to Vote?" When the trial was moved to a different county, she spoke there in every district. In the end, Anthony's efforts to reach potential jurors were thwarted when the judge issued a directed verdict of guilty and ordered her to pay a fine of one hundred dollars. True to her character, Anthony never paid that fine.

Perhaps Anthony just got tired of arguing for women's suffrage and decided to take matters into her own hands. She used the Fourteenth Amendment's clause stating that "All persons born or naturalized in the United States are citizens" to urge women simply to claim their citizens' rights at the polls. More likely, casting this ballot (for Ulysses S. Grant) was a carefully planned maneuver in support of the cause Anthony worked for single-mindedly: a constitutional amendment granting women the right to vote. Along with her close friend Elizabeth Cady Stanton, Anthony spoke and wrote tirelessly for women's rights and suffrage all her life, although after the Civil War, their single-mindedness led them to place white women's rights above those of African American men. Anthony did not live to see her dreams of equal representation fulfilled, dying fourteen years before women received the vote, but she never wavered in her belief that this right would come. On her seventy-fourth birthday, speaking before the annual convention of the National American Women's Suffrage Association (which she and Stanton had founded in 1869, with Anthony serving as president until 1900), Anthony spoke of the future: "We shall some day be heeded, and when we shall have our amendment to the Constitution, everybody will think it was always so. [They will] have no idea of how every single inch of ground that she stands upon has been gained by the hard work of some little handful of women in the past" (*History of Woman Suffrage* 4:223).

The account of Anthony's trial on the charge of voting while being a woman gives us a glimpse into some of that hard work. The exchange reprinted here also clearly demonstrates Anthony's strength and wit as a rhetor. Consistently interrupted by the judge, Anthony continues to make her case, reminding him that she was not permitted to speak on her own behalf during the trial. She draws on arguments of law as a "citizen" of the United States and makes appeals for humanity and equality, building on her experience as an abolitionist. This impromptu speech captures a highly charged moment in women's rhetorical history, revealing the risks Anthony took on our behalf and the resilience of an orator who never retreated from the struggle for enfranchisement.

From *The United States of America v. Susan B. Anthony*

1873

The Prosecution

D. A. Richard Crowley: May it please the Court and Gentlemen of the Jury: . . . The defendant, Miss Susan B. Anthony . . . voted for a representative in the Congress of the United States, to represent the 29th Congressional District of this State, and also for a representative at large for the State of New York to represent the State in the Congress of the United States. At that time she was a woman. I suppose there will be no question about that . . . whatever Miss Anthony's intentions may have been—whether they were good or otherwise—she did not have a right to vote upon that question, and if she did vote without having a lawful right to vote, then there is no question but what she is guilty of violating a law of the United States. . . .

Conceded, that on the 5th day of November, 1872, Miss Susan B. Anthony was a woman.

The Inspectors' Testimony

Q: Did you see her vote?
A: [Beverly W. Jones]: Yes, sir. . . .
Q: She was not challenged on the day she voted?
A: No, sir.

Cross-examination by Defense Attorney, Judge Henry Selden

Q: Prior to the election, was there a registry of voters in that district made?
A: Yes, sir.
Q: Were you one of the officers engaged in making that registry?
A: Yes, sir.
Q: When the registry was being made did Miss Anthony appear before the Board of Registry and claim to be registered as a voter?

Reprinted from *An Account of the Proceedings on the Trial of Susan B. Anthony, on the Charge of Illegal Voting, at the Presidential Election in Nov., 1872*, 68–85. Rochester: Daily Democrat and Chronicle Book Print, 1874.

A: She did.

Q: Was there any objection made, or any doubt raised as to her right to vote?

A: There was.

Q: On what ground?

A: On the ground that the Constitution of the State of New York did not allow women to vote.

Q: What was the defect in her right to vote as a citizen?

A: She was not a male citizen.

Q: That she was a woman?

A: Yes, sir. . . .

Q: Did the Board consider the question of her right to registry, and decide that she was entitled to registry as a voter?

A: Yes, sir.

Q: And she was registered accordingly?

A: Yes, sir. . . .

Q: Won't you state what Miss Anthony said, if she said anything, when she came there and offered her name for registration?

A: She stated that she did not claim any rights under the Constitution of the State of New York; she claimed her right under the Constitution of the United States.

Q: Did she name any particular amendment?

A: Yes, sir; she cited the XIV amendment.

Q: Under that she claimed her right to vote?

A: Yes, sir. . . .

The Defense

Attorney, Judge Henry R. Selden: The only alleged ground of illegality of the defendant's vote is that she is a woman. If the same act had been done by her brother under the same circumstances, the act would have been not only innocent, but honorable and laudable; but having been done by a woman it is said to be a crime. . . . I believe this is the first instance in which a woman has been arraigned in a criminal court merely on account of her sex. . . . Another objection is, that the right to hold office must attend the right to vote, and that women are not qualified to discharge the duties of responsible offices. I beg leave to answer this objection by asking one or more questions. How many of the male bipeds who do our voting are qualified to hold high offices? . . . Another objection is that engaging in political controversies is not consistent with the feminine character. Upon that subject, women themselves are the best judges, and if political duties should be found inconsistent with female delicacy, we may rest assured that women will either effect a change in the character of political contests, or decline to engage in them. . . .

The Judge

The Court: The question, gentlemen of the jury . . . is wholly a question or questions of law, and I have decided as a question of law, in the first place, that under the XIV Amendment, which Miss Anthony claims protects her, she was not protected in a right to vote. And I have decided also that her belief and the advice which she took do not protect her in the act which she committed. If I am right in this, the result must be a verdict on your part of guilty, and I therefore direct that you find a verdict of guilty.

Mr. Selden: That is a direction no Court has power to make in a criminal case.

The Court: Take the verdict, Mr. Clerk.

The Clerk: Gentlemen of the jury, hearken to your verdict as the Court has recorded it. You say you find the defendant guilty of the offense whereof she stands indicted, and so say you all? . . .

Mr. Selden: I don't know whether an exception is available, but I certainly must except to the refusal of the Court to submit those propositions, and especially to the direction of the Court that the jury should find a verdict of guilty. I claim that it is a power that is not given to any Court in a criminal case. Will the Clerk poll the jury?

The Court: No. Gentlemen of the jury, you are discharged.

The Next Day

The Court: The prisoner will stand up. Has the prisoner anything to say why sentence shall not be pronounced?

Miss Anthony: Yes, your honor, I have many things to say; for in your ordered verdict of guilty, you have trampled underfoot every vital principle of our government. My natural rights, my civil rights, my political rights, are all alike ignored. Robbed of the fundamental privilege of citizenship, I am degraded from the status of a citizen to that of a subject; and not only myself individually, but all of my sex, are, by your honor's verdict, doomed to political subjection under this so-called Republican government.

Judge Hunt: The Court can not listen to a rehearsal of arguments the prisoner's counsel has already consumed three hours in presenting.

Miss Anthony: May it please your honor, I am not arguing the question, but simply stating the reasons why sentence can not, in justice, be pronounced against me. Your denial of my citizen's right to vote is the denial of my right of consent as one of the governed, the denial of my right of representation as one of the taxed, the denial of my right to a trial by a jury of my peers as an offender against the law, therefore, the denial of my sacred rights to life, liberty, property, and—

Judge Hunt: The Court can not allow the prisoner to go on.

Miss Anthony: But your honor will not deny me this one and only poor privilege of protest against this high-handed outrage upon my citizen's rights. May it please the Court to remember that since the day of my arrest last November, this is the first time that either myself or any person of my disfranchised class has been allowed a word of defense before judge or jury—

Judge Hunt: The prisoner must sit down; the Court can not allow it.

Miss Anthony: All my prosecutors, from the 8th Ward corner grocery politician, who entered the complaint, to the United States Marshal, Commissioner, District Attorney, District Judge, your honor on the bench, not one is my peer, but each and all are my political sovereigns; and had your honor submitted my case to the jury, as was clearly your duty, even then I should have had just cause of protest, for not one of those men was my peer; but, native or foreign, white or black, rich or poor, educated or ignorant, awake or asleep, sober or drunk, each and every man of them was my political superior; hence, in no sense, my peer. . . .

Judge Hunt: The Court must insist—the prisoner has been tried according to the established forms of law.

Miss Anthony: Yes, your honor, but by forms of law all made by men, interpreted by men, administered by men, in favor of men, and against women; and hence, your honor's ordered verdict of guilty, against a United States citizen for the exercise of "that citizen's right to vote," simply because that citizen was a woman and not a man. But, yesterday, the same manmade forms of law declared it a crime punishable with $1,000 fine and six months' imprisonment, for you, or me, or any of us, to give a cup of cold water, a crust of bread, or a night's shelter to a panting fugitive as he was tracking his way to Canada. And every man or woman in whose veins coursed a drop of human sympathy violated that wicked law, reckless of consequences, and was justified in so doing. As then the slaves who got their freedom must take it over, or under, or through the unjust forms of law, precisely so now must women, to get their right to a voice in this Government, take it; and I have taken mine, and mean to take it at every possible opportunity.

Judge Hunt: The Court orders the prisoner to sit down. It will not allow another word.

Miss Anthony: When I was brought before your honor for trial, I hoped for a broad and liberal interpretation of the Constitution and its recent amendments, that should declare all United States citizens under its protecting aegis—that should declare equality of rights the national guarantee to all persons born or naturalized in the United States. But failing to get this justice—failing, even, to get a trial by a jury *not* of my peers—I ask not leniency at your hands—but rather the full rigors of the law.

Judge Hunt: The Court must insist—*[Here the prisoner sat down.]* The prisoner will stand up. *[Here Miss Anthony arose again.]* The sentence of the Court is that you pay a fine of $100 and the costs of the prosecution.

Miss Anthony: May it please your honor, I shall never pay a dollar of your unjust penalty. All the stock in trade I possess is a $10,000 debt, incurred by publishing my paper—*The Revolution*—four years ago, the sole object of which was to educate all women to do precisely as I have done, rebel against your man-made, unjust, unconstitutional forms of law, that tax, fine, imprison, and hang women, while they deny them the right of representation in the Government; and I shall work on with might and main to pay every dollar of that honest debt, but not a penny shall go to this unjust claim. And I shall earnestly and persistently continue to urge all women to the practical recognition of the old revolutionary maxim that "Resistance to tyranny is obedience to God."

Judge Hunt: Madam, the Court will not order you committed until the fine is paid.

—Trial, 1873

FOR FURTHER READING

Lutz, Alma. *Susan B. Anthony: Rebel, Crusader, Humanitarian.* Boston: Beacon Press, 1959.

Sherr, Lynn. *Failure is Impossible: Susan B. Anthony in Her Own Words.* New York: Random House, 1995.

Stanton, Elizabeth Cady, Susan B. Anthony, and Matilda Joslyn Gage, eds. *History of Woman Suffrage, Vol. 4 (1883–1900).* New York: Fowler and Wells, 1881.

Sarah Winnemucca

1844–1891

Sarah Winnemucca is a complex figure standing as a translator and go-between for both Native American and European American cultures and as the only Native woman to write a personal and tribal history in the nineteenth century. Malea Powell writes that Winnemucca's rhetorical strategies "authenticate and authorize herself as that most contradictory of subjects—a *civilized Indian* . . . through a textual representation of herself in *Life Among the Piutes* as a literate practitioner of Euroamerican cultural discourse [and] at the same time . . . as a Paiute" (3).

Winnemucca was born in Nevada, the granddaughter of Truckee, the chief of the Paiutes. As a child she taught herself to read and write in English while she worked as a domestic servant. Later she served as an interpreter for the U.S. Army and the Bureau of Indian Affairs and as a teacher in "Indian" schools. In 1879, she began a series of public lectures to expose the mistreatment of the Paiutes by Indian agents, especially by William V. Rinehart at the Malheur Reservation, where the Paiutes were contained in eastern Oregon. During the Bannock War of 1878, an uprising in which the Paiutes joined the Bannocks in resisting reservation conditions for which Rinehart is blamed, Winnemucca was asked to serve as interpreter and go-between for the U.S. Army. She used the money she earned to travel to San Francisco to begin her lectures; because of their success she received financial support from well-known suffragist and reform advocate Elizabeth Peabody to give a series of three hundred highly successful lectures in the East in 1883 and 1884. With Peabody's support Winnemucca wrote her book, *Life Among the Piutes*, published in 1884. The Bureau of Indian Affairs immediately tried to discredit it by attacking her character, calling her the "Amazonian Champion of the Army." Nevertheless, with Peabody's continued financial backing, Winnemucca founded a school for Paiute children in Nevada.

Life Among the Piutes is framed as an autobiography, but it is also a public, historical account of Winnemucca's tribe's history and a passionate argument for change in nineteenth-century governmental policies toward Native people. In that respect, Winnemucca follows the strategy of many women rhetoricians who elide the boundaries between the personal and public spheres in writing. The passage from *Life Among the Piutes* that we include here describes an episode after the Bannock War when the Paiutes were to be moved in the middle of the winter across the Columbia River into the Yakima Valley of Washington, a move that constituted a breach of promise on the part of the U.S. government and therefore set Winnemucca herself in a difficult position as translator of governmental policy to her people. In a speech crucial to this episode, Winnemucca uses her audience's Christian values and her knowledge of Biblical rhetoric to chastise her white listeners and to challenge self-righteous patriotic narratives. Like other women rhetoricians of the nineteenth century, including Frances Ellen Watkins Harper, she draws on her audience's belief in justice, freedom, and righteousness to show that in undermining these principles the whites degrade themselves as well as the Native people she represents.

From *Life Among the Piutes*

1883

One day the commanding officer sent for me. Oh, how my heart did jump! I said to Mattie, "There is bad news." Truly I had not felt like this since the night Egan was killed by the Umatillas. I got ready and went down to the office, trembling as if something fearful was waiting for me. I walked into the office. Then the officer said to me,—

Sarah, I have some news to tell you and I want you to keep it still until we are sure if it will be true."

I then promised I would keep it still if it was not too awful bad news.

He said, "It is pretty bad." He looked at me and said, "Sarah, you look as if you were ready to die. It is nothing about you; it is about your people. Sarah, an order is issued that your people are to be taken to Yakima Reservation, across the Columbia River."

I said, "All of my people?"

"No, not your father's, but all that are here." I asked, "What for?"

He said he did not know.

I said, "Major, my people have not done anything, and why should they be sent away from their own country? If there are any to be sent away, let it be Oytes and his men, numbering about twenty-five men in all, and the few Bannocks that are with them. Oh, Major! if you knew what I have promised my people, you would leave nothing undone but what you would try not to have them sent away. Oh, Major! my people will never believe me again."

"Well, Sarah, I will do all I can. I will write to the President and see what he thinks about it. I will tell him all you have said about your people."

I was crying. He told me to keep up a good heart, and he would do all he could for me.

Reprinted from Hopkins, Sarah Winnemucca. *Life Among the Piutes Their Wrongs and Claims,* 203–10. New York: G. P. Putnam's Sons, 1883. Lincoln: University of Nebraska-Lincoln. Microfilm.

I went home and told Mattie all, and she said, "Well, sister, we cannot help it if the white people won't keep their word. We can't help it. We have to work for them and if they get our people not to love us, by telling what is not true to them, what can we do? It is they, not us."

I said, "Our people won't think so because they will never know that it was they who told the lie. Oh! I know all our people will say we are working against them and are getting money for all this."

In the evening Mattie and I took a walk down to their camp. There they were so happy; singing here, singing there and everywhere. I thought to myself, "My poor, poor people, you will be happy to-day; to-morrow or next week your happiness will be turned to weeping." Oh, how sad I was for them! I could not sleep at night, for the sad thing that had come.

At last one evening I was sent for by the commanding officer. Oh how can I tell it? My poor heart stood still. I said to Mattie, "Mattie, I wish this was my last day in this cruel world."

I came to myself and I said, "No, Mattie, I don't mean the world. I mean the cruel—yes, the cruel, wicked, white people, who are going to drive us to some foreign country, away from our own. Mattie, I feel so badly I don't think I can walk down there."

Mattie said, "I will go with you."

We then went down, and Major Cochran met us at the door and said, "Sarah, are you sick? You look so badly."

I said, "No."

He then replied, "Sarah, I am heartily sorry for you, but we cannot help it. We are ordered to take your people to Yakima Reservation."

It was just a little before Christmas. My people were only given one week to get ready in.

I said, "What! In this cold winter and in all this snow, and my people have so many little children? Why, they will all die. Oh, what can the President be thinking about? Oh, tell me, what is he? Is he man or beast? Yes, he must be a beast; if he has no feeling for my people, surely he ought to have some for the soldiers."

"I have never seen a president in my life and I want to know whether he is made of wood or rock, for I cannot for once think that he can be a human being. No human being would do such a thing as that,—send people across a fearful mountain in midwinter."

I was told not to say anything till three days before starting. Every night I imagined I could see the thing called President. He had long ears, he had big eyes and long legs, and a head like a bull-frog or something like that. I could not think of anything that could be so inhuman as to do such a thing—send people across mountains with snow so deep.

Mattie and I got all the furs we could; we had fur caps, fur gloves, and fur overshoes.

At last the time arrived. The commanding-officer told me to tell Leggins to come to him. I did so. He came, and Major Cochrane told me to tell him that he wanted him to tell which of the Bannock men were the worst, or which was the leader in the war. Leggins told him, and counted out twelve men to him. After this talk, Major Cochrane asked me to go and tell these men to come up to the office. They were Oytes, Bannock Joe, Captain Bearskin, Paddy Cap, Boss, Big John, Eagle Eye, Charley, D. E. Johnson, Beads, and Oytes' son-in-law, called Surger. An officer was sent with me. I called out the men by their names. They all came out to me. I said to Oytes,

"Your soldier-father wants you all to go up to see him." We went up, and Oytes asked me many things. We had to go right by the guard-house. Just as we got near it, the soldier on guard came out and headed us off and took the men and put them into the guard-house. After they were put in there the soldiers told me to tell them they must not try to get away, or they would be shot.

"We put you in here for safe-keeping," they said. "The citizens are coming over here from Canyon City to arrest you all, and we don't want them to take you; that is why we put you in here."

Ten soldiers were sent down to guard the whole encampment—not Leggins' band, only Oytes' and the Bannocks. I was then ordered to tell them to get ready to go to Yakima Reservation.

Oh, how sad they were! Women cried and blamed their husbands for going with the Bannocks; but Leggins and his band were told they were not going with the prisoners of war, and that he was not going at all.

Then Leggins moved down the creek about two miles. At night some would get out and go off. Brother Lee and Leggins were sent out to bring them back again. One afternoon Mattie and I were sent out to get five women who got away during the night, and an officer was sent with us. We were riding very fast, and my sister Mattie's horse jumped on one side and threw her off and hurt her. The blood ran out of her mouth, and I thought she would die right off; but, poor dear, she went on, for an ambulance was at our command. She had great suffering during our journey.

Oh, for shame! You who are educated by a Christian government in the art of war; the practice of whose profession makes you natural enemies of the savages, so called by you. Yes, you, who call yourselves the great civilization; you who have knelt upon Plymouth Rock, covenanting with God to make this land the home of the free and the brave. Ah, then you rise from your bended knees and seizing the welcoming hands of those who are the owners of this land, which you are not, your carbines rise upon the bleak shore, and your so-called civilization sweeps inland from the ocean wave; but, oh, my God! leaving its pathway marked by crimson lines of blood, and strewed by the bones of two races, the inheritor and the invader; and I am crying out to you for justice—yes, pleading for the far-off plains of the West, for the dusky mourner, whose tears of love are pleading for her husband, or for their children, who are sent far away from them. Your Christian minister will hold my people against their will; not because he loves them—no, far from it—but because it puts money in his pockets.

Now we are ready to start for Yakima. Fifty wagons were brought, and citizens were to take us there. Some of the wagons cost the government from $10 to $15 per day. We got to Canyon City, and while we camped there Captain Winters got a telegram from Washington, telling him he must take Leggins' band too. So we had to wait for them to overtake us. While we were waiting, our dear good father and mother, Mr. Charles W. Parrish, came with his wife and children to see us. My people threw their arms round him and his wife, crying, "Oh, our father and mother, if you had stayed with us we would not suffer this."

Poor Mrs. Parrish could not stop her tears at seeing the people who once loved her, the children whom she had taught—yes, the savage children who once called her their white-lily mother, the children who used to bring her wild flowers, with happy faces, now ragged, no clothes whatever. They all cried out to him and his wife, saying, "Oh, good father and mother, talk for us! Don't let them take us away; take us back to our home!" He told them he could do nothing for them. They asked him where his brother, Sam Parrish, was. He told them he was a long way off; and then they bade us good-by, and that was the last they saw of him.

While we were waiting for Leggins, it snowed all the time. In two days the rest of my people overtook us. It was so very cold some of them had to be left on the road; but they came in later. That night an old man was left in the road in a wagon. The next morning they went back to get the wagon, and found the old man frozen to death. The citizen who owned the wagon did not bring him to the camp; but threw him out of his wagon and left him. I thought it was the most fearful thing I ever saw in my life.

Early the next morning, the captain sent me to tell Leggins that he wanted him to help the soldiers guard the prisoners and see that none of them got away. He said the Big Father in Washington wanted him to do this, and then he and his people could come back in the spring. I went to tell Leggins; but he would not speak to me, neither would my brother Lee. I told him all and went away. When I got back, the captain asked me what he said. I told him he would not speak to me.

"Did you tell him what I told you to?"

"I did."

"Go and tell the prisoners to be ready to march in half an hour."

We travelled all day. It snowed all day long. We camped, and that night a woman became a mother; and during the night the baby died, and was put under the snow. The next morning the mother was put into the wagon. She was almost dead when we went into camp. That night she too was gone, and left on the roadside, her poor body not even covered with the snow.

In five days three more children were frozen to death, and another woman became a mother. Her child lived three days, but the mother lived. We then crossed Columbia River. All the time my poor dear little Mattie was dying little by little.

At last we arrived in Yakima on the last day of the month. Father Wilbur and the chief of the Yakima Indians came to meet us. We came into camp about thirty miles from where the agency buildings are, and stayed at this place for ten days. Another one of my people died here, but oh, thanks be to the Good Father in the Spirit-land, he was buried as if he were a man. At the end of the ten days we were turned over to Father Wilbur and his civilized Indians, as he called them. Well, as I was saying, we were turned over to him as if we were so many horses or cattle. After he received us he had some of his civilized Indians come with their wagons to take us up to Fort Simcoe. They did not come because they loved us, or because they were Christians. No; they were just like all civilized people; they came to take us up there because they were to be paid for it. They had a kind of shed made to put us in. You know what kind of shed you make for your stock in winter time. It was that kind. Oh, how we did suffer with cold. There was no wood, and the snow was waist-deep, and many died off just as cattle or horses do after travelling so long in the cold.

FOR FURTHER READING

Canfield, G. W. *Sarah Winnemucca of the Northern Paiutes.* Norman: University of Oklahoma Press, 1983.

Powell, Malea. "This Indian Is Not a Princess: Sarah Winnemucca Hopkins' *Life Among the Piutes.*" Paper presented at the Second Biennial Conference on Feminism(s) and Rhetoric(s), Minneapolis, Minn., October 1999.

Anna Julia Cooper

1858–1964

Anna Julia Cooper's remarkable life spanned the history of race relations in the nineteenth and twentieth centuries. She was born in the antebellum South and died at the height of the Civil Rights Movement of the 1960s. In between she rose to become a celebrated educator, an accomplished speaker and writer, and a passionate defender of the rights of all women.

Cooper was born in Raleigh, North Carolina, on August 10, 1858, to Hannah Stanley Haywood. Her father was most likely the slaveholder George Washington Haywood. After the Civil War, she received a scholarship to Saint Augustine Normal School, where she demanded admission to the all-male Greek classes. The teacher, George Cooper, married Anna in 1877. Two years later George Cooper died. Anna Cooper left Saint Augustine in 1881 to study at Oberlin College, receiving her B.A. in 1884 and her M.A. in 1887. She moved to Washington, D.C., in 1887 to become a math, science, and Latin teacher at the Washington Colored School, where she served as principal from 1902 to 1906. At the same time, she wrote essays and traveled around the country and the world giving speeches on women's and civil rights. In 1915, she adopted five great-nephews and great-nieces. While she raised these children, Cooper became the fourth African American woman to earn a Ph.D., earning hers from the University of Paris in 1925. After retiring from public school teaching in 1930, Cooper became president of Frelinghuysen University, a school for working-class adults, and devoted the rest of her life to this school, until her death in 1964 at the age of 105.

In *A Voice from the South by a Black Woman of the South,* her only published work, Cooper dramatically challenges prevailing ideas about women, particularly black women. In her introduction to this text, Mary Helen Washington explains that because Cooper saw the black woman as the "least likely to be among the eminent and the most likely to be responsible for the nurturing of families, it is she, according to Cooper, who represents the entire race" (xxviii–xxix). Thus, in a famous line near the beginning of her book, Cooper says: "Only the BLACK WOMAN can say 'when and where I enter, in the quiet, undisputed dignity of my womanhood, without violence and without suing or special patronage, then and there the whole *Negro race enters with* me'" (31). Cooper's teaching, writing, and activism all demonstrated that peaceful dignity and her belief that educating the least privileged in society was her highest calling.

In the chapter excerpted here, "The Higher Education of Women," Cooper argues that "the feminine half of the world's truth" must become a part of learning. She claims, in prose that is both scholarly and elegant, that the dominating and all-too-often violent tendencies of men—specifically white men—run counter to the professed goals of higher education. She also reveals the nature of her own hard-won education at a time when there was little encouragement for female intellectuals. Some scholars argue that Cooper's prose betrays her submission to the nineteenth-century cult of true womanhood, with its themes of domesticity, gentility, and sympathy. But Washington names *A Voice from the South* as the "most precise, forceful well-argued statement of black feminist thought to come out of the nineteenth century" (li). Today, Cooper's confident hope for the twentieth century still resonates with urgency: "you will not find the law of love shut out from the affairs of men" once all women have full access to education.

"The Higher Education of Women"

1892

In the very first year of our century, the year 1801, there appeared in Paris a book by Silvain Marechal, entitled "Shall Woman Learn the Alphabet." The book proposes a law prohibiting the alphabet to women, and quotes authorities weighty and various, to prove that the woman who knows the alphabet has already lost part of her womanliness. The author declares that woman can use the alphabet only as Moliere predicted they would, in spelling out the verb *amo;* that they have no occasion to peruse Ovid's *Ars Amoris,* since that is already the ground and limit of their intuitive furnishing; that Madame Guion would have been far more adorable had she remained a beautiful ignoramus as nature made her; that Ruth, Naomi, the Spartan woman, the Amazons, Penelope, Andromache, Lucretia, Joan of Arc, Petrarch's Laura, the daughters of Charlemagne, could not spell their names; while Sappho, Aspasia, Madame de Maintenon, and Madame de Stael could read altogether too well for their good; finally, that if women were once permitted to read Sophocles and work with logarithms, or to nibble at any side of the apple of knowledge, there would be an end forever to their sewing on buttons and embroidering slippers.

Please remember this book was published at the *beginning* of the 19th Century. At the end of its first third, (in the year 1833) one solitary college in America decided to admit women within its sacred precincts, and organized what was called a "Ladies' Course" as well as the regular B.A. or Gentlemen's course.

Reprinted from Cooper, Anna Julia. *A Voice from the South by a Black Woman of the South,* introduced by Mary Helen Washington, 48–61. New York: Oxford University Press, 1988.

It was felt to be an experiment—a rather dangerous experiment—and was adopted with fear and trembling by the good fathers, who looked as if they had been caught secretly mixing explosive compounds and were guiltily expecting every moment to see the foundations under them shaken and rent and their fair superstructure shattered into fragments.

But the girls came, and there was no upheaval. They performed their tasks modestly and intelligently. Once in a while one or two were found choosing the gentlemen's course. Still no collapse; and the dear, careful, scrupulous, frightened old professors were just getting their hearts out of their throats and preparing to draw one good free breath, when they found they would have to change the names of those courses; for there were as many ladies in the gentlemen's course as in the ladies', and a distinctively Ladies' Course, inferior in scope and aim to the regular classical course, did not and could not exist.

Other colleges gradually fell into line, and to-day there are 198 colleges for women, and 207 coeducational colleges and universities in the United States alone offering the degree of B.A. to women, and sending out yearly into the arteries of this nation a warm, rich flood of strong, brave, active, energetic, well-equipped, thoughtful women—women quick to see and eager to help the needs of this needy world—women who can think as well as feel, and who feel none the less because they think—women who are none the less tender and true for the parchment scroll they bear in their hands—women who have given a deeper, richer, nobler and grander meaning to the word "womanly" than any one-sided masculine definition could ever have suggested or inspired—women whom the world has long waited for in pain and anguish till there should be at last added to its forces and allowed to permeate its thought the complement of that masculine influence which has dominated it for fourteen centuries.

Since the idea of order and subordination succumbed to barbarian brawn and brutality in the fifth century, the civilized world has been like a child brought up by his father. It has needed the great mother heart to teach it to be pitiful, to love mercy, to succor the weak and care for the lowly.

Whence came this apotheosis of greed and cruelty? Whence this sneaking admiration we all have for bullies and prize-fighters? Whence the self-congratulation of "dominant" races, as if "dominant" meant "righteous" and carried with it a title to inherit the earth? Whence the scorn of so-called weak or unwarlike races and individuals, and the very comfortable assurance that it is their manifest destiny to be wiped out as vermin before this advancing civilization? As if the possession of the Christian graces of meekness, non-resistance and forgiveness, were incompatible with a civilization professedly based on Christianity, the religion of love! Just listen to this little bit of Barbarian brag:

"As for Far Orientals, they are not of those who will survive. Artistic attractive people that they are, their civilization is like their own tree flowers, beautiful blossoms destined never to bear fruit. If these people continue in their old course, their earthly career is closed. Just as surely as morning passes into afternoon, so surely are these races' of the Far East, if unchanged, destined to disappear before the advancing nations of the West. Vanish, they will, off the face of the earth, and leave our planet the eventual possession of the dwellers where the day declines. Unless their newly imported ideas really take root, it is from this whole world that Japanese and Koreans, as well as Chinese, will inevitably be excluded. Their Nirvana is already being realized; already, it has wrapped Far Eastern Asia in its winding sheet."—*Soul of the Far East—P. Lowell.*

Delightful reflection for "the dwellers where day declines." A spectacle to make the gods laugh, truly, to see the scion of an upstart race by one sweep of his generalizing pen consigning to annihilation one-third the inhabitants of the globe—a people whose civilization was hoary headed before the parent elements that begot his race had advanced beyond nebulosity.

How like Longfellow's Iagoo, we Westerners are, to be sure! In the few hundred years, we have had to strut across our allotted territory and bask in the afternoon sun, we imagine we have exhausted the possibilities of humanity. Verily, we are the people, and after us there is none other. Our God is power; strength, our standard of excellence, inherited from barbarian ancestors through a long line of male progenitors, the Law Salic permitting no feminine modifications.

Says one, "The Chinaman is not popular with us, and we do not like the Negro. It is not that the eyes of the one are set bias, and the other is dark-skinned; but the Chinaman, the Negro is weak—*and Anglo Saxons don't like weakness.*"

The world of thought under the predominant man-influence, unmollified and unrestrained by its complementary force, would become like Daniel's fourth beast: "dreadful and terrible, and *strong* exceedingly;" "it had great iron teeth; it devoured and brake in pieces, and stamped the residue with the feet of it;" and the most independent of us find ourselves ready at times to fall down and worship this incarnation of power.

Mrs. Mary A. Livermore, a woman whom I can mention only to admire, came near shaking my faith a few weeks ago in my theory of the thinking woman's mission to put in the tender and sympathetic chord in nature's grand symphony, and counteract, or better, harmonize the diapason of mere strength and might.

She was dwelling on the Anglo-Saxon genius for power and his contempt for weakness, and described a scene in San Francisco which she had witnessed.

The incorrigible animal known as the American small-boy, had pounced upon a simple, unoffending Chinaman, who was taking home his work, and had emptied the beautifully laundried contents of his basket into the ditch. "And," said she, "when that great man stood there and blubbered before that crowd of lawless urchins, to any one of whom he might have taught a lesson with his two fists, *I didn't much care.*

This is said like a man! It grates harshly. It smacks of the worship of the beast. It is contempt for weakness, and taken out of its setting it seems to contradict my theory. It either shows that one of the highest exponents of the Higher Education can be at times untrue to the instincts I have ascribed to the thinking woman and to the contribution she is to add to the civilized world, or else the influence she wields upon our civilization may be potent without being necessarily and always direct and conscious. The latter is the case. Her voice may strike a false note, but her whole being is musical with the vibrations of human suffering. Her tongue may parrot over the cold conceits that some man has taught her, but her heart is aglow with sympathy and loving kindness, and she cannot be true to her real self without giving out these elements into the forces of the world.

No one is in any danger of imagining Mark Antony "a plain blunt man," nor Cassius a sincere one—whatever the speeches they may make.

As individuals, we are constantly and inevitably, whether we are conscious of it or not, giving out our real selves into our several little worlds, inexorably adding our own true ray to the flood of starlight, quite independently of our professions and our masquerading; and so in the world of thought, the influence of thinking woman far transcends her feeble declamation and may seem at times even opposed to it.

A visitor in Oberlin once said to the lady principal, "Have you no rabble in Oberlin? How is it I see no police here, and yet the streets are as quiet and orderly as if there were an officer of the law standing on every corner."

Mrs. Johnston replied, "Oh, yes; there are vicious persons in Oberlin just as in other towns—*but our girls are our police.*"

With from five to ten hundred pure-minded young women threading the streets of the village every evening unattended, vice must slink away, like frost before the rising sun: and yet I venture to say there was not one in a hundred of those girls who would not have run from a street brawl as she would from a mouse, and who would not have declared she could never stand the sight of blood and pistols.

There is, then, a real and special influence of woman. An influence subtle and often involuntary, an influence so intimately interwoven in, so intricately interpenetrated by the masculine influence of the time that it is often difficult to extricate the delicate meshes and analyze and identify the closely clinging fibers. And yet, without this influence—so long as woman sat with bandaged eyes and manacled hands, fast bound in the clamps of ignorance and inaction, the world of thought moved in its orbit like the revolutions of the moon; with one face (the man's face) always out, so that the spectator could not distinguish whether it was disc or sphere.

Now I claim that it is the prevalence of the Higher Education among women, the making it a common everyday affair for women to reason and think and express their thought, the training and stimulus which enable and encourage women to administer to the world the bread it needs as well as the sugar it cries for; in short it is the transmitting the potential forces of her soul into dynamic factors that has given symmetry and completeness to the world's agencies. So only could it be consummated that Mercy, the lesson she teaches, and Truth, the task man has set himself, should meet together: that righteousness, or *rightness,* man's ideal,—and *peace,* its necessary 'other half,' should kiss each other.

We must thank the general enlightenment and independence of woman (which we may now regard as a *fait accompli*) that both these forces are now at work in the world, and it is fair to demand from them for the 20th century a higher type of civilization than any attained in the 19th. Religion, science, art, economics, have all needed the feminine flavor; and literature, the expression of what is permanent and best in all of these, may be gauged at any time to measure the strength of the feminine ingredient. You will not find theology consigning infants to lakes of unquenchable fire long after women have had a chance to grasp, master, and wield its dogmas. You will not find science annihilating personality from the government of the Universe and making of God an ungovernable, unintelligible, blind, often destructive physical force; you will not find jurisprudence formulating as an axiom the absurdity that man and wife are one, and that one the man—that the married woman may not hold or bequeath her own property save as subject to her husband's direction; you will not find political economists declaring that the only possible adjustment between laborers and capitalists is that of selfishness and rapacity—that each must get all he can and keep all that he gets, while the world cries *laissez faire* and the lawyers explain, "it is the beautiful working of the law of supply and demand"; in fine, you will not find the law of love shut out from the affairs of men after the feminine half of the world's truth is completed.

Nay, put your ear now close to the pulse of the time. What is the key-note of the literature of these days? What is the banner cry of all the activities of the last half decade? What is the dominant seventh which is to add richness and tone to the final cadences of this century and lead by a grand modulation into the triumphant harmonies of the next? Is it not compassion for the poor and unfortunate, and, as Bellamy has expressed it, "indignant outcry against the failure of the social machinery as it is, to ameliorate the miseries of men!" Even Christianity is being brought to the bar of humanity and tried by the standard of its ability to alleviate the world's suffering and lighten and brighten its woe. What else can be the meaning of Matthew Arnold's saddening protest, "We cannot do without Christianity," cried he, "and we cannot endure it as it is."

When went there by an age, when so much time and thought, so much money and labor were given to God's poor and God's invalids, the lowly and unlovely, the sinning as well as the suffering—homes for inebriates and homes for lunatics, shelter for the aged and shelter for babes, hospitals for the sick, props and braces for the falling, reformatory prisons and prison reformatories, all show that a "mothering" influence from some source is leavening the nation.

Now please understand me. I do not ask you to admit that these benefactions and virtues are the exclusive possession of women, or even that women are their chief and only advocates. It may be a man who formulates and makes them vocal. It may be, and often is, a man who weeps over the wrongs and struggles for the amelioration: but that man has imbibed those impulses from a mother rather than from a father and is simply materializing and giving back to the world in tangible form the ideal love and tenderness, devotion and care that have cherished and nourished the helpless period of his own existence.

All I claim is that there is a feminine as well as a masculine side to truth; that these are related not as inferior and superior, not as better and worse, not as weaker and stronger, but as complements—complements in one necessary and symmetric whole. That as the man is more noble in reason, so the woman is more quick in sympathy. That as he is indefatigable in pursuit of abstract truth, so is she in caring for the interests by the way—striving tenderly and lovingly that not one of the least of these 'little ones' should perish. That while we not unfrequently see women who reason, we say, with the coolness and precision of a man, and men as considerate of helplessness as a woman, still there is a general consensus of mankind that the one trait is essentially masculine and the other as peculiarly feminine. That both are needed to be worked into the training of children, in order that our boys may supplement their virility by tenderness and sensibility, and our girls may round out their gentleness by strength and self-reliance. That, as both are alike necessary in giving symmetry to the individual, so a nation or a race will degenerate into mere emotionalism on the one hand, or bullyism on the other, if dominated by either exclusively; lastly, and most emphatically, that the feminine factor can have its proper effect only through woman's development and education so that she may fitly and intelligently stamp her force on the forces of her day, and add her modicum to the riches of the world's thought.

> "For woman's cause is man's: they rise or sink
> Together, dwarfed or godlike, bond or free:
> For she that out of Lethe scales with man
> The shining steps of nature, shares with man
> His nights, his days, moves with him to one goal.
> If she be small, slight-natured, miserable,
> How shall men grow?
> * * * Let her make herself her own
> To give or keep, to live and learn and be
> All that not harms distinctive womanhood.
> For woman is not undeveloped man. . . .

FOR FURTHER READING

Giddings, Paula. *When and Where I Enter: The Impact of Black Women on Race and Sex in America.* New York: William Morrow, 1984.

Logan, Shirley Wilson. *"We Are Coming": The Persuasive Discourse of Nineteenth-Century Black Women.* Carbondale: Southern Illinois University Press, 1999.

———, ed. *With Pen and Voice: A Critical Anthology of Nineteenth-Century African-American Women.* Carbondale: Southern Illinois University Press, 1995.

Royster, Jacqueline Jones. *Traces of a Stream: Literacy and Social Change Among African American Women.* Pittsburgh: University of Pittsburgh Press, 2000.

Elizabeth Cady Stanton

1815–1902

Can a woman be a free individual? Elizabeth Cady Stanton, one of the founding mothers of the women's movement in the United States, eloquently presents her answer to this question in her speech, "The Solitude of Self." In doing so, she inserts women's voices into the American political and philosophical discourse about freedom and individual autonomy. Her definition is unique and groundbreaking because all previous formulations of individualism make the implicit assumption that the individual is male (Kerber 201).

Stanton delivered this speech in three settings at the climax of her fifty-year speaking career, as she withdrew from the divisive struggles that had exposed her race and class biases, especially during the debates over women's suffrage and black male suffrage. In some respects her rhetorical strategy is akin to that of the Seneca Falls "Declaration of Sentiments and Resolutions" of 1848, in which the authors revise the rhetoric of freedom and liberty in terms of women's lives. This speech recasts the rhetoric of individualism in terms of women's experiences, asserting a deeply psychological understanding of women's need for freedom if they are to face inevitable solitude: "[T]he fierce storms of life . . . beat on her from every point of the compass, just as they do on man, and with more fatal results, for he has been trained to protect himself, to resist, and to conquer."

Some critics suggest that this speech violated all traditional rhetorical conventions, in part because Stanton realized that her audiences were all well aware of the arguments for women's suffrage and no longer needed to hear them again. "The Solitude of Self" does not provide a dramatic recitation of evidence supporting women's rights but instead moves to make a more radical philosophical argument, dramatizing the fundamental, existential condition of human solitude in all phases of women's lives and linking this condition to the humanistic values that demand the rights of women as part of their fundamental "natural rights" as human beings. The personal, intimate, lyrical tone of the speech is more soliloquy than political speech, and the metaphors of solitary voyager and lonely fighter create a sense of solemnity and muted pathos rather than passionate argument. Nevertheless, with her indomitable *ethos*, Stanton held her audience, "looking as if she should be the Lord Chief Justice with her white hair puffed all over her head, and her amiable and intellectual face marked with lines of wisdom," (Campbell 137). Susan B. Anthony, her lifelong friend and collaborator, later said, "It is the strongest and most unanswerable argument and appeal ever made by mortal pen or tongue for the full freedom and franchise of women" (Ward and Burns 189). Frederick Douglass, the great orator who had supported the women's suffrage resolution in the 1848 "Declaration of Sentiments," but who had opposed Stanton's stand against the Fifteenth Amendment, remarked: "After her—silence" (Campbell 135).

From "The Solitude of Self"

1892

The point I wish plainly to bring before you on this occasion is the individuality of each human soul; our Protestant idea, the right of individual conscience and judgment; our republican idea, individual citizenship. In discussing the rights of woman, we are to consider, first, what belongs to her as an individual, in a world of her own, the arbiter of her own destiny, an imaginary Robinson Crusoe, with her woman Friday on a solitary island. Her rights under such circumstances are to use all her faculties for her own safety and happiness.

Secondly, if we consider her as a citizen, as a member of a great nation, she must have the same rights as all other members, according to the fundamental principles of our government.

Thirdly, viewed as a woman, an equal factor in civilization, her rights and duties are still the same; individual happiness and development.

Fourthly, it is only the incidental relations of life, such as mother, wife, sister, daughter, that may involve some special duties and training. In the usual discussion in regard to woman's sphere, such men as Herbert Spencer, Frederic Harrison and Grant Allen, uniformly subordinate her rights and duties as an individual, as a citizen, as a woman, to the necessities of these incidental relations, neither of which a large class of women may ever assume. In discussing the sphere of man, we do not decide his rights as an individual, as a citizen, as a man, by his duties as a father, a husband, a brother or a son, relations he may never fill. Moreover, he would be better fitted for these very relations, and whatever special work he might choose to do to earn his bread, by the complete development of all his faculties as an individual.

Just so with woman. The education that will fit her to discharge the duties in the largest sphere of human usefulness will best fit her for whatever special work she may be compelled to do.

The isolation of every human soul, and the necessity of self-dependence, must give each individual the right to choose his own surroundings.

Reprinted from Stanton, Elizabeth Cady. "The Solitude of Self." *The Woman's Journal* (23 January 1892): 1–32.

The strongest reason for giving woman all the opportunities for higher education, for the full development of her faculties, forces of mind and body; for giving her the most enlarged freedom of thought and action; a complete emancipation from all forms of bondage, of custom, dependence, superstition; from all the crippling influences of fear—is the solitude and personal responsibility of her own individual life. The strongest reason why we ask for woman a voice in the government under which she lives; in the religion she is asked to believe; equality in social life, where she is the chief factor; a place in the trades and professions, where she may earn her bread, is because of her birthright to self-sovereignty; because, as an individual, she must rely on herself. No matter how much women prefer to lean, to be protected and supported, nor how much men desire to have them to do so, they must make the voyage of life alone, and for safety in an emergency, they must know something of the laws of navigation. To guide our own craft, we must be captain, pilot, engineer; with chart and compass to stand at the wheel; to watch the winds and waves, and know when to take in the sail, and to read the signs in the firmament over all. It matters not whether the solitary voyager is man or woman; nature, having endowed them equally, leaves them to their own skill and judgment in the hour of danger, and, if not equal to the occasion, alike they perish.

To appreciate the importance of fitting every human soul for independent action, think for a moment of the immeasurable solitude of self. We come into the world alone, unlike all who have gone before us; we leave it alone, under circumstances peculiar to ourselves. No mortal ever has been, no mortal ever will be like the soul just launched on the sea of life. There can never again be just such a combination of prenatal influences; never again just such environments as make up the infancy, youth and manhood of this one. Nature never repeats herself, and the possibilities of one human soul will never be found in another. No one has ever found two blades of ribbon grass alike, and no one will ever find two human beings alike. Seeing, then, what must be the infinite diversity in human character, we can in a measure appreciate the loss to a nation when any large class of the people is uneducated and unrepresented in the government.

We ask for the complete development of every individual, first, for his own benefit and happiness. In fitting out an army, we give each soldier his own knapsack, arms, powder, his blanket, cup, knife, fork and spoon. We provide alike for all their individual necessities; then each man bears his own burden.

Again, we ask complete individual development for the general good; for the consensus of the competent on the whole round of human interests, on all questions of national life; and here each man must bear his share of the general burden. It is sad to see how soon friendless children are left to bear their own burdens, before they can analyze their feelings; before they can even tell their joys and sorrows, they are thrown on their own resources. The great lesson that nature seems to teach us at all ages is self-dependence, self-protection, self-support. What a touching instance of a child's solitude, of that hunger of the heart for love and recognition, in the case of the little girl who helped to dress a Christmas tree for the children of the family in which she served. On finding there was no present for herself, she slipped away in the darkness and spent the night in an open field sitting on a stone, and when found in the morning was weeping as if her heart would break. No mortal will ever know the thoughts that passed through the mind of that friendless child in the long hours of that cold night, with only the silent stars to keep her company. The mention of her case in the daily papers moved many generous hearts to send her presents, but in the hours of her keenest suffering she was thrown wholly on herself for consolation. . . .

We ask no sympathy from others in the anxiety and agony of a broken friendship or shattered love. When death sunders our nearest ties, alone we sit in the shadow of our affliction. Alike amid the greatest triumphs and darkest tragedies of life, we walk alone. On the divine heights of human attainment, eulogized and worshipped as a hero or saint, we stand alone. In ignorance, poverty and vice, as a pauper or criminal, alone we starve or steal; alone we suffer the sneers and rebuffs of our fellows; alone we are hunted and hounded through dark courts and alleys, in by-ways and highways; alone we stand in the judgment seat; alone in the prison cell we lament our crimes and misfortunes; alone we expiate them on the gallows. In hours like these we realize the awful solitude of individual life, its pains, its penalties, its responsibilities; hours in which the youngest and most helpless are thrown on their own resources for guidance and consolation. Seeing, then, that life must ever be a march and a battle, that each soldier must be equipped for his own protection, it is the height of cruelty to rob the individual of a single natural right.

To throw obstacles in the way of a complete education is like putting out the eyes; to deny the rights of property, like cutting off the hands. To deny political equality is to rob the ostracised of all self-respect; of credit in the market place; of recompense in the world of work; of a voice in those who make and administer the law; a choice in the jury before whom they are tried, and in the judge who decides their punishment. Shakespeare's play of "Titus Andronicus" contains a terrible satire on woman's position in the 19th century. Rude men (the play tells us) seized the king's daughter, cut out her tongue, cut off her hands, and then bade her go call for water and wash her hands. What a picture of woman's position! Robbed of her natural rights, handicapped by law and custom at every turn, yet compelled to fight her own battles, and in the emergencies of life to fall back on herself for protection.

The girl of sixteen, thrown on the world to support herself, to make her own place in society, to resist the temptations that surround her and maintain a spotless integrity, must do all this by native force or superior education. She does not acquire this power by being trained to trust others and distrust herself. If she wearies of the struggle, finding it hard work to swim up stream, and allows herself to drift with the current, she will find plenty of company, but not one to share her misery in the hour of her deepest humiliation. If she tries to re-trieve her position, to conceal the past, her life is hedged about with fears lest willing hands should tear the veil from what she fain would hide. Young and friendless, she knows the bitter solitude of self.

How the little courtesies of life on the surface of society, deemed so impor-tant from man towards woman, fade into utter insignificance in view of the deeper tragedies in which she must play her part alone, where no human aid is possible!

The young wife and mother, at the head of some establishment, with a kind husband to shield her from the adverse winds of life, with wealth, fortune and position, has a certain harbor of safety, secure against the ordinary ills of life. But to manage a household, have a desirable influence in society, keep her friends and the affections of her husband, train her children and servants well, she must have rare common sense, wisdom, diplomacy, and a knowledge of hu-man nature. To do all this, she needs the cardinal virtues and the strong points of character that the most successful statesman possesses. An uneducated woman trained to dependence, with no resources in herself, must make a fail-ure of any position in life. But society says women do not need a knowledge of the world, the liberal training that experience in public life must give, all the advantages of collegiate education, but when for the lack of all this, the woman's happiness is wrecked, alone she bears her humiliation; and the soli-tude of the weak and the ignorant is indeed pitiable. In the wild chase for the prizes of life, they are ground to powder. . . .

The more fully the faculties of the mind are developed and kept in use, the longer the period of vigor and active interest in all around us continues. If, from a life-long participation in public affairs, a woman feels responsible for the laws regulating our system of education, the discipline of our jails and prisons, the sanitary condition of our private homes, public buildings and thoroughfares, an interest in commerce, finance, our foreign relation in any or all these ques-tions, her solitudes will at least be respectable, and she will not be driven to gossip or scandal for entertainment. . . .

Inasmuch, then, as woman shares equally the joys and sorrows of time and eternity, is it not the height of presumption in man to propose to represent her at the ballot box and the throne of grace, to do her voting in the State, her pray-ing in the church, and to assume the position of High Priest at the family altar?

Nothing strengthens the judgment and quickens the conscience like individ-ual responsibility; nothing adds such dignity to character as the recognition of one's self-sovereignty; the right to an equal place, everywhere conceded; a place earned by personal merit, not an artificial attainment by inheritance, wealth, family and position. Seeing, then, that the responsibilities of life rest equally on man and woman, that their destiny is the same, they need the same preparation for time and eternity. The talk of sheltering woman from the fierce storms of life is the sheerest mockery, for they beat on her from every point of the compass, just as they do on man, and with more fatal results, for he has been trained to protect himself, to resist, and to conquer. Such are the facts in human experience, the responsibilities of individual sovereignty. Rich and poor, intelligent and ignorant, wise and foolish, virtuous and vicious, man and woman; it is ever the same, each soul must depend wholly on itself.

Whatever the theories may be of woman's dependence on man, in the supreme moments of her life, he cannot bear her burdens. Alone she goes to the gates of death to give life to every man that is born into the world; no one can share her fears, no one can mitigate her pangs; and if her sorrow is greater than she can bear, alone she passes beyond the gates into the vast unknown. . . .

But when all artificial trammels are removed, and women are recognized as individuals, responsible for their own environments, thoroughly educated for all positions in life they may be called to fill; with all the resources in themselves that liberal thought and broad culture can give; guided by their own conscience and judgment, trained to self-protection, by a healthy development of the muscular system, and skill in the use of weapons of defense; and stimulated to self-support by a knowledge of the business world and the pleasure that pecuniary independence must ever give; when women are trained in this way, they will in a measure be fitted for those hours of solitude that come alike to all, whether prepared or otherwise. As in our extremity we must depend on ourselves, the dictates of wisdom point to complete individual development.

In talking of education, how shallow the argument that each class must be educated for the special work it proposes to do, and that all those faculties not needed in this special walk must lie dormant and utterly wither for want of use, when, perhaps, these will be the very faculties needed in life's greatest emergencies! Some say, Where is the use of drilling girls in the languages, the sciences, in law, medicine, theology? As wives, mothers, housekeepers, cooks, they need a different curriculum from boys who are to fill all positions. The chief cooks in our great hotels and ocean steamers are men. In our large cities, men run the bakeries; they make our bread, cake and pies. They manage the laundries; they are now considered our best milliners and dressmakers. Because some men fill these departments of usefulness, shall we regulate the curriculum in Harvard and Yale to their present necessities? If not, why this talk in our best colleges of a curriculum for girls who are crowding into the trades and professions, teachers in all our public schools, rapidly filling many lucrative and honorable positions in life? . . .

Women are already the equals of men in the whole realm of thought, in art, science, literature and government. With telescopic vision they explore the starry firmament and bring back the history of the planetary spheres. With chart and compass they pilot ships across the mighty deep, and with skillful fingers send electric messages around the world. In galleries of art the beauties of nature and the virtues of humanity are immortalized by them on canvas, and by their inspired touch dull blocks of marble are transformed into angels of light. In music they speak again the language of Mendelssohn, Beethoven, Chopin, Schumann, and are worthy interpreters of their great thoughts. The poetry and novels of the century are theirs, and they have touched the keynote of reform, in religion, politics and social life. They fill the editor's and professor's chair, and plead at the bar of justice; walk the wards of the hospital, and speak from the pulpit and the platform. Such is the type of womanhood that an enlightened public sentiment welcomes to-day, and such the triumph of the facts of life over the false theories of the past.

Is it, then, consistent to hold the developed woman of this day within the same narrow political limits as the dame with the spinning-wheel and knitting-needle occupied in the past? No! no! Machinery has taken the labors of woman, as well as man, on its tireless shoulders, the loom and the spinning wheel are but dreams of the past; the pen, the brush, the easel, the chisel, have taken their places, while the hopes and ambitions of women are essentially changed.

We see reason sufficient in the outer conditions of human beings for individual liberty and development, but when we consider the self-dependence of every human soul we see the need of courage, judgment and the exercise of every faculty of mind and body, strengthened and developed by use, in woman as well as man.

Whatever may be said of man's protecting power in ordinary conditions, amid all the terrible disasters by land and sea, in the supreme moments of danger, alone woman must ever meet the horrors of the situation. The Angel of Death even makes no royal pathway for her. Man's love and sympathy enter only into the sunshine of our lives. In that solemn solitude of self, that links us with the immeasurable and the eternal, each soul lives alone forever. . . .

And yet, there is a solitude which each and every one of us has always carried with him, more inaccessible than the ice-cold mountains, more profound than the midnight sea; the solitude of self. Our inner being which we call ourself, no eye nor touch of man or angel has ever pierced. It is more hidden than the caves of the gnome; the sacred adytum of the oracle; the hidden chamber of Eleusinian mystery, for to it only Omniscience is permitted to enter.

Such is individual life. Who, I ask you, can take, dare take on himself the rights, the duties, the responsibilities of another human soul?

FOR FURTHER READING

Campbell, Karlyn Kohrs, ed. *Key Texts of the Early Feminists.* Vol. 2 of *Man Cannot Speak for Her.* New York: Praeger, 1989.

Giddings, Paula. *When and Where I Enter: The Impact of Black Women on Race and Sex in America.* New York: William Morrow, 1984.

Kerber, Linda K. *Toward an Intellectual History of Women*. Chapel Hill: University of North Carolina Press, 1997.

Stanton, Elizabeth Cady. *Eighty Years and More: Reminiscences, 1815–1897*. Boston: Northeastern University Press, 1991.

Stanton, Theodore, and Harriot Stanton Blatch, eds. *Elizabeth Cady Stanton*. 2 vols. New York: Arno Press, 1969.

Ward, Geoffrey C., and Ken Burns. *Not for Ourselves Alone: The Story of Elizabeth Cady Stanton and Susan B. Anthony*. New York: Alfred A. Knopf, 1999.

Fannie Barrier Williams

1855–1944

Fannie Barrier Williams is frequently described as a "lecturer and club woman," but perhaps she would be more accurately described as an educator and reformer who fought to raise consciousness about the poor social, economic, and political conditions of African American women and to take back and reconstruct representations of African American women in antebellum United States culture.

Born to a well-established family in Brockport, New York, Williams left New York after graduating from the State Normal School at Brockport in 1879 to teach freed slaves in the Deep South, where Jim Crow laws were in effect. Finding the racism of the South intolerable, she quickly secured a teaching job in the public schools of Washington, D.C., where she stayed for ten years. Williams met and married the attorney S. Laing Williams, a protégé of Booker T. Washington and a colleague of Ferdinand Barnett, the future husband of Ida B. Wells.

Williams's achievements in the fight for equality for African American women were groundbreaking. In 1891 she helped to organize Provident Hospital, the first African American–owned interracial hospital in the United States, and its School for Nurses. She was the first African American woman to be nominated for and inducted into the Chicago Women's Club. Her membership was contested for over a year, with several members of the club resigning upon her admission in 1895, but Williams subsequently became an active reformer of the women's club movement. Williams also worked as a correspondent for the national monthly, *Women's Era*, which covered the issues facing African American women, and wrote for the *Chicago Record-Herald* and the *New York Age*. One of her most important contributions came in 1893, when she cofounded the National League of Colored Women (now the National Association of Colored Women).

As early as 1891, Williams argued for more representation for African American women in the World's Congress of Representative Women in Chicago (part of the Colombian Exposition). In all, six African American women were granted speaking roles in the Congress, including Williams, Anna Julia Cooper, and Frances Ellen Watkins Harper. According to Shirley Wilson Logan and Hazel Carby, Williams and her five contemporaries may have been included in the program as exotic tokens, "as anomalies to contemporary views of blacks" (*"We Are Coming"* 103).

"The Intellectual Progress of the Colored Women of the United States since the Emancipation Proclamation," which Williams delivered to the Congress of

Representative Women, was her first address to a non–African American audience. In this context—speaking to an audience of women who had been reluctant to hear her—Williams, like Frances Ellen Watkins Harper thirty years earlier, sought to create a sense of their shared values as women. She provides evidence of the moral, religious, and intellectual stature of African American women by drawing parallels with the moral stature of white women. But then, also like Harper, she turns to challenge white women's misconceptions and misrepresentation of African American women. She places the responsibility for their condition on white male power and slavery's legacy of rape and exploitation, which continued to degrade black women and deny them opportunities for decent work, education, and respectful treatment. Paula Giddings has written that by confronting this issue openly, Williams challenged the Victorian values and discourses about women that kept both white and black women subservient. She challenged American notions of citizenship and equality, pushing her audience to understand that these American ideals are hollow unless they apply to all Americans and to recognize that they are implicated in African American women's conditions. She argues: "Women of the dominant race can not afford to be responsible for the wrongs we suffer, since those who do injustice can not escape a certain penalty."

From "The Intellectual Progress of the Colored Women of the United States since the Emancipation Proclamation"

1893

Less than 30 years ago the term progress as applied to colored women of African descent in the United States would have been an anomaly. The recognition of that term today as appropriate is a fact full of interesting significance. That the discussion of progressive womanhood in this great assemblage of the representative women of the world is considered incomplete without some account of the colored women's status is a most noteworthy evidence that we have not failed to impress ourselves on the higher side of American life.

Less is known of our women than of any other class of Americans.

No organization of far-reaching influence for their special advancement, no conventions of women to take note of their progress, and no special literature reciting the incidents, the events, and all things interesting and instructive concerning them are to be found among the agencies directing their career. There

Reprinted from Williams, Fannie Barrier. "The Intellectual Progress of the Colored Women of the United States since the Emancipation Proclamation." In *The World's Congress of Representative Women*, edited by May Wright Sewell, 696–711. Chicago: Rand, McNally, and Company, 1894.

has been no special interest in their peculiar condition as native-born American women. Their power to affect the social life of America, either for good or for ill, has excited not even a speculative interest.

Though there is much that is sorrowful, much that is wonderfully heroic, and much that is romantic in a peculiar way in their history, none of it has as yet been told as evidence of what is possible for these women. How few of the happy, prosperous, and eager living Americans can appreciate what it all means to be suddenly changed from irresponsible bondage to the responsibility of freedom and citizenship!

The distress of it all can never be told, and the pain of it all can never be felt except by the victims, and by those saintly women of the white race who for thirty years have been consecrated to the uplifting of a whole race of women from a long-enforced degradation.

The American people have always been impatient of ignorance and poverty. They believe with Emerson that "America is another word for opportunity," and for that reason success is a virtue and poverty and ignorance are inexcusable. This may account for the fact that our women have excited no general sympathy in the struggle to emancipate themselves from the demoralization of slavery. This new life of freedom, with its far-reaching responsibilities, had to be learned by these children of darkness mostly without a guide, a teacher, or a friend. In the mean vocabulary of slavery there was no definition of any of the virtues of life. The meaning of such precious terms as marriage, wife, family, and home could not be learned in a school-house. The blue-back speller, the arithmetic, and the copy-book contain no magical cures for inherited inaptitudes for the moralities. Yet it must ever be counted as one of the most wonderful things in human history how promptly and eagerly these suddenly liberated women tried to lay hold upon all that there is in human excellence. There is a touching pathos in the eagerness of these millions of new homemakers to taste the blessedness of intelligent womanhood. The path of progress in the picture is enlarged so as to bring to view these trustful and zealous students of freedom and civilization striving to overtake and keep pace with women whose emancipation has been a slow and painful process for a thousand years. The longing to be something better than they were when freedom found them has been the most notable characteristic in the development of these women. This constant striving for equality has given an upward direction to all the activities of colored women.

Freedom at once widened their vision beyond the mean cabin life of their bondage. Their native gentleness, good cheer, and hopefulness made them susceptible to those teachings that make for intelligence and righteousness. Sullenness of disposition, hatefulness, and revenge against the master class because of two centuries of ill-treatment are not in the nature of our women.

But a better view of what our women are doing and what their present status is may be had by noticing some lines of progress that are easily verifiable.

First it should be noticed that separate facts and figures relative to colored women are not easily obtainable. Among the white women of the country independence, progressive intelligence, and definite interests have done so much that nearly every fact and item illustrative of their progress and status is classified and easily accessible. Our women, on the contrary, have had no advantage of interests peculiar and distinct and separable from those of men that have yet excited public attention and kindly recognition.

In their religious life, however, our women show a progressiveness parallel in every important particular to that of white women in all Christian churches. It has always been a circumstance of the highest satisfaction to the missionary efforts of the Christian church that the colored people are so susceptible to a religion that marks the highest point of blessedness in human history. . . .

Close allied to this religious development is their progress in the work of education in schools and colleges. For thirty years education has been the magic word among the colored people of this country. That their greatest need was education in its broadest sense was understood by these people more strongly than it could be taught to them. It is the unvarying testimony of every teacher in the South that the mental development of the colored women as well as men has been little less than phenomenal. In twenty-five years, and under conditions discouraging in the extreme, thousands of our women have been educated as teachers. They have adapted themselves to the work of mentally lifting a whole race of people so eagerly and readily that they afford an apt illustration of the power of self-help. Not only have these women become good teachers in less than twenty-five years, but many of them are the prize teachers in the mixed schools of nearly every Northern city.

These women have also so fired the hearts of the race for education that colleges, normal schools, industrial schools, and universities have been reared by a generous public to meet the requirements of these eager students of intelligent citizenship. As American women generally are fighting against the 19th century narrowness that still keeps women out of the higher institutions of learning, so our women are eagerly demanding the best of education open to their race. . . .

Benevolence is the essence of most of the colored women's organizations. The humane side of their natures has been cultivated to recognize the duties they owe to the sick, the indigent and ill-fortuned. No church, school, or charitable institution for the special use of colored people has been allowed to languish or fail when the associated efforts of the women could save it.

It is highly significant and interesting to note that these women, whose hearts have been wrung by all kinds of sorrows, are abundantly manifesting those gracious qualities of heart that characterize women of the best type. These kinder sentiments arising from mutual interests that are lifting our women into purer and tenderer relationship to each other, and are making the meager joys and larger griefs of our conditions known to each other, have been a large part of their education.

The hearts of Afro-American women are too warm and too large for race hatred. Long suffering has so chastened them that they are developing a special sense of sympathy for all who suffer and fail of justice. All the associated interests of church, temperance, and social reform in which American women are winning distinction can be wonderfully advanced when our women shall be welcomed *as co-workers,* and estimated solely by what they are worth to the moral elevation of all the people.

I regret the necessity of speaking to the question of the moral progress of our women, because the morality of our home life has been commented upon so disparagingly and meanly that we are placed in the unfortunate position of being defenders of our name.

It is proper to state, with as much emphasis as possible, that all questions relative to the moral progress of the colored women of America are impertinent and unjustly suggestive when they relate to the thousands of colored women in the North who were free from the vicious influences of slavery. They are also meanly suggestive as regards thousands of our women in the South whose force of character enabled them to escape the slavery taints of immorality. The question of the moral progress of colored women in the United States has force and meaning in this discussion only so far as it tells the story of how the once-enslaved women have been struggling for twenty-five years to emancipate themselves from the demoralization of their enslavement.

While I duly appreciate the offensiveness of all references to American slavery, it is unavoidable to charge to that system every moral imperfection that mars the character of the colored American. The whole life and power of slavery depended upon an enforced degradation of everything human in the slaves. The slave code recognized only animal distinctions between the sexes, and ruthlessly ignored those ordinary separations that belong to the social state.

It is a great wonder that two centuries of such demoralization did not work a complete extinction of all the moral instincts. But the recuperative power of these women to regain their moral instincts and to establish a respectable relationship to American womanhood is among the earlier evidences of their moral ability to rise above their conditions. In spite of a cursed heredity that bound them to the lowest social level, in spite of everything that is unfortunate and unfavorable, these women have continually shown an increasing degree of teachableness as to the meaning of woman's relationship to man.

Out of this social purification and moral uplift have come a chivalric sentiment and regard from the young men of the race that give to the young women a new sense of protection. I do not wish to disturb the serenity of this conference by suggesting why this protection is needed and the kind of men against whom it is needed.

It is sufficient for us to know that the daughters of women who thirty years ago were not allowed to be modest, not allowed to follow the instincts of moral rectitude, who could cry for protection to no living man, have so elevated the moral tone of their social life that new and purer standards of personal worth have been created, and new ideals of womanhood, instinct with grace and delicacy, are everywhere recognized and emulated.

This moral regeneration of a whole race of women is no idle sentiment—it is a serious business; and everywhere there is witnessed a feverish anxiety to be free from the mean suspicions that have so long underestimated the character strength of our women.

These women are not satisfied with the unmistakable fact that moral progress has been made, but they are fervently impatient and stirred by a sense of outrage under the vile imputations of a diseased public opinion.

Loves that are free from the dross of coarseness, affections that are unsullied, and a proper sense of all the sanctities of human intercourse felt by thousands of these women all over the land plead for the recognition of their fitness to be judged, not by the standards of slavery, but by the higher standards of freedom and of twenty-five years of education, culture, and moral contact.

The moral aptitudes of our women are just as strong and just as weak as those of any other American women with like advantages of intelligence and environment.

It may now perhaps be fittingly asked, What mean all these evidences of mental, social, and moral progress of a class of American women of whom you know so little? Certainly you can not be indifferent to the growing needs and importance of women who are demonstrating their intelligence and capacity for the highest privileges of freedom.

The most important thing to be noted is the fact that the colored people of America have reached a distinctly new era in their career so quickly that the American mind has scarcely had time to recognize the fact, and adjust itself to the new requirements of the people in all things that pertain to citizenship.

Thirty years ago public opinion recognized no differences in the colored race. To our great misfortune public opinion has changed but slightly. History is full of examples of the great injustice resulting from the perversity of public opinion, and its tardiness in recognizing new conditions.

It seems to daze the understanding of the ordinary citizen that there are thousands of men and women everywhere among us who in twenty-five years have progressed as far away from the non-progressive peasants of the "black belt" of the South as the highest social life in New England is above the lowest levels of American civilization.

This general failure of the American people to know the new generation of colored people, and to recognize this important change in them, is the cause of more injustice to our women than can well be estimated. Further progress is everywhere seriously hindered by this ignoring of their improvement.

Our exclusion from the benefits of the fair play sentiment of the country is little less than a crime against the ambitions and aspirations of a whole race of women. The American people are but repeating the common folly of history in thus attempting to repress the yearnings of progressive humanity.

In the item of employment colored women bear a distressing burden of mean and unreasonable discrimination. A Southern teacher of thirty years' experience in the South writes that "one million possibilities of good through black womanhood all depend upon an opportunity to make a living."

It is almost literally true that, except teaching in colored schools and menial work, colored women can find no employment in this free America. They are the only women in the country for whom real ability, virtue, and special talents count for nothing when they become applicants for respectable employment. Taught everywhere in ethics and social economy that merit always wins, colored women carefully prepare themselves for all kinds of occupation only to meet with stern refusal, rebuff, and disappointment. . . .

This question of employment for the trained talents of our women is a most serious one. Refusal of such employment because of color belies every maxim of justice and fair play. Such refusal takes the blessed meaning out of all the teachings of our civilization, and sadly confuses our conceptions of what is just, humane, and moral.

Can the people of this country afford to single out the women of a whole race of people as objects of their special contempt? Do these women not belong to a race that has never faltered in its support of the country's flag in every war since Attucks fell in Boston's streets?

Are they not the daughters of men who have always been true as steel against treason to everything fundamental and splendid in the republic? In short, are these women not as thoroughly American in all the circumstances of citizenship as the best citizens of our country?

If it be so, are we not justified in a feeling of desperation against that peculiar form of Americanism that shows respect for our women as servants and contempt for them when they become women of culture? We have never been taught to understand why the unwritten law of chivalry, protection, and fair play that are everywhere the conservators of women's welfare must exclude every woman of a dark complexion.

We believe that the world always needs the influence of every good and capable woman, and this rule recognizes no exceptions based on complexion. In their complaint against hindrances to their employment colored women ask for no special favors.

They are even willing to bring to every position fifty percent more of ability than is required of any other class of women. They plead for opportunities untrammeled by prejudice. They plead for the right of the individual to be judged, not by tradition and race estimate, but by the present evidences of individual worth. We believe this country is large enough and the opportunities for all kinds of success are great enough to afford our women a fair chance to earn a respectable living, and to win every prize within the reach of their capabilities.

Another, and perhaps more serious, hindrance to our women is that night-mare known as "social equality." The term equality is the most inspiring word in the vocabulary of citizenship. It expresses the leveling quality in all the splendid possibilities of American life. It is this idea of equality that has made room in this country for all kinds and conditions of men, and made personal merit the supreme requisite for all kinds of achievement.

When the colored people became citizens, and found it written deep in the organic law of the land that they too had the right to life, liberty, and the pursuit of happiness, they were at once suspected of wishing to interpret this maxim of equality as meaning social equality. . . .

We know, without being exceptional students of history, that the social relationship of the two races will be adjusted equitably in spite of all fear and injustice, and that there is a social gravitation in human affairs that eventually overwhelms and crushes into nothingness all resistance based on prejudice and selfishness.

Our chief concern in this false social sentiment is that it attempts to hinder our further progress toward the higher spheres of womanhood. On account of it, young colored women of ambition and means are compelled in many instances to leave the country for training and education in the salons and studios of Europe. On many of the railroads of this country women of refinement and culture are driven like cattle into human cattle-cars lest the occupying of an individual seat paid for in a first-class car may result in social equality. This social quarantine on all means of travel in certain parts of the country is guarded and enforced more rigidly against us than the quarantine regulations against cholera.

Without further particularizing as to how this social question opposes our advancement, it may be stated that the contentions of colored women are in kind like those of other American women for greater freedom of development. Liberty to be all that we can be, without artificial hindrances, is a thing no less precious to us than to women generally.

We come before this assemblage of women feeling confident that our progress has been along high levels and rooted deeply in the essentials of intelligent humanity. We are so essentially American in speech, in instincts, in sentiments and destiny that the things that interest you equally interest us.

We believe that social evils are dangerously contagious. The fixed policy of persecution and injustice against a class of women who are weak and defenseless will be necessarily hurtful to the cause of all women. Colored women are becoming more and more a part of the social forces that must help to determine the questions that so concern women generally. In this Congress we ask to be known and recognized for what we are worth. If it be the high purpose of these deliberations to lessen the resistance to woman's progress, you can not fail to be interested in our struggles against the many oppositions that harass us.

Women who are tender enough in heart to be active in humane societies, to be foremost in all charitable activities, who are loving enough to unite Christian womanhood everywhere against the sin of intemperance, ought to be instantly concerned in the plea of colored women for justice and humane treatment. Women of the dominant race can not afford to be responsible for the wrongs we suffer, since those who do injustice can not escape a certain penalty.

But there is no wish to overstate the obstacles to colored women or to picture their status as hopeless. There is no disposition to take our place in this Congress as faultfinders or suppliants for mercy. As women of a common country, with common interests, and a destiny that will certainly bring us closer to each other, we come to this altar with our contribution of hopefulness as well as with our complaints.

When you learn that womanhood everywhere among us is blossoming out into greater fullness of everything that is sweet, beautiful, and good in women; when you learn that the bitterness of our experience as citizen-women has not hardened our finer feelings of love and pity for our enemies; when you learn that fierce opposition to the widening spheres of our employment has not abated the aspirations of our women to enter successfully into all the professions and arts open only to intelligence, and that everywhere in the wake of enlightened womanhood our women are seen and felt for the good they diffuse, this Congress will at once see the fullness of our fellowship, and help us to avert the arrows of prejudice that pierce the soul because of the color of our bodies.

If the love of humanity more than the love of races and sex shall pulsate throughout all the grand results that shall issue to the world from this parliament of women, women of African descent in the United States will for the first time begin to feel the sweet release from the blighting thrall of prejudice.

The colored women, as well as all women, will realize that the inalienable right to life, liberty, and the pursuit of happiness is a maxim that will become more blessed in its significance when the hand of woman shall take it from its sepulture in books and make it the gospel of every-day life and the unerring guide in the relations of all men, women, and children.

FOR FURTHER READING

Carby, Hazel. *Reconstructing Womanhood: The Emergence of the Afro-American Woman Novelist.* New York: Oxford University Press, 1987.

Giddings, Paula. *When and Where I Enter: The Impact of Black Women on Race and Sex.* New York: William Morrow, 1984.

Logan, Shirley Wilson. *"We Are Coming": The Persuasive Discourse of Nineteenth-Century Black Women.* Carbondale: Southern Illinois University Press, 1999.

————, ed. *With Pen and Voice: A Critical Anthology of Nineteenth-Century African-American Women.* Carbondale: Southern Illinois University Press, 1995.

Royster, Jacqueline Jones. *Traces of a Stream: Literacy and Social Change Among African American Women.* Pittsburgh: University of Pittsburgh Press, 2000.

Ida B. Wells

1862–1931

Ida B. Wells might be considered one of the first women investigative reporters in the United States. Her campaign against lynching in the South relied on careful research, firsthand accounts, and meticulous reporting of the systematic horror of what she named "mob rule" in the South at the end of the nineteenth century and well into the twentieth. Despite threats on her own life for reporting the facts of systematic lynching across the Southern states, and despite experiencing the loss of her own friends to lynch mobs, Wells always maintained the tone of a journalist; she insisted that the facts must be brought to light, and she believed that the facts would speak for themselves. This optimism about her audiences and about the impact of knowledge came from Wells's parents, who believed that education was the key to progress for all races. Born a slave in 1862 in Holly Springs, Mississippi, and the oldest of eight children, Wells grew up in a family that embraced what Jacqueline Jones Royster calls "a spirit of activism and achievement" (14). After the Civil War, Wells attended Freedman's Bureau schools, commenting later on her family's commitment to education: "our job was to go to school and learn all we could" in order to fulfill her parents' "great expectations for a future in freedom" (Royster 14).

Wells also learned early how to be independent. Her parents and youngest brother died of yellow fever when Wells was sixteen; Wells left school, somehow made herself look older than her years, passed the teaching exam, and began teaching at a school six miles away while a friend of the family looked after the children. A year later, her aunt invited her to move to Memphis, Tennessee. Wells brought the children, continued to teach in the public schools, and began her career in public life. Her sense of social responsibility led her to participate in the African Methodist Episcopal (A.M.E.) Church, as well as in a lyceum of teachers who met regularly to read and discuss issues of the day. This group published a newsletter, the *Evening Star,* which Wells began to edit in 1886. Also during this time, Wells filed a lawsuit against the Chesapeake Railroad because on a trip from Memphis to her school she had been forcibly removed from the "ladies' car" and taken to the smoking car. Wells won her lawsuit, but the Tennessee Supreme Court overruled the verdict when the railroad appealed. The case, however, made Wells a public name in Memphis and fueled her passion for plainly speaking the facts of racism. She was asked to write a nationally syndicated column for the *Living Way,* a religious newspaper, and in 1889 she became co-owner of the Memphis *Free Speech and Headlight.* Because she wrote an editorial condemning the inferior conditions of the black schools in Memphis, Wells was fired from her teaching job and thus became a full-time journalist.

In May of 1892, three of Wells's friends were murdered by a white mob in Memphis, a community that Wells had believed was "civilized." Deeply hurt by this event, Wells wrote an editorial that not only condemned lynching but also raised questions about the "threadbare lie that Negro men rape white women" and the "moral reputation" of white women. The next day she left for the national A.M.E. Convention in Philadelphia, then traveled on to New York City, where she learned that her offices had been destroyed, that her partner had fled in fear for his life, and that white men in Memphis were threatening to kill her if she returned to Tennessee. Wells would not go to the South for another thirty years; she became a reporter for the *New York Age* and began to systematically expose the facts of Southern white-mob rule. She says in her autobiography: "Having lost my paper, had a price put on my life, and been made an exile from home for hinting at the truth, I felt that I owed it to myself and to my race to tell the whole truth now that I was where I could do so freely" (69).

Thus began Wells's international anti-lynching campaign. The speech included here was delivered at the Tremont Temple on February 13, 1893, at the invitation of the Boston Monday Lectureship, a group of white clergy and prominent leaders of Boston's intelligentsia. Speaking as an investigative reporter, Wells piles fact upon fact, narrating her own story and many other instances of horror so that her audience might become informed. Restraining from any emotional appeal, even when recounting her own shock, fear, and exile, Wells demonstrates her belief in *logos* and in her hearers—who, she argues, were simply ignorant of the "true situation"—even as she subtly indicts her white audience by implying that if they knew about the horrible injustices of lynching, they would surely have acted to stop it. For the rest of her life, Wells carried on what Royster calls a "one-woman" campaign against lynching, publishing several pamphlets and taking her case to Europe as well as across the United States, trying to "intervene in public discourse and change public opinion" (40).

"Lynch Law in All its Phases"

1893

I am before the American people to-day through no inclination of my own, but because of a deep-seated conviction that the country at large does not know the extent to which lynch law prevails in parts of the Republic, nor the conditions

Reprinted from Wells, Ida B. "Lynch Law in All its Phases." *Our Day: A Record and Review of Current Reform* 11 (January–June 1893): 333–47.

which force into exile those who speak the truth. I cannot believe that the apathy and indifference which so largely obtains regarding mob rule is other than the result of ignorance of the true situation. And yet, the observing and thoughtful must know that in one section, at least, of our common country, a government of the people, by the people, and for the people, means a government by the mob; where the land of the free and home of the brave means a land of lawlessness, murder and outrage; and where liberty of speech means the license of might to destroy the business and drive from home those who exercise this privilege contrary to the will of the mob. Repeated attacks on the life, liberty and happiness of any citizen or class of citizens are attacks on distinctive American institutions; such attacks imperiling as they do the foundation of government, law and order, merit the thoughtful consideration of far-sighted Americans; not from a standpoint of sentiment, not even so much from a standpoint of justice to a weak race, as from a desire to preserve our institutions.

The race problem or negro question, as it has been called, has been omnipresent and all-pervading since long before the Afro-American was raised from the degradation of the slave to the dignity of the citizen. It has never been settled because the right methods have not been employed in the solution. It is the Banquo's ghost of politics, religion, and sociology which will not down at the bidding of those who are tormented with its ubiquitous appearance on every occasion. Times without number, since invested with citizenship, the race has been indicted for ignorance, immorality and general worthlessness—declared guilty and executed by its self-constituted judges. The operations of law do not dispose of negroes fast enough, and lynching bees have become the favorite pastime of the South. As excuse for the same, a new cry, as false as it is foul, is raised in an effort to blast race character, a cry which has proclaimed to the world that virtue and innocence are violated by Afro-Americans who must be killed like wild beasts to protect womanhood and childhood.

Born and reared in the South, I had never expected to live elsewhere. Until this past year I was one among those who believed the condition of the masses gave large excuse for the humiliations and proscriptions under which we labored; that when wealth, education and character became more general among us, the cause being removed the effect would cease, and justice be accorded to all alike. I shared the general belief that good newspapers entering regularly the homes of our people in every state could do more to bring about this result than any agency. Preaching the doctrine of self-help, thrift and economy every week, they would be the teachers to those who have been deprived of school advantages, yet were making history every day—and train to think for themselves our mental children of a larger growth. And so, three years ago last June, I became editor and part owner of the *Memphis Free Speech*. As editor, I had occasion to criticize the city School Board's employment of inefficient teachers and poor school-buildings for Afro-American children. I was in the employ of that board at the time, and at the close of that school-term one year ago, was not re-elected to a position I had held in the city schools for seven years. Accepting the decision of the Board of Education, I set out to make a race newspaper pay—a thing which older and wiser heads said could not be done. But there were enough of our people in Memphis and surrounding territory to support a paper, and I believed they would do so. With nine months' hard work the circulation increased from 1,500 to 3,500; in twelve months it was on a good paying basis. Throughout the Mississippi Valley in Arkansas, Tennessee and Mississippi on plantations and in towns, the demand for and interest in the paper increased among the masses. The newsboys who would not sell it on the trains, voluntarily testified that they had never known colored people to demand a paper so eagerly.

To make the paper a paying business I became advertising agent, solicitor, as well as editor, and was continually on the go. Wherever I went among the people, I gave them in church, school, public gatherings, and home, the benefit of my honest conviction that maintenance of character, money getting and education would finally solve our problem and that it depended on us to say how soon this would be brought about. This sentiment bore good fruit in Memphis. We had nice homes, representatives in almost every branch of business and profession, and refined society. We had learned that helping each other helped all, and every well-conducted business by Afro-Americans prospered. With all our proscription in theatres, hotels and on railroads, we had never had a lynching and did not believe we could have one. There had been lynchings and brutal outrages of all sorts in our own state and those adjoining us, but we had confidence and pride in our city and the majesty of its laws. So far in advance of other Southern cities was ours, we were content to endure the evils we had, to labor and to wait.

But there was a rude awakening. On the morning of March 9, the bodies of three of our best young men were found in an old field horribly shot to pieces. These young men had owned and operated the "People's Grocery," situated at what was known as the Curve—a suburb made up almost entirely of colored people—about a mile from city limits. Thomas Moss, one of the oldest letter-carriers in the city, was president of the company, Calvin McDowell was manager and Will Stewart was a clerk. There were about ten other stockholders, all colored men. The young men were well known and popular and their business flourished, and that of Barrett, a white grocer who kept store there before the "People's Grocery" was established, went down. One day an officer came to the "People's Grocery" and inquired for a colored man who lived in the neighborhood, and for whom the officer had a warrant. Barrett was with him and when McDowell said he knew nothing as to the whereabouts of the man for whom they were searching, Barrett, not the officer, then accused McDowell of harboring the man, and McDowell gave the lie. Barrett drew his pistol and struck McDowell with it; thereupon McDowell, who was a tall, fine-looking six-footer, took Barrett's pistol from him, knocked him down and gave him a good thrashing, while Will Stewart, the clerk, kept the special officer at bay. Barrett went to town, swore out a warrant for their arrest on a charge of assault and battery. McDowell went before the Criminal Court, immediately gave bond and returned to his store. Barrett then threatened (to use his own words) that he was going to clean out the whole store. Knowing how anxious he was to destroy their business, these young men consulted a lawyer who told them they were justified in defending themselves if attacked, as they were a mile beyond city limits and police protection. They accordingly armed several of their friends not to assail, but to resist the threatened Saturday night attack.

When they saw Barrett enter the front door and a half dozen men at the rear door at 11 o'clock that night, they supposed the attack was on and immediately fired into the crowd, wounding three men. These men, dressed in citizen's clothes, turned out to be deputies who claimed to be hunting another man for whom they had a warrant, and whom any one of them could have arrested without trouble. When these men found they had fired upon officers of the law, they threw away their firearms and submitted to arrest, confident they should establish their innocence of intent to fire upon officers of the law. The daily papers inflaming headlines roused the evil passions of the whites, denounced these poor boys in unmeasured terms, nor permitted them a word in their own defense.

The neighborhood of the Curve was searched next day, and about thirty persons were thrown into jail, charged with conspiracy. No communication was to be had with friends any of the three days these men were in jail; bail was refused and Thomas Moss was not allowed to eat the food his wife prepared for him. The judge is reported to have said, "Any one can see them after three days." They were seen after three days, but they were no longer able to respond to the greetings of friends. On Tuesday following the shooting at the grocery, the papers which had made much of the sufferings of the wounded deputies, and promised it would go hard with those who did the shooting, if they died, announced that the officers were all out of danger, and would recover. The friends of the prisoners breathed more easily and relaxed their vigilance. They felt that as the officers would not die, there was no danger that in the heat of passion the prisoners would meet violent death at the hands of the mob. Besides, we had such confidence in the law. But the law did not provide capital punishment for shooting which did not kill. So the mob did what the law could not be made to do, as a lesson to the Afro-American that he must not shoot a white man, no matter what the provocation. The same night after the announcement was made in the papers that the officers would get well, the mob, in obedience to a plan known to every prominent white man in the city, went to the jail between two and three o'clock in the morning, dragged out these young men, hatless and shoeless, put them on the yard engine of the railroad which was in waiting just behind the jail, carried them a mile north of city limits and horribly shot them to death while the locomotive at a given signal let off steam and blew the whistle to deaden the sound of the firing.

"It was done by unknown men," said the jury, yet the *Appeal Avalanche*, which goes to press at 3 a.m., had a two-column account of the lynching. The papers also told how McDowell got hold of the guns of the mob, and as his grasp count not be loosened, his hand was shattered with a pistol ball and all the lower part of his face was torn away. There were four pools of blood found and only three bodies. It was whispered that he, McDowell, killed one of the lynchers with his gun, and it is well known that a policeman who was seen on the street a few days previous to the lynching, died very suddenly the next day.

"It was done by unknown parties," said the jury, yet the papers told how Tom Moss begged for his life, for the sake of his wife, his little daughter and his unborn infant. They also told us that his last words were, "If you will kill us, turn our faces to the West "

All this we learned too late to save these men, even if the law had not been in the hands of their murderers. When the colored people realized that the flower of our young manhood had been stolen away at night and murdered, there was a rush for firearms to avenge the wrong, but no house would sell a colored man a gun; the armory of the Tennessee Rifles, our only colored military company, and of which McDowell was a member, was broken into by order of the Criminal Court judge, and its guns taken. One hundred men and irresponsible boys from fifteen years and up were armed by order of the authorities and rushed out to the Curve, where it was reported that the colored people were massing, and at point of the bayonet dispersed these men who could do nothing but talk. The cigars, wines, etc., of the grocery stock were freely used by the mob, who possessed the place on pretence of dispersing the conspiracy. The money drawer was broken into and contents taken. The trunk of Calvin McDowell, who had a room in the store, was broken open, and his clothing, which was not good enough to take away, was thrown out and trampled on the floor.

These men were murdered, their stock was attached by creditors and sold for less than one-eighth of its cost to that same man Barrett, who is today running his grocery in the same place. He had indeed kept his word, and by aid of the authorities destroyed the People's Grocery Company root and branch. The relatives of Will Stewart and Calvin McDowell are bereft of their protectors. The baby daughter of Tom Moss, too young to express how she misses her father, toddles to the wardrobe, seizes the legs of the trousers of his letter-carrier uniform, hugs and kisses them with evident delight and stretches up her little hands to be taken up into the arms which will nevermore clasp his daughter's form. His wife holds Thomas Moss, Jr., in her arms, upon whose unconscious baby face the tears fall thick and fast when she is thinking of the sad fate of the father he will never see, and of the two helpless children who cling to her for the support she cannot give. Although these men were peaceable, law-abiding citizens of this country, we are told there can be no punishment for their murderers nor indemnity for their relatives.

I have no power to describe the feeling of horror that possessed every member of the race in Memphis when the truth dawned upon us that the protection of the law which we had so long enjoyed was no longer ours; all this had been destroyed in a night, and the barriers of the law had been thrown down, and the guardians of the public peace and confidence scoffed away into the shadows, and all authority given into the hands of the mob, and innocent men cut down as if they were brutes—the first feeling was one of utter dismay, then intense indignation. Vengeance was whispered from ear to ear, but sober reflection brought the conviction that it would be extreme folly to seek vengeance when such action meant certain death for the men, and horrible slaughter for the women and children, as one of the evening papers took care to remind us. The power of the State, country and city, the civil authorities and the strong arm of the military power were all on the side of the mob and of lawlessness. Few of our men possessed firearms, our only company's guns were confiscated, and the only white man who would sell a colored man a gun, was himself jailed, and his store closed. We were helpless in our great strength. It was our first object lesson in the doctrine of white supremacy; an illustration of the South's cardinal principle that no matter what the attainments, character or standing of an Afro-American, the laws of the South will not protect him against a white man.

There was only one thing we could do, and a great determination seized upon the people to follow the advice of the martyred Moss, and "turn our faces to the West," whose laws protect all alike. The *Free Speech* supported by our ministers and leading business men advised the people to leave a community whose laws did not protect them. Hundreds left on foot to walk four hundred miles between Memphis and Oklahoma. A Baptist minister went to the territory, built a church, and took his entire congregation out in less than a month. Another minister sold his church and took his flock to California, and still another has settled in Kansas. In two months, six thousand persons had left the city and every branch of business began to feel this silent resentment of the outrage, and failure of the authorities to punish the lynchers. There were a number of business failures and blocks of houses were for rent. The superintendent and treasurer of the street railway company called at the office of the *Free Speech*, to have us urge the colored people to ride again on the street cars. A real estate dealer said to a colored man who returned some property he had been buying on the installment plan: "I don't see what you 'niggers' are cutting up about. You got off light. We first intended to kill every one of those thirty-one 'niggers' in jail, but concluded to let all go but the 'leaders.'" They did let all go to the penitentiary. These so-called rioters have since been tried in the Criminal Court for the conspiracy of defending their property, and are now serving terms of three, eight, and fifteen years each in the Tennessee State prison.

To restore the equilibrium and put a stop to the great financial loss, the next move was to get rid of the *Free Speech,* the disturbing element which kept the waters troubled; which would not let the people forget, and in obedience to whose advice nearly six thousand persons had left the city. In casting about for an excuse, the mob found it in the following editorial which appeared in the Memphis *Free Speech,* May 21, 1892:

> Eight negroes lynched in one week. Since last issue of the *Free Speech* one was lynched at Little Rock, Ark., where the citizens broke into the penitentiary and got their man; three near Anniston, Ala., and one in New Orleans, all on the same charge, the new alarm of assaulting white women and three near Clarksville, Ga., for killing a white man. The same program of hanging then shooting bullets into the lifeless bodies was carried out to the letter. Nobody in this section of the country believes the old threadbare lie that negro men rape white women. If Southern white men are not careful they will overreach themselves, and public sentiment will have a reaction. A conclusion will then be reached which will be very damaging to the moral reputation of their women.

Commenting on this, *The Daily Commercial* of Wednesday following said:

> Those negroes who are attempting to make lynching of individuals of their race a means for arousing the worst passions of their kind, are playing with a dangerous sentiment. The negroes may as well understand that there is no mercy for the negro rapist, and little patience with his defenders. A negro organ printed in this city in a recent issue published the following atrocious paragraph: "Nobody in this section believes the old threadbare lie that negro men rape white women. If Southern white men are not careful they will overreach themselves and public sentiment will have a reaction. A conclusion will be reached which will be very damaging to the moral reputation of their women." The fact that a black scoundrel is allowed to live and utter such loathsome and repulsive calumnies is a volume of evidence as to the wonderful patience of Southern whites. There are some things the Southern white man will not tolerate, and the obscene intimidation of the foregoing has brought the writer to the very utter-most limit of public patience. We hope we have said enough.

The *Evening Scimitar* of the same day copied this leading editorial and added this comment: "Patience under such circumstances is not a virtue. If the negroes themselves do not apply the remedy without delay, it will be the duty of those he has attacked, to tie the wretch who utters these calumnies to a stake at the intersection of Main and Madison streets, brand him in the forehead with a hot iron and—"

Such open suggestions by the leading daily papers of the progressive city of Memphis were acted upon by the leading citizens and a meeting was held at the Cotton Exchange that evening. *The Commercial* two days later had the following account of it:

ATROCIOUS BLACKGUARDISM.

There will be no Lynching and no Repetition of the Offense.

In its issue of Wednesday *The Commercial* reproduced and commented upon an editorial which appeared a day or two before in a negro organ known as the *Free Speech.* The article was so insufferably and indecently slanderous that the whole city awoke to a feeling of intense resentment which came within an ace of culminating in one of those occurrences whose details are so eagerly seized and so prominently published by Northern newspapers. Conservative counsels, however, prevailed, and no extreme measures were resorted to. On Wednesday afternoon a meeting of citizens was held. It was not an assemblage of hoodlums or irresponsible fire-eaters, but solid, substantial business men who knew exactly what they were doing and who were far more indignant at the villainous insult to the women of the South than they would have been at any injury done themselves. This meeting appointed a committee to seek the author of the infamous editorial and warn him quietly that upon repetition of the offense he would find some other part of the country a good deal safer and pleasanter place of residence than this. The committee called a negro preacher named Nightingale, but he disclaimed responsibility and convinced the gentlemen that he had really sold out his paper to a woman named Wells. This woman is not in Memphis at present. It was finally learned that one Fleming, a negro who was driven out of Crittenden Co. during the trouble there a few years ago, wrote the paragraph. He had, however, heard of the meeting, and fled from a fate which he feared was in store for him, and which he knew he deserved. His whereabouts could not be ascertained, and the committee so reported. Later on, a communication from Fleming to a prominent Republican politician, and that politician's reply were shown to one or two gentlemen. The former was an inquiry as to whether the writer might safely return to Memphis, the latter was an emphatic answer in the negative, and Fleming is still in hiding. Nothing further will be done in the matter. There will be no lynching, and it is very certain there will be no repetition of the outrage. If there should be Friday, May 25.

The only reason there was no lynching of Mr. Fleming who was business manager and half owner of the *Free Speech,* and who did not write the editorial, was because this same white Republican told him the committee was coming, and warned him not to trust them, but get out of the way. The committee scoured the city hunting him, and had to be content with Mr. Nightingale who was dragged to the meeting, shamefully abused (although it was known he had sold out his interest in the paper six months before). He was struck in the face and forced at the pistol's point to sign a letter which was written by them, in which he denied all knowledge of the editorial, denounced and condemned it as slander on white women. I do not censure Mr. Nightingale for his action because, having never been at the pistol's point myself, I do not feel that I am

competent to sit in judgment on him, or say what I would do under such circumstances.

I had written that editorial with other matter for the week's paper before
leaving home the Friday previous for the General Conference of the A.M.E.
Church in Philadelphia. Conference adjourned Tuesday, and Thursday, May 25,
at 3 p.m., I landed in New York City for a few days' stay before returning home,
and there learned from the papers that my business manager had been driven
away and the paper suspended. Telegraphing for news, I received telegrams and
letters in return informing me that the trains were being watched, that I was to
be dumped into the river and beaten, if not killed; it had been learned that I
wrote the editorial and I was to be hanged in front of the court-house and my
face bled if I returned, and I was implored by my friends to remain away. The
creditors attached the office in the meantime and the outfit was sold without
more ado, thus destroying effectively that which it had taken years to build.
One prominent insurance agent publicly declares he will make it his business to
shoot me down on sight if I return to Memphis in twenty years, while a leading
white lady had remarked that she was opposed to the lynching of those three
men in March, but she did wish there was some way by which I could be gotten
back and lynched.

I have been censured for writing that editorial, but when I think of the five
men who were lynched that week for assault on white women and that not a
week passes but some poor soul is violently ushered into eternity on this
trumped-up charge, knowing the many things I do, and part of which I tried to
tell in the New York Age of June 25, (and in the pamphlets I have with me) seeing
that the whole race in the South was injured in the estimation of the world because of these false reports, I could no longer hold my peace, and I feel, yes, I am
sure, that if it had to be done over again (provided no one else was the loser save
myself) I would do and say the very same again.

The lawlessness here described is not confined to one locality. In the past ten
years over a thousand colored men, women and children have been butchered,
murdered and burnt in all parts of the South. The details of these horrible outrages seldom reach beyond the narrow world where they occur. Those who
commit the murders write the reports, and hence these lasting blots upon the
honor of a nation cause but a faint ripple on the outside world. They arouse no
great indignation and call forth no adequate demand for justice. The victims
were black, and the reports are so written as to make it appear that the helpless
creatures deserved the fate which overtook them.

Not so with the Italian lynching of 1891. They were not black men, and three
of them were not citizens of the Republic, but subjects of the King of Italy. The
chief of police of New Orleans was shot and eleven Italians were arrested
charged with the murder; they were tried and the jury disagreed; the good, law-
abiding citizens of New Orleans thereupon took them from the jail and lynched

them at high noon. A feeling of horror ran through the nation at this outrage. All Europe was amazed. The Italian government demanded thorough investigation and redress, and the Federal Government promised to give the matter the consideration which was its due. The diplomatic relations between the two countries became very much strained and for a while war talk was freely indulged. Here was a case where the power of the federal Government to protect its own citizens and redeem its pledges to a friendly power was put to the test. When our State Department called upon the authorities of Louisiana for investigation of the crime and punishment of the criminals, the United States government was told that the crime was strictly within the authority of the State of Louisiana, and Louisiana would attend to it. After a farcical investigation, the usual verdict in such cases was rendered: "Death at the hand of parties unknown to the jury," the same verdict which has been pronounced over the bodies of over 1,000 colored persons! Our general government has thus admitted that it has no jurisdiction over the crimes committed at New Orleans upon citizens of the country, nor upon those citizens of a friendly power to whom the general government and not the State government has pledged protection. Not only has our general government made the confession that one of the states is greater than the Union, but the general government has paid $25,000 of the people's money to the King of Italy for the lynching of those three subjects, the evil-doing of one State, over which it has no control, but for whose lawlessness the whole country must pay. The principle involved in the treaty power of the government has not yet been settled to the satisfaction of foreign powers; but the principle involved in the right of State jurisdiction in such matters, was settled long ago by the decision of the United States Supreme Court.

I beg your patience while we look at another phase of the lynching mania. We have turned heretofore to the pages of ancient and medieval history, to Roman tyranny, the Jesuitical Inquisition of Spain for the spectacle of a human being burnt to death. In the past ten years three instances, at least, have been furnished where men have literally been roasted to death to appease the fury of Southern mobs. The Texarkana instance of last year and the Paris, Texas, case of this month are the most recent as they are the most shocking and repulsive. Both were charged with crimes from which the laws provide adequate punishment. The Texarkana man, Ed Coy, was charged with assaulting a white woman. A mob pronounced him guilty, strapped him to a tree, chipped the flesh from his body, poured coal oil over him and the woman in the case set fire to him. The country looked on and in many cases applauded, because it was published that this man had violated the honor of the white woman, although he protested his innocence to the last. Judge Tourgee in the Chicago *Inter Ocean* of recent date says investigation has shown that Ed Coy had supported this woman, (who was known to be of bad character,) and her drunken husband for over a year previous to the burning.

The Paris, Texas, burning of Henry Smith, February 1st, has exceeded all the others in its horrible details. The man was drawn through the streets on a float, as the Roman generals used to parade their trophies of war, while the scaffold ten feet high, was being built, and irons were heated in the fire. He was bound on it, and red-hot irons began at his feet and slowly branded his body, while the mob howled with delight at his shrieks. Red hot irons were run down his throat and cooked his tongue; his eyes were burned out, and when he was at last unconscious, cotton seed hulls were placed under him, coal oil poured over him, and a torch applied to the mass. When the flames burned away the ropes which bound Smith and scorched his flesh, he was brought back to sensibility and burned and maimed and sightless as he was, he rolled off the platform and away from the fire. His half-cooked body was seized and trampled and thrown back into the flames while a mob of twenty thousand persons who came from all over the country howled with delight, and gathered up some buttons and ashes after all was over to preserve for relics. This man was charged with outraging and murdering a four-year-old white child, covering her body with brush, sleeping beside her through the night, then making his escape. If true, it was the deed of a mad-man, and should have been clearly proven so. The fact that no time for verification of the newspaper reports was given, is suspicious, especially when I remember that a negro was lynched in Indianola, Sharkey Co., Miss., last summer. The dispatches said it was because he had assaulted the sheriff's eight-year-old daughter. The girl was more than eighteen years old and was found by her father in this man's room, who was a servant on the place.

These incidents have been made the basis of this terrible story because they overshadow all others of a like nature in cruelty and represent the legal phases of the whole question. They could be multiplied without number and each outrival the other in the fiendish cruelty exercised, and the frequent awful lawlessness exhibited. The following table shows the number of black men lynched from January 1, 1882, to January 1, 1892: In 1882, 52; 1883, 39; 1884, 53; 1885, 77; 1886, 73; 1887, 70; 1888, 72; 1889, 95; 1890, 100; 1891, 169. Of these 728 black men who were murdered, 269 were charged with rape, 253 with murder, 44 with robbery, 37 with incendiarism, 32 with reasons unstated (it was not necessary to have a reason), 27 with race prejudice, 13 with quarreling with white men, 10 with making threats, 7 with rioting, 5 with miscegenation, 4 with burglary. One of the men lynched in 1891 was Will Lewis, who was lynched because "he was drunk and saucy to white folks." A woman who was one of the 73 victims in 1886, was hung in Jackson, Tenn., because the white woman for whom she cooked, died suddenly of poisoning. An examination showed arsenical poisoning. A search in the cook's room found rat poison. She was thrown into jail, and when the mob had worked itself up to the lynching pitch, she was dragged out, every stitch of clothing torn from her body, and was hung in the public court house square in sight of everybody. That white woman's husband has since died, in the insane asylum, a raving maniac, and his ravings have led to the conclusion that he and not the cook, was the poisoner of his wife. A fifteen-year-old colored girl was lynched last spring, at Rayville, La., on the same charge of poisoning. A woman was also lynched at Hollendale, Miss., last spring, charged with being an accomplice in the murder of her white paramour who had abused her. These were only two of the 159 persons lynched in the South from January 1, 1892, to January 1, 1893. Over a dozen black men have been lynched already since this new year set in, and the year is not yet two months old.

It will thus be seen that neither age, sex nor decency are spared. Although the impression has gone abroad that most of the lynchings take place because of assaults on white women only one-third of the number lynched in the past ten years have been charged with that offense, to say nothing of those who were not guilty of the charge. And according to law none of them were guilty until proven so. But the unsupported word of any white person for any cause is sufficient to cause a lynching. So bold have the lynchers become, masks are laid aside, the temples of justice and strong-holds of law are invaded in broad daylight and prisoners taken out and lynched, while governors of states and officers of law stand by and see the work well done.

And yet this Christian nation, the flower of the nineteenth century civilization, says it can do nothing to stop this inhuman slaughter. The general government is willingly powerless to send troops to protect the lives of its black citizens, but the state governments are free to use state troops to shoot them down like cattle, when in desperation the black men attempt to defend themselves, and then tell the world that it was necessary to put down a "race war."

Persons unfamiliar with the condition of affairs in the Southern States do not credit the truth when it is told them. They cannot conceive how such a condition of affairs prevails so near them with steam power, telegraph wires and printing presses in daily and hourly touch with the localities where such disorder reigns. In a former generation the ancestors of these same people refused to believe that slavery was the "league with death and the covenant with hell." Wm. Lloyd Garrison declared it to be, until he was thrown into a dungeon in Baltimore, until the signal lights of Nat Turner lit the dull skies of Northampton County, and until sturdy old John Brown made his attack on Harper's Ferry. When freedom of speech was martyred in the person of Elijah Lovejoy at Alton, when the liberty of free-discussion in Senate of the Nation's Congress was struck down in the person of the fearless Charles Sumner, the Nation was at last convinced that slavery was not only a monster but a tyrant. That same tyrant is at work under a new name and guise. The lawlessness which has been here described is like unto that which prevailed under slavery. *The very same forces are at work now as then.* The attempt is being made to subject to a condition of civil and industrial dependence, those whom the Constitution declares to be free men. The events which have led up to the present wide-spread lawlessness in the South can be traced to the very first year Lee's conquered veterans marched from Appomattox to their homes in the Southland. They were conquered in war, but not in spirit. They believed as firmly as ever that it was their right to rule black men and dictate to the National Government. The Knights of White Liners, and the Ku Klux Klans were composed of veterans of the Confederate army who were determined to destroy the effect of all the slave had gained by the war. They finally accomplished their purpose in 1876. The right of the Afro-American to vote and hold office remains in the Federal Constitution, but is destroyed in the constitution of the Southern states. Having destroyed the citizenship of the man, they are now trying to destroy the manhood of the citizen. All their laws are shaped to this end, school laws, railroad car regulations, those governing labor liens on crops, every device is adopted to make slaves of free men and rob them of their wages. Whenever a malicious law is violated in any of its parts, any farmer, any railroad conductor, or merchant can call together a posse of his neighbors and punish even with death the black man who resists and the legal authorities sanction what is done by failing to prosecute and punish the murderers. The Repeal of the Civil Rights Law removed their last barrier and the black man's last bulwark and refuge. The rule of the mob is absolute.

Those who know this recital to be true, say there is nothing they can do—they cannot interfere and vainly hope by further concession to placate the imperious and dominating part of our country in which this lawlessness prevails. Because this country has been almost rent in twain by internal dissension, the other sections seem virtually to have agreed that the best way to heal the breach is to permit the taking away of civil, political, and even human rights, to stand by in silence and utter indifference while the South continues to wreak fiendish vengeance on the irresponsible cause. They pretend to believe that with all the machinery of law and government in its hands; with the jails and penitentiaries and convict farms filled with petty race criminals; with the well-known fact that no negro has ever been known to escape conviction and punishment for any crime in the South—still there are those who try to justify and condone the lynching of over a thousand black men in less than ten years—an average of one hundred a year. The public sentiment of the country, by its silence in press, pulpit and in public meetings has encouraged this state of affairs, and public sentiment is stronger than law. With all the country's disposition to condone and temporize with the South and its methods; with its many instances of sacrificing principle to prejudice for the sake of making friends and healing the breach made by the late war; of going into the lawless country with capital to build up its waste places and remaining silent in the presence of outrage and wrong the South is as vindictive and bitter as ever. She is willing to make friends as long as she is permitted to pursue unmolested and uncensored, her course of proscription, injustice, outrage and vituperation. The malignant misrepresentation of General Butler, the uniformly indecent and abusive assault of this dead man whose only crime was a defense of his country, is a recent proof that the South has lost none of its bitterness. *The Nashville American*, one of the leading papers of one of the leading southern cities, gleefully announced editorially that "'The Beast is dead.' Early yesterday morning, acting under the devil's orders, the angel of Death took Ben Butler and landed him in the lowest depths of hell, and we pity even the devil the possession he has secured." The men who wrote these editorials are without exception young men who know nothing of slavery and scarcely anything of the war. The bitterness and hatred have been instilled in and taught them by their parents, and they are men who make and reflect the sentiment of their section. The South spares nobody else's feelings, and it seems a queer logic that when it comes to a question of right, involving lives of citizens and the honor of the government, the South's feelings must be respected and spared.

Do you ask the remedy? A public sentiment strong against lawlessness must be aroused. Every individual can contribute to this awakening. When a sentiment against lynch law as strong, deep and mighty as that roused against slavery prevails, I have no fear of the result. It should be already established as a fact and not as a theory, that every human being must have a fair trial for his life and liberty, no matter what the charge against him. When a demand goes up from fearless and persistent reformers from press and pulpit, from industrial and moral associations that this shall be so from Maine to Texas and from ocean to ocean, a way will be found to make it so.

In deference to the few words of condemnation uttered at the M.E. General Conference last year, and by other organizations, Governors Hogg of Texas, Northern of Georgia, and Tillman of South Carolina, have issued proclamations offering rewards for the apprehension of lynchers. These rewards have never been claimed, and these governors knew they would not be when offered. In many cases they knew the ring-leaders of the mobs. The prosecuting attorney of Shelby County, Tenn., wrote Governor Buchanan to offer a reward for the arrest of the lynchers of three young men murdered in Memphis. Everybody in that city and state knew well that the letter was written for the sake of effect and the governor did not even offer the reward. But the country at large deluded itself with the belief that the officials of the South and the leading citizens condemned lynching. The lynchings go on in spite of offered rewards, and in face of Governor Hogg's vigorous talk, the second man was burnt alive in his state with the utmost deliberation and publicity. Since he sent a message to the legislature the mob found and hung Henry Smith's stepson, because he refused to tell where Smith was when they were hunting for him. Public sentiment which shall denounce these crimes in season and out; public sentiment which turns capital and immigration from a section given over to lawlessness; public sentiment which insists on the punishment of criminals and lynchers by law must be aroused.

It is no wonder in my mind that the party which stood for thirty years as the champion of human liberty and human rights, the party of great moral ideas, should suffer overwhelming defeat when it has proven recreant to its professions and abandoned a position it created; when although its followers were being out-raged in every sense, it was afraid to stand for the right, and appeal to the American people to sustain them in it. It put aside the question of a free ballot and fair count of every citizen and gave its voice and influence for the protection of the coat instead of the man who wore it, for the product of labor instead of the laborer; for the seal of citizenship rather than the citizen, and insisted upon the evils of free trade instead of the sacredness of free speech. I am no politician but I believe if the Republican party had met the issues squarely for human rights instead of the tariff it would have occupied a different position to-day. The voice of the people is the voice of God, and I long with all the intensity of my soul for the Garrison, Douglas[s], Sumner, W[h]ittier and Phillips who shall rouse this nation to a demand that from Greenland's icy mountains to the coral reefs of the Southern seas, mob rule shall be put down and equal and exact justice be accorded to every citizen of whatever race, who finds a home within the borders of the land of the free and the home of the brave.

Then no longer will our national hymn be sounding brass and a tinkling cymbal, but every member of this great composite nation will be a living, harmonious illustration of the words, and all can honestly and gladly join in singing:

My country! 'tis of thee,
Sweet land of liberty
Of thee I sing.
Land where our fathers died,
Land of the Pilgrim's pride,
From every mountain side
Freedom does ring.

FOR FURTHER READING

Giddings, Paula. "The Last Taboo." In *Race-ing Justice, En-gendering Power*, edited by Toni Morrison, 441–65. New York: Pantheon Books, 1992.

Logan, Shirley Wilson. *"We Are Coming": The Persuasive Discourse of Nineteenth-Century Black Women*. Carbondale: Southern Illinois University Press, 1999.

———, ed. *With Pen and Voice: A Critical Anthology of Nineteenth-Century African-American Women*. Carbondale: Southern Illinois University Press, 1995.

Royster, Jacqueline Jones. *Traces of a Stream: Literacy and Social Change Among African American Women*. Pittsburgh: University of Pittsburgh Press, 2000.

Wells, Ida B. *Crusade for Justice: The Autobiography of Ida B. Wells*. Edited by Alfreda Duster. Chicago: University of Chicago Press, 1970.

———. *Southern Horrors and Other Writings: The Anti-Lynching Campaign of Ida B. Wells, 1892–1900*. Edited by Jacqueline Jones Royster. Boston: Bedford Books of St. Martin's Press, 1997.

Charlotte Perkins Gilman

1860–1935

Although she is now best known for her short story "The Yellow Wallpaper," Charlotte Perkins Gilman was one of the most important feminist social theorists and philosophers of her time, attacking "masculinist" social structures and especially the economic relations that kept women economically dependent and tied to subservient and straitjacketed domestic roles. Although she was part of the renowned Beecher family (her great aunt was Harriet Beecher Stowe), Charlotte Perkins Gilman grew up in poverty after her father left the family. Gilman was largely self-educated; her father sent her brother to M.I.T. but provided Gilman with only two years of advanced education in art. Yet her writing demonstrates a wide knowledge of philosophy, history, and social theory. Despite her strong views on women's economic and social status, she did not want to be called a feminist and referred to herself as a sociologist.

The birth of a child after her first marriage caused an emotional breakdown that might now be attributed to postpartum depression. This trauma led her to leave her husband and provided the experience on which she based "The Yellow Wallpaper." Until she remarried, she supported herself as a speaker, activist, writer, and editor of her monthly magazine, *The Forerunner*. The magazine became a platform for her writing about the status and roles women should have in industrial and urban culture, and it also enabled her to expound upon the utopian view of a matriarchal culture that she had expressed in her novel, *Herland*.

The social theory Gilman enunciated in *Women and Economics*—a mixture of socialism, Darwinism, and democratic theory—was so popular that several editions of the book were published, and it was translated into seven languages. *Women and Economics* outlines the causes of women's subservience and its negative consequences for women and for the progress of human society. In the preface she asserts that the conditions in which women live are not natural but are the result of "arbitrary conditions of our own adoption" (xxxix). She especially defines her audience as women and states her goal as to "urge upon them a new sense, not only of their social responsibility as individuals, but of their measureless racial importance as makers of men" (xxxix).

In the excerpt included here Gilman draws on Darwinian theory to develop the form of argument that characterizes her work, in which she customarily draws analogies between human and animal cultures, makes anthropological and historical observations, and points out the contrasts between the everyday lives of men and of women. Gilman continued throughout her life not only to attempt to devise alternatives to the traditional women's roles of household work and childrearing but also to promote the principles she found most beneficial in women's social structures: cooperation, nurture, and care. Gilman's arguments presaged and were as groundbreaking as the later writing of Simone de Beauvoir, Betty Friedan, and Angela Davis.

In print, Gilman took on the role of strong-willed iconoclast, but in person, she often surprised her audiences by being small and soft-spoken, leading one reporter to call her "a militant madonna" (Degler xvii). When Gilman discovered that she had breast cancer, she returned to live with her daughter but continued to write and lecture energetically. When she was no longer able to function she purchased chloroform and ended her life. "I have preferred chloroform to cancer," she wrote (Degler xvii).

From *Women and Economics*

1898

Without touching yet upon the influence of the social factors, treating the human being merely as an individual animal, we see that he is modified most by his economic conditions, as is every other animal. Differ as they may in color and size, in strength and speed, in minor adaptation to minor conditions, all animals that live on grass have distinctive traits in common, and all animals that eat flesh have distinctive traits in common, so distinctive and so common that it is by teeth, by nutritive apparatus in general, that they are classified, rather than by means of defence or locomotion. The food supply of the animal is the largest passive factor in his development; the processes by which he obtains his food supply, the largest active factor in his development. . . .

The human animal is no exception to this rule. Climate affects him, weather affects him, enemies affect him; but most of all he is affected, like every other living creature, by what he does for his living. Under all the influence of his later and wider life, all the reactive effect of social institutions, the individual is still inexorably modified by his means of livelihood: "The hand of the dyer is subdued to what he works in."

In view of these facts, attention is now called to a certain marked and peculiar economic condition affecting the human race, and unparalleled in the organic world. We are the only animal species in which the female depends on the male for food, the only animal species in which the sex-relation is also an economic relation. With us an entire sex lives in a relation of economic dependence upon the other sex, and the economic relation is combined with the

Reprinted from Gilman, Charlotte Perkins. *Women and Economics: A Study of the Economic Relation Between Men and women as a Factor in Social Evolution*, 2–17. Boston: Small, Maynard, 1898.

sex-relation. The economic status of the human female is relative to the sex-relation.

It is commonly assumed that this condition also obtains among other animals, but such is not the case. There are many birds among which, during the nesting season, the male helps the female feed the young, and partially feeds her; and, with certain of the higher carnivora, the male helps the female feed the young, and partially feeds her. In no case does she depend on him absolutely, even during this season, save in that of the hornbill, where the female, sitting on her nest in a hollow tree, is walled in with clay by the male, so that only her beak projects; and then he feeds her while the eggs are developing. But even the female hornbill does not expect to be fed at any other time. The female bee and ant are economically dependent, but not on the male. The workers are females, too, specialized to economic functions solely. And with the carnivora, if the young are to lose one parent, it might far better be the father: the mother is quite competent to take care of them herself. With many species, as in the case of the common cat, she not only feeds herself and her young, but has to defend the young against the male as well. In no case is the female throughout her life supported by the male.

In the human species the condition is permanent and general, though there are exceptions, and though the present century is witnessing the beginnings of a great change in this respect. We have not been accustomed to face this fact beyond our loose generalization that it was "natural," and that other animals did so, too.

To many this view will not seem clear at first; and the case of working peasant women or females of savage tribes, and the general household industry of women, will be instanced against it. Some careful and honest discrimination is needed to make plain to ourselves the essential facts of the relation, even in these cases. The horse, in his free natural condition, is economically independent. He gets his living by his own exertions, irrespective of any other creature. The horse, in his present condition of slavery, is economically dependent. He gets his living at the hands of his master; and his exertions, though strenuous, bear no direct relation to his living. . . . His living comes through another. He is economically dependent. So with the hard-worked savage or peasant women. Their labor is the property of another: they work under another will; and what they receive depends not on their labor, but on the power and will of another. They are economically dependent. This is true of the human female both individually and collectively.

In studying the economic position of the sexes collectively, the difference is most marked. As a social animal, the economic status of man rests on the combined and exchanged services of vast numbers of progressively specialized individuals. The economic progress of the race, its maintenance at any period, its continued advance, involve the collective activities of all the trades, crafts, arts, manufactures, inventions, discoveries, and all the civil and military institutions that go to maintain them. The economic status of any race at any time, with its involved effect on all the constituent individuals, depends on their world-wide labors and their free exchange. Economic progress, however, is almost exclusively masculine. Such economic processes as women have been allowed to exercise are of the earliest and most primitive kind. Were men to perform no economic services save such as are still performed by women, our racial status in economics would be reduced to most painful limitations.

To take from any community its male workers would paralyze it economically to a far greater degree than to remove its female workers. The labor now performed by the women could be performed by the men, requiring only the setting back of many advanced workers into earlier forms of industry; but the labor now performed by the men could not be performed by the women without generations of effort and adaptation. Men can cook, clean, and sew as well as women; but the making and managing of the great engines of modern industry, the threading of earth and sea in our vast systems of transportation, the handling of our elaborate machinery of trade, commerce, government—these things could not be done so well by women in their present degree of economic development.

This is not owing to lack of the essential human faculties necessary to such achievements, nor to any inherent disability of sex, but to the present condition of woman, forbidding the development of this degree of economic ability. The male human being is thousands of years in advance of the female in economic status. Speaking collectively, men produce and distribute wealth; and women receive it at their hands. As men hunt, fish, keep cattle, or raise corn, so do women eat game, fish, beef, or corn. As men go down to the sea in ships, and bring coffee and spices and silks and gems from far away, so do women partake of the coffee and spices and silks and gems the men bring.

The economic status of the human race in any nation, at any time, is governed mainly by the activities of the male: the female obtains her share in the racial advance only through him. . . . And, when the woman, left alone with no man to "support" her, tries to meet her own economic necessities, the difficulties which confront her prove conclusively what the general economic status of the woman is. None can deny these patent facts—that the economic status of women generally depends upon that of men generally, and that the economic status of women individually depends upon that of men individually, those men to whom they are related. But we are instantly confronted by the commonly received opinion that, although it must be admitted that men make and distribute the wealth of the world, yet women earn their share of it as wives. This assumes either that the husband is in the position of employer and the wife as employee, or that marriage is a "partnership," and the wife an equal factor with the husband in producing wealth. . . .

She is in no sense a business partner, unless she contributes capital or experience or labor, as a man would in like relation. Most men would hesitate very seriously before entering a business partnership with any woman, wife or not.

If the wife is not, then, truly a business partner, in what way does she earn from her husband the food, clothing, and shelter she receives at his hands? By house service, it will be instantly replied. This is the general misty idea upon the subject—that women earn all they get, and more, by house service. Here we come to a very practical and definite economic ground. Although not producers of wealth, women serve in the final processes of preparation and distribution. Their labor in the household has a genuine economic value.

For a certain percentage of persons to serve other persons, in order that the ones so served may produce more, is a contribution not to be overlooked. The labor of women in the house, certainly, enables men to produce more wealth than they otherwise could; and in this way women are economic factors in society. But so are horses. The labor of horses enables men to produce more wealth than they otherwise could. The horse is an economic factor in society. But the horse is not economically independent, nor is the woman. If a man plus a valet can perform more useful service than he could minus a valet, then the valet is performing useful service. But, if the valet is the property of the man, is obliged to perform this service, and is not paid for it, he is not economically independent.

The labor which the wife performs in the household is given as part of her functional duty, not as employment. The wife of the poor man, who works hard in a small house, doing all the work for the family, or the wife of the rich man, who wisely and gracefully manages a large house and administers its functions, each is entitled to fair pay for services rendered.

To take this ground and hold it honestly, wives, as earners through domestic service, are entitled to the wages of cooks, housemaids, nursemaids, seamstresses, or housekeepers, and to no more. This would of course reduce the spending money of the wives of the rich, and put it out of the power of the poor man to "support" a wife at all, unless, indeed, the poor man faced the situation fully, paid his wife her wages as house servant, and then she and he combined their funds in the support of their children. He would be keeping a servant: she would be helping keep the family. But nowhere on earth would there be "a rich woman" by these means. Even the highest class of private housekeeper, useful as her services are, does not accumulate a fortune. She does not buy diamonds and sables and keep a carriage. Things like these are not earned by house service.

But the salient fact in this discussion is that, whatever the economic value of the domestic industry of women is, they do not get it. The women who do the most work get the least money, and the women who have the most money do the least work. Their labor is neither given nor taken as a factor in economic exchange. It is held to be their duty as women to do this work; and their economic status bears no relation to their domestic labors, unless an inverse one. Moreover, if they were thus fairly paid,—given what they earned, and no more,—all women working in this way would be reduced to the economic status of the house servant. Few women—or men either—care to face this condition. The ground that women earn their living by domestic labor is instantly forsaken, and we are told that they obtain their livelihood as mothers. This is a peculiar position. We speak of it commonly enough, and often with deep feeling, but without due analysis.

In treating of an economic exchange, asking what return in goods or labor women make for the goods and labor given them—either to the race collectively or to their husbands individually—what payment women make for their clothes and shoes and furniture and food and shelter, we are told that the duties and services of the mother entitle her to support.

If this is so, if motherhood is an exchangeable commodity given by women in payment for clothes and food, then we must of course find some relation between the quantity or quality of the motherhood and the quantity and quality of the pay. This being true, then the women who are not mothers have no economic status at all; and the economic status of those who are must be shown to be relative to their motherhood. This is obviously absurd. The childless wife has as much money as the mother of many—more; for the children of the latter consume what would otherwise be hers; and the inefficient mother is no less provided for than the efficient one. Visibly, and upon the face of it, women are not maintained in economic prosperity proportioned to their motherhood. Motherhood bears no relation to their economic status. Among primitive races, it is true—in the patriarchal period, for instance—there was some truth in this position. Women being of no value whatever save as bearers of children, their favor and indulgence did bear direct relation to maternity; and they had reason to exult on more grounds than one when they could boast a son. To-day, however, the maintenance of the woman is not conditioned upon this. A man is not allowed to discard his wife because she is barren. The claim of motherhood as a factor in economic exchange is false to-day. But suppose it were true. Are we willing to hold this ground, even in theory? Are we willing to consider motherhood as a business, a form of commercial exchange? Are the cares and duties of the mother, her travail and her love, commodities to be exchanged for bread?

It is revolting so to consider them; and, if we dare face our own thoughts, and force them to their logical conclusion, we shall see that nothing could be more repugnant to human feeling, or more socially and individually injurious, than to make motherhood a trade. Driven off these alleged grounds of women's economic independence; shown that women, as a class, neither produce nor distribute wealth; that women, as individuals, labor mainly as house servants, are not paid as such, and would not be satisfied with such an economic status if they were so paid; that wives are not business partners or co-producers of wealth with their husbands, unless they actually practise the same profession;

that they are not salaried as mothers, and that it would be unspeakably degrading if they were—what remains to those who deny that women are supported by men? This (and a most amusing position it is)—that the function of maternity unfits a woman for economic production, and, therefore, it is right that she should be supported by her husband.

FOR FURTHER READING

Degler, Carl N. Introduction to *Women and Economics: A Study of the Economic Relation Between Men and Women as a Factor in Social Evolution*, by Charlotte Perkins Gilman. 1898; New York: Torchbooks, 1966.

Egan, Maureen L. "Evolutionary Theory in the Social Philosophy of Charlotte Perkins Gilman." In *Hypatia's Daughters: Fifteen Hundred Years of Women Philosophers*, edited by Linda Lopez McAlister, 248–66. Bloomington: Indiana University Press, 1996.

Gilman, Charlotte Perkins. *The Charlotte Perkins Gilman Reader*. Edited by Ann J. Lane. Charlottesville: University of Virginia Press, 1999.

———. *Herland: A Lost Feminist Utopian Novel*. New York: Pantheon Books, 1979.

———. *The Living of Charlotte Perkins Gilman: An Autobiography*. 1935; Madison: University of Wisconsin Press, 1991.

Rudd, Jill, and Val Gough, eds. *Charlotte Perkins Gilman: Optimist Reformer*. Iowa City: University of Iowa Press, 1999.

Gertrude Buck

1871–1922

Gertrude Buck once described herself as "a hopeless radical" (Campbell xlii) because she spent her whole life teaching writing and literature that challenged the cold, mechanistic methods of composition instruction popular in the late nineteenth and early twentieth centuries. She was an accomplished and passionate teacher, scholar, and rhetorical theorist; her ideas ran counter to mainstream ideas of writing instruction that were more concerned with grammar, mechanics, and correct form. "So radically different an approach to one of the rhetorical staples could not be assimilated by rhetoricians contemporary with her," according to Albert R. Kitzhaber (289).

Buck was part of the first generation of privileged white women who engaged in formal university study and devoted their lives to academic pursuits. This dramatic increase in the number of women gaining access to higher education (usually at elite women's colleges) signals an important advance in women's access to the academic contexts in which they could contribute to rhetorical theory. Buck attended the University of Michigan, where she earned a Ph.D. in rhetoric in 1898, studying with the well-known educator Fred Newton Scott. Following graduation, Buck took a position teaching composition, rhetoric, and literary theory at Vassar College. There, in addition to teaching, she wrote textbooks, articles, poems, plays, and rhetorical theory and took an active role in administration as well as community social issues. Her scholarly work focused on developing a theory of teaching writing designed to promote the cooperation of the individual and the social community in the ethical pursuit of truth. In developing this theory, Buck enacted what now might be considered a feminist rhetoric, which relied on cooperation, collaboration, and social responsibility.

In the short essay included here, "The Present Status of Rhetorical Theory," Buck outlines her social theory of rhetoric. Subscribing to current interpretations of the pre-Socratic sophists, Buck defines sophistic rhetoric as violent and manipulative, furthering the aims of the speaker and with little regard for the good of the listener. This type of discourse, she writes, "is purely predatory—a primitive aggression of the strong upon the weak. The art of rhetoric is the art of war." Buck sees this type of rhetoric as "socially irresponsible." She calls instead for "a real communication between speaker and hearer, to the equal advantage of both, and thus a real function of the social organism." She argues for a "Platonic" understanding of discourse, whose goal is to establish equality between speaker and hearer in a democratic effort to advance the common good.

Buck's essay is one of the earliest statements of rhetorical theory written by a woman. Although she does not explore the differences in privilege and power that occur within any community, with her emphasis on collaboration and the pursuit of a democratic and ethical rhetoric, Buck creates, according to JoAnn Campbell, a feminist rhetoric that is still being developed eighty years after her death.

"The Present Status of Rhetorical Theory"

1900

Two opposing conceptions of the nature of discourse bequeathed to us from classic times still struggle for dominance in our modern rhetorical theory—the social conception of Plato and the anti-social conception of the Sophists. The latter, though known to us only fragmentarily from allusions and quotations in later treatises, can be, in its essential outlines, easily reconstructed. According to the sophistic teaching, discourse was simply a process of persuading the hearer to a conclusion which the speaker, for any reason, desired him to accept. Analyzed further, this familiar definition discloses certain significant features.

First of all it conveys, though somewhat indirectly, a notion of the ultimate end of the process of discourse. Why should discourse take place at all? Why should the hearer be persuaded? Because, answers the definition, the speaker wishes to persuade him. And, to pursue the inquiry still further, the speaker wishes to persuade the hearer to a certain belief presumably because he recognizes some advantage to himself in doing so. We should conclude, therefore, from examination of the definition before us, that discourse is for the sake of the speaker.

Nor is this conclusion threatened by further investigation into the pre-Platonic philosophy of discourse. It is true that the practical precepts of the sophistic rhetoricians pay great deference to the hearer, even seeming, at first glance, to exalt him over the speaker. Every detail of the speech is to be sedulously "adapted" to the hearer. Nothing is to be done without reference to him. His tastes are to be studied, his prejudices regarded, his little jealousies and chagrins written down in a book—but all this, be it remembered, in order simply that he may the more completely be subjugated to the speaker's will. As the definition has previously suggested, the hearer's ultimate importance to discourse is of the slightest. To his interests the process of discourse is quite indifferent.

But not only does persuasion, according to the sophistic notion, fail to con-

Reprinted from Buck, Gertrude. "The Present Status of Rhetorical Theory." *Modern Language Notes* 15 (March 1900): 84–87.

sider the interests of the hearer; frequently it even assails them. In fact, the sophistic precepts bristle with implications that the hearer's part in discourse is virtually to be spoiled. The hearer is to be persuaded for the sake of some advantage to the speaker. If his own advantage should chance to lie in the same direction with that of the speaker, the utmost that the process of discourse could do would be merely to point out this fact to the hearer. In such a case little persuasive art is demanded. It is rather when the interests of the hearer, if rightly understood by him, oppose his acceptance of the conclusion urged by the speaker that real rhetorical skill comes into play. Then is the speaker confronted by a task worthy of his training—that of making the acceptance of this conclusion, which is really inimical to the hearer's interests, seem to him advantageous. In plainest statement, the speaker must by finesse assail the hearer's interests for the sake of his own.

This is a typical case of discourse, according to the sophistic conception. Its essentially anti-social character appears both in its conscious purpose and in its unrecognized issues. We have seen that the end it seeks is exclusively individual, sanctioned only by that primitive ethical principle of the dominance of the strong. The speaker through discourse secures his own advantage simply because he is able to do so. The meaning of his action to the hearer or to society as a whole, is purely a moral question with which rhetoric is not directly concerned. There is, in the rhetorical theory of the sophists, no test for the process of discourse larger than the success of the speaker in attaining his own end.

But further, the sophistic conception of discourse is antisocial in its outcome. Instead of levelling conditions between the two parties to the act, as we are told is the tendency in all true social functioning, discourse renders these conditions more unequal than they were before it took place. The speaker, superior at the outset, by virtue at least of a keener perception of the situation, through the process of discourse, comes still further to dominate the hearer. As in primitive warfare the stronger of two tribal organizations subdues and eventually enslaves the weaker, so in discourse the initial advantage of the speaker returns to him with usury.

This anti-social character of the sophistic discourse, as seen both in its purpose and in its outcome, may be finally traced to the fact that the process, as we have analyzed it, just fails of achieving complete communication between speaker and hearer. Some conclusion is, indeed, established in the mind of the hearer, but not necessarily the conclusion which the speaker himself has reached upon this subject. It may, in fact, oppose all his own experience and thought, and thus hold no organic relation to his own mind. But wishing the hearer to believe it, he picks it up somewhere and proceeds to insert it into the hearer's mind.

This absence of a vital relationship between the normal activities of the speaker's mind and the action by which he seeks to persuade the hearer, breaks the line of communication between the two persons concerned. Conditions at the ends of the circuit cannot be equalized, as in true social functioning, because the current is thus interrupted.

This conception of the process of discourse might be graphically represented in Figure 1.

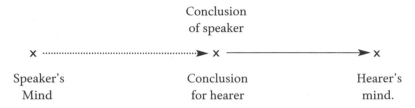

The sophistic account of discourse, then, makes it a process essentially individualistic, and thus socially irresponsible. It secures the advantage of the speaker without regard to that of the hearer, or even in direct opposition to it. Because this conception leaves a gap in the chain of communication between the minds of speaker and hearer, it fails to equalize conditions between them. The speaker wins and the hearer loses continually. Discourse is purely predatory—a primitive aggression of the strong upon the weak. The art of rhetoric is the art of war.

Against this essentially crude and anti-social conception of discourse, Plato seems to have raised the first articulate protest. Discourse is not an isolated phenomenon, he maintained, cut off from all relations to the world in which it occurs, and exempt from the universal laws of justice and right. The speaker has certain obligations, not perhaps directly to the hearer, but to the absolute truth of which he is but the mouthpiece, to the entire order of things which nowadays we are wont to call society. Discourse is, indeed, persuasion, but not persuasion to any belief the speaker pleases. Rather is it persuasion to the truth, knowledge of which, on the part of the hearer, ultimately advantages both himself and the speaker as well. The interests of both are equally furthered by legitimate discourse. In fact the interests of both are, when rightly understood, identical; hence there can be no antagonism between them.

In respect, then, to the advantage gained by each party to the act of discourse, speaker and hearer stand on a footing of at least approximate equality. In fact the ultimate end of discourse must be, from the Platonic premises, to establish equality between them. Before discourse takes place the speaker has a certain advantage over the hearer. He perceives a truth as yet hidden from the hearer, but necessary for him to know. Since the recognition of this truth on the part of the hearer must ultimately serve the speaker's interests as well, the speaker, through the act of discourse, communicates to the hearer his own vision. This done, the original inequality is removed, the interests of both speaker and hearer are furthered, and equilibrium is at this point restored to the social organism.

It is plain that the circuit of communication between speaker and hearer is in Plato's conception of discourse continuous. The speaker having himself come to a certain conclusion, does not set about establishing another in the hearer's mind, but simply transmits his own belief into the other's consciousness. The connection between the two minds is living and unbroken. The Platonic notion of the process of discourse may be thus illustrated as in Figure 2.

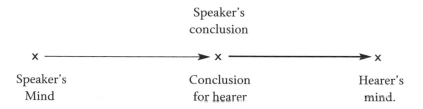

Thus have been hastily reviewed the two opposing conceptions of discourse delivered to us by the earliest rhetoricians. The changes which they have suffered in the lapse of centuries are surprisingly slight. We find implicit in many of our modern text-books practically the same conception of discourse which was held by the pre-Platonic teachers of rhetoric—a conception which regards discourse as an act performed by the speaker upon the hearer for the advantage of the speaker alone. It is true that the present-day sophists include in the end of discourse not persuasion alone, but the production of any desired effect upon the hearer. This fact does not, however, modify fundamentally the nature of the process itself. The hearer (or reader as he has now become) is to be interested or amused, or reduced to tears, or overborne with a sense of the sublime, not indeed because the writer himself has previously been interested or amused and, in obedience to the primal social instinct, would communicate his experience to another, but because—well, because the writer wishes to produce this effect upon the reader. Thus wishing, and being able to gratify his desire, the act of discourse results—an act still individualistic and one-sided, serving no ends but those of the speaker himself. The effect to be produced upon the hearer, being wholly external to the experience of the speaker, leaves unjoined the old break between speaker and hearer in the process of communication. We have again, in but slightly altered guise, the sophistic conception of discourse.

But in spite of the persistence of this outworn conception in even some recent text-books, there are not wanting many evidences that the Platonic theory of discourse is at last coming home to the modern consciousness. It is doubtless true that the later social theory of rhetoric would not venture to define the end of discourse as that of declaring to another the absolute and universal truth.

There may be two reasons for this. In the first place we are not now-a-days on such joyfully intimate terms with the absolute truth as was Plato. And, again, the practical value of even a little relative and perhaps temporary truth has become clearer to us—such truth as touches us through our personal experiences and observations. Yet it must be remembered that Plato himself allowed the subject-matter of discourse to be the speaker's own vision of the absolute truth, thus individualizing the abstraction until we cannot regard it as fundamentally alien from our modern conception of experience, in the largest sense of the word.

Granting this substantial identity, then, we have only to prove that Plato's idea of personal experience as the subject-matter of discourse is a real factor in modern rhetorical theory. For this no long argument is required. We find this idea theoretically expressed in rhetorical treatises even as far back as Quintilian, in the implied definition of discourse as self-expression, a conception recently popularized by such writers as Arnold and Pater. This notion of discourse, neglecting that part of the process of communication by which an experience is set up in the mind of the writer, emphasized exclusively that segment which develops the experience of the writer into articulate form. Being thus incomplete as was the sophistic theory of discourse, it served only to supplement that by bringing out into clear consciousness the Platonic truth that the subject-matter of discourse has a direct relation to the mental processes of the writer.

On the practical side this truth has appeared in the comparatively recent decay of formal instruction in rhetoric, and the correlative growth of composition work in our schools. This practical study of composition, in so far as it deserved its name, displaced the writing of biographical essays, largely drawn from encyclopediac sources, and of treatises on abstract subjects far removed from any natural interests of the student who wrote. Both these lines of effort proving relatively profitless, the experiment was tried of drawing the material for writing directly from the every-day experience, observation and thinking of the student—an experiment whose results proved so successful that the practice has long been established in most of our schools. This is a piece of history so recent and so well-known that it need not be dwelt upon. Its import, however, is worth noting. It means the practical, though perhaps unconscious, acceptance of Plato's principle that the subject-matter of discourse bears a vital relation to the mind of the speaker. And by virtue of this, it means the complete closing of the circuit of communication between speaker and hearer.

So far, then, the rising modern rhetorical theory agrees with the doctrine of Plato. It may, perhaps, differ from him in making discourse a process somewhat less self-conscious than he seems to have conceived it, arising from the speaker's primitive social instinct for sympathy, or (to put it more technically) for closer relations with his environment, rather than from any explicit desire to communicate his own vision of the truth to another. But this modification affects neither the nature of the process itself nor its ultimate outcome. Both the Platonic and the modern theory of discourse make it not an individualistic and isolate process for the advantage of the speaker alone, but a real communication between speaker and hearer, to the equal advantage of both, and thus a real function of the social organism.

This conception of discourse is rich in implications which Plato never saw, and which no modern has yet formulated. To this formulation, however, our practical teaching of English with all its psychologic and sociological import, is daily bringing us nearer. It cannot be long before we shall recognize a modern theory of discourse as large in its outlines as Plato's and far better defined in its details; a theory which shall complete the social justification which rhetoric has so long been silently working out for itself.

FOR FURTHER READING

Allen, Virginia. "Gertrude Buck and the Emergence of Composition in the United States." *Educational Biography, Vitae Scholasticae* 5 (1986): 141–59.

Brody, Miriam. *Manly Writing: Gender, Rhetoric, and the Rise of Composition.* Carbondale: Southern Illinois University Press, 1993.

Burke, Rebecca J. "Gertrude Buck's Rhetorical Theory." In *Occasional Papers in Composition History and Theory,* edited by Donald C. Stewart, 1–26. Manhattan: Kansas State University, 1978.

Campbell, JoAnn, ed. *Toward a Feminist Rhetoric: The Writings of Gertrude Buck.* Pittsburgh: University of Pittsburgh Press, 1996

Kitzhaber, Albert R. "Rhetoric in American College, 1850–1900." Ph D. diss., University of Washington, 1953.

Mulderig, Gerald. "Gertrude Buck's Rhetorical Theory and Modern Composition Teaching." *Rhetoric Society Quarterly* 14 (1984): 96–104.

Mary Augusta Jordan

1855–1941

When financial constraints permitted Mary Augusta Jordan's father to send only one of his three children to college, he made the unorthodox decision of selecting his daughter rather than his son. This story is prophetic because it foreshadows the way in which Jordan, throughout her entire life, was able to invade the male-dominated world of academe and leave her own mark as a teacher, a scholar, a writer, and an accomplished rhetorician.

Jordan graduated from Vassar College in 1876, and from 1884 to 1921 she taught English at Smith College. Like Gertrude Buck, she initiated the vital and unconventional attention to rhetorical pedagogy that women's colleges provided the privileged women who could attend them. Her goal was to prepare women to enter public life, to encourage them to become "restless disturbers" even though the opportunities still did not exist for their full participation alongside men (Wagner 198). Jordan also traveled widely throughout New England giving lectures on rhetorical theory, and she led and participated in women's study groups.

Her book *Correct Speaking and Writing*, published in 1904, was written for educated women and attempted to challenge the correctness-obsessed strictures that limited women's expression and that consequently circumscribed their thinking. She argues for an intelligent, flexible, and ethical consideration of audience and occasion in making choices about rhetorical approaches rather than a reliance on slavish adherence to rules and formulas. The selection from *Correct Speaking and Writing* included here is evidence of Jordan's crusade toward demystification of academic writing. It is an example of rhetorical theory and pedagogy that also serves as a demonstration of rhetorical facility. Jordan uses the history of the English language to show that any notion of a "standard" English usage is arbitrary at best; the English language is always changing, she tells her audience, and the notion of it being static is absurd. In elegant prose peppered with humor and sarcasm, Jordan uses her *ethos* as an English teacher and scholar to encourage her female audience to use their intelligence in making rhetorical choices and even in taking rhetorical risks that would allow them to be effective participants in public and academic realms.

From *Correct Writing and Speaking*

1904

The desire for rules and standards is an expression of human nature in one or more of its aspiring, its self-satisfied, or its despairing moods. Rules and standards may point to perfection, may rest in the easily attainable, or may make the best of a bad matter. Or, in still other words, rules and standards may be ideals, or conventions, or observed facts.

From this difference of meaning springs much confusion of thought in all subjects where rules and standards are applicable. Rule is made to stand for at once too much or too little. Standards are treated now as foot rules, now as ever advancing aims. Nowhere is this confusion more fertile in mischief than in the practical interests of speaking and writing. It is not limited in its influence to those who instruct or to those who wish for instruction. Like a shifting mist, it sways and swings over both companies, and disguises not only one from the other, but the members of each from all the rest.

To a man satisfied in the faith that a rule at its best approximates to a moving and advancing ideal, the demand for easy and precise accuracy seems so unreasonable that it blinds him to the natural disappointment of those who believed that he would provide them with ascertained weights and measures. The stupid and the children of genius alike emancipate themselves from conventions, and yet the discussion about correct speech, good English, and faultless grammar goes on. It is at least encouraging to know that it goes off much as it has always gone on.

In this respect matters are no worse than they have been in the past. We are not forced to bring action against human nature in our generation, as more incompetent and more muddle-headed and tongue-tied than it was before our evil days. It is safe to say that we are not degenerate. There is some ground for belief that we are holding our own fairly well amidst a Babel of interests and words second only to the first great recorded confusion of tongues. It is with a spirit of good cheer that one undertakes to find out what is meant by correct English and how it is to be acquired in speaking and in writing.

There is a general impression that correct English is something that the ordinary, plain person may reasonably hope to secure. It is a well-defined, safe territory in which the painstaking need not err. It is believed that correct English is the passport to good society where, on a level plain of expression, the gently bred exercise their minds. To speak like persons of intelligence is the goal that most of us set up as reasonable and desirable. And certainly the aim

Reprinted from Jordan, Mary A. *Correct Writing and Speaking*, 7–10, 12–15, 25, 36. The Woman's Home Library series, ed. Margaret E. Sangster. New York: A. S. Barnes and Company, 1904.

seems within reach. But a little effort shows us that reaching our goal is about our only evidence that it is within reach. There are so many ways that persons of intelligence have of expressing themselves. Some of these ways have little in common, many of them are contradictory in method, most of them differ in the effect aimed at, or the impression made. In despair the student of English decides to adopt a classification that will relieve him from some of his embarrassment. He will use a self-consistent form of English that shall avoid what Dryden called gross error; and he will exact of others no more than he requires of himself. But the first effort that he makes to secure consistency brings him into open rebellion against the idioms that he has used all his life and that are as dear to him as his home, his church, and his dead. Is idiom part of correctness, or is it flat defiance of it, or is it better than correctness—a sort of Sunday-best, to be used for every-day only when it is outgrown or threadbare?

The like happens to the inquirer concerning the typical English voice. Is it to be found in England, Scotland, Ireland, or Wales? In the United States, Canada, Australia, or India? With what authority does the voice speak when it is found? . . .

If finally we are willing to replace "United States" by "English," what English shall we choose? How shall we get it? The state of mind naturally following upon these questions instructs us concerning the folly of any demand for absolute precision. The desire for it is natural, and so excusable, if not laudable, but satisfaction is no part of its history. In this condition of affairs inquirers often fall into the mistake of thinking that English is a tongue exceptional in its history and eccentric in its structure. It is often described as the spoiled child of the linguistic family. The result of the acceptance of this view of English speech and writing is unfortunate. The student can hardly fail to be depressed at the seeming necessity of dealing with his subject in a spirit quite apart from that directing his other efforts at expression. Nor can he readily get his own consent to study in an orderly way what is confessedly a realm of disorder. So whim will call out whim, and individuality which charms without rule will become eccentricity without rule or charm.

Clearly the case is a hard one for the seeker after truth about standard English. It has not precision enough to do his work without his will, but it has too much precision to let him have his will entirely with it. It is of course quite possible to put the whole matter out of mind as an overstrained counsel of perfection. It is possible to dispose of it as a pure abstraction, expensive and tantalizing, like the principle of life or the existence of the soul. But English speech and writing resist this treatment. They are so closely entangled with those social relations which make existence intelligible, endurable, or enjoyable that we hate to waste time and strength in costly experiment about the best way of employing them.

It is deplorable to make false starts, lose the clew, and get into no-thoroughfares, when the right road would have led into the noble estate of self-mastery and the pleasant country of human brotherhood. We want to know, and we need to know, English. Must we then assume that it is a gift like that of personal beauty? That, therefore, its excellence is indeed a superlative which may not be acquired as such, but must be gratefully accepted and joyfully acknowledged as of the beneficence of nature? Is this the only English speaking and writing in which precision is possible; this all that affords the conditions of standard expression, beside which everything else is known by its defect? Must we adopt a "great man" theory in English expression, and explain all attainments of the less imposing representatives of the race by the much or little that they derive from him as he appears at intervals in history? This doctrine has not been without its supporters. The use of the masterpieces of literature and the influence of great orators and actors has been cited in evidence of its validity.

But the result has been the thing known as a school—a thing so definite and so much apart from the normal progress and development of expression, whether in English or in French, or Latin, or Greek, that a clear statement of the theory is all that is necessary for its refutation.

The teacher of speech or writing who imparts few or many of his own devices and makes a series of incomplete editions of himself does not, in the old phrases, "ascertain the tongue" or "*extend* the powers of language." He makes men into puppets and supplies them in their memory and habit with a superior sort of string to work themselves by. Likewise if they unconsciously imitate him their use of his powers is but mimicry, unless they unconsciously or consciously use it as a point of departure for something in their own talent or genius. . . . The precision that is gained by imitation of the ancients, the classics, or the popular idol is misleading. The standard we are looking for is not a graduated series of lengths from the admirably great to the little admirable, whatever else it may be. Then it seems likely that what is ordinarily known as precision is not in any high degree characteristic of English speaking and writing.

The standard form, the exemplary instances, are not readily discovered. The body of doctrine, the recipe for manufacture, are not close at hand for use. . . .

Most speakers naturally incline to agree with Ben Jonson's Morose: "All discourses but my own afflict me; they seem harsh, impertinent, and irksome." Without too close scrutiny our own delivery passes for sweet, pointed, and entertaining, but only because we assume that our outward show is what we would have it, not because we aim intelligently at any precise effect, not because we know the means that we habitually employ to effect the results we actually secure.

So the theory of a standard pronunciation is kept for the most part in reserve for use when we wish to silence opposition or to confirm our own judgment in our own behalf. . . .

There certainly is at present, then, no standard English, either in writing or in speaking, that is easily and cheaply available. There is no one correct way of writing or of speaking English. Within certain limits there are many ways of attaining correctness. What these limits are and how they are to be employed and what their interrelations are, it is the purpose of the later chapters of this book to indicate.

FOR FURTHER READING

Jordan, Mary Augusta. "The Higher Education: A Social Necessity for Women." Paper presented to the Rhode Island branch of the Association of Collegiate Alumnae at Brown University, Providence, Rhode Island, 4 November 1892. Mary Jordan folder, Smith College Archives, Northampton, Mass.

Kates, Susan. "The History of Language Conventions in Mary Augusta Jordan's Rhetoric Text, *Correct Writing and Speaking* (1904)." In *Making and Unmaking the Prospects of Rhetoric*, edited by Theresa Enos, 109–14. Mahwah, N.J.: Erlbaum, 1997.

———. "Subversive Feminism: The Politics of Correctness in Mary Augusta Jordan's *Correct Writing and Speaking* (1904)." *College Composition and Communication* 48.4 (1997): 501–17.

Martin, Theodora Penny. *The Sound of Our Own Voices: Women's Study Clubs 1860–1910*. Boston: Beacon Press, 1987.

Wagner, Joanne. "Intelligent Members or Restless Disturbers? Women's Rhetorical Styles, 1880–1920." In *Reclaiming Rhetorica: Women in the Rhetorical Tradition*, edited by Andrea A. Lunsford, 185–202. Pittsburgh: University of Pittsburgh Press, 1995.

Margaret Sanger

1879–1966

Most famous for founding the Birth Control Federation of America (now known as Planned Parenthood) in 1939, Margaret Sanger was born Margaret Louise Higgins, the sixth of eleven children. (Sanger reportedly blamed her mother's premature death, in part, on the strain of childbearing.) She began her revolutionary career as an activist for women's reproductive rights by attending college with the financial support of her sisters. Sanger then entered nursing school in 1900, married William Sanger in 1902, and bore three children. By 1910, Sanger and her family were living in New York City, where she was active in a variety of political clubs, including the Women's Committee of the New York Socialist Party. Influenced by the artistic and intellectual climate of Greenwich Village before the war, Sanger's activist work took many forms.

Sanger began a feminist monthly newspaper in 1914 called *The Woman Rebel* that served as a forum for discussion of feminist issues and concerns, particularly contraception. Like Ida B. Wells, Sanger believed that the dissemination of facts and information was the surest vehicle for social change. However, Sanger soon fell prey to the Comstock Law of New York, which criminalized the distribution of information about contraception and abortion. She was arrested and released on bail. Choosing not to waste precious time serving a jail sentence, Sanger fled to England after instructing her supporters in the United States to release one hundred thousand copies of her pamphlet "Family Limitation." (She references the pamphlet in the letter below.) The controversial contents of this pamphlet include steps for preventing conception such as douching, ingesting herbs and quinine, and using pessaries (an early European form of the diaphragm). In "Family Limitation" Sanger declares that "Contraception is the only cure for abortions."

Margaret Sanger's "Letter to the Readers of *The Woman Rebel*" was written directly before she fled to England, as evidenced by her inscription, "En Route to Exile." It is representative of her urgent, entreating rhetorical style. In the letter she explains how she developed into an advocate for birth control and speaks to the plight of disenfranchised women who seek birth control yet are denied access. She relies on statistics—one of her customary rhetorical strategies—to illustrate the pressing material circumstances of women who often had only two choices: to die as the result of an illegal abortion or to raise children in poverty. She also enhances her journalistic style with a more *pathetic* rhetorical appeal—repeated and increasingly urgent questions, which Sanger believed demanded answers.

She returned to the United States in 1916 only to be arrested again and jailed for thirty days for opening the first birth-control clinic in the United States. After her release, she continued agitating for women's reproductive rights and founded the *Birth Control Review* (1917), the American Birth Control League (1921), and the Birth Control Clinical Research Bureau (1923). She expanded the Birth Control Federation internationally in 1952, and in 1965, the year before her death, birth control was legalized for married couples in the United States. As a shaper of U.S. reproductive history, Sanger spoke words that are powerful and familiar even today: "We now know that there never can be a free humanity until woman is freed from ignorance, and we know, too, that woman can never call herself free until she is mistress of her own body" ("Morality and Birth Control" 11).

"Letter to the Readers of *The Woman Rebel*"

1914

En Route to Exile
October 28, 1914
Comrades and Friends,—
Every paper published should have a message for its readers. It should deliver it and be done. *The Woman Rebel* had for its aim the imparting of information for the prevention of conception. (None of the suppressed issues contained such information.) It was not the intention to labor for years advocating the idea, but to give the information directly to those who desired it. The March, May, July, August, September, and October issues have been suppressed and confiscated by the Post Office. They have been mailed regularly to all subscribers. If you have not received your copies, it has been because the U.S. Post Office has refused to carry them on to you.

My work in the nursing field for the past fourteen years has convinced me that the workers desire the knowledge of the prevention of conception. My work among women of the working class proved to me sufficiently that it is they who are suffering because of the law which forbids the imparting of information. To wait for this law to be repealed would be years and years hence. Thousand of unwanted children may be brought into the world in the meantime, thousands of women made miserable and unhappy.

Why should we wait?

Reprinted from Sanger, Margaret. *The Woman Rebel* (October 1914). Reprinted with permission from the Mary Ware Dennett Papers, Schlesinger Library, Radcliffe Institute, Harvard College, Cambridge, Mass.

Shall we who have heard the cries and seen the agony of dying women respect the law which has caused their deaths?

Shall we watch in patience the murdering of 25,000 women each year in the United States from criminal abortions?

Shall we fold our hands and wait until a body of sleek and well fed politicians get ready to abolish the cause of such slaughter?

Shall we look upon a piece of parchment as greater than human happiness, greater than human life?

Shall we let it destroy our womanhood, or hold millions of workers in bondage and slavery? Shall we who respond to the throbbing pulse of human needs concern ourselves with indictments, courts, and judges, or shall we do our work first and settle with these evils after?

This law has caused the perpetuation of quackery. It has created the fake and quack who benefited by its existence.

Jail has not been my goal. There is special work to be done and I shall do it first. If jail comes after, I shall call upon all to assist me. In the meantime, I shall attempt to nullify the law by direct action and attend to the consequences afterward.

Over 100,000 working men and women in the United States shall hear from me.

The Boston Tea Party was a defiant and revolutionary act in the eyes of the British Government, but to the American Revolutionist it was but an act of courage and justice.

Yours fraternally,
Margaret Sanger

FOR FURTHER READING

Baskin, Alex, ed. *The Woman Rebel.* New York: Archives of Social History, 1976.

Sanger, Margaret. *The Case for Birth Control: A Supplementary Brief and Statement of the Facts.* New York: Modern Art Printing Company, 1917.

———. *Margaret Sanger: An Autobiography.* New York, W. W. Norton and Company, 1938.

———. "Morality and Birth Control." *Birth Control Review* (February–March 1918): 11, 14.

———. *My Fight for Birth Control.* New York: Farrar and Rinehardt, 1931.

———. *What Every Girl Should Know.* New York: M. N. Maisel, 1920.

———. *Woman and the New Race.* New York: Brentano's, 1920.

Emma Goldman

"One cannot be too extreme in dealing with social ills; besides, the extreme thing is usually the true thing," writes Emma Goldman in the preface to *Anarchism and Other Essays*, the collection from which we have chosen our selection, "Marriage and Love." Goldman suffered from accusations of extremism all her life. It might be more accurate to say that Goldman, an early advocate of free speech, birth control, women's rights, labor unions, and the eight-hour workday, suffered from extreme reactions to these positions.

Born in the Russian province of Kovno to German-speaking Jewish parents, Goldman spent her early life in Saint Petersburg, then the capital of Russia. During her teenage years, she studied Russian and committed herself to the revolutionary spirit brewing in the capital at that time. When she was seventeen, she became a worker in a corset factory, but she soon emigrated to the United States with her sister Helene. In Rochester, New York, Goldman found work in another clothing factory, where she first experienced the drudgery and exploitation of unregulated labor. The long hours, dim light, and physical demands made her ill, and in 1889, she moved to New York City, joined the anarchist movement, and began to speak out in public for more just labor practices and women's rights.

In New York, Goldman met and came to love (though never married) the Russian anarchist Alexander Berkman. In 1892 he was sentenced to a twenty-two-year prison term for his attempted assassination of the industrialist Henry Clay Frick during the Homestead steel strike in Pittsburgh, Pennsylvania. Goldman continued her activities as an advocate for workers and fair labor practices. In 1893, Goldman led several marches of the unemployed and hungry, repeating her belief that workers have a right to "ask for work. If they do not give you work, ask for bread. If they do not give you work or bread, then take mead" (Havel 21). She was arrested after this speech for inciting a riot, convicted, and sentenced to a year in jail.

After Berkman received an early release in 1906, he and Goldman continued to speak out on labor issues, publishing the anarchist magazine *Mother Earth* until 1917, when they were arrested for opposing the military draft in World War I and served two years in prison. They were deported to Russia in 1919. For the rest of her life, until her death in 1940, Goldman participated in the social and political movements of her age, including the Russian Revolution and the Spanish Civil War. Often homeless and hounded by both the press and the police, Goldman continued to write and speak on the principles of anarchism.

Our selection here, "Marriage and Love," applies Goldman's theory of anarchism—which derives from the Greek words meaning "without rule"—to marriage. Influenced by and reminiscent of Margaret Fuller's *Woman in the Nineteenth Century,* this essay dramatically argues the case that marriage is a prison for women, an economic exchange for which "woman pays with her name, her privacy, her self-respect, her very life." Goldman worked for money all her life—in garment factories; as a nurse, a tour guide, a cook. In this essay she urges women not to fall into the trap of being "protected" in a "home" that has more "solid doors and bars" than a prison, where women's "wage-slavery" only increases. Goldman compares marriage to capitalism—that "other paternal arrangement"—arguing that both deprive men and women of self-respect and freedom. Goldman's rhetorical style is bold, direct, and vivid; she makes use of many dramatic devices, peppering her argument with exclamation points, many *ohs* and *yeses,* vivid adjectives and verbs, repetition of opening lines and sentence structure, as well as questions that read as if they are shouted. The essay moves at a fast pace, too, adding to the rhetorical sense of frustration and urgency, two attributes that Goldman shares with many of the women rhetors in this collection.

From "Marriage and Love"

1914

Marriage is primarily an economic arrangement, an insurance pact. It differs from the ordinary life insurance agreement only in that it is more binding, more exacting. Its returns are insignificantly small compared with the investments. In taking out an insurance policy one pays for it in dollars and cents, always at liberty to discontinue payments. If, however, woman's premium is a husband, she pays for it with her name, her privacy, her self-respect, her very life, "until death doth part." Moreover, the marriage insurance condemns her to life-long dependency, to parasitism, to complete uselessness, individual as well as social. Man, too, pays his toll, but as his sphere is wider, marriage does not limit him as much as woman. He feels his chains more in an economic sense. . . .

. . . [B]ehind every marriage stands the life-long environment of the two sexes; an environment so different from each other that man and woman must remain strangers. Separated by an insurmountable wall of superstition, custom, and habit, marriage has not the potentiality of developing knowledge of, and respect for, each other, without which every union is doomed to failure.

Reprinted from Goldman, Emma. "Marriage and Love." In *Anarchism and Other Essays,* 233–47. New York: Mother Earth Publishing Association, 1911.

Henrik Ibsen, the hater of all social shams, was probably the first to realize this great truth. Nora leaves her husband, not—as the stupid critic would have it—because she is tired of her responsibilities or feels the need of woman's rights, but because she has come to know that for eight years she had lived with a stranger and borne him children. Can there be anything more humiliating, more degrading than a life-long proximity between two strangers? No need for the woman to know anything of the man, save his income. As to the knowledge of the woman—what is there to know except that she has a pleasing appearance? We have not yet outgrown the theologic myth that woman has no soul, that she is a mere appendix to man, made out of his rib just for the convenience of the gentleman who was so strong that he was afraid of his own shadow.

Perchance the poor quality of the material whence woman comes is responsible for her inferiority. At any rate, woman has no soul—what is there to know about her? Besides, the less soul a woman has the greater her asset as a wife, the more readily will she absorb herself in her husband. It is this slavish acquiescence to man's superiority that has kept the marriage institution seemingly intact for so long a period. Now that woman is coming into her own, now that she is actually growing aware of herself as a being outside of the master's grace, the sacred institution of marriage is gradually being undermined, and no amount of sentimental lamentation can stay it.

From infancy, almost, the average girl is told that marriage is her ultimate goal; therefore her training and education must be directed towards that end. Like the mute beast fattened for slaughter, she is prepared for that. Yet, strange to say, she is allowed to know much less about her function as wife and mother than the ordinary artisan of his trade. It is indecent and filthy for a respectable girl to know anything of the marital relation. Oh, for the inconsistency of respectability, that needs the marriage vow to turn something which is filthy into the purest and most sacred arrangement that none dare question or criticize. Yet that is exactly the attitude of the average upholder of marriage. The prospective wife and mother is kept in complete ignorance of her only asset in the competitive field—sex. Thus she enters into life-long relations with a man only to find herself shocked, repelled, outraged beyond measure by the most natural and healthy instinct, sex. It is safe to say that a large percentage of the unhappiness, misery, distress, and physical suffering of matrimony is due to the criminal ignorance in sex matters that is being extolled as a great virtue. Nor is it at all an exaggeration when I say that more than one home has been broken up because of this deplorable fact.

If, however, woman is free and big enough to learn the mystery of sex without the sanction of State or Church, she will stand condemned as utterly unfit to become the wife of a "good" man, his goodness consisting of an empty head and plenty of money. Can there be anything more outrageous than the idea that a healthy, grown woman, full of life and passion, must deny nature's demand, must subdue her most intense craving, undermine her health and break her spirit, must stunt her vision, abstain from the depth and glory of sex experience until a "good" man comes along to take her unto himself as a wife? That is precisely what marriage means. How can such an arrangement end except in failure? This is one, though not the least important, factor of marriage, which differentiates it from love.

Ours is a practical age. The time when Romeo and Juliet risked the wrath of their fathers for love, when Gretchen exposed herself to the gossip of her neighbors for love, is no more. If, on rare occasions, young people allow themselves the luxury of romance, they are taken in care by the elders, drilled and pounded until they become "sensible."

The moral lesson instilled in the girl is not whether the man has aroused her love, but rather is it, "How much?" The important and only God of practical American life: Can the man make a living? Can he support a wife? That is the only thing that justifies marriage. Gradually this saturates every thought of the girl; her dreams are not of moonlight and kisses, of laughter and tears; she dreams of shopping tours and bargain counters. This soul-poverty and sordidness are the elements inherent in the marriage institution. The State and the Church approve of no other ideal, simply because it is the one that necessitates the State and Church control of men and women.

Doubtless there are people who continue to consider love above dollars and cents. Particularly is this true of that class whom economic necessity has forced to become self-supporting. The tremendous change in woman's position, wrought by that mighty factor, is indeed phenomenal when we reflect that it is but a short time since she has entered the industrial arena. Six million women wage workers; six million women, who have the equal right with men to be exploited, to be robbed, to go on strike; aye, to starve even. Anything more, my lord? Yes, six million wage workers in every walk of life, from the highest brain work to the mines and the railroad tracks; yes, even detectives and policemen. Surely the emancipation is complete.

Yet with all that, but a very small number of the vast army of women wage workers look upon work as a permanent issue, in the same light as does man. No matter how decrepit the latter, he has been taught to be independent, self-supporting. Oh, I know that no one is really independent in our economic treadmill; still, the poorest specimen of a man hates to be a parasite; to be known as such, at any rate.

The woman considers her position as worker transitory, to be thrown aside for the first bidder. That is why it is infinitely harder to organize women than men. "Why should I join a union? I am going to get married, to have a home." Has she not been taught from infancy to look upon that as her ultimate calling? She learns soon enough that the home, though not so large a prison as the factory, has more solid doors and bars. It has a keeper so faithful that naught can escape him. The most tragic part, however, is that the home no longer frees her from wage slavery; it only increases her task.

According to the latest statistics submitted before a Committee "on labor and wages, and congestion of population," ten per cent of the wage workers in New York City alone are married, yet they must continue to work at the most poorly paid labor in the world. Add to this horrible aspect the drudgery of housework, and what remains of the protection and glory of the home? As a matter of fact, even the middle-class girl in marriage can not speak of her home, since it is the man who creates her sphere. It is not important whether the husband is a brute or a darling. What I wish to prove is that marriage guarantees woman a home only by the grace of her husband. There she moves about in *his* home, year after year, until her aspect of life and human affairs becomes as flat, narrow, and drab as her surroundings. Small wonder if she becomes a nag, petty, quarrelsome, gossipy, unbearable, thus driving the man from the house. She could not go, if she wanted to; there is no place to go. Besides, a short period of married life, of complete surrender of all faculties, absolutely incapacitates the average woman for the outside world. She becomes reckless in appearance, clumsy in her movements, dependent in her decisions, cowardly in her judgment, a weight and a bore, which most men grow to hate and despise. Wonderfully inspiring atmosphere for the bearing of life, it is not?

But the child, how is it to be protected, if not for marriage? After all, is not that the most important consideration? The shame, the hypocrisy of it! Marriage protecting the child, yet thousands of children destitute and homeless. Marriage protecting the child, yet orphan asylums and reformatories overcrowded. . . . Oh, the mockery of it! . . .

As to the protection of the women,—therein lies the curse of marriage. Not that it really protects her, but the very idea is so revolting, such an outrage and insult on life, so degrading to human dignity, as to forever condemn this parasitic institution.

It is like that other paternal arrangement—capitalism. It robs man of his birthright, stunts his growth, poisons his body, keeps him in ignorance, in poverty and dependence, and then institutes charities that thrive on the last vestiges of man's self-respect.

The institution of marriage makes a parasite of woman, an absolute dependent. It incapacitates her for life's struggle, annihilates her social consciousness, paralyzes her imagination, and then imposes its gracious protection, which is in reality a snare, a travesty on human character.

If motherhood is the highest fulfillment of woman's nature, what other protection does it need save love and freedom? Marriage but defiles, outrages, and corrupts her fulfillment. Does it not say to woman, Only when you follow me shall you bring forth life? Does it not condemn her to the block, does it not degrade and shame her if she refuses to buy her right to motherhood by selling herself? Does not marriage only sanction motherhood, even though conceived in hatred, in compulsion? Yet, if motherhood be of free choice, of love, of ecstasy, of defiant passion, does it not place a crown of thorns upon an innocent head and carve in letters of blood the hideous epithet, Bastard? Were marriage to contain all the virtues claimed for it, its crimes against motherhood would exclude it forever from the realm of love.

Love, the strongest and deepest element in all life, the harbinger of hope, of joy, of ecstasy; love, the defier of all laws, of all conventions; love, the freest, the most powerful moulder of human destiny; how can such an all-compelling force be synonymous with that poor little State and Church-begotten weed, marriage?

Free love? As if love is anything but free! Man has bought brains, but all the millions in the world have failed to buy love. Man has subdued bodies, but all the power on earth has been unable to subdue love. Man has conquered whole nations, but all his armies could not conquer love. Man has chained and fettered the spirit, but he has been utterly helpless before love. High on a throne, with all the splendor and pomp his gold can command, man is yet poor and desolate, if love passes him by. And if it stays, the poorest hovel is radiant with warmth, with life and color. Thus love has the magic power to make of a beggar a king. Yes, love is free; it can dwell in no other atmosphere. In freedom it gives itself unreservedly, abundantly, completely. All the laws on the statutes, all the courts in the universe, cannot tear it from the soil, once love has taken root. If, however, the soil is sterile, how can marriage make it bear fruit? It is like the last desperate struggle of fleeting life against death.

Love needs no protection; it is its own protection. So long as love begets life no child is deserted, or hungry, or famished for the want of affection. I know this to be true. I know women who became mothers in freedom by the men they loved. Few children in wedlock enjoy the care, the protection, the devotion free motherhood is capable of bestowing. . . .

Some day, some day men and women will rise, they will reach the mountain peak, they will meet big and strong and free, ready to receive, to partake, and to bask in the golden rays of love. What fancy, what imagination, what poetic genius can foresee even approximately the potentialities of such a force in the life of men and women. If the world is ever to give birth to true companionship and oneness, not marriage, but love will be the parent.

FOR FURTHER READING

Goldman, Emma. *Living My Life*. New York, Alfred A. Knopf, 1931. Reprint, Salt Lake City: G. M. Smith, 1982.
———. *My Disillusionment in Russia*. Garden City, N.Y.: Doubleday, Page and Company, 1923.
———. *Nowhere at Home: Letters from Exile of Emma Goldman and Alexander Berkman*. Edited by Richard Drinnon and Anna Maria Drinnon. New York: Schocken Books, 1975.

————. *Red Emma Speaks: An Emma Goldman Reader.* Edited by Alix Kates Shulman. New York: Schocken Books, 1983.

————. *Vision on Fire: Emma Goldman on the Spanish Revolution.* Edited by David Porter. New Paltz, N.Y.: Commonground Press, 1983.

Havel, Hippolyte. "Biographic Sketch." In *Anarchism and Other Essays,* by Emma Goldman, 1–41. New York: Dover Publications, Inc., 1969.

Alice Dunbar Nelson

1875–1935

Best known as a poet, dramatist, and fiction writer, Alice Dunbar Nelson was also a respected journalist and activist of the Harlem Renaissance. Born in New Orleans, she later wrote movingly in her essay "Brass Ankles Speak" about the pain she suffered as a child because of Creole, Indian, black, and white ancestry. Although she was a prolific writer, she supported herself as a teacher, stenographer, secretary, editor, newspaper columnist, and campaign manager. Dunbar Nelson was an outspoken advocate of racial equality, participating in the women's club movement, working for the Dyer Anti Lynching Bill, and founding the Industrial School for Colored Girls. This activism did not appear in her fiction and poetry. In fact, biographer and critic Gloria T. Hull says that Dunbar Nelson's stratified notions of genre kept race muted in these works. "The 'real' Dunbar-Nelson . . . 'stands up' in her newspaper columns," according to Hull (li). These were not typical "woman's" columns, however. Dunbar Nelson wrote about everything from dramatic productions and the current social scene to race relations, the black presence in elections, the declining birthrate among African Americans, and working conditions for domestic servants. She articulated her feminist and political ideals in the persona of the urbane, witty, irreverent, and even "sassy" journalist, in the tradition of Ida B. Wells and other women of the previous generation.

In "Facing Life Squarely," published in *The Messenger*, one of the most important black journals of her day, Dunbar Nelson speaks forthrightly from her position as a black woman to other black women. The essay challenges the complacency of Northern, educated African Americans about the "progress" their people are making and argues strongly that until less educated, poor, Southern African Americans are released from the Jim Crow conditions of the South, no one can rest easily with a sense of "progress." Dunbar Nelson begins the essay by gently citing the advances women had made from the Victorian social restrictions of their mothers, but she moves quickly to describe the realities of life for Southern black men and women. With biting sarcasm she announces that "there is no progress" worth "sobbing for joy" over in the "spectacle of two or three ordinary Southern white women sitting down to talk with several very high class black women." Nor, she says, are the educational achievements of African Americans a sign of progress while schools remain segregated with lower standards for black children. At the end of the essay, evoking the spirit of Anna Julia Cooper's call for "lifting as we climb," Dunbar Nelson challenges women

to recognize that these signs of progress are instances of self-deception. She exhorts women to challenge men to "face life squarely."

"Facing Life Squarely"

1927

The Girl Reserves in their beautiful ritual promise to "face life squarely." Surely,
a most essential thing for all young girls to know; to learn to look with honest,
clear-eyed vision at life, stripping away shams and non-essentials, facing facts
and not being lured from the truth by silly reticences and repressions.

I wish that every girl of our race could learn the code of the Girl Reserves—
at least that one part of it. And I wish that every Aframerican woman in this
country could take as the essential basic element of her life this one thing—to
face life squarely. We have come a long way from the Victorian days of repressions and hidings of the truth, and silences about what everyone knew was
true, and pretences and shams, when the mention of any portion of anatomy
but the face was silenced with blushes, and no respectable woman wore silk
stockings. But we still love to deceive ourselves, and while we are less prudish
than our Victorian mothers, we are still afraid of the truth as it touches the fabric of society. And we love to make high-sounding phrases which mean nothing, and to talk glibly about progress and changes in the social order and the
superiority of the age, and how mankind is marching on, and kindred banal
stuff. And the mere mention of a question which might puncture the gossamer
veil of pretense cloaking the meaningless words causes consternation.

Let me illustrate. We are fond of talking nowadays about "Progress in Race
Relations." It is a phrase that is on the tongues of white and black—those interested in sociology and economics. We are deluged with releases giving statistics
of the increased good will between the races. Headlines of startling height in
some of our papers record touching instances of affection and love between
Nordics and Aframericans.

Much is doubtless true. Southern colleges and universities are studying the
Negro as never before. Men and women of our race appear before their student
bodies, and in the classrooms, getting respectful and interested hearings. A
thing unthinkable in any term twenty-five years ago. The Negro just now is the
pet subject of litterateurs and sociologists. He is in the hey-day of an unprecedented era of popularity. And so his emissaries are given eager attention; his
books are read avidly, and best of all, bought and circulated. Gatherings and

Reprinted from Dunbar Nelson, Alice. "Facing Life Squarely." In *The Works of Alice Dunbar-
Nelson*, vol. 2, edited by Gloria T. Hull, 297–301. The Schomburg Library of Nineteenth-Century Black Women Writers. New York: Oxford University Press, 1988.

meetings and conferences between the races in the South are common occurrences, and there is no longer fear and wonder on the part of the Southern white women lest fire from Heaven descend upon them in wrath at meeting black men on a quasi equality.

But—let us face the situation squarely. We are apt to be lulled to sleep by the beautiful and touching instances of Christian amity between our people and those of the Nordic race. And yet we ought to know that behind the web of honeyed words, under the skin of every Southern white man and woman there lies the venom of race hatred. As in older days it was said that if you scratch any Russian, you would find a Tartar. We may amend the proverb to say scratch every Nordic and you find a cracker.

The Mississippi Flood is a case in point. While Nature has unloosed the torrent of her wrath upon a hapless land and wrought devastation untold and horror inescapable, similar demons have been unleashed in the souls of the white men in the path of destruction. If there ever were truth in the statement that "one touch of nature makes the whole world kin," it has lost its applicability in this instance. If the progress in race relations had kept pace with its advertisements, we should not hear the pitiful tales which filter through from the Southland. The thin veneer of civilization has sloughed off the white men and the old slave-driving, whip-cracking, black-women-raping, antebellum, plantation overseer herds the helpless blacks to his own liking, and a virtual slavery exists in the vast flood area.

Let us face this fact squarely. True the plantation owners of Mississippi, Louisiana and Arkansas are not the highest type of Nordics. They are not the ones who got to colleges of universities, or are interested in lectures or literature. The only race relations they ever heard of are the relations of black man and white master, or black woman and white ravisher. But until the Negroes of the backwoods are safe in the knowledge of their own freedom; until peonage ceases to be winked at by the law; until the chain gang is abolished and simple, elemental justice is dealt the ignorant blacks, we are hiding our heads in the sand. And the women of our race must realize that there is no progress in sobbing with joy over the spectacle of two or three ordinary Southern white women sitting down to talk with several very high class black women over the race problem. We are deluding ourselves if we feel we are getting anywhere by having conferences, when hundreds of black women are wringing their hands because their men have been driven over the crumbling levee to certain death, while the white men stand out of the danger zone.

We have learned to face the issue of lynching squarely. We are no longer hoodwinked by unsupported statements. We know that there have been more lynchings in the present year thus far than in the past. But this phase of the question is a good one for the women to look firmly in the face. Lynchings only occur where Negroes are afraid. When they cease to fear, the white man turns tail and skulks away.

We talk much about the army of graduates who step forth proudly this month ready for their conquering march through life. And we quote statistics to show our remarkable progress and expansion educationally. But if we would face this educational question squarely, we would see that the problem is to keep the standard where it belongs. For as long as we have segregated schools, as long as our educational system in this country is a biracial one, unless every nerve of every one of us is strained to the uttermost, we will have a biracial standard, and the Negro one will inevitably be lower. We cannot afford to deceive ourselves; for the sake of the children we should fight segregation in schools as if it were a poisonous viper attacking the very heart of our race. To face this problem squarely we must admit that the schools are primarily for the children and not for the teachers, and that it were far better that our youngsters be thrown into competition with all races in schools, where no quarter is given, and the rate must be kept high, and from whence if they get through, they can emerge strong from the battle, and with respect for their own ability to stand up in a contest of wits, than that they be swathed in the inevitable paternalism of a strictly "colored" school. The job for women of the race is to abolish the double standard of measurement and achievement of the child. And we do not need to deceive ourselves by averring that such a double stand does not exist.

Perhaps the place at which we are apt to deceive ourselves most blatantly is at the point of political independence. The political independence of any American citizen is a joke. And not only the political independence, but the political participation of the Negro in the affairs of the body politic is something to make high Olympus howl with mirth. Even in New York where the Aframerican is largely Tammanyized, he is no free agent. For being wise, he is an opportunist and slips into the well-worn groove of the perfectly obvious.

But now and then we hear of groups among us having conferences, the women as well as the men. And we talk wisely about what will be done to candidates when they dare to rear their heads. And if we were honest enough with ourselves to face the issue squarely, we'd all go home and admit that we will all file in line, march to the ballot box and vote as we are told at the crack of the boss's whip.

I might go on and multiply instances in our racial and national life where endless confusion of thought and action are caused by our refusing to look situations in the face; by self- and racial-deception, by weak acceptance of the obvious explanation —by "going along" in other words.

Oh, that the girls may teach the women and the boys teach the men the wisdom of "facing life squarely."

FOR FURTHER READING

Giddings, Paula. *Where and When I Enter: The Impact of Black Women on Race and Sex in America.* New York: William Morrow, 1984.
Hull, Gloria T. *Color, Sex, and Poetry: Three Women Writers of the Harlem Renaissance.* Bloomington: Indiana University Press, 1987.

Dorothy Day

1897–1980

Writing and activism were inseparable for Dorothy Day. "Both can be . . . an ethical response to the world," she wrote (Ellsberg xvi). Day began her career with a socialist daily newspaper in New York, interviewing activists like Leon Trotsky and Margaret Sanger and writing stories about labor strikes and the poor immigrants who were her neighbors on the Lower East Side. When the next paper she worked for was suppressed by the U.S. government, she joined suffragist protesters picketing the White House. After one protest, she was arrested and sent to prison, where she was placed in solitary confinement for participating in a hunger strike.

By 1933, her transformation from secular political activist to religious and spiritual activist had culminated in her founding of the *Catholic Worker*. The paper was the first part of her effort to reconnect politics, economics, and social justice with a sense of reverence and sacrifice derived from the Christian Gospels. The second part of her Catholic Worker program, establishing Houses of Hospitality, began soon after. In her work with the poor, Day joined radical politics, socialism, anarchism, pacifism, and conservative theology to become, as Robert Ellsberg notes in his introduction to her *Selected Writings*, "the most significant, interesting, and influential person in the history of American Catholicism" (xvii), and yet her work never gained wide acceptance. Day herself lived a life of voluntary poverty, believing that true activism emerged "little by little," in small daily acts of mercy—feeding the hungry, giving shelter to the homeless, supporting the struggling worker. Her radical mixture of religion, pacifism, and social activism made the Catholic Worker movement subject to investigation by the F.B.I. Several times over the next thirty years, J. Edgar Hoover attempted to bring charges of sedition against her.

Her regular columns for the *Catholic Worker* were a hybrid of journalistic report, editorial, diary, and meditation. Motivated by her commitment to give a vivid face to poverty and oppression and her belief "in the sacramentality, the holy sublimity of the everyday" (Ellsberg xii), she attempted to represent the lives and the struggles of the worker. Although some criticized her pieces in the *Worker* for digression, repetition, and lack of focus, her writing—whether about abstract political issues or about a particular event—had a personal and immediate quality that led the 150,000 subscribers to the *Catholic Worker* to call her "Dorothy." Despite her commitment to writing as activism, she felt conflicted and very humble about her work. In the epigram to her *Selected Writings*, she notes: "The sustained effort of writing, of putting pen to paper so many hours a day when there are human beings around who need me, when there is sickness, and hunger, and sorrow, is a harrowingly painful job. I feel that I have done nothing well. But I have done what I could."

"Memorial Day in Chicago"

1937

On Memorial Day, May 30, 1937, police opened fire on a parade of striking steel workers and their families at the gate of the Republic Steel Company, in South Chicago. Fifty people were shot, of whom 10 later died; 100 others were beaten with clubs.

Have you ever heard a man scream as he was beaten over the head by two or three policemen with clubs and cudgels? Have you ever heard the sickening sounds of blows and seen people with their arms upraised, trying to protect their faces, stumbling blindly to get away, failing and rising again to be beaten down? Did you ever see a man shot in the back, being dragged to his feet by policemen who tried to force him to stand, while his poor body crumpled, paralyzed by a bullet in the spine?

We are sickened by stories of brutality in Germany and Russia and Italy. A priest from Germany told me of one man who came to him whose back was ridged "like a washboard," by the horrible beatings he had received at the hands of the German police in concentration camps. I shudder with horror at the thought of the tortures inflicted on Catholics, Protestants, Jews, and Communists in Germany today.

And here in America, last month, there was a public exhibition of such brutality that the motion-picture film, taken by a Paramount photographer in a sound truck, was suppressed by the company for fear that it would cause riots and mass hysteria, it was so unutterably horrible.

I am trying to paint a picture of it for our readers because so many did not read the story of the Memorial Day "riot" in Chicago in front of the Republic Steel Mills.

Try to imagine this mass of people—men, women, and children—picketing, as they have a right to do, coming up to the police line and being suddenly shot into, not by one hysterical policeman, but by many. Ten were killed and 100 were taken to the hospital wounded. Tear gas and clubs supplied by the Republic Steel Company were used.

I am trying to picture this scene to our readers because I have witnessed these things firsthand, and I know the horror of them. I was on a picket line when the "radical" squad shot into the line and pursued the fleeing picketers down the streets, knocking them down and kicking and beating them. I, too, have fled down streets to escape the brutality and vicious hatred of the "law" for those whom they consider "radical." And by the police anyone who protests injustice, who participates in labor struggles, is considered a radical.

Two years ago I wrote an account in *The Catholic Worker* of two plainclothesmen beating up a demonstrator. I told of the screams and the crumpling body of the man as two men who had dragged him into a hallway beat him up against the wall, aiming well-directed blows at his face, smashing it to a pulp.

We protested this to the Police Commissioner, and our protest was respected and acted upon.

We are repeating the protest against the Chicago massacre because the only way to stop such brutality is to arouse a storm of protest against it

On whom shall the blame be laid for such a horrible spectacle of violence? Of course, the police and the press in many cases lay the blame on the strikers. But I have lived with these people, I have eaten with them and talked to them day after day. Many of them have never been in a strike before, many of them were marching in the picket line, as in a supplicatory procession, for the first time in their lives. They even brought children on that line in Chicago.

Shall we blame only the police? Or shall we blame just Tom Girdler of the Republic Steel Company? God knows how he can sleep comfortably in his bed at night with the cries of those strikers, of their wives and children, in his ears. He may not hear them now in the heat of battle, but he will hear them, as there is a just God.

Or shall we blame the press, the pulpit, and all those agencies who form public opinion, who have neglected to raise up their voices in protest at injustice and so have permitted it? In some cases the press have even instigated it so that it would come to pass. Inflammatory, hysterical headlines about mobs, about expected riots, do much to arouse the temper of the police to prepare them for just what occurred. The calm, seemingly reasonable stories of such papers as the *Herald Tribune* and the *Times,* emphasizing the violence and the expectation of violence, do much to prepare the public to accept such violence when it comes to pass.

In that case we all are guilty inasmuch as we have not "gone to the workingman" as the Holy Father pleads and repeats. Inasmuch as we have not inclined our hearts to him, and sought to incline his to us, so that we could work together for peace instead of war, inasmuch as we have not protested such murder as was committed in Chicago—then we are guilty.

One more sin, suffering Christ, worker Yourself, for You to bear. In the garden of Gethsemane, You bore the sins of all the world—You took them on Yourself, the sins of those police, the sins of the Girdlers and the Schwabs, of the

Graces of this world. In committing them, whether ignorantly or of their own free will, they piled them on Your shoulders, bowed to the ground with the weight of the guilt of the world, which You assumed because You loved each of us so much. You took them on Yourself, and You died to save us all. Your Precious Blood was shed even for that policeman whose cudgel smashed again and again the skull of that poor striker, whose brains lay splattered on the undertaker's slab.

And the sufferings of those strikers' wives and children are completing Your suffering today.

Have pity on us all, Jesus of Gethsemane—on Tom Girdler, those police, the souls of the strikers, as well as on all of us who have not worked enough for "a new heaven and a new earth wherein justice dwelleth."

FOR FURTHER READING

Day, Dorothy. *Loaves and Fishes.* New York: Harper and Row, 1963. Reprint, Maryknoll, N.Y.: Orbis Books, 1997.
———. *The Long Loneliness: An Autobiography.* 1952; New York: Harper and Row, 1997.
Ellsberg, Robert. Introduction to *Dorothy Day: Selected Writings,* by Dorothy Day. Maryknoll, N.Y.: Orbis Books, 1992.

Virginia Woolf

1882–1941

"A woman must have money and a room of her own if she is to write," declared Virginia Woolf in *A Room of One's Own* in 1929 (4). She was referring to the writing of fiction in this famous line, but her words speak to the many forms of women's writing in this anthology, as well to women's struggles to claim a voice. Now seen as one of the foremothers of feminist theories of writing, Woolf was both a novelist and a critic, one of the few women authors admitted to the canon of modern literature as early the 1930s. She did have money and a room of her own. Educated at home by her father, Sir Leslie Stephen, she married Leonard Woolf in 1912, and in 1917 they founded the Hogarth Press, which published her books.

In all her fiction, Woolf experimented with time, consciousness, and setting. In *Mrs. Dalloway* (1925) and *To the Lighthouse* (1927), her most famous novels, Woolf plays with present and past in order to convey a more realistic sense of how people's minds and emotions work on ideas and feelings and how circumstances affect consciousness. Woolf struggled with her own mind all her life. In 1941, when the mental illness she had fought for years returned, she drowned herself in the Ouse River near her cottage in Rodnell, England.

In *A Room of One's Own*, Woolf imagines that Shakespeare had a sister, as talented a writer as her brother, but "alas, she never wrote a word" (117). But Woolf concludes by saying that Shakespeare's sister "lives in you and in me, and in many other women who are not here tonight, for they are washing up the dishes and putting the children to bed" (117). She predicted that "continuing presences" like this phantom poet could live again "if we have the habit of freedom and the courage to write exactly what we think. . . . I maintain that she would come again if we worked for her" (117). "Professions for Women," originally delivered to the Women's Service League, describes what such work entails. In this essay, Woolf discusses two "adventures" in her professional life as a writer. She describes herself with a "bedroom and an inkpot" (two things Shakespeare's sister did not own) but still argues that in order to write, she must complete two more important tasks. She must first "kill the Angel in the House"—the "phantom" who lures her into the cult of true womanhood; into self-sacrifice, self-deprecation; and above all, into hiding the fact that she has her own mind. Readers may find traces of this Angel in many of the other selections in this anthology; claiming the right to speak, throughout the centuries, has remained a formidable obstacle for a woman rhetor.

Woolf describes her success in murdering this Angel, but she still faces a second, more daunting obstacle: "telling the truth about my own experiences as a body." Hauntingly, she raises this topic—"something about the body, about the passions. Which it was unfitting for a woman to say"—and lets it go just as quickly. Woolf speculates that the "extreme conventionality" of men, who participate in ideals of true womanhood, inhibits women from writing exactly what they experience. Yet, as Alice Walker points out in "In Search of Our Mothers' Gardens," Woolf ignores other barriers to women's writing, particularly writing by women of color. In tentatively laying out one of the early statements of women's rhetorical theory, she also struggles with her own meaning in this essay (as Adrienne Rich points out in "When We Dead Awaken"), finding the problems of writing about her own body difficult even to define and groping for words in which to express the obstacles she faces. However tentative she is, though, Woolf was one of the first women rhetors to suggest that women must "write the body" in order to forge weapons against Angels in the House—or the School, the Media, the Marketplace, or the Profession.

"Professions for Women"

1942

When your secretary invited me to come here, she told me that your Society is concerned with the employment of women and she suggested that I might tell you something about my own professional experiences. It is true I am a woman; it is true I am employed; but what professional experiences have I had? It is difficult to say. My profession is literature; and in that profession there are fewer experiences for women than in any other, with the exception of the stage— fewer, I mean, that are peculiar to women. For the road was cut many years ago—by Fanny Burney, by Aphra Behn, by Harriet Martineau, by Jane Austen, by George Eliot—many famous women, and many more unknown and forgotten, have been before me, making the path smooth, and regulating my steps. Thus, when I came to write, there were very few material obstacles in my way. Writing was a reputable and harmless occupation. The family peace was not broken by the scratching of a pen. No demand was made upon the family purse. For ten and sixpence one can buy paper enough to write all the plays of Shakespeare—if one has a mind that way. Pianos and models, Paris, Vienna and Berlin, masters and mistresses, are not needed by a writer. The cheapness of writing paper is, of course, the reason why women have succeeded as writers before they have succeeded in the other professions.

But to tell you my story—it is a simple one. You have only got to figure to yourselves a girl in a bedroom with a pen in her hand. She had only to move that pen from left to right—from ten o'clock to one. Then it occurred to her to do what is simple and cheap enough after all—to slip a few of those pages into an envelope, fix a penny stamp in the corner, and drop the envelope into the red box at the corner. It was thus that I became a journalist; and my effort was rewarded on the first day of the following month—a very glorious day it was for me—by a letter from an editor containing a cheque for one pound ten shillings and sixpence. But to show you how little I deserve to be called a professional woman, how little I know of the struggles and difficulties of such lives, I have to admit that instead of spending that sum upon bread and butter, rent, shoes and stockings, or butcher's bills, I went out and bought a cat—a beautiful cat, a Persian cat, which very soon involved me in bitter disputes with my neighbours.

What could be easier than to write articles and to buy Persian cats with the profits? But wait a moment. Articles have to be about something. Mine, I seem to remember, was about a novel by a famous man. And while I was writing this review, I discovered that if I were going to review books I should need to do battle with a certain phantom. And the phantom was a woman, and when I came to know her better I called her after the heroine of a famous poem, The Angel in the House. It was she who used to come between me and my paper when I was writing reviews. It was she who bothered me and wasted my time and so tormented me that at last I killed her. You who come of a younger and happier generation may not have heard of her—you may not know what I mean by the Angel in the House. I will describe her as shortly as I can. She was intensely sympathetic. She was immensely charming. She was utterly unselfish. She excelled in the difficult arts of family life. She sacrificed herself daily. If there was chicken, she took the leg; if there was a draught she sat in it—in short she was so constituted that she never had a mind or a wish of her own, but preferred to sympathize always with the minds and wishes of others. Above all—I need not say it—she was pure. Her purity was supposed to be her chief beauty—her blushes, her great grace. In those days—the last of Queen Victoria—every house had its Angel. And when I came to write I encountered her with the very first words. The shadow of her wings fell on my page; I heard the rustling of her skirts in the room. Directly, that is to say, I took my pen in hand to review that novel by a famous man, she slipped behind me and whispered: "My dear, you are a young woman. You are writing about a book that has been written by a man. Be sympathetic; be tender; flatter; deceive; use all the arts and wiles of our sex. Never let anybody guess that you have a mind of your own. Above all, be pure." And she made as if to guide my pen. I now record the one act for which I take some credit to myself, though the credit rightly belongs to some excellent ancestors of mine who left me a certain sum of money—shall we say five hundred pounds a year?—so that it was not necessary for me to depend solely on charm for my living. I turned upon her and caught her by the throat. I did my best to kill her. My excuse, if I were to be had up in a court of law, would be that I acted in self-defence. Had I not killed her she would have killed me. She would have plucked the heart out of my writing. For, as I found, directly I put pen to paper, you cannot review even a novel without having a mind of your own, without expressing what you think to be the truth about human relations, morality, sex. And all these questions, according to the Angel in the House, cannot be dealt with freely and openly by women; they must charm, they must conciliate, they must—to put it bluntly—tell lies if they are to succeed. Thus, whenever I felt the shadow of her wing or the radiance of her halo upon my page, I took up the inkpot and flung it at her. She died hard. Her fictitious nature was of great assistance to her. It is far harder to kill a phantom than a reality. She was always creeping back when I thought I had despatched her. Though I flatter myself that I killed her in the end, the struggle was severe; it took much time that had better have been spent upon learning Greek grammar; or in roaming the world in search of adventures. But it was a real experience; it was an experience that was bound to befall all women writers at that time. Killing the Angel in the House was part of the occupation of a woman writer.

But to continue my story. The Angel was dead; what then remained? You may say that what remained was a simple and common object—a young woman in a bedroom with an inkpot. In other words, now that she had rid herself of falsehood, that young woman had only to be herself. Ah, but what is "herself"? I mean, what is a woman? I assure you, I do not know. I do not believe that you know. I do not believe that anybody can know until she has expressed herself in all the arts and professions open to human skill. That indeed is one of the reasons why I have come here—out of respect for you, who are in process of showing us by your experiments what a woman is, who are in process of providing us, by your failures and successes, with that extremely important piece of information.

But to continue the story of my professional experiences. I made one pound ten and six by my first review; and I bought a Persian cat with the proceeds. Then I grew ambitious. A Persian cat is all very well, I said; but a Persian cat is not enough. I must have a motor car. And it was thus that I became a novelist— for it is a very strange thing that people will give you a motor car if you will tell them a story. It is a still stranger thing that there is nothing so delightful in the world as telling stories. It is far pleasanter than writing reviews of famous novels. And yet, if I am to obey your secretary and tell you my professional experiences as a novelist, I must tell you about a very strange experience that befell me as a novelist. And to understand it you must try first to imagine a novelist's state of mind. I hope I am not giving away professional secrets if I say that a novelist's chief desire is to be as unconscious as possible. He has to induce in himself a state of perpetual lethargy. He wants life to proceed with the utmost quiet and regularity. He wants to see the same faces, to read the same books, to do the same things day after day, month after month, while he is writing, so that nothing may break the illusion in which he is living—so that nothing may disturb or disquiet the mysterious nosings about, feelings round, darts, dashes and sudden discoveries of that very shy and illusive spirit, the imagination. I suspect that this state is the same both for men and women. Be that as it may, I want you to imagine me writing a novel in a state of trance. I want you to figure to yourselves a girl sitting with a pen in her hand, which for minutes, and indeed for hours, she never dips into the inkpot. The image that comes to my mind when I think of this girl is the image of a fisherman lying sunk in dreams on the verge of a deep lake with a rod held out over the water. She was letting her imagination sweep unchecked round every rock and cranny of the world that lies submerged in the depths of our unconscious being. Now came the experience, the experience that I believe to be far commoner with women writers than with men. The line raced through the girl's fingers. Her imagination had rushed away. It had sought the pools, and depths, the dark places where the largest fish slumber. And then there was a smash. There was an explosion. There was foam and confusion. The imagination had dashed itself against something hard. The girl was roused from her dream. She was indeed in a state of the most acute and difficult distress. To speak without figure she had thought of something, something about the body, about the passions which it was unfitting for her as a woman to say. Men, her reason told her, would be shocked. The consciousness of what men will say of a woman who speaks the truth about her passions had roused her from her artist's state of unconsciousness. She could write no more. The trance was over. Her imagination could work no longer. This I believe to be a very common experience with women writers—they are impeded by the extreme conventionality of the other sex. For though men sensibly allow themselves great freedom in these respects, I doubt that they realize or can control the extreme severity with which they condemn such freedom in women.

These then were two very genuine experiences of my own. These were two of the adventures of my professional life. The first—killing the Angel in the House—I think I solved. She died. But the second, telling the truth about my own experiences as a body, I do not think I solved. I doubt that any woman has solved it yet. The obstacles against her are still immensely powerful—and yet they are very difficult to define. Outwardly, what is simpler than to write books? Outwardly, what obstacles are there for a woman rather than for a man? Inwardly, I think, the case is very different; she has still many ghosts to fight, many prejudices to overcome. Indeed it will be a long time still, I think, before a woman can sit down to write a book without finding a phantom to be slain, a rock to be dashed against. And if this is so in literature, the freest of all professions for women, how is it in the new professions which you are now for the first time entering?

Those are the questions that I should like, had I time, to ask you. And indeed, if I have laid stress upon these professional experiences of mine, it is because I believe that they are, though in different forms, yours also. Even when the path is nominally open—when there is nothing to prevent a woman from being a doctor, a lawyer, a civil servant—there are many phantoms and obstacles, as I believe, looming in her way. To discuss and define them is I think of great value and importance; for thus only can the labour be shared, the difficulties be solved. But besides this, it is necessary also to discuss the ends and the aims for which we are fighting, for which we are doing battle with these formidable obstacles. Those aims cannot be taken for granted; they must be perpetually questioned and examined. The whole position, as I see it—here in this hall surrounded by women practising for the first time in history I know not how many different professions—is one of extraordinary interest and importance. You have won rooms of your own in the house hitherto exclusively owned by men. You are able, though not without great labour and effort, to pay the rent. You are earning your five hundred pounds a year. But this freedom is only a beginning; the room is your own, but it is still bare. It has to be furnished; it has to be decorated; it has to be shared. How are you going to furnish it, how are you going to decorate it? With whom are you going to share it, and upon what terms? These, I think are questions of the utmost importance and interest. For the first time in history you are able to ask them; for the first time you are able to decide for yourselves what the answers should be. Willingly would I stay and discuss those questions and answers—but not tonight. My time is up; and I must cease.

FOR FURTHER READING

Ratcliffe, Krista. *Anglo-American Challenges to the Rhetorical Tradition: Virginia Woolf, Mary Daly, and Adrienne Rich.* Carbondale: Southern Illinois University Press, 1996.

Walker, Alice. "In Search of Our Mothers' Gardens." In *In Search of Our Mothers' Gardens: Womanist Prose,* 231–43. New York: Harcourt Brace Jovanovich, 1974.

Woolf, Virginia. *The Common Reader.* New York: Harcourt Brace, 1925.

———. *The Diary of Virginia Woolf.* Edited by Anne Oliver Bell. Introduction by Quentin Bell. London: Hogarth Press, 1977. New York: Harcourt Brace Jovanovich, 1984.

———. *Flight of the Mind: The Letters of Virginia Woolf.* Edited by Nigel Nicolson. New York : Harcourt Brace Jovanovich, 1975.

———. *A Room of One's Own.* New York: Harcourt, Brace and Co., 1929.

———. *The Second Common Reader.* New York: Harcourt, Brace and Co., 1932.

———. *Three Guineas.* New York, Harcourt, Brace and Co., 1938.

Zora Neale Hurston

1901 (?)–1960

Alice Walker says of Zora Neale Hurston's 1937 novel *Their Eyes Were Watching God*, "There is no book more important to me than this one" (86). A novelist, anthropologist, folklorist, journalist, critic, and autobiographer, Hurston was the most prolific African American woman writing between 1920 and 1950. She paved the way for later writers such as Toni Morrison and Walker herself, yet she died in poverty and obscurity, buried in 1960 in a grave that was unmarked until Walker placed a memorial stone there in 1973. Her sensuous imagery, drawn from what bell hooks would call her "homeplace"; her insistence that writers capture the sense of their subjects; and her raucous sense of humor took her on a roller-coaster ride from fame to obscurity and, after her death, back again to fame.

During her life Zora Neale Hurston claimed her birth date as January 7, 1901, and her birthplace as Eatonville, Florida, although there is some evidence that she was actually born ten years earlier in Alabama. When she was very young, in any case, her family moved to all-black Eatonville, and this location influenced all her writing. Her father, a carpenter and a preacher, served as mayor of Eatonville. Her mother died in 1904. Soon after, Hurston joined a traveling theatrical company and finished high school in Baltimore. Hurston entered Howard University in 1920 and studied there off and on for the next four years while working as a manicurist to support herself. In the later 1920s, she moved to New York City during the height of the flourishing of African American arts and culture known as the Harlem Renaissance. Here she became part of that Renaissance, coauthoring the play *Mule Bone* with Langston Hughes and writing her first novel, *Jonah's Gourd Vine*.

Hurston also took classes at Barnard College, studying anthropology under the renowned scholar Franz Boas. She specialized in folklore, and her hometown provided her both with data for scholarly study and with rich material for her fiction and commentary. In her fieldwork in anthropology, Hurston interviewed storytellers in Florida and voodoo doctors in Haiti, all of which would feed into her writing. In her second book, *Mules and Men*, Hurston published the material she had found in her trips in the South. Like Ruth Behar, Hurston insisted that anthropology and folklore must capture the richness of a culture and represent the feel of subjects in context rather than report from an objective, scientific stance.

Hurston always made her position as a writer clear, using her voice itself as one of her most powerful methods of argument—in any genre. Her political commentary, "Crazy for This Democracy" reveals Hurston's feisty tone, her ironic humor, and her willingness to speak from her own unique position. Playing off the "democratic" frenzy that accompanied the U.S. victories in 1945, Hurston uses an ironic logical appeal to suggest that the "arsenal" (or as she terms it, "ass-and-all") of democracy be commandeered for all U.S. citizens. Her arguments are logical, but Hurston was savvy enough to know that she was facing an illogical monster in racism; her biting sarcasm makes her own voice, her *ethos*, carry the weight of her argument—no small feat for working-class African American woman at the end of World War II. Moreover, Hurston's sense of audience in this text is expansive; her call for repeal of the Jim Crow laws speaks not only to the Southern United States but to the world.

"Crazy for This Democracy"

1945

They tell me this democracy form of government is a wonderful thing. It has freedom, equality, justice, in short, everything! Since 1937 nobody has talked about anything else.

The late Franklin D. Roosevelt sort of re-decorated it, and called these United States the boastful name of "The Arsenal of Democracy."

The radio, the newspapers, and the columnists inside the newspapers, have said how lovely it was.

All this talk and praise-giving has got me in the notion to try some of the stuff. All I want to do is to get hold of a sample of the thing, and I declare, I sure will try it. I don't know for myself, but I have been told that it is really wonderful.

Like the late Will Rogers, all I know is what I see by the papers. It seems like now, I do not know geography as well as I ought to, or I would not get the wrong idea about so many things. I heard so much about "global" "world-freedom" and things like that, that I must have gotten mixed up about oceans.

I thought that when they said Atlantic Charter, that meant me and everybody in Africa and Asia and everywhere. But it seems like the Atlantic is an ocean that does not touch anywhere but North America and Europe.

Just the other day, seeing how things were going in Asia, I went out and bought myself an atlas and found out how narrow this Atlantic ocean was. No wonder that those Four Freedoms couldn't get no further than they did! Why, that poor little ocean can't even wash up some things right here in America, let

Reprinted from Hurston, Zora Neale. "Crazy for This Democracy." *The Negro Digest* (December 1945): 45–48. Used with the kind permission of the estate of Zora Neale Hurston.

alone places like India, Burma, Indo-China, and the Netherlands East Indies. We need two more whole oceans for that.

Maybe, I need to go out and buy me a dictionary, too. Or perhaps a spelling-book would help me out a lot. Or it could be that I just mistook the words. Maybe I mistook a British pronunciation for a plain American word. Did F.D.R., aristocrat from Groton and Harvard, using the British language say "arse-and-all" of Democracy when I thought he said plain arsenal? Maybe he did, and I have been mistaken all this time. From what is going on, I think that is what he must have said.

That must be what he said, for from what is happening over on that other, unmentioned ocean, we look like the Ass-and-All of Democracy. Our weapons, money, and the blood of millions of our men have been used to carry the English, French and Dutch and lead them back on the millions of unwilling Asiatics. The Ass-and-all-he-has has been very useful.

The Indo-Chinese are fighting the French now in Indo-China to keep the freedom that they have enjoyed for five or six years now. The Indonesians are trying to stay free from the Dutch, and the Burmese and Malayans from the British.

But American soldiers and sailors are fighting along with the French, Dutch and English to rivet these chains back on their former slaves. How can we so admire the fire and determination of Toussaint Louverture to resist the orders of Napoleon to "Rip the gold braids off those Haitian slaves and put them back to work" after four years of freedom, and be indifferent to these Asiatics for the same feelings under the same circumstances?

Have we not noted that not one word has been uttered about the freedom of the Africans? On the contrary, there have been mutterings in undertones about being fair and giving different nations sources of raw materials there? The Ass-and-All of Democracy has shouldered the load of subjugating the dark world completely.

The only Asiatic power able to offer any effective resistance has been double-teened by the combined powers of the Occident and rendered incapable of offering or encouraging resistance, and likewise removed as an example to the dark people of the world.

The inference is, that God has restated the superiority of the West. God always does like that when a thousand white people surround one dark one. Dark people are always "bad" when they do not admit the Divine Plan like that. A certain Javanese man who sticks up for Indonesian Independence is very low-down by the papers, and suspected of being a Japanese puppet. Wanting the Dutch to go back to Holland and go to work for themselves! The very idea! A very, very bad man, that Javanese.

As for me, I am just as skeptical as this contrary Javanese. I accept this idea of Democracy. I am all for trying it out. It must be a good thing if everybody

praises it like that. If our government has been willing to go to war and to sacrifice billions of dollars and millions of men for the idea, I think that I ought to
give the thing a trial.

The only thing that keeps me from pitching headlong into the thing is the
presence of numerous Jim Crow laws on the statute books of the nation. I am
crazy about the idea of this Democracy. I want to see how it feels. Therefore, I
am all for the repeal of every Jim Crow law in the nation here and now. Not in
another generation or so. The Hurstons have already been waiting eighty years
for that. I want it here and now.

And why not? A lot of people in these United States have been saying all this
time that things ought to be equal. Numerous instances of inequality have been
pointed out, and fought over in the courts and in the newspapers. That seems
like a waste of time to me.

The patient has the small-pox. Segregation and things like that are the
bumps and blisters on the skin, and not the disease, but evidence and symptoms of the sickness. The doctors around the bedside of the patient are desperately picking bumps. Some assume that the opening of one blister will cure the
case. Some strangely assert that a change of climate is all that is needed to kill
the virus in the blood!

But why this sentimental oversimplification in diagnosis? Do the doctors
not know anything about the widespread occurrence of this disease? It is NOT
peculiar to the South. Canada, once the refuge of escaping slaves, has now its
denomination of second-class citizens, and they are the Japanese and other
non-Caucasians. The war cannot explain it, because enemy Germans are not
put in that second class.

Jim Crow is the rule in South Africa, and is even more extensive than in
America. More rigid and grinding. No East Indian may ride first-class in the
trains of British-held India. Jim Crow is common in all colonial Africa, Asia and
the Netherlands East Indies. There, too, a Javanese male is punished for flirting
back at a white female. So why this stupid assumption that "moving North"
will do away with social smallpox? Events in the northern cities do not bear out
this juvenile contention.

So why the waste of good time and energy, and further delay the recovery of
the patient by picking him over bump by bump and blister to blister? Why not
the shot of serum that will kill the thing in the blood? The bumps are symptoms. The symptoms cannot disappear until the cause is cured.

These Jim Crow laws have been put on the books for a purpose, and that purpose is psychological. It has two edges to the thing. By physical evidence, back
seats in trains, backdoors of houses, exclusion from certain places and activities, to promote in the mind of the smallest white child the conviction of First
by Birth, eternal and irrevocable like the place assigned to the Levites by Moses
over the other tribes of the Hebrews. Talent, capabilities, nothing has anything
to do with the case. Just FIRST BY BIRTH.

No one of darker skin can ever be considered an equal. Seeing the daily humiliations of the darker people confirms the child in its superiority, so that it comes to feel it the arrangement of God. By the same means, the smallest dark child is to be convinced of its inferiority, so that it is to be convinced that competition is out of the question, and against all nature and God.

All physical and emotional things flow from this premise. It perpetuates itself. The unnatural exaltation of one ego, and the equally unnatural grinding down of the other. The business of some whites to help pick a bump or so is even part of the pattern. Not a human right, but a concession from the throne has been made. Otherwise why do they not take the attitude of Robert Ingersoll that all of it is wrong? Why the necessity for the little concession? Why not go for the underskin injection? Is it a bargaining with a detail to save the whole intact? It is something to think about.

As for me, I am committed to the hypodermic and the serum. I see no point in the picking of a bump. Others can erupt too easily. That same one can burst out again. Witness the easy scrapping of FEPC. No, I give my hand, my heart and my head to the total struggle. I am for complete repeal of All Jim Crow Laws in the United States once and for all, and right now. For the benefit of this nation and as a precedent to the world.

I have been made to believe in this democracy thing, and I am all for tasting this democracy out. The flavor must be good. If the Occident is so intent in keeping the taste out of darker mouths that it spends all those billions and expends all those millions of lives, colored ones too, to keep it among themselves, then it must be something good. I crave to sample this gorgeous thing. So I cannot say anything different from repeal of all Jim Crow laws! Not in some future generation, but repeal *now* and forever!!

FOR FURTHER READING

Hurston, Zora Neale. *Dust Tracks on a Road: An Autobiography.* Philadelphia: J. B. Lippencott Company, 1942. Reprint, New York: Perennial Library, 1996.

————. *Go Gator and Muddy the Water: Writings by Zora Neale Hurston from the Federal Writers' Project.* Edited by Pamela Bordelon. New York: W. W. Norton and Company, 1999.

————. *I Love Myself When I am Laughing . . . And Then Again When I am Looking Mean and Impressive: A Zora Neale Hurston Reader.* Edited by Alice Walker. New York: The Feminist Press, 1979.

————. *Mules and Men.* Preface by Franz Boas. 1935; Bloomington: Indiana University Press, 1978.

————. *Tell My Horse: Voodoo and Life in Haiti and Jamaica.* 1938; New York: Perennial Library, 1990.

————. *Their Eyes Were Watching God.* New York: Perennial Library, 1990.

Walker, Alice. "Zora Neale Hurston: A Cautionary Tale and Partisan View." In *In Search of Our Mothers' Gardens: Womanist Prose,* 83–92. New York Harcourt Brace Jovanovich, 1974.

Simone de Beauvoir

1908–1986

"One is not born, but rather becomes, a woman" is perhaps the most famous line associated with French feminist existentialist Simone de Beauvoir (*The Second Sex* 301). Written in the late 1940s, *The Second Sex* was one of the philosophical inspirations for the second wave of feminism throughout the world and secured de Beauvoir's place as an outspoken defender of women's rights long before they became a cause in France. *The Second Sex* challenged the belief that innate female traits created "woman" and asserted instead that "woman" is a social construct, not a biological one.

De Beauvoir studied philosophy at the Sorbonne and gained prominence because of her standing on the highly competitive examination, the *agrégation*. She was second only to the philosopher Jean-Paul Sartre. She went on to teach philosophy in Marseilles, Rouen, and Paris, but in 1944 she declared that she was a writer rather than a philosopher. Setting aside philosophy because of its abstractness, de Beauvoir asserted the importance of the reality that exists within the lived experience of people. Her subtle form of existentialism valued the complexity of human experience, especially the ambiguity of human life, which resists essentialism and rigid categories.

When asked what prompted her to begin the study that culminated in *The Second Sex*, de Beauvoir said: "Because I wanted to talk about myself and because I realized that in order to talk about myself I had to understand the fact that I was a woman" (Wenzel 27). Her inquiry became the most comprehensive feminist philosophical/historical/theological treatise available to the contemporary world.

De Beauvoir begins her introduction to *The Second Sex* with the simple question, "What is woman?" She asks why "woman" is perceived and constructed as the "other"—the "second sex"—and demonstrates that biology is not an adequate explanation for the existing sexual hierarchy. Grounded in philosophy, her analysis asserts that human consciousness organizes reality in terms of binaries, the most fundamental of which is the human propensity to set self in opposition to "other." And woman is the "other." De Beauvoir's book not only explains how that position is sustained by patriarchy, but it also explains women's complicity in their own "othering." De Beauvoir is painstakingly thorough in her explanation of her perspective and ideas. Using vivid examples drawn from history, religion, mythology, anthropology, and economics, she outlines then-prevailing biological and philosophical assumptions, or "truths," and then carefully deconstructs them, creating new systems of belief and models of reality. Her existentialist beliefs support her assertion throughout *The Second Sex* that women should be measured not by the limitations and constrictions patriarchy imposes on them but by whom they shall or can become when freed from patriarchy.

Although she spent her life in the shadow of the philosopher Jean-Paul Sartre, many scholars believe that in the breadth of her thought in both *Ethics of Ambiguity* and *The Second Sex* de Beauvoir superseded Sartre. She is no longer regarded as "second."

From the Introduction to *The Second Sex*

1952

For a long time I have hesitated to write a book on woman. The subject is irritating, especially to women; and it is not new. Enough ink has been spilled in the quarreling over feminism, now practically over, and perhaps we should say no more about it. It is still talked about, however, for the voluminous nonsense uttered during the last century seems to have done little to illuminate the problem. After all, is there a problem? And if so, what is it? Are there women, really? Most assuredly the theory of the eternal feminine still has its adherents who will whisper in your ear: Even in Russia women still are *women;* and other erudite persons—sometimes the very same—say with a sigh: Woman is losing her way, woman is lost. One wonders if women still exist, if they will always exist, whether or not it is desirable that they should, what place they occupy in this world, what their place should be. What has become of women? was asked recently in an ephemeral magazine.

But first we must ask: what is a woman? *"Tota mulier in utero,"* says one, "woman is a womb." But in speaking of certain women, connoisseurs declare that they are not women, although they are equipped with a uterus like the rest. All agree in recognizing the fact that females exist in the human species; today as always they make up about one half of humanity. And yet we are told that femininity is in danger; we are exhorted to be women, remain women, become women. It would appear, then, that every female human being is not necessarily a woman; to be so considered she must share in that mysterious and threatened reality known as femininity. Is this attribute something secreted by the ovaries? Or is it a Platonic essence, a product of the philosophic imagination? Is a rustling petticoat enough to bring it down to earth? Although some women try zealously to incarnate this essence, it is hardly patentable. It is frequently described in vague and dazzling terms that seem to have been borrowed from the vocabulary of the seers, and indeed in the times of St. Thomas it was considered an essence as certainly defined as the somniferous virtue of the poppy.

But conceptualism has lost ground. The biological and social sciences no longer admit the existence of unchangeably fixed entities that determine given characteristics, such as those ascribed to woman, the Jew, or the Negro. Science regards any characteristic as a reaction dependent in part upon a *situation*. If today femininity no longer exists, then it never existed. But does the word *woman*, then, have no specific content? This is stoutly affirmed by those who hold to the philosophy of the enlightenment, of rationalism, of nominalism; women, to them, are merely the human beings arbitrarily designated by the word *woman*. Many American women particularly are prepared to think that there is no longer any place for woman as such; if a backward individual still takes herself for a woman, her friends advise her to be psychoanalyzed and thus get rid of this obsession. In regard to a work, *Modern Woman: The Lost Sex*, which in other respects has its irritating features, Dorothy Parker has written: "I cannot be just to books which treat of woman as woman . . . My idea is that all of us, men as well as women, should be regarded as human beings." But nominalism is a rather inadequate doctrine, and the antifeminists have had no trouble in showing that women simply *are not* men. Surely woman is, like man, a human being; but such a declaration is abstract. The fact is that every concrete human being is always a singular, separate individual. To decline to accept such notions as the eternal feminine, the black soul, the Jewish character, is not to deny that Jews, Negroes, women exist today—this denial does not represent a liberation for those concerned, but rather a flight from reality. Some years ago a well-known woman writer refused to permit her portrait to appear in a series of photographs especially devoted to women writers; she wished to be counted among the men. But in order to gain this privilege she made use of her husband's influence! Women who assert that they are men lay claim none the less to masculine consideration and respect. I recall also a young Trotskyite standing on a platform at a boisterous meeting and getting ready to use her fists, in spite of her evident fragility. She was denying her feminine weakness; but it was for love of a militant male whose equal she wished to be. The attitude of defiance of many American women proves that they are haunted by a sense of their femininity. In truth, to go for a walk with one's eyes open is enough to demonstrate that humanity is divided into two classes of individuals whose clothes, faces, bodies, smiles, gaits, interests, and occupations are manifestly different. Perhaps these differences are superficial, perhaps they are destined to disappear. What is certain is that right now they do most obviously exist.

If her functioning as a female is not enough to define woman, if we decline

also to explain her through "the eternal feminine," and if nevertheless we admit, provisionally, that women do exist, then we must face the question: what
is a woman?

To state the question is, to me, to suggest, at once, a preliminary answer. The
fact that I ask it is in itself significant. A man would never get the notion of
writing a book on the peculiar situation of the human male. But if I wish to define myself, I must first of all say: "I am a woman"; on this truth must be based
all further discussion. A man never begins by presenting himself as an individual of a certain sex; it goes without saying that he is a man. The terms *masculine*
and *feminine* are used symmetrically only as a matter of form, as on legal papers.
In actuality the relation of the two sexes is not quite like that of two electrical
poles, for man represents both the positive and the neutral, as is indicated by
the common use of man to designate human beings in general; whereas woman
represents only the negative, defined by limiting criteria, without reciprocity.
In the midst of an abstract discussion it is vexing to hear a man say: "You think
thus and so because you are a woman"; but I know that my only defense is to
reply: "I think thus and so because it is true," thereby removing my subjective
self from the argument. It would be out of the question to reply: "And you think
the contrary because you are a man," for it is understood that the fact of being a
man is no peculiarity. A man is in the right in being a man; it is the woman who
is in the wrong. It amounts to this: just as for the ancients there was an absolute
vertical with reference to which the oblique was defined, so there is an absolute
human type, the masculine. Woman has ovaries, a uterus; these peculiarities
imprison her in her subjectivity, circumscribe her within the limits of her own
nature. It is often said that she thinks with her glands. Man superbly ignores
the fact that his anatomy also includes glands, such as the testicles, and that
they secrete hormones. He thinks of his body as a direct and normal connection
with the world, which he believes he apprehends objectively, whereas he regards the body of woman as a hindrance, a prison, weighed down by everything
peculiar to it. "The female is a female by virtue of a certain *lack* of qualities,"
said Aristotle; "we should regard the female nature as afflicted with a natural
defectiveness." And St. Thomas for his part pronounced woman to be an "imperfect man," an "incidental" being. This is symbolized in Genesis where Eve is
depicted as made from what Bossuet called "a supernumerary bone" of Adam.

Thus humanity is male and man defines woman not in herself but as relative
to him; she is not regarded as an autonomous being. Michelet writes: "Woman,
the relative being . . ." And Benda is most positive in his Rapport d' Uriel: "The
body of man makes sense in itself quite apart from that of woman, whereas the
latter seems wanting in significance by itself . . . Man can think of himself without woman. She cannot think of herself without man." And she is simply what
man decrees; thus she is called "the sex," by which is meant that she appears essentially to the male as a sexual being. For him she is sex—absolute sex, no less.

She is defined and differentiated with reference to man and not he with reference to her; she is the incidental, the inessential as opposed to the essential. He is the Subject, he is the Absolute—she is the Other.

The category of the *Other* is as primordial as consciousness itself. In the most primitive societies, in the most ancient mythologies, one finds the expression of a duality—that of the Self and the Other. This duality was not originally attached to the division of the sexes; it was not dependent upon any empirical facts. It is revealed in such works as that of Granet on Chinese thought and those of Dumézil on the East Indies and Rome. The feminine element was at first no more involved in such pairs as Varuna-Mitra, Uranus-Zeus, Sun-Moon, and Day-Night than it was in the contrasts between Good and Evil, lucky and unlucky auspices, right and left, God and Lucifer. Otherness is a fundamental category of human thought.

Thus it is that no group ever sets itself up as the One without at once setting up the Other over against itself. If three travelers chance to occupy the same compartment, that is enough to make vaguely hostile "others" out of all the rest of the passengers on the train. In small-town eyes all persons not belonging to the village are "strangers" and suspect; to the native of a country all who inhabit other countries are "foreigners"; Jews are "different" for the anti-Semite, Negroes are "inferior" for American racists, aborigines are "natives" for colonists, proletarians are the "lower class" for the privileged.

Lévi-Strauss, at the end of a profound work on the various forms of primitive societies, reaches the following conclusion: "Passage from the state of Nature to the state of Culture is marked by man's ability to view biological relations as a series of contrasts; duality, alteration, opposition, and symmetry, whether under definite or vague forms, constitute not so much phenomena to be explained as fundamental and immediately given data of social reality." These phenomena would be incomprehensible if in fact human society were simply a *Mitsein* or fellowship based on solidarity and friendliness. Things become clear, on the contrary, if, following Hegel, we find in consciousness itself a fundamental hostility toward every other consciousness; the subject can be posed only in being opposed—he sets himself up as the essential, as opposed to the other, the inessential, the object.

But the other consciousness, the other ego, sets up a reciprocal claim. The native traveling abroad is shocked to find himself in turn regarded as a "stranger" by the natives of neighboring countries. As a matter of fact, wars, festivals, trading, treaties, and contests among tribes, nations, and classes tend to deprive the concept *Other* of its absolute sense and to make manifest its relativity; willy-nilly, individuals and groups are forced to realize the reciprocity of their relations. How is it, then, that this reciprocity has not been recognized between the sexes, that one of the contrasting terms is set up as the sole essential, denying any relativity in regard to its correlative and defining the latter as pure otherness? Why is it that women do not dispute male sovereignty? No subject will readily volunteer to become the object, the inessential; it is not the Other who, in defining himself as the Other, establishes the One. The Other is posed as such by the One in defining himself as the One. But if the Other is not to regain the status of being the One, he must be submissive enough to accept this alien point of view. Whence comes this submission in the case of woman?

The reason for this is that women lack concrete means for organizing them-selves into a unit which can stand face to face with the correlative unit. They have no past, no history, no religion of their own; and they have no such soli-darity of work and interest as that of the proletariat. They are not even promis-cuously herded together in the way that creates community feeling among the American Negroes, the ghetto Jews, the workers of Saint-Denis, or the factory hands of Renault. They live dispersed among the males, attached through res-idence, housework, economic condition, and social standing to certain men—fathers or husbands—more firmly than they are to other women. . . . The bond that unites her to her oppressors is not comparable to any other. The division of the sexes is a biological fact, not an event in human history. Male and female stand opposed within a primordial *Mitsein*, and woman has not broken it. The couple is a fundamental unity with its two halves riveted together, and the cleavage of society along the line of sex is impossible. Here is to be found the basic trait of woman: she is the Other in a totality of which the two compo-nents are necessary to one another.

One could suppose that this reciprocity might have facilitated the liberation of woman. . . . In truth woman has not been socially emancipated through man's need—sexual desire and the desire for offspring—which makes the male dependent for satisfaction upon the female.

And even today woman is heavily handicapped though her situation is be-ginning to change. Almost nowhere is her legal status the same as man's, and frequently it is much to her disadvantage. Even when her rights are legally rec-ognized in the abstract, long-standing custom prevents their full expression in mores. . . . To decline to be the Other, to refuse to be party to the deal—this would be for women to renounce all the advantages conferred upon them by their alliance with the superior caste. Man-the-sovereign will provide woman-the-liege with material protection and will undertake the moral justification of her existence; thus she can evade at once both economic risk and the meta-physical risk of a liberty in which ends and aims must be contrived without as-sistance. . . . But it is an easy road; on it one avoids the strain involved in under-taking an authentic existence. When man makes woman the *Other*, he may, then, expect her to manifest deep-seated tendencies toward complicity. Thus, woman may fail to lay claim to the status of subject because she lacks definite resources, because she feels the necessary bond that ties her to man regardless of reciprocity, and because she is often very well pleased with her role as the *Other*.

FOR FURTHER READING

de Beauvoir, Simone. *Adieu: A Farewell to Sartre*. New York: Pantheon Books, 1984.
———. *The Ethics of Ambiguity*. Translated by Bernard Frechtman. New York: Citadel Press, 1970.
———. *Memoirs of a Dutiful Daughter*. Cleveland: World Publishing Company, 1959.
Moi, Toril. *Simone de Beauvoir: The Making of an Intellectual Woman*. Oxford: Blackwell, 1994.
———. *What Is a Woman? And Other Essays*. Oxford: Oxford University Press, 1999.
Wenzel, Helene Vivienne. *Simone de Beauvoir: Witness to a Century*. New Haven: Yale University Press, 1986.

Rachel Carson

1907–1964

When Carson testified before Congress in 1963 on the dangers of pesticides, Senator Abraham Ribicoff welcomed her by noting, "Miss Carson, you are the lady who started all this" (Gore xix). Ribicoff's greeting almost exactly echoes the words uttered by President Abraham Lincoln to Harriet Beecher Stowe in the White House one hundred years earlier. The impact of Rachel Carson's 1962 book, *Silent Spring*, has often been compared to the impact Stowe's *Uncle Tom's Cabin* had as a harbinger of social change. While Rachel Carson has earned a spot as a pioneer in the environmental movement, the writing and speeches she left behind also reveal a very strong, sophisticated rhetor.

Born in 1907 in Springdale, Pennsylvania, Carson received from her mother a lifelong love of nature. After earning a degree in marine biology from the Pennsylvania College for Women in 1929, she studied at the Woods Hole Marine Biological Laboratory and earned an M.A. in zoology from Johns Hopkins University in 1932. For several years she worked for the federal government as a scientist and editor for the U.S. Fish and Wildlife Service, wrote pamphlets on environmental conservation, and wrote feature articles on natural history for the *Baltimore Sun*. In the decade following World War II, Carson became increasingly disturbed by profligate use of chemical pesticides and subsequently turned her focus to warning the public about the dangers of these pesticides. The result was *Silent Spring*, a book that challenged the practices of agricultural scientists and the government. Carson was attacked by the chemical industry and by some in the government as an alarmist, but she courageously spoke out. She testified to Congress in 1963, calling for new policies to protect human health and the environment. She died in 1964 after a long battle with cancer.

The excerpt included here is chapter 1 of *Silent Spring*, "A Fable for Tomorrow." Carson shows a sophisticated grasp of multiple modes of persuasion. She uses the fable as a rhetorical device to make an emotional appeal that will draw nonscientist readers into her argument about the importance of the delicate balance of nature. Here, she also juxtaposes sound and silence to reinforce her purpose: to expose the chemical industry and to break through the "silence" of the American people, government, and businesses on the dangers of pesticides.

"A Fable for Tomorrow"

1962

There was once a town in the heart of America where all life seemed to live in harmony with its surroundings. The town lay in the midst of a checkerboard of prosperous farms, with fields of grain and hillsides of orchards where, in spring, white clouds of bloom drifted above the green fields. In autumn, oak and maple and birch set up a blaze of color that flamed and flickered across a backdrop of pines. Then foxes barked in the hills and deer silently crossed the fields, half hidden in the mists of the fall mornings.

Along the roads, laurel, viburnum and alder, great ferns and wildflowers delighted the traveler's eye through much of the year. Even in winter the roadsides were places of beauty, where countless birds came to feed on the berries and on the seed heads of the dried weeds rising above the snow. The countryside was, in fact, famous for the abundance and variety of its bird life, and when the flood of migrants was pouring through in spring and fall people traveled from great distances to observe them. Others came to fish the streams, which flowed clear and cold out of the hills and contained shady pools where trout lay. So it had been from the days many years ago when the first settlers raised their houses, sank their wells, and built their barns.

Then a strange blight crept over the area and everything began to change. Some evil spell had settled on the community: mysterious maladies swept the flocks of chickens; the cattle and sheep sickened and died. Everywhere was a shadow of death. The farmers spoke of much illness among their families. In the town the doctors had become more and more puzzled by new kinds of sickness appearing among their patients. There had been several sudden and unexplained deaths, not only among adults but even among children, who would be stricken suddenly while at play and die within a few hours.

There was a strange stillness. The birds, for example—where had they gone? Many people spoke of them, puzzled and disturbed. The feeding stations in the backyards were deserted. The few birds seen anywhere were moribund; they trembled violently and could not fly. It was a spring without voices. On the mornings that had once throbbed with the dawn chorus of robins, catbirds, doves, jays, wrens, and scores of other bird voices there was now no sound; only silence lay over the fields and woods and marsh.

On the farms the hens brooded, but no chicks hatched. The farmers complained that they were unable to raise any pigs—the litters were small and the young survived only a few days. The apple trees were coming into bloom but no bees droned among the blossoms, so there was no pollination and there would be no fruit.

The roadsides, once so attractive, were now lined with browned and withered vegetation as though swept by fire. These, too, were silent, deserted by all living things. Even the streams were now lifeless. Anglers no longer visited them, for all the fish had died.

In the gutters under the eaves and between the shingles of the roofs, a white granular powder still showed a few patches; some weeks before it had fallen like snow upon the roofs and the lawns, the fields and streams.

No witchcraft, no enemy action had silenced the rebirth of new life in this stricken world. The people had done it themselves.

This town does not actually exist, but it might easily have a thousand counterparts in America or elsewhere in the world. I know of no community that has experienced all the misfortunes I describe. Yet every one of these disasters has actually happened somewhere, and many real communities have already suffered a substantial number of them. A grim specter has crept upon us almost unnoticed, and this imagined tragedy may easily become a stark reality we all shall know.

What has already silenced the voices of spring in countless towns in America? This book is an attempt to explain.

FOR FURTHER READING

Carson, Rachel. *The Edge of the Sea*. Boston: Houghton Mifflin, 1955.
————. *Lost Woods: The Discovered Writing of Rachel Carson*. Edited by Linda Lear. Boston: Beacon Press, 1998.
————. *The Sea Around Us*. 1951; New York: Oxford University Press, 1991.
————. *The Sense of Wonder*. 1965; New York: Harper Collins, 1998.
Freeman, Martha, ed. *Always, Rachel: The Letters of Rachel Carson and Dorothy Freeman, 1952–1964*. Boston: Beacon Press, 1995.
Gore, Albert. Introduction to *Silent Spring*, by Rachel Carson, xv–xxvi. Boston: Houghton Mifflin, 1994.
Lear, Linda. *Rachel Carson: Witness for Nature*. New York: Henry Holt, 1997.
Waddell, Craig, ed. *And No Birds Sing: Rhetorical Analyses of Silent Spring*. Carbondale: Southern Illinois University Press, 2000.

Fannie Lou Hamer

1917–1977

Fannie Lou Hamer's headstone displays her most famous remark: "I am sick and tired of being sick and tired." These words capture the typically blunt and candid speaking style of a woman who had good reason to be sick and tired. She started picking cotton at the age of six, working in the fields until she was fired at the age of forty-five for registering to vote in the state of Mississippi. At that time voter reading and writing tests existed to prevent poor, uneducated blacks from registering and voting. Hamer failed the written tests two times before she was allowed to register. In the fall of 1963, when Hamer went to vote for the first time, she was again denied her right because she did not have the money to pay the poll tax.

From that point, Hamer became a tireless grassroots activist who worked for integration, civil rights, and the poor in her home county and the world. For her efforts at integrating restaurants and registering voters, she was repeatedly jailed and beaten while in police custody. Hamer suffered permanent damage to her feet, her kidneys, and one eye from police beatings. One of the most vivid images of the Civil Rights Movement is from a black-and-white newsreel of Hamer, recently released from jail and on her way to a civil rights rally. The film clip shows her standing strong, head tipped back to display her swollen black-and-blue face, singing "This Little Light of Mine."

Hamer, denied a formal education because of poverty and the color of her skin, came to symbolize the strength, perseverance, and communal work of the Civil Rights Movement. As a field leader for the Student Nonviolent Coordinating Committee, she helped organize the Mississippi Democratic Freedom Party, an organization committed to challenging white domination of the Democratic Party. She was one of its spokespersons at the 1964 Democratic National Convention in Atlantic City, where the M.D.F.P. challenged the all-white delegation and raised the issue of Southern Jim Crow culture in the international arena. She ran for Congress in Mississippi that same year, receiving over thirty thousand votes. Hamer also devoted a good deal of her physical and rhetorical energy to the Freedom Farmers Cooperative in Mississippi, which was dedicated to ensuring housing and land to farm for the poor in her rural area.

In this speech, delivered to the NAACP Legal Defense Fund, Hamer uses her characteristic no-nonsense rhetoric—always with a spoken and down-to-earth tone—to, in the words of 1971, "tell it like it is." She speaks first to white women, who, she says, have been persuaded that they are "angels" who deserve their privileges, telling them the truth about the costs of those privileges. She also has a message for black women: that they should not to be lured into thinking that their problem is liberation from black men but should work for liberation from racism and poverty. Hamer uses humor and candid language to talk straight about the most crucial issues—issues that are often glossed over in a rhetoric of unity and common purpose. She leaves both groups of women in her audience with the message that they alone are responsible for their actions, using the same well-known African American folk story that Toni Morrison used in her Nobel Prize acceptance speech.

"The Special Plight and the Role of The Black Woman"

1971

The special plight and the role of black women is not something that just happened three years ago. We've had a special plight for 350 years. My grandmother had it. My grandmother was a slave. She died in 1960. She was 136 years old. She died in Mount Bayou, Mississippi.

It's been a special plight for the black woman. I remember my uncles and some of my aunts—and that's why it really tickled me when you talked about integration. Because I'm very black, but I remember some of my uncles and some of my aunts was as white as anybody in here, and blue-eyed, and some kind of green-eyed—and my grandfather didn't do it, you know. So what the folks is fighting at this point is what they started. They started unloading the slave ships of Africa, that's when they started. And right now, sometimes, you know I work for the liberation of all people, because when I liberate myself, I'm liberating other people. But you know, sometimes I really feel more sorrier for the white woman than I feel for ourselves because she been caught up in this thing, caught up feeling very special, and folks, I'm going to put it on the line, because my job is not to make people feel comfortable—(drowned out by applause). You've been caught up in this thing because, you know, you worked my grandmother, and after that you worked my mother, and then finally you got hold of me. And you really thought, people—you might try and cool it now, but I been watching you, baby. You thought that you was *more* because you was a woman, and especially a white woman, you had this kind of angel feeling that you were untouchable. You know that? There's nothing under the sun that made you believe that you was just like me, that under this white pigment of skin is red blood, just like under this black skin of mine. So we was used as black women over and over and over. You know, I remember a time when I was working around white people's house, and one thing that would make me mad

Reprinted from Hamer, Fannie Lou. "The Special Plight and the Role of Black Woman." Speech given at NAACP Legal Defense Fund Institute, New York City, 7 May 1971.

as hell, after I would be done slaved all day long, this white woman would get on the phone, calling some of her friends, and said, "You know, I'm tired, because *we* have been working," and I said, "That's a damn lie." You're not used to that kind of language, honey, but I'm gone tell you where it's *at*. So all of these things was happening because you *had* more. You had been put on a pedestal, and then not only put on a pedestal, but you had been put in something like a ivory castle. So what happened to you, we have busted the castle open and whacking like hell for the pedestal. And when you hit the ground, you're gone have to fight like hell, like we've been fighting all this time.

In the past, I don't care how poor this white woman was, in the South she still felt like she was more than us. In the North, I don't care how poor or how rich this white woman has been, she still felt like she was more than us. But coming to the realization of the thing, her freedom is shackled in chains to mine, and she realizes for the first time that she is not free until I am free. The point about it, the male influence in this country—you know the white male, he didn't go and brainwash the black man and the black woman, he brainwashed his wife too. . . . He made her think that she was a angel. You know the reason I can say it, folks, I been watching. And there's a lot of people been watching. That's why it's such a shock wherever we go throughout this country, it's a great blow. White Americans today don't know what in the world to do because when they put us *behind* them, that's where they made their mistake. If they had put us in front, they wouldn't have *let* us look back. But they put us behind them, and we watched every move they made. . . .

And this is the reason I tell the world, as I travel to and fro, I'm not fighting for equal rights. What do I want to be equal to [Senator] Eastland for? Just tell me that. But we are not only going to liberate ourselves. I think it's a responsibility. I think we're special people, God's children is going to help in the survival of this country if it's not too late. We're a lot sicker than people realize we are. And what we are doing now in the South, in politics, in gaining seats for black people and concerned whites in the state of Mississippi, is going to have an effect on what happens throughout this country. You know, I used to think that if I could go North and tell people about the plight of the black folk in the state of Mississippi, everything would be all right. But traveling around, I found one thing for sure: it's up-South and down-South, and it's no different. The man shoot me in the face in Mississippi, and you turn around he'll shoot you in the back here [in New York]. We have a problem, folks, and we want to try to deal with the problem in the only way that we can deal with the problem as far as black women. And you know, I'm not hung up on this about liberating myself from the black man, I'm not going to try that thing. I got a black husband, six feet three, two hundred and forty pounds, with a 14 shoe, that I don't *want* to be liberated from. But we are here to work side by side with this black man in trying to bring liberation to all people.

Sunflower County is one of the poorest counties, one of the poorest counties on earth, while Senator James O. Eastland—you know, people tells you, don't talk politics, but the air you breathe is polluted air, it's political polluted air. The air you breathe is politics. So you have to be involved. You have to be involved in trying to elect people that's going to help do something about the liberation of all people.

Sunflower County, the county where I'm from, is Senator Eastland's county that owns 5,800 acres of some of the richest black fertile soil in Mississippi, and where kids, there in Sunflower County, suffer from malnutrition. But I want to tell you one of the things that we're doing, right now in Sunflower County. In 1969 I founded the Freedom Farm Coop. We started off with 40 acres of land. Nineteen-seventy in Sunflower County, we fed 1500 people from this 40 acres of land. Nineteen-seventy I've become involved with Y.W.D.—Young World Developers. On the 14th of January 1971, we put $85,400 on 640 acres of land, giving us the total of 680 acres of land. We also have 68 houses. We hope sometime in '71 we will build another hundred houses on a hundred of the 640 acres.

This coming Saturday . . . young people will be walking throughout the world against hunger and poverty. It will be forty countries walking, millions of people throughout the world. In the United States it will be over 377 walks. These walkers are young people that really care about what's going on. . . . And out of this walk—people will pay so much per mile for the kids that'll be walking—and out of this walk we hope to get a million dollars for Sunflower County. . . . If we get the kind of economic support that we need in Sunflower County, in two more years . . . We'll have the tools to produce food ourselves.

A couple of weeks ago, we moved the first poor white family into Freedom Farm in the history of the state of Mississippi. A white man came to me and said, "I got five children and I don't have nowhere to live. I don't have food. I don't have anything. And my children, some of them, is sick." And we gave this man a house. . . .

We have a job as black women, to support whatever is right, and to bring in justice where we've had so much injustice. Some people say, well, I work for $24 per week. That's not true in my case, I work sometimes for $15 per week. I remember my mother working for 25 and 30 cents per day. But we are organizing ourselves now, because we don't have any other choice. Sunflower County is one of the few counties in the state of Mississippi where in that particular area we didn't lose one black teacher. Because . . . I went in and told the judge, I said, "Judge, we're not going to stand by and see you take a man with a master's degree and bring him down to janitor help. So if we don't have the principal . . . there ain't gonna *be* no school, private or public." These are the kinds of roles.

A few years ago throughout the country the middle-class black woman—I used to say not really black women, but the middle-class colored women, c-u-l-l-u-d, didn't even respect the kind of work that I was doing. But you see now, baby, whether you have a Ph.D., D.D., or no D, we're in this bag together. And whether you're from Morehouse or Nohouse, we're still in this bag together. Not to fight to try to liberate ourselves from the men—this is another trick to get us fighting among ourselves—but to work together with the black man, then we will have a better chance to just act as human beings, and to be treated as human beings in our sick society.

I would like to tell you in closing a story of an old man. This old man was very wise, and he could answer questions that was almost impossible for people to answer. So some people went to him one day, two young people, and said, "We're going to trick this guy today. We're going to catch a bird and we're going to carry it to this old man. And we're going to ask him, 'This that we hold in our hands today, is it alive or is it dead?' If he says 'Dead,' we're going to turn it loose and let it fly. But if he says, 'Alive,' we're going to crush it." So they walked up to this old man, and they said, "This that we hold in our hands today, is it alive or is it dead?" He looked at the young people and he smiled. And he said, "It's in your hands."

FOR FURTHER READING

Jordan, June. *Fannie Lou Hamer*. New York: Cromwell, 1972.

Lee, Chana Kai. *For Freedom's Sake: The Life of Fannie Lou Hamer*. Urbana: University of Illinois Press, 1999.

Mills, Kay. *This Little Light of Mine: The Life of Fannie Lou Hamer*. New York: E. P. Dutton, 1993.

Adrienne Rich

1929–

Adrienne Rich—poet, essayist, critic, activist, and teacher—says that "you must write, and read, as if your life depended on it" (*What Is Found There* 32). She has published over eighteen books of poetry, essays, and speeches. Among the many awards she has won for her writing, she won the 1974 National Book Award, which she rejected as an individual but accepted "in the name of all women" in a statement cowritten with nominees Alice Walker and Audre Lorde. Her work explores her own locations as a white, female, lesbian, Jewish American and analyzes interconnections among the political and social impli cations of writing, culture, and citizenship.

Adrienne Rich's 1971 essay included here almost immediately became a landmark for the emerging disciplines of both women's studies and composition studies. Scholars in both fields used this essay to argue for the integral connections among an individual's life, location, and writing. Rich's exhilarating and spirited call for seeing writing as exploration reconnects the rhetorical concepts of invention, arrangement, and style through her concept of revision. Rather than correcting or setting in final form, "[r]e-vision—the act of looking back, of seeing with fresh eyes, of entering an old text from a new critical direction—is for women more than a chapter in cultural history: it is an act of survival." Rich's redefinition of writing captured and made public for her audience of teachers and scholars the changing ground upon which they read, wrote, and taught. Rich juxtaposes her own personal creative history with the field of literature, a radical move at a time when only the "text" was considered a worthy object of attention. She rejects the impersonal, objective tone of most academic performances in favor of language that spills and rolls over her audience, so that her argument that style and substance cannot be separated is in fact enacted in her own writing. Even her footnotes are a blend of scholarly citation and personal observation. Rich's challenge that "[a]s women, we have our work cut out for us," reminds us that complacency is always a threat, that change and critical consciousness are always in process, and that writing only leads in such directions when writers pay attention to their own words and how those words reflect, resist, or revise the lives around them.

"When We Dead Awaken: Writing as Re-Vision"

1971

The Modern Language Association is both marketplace and funeral parlor for the professional study of Western literature in North America. Like all gatherings of the professions, it has been and remains a "procession of the sons of educated men" (Virginia Woolf): a congeries of old-boys' networks, academicians rehearsing their numb canons in sessions dedicated to the literature of white males, junior scholars under the lash of "publish or perish" delivering papers in the bizarrely lit drawing-rooms of immense hotels: a ritual competition veering between cynicism and desperation.

However, in the interstices of these gentlemanly rites (or, in Mary Daly's words, on the boundaries of this patriarchal space),* some feminist scholars, teachers and graduate students, joined by feminist writers, editors, and publishers, have for a decade been creating more subversive occasions, challenging the sacredness of the gentlemanly canon, sharing the rediscovery of buried works by women, asking women's questions, bringing literary history and criticism back to life in both senses. The Commission on the Status of Women in the Profession was formed in 1969, and held its first public event in 1970. In 1971 the Commission asked Ellen Peck Killoh, Tillie Olsen, Elaine Reuben, and myself, with Elaine Hedges as moderator, to talk on "The Woman Writer in the Twentieth Century." The essay that follows was written for that forum, and later published, along with the other papers from the forum and workshops, in an issue of *College English* edited by Elaine Hedges ("Women Writing and Teaching," vol. 34, no. 1, October 1972.) With a few revisions, mainly updating, it was reprinted in *American Poets* in 1976, edited by William Heyen (New York: Bobbs-Merrill, 1976). That later text is the one published here.

The challenge flung by feminists at the accepted literary canon, at the methods of teaching it, and at the biased and astigmatic view of male "literary schol-

---

* Mary Daly, *Beyond God the Father* (Boston: Beacon, 1971), pp. 40–41.

arship," has not diminished in the decade since the first Women's Forum; it has become broadened and intensified more recently by the challenges of black and lesbian feminists pointing out that feminist literary criticism itself has overlooked or held back from examining the work of black women and lesbians. The dynamic between a political vision and the demand for a fresh vision of literature is clear; without a growing feminist movement, the first inroads of feminist scholarship could not have been made; without the sharpening of a black feminist consciousness, black women's writing would have been left in limbo between misogynist black male critics and white feminists still struggling to unearth a white women's tradition; without an articulate lesbian/feminist movement, lesbian writing would still be lying in that closet where many of us used to sit reading forbidden books "in a bad light."

Much, much more is yet to be done; and university curricula have of course changed very little as a result of all this. What *is* changing is the availability of knowledge, of vital texts, the visible effects on women's lives of seeing, hearing our wordless or negated experience affirmed and pursued further in language.

Ibsen's *When We Dead Awaken* is a play about the use that the male artist and thinker—in the process of creating culture as we know it—has made of women, in his life and in his work; and about a woman's slow struggling awakening to the use to which her life has been put. Bernard Shaw wrote in 1900 of this play:

> [Ibsen] shows us that no degradation ever devized or permitted is as disastrous as this degradation; that through it women can die into luxuries for men and yet can kill them; that men and women are becoming conscious of this; and that what remains to be seen as perhaps the most interesting of all imminent social developments is what will happen "when we dead awaken."[1]

It's exhilarating to be alive in a time of awakening consciousness; it can also be confusing, disorienting, and painful. This awakening of dead or sleeping consciousness has already affected the lives of millions of women, even those who don't know it yet. It is also affecting the lives of men, even those who deny its claims upon them. The argument will go on whether an oppressive economic class system is responsible for the oppressive nature of male/female relations, or whether, in fact, patriarchy—the domination of males—is the original model of oppression on which all others are based. But in the last few years the women's movement has drawn inescapable and illuminating connections between our sexual lives and our political institutions. The sleepwalkers are coming awake, and for the first time this awakening has a collective reality; it is no longer such a lonely thing to open one's eyes.

Re-vision—the act of looking back, of seeing with fresh eyes, of entering an old text from a new critical direction—is for women more than a chapter in cul-

1. G. B. Shaw. *The Quintessence of Ibsenism* (New York: Hill and Wang, 1922), p. 139.

tural history: it is an act of survival. Until we can understand the assumptions in which we are drenched we cannot know ourselves. And this drive to self-knowledge, for women, is more than a search for identity: it is part of our refusal of the self-destructiveness of male-dominated society. A radical critique of literature, feminist in its impulse, would take the work first of all as a clue to how we live, how we have been living, how we have been led to imagine ourselves, how our language has trapped as well as liberated us, how the very act of naming has been till now a male prerogative, and how we can begin to see and name—and therefore live—afresh. A change in the concept of sexual identity is essential if we are not going to see the old political order reassert itself in every new revolution. We need to know the writing of the past, and know it differently than we have ever known it; not to pass on a tradition but to break its hold over us.

For writers, and at this moment for women writers in particular, there is the challenge and promise of a whole new psychic geography to be explored. But there is also a difficult and dangerous walking on the ice, as we try to find language and images for a consciousness we are just coming into, and with little in the past to support us. I want to talk about some aspects of this difficulty and this danger.

Jane Harrison, the great classical anthropologist, wrote in 1914 in a letter to her friend Gilbert Murray:

> By the by, about "Women," it has bothered me often—why do women never want to write poetry about Man as a sex—why is Woman a dream and a terror to man and not the other way around? . . . Is it mere convention and propriety, or something deeper?[2]

I think Jane Harrison's question cuts deep into the myth-making tradition, the romantic tradition; deep into what women and men have been to each other; and deep into the psyche of the woman writer. Thinking about that question, I began thinking of the work of two twentieth-century women poets, Sylvia Plath and Diane Wakoski. It strikes me that in the work of both Man appears as, if not a dream, a fascination and a terror; and that the source of the fascination and the terror is, simply, Man's power—to dominate, tyrannize, choose, or reject the woman. The charisma of Man seems to come purely from his power over her and his control of the world by force, not from anything fertile or life-giving in him. And, in the work of both these poets, it is finally the woman's sense of *herself*—embattled, possessed—that gives the poetry its dynamic charge, its rhythms of struggle, need, will, and female energy. Until recently this female anger and this furious awareness of the Man's power over her were not available materials to the female poet, who tended to write of Love as the source of her suffering, and to view that victimization by Love as an almost

2. J. G. Stewart, *Jane Ellen Harrison: A Portrait from Letters* (London: Merlin, 1959), p. 140.

inevitable fate. Or, like Marianne Moore and Elizabeth Bishop, she kept sexuality at a measured and chiseled distance in her poems.

One answer to Jane Harrison's question has to be that historically men and women have played very different parts in each others' lives. Where woman has been a luxury for man, and has served as the painter's model and the poet's muse, but also as comforter, nurse, cook, bearer of his seed, secretarial assistant, and copyist of manuscripts, man has played a quite different role for the female artist. Henry James repeats an incident which the writer Prosper Mérimée described, of how, while he was living with George Sand,

> he once opened his eyes, in the raw winter dawn, to see his companion, in a dressing-gown, on her knees before the domestic hearth, a candlestick beside her and a red *madras* round her head, making bravely, with her own hands the fire that was to enable her to sit down betimes to urgent pen and paper. The story represents him as having felt that the spectacle chilled his ardor and tried his taste; her appearance was unfortunate, her occupation an inconsequence, and her industry a reproof—the result of all which was a lively irritation and an early rupture.[3]

The specter of this kind of male judgment, along with the misnaming and thwarting of her needs by a culture controlled by males, has created problems for the woman writer: problems of contact with herself, problems of language and style, problems of energy and survival.

In rereading Virginia Woolf's *A Room of One's Own* (1929) for the first time in some years, I was astonished at the sense of effort, of pains taken, of dogged tentativeness, in the tone of that essay. And I recognized that tone. I had heard it often enough, in myself and in other women. It is the tone of a woman almost in touch with her anger, who is determined not to appear angry, who is *willing* herself to be calm, detached, and even charming in a roomful of men where things have been said which are attacks on her very integrity. Virginia Woolf is addressing an audience of women, but she is acutely conscious—as she always was—of being overheard by men: by Morgan and Lytton and Maynard Keynes and for that matter by her father, Leslie Stephen.[4] She drew the language out into an exacerbated thread in her determination to have her own sensibility yet protect it from those masculine presences. Only at rare moments in that essay do you hear the passion in her voice; she was trying to sound as cool as Jane

3. Henry James, "Notes on Novelists," in *Selected Literary Criticism of Henry James*, Morris Shapira, ed. (London: Heinemann, 1963), pp. 157–158.

4. *A.R., 1978:* This intuition of mine was corroborated when, early in 1978, I read the correspondence between Woolf and Dame Ethel Smyth (Henry W. and Albert A. Berg Collection, The New York Public Library, Astor, Lenox and Tilden Foundation); in a letter dated June 8, 1933, Woolf speaks of having kept her own personality out of *A Room of One's Own* lest she not be taken seriously: " . . . how personal, so will they say, rubbing their hands with glee, women always are; *I even hear them as I write.*" (Italics mine.)

Austen, as Olympian as Shakespeare, because that is the way the men of the culture thought a writer should sound.

No male writer has written primarily or even largely for women, or with the sense of women's criticism as a consideration when he chooses his materials, his theme, his language. But to a lesser or greater extent, every woman writer has written for men even when, like Virginia Woolf, she was supposed to be addressing women. If we have come to the point when this balance might begin to change, when women can stop being haunted, not only by "convention and propriety" but by internalized fears of being and saying themselves, then it is an extraordinary moment for the woman writer—and reader.

I have hesitated to do what I am going to do now, which is to use myself as an illustration. For one thing, it's a lot easier and less dangerous to talk about other women writers. But there is something else. Like Virginia Woolf, I am aware of the women who are not with us here because they are washing the dishes and looking after the children. Nearly fifty years after she spoke, that fact remains largely unchanged. And I am thinking also of women whom she left out of the picture altogether—women who are washing other people's dishes and caring for other people's children, not to mention women who went on the streets last night in order to feed their children. We seem to be special women here, we have liked to think of ourselves as special, and we have known that men would tolerate, even romanticize us as special, as long as our words and actions didn't threaten their privilege of tolerating or rejecting us and our work according to *their* ideas of what a special woman ought to be. An important insight of the radical women's movement has been how divisive and how ultimately destructive is this myth of the special woman, who is also the token woman. Every one of us here in this room has had great luck—we are teachers, writers, academicians; our own gifts could not have been enough, for we all know women whose gifts are buried or aborted. Our struggles can have meaning and our privileges—however precarious under patriarchy—can be justified only if they can help to change the lives of women whose gifts—and whose very being—continue to be thwarted and silenced.

My own luck was being born white and middle-class into a house full of books, with a father who encouraged me to read and write. So for about twenty years I wrote for a particular man, who criticized and praised me and made me feel I was indeed "special." The obverse side of this, of course, was that I tried for a long time to please him, or rather, not to displease him. And then of course there were other men—writers, teachers—the Man, who was not a terror or a dream but a literary master and a master in other ways less easy to acknowledge. And there were all those poems about women, written by men: it seemed to be a given that men wrote poems and women frequently inhabited them. These women were almost always beautiful, but threatened with the loss of beauty, the loss of youth—the fate worse than death. Or, they were beautiful and died young, like Lucy and Lenore. Or, the woman was like Maud Gonne, cruel and disastrously mistaken, and the poem reproached her because she had refused to become a luxury for the poet.

A lot is being said today about the influence that the myths and images of women have on all of us who are products of culture. I think it has been a peculiar confusion to the girl or woman who tries to write because she is peculiarly susceptible to language. She goes to poetry or fiction looking for *her* way of being in the world, since she too has been putting words and images together; she is looking eagerly for guides, maps, possibilities; and over and over in the "words' masculine persuasive force" of literature she comes up against something that negates everything she is about: she meets the image of Woman in books written by men. She finds a terror and a dream, she finds a beautiful pale face, she finds La Belle Dame Sans Merci, she finds Juliet or Tess or Salomé, but precisely what she does not find is that absorbed, drudging, puzzled, sometimes inspired creature, herself, who sits at a desk trying to put words together.

So what does she do? What did I do? I read the older women poets with their peculiar keenness and ambivalence: Sappho, Christina Rossetti, Emily Dickinson, Elinor Wylie, Edna Millay, H. D. I discovered that the woman poet most admired at the time (by men) was Marianne Moore, who was maidenly, elegant, intellectual, discreet. But even in reading these women I was looking in them for the same things I had found in the poetry of men, because I wanted women poets to be the equals of men, and to be equal was still confused with sounding the same.

I know that my style was formed first by male poets: by the men I was reading as an undergraduate—Frost, Dylan Thomas, Donne, Auden, MacNiece, Stevens, Yeats. What I chiefly learned from them was craft.[5] But poems are like dreams: in them you put what you don't know you know. Looking back at poems I wrote before I was twenty-one, I'm startled because beneath the conscious craft are glimpses of the split I even then experienced between the girl who wrote poems, who defined herself in writing poems, and the girl who was to define herself by her relationships with men. "Aunt Jennifer's Tigers" (1951), written while I was a student, looks with deliberate detachment at this split.[6]

> Aunt Jennifer's tigers stride across a screen,
> Bright topaz denizens of a world of green.
> They do not fear the men beneath the tree;
> They pace in sleek chivalric certainty.

5. *A.R., 1978:* Yet I spent months, at sixteen, memorizing and writing imitations of Millay's sonnets; and in notebooks of that period I find what are obviously attempts to imitate Dickinson's metrics and verbal compression. I knew H.D. only through anthologized lyrics; her epic poetry was not then available to me.

6. *A.R., 1978:* Text of poetry quoted herein can be found in A.R., *Poems Selected and New, 1950–1974* (New York: Norton, 1975).

Aunt Jennifer's fingers fluttering through her wool
Find even the ivory needle hard to pull.
The massive weight of Uncle's wedding band
Sits heavily upon Aunt Jennifer's hand.

When Aunt is dead, her terrified hands will lie
Still ringed with ordeals she was mastered by.
The tigers in the panel that she made
Will go on striding, proud and unafraid.

In writing this poem, composed and apparently cool as it is, I thought I was creating a portrait of an imaginary woman. But this woman suffers from the opposition of her imagination, worked out in tapestry, and her life-style, "ringed with ordeals she was mastered by." It was important to me that Aunt Jennifer was a person as distinct from myself as possible—distanced by the formalism of the poem, by its objective, observant tone—even by putting the woman in a different generation.

In those years formalism was part of the strategy—like asbestos gloves, it allowed me to handle materials I couldn't pick up barehanded. A later strategy was to use the persona of a man, as I did in "The Loser" (1958):

A man thinks of the woman he once loved: first, after her
wedding, and then nearly a decade later.

I

I kissed you, bride and lost, and went
home from that bourgeois sacrament,
your cheek still tasting cold upon
my lips that gave you benison
with all the swagger that they knew—
as losers somehow learn to do.

Your wedding made my eyes ache; soon
the world would be worse off for one
more golden apple dropped to ground
without the least protesting sound,
and you would windfall lie, and we
forget your shimmer on the tree.

Beauty is always wasted: if
not Mignon's song sung to the deaf,
at all events to the unmoved.
A face like yours cannot be loved
long or seriously enough.
Almost, we seem to hold it off.

II

Well, you are tougher than I thought.
Now when the wash with ice hangs taut
this morning of St. Valentine,
I see you strip the squeaking line,
your body weighed against the load,
and all my groans can do no good.

Because you are still beautiful,
though squared and stiffened by the pull
of what nine windy years have done.
You have three daughters, lost a son.
I see all your intelligence
flung into that unwearied stance.

My envy is of no avail.
I turn my head and wish him well
who chafed your beauty into use
and lives forever in a house
lit by the friction of your mind.
You stagger in against the wind.

I finished college, published my first book by a fluke, as it seemed to me, and
broke off a love affair. I took a job, lived alone, went on writing, fell in love. I
was young, full of energy, and the book seemed to mean that others agreed I
was a poet. Because I was also determined to prove that as a woman poet I
could also have what was then defined as a "full" woman's life, I plunged in my
early twenties into marriage and had three children before I was thirty. There
was nothing overt in the environment to warn me: these were the fifties, and in
reaction to the earlier wave of feminism, middle-class women were making ca-
reers of domestic perfection, working to send their husbands through professional schools, then retiring to raise large families. People were moving out to
the suburbs, technology was going to be the answer to everything, even sex; the
family was in its glory. Life was extremely private; women were isolated from
each other by the loyalties of marriage. I have a sense that women didn't talk to
each other much in the fifties—not about their secret emptinesses, their frustrations. I went on trying to write; my second book and first child appeared in
the same month. But by the time that book came out I was already dissatisfied
with those poems, which seemed to me mere exercises for poems I hadn't
written. The book was praised, however, for its "gracefulness"; I had a marriage
and a child. If there were doubts, if there were periods of null depression or active despairing, these could only mean that I was ungrateful, insatiable, perhaps
a monster.

About the time my third child was born, I felt that I had either to consider myself a failed woman and a failed poet, or to try to find some synthesis by which to understand what was happening to me. What frightened me most was the sense of drift, of being pulled along on a current which called itself my destiny, but in which I seemed to be losing touch with whoever I had been, with the girl who had experienced her own will and energy almost ecstatically at times, walking around a city or riding a train at night or typing in a student room. In a poem about my grandmother I wrote (of myself): "A young girl, thought sleeping, is certified dead" ("Halfway"). I was writing very little, partly from fatigue, that female fatigue of suppressed anger and loss of contact with my own being; partly from the discontinuity of female life with its attention to small chores, errands, work that others constantly undo, small children's constant needs. What I did write was unconvincing to me; my anger and frustration were hard to acknowledge in or out of poems because in fact I cared a great deal about my husband and my children. Trying to look back and understand that time I have tried to analyze the real nature of the conflict. Most, if not all, human lives are full of fantasy—passive day-dreaming which need not be acted on. But to write poetry or fiction, or even to think well, is not to fantasize, or to put fantasies on paper. For a poem to coalesce, for a character or an action to take shape, there has to be an imaginative transformation of reality which is in no way passive. And a certain freedom of the mind is needed—freedom to press on, to enter the currents of your thought like a glider pilot, knowing that your motion can be sustained, that the buoyancy of your attention will not be suddenly snatched away. Moreover, if the imagination is to transcend and transform experience it has to question, to challenge, to conceive of alternatives, perhaps to the very life you are living at that moment. You have to be free to play around with the notion that day might be night, love might be hate; nothing can be too sacred for the imagination to turn into its opposite or to call experimentally by another name. For writing is re-naming. Now, to be maternally with small children all day in the old way, to be with a man in the old way of marriage, requires a holding-back, a putting-aside of that imaginative activity, and demands instead a kind of conservatism. I want to make it clear that I am *not* saying that in order to write well, or think well, it is necessary to become unavailable to others, or to become a devouring ego. This has been the myth of the masculine artist and thinker; and I do not accept it. But to be a female human being trying to fulfill traditional female functions in a traditional way *is* in direct conflict with the subversive function of the imagination. The word traditional is important here. There must be ways, and we will be finding out more and more about them, in which the energy of creation and the energy of relation can be united. But in those years I always felt the conflict as a failure of love in myself. I had thought I was choosing a full life: the life available to most men, in which sexuality, work, and parenthood could coexist. But I felt, at twenty-nine, guilt toward the people closest to me, and guilty toward my own being.

I wanted, then, more than anything, the one thing of which there was never enough: time to think, time to write. The fifties and early sixties were years of rapid revelations: the sit-ins and marches in the South, the Bay of Pigs, the early antiwar movement, raised large questions—questions for which the masculine world of the academy around me seemed to have expert and fluent answers. But I needed to think for myself—about pacifism and dissent and violence, about poetry and society, and about my own relationship to all these things. For about ten years I was reading in fierce snatches, scribbling in notebooks, writing poetry in fragments; I was looking desperately for clues, because if there were no clues then I thought I might be insane. I wrote in a notebook about this time:

> Paralyzed by the sense that there exists a mesh of relationships—e.g., between my anger at the children, my sensual life, pacifism, sex (I mean sex in its broadest significance, not merely sexual desire)—an interconnectedness which, if I could see it, make it valid, would give me back myself, make it possible to function lucidly and passionately. Yet I grope in and out among these dark webs.

I think I began at this point to feel that politics was not something "out there" but something "in here" and of the essence of my condition.

In the late fifties I was able to write, for the first time, directly about experiencing myself as a woman. The poem was jotted in fragments during children's naps, brief hours in a library, or at 3:00 A.M. after rising with a wakeful child. I despaired of doing any continuous work at this time. Yet I began to feel that my fragments and scraps had a common consciousness and a common theme, one which I would have been very unwilling to put on paper at an earlier time because I had been taught that poetry should be "universal," which meant, of course, nonfemale. Until then I had tried very much *not* to identify myself as a female poet. Over two years I wrote a ten-part poem called "Snapshots of a Daughter-in-Law" (1958–1960), in a longer looser mode than I'd ever trusted myself with before. It was an extraordinary relief to write that poem. It strikes me now as too literary, too dependent on allusion; I hadn't found the courage yet to do without authorities, or even to use the pronoun "I"—the woman in the poem is always "she." One section of it, No. 2, concerns a woman who thinks she is going mad; she is haunted by voices telling her to resist and rebel, voices which she can hear but not obey.

2.

Banging the coffee-pot into the sink
she hears the angels chiding, and looks out
past the raked gardens to the sloppy sky.
Only a week since They said: *Have no patience.*

The next time it was: *Be insatiable.*
Then: *Save yourself; others you cannot save.*
Sometimes she's let the tapstream scald her arm,
a match burn to her thumbnail,

or held her hand above the kettle's snout
right in the woolly steam. They are probably angels,
since nothing hurts her anymore, except
each morning's grit blowing into her eyes.

The poem "Orion," written five years later, is a poem of reconnection with a part of myself I had felt I was losing—the active principle, the energetic imagination, the "half-brother" whom I projected, as I had for many years, into the constellation Orion. It's no accident that the words "cold and egotistical" appear in this poem, and are applied to myself.

Far back when I went zig-zagging
through tamarack pastures
you were my genius, you
my cast-iron Viking, my helmed
lion-heart king in prison.
Years later now you're young

my fierce half-brother, staring
down from that simplified west
your breast open, your belt dragged down
by an oldfashioned thing, a sword
the last bravado you won't give over
though it weighs you down as you stride

and the stars in it are dim
and maybe have stopped burning.
But you burn, and I know it;
as I throw back my head to take you in
an old transfusion happens again:
divine astronomy is nothing to it.

Indoors I bruise and blunder,
break faith, leave ill enough
alone, a dead child born in the dark.
Night cracks up over the chimney,
pieces of time, frozen geodes
come showering down in the grate.

A man reaches behind my eyes
and finds them empty

a woman's head turns away
from my head in the mirror
children are dying my death
and eating crumbs of my life.

Pity is not your forte.
Calmly you ache up there
pinned aloft in your crow's nest,
my speechless pirate!
You take it all for granted
and when I look you back

it's with a starlike eye
shooting its cold and egotistical spear
where it can do least damage.
Breathe deep! No hurt, no pardon
out here in the cold with you
you with your back to the wall.

The choice still seemed to be between "love"—womanly, maternal love, altruis-
tic love—a love defined and ruled by the weight of an entire culture; and ego-
tism—a force directed by men into creation, achievement, ambition, often at
the expense of others, but justifiably so. For weren't they men, and wasn't that
their destiny as womanly, selfless love was ours? We know now that the alternatives are false ones—that the word "love" is itself in need of re-vision.

There is a companion poem to "Orion," written three years later, in which at
last the woman in the poem and the woman writing the poem become the same
person. It is called "Planetarium," and it was written after a visit to a real planetarium, where I read an account of the work of Caroline Herschel, the astronomer, who worked with her brother William, but whose name remained obscure, as his did not.

Thinking of Caroline Herschel, 1750–1848, astronomer, sister of William;
  and others

A woman in the shape of a monster
a monster in the shape of a woman
the skies are full of them
a woman   "in the snow
among the Clocks and instruments
or measuring the ground with poles"

in her 98 years to discover
8 comets
she whom the moon ruled
like us

levitating into the night sky
riding the polished lenses

Galaxies of women, there
doing penance for impetuousness
ribs chilled
in those   spaces of the mind

An eye,
        "virile, precise and absolutely certain"
        from the mad webs of Uranisborg
                encountering the NOVA

every impulse of light exploding
from the core
as life flies out of us
        Tycho whispering at last
        "Let me not seem to have lived in vain"

What we see, we see
and seeing is changing

the light that shrivels a mountain
and leaves a man alive

Heartbeat of the pulsar
heart sweating through my body

The radio impulse
pouring in from Taurus

        I am bombarded   yet I stand

I have been standing all my life in the
direct path of a battery of signals
the most accurately transmitted most
untranslateable language in the universe
I am a galactic cloud so deep so involuted
that a light wave could take 15
years to travel through me   And has
taken   I am an instrument in the shape
of a woman trying to translate pulsations
into images   for the relief of the body
and the reconstruction of the mind.

In closing I want to tell you about a dream I had last summer. I dreamed I
was asked to read my poetry at a mass women's meeting, but when I began to

read, what came out were the lyrics of a blues song. I share this dream with you because it seemed to me to say something about the problems and the future of the woman writer, and probably of women in general. The awakening of consciousness is not like the crossing of a frontier—one step and you are in another country. Much of woman's poetry has been of the nature of the blues song: a cry of pain, of victimization, or a lyric of seduction.⁷ And today, much poetry by women—and prose for that matter—is charged with anger. I think we need to go through that anger, and we will betray our own reality if we try, as Virginia Woolf was trying, for an objectivity, a detachment, that would make us sound more like Jane Austen or Shakespeare. We know more than Jane Austen or Shakespeare knew: more than Jane Austen because our lives are more complex, more than Shakespeare because we know more about the lives of women—Jane Austen and Virginia Woolf included.

Both the victimization and the anger experienced by women are real, and have real sources, everywhere in the environment, built into society, language, the structures of thought. They will go on being tapped and explored by poets, among others. We can neither deny them, nor will we rest there. A new generation of women poets is already working out of the psychic energy released when women begin to move out towards what the feminist philosopher Mary Daly has described as the "new space" on the boundaries of patriarchy.⁸ Women are speaking to and of women in these poems, out of a newly released courage to name, to love each other, to share risk and grief and celebration.

To the eye of a feminist, the work of Western male poets now writing reveals a deep, fatalistic pessimism as to the possibilities of change, whether societal or personal, along with a familiar and threadbare use of women (and nature) as redemptive on the one hand, threatening on the other; and a new tide of phallocentric sadism and overt woman-hating which matches the sexual brutality of recent films. "Political" poetry by men remains stranded amid the struggles for power among male groups; in condemning U.S. imperialism or the Chilean junta the poet can claim to speak for the oppressed while remaining, as male, part of a system of sexual oppression. The enemy is always outside the self, the struggle somewhere else. The mood of isolation, self-pity, and self-imitation that pervades "nonpolitical" poetry suggests that a profound change in masculine consciousness will have to precede any new male poetic—or other—inspiration. The creative energy of patriarchy is fast running out; what remains is its self-generating energy for destruction. As women, we have our work cut out for us.

7. *A.R., 1978:* When I dreamed that dream, was I wholly ignorant of the tradition of Bessie Smith and other women's blues lyrics which transcended victimization to sing of resistance and independence?

8. Mary Daly, *Beyond God the Father: Towards a Philosophy of Women's Liberation* (Boston: Beacon, 1973).

FOR FURTHER READING

"An Interview: Audre Lorde and Adrienne Rich." In *Sister Outsider: Essays and Speeches*, by
   Audre Lorde, 81–90. Freedom, Calif.: The Crossing Press, 1984.
Ratcliffe, Krista. *Anglo-American Challenges to the Rhetorical Tradition: Virginia Woolf, Mary
   Daly, and Adrienne Rich*. Carbondale: Southern Illinois University Press, 1996.
Rich, Adrienne. *Blood, Bread, and Poetry: Selected Prose 1979–1985*. New York: W. W. Nor-
   ton and Company, 1986.
———. *Of Woman Born: Motherhood As Experience and Institution*. New York, W. W. Nor-
   ton and Company, 1976.
———. *On Lies, Secrets, and Silence: Selected Prose 1966–1978*. New York: W. W. Norton and
   Company, 1979.
———. *What is Found There: Notebooks on Poetry and Politics*. New York: W. W. Norton and
   Company, 1993.

Hélène Cixous

1937–

Considered one of the three most famous "French feminists" (along with Luce Irigaray and Julia Kristeva), Hélène Cixous has been at the center of contemporary discussions of women's writing, feminism, and women's rhetoric. Cixous has written thirty books of fiction, many critical essays, and eight plays. She is professor of literature at the Université de Paris VIII, an experimental university she helped found in 1968.

Published in France in 1975, "Sorties" first appeared in English in 1986. Like Cixous's essay "The Laugh of the Medusa"—also one of the most widely recognized pieces of feminist rhetorical theory in the second-wave feminist movement—"Sorties" gave voice to a dramatic feminist activist movement and resonated with academic feminist ideas. As feminist activists were marching in the streets for women's rights (the Equal Rights Amendment in America and similar legislation in France and England) and celebrating reproductive freedom (legalized abortion and the Pill), women writers were also beginning to be published; this new material allowed academic feminists the opportunity to read, research, and write about women writers—and speak openly about writing as women.

In "Sorties," Cixous provides an extensive rhetorical analysis of women's relationship to masculine discourse and of their restricted use of language. In addition, like Virginia Woolf, she gives strong rhetorical advice, challenging women to speak their realities, to burst through conventions, to rupture cultural and rhetorical restraints, to move into the "elsewhere." In this selection from "Sorties," Cixous follows de Beauvoir in examining the position of women writers within the dualistic, hierarchical strategies of Western philosophy, where the "not-I" is always in the position of "other." To the "other" we ascribe everything hidden, shameful, inferior—the very qualities we prefer not to claim for ourselves. The body has also taken this suspect position in Western discourse, always inferior to mind and reason. Cixous says, "We have turned away from our bodies. Shamefully, we have been taught to be unaware of them." Cixous again urges women to reclaim their physical and rhetorical voices. It is in this connection between their bodies and their sexuality that women can "exceed" the discourse that "governs the phallocentric system." From a contemporary feminist perspective, this idea may seem problematic when we realize the historical problems feminists have had in searching for common ground in a movement that desperately needed to support, discover, and recognize the diverse issues of different women's locations and experiences. But Cixous is writing from a political space (the academy) at a time when there were few voices of women and even fewer voices of women's experiences represented in writing.

Cixous's body-rhetoric helped to initiate the French feminist theory of *ecriture feminine*, defining, yet recognizing as indefinable, a feminine practice of writing through writing of the female experience, the reclamation of female voice by articulating experience of the female body. *Ecriture feminine* cannot be limited to a purely theoretical concept. It articulates the connections among the physical, discursive, and political realities of women—their physical bodies, their experiences as women. The unique feminine perspective is represented via the written word and via the embodied voice of women. Cixous's rhetoric in this essay is full of sarcasm, word-play, lyricism, and exhortation. In the cadence of sentences and the flood of words, Cixous enacts the rushing, explosive, careening, singing energy of women breaking from the bondage of the patriarchal version of "woman" and reclaiming their physical bodies and spiritual identities, forming a community of women that can change the world.

From "Sorties"

1975

Writing femininity tranformation:

And there is a link between the economy of femininity—the open, extravagant subjectivity, that relationship to the other in which the gift doesn't calculate its influence—and the possibility of love; and a link today between this "libido of the other" and writing.

At the present time, *defining* a feminine practice of writing is impossible with an impossibility that will continue; for this practice will never be able to be *theorized*, enclosed, coded, which does not mean it does not exist. But it will always exceed the discourse governing the phallocentric system; it takes place and will take place somewhere other than in the territories subordinated to philosophical-theoretical domination. It will not let itself think except through subjects that break automatic functions, border runners never subjugated by any authority. But one can begin to speak. Begin to point out some effects, some elements of unconscious drives, some relations of the feminine Imaginary to the Real, to writing.

What I have to say about it is also only a beginning, because right from the start these features affect me powerfully.

From: *The Newly Born Woman*. Trans. Betsy Wing. Minneapolis: University of Minnesota Press, 1986. 91–100. Original, French language edition copyright 1975 by Union Generale d'Editions, Paris. English translation copyright by the University of Minnesota.

First I sense femininity in writing by: a privilege of *voice: writing and voice* are entwined and interwoven and writing's continuity/voice's rhythm take each other's breath away through interchanging, make the text gasp or form it out of suspenses and silences, make it lose its voice or rend it with cries.

In a way, feminine writing never stops reverberating from the wrench that the acquisition of speech, speaking out loud, is for her—"acquisition" that is experienced more as tearing away, dizzying flight and flinging oneself, diving. Listen to woman speak in a gathering (if she is not painfully out of breath): she doesn't "speak," she throws her trembling body into the air, she lets herself go, she flies, she goes completely into her voice, she vitally defends the "logic" of her discourse with her body; her flesh speaks true. She exposes herself. Really she makes what she thinks materialize carnally, she conveys meaning with her body. She *inscribes* what she is saying because she does not deny unconscious drives the unmanageable part they play in speech.

Her discourse, even when "theoretical" or political, is never simple or linear or "objectivized," universalized; she involves her story in history.

Every woman has known the torture of beginning to speak aloud, heart beating as if to break, occasionally falling into loss of language, ground and language slipping out from under her, because for woman speaking—even just opening her mouth—in public is something rash, a transgression.

A double anguish, for even if she transgresses, her word almost always falls on the deaf, masculine ear, which can only hear language that speaks in the masculine.

We are not culturally accustomed to speaking, throwing signs out toward a scene, employing the suitable rhetoric. Also, it is not where we find our pleasure: indeed, one pays a certain price for the use of a discourse. The logic of communication requires an economy both of signs—of signifiers—and of subjectivity. The orator is asked to unwind a thin thread, dry and taut. We like uneasiness, questioning. There is waste in what we say. We need that waste. To write is always to make allowances for superabundance and uselessness while slashing the exchange value that keeps the spoken word on its track. That is why writing is good, letting the tongue try itself out—as one attempts a caress, taking the time a phrase or a thought needs to make oneself loved, to make oneself reverberate.

It is in writing, from woman and toward woman, and in accepting the challenge of the discourse controlled by the phallus, that woman will affirm woman somewhere other than in silence, the place reserved for her in and through the Symbolic. May she get out of booby-trapped silence! And not have the margin or the harem foisted on her as her domain!

In feminine speech, as in writing, there never stops reverberating something that, having once passed through us, having imperceptibly and deeply touched us, still has the power to affect us—song, the first music of the voice of love, which every woman keeps alive.

The Voice sings from a time before law, before the Symbolic took one's breath away and re-appropriated it into language under its authority of separation. The deepest, the oldest, the loveliest Visitation. Within each woman the first, nameless love is singing.

In woman there is always, more or less, something of "the mother" repairing and feeding, resisting separation, a force that does not let itself be cut off but that runs codes ragged. The relationship to childhood (the child she was, she is, she acts and makes and starts anew, and unties at the place where, as a same she even others herself), is no more cut off than is the relationship to the "mother," *as it consists of* delights and violences. Text, my body: traversed by lilting flows; listen to me, it is not a captivating, clinging "mother"; it is the equivoice that, touching you, affects you, pushes you away from your breast to come to language, that summons *your* strength; it is the rhyth-me that laughs you; the one intimately addressed who makes all metaphors, all body (?)—bodies (?)—possible and desirable, who is no more describable than god, soul, or the Other; the part of you that puts space between yourself and pushes you to inscribe your woman's style in language. Voice: milk that could go on forever. Found again. The lost mother/bitter-lost. Eternity: is voice mixed with milk.

Not the origin: she doesn't go back there. A boy's journey is the return to the native land, the *Heimweh* Freud speaks of, the nostalgia that makes man a being who tends to come back to the point of departure to appropriate it for himself and to die there. A girl's journey is farther—to the unknown, to invent.

How come this privileged relationship with voice? Because no woman piles up as many defenses against instinctual drives as a man does. You don't prop things up, you don't brick things up the way he does, you don't withdraw from pleasure so "prudently." Even if phallic mystification has contaminated good relations in general, woman is never far from the "mother" (I do not mean the role but the "mother" as no-name and as source of goods). There is always at least a little good mother milk left in her. She writes with white ink.

Voice! That, too, is launching forth and effusion without return. Exclamation, cry, breathlessness, yell, cough, vomit, music. Voice leaves. Voice loses. She leaves. She loses. And that is how she writes, as one throws a voice—forward, into the void. She goes away, she goes forward, doesn't turn back to look at her tracks. Pays no attention to herself. Running breakneck. Contrary to the self-absorbed, masculine narcissism, making sure of its image, of being seen, of seeing itself, of assembling its glories, of pocketing itself again. The reductive look, the always divided look returning, the mirror economy; he needs to love himself. But she launches forth; she seeks to love. Moreover, this is what Valéry sensed, marking his Young Fate in search of herself with ambiguity, masculine in her jealousy of herself: "seeing herself see herself," the motto of all phallocentric speculation/specularization, the motto of every Teste; and feminine in the frantic descent deeper deeper to where a voice that doesn't know itself is lost in the sea's churning.

Voice-cry. Agony—the spoken "word" exploded, blown to bits by suffering and anger, demolishing discourse: this is how she has always been heard before, ever since the time when masculine society began to push her offstage, expulsing her, plundering her. Ever since Medea, ever since Electra.

Voice: unfastening, fracas. Fire! She shoots, she shoots away. Break. From their bodies where they have been buried, shut up and at the same time forbidden to take pleasure. Women have almost everything to write about femininity: about their sexuality, that is to say, about the infinite and mobile complexity of their becoming erotic, about the lightning ignitions of such a minuscule-vast region of their body, not about destiny but about the adventure of such an urge, the voyages, crossings, advances, sudden and slow awakenings, discoveries of a formerly timid region that is just now springing up. Woman's body with a thousand and one fiery hearths, when—shattering censorship and yokes—she lets it articulate the proliferation of meanings that runs through it in every direction. It is going to take much more than language for him to make the ancient maternal tongue sound in only one groove.

We have turned away from our bodies. Shamefully we have been taught to be unaware of them, to lash them with stupid modesty; we've been tricked into a fool's bargain: each one is to love the other sex. I'll give you your body and you will give me mine. But which men give women the body that they blindly hand over to him? Why so few texts? Because there are still so few women winning back their bodies. Woman must write her body, must make up the unimpeded tongue that bursts partitions, classes, and rhetorics, orders and codes, must inundate, run through, go beyond the discourse with its last reserves, including the one of laughing off the word "silence" that has to be said, the one that, aiming for the impossible, stops dead before the word "impossible" and writes it as "end."

In body/Still more: woman is body more than man is. Because he is invited to social success, to sublimation. More body hence more writing. For a long time, still, bodily, within her body she has answered the harassment, the familial conjugal venture of domestication, the repeated attempts to castrate her. Woman, who has run her tongue ten thousand times seven times around her mouth before not speaking, either dies of it or knows her tongue and her mouth better than anyone. Now, I-woman am going to blow up the Law: a possible and inescapable explosion from now on; let it happen, right now, in language.

When "*The* Repressed" of their culture and their society come back, it is an explosive return, which is *absolutely* shattering, staggering, overturning, with a force never let loose before, on the scale of the most tremendous repressions: for at the end of the Age of the Phallus, women will have been either wiped out or heated to the highest, most violent, white-hot fire. Throughout their deafening dumb history, they have lived in dreams, embodied but still deadly silent, in silences, in voiceless rebellions. . . .

If woman has always functioned "within" man's discourse, a signifier referring always to the opposing signifier that annihilates its particular energy, puts down or stifles its very different sounds, now it is time for her to displace this "within," explode it, overturn it, grab it, make it hers, take it in, take it into her women's mouth, bite its tongue with her women's teeth, make up her own tongue to get inside of it. And you will see how easily she will well up, from this "within" where she was hidden and dormant, to the lips where her foams will overflow.

It is not a question of appropriating their instruments, their concepts, their places for oneself or of wishing oneself in their position of mastery. Our knowing that there is a danger of identification does not mean we should give in. Leave that to the worriers, to masculine anxiety and its obsessional relationship to workings they must control—knowing "how it runs" in order to "make it run." Not taking possession to internalize or manipulate but to shoot through and smash the walls. . . .

To fly/steal is woman's gesture, to steal into language to make it fly. We have all learned flight/theft, the art with many techniques, for all the centuries we have only had access to having by stealing/flying; we have lived in a flight/theft, stealing/flying, finding the close, concealed ways-through of desire. It's not just luck if the word "voler" volleys between the "vol" of theft and the "vol" of flight, pleasuring in each and routing the sense police. It is not just luck: woman partakes of bird and burglar, just as the burglar partakes of woman and bird: hesheits pass, hesheits fly by, hesheits pleasure in scrambling spatial order, disorienting it, moving furniture, things, and values around, breaking in, emptying structures, turning the selfsame, the proper upside down.

What woman has not stolen? Who has not dreamed, savored, or done the thing that jams sociality? Who has not dropped a few red herrings, mocked her way around the separating bar, inscribed what makes a difference with her body, punched holes in the system of couples and positions, and with a transgression screwed up whatever is successive, chain-linked, the fence of circumfusion?

A feminine text cannot not be more than subversive: if it writes itself it is in volcanic heaving of the old "real" property crust. In ceaseless displacement. She must write herself because, when the time comes for her liberation, it is the invention of a *new, insurgent* writing that will allow her to put the breaks and indispensable changes into effect in her history. At first, individually, on two inseparable levels:—woman, writing herself, will go back to this body that has been worse than confiscated, a body replaced with a disturbing stranger, sick or dead, who so often is a bad influence, the cause and place of inhibitions. By censuring the body, breath and speech are censored at the same time.

To write—the act that will "realize" the un-censored relationship of woman to her sexuality, to her woman-being giving her back access to her own forces; that will return her goods, her pleasures, her organs, her vast bodily territories

kept under seal; that will tear her out of the superegoed, over-Mosesed structure where the same position of guilt is always reserved for her (guilty of everything, every time: of having desires, of not having any; of being frigid, of being
"too" hot; of not being both at once; of being too much of a mother and not
enough; of nurturing and of not nurturing . . .). Write yourself: your body must
make itself heard. Then the huge resources of the unconscious will burst out.
Finally the inexhaustible feminine Imaginary is going to be deployed. Without
gold or black dollars, our naphtha will spread values over the world, un-quoted
values that will change the rules of the old game.

In the Selfsame Empire, where will the displacement's person find somewhere to lose herself, to write her not-taking-place, her permanent availability.

But somewhere else? There will be some elsewhere where the other will no
longer be condemned to death. But has there ever been any elsewhere, is there
any? While it is not yet "here," it is there by now—in this other place that disrupts social order, where desire makes fiction exist. Not any old fiction, for, of
course, there is classical fiction caught in the oppositions of the system, and literary history has been homogeneous with phallocentric tradition, to the point
of being phallocentrism-looking-at-itself, taking pleasure in repeating itself.

But I move toward something that only exists in an elsewhere, and I search
in the thought that writing has uncontrollable resources. That writing is what
deals with the no-deal, relates to what gives no return. That something else
(what history forbids, what reality excludes or doesn't admit) can manifest itself there: some other. With the desire to keep this other alive—hence some living feminine—some difference—and some love; for example a desire, like the
one that can unleash a woman, that goes all the way and does not let itself be
subjugated by anything. That imposes its necessity as a value without letting itself be intimidated by cultural blackmail, the sacrosanction of social structures.
That does not organize life around the threat of death; because a life that has
given up can no longer call itself life.

Hence, a "place" of intransigence and of passion. A place of lucidity where
no one takes what is a pretense of existence for life. Desire is clearly there like a
stroke of fire, it shoots the night through with something. Lightning! that way!
I don't have it wrong. Life is right here. Afterward, it's death. . . .

It is then that writing makes love other. It is itself this love. Other-Love is
writing's first name.

At the beginnings of *Other-Love* there are differences. The new love dares the
other, wants it, seems in flight, be-leaves, does some stealing between knowing
and making up. She, the one coming from forever, doesn't stand still, she goes
all over, she exchanges, she is desire-that-gives. Not shut up inside the paradox
of the gift-that-takes or in the illusion of onely uniting. She enters, she be-
tweens—she mes and thees between the other me where one is always infinitely more than one and more than me, without fearing ever to reach a limit:
sensualist in our be-coming. We'll never be done with it! She runs through de-

fensive loves, motherings and devourings. She runs her risks beyond stingy nar-cissism, in moving, open, transitional space. Beyond the back-to-bed of war-love that claims to represent exchange, she mocked the dynamics of Eros which is fed by hate—hate: an inheritance, a leftover, a deceiving subservience to the phallus—to love, to regard-think-seek the other in the other, to de-specularize, to de-speculate. She doesn't enter where history still works as the story of death. Still, having a present does not prevent woman's beginning the story of life elsewhere. Elsewhere, she gives. She doesn't measure what she is giving, but she gives neither false leads nor what she doesn't have. She gives cause to live, to think, to transform. That "economy" can no longer be expressed as an eco-nomic term. Wherever she loves, all the ideas of the old management are sur-passed. I am for you what you want me to be at the moment in which you look at me as if you have never before seen me so: every moment. When I write, all those that we don't know we can be write themselves from me, without exclu-sion, without prediction, and everything that we will be calls us to the tireless, intoxicating, tender-costly-search for love. We will never lack ourselves.

FOR FURTHER READING

Cixous, Hélène. *The Book of Promethea*. Lincoln: University of Nebraska Press, 1991.
———. *"Coming to Writing" and Other Essays*. Cambridge: Harvard University Press, 1991.
———. "The Laugh of the Medusa." In *New French Feminisms: An Anthology*, edited by Elaine Marks and Isabelle de Courtivron, 245–64. New York: Schocken Books, 1981.
———. *Stigmata: Escaping Texts*. New York: Routledge, 1998.
Cixous, Hélène, and Mireille Calle-Gruber. *Rootprints: Memory and Life Writing*. New York: Routledge, 1997.

Combahee River Collective

1977

"We examined our own lives and found that everything out there was kicking our behinds—race, class, sex, and homophobia" (*Home Girls* xxxiv). Barbara Smith's words describe the desperate circumstances of many black women in 1977. As black lesbian feminists active in the Combahee River Collective, Barbara Smith, her twin sister, Beverly, and Demita Frazier drafted the "Combahee River Collective Statement" in 1977. First published in Zillah Eisenstein's collection, *Capitalist Patriarchy: The Case for Social Feminism,* the statement motivated black feminists to work against their multilayered oppression and challenged white feminists to acknowledge their exclusion of women of color and working-class women in the feminist movement.

As a grassroots organization formed in conjunction with New York's National Black Feminist Organization (NBFO), the Combahee River Collective worked for six years in Boston. They borrowed their name from Harriet Tubman's organized action during the Civil War that freed over 750 slaves. It was an appropriate name for their 1970s organization that sought to raise consciousness among black women. Among other issues, the Collective addressed the racism of white feminists in the women's movement—the racism that forced many black women to reject feminism altogether. The Combahee River Collective called the feminism they fought for "Black feminism," which Barbara Smith says builds on history: "It is used to characterize Black women's tradition of courage, independence, and pragmatism under the brutal conditions of slavery and institutionalized racism" (Mankiller et al. 202). The Combahee River Collective also organized retreats for black feminists and challenged homophobia, sexual harassment, and classism in the black community.

Perhaps the most revolutionary and influential premise of the "Combahee River Collective Statement" is that the oppression of black women is multilayered and simultaneous. This antihierarchical view of the oppression of black women places racism, but also sexism, classism, and homophobia into the center of feminist critique. Smith, Smith, and Frazier write, "The synthesis of these oppressions creates the conditions of our lives."

The first of the four parts of the statement narrates the origin of the Combahee River Collective and the history of black feminism by drawing on both the mundane and politically active experiences of black women in America. The first section acknowledges the rhetorical tradition on which they build: the speeches, essays, and manifestos of Sojourner Truth, Frances Ellen Watkins Harper, and Ida B. Wells. The authors validate their combination of feminist, antiracist, and socialist perspectives in the second section and reject what they call "Lesbian separatism" because it does not account for the effects of class and race. They argue for a collective approach to battling sex oppression that includes people of multiple locations in the black community. The rhetoric in this section is forceful, as the authors sketch their convictions about contentious issues, including their relationships with other feminists and black males. The authors assert the importance of rhetorical forms such as consciousness-raising and what they claim as "women's style of talking/testifying in Black language." In the third section, the authors delve deeper into the struggles of organizing the collective, bringing the different ideological stances of the members to the fore. The final section outlines the projects in which the collective was involved and its future directions.

The works of many feminist rhetors in *Available Means* were born in crisis, in times when women were compelled to fight for their rights, for their lives. The "Combahee River Collective Statement" is the embodiment of this urgency. In a 1979 diary entry about the murder of twelve black women in Boston, Barbara Smith captures the urgency with which the "Combahee River Collective Statement" was written. She writes, "We are dying. Again the truth I've always talked about, that at bottom Black feminism is about keeping Black women from dying, is made frighteningly real" ("Boston Murders" 319).

"The Combahee River Collective Statement"

1977

We are a collective of Black feminists who have been meeting together since 1974. During that time we have been involved in the process of defining and clarifying our politics, while at the same time doing political work within our own group and in coalition with other progressive organizations and movements. The most general statement of our politics at the present time would be that we are actively committed to struggling against racial, sexual, heterosexual, and class oppression, and see as our particular task the development of integrated analysis and practice based upon the fact that the major systems of oppression are interlocking. The synthesis of these oppressions creates the conditions of our lives. As Black women we see Black feminism as the logical political movement to combat the manifold and simultaneous oppressions that all women of color face.

Reprinted from Smith, Barbara. "The Combahee River Collective Statement." In *Home Girls: A Black Feminist Anthology*, edited by Barbara Smith, 266–74. New Brunswick: Rutgers University Press, 2000. Reprinted by permission of Rutgers University Press.

We will discuss four major topics in the paper that follows: (1) the genesis of contemporary Black feminism; (2) what we believe, i.e., the specific province of our politics; (3) the problems in organizing Black feminists, including a brief herstory of our collective; and (4) Black feminist issues and practice.

1. The Genesis of Contemporary Black Feminism

Before looking at the recent development of Black feminism we would like to affirm that we find our origins in the historical reality of Afro-American women's continuous life-and-death struggle for survival and liberation. Black women's extremely negative relationship to the American political system (a system of white male rule) has always been determined by our membership in two oppressed racial and sexual castes. As Angela Davis points out in "Reflections on the Black Woman's Role in the Community of Slaves," Black women have always embodied, if only in their physical manifestation, an adversary stance to white male rule and have actively resisted its inroads upon them and their communities in both dramatic and subtle ways. There have always been Black women activists—some known, like Sojourner Truth, Harriet Tubman, Frances E. W. Harper, Ida B. Wells Barnett, and Mary Church Terrell, and thousands upon thousands unknown—who have had a shared awareness of how their sexual identity combined with their racial identity to make their whole life situation and the focus of their political struggles unique. Contemporary Black feminism is the outgrowth of countless generations of personal sacrifice, militancy, and work by our mothers and sisters.

A Black feminist presence has evolved most obviously in connection with the second wave of the American women's movement beginning in the late 1960s. Black, other Third World, and working women have been involved in the feminist movement from its start, but both outside reactionary forces and racism and elitism within the movement itself have served to obscure our participation. In 1973, Black feminists, primarily located in New York, felt the necessity of forming a separate Black feminist group. This became the National Black Feminist Organization (NBFO).

Black feminist politics also have an obvious connection to movements for Black liberation, particularly those of the 1960s and 1970s. Many of us were active in those movements (Civil Rights, Black nationalism, the Black Panthers), and all of our lives were greatly affected and changed by their ideologies, their goals, and the tactics used to achieve their goals. It was our experience and disillusionment within these liberation movements as well as experience on the periphery of the white male left, that led to the need to develop a politics that was anti-racist, unlike those of white women, and anti-sexist, unlike those of Black and white men.

There is also undeniably a personal genesis for Black feminism, that is, the political realization that comes from the seemingly personal experiences of individual Black women's lives. Black feminists and many more Black women who do not define themselves as feminists have all experienced sexual oppression as a constant factor in our day-to-day existence. As children we realized that we were different from boys and that we were treated differently. For example, we were told in the same breath to be quiet both for the sake of being "ladylike" and to make us less objectionable in the eyes of white people. As we grew older we became aware of the threat of physical and sexual abuse by men. However, we had no way of conceptualizing what was so apparent to us, what we *knew* was really happening.

Black feminists often talk about their feelings of craziness before becoming conscious of the concepts of sexual politics, patriarchal rule, and most importantly, feminism, the political analysis and practice that we women use to struggle against our oppression. The fact that racial politics and indeed racism are pervasive factors in our lives did not allow us, and still does not allow most Black women, to look more deeply into their own experiences and, from the sharing and growing consciousness, to build a politics that will change our lives and inevitably end our oppression. Our development must also be tied to the contemporary economic and political position of Black people. The post World War II generation of Black youth was the first to be able to minimally partake of certain educational and employment options, previously closed completely to Black people. Although our economic position is still at the very bottom of the American capitalistic economy, a handful of us have been able to gain certain tools as a result of tokenism in education and employment which potentially enable us to more effectively fight our oppression.

A combined anti-racist and anti-sexist position drew us together initially, and as we developed politically we addressed ourselves to heterosexism and economic oppression under capitalism.

2. What We Believe

Above all else, our politics initially sprang from the shared belief that Black women are inherently valuable, that our liberation is a necessity not as an adjunct to somebody else's but because of our need as human persons for autonomy. This may seem so obvious as to sound simplistic, but it is apparent that no other ostensibly progressive movement has ever considered our specific oppression as a priority or worked seriously for the ending of that oppression. Merely naming the pejorative stereotypes attributed to Black women (e.g., mammy, matriarch, Sapphire, whore, bulldagger), let alone cataloguing the cruel, often murderous, treatment we receive, indicates how little value has been placed upon our lives during four centuries of bondage in the Western hemisphere. We realize that the only people who care enough about us to work consistently for our liberation are us. Our politics evolve from a healthy love for ourselves, our sisters and our community which allows us to continue our struggle and work.

This focusing upon our own oppression is embodied in the concept of identity politics. We believe that the most profound and potentially most radical politics come directly out of our own identity, as opposed to working to end somebody else's oppression. In the case of Black women this is a particularly repugnant, dangerous, threatening, and therefore revolutionary concept because it is obvious from looking at all the political movements that have preceded us that anyone is more worthy of liberation than ourselves. We reject pedestals, queenhood, and walking ten paces behind. To be recognized as human, levelly human, is enough.

We believe that sexual politics under patriarchy is as pervasive in Black women's lives as are the politics of class and race. We also often find it difficult to separate race from class from sex oppression because in our lives they are most often experienced simultaneously. We know that there is such a thing as racial-sexual oppression which is neither solely racial nor solely sexual, e.g., the history of rape of Black women by white men as a weapon of political repression.

Although we are feminists and Lesbians, we feel solidarity with progressive Black men and do not advocate the fractionalization that white women who are separatists demand. Our situation as Black people neccessitates that we have solidarity around the fact of race, which white women of course do not need to have with white men, unless it is their negative solidarity as racial oppressors. We struggle together with Black men against racism, while we also struggle with Black men about sexism.

We realize that the liberation of all oppressed peoples necessitates the destruction of the political-economic systems of capitalism and imperialism as well as patriarchy. We are socialists because we believe that work must be organized for the collective benefit of those who do the work and create the products, and not for the profit of the bosses. Material resources must be equally distributed among those who create these resources. We are not convinced, however, that a socialist revolution that is not also a feminist and anti-racist revolution will guarantee our liberation. We have arrived at the necessity for developing an understanding of class relationships that takes into account the specific class position of Black women who are generally marginal in the labor force, while at this particular time some of us are temporarily viewed as doubly desirable tokens at white-collar and professional levels. We need to articulate the real class situation of persons who are not merely raceless, sexless workers, but for whom racial and sexual oppression are significant determinants in their working/economic lives. Although we are in essential agreement with Marx's theory as it applied to the very specific economic relationships he analyzed, we know that his analysis must be extended further in order for us to understand our specific economic situation as Black women.

A political contribution which we feel we have already made is the expansion of the feminist principle that the personal is political. In our consciousness-raising sessions, for example, we have in many ways gone beyond white women's revelations because we are dealing with the implications of race and class as well as sex. Even our Black women's style of talking/testifying in Black language about what we have experienced has a resonance that is both cultural and political. We have spent a great deal of energy delving into the cultural and experiential nature of our oppression out of necessity because none of these matters has ever been looked at before. No one before has ever examined the multilayered texture of Black women's lives. An example of this kind of revelation/conceptualization occurred at a meeting as we discussed the ways in which our early intellectual interests had been attacked by our peers, particularly Black males. We discovered that all of us, because we were "smart" had also been considered "ugly," i.e., "smart-ugly." "Smart-ugly" crystallized the way in which most of us had been forced to develop our intellects at great cost to our "social" lives. The sanctions in the Black and white communities against Black women thinkers are comparatively much higher than for white women, particularly ones from the educated middle and upper classes.

As we have already stated, we reject the stance of Lesbian separatism because it is not a viable political analysis or strategy for us. It leaves out far too much and far too many people, particularly Black men, women, and children. We have a great deal of criticism and loathing for what men have been socialized to be in this society: what they support, how they act, and how they oppress. But we do not have the misguided notion that it is their maleness, per se—i.e., their biological maleness—that makes them what they are. As Black women we find any type of biological determinism a particularly dangerous and reactionary basis upon which to build a politic. We must also question whether Lesbian separatism is an adequate and progressive political analysis and strategy, even for those who practice it, since it so completely denies any but the sexual sources of women's oppression, negating the facts of class and race.

3. Problems in Organizing Black Feminists

During our years together as a Black feminist collective we have experienced success and defeat, joy and pain, victory and failure. We have found that it is very difficult to organize around Black feminist issues, difficult even to announce in certain contexts that we are Black feminists. We have tried to think about the reasons for our difficulties, particularly since the white women's movement continues to be strong and to grow in many directions. In this section we will discuss some of the general reasons for the organizing problems we face and also talk specifically about the stages in organizing our own collective.

The major source of difficulty in our political work is that we are not just trying to fight oppression on one front or even two, but instead to address a whole range of oppressions. We do not have racial, sexual, heterosexual, or class privilege to rely upon, nor do we have even the minimal access to re-

sources and power that groups who possess any one of these types of privilege
have.

The psychological toll of being a Black woman and the difficulties this presents in reaching political consciousness and doing political work can never be
underestimated. There is a very low value placed upon Black women's psyches
in this society, which is both racist and sexist. As an early group member once
said, "We are all damaged people merely by virtue of being Black women." We
are dispossessed psychologically and on every other level, and yet we feel the
necessity to struggle to change the condition of all Black women. In "A Black
Feminist's Search for Sisterhood," Michele Wallace arrives at this conclusion:

> We exist as women who are Black who are feminists, each stranded for the mo-
> ment, working independently because there is not yet an environment in this
> society remotely congenial to our struggle—because, being on the bottom, we
> would have to do what no one else has done: we would have to fight the world.

Wallace is pessimistic but realistic in her assessment of Black feminists' position, particularly in her allusion to the nearly classic isolation most of us face.
We might use our position at the bottom, however, to make a clear leap into
revolutionary action. If Black women were free, it would mean that everyone
else would have to be free since our freedom would necessitate the destruction
of all the systems of oppression.

Feminism is, nevertheless, very threatening to the majority of Black people
because it calls into question some of the most basic assumptions about our existence, i.e., that sex should be a determinant of power relationships. Here is
the way male and female roles were defined in a Black nationalist pamphlet
from the early 1970s:

> We understand that it is and has been traditional that the man is the head of the
> house. He is the leader of the house/nation because his knowledge of the world
> is broader, his awareness is greater, his understanding is fuller and his applica-
> tion of this information is wiser . . . After all, it is only reasonable that the man
> be the head of the house because he is able to defend and protect the devel-
> opment of his home . . . Women cannot do the same things as men—they are
> made by nature to function differently. Equality of men and women is some-
> thing that cannot happen even in the abstract world. Men are not equal to other
> men, i.e. ability, experience or even understanding. The value of men and
> women can be seen as in the value of gold and silver—they are not equal but
> both have great value. We must realize that men and women are a complement
> to each other because there is no house/family without a man and his wife.
> Both are essential to the development of any life.

The material conditions of most Black women would hardly lead them to
upset both economic and sexual arrangements that seem to represent some stability in their lives. Many Black women have a good understanding of both sex-

ism and racism, but because of the everyday constrictions of their lives, cannot risk struggling against them both.

The reaction of Black men to feminism has been notoriously negative. They are, of course, even more threatened than Black women by the possibility that Black feminists might organize around our own needs. They realize that they might not only lose valuable and hardworking allies in their struggles but that they might also be forced to change their habitually sexist ways of interacting with and oppressing Black women. Accusations that Black feminism divides the Black struggle are powerful deterrents to the growth of an autonomous Black women's movement.

Still, hundreds of women have been active at different times during the three-year existence of our group. And every Black woman who came, came out of a strongly-felt need for some level of possibility that did not previously exist in her life.

When we first started meeting early in 1974 after the NBFO first eastern regional conference, we did not have a strategy for organizing, or even a focus. We just wanted to see what we had. After a period of months of not meeting, we began to meet again late in the year and started doing an intense variety of consciousness-raising. The overwhelming feeling that we had is that after years and years we had finally found each other. Although we were not doing political work as a group, individuals continued their involvement in Lesbian politics, sterilization abuse and abortion rights work, Third World Women's International Women's Day activities, and support activity for the trials of Dr. Kenneth Edelin, Joan Little, and Inéz Garcia. During our first summer, when membership had dropped off considerably, those of us remaining devoted serious discussion to the possibility of opening a refuge for battered women in a Black community. (There was no refuge in Boston at that time.) We also decided around that time to become an independent collective since we had serious disagreements with NBFO's bourgeois-feminist stance and their lack of a clear political focus.

We also were contacted at that time by socialist feminists, with whom we had worked on abortion rights activities, who wanted to encourage us to attend the National Socialist Feminist Conference in Yellow Springs. One of our members did attend and despite the narrowness of the ideology that was promoted at that particular conference, we became more aware of the need for us to understand our own economic situation and to make our own economic analysis.

In the fall, when some members returned, we experienced several months of comparative inactivity and internal disagreements which were first conceptualized as a Lesbian-straight split but which were also the result of class and political differences. During the summer those of us who were still meeting had determined the need to do political work and to move beyond consciousness-raising and serving exclusively as an emotional support group. At the beginning of 1976, when some of the women who had not wanted to do political work and who also had voiced disagreements stopped attending of their own accord, we again looked for a focus. We decided at that time, with the addition of new members, to become a study group. We had always shared our reading with each other, and some of us had written papers on Black feminism for group discussion a few months before this decision was made. We began functioning as a study group and also began discussing the possibility of starting a Black feminist publication. We had a retreat in the late spring which provided a time for both political discussion and working out interpersonal issues. Currently we are planning to gather together a collection of Black feminist writing. We feel that it is absolutely essential to demonstrate the reality of our politics to other Black women and believe that we can do this through writing and distributing our work. The fact that individual Black feminists are living in isolation all over the country, that our own numbers are small, and that we have some skills in writing, printing, and publishing makes us want to carry out these kinds of projects as a means of organizing Black feminists as we continue to do political work in coalition with other groups.

4. Black Feminist Issues and Projects

During our time together we have identified and worked on many issues of particular relevance to Black women. The inclusiveness of our politics makes us concerned with any situation that impinges upon the lives of women, Third World and working people. We are of course particularly committed to working on those struggles in which race, sex and class are simultaneous factors in oppression. We might, for example, become involved in workplace organizing at a factory that employs Third World women or picket a hospital that is cutting back on already inadequate health care to a Third World community, or set up a rape crisis center in a Black neighborhood. Organizing around welfare and daycare concerns might also be a focus. The work to be done and the countless issues that this work represents merely reflect the pervasiveness of our oppression.

Issues and projects that collective members have actually worked on are sterilization abuse, abortion rights, battered women, rape and health care. We have also done many workshops and educationals on Black feminism on college campuses, at women's conferences, and most recently for high school women.

One issue that is of major concern to us and that we have begun to publicly address is racism in the white women's movement. As Black feminists we are made constantly and painfully aware of how little effort white women have made to understand and combat their racism, which requires among other things that they have a more than superficial comprehension of race, color, and Black history and culture. Eliminating racism in the white women's movement is by definition work for white women to do, but we will continue to speak to and demand accountability on this issue.

In the practice of our politics we do not believe that the end always justifies the means. Many reactionary and destructive acts have been done in the name of achieving "correct" political goals. As feminists we do not want to mess over people in the name of politics. We believe in collective process and a nonhierarchical distribution of power within our own group and in our vision of a revolutionary society. We are committed to a continual examination of our politics as they develop through criticism and self-criticism as an essential aspect of our practice. In her introduction to *Sisterhood is Powerful* Robin Morgan writes:

> I haven't the faintest notion what possible revolutionary role white heterosexual men could fulfill, since they are the very embodiment of reactionary-vested-interest-power.

As Black feminists and Lesbians we know that we have a very definite revolutionary task to perform and we are ready for the lifetime of work and struggle before us.

FOR FURTHER READING

Eisenstein, Zillah, ed. *Capitalist Patriarchy: The Case for Social Feminism.* New York: Monthly Review Press, 1978.

Hull, Gloria, Patricia Bell-Scott, and Barbara Smith. *All the Women Are White, All the Blacks Are Men, But Some of Us Are Brave: Black Women's Studies.* New York: The Feminist Press, 1982.

Mankiller, Wilma, Gwendolyn Mink, Marysa Navarro, Barbara Smith, and Gloria Steinem, eds. *The Reader's Companion to U.S. Women's History.* Boston: Houghton Mifflin, 1998.

Smith, Barbara. "The Boston Murders." In *Life Notes: Personal Writings by Contemporary Black Women,* edited by Patricia Bell-Scott, 315–20. New York: W. W. Norton and Company, 1994.

———. *The Truth That Never Hurts: Writings on Race, Gender and Freedom.* New Brunswick: Rutgers University Press: 1998.

———, ed. *Home Girls: A Black Feminist Anthology.* New Brunswick: Rutgers University Press, 2000.

Audre Lorde

1934–1992

"Because I am woman, because I am Black, because I am lesbian, because I am myself—a Black woman warrior poet doing my work—come to ask you, are you doing yours?" These powerful words of Audre Lorde embody her constant resistance to the politics of racism, homophobia, and separatism and her insistence on the necessity of action. From her earliest collection of poetry, *The First Cities* (1968), to her biomythography, *Zami: A New Spelling of My Name* (1982), she showed how women can use their differences to construct a stronger community. Her poetry and prose reverberate with concern about the distance between white women and women of color, insisting that white women become conscious of their privilege and attend to the different material conditions of women of color. Lorde does not name these differences to separate women from one another; rather, she names them so that women can use and build upon their differences. By this act of naming, Lorde actively negates the collective silence that she says keeps women apart: "for it is not difference which immobilizes us, but silence. And there are so many silences to be broken."

A self-described "warrior" and "casualty," Lorde died in 1992 from breast cancer. In this speech, which was first delivered as part of the "Lesbian and Literature Panel" at the 1977 Modern Language Association Conference, she speaks of her initial diagnosis and surgery to an academic audience invested in public, academic discourse. She breaks with convention by delivering a public speech that deals, in part, with the intensely private issue of breast cancer. Not only does she challenge the academic notion of public discourse in all of her work, but she also establishes theories of the erotic and the emotions, creating a feminist rhetoric that does not separate the body from language, nor anger from reason.

She offers her personal experience in this inspiring speech to urge women to break the silences in their lives. The speech serves as a model for breaking the silence as Lorde traces her realization that "I was going to die, if not sooner then later, whether or not I had ever spoken myself. My silences had not protected me." For Lorde, claiming the right to speak means survival, while silence equals death.

"The Transformation of Silence into Language and Action"

1977

I have come to believe over and over again that what is most important to me must be spoken, made verbal and shared, even at the risk of having it bruised or misunderstood. That the speaking profits me, beyond any other effect. I am standing here as a black lesbian poet, and the meaning of all that waits upon the fact that I am still alive, and might not have been. Less than two months ago I was told by doctors, one female and one male, that I would have to have breast surgery, and that there was a 60 to 80 percent chance that the tumor was malignant. Between that telling and the actual surgery, there was a three-week period of the agony of an involuntary reorganization of my entire life. The surgery was completed, and the growth was benign.

But within those three weeks, I was forced to look upon myself and my living with a harsh and urgent clarity that has left me still shaken but much stronger. This is a situation faced by many women, by some of you here today. Some of what I experienced during that time has helped elucidate for me much of what I feel concerning the transformation of silence into language and action.

In becoming forcibly and essentially aware of my mortality, and of what I wished and wanted for my life, however short it might be, priorities and omissions became strongly etched in a merciless light, and what I most regretted were my silences. Of what had I *ever* been afraid? To question or to speak as I believed could have meant pain, or death. But we all hurt in so many different ways, all the time, and pain will either change or end. Death, on the other hand, is the final silence. And that might be coming quickly, now, without regard for whether I had ever spoken what needed to be said, or had only betrayed myself into small silences, while I planned someday to speak, or waited for someone else's words. And I began to recognize a source of power within myself that comes from the knowledge that while it is most desirable not to be afraid, learning to put fear into a perspective gave me great strength.

I was going to die, if not sooner then later, whether or not I had ever spoken myself. My silences had not protected me. Your silence will not protect you. But for every real word spoken, for every attempt I had ever made to speak those truths for which I am still seeking, I had made contact with other women while we examined the words to fit a world in which we all believed, bridging our differences. And it was the concern and caring of all those women which gave me strength and enabled me to scrutinize the essentials of my living.

The women who sustained me through that period were Black and white, old and young, lesbian, bisexual, and heterosexual, and we all shared a war against the tyrannies of silence. They all gave me a strength and concern without which I could not have survived intact. Within those weeks of acute fear came the knowledge—within the war we are all waging with the forces of death, subtle and otherwise, conscious or not—I am not only a casualty, I am also a warrior.

What are the words you do not yet have? What do you need to say? What are the tyrannies you swallow day by day and attempt to make your own, until you will sicken and die of them, still in silence? Perhaps for some of you here today, I am the face of one of your fears. Because I am woman, because I am Black, because I am lesbian, because I am myself—a Black woman warrior poet doing my work—come to ask you, are you doing yours?

And of course I am afraid, because the transformation of silence into language and action is an act of self-revelation, and that always seems fraught with danger. But my daughter, when I told her of our topic and my difficulty with it, said, "Tell them about how you're never really a whole person if you remain silent, because there's always that one little piece inside you that wants to be spoken out, and if you keep ignoring it, it gets madder and madder and hotter and hotter, and if you don't speak it out one day it will just up and punch you in the mouth from the inside."

In the cause of silence, each of us draws the face of her own fear—fear of contempt, of censure, or some judgment, or recognition, of challenge, of annihilation. But most of all, I think, we fear the visibility without which we also cannot truly live. Within this country where racial difference creates a constant, if unspoken, distortion of vision, black women have on one hand always been highly visible, and so, on the other hand, have been rendered invisible through the depersonalization of racism. Even within the women's movement, we have had to fight, and still do, for that very visibility which also renders us most vulnerable, our Blackness. For to survive in the mouth of this dragon we call america, we have had to learn this first and most vital lesson—that we were never meant to survive. Not as human beings. And neither were most of you here today, Black or not. And that visibility which makes us most vulnerable is that which also is the source of our greatest strength. Because the machine will try to grind you into dust anyway, whether or not we speak. We can sit in our corners mute forever while our sisters and our selves are wasted, while our children are distorted and destroyed, while our earth is poisoned; we can sit in our safe corners mute as bottles, and we still will be no less afraid.

In my house this year we are celebrating the feast of Kwanza, the African-american festival of harvest which begins the day after Christmas and lasts for seven days. There are seven principles of Kwanza, one for each day. The first principle is Umoja, which means unity, the decision to strive for and maintain unity in self and community. The principle for yesterday, the second day, was

Kujichagulia—self-determination—the decision to define ourselves, name ourselves, and speak for ourselves, instead of being defined and spoken for by others. Today is the third day of Kwanza, and the principle for today is Ujima—collective work and responsibility—the decision to build and maintain ourselves and our communities together and to recognize and solve our problems together.

Each of us is here now because in one way or another we share a commitment to language and to the power of language, and to the reclaiming of that language which has been made to work against us. In the transformation of silence into language and action, it is vitally necessary for each one of us to establish or examine her function in that transformation and to recognize her role as vital within that transformation.

For those of us who write, it is necessary to scrutinize not only the truth of what we speak, but the truth of that language by which we speak it. For others, it is to share and spread also those words that are meaningful to us. But primarily for us all, it is necessary to teach by living and speaking those truths which we believe and know beyond understanding. Because in this way alone we can survive, by taking part in a process of life that is creative and continuing, that is growth.

And it is never without fear—of visibility, of the harsh light of scrutiny and perhaps judgment, of pain, of death. But we have lived through all of those already, in silence, except death. And I remind myself all the time now that if I were to have been born mute, or had maintained an oath of silence my whole life long for safety, I would still have suffered, and I would still die. It is very good for establishing perspective.

And where the words of women are crying to be heard, we must each of us recognize our responsibility to seek those words out, to read them and share them and examine them in their pertinence to our lives. That we not hide behind the mockeries of separations that have been imposed upon us and which so often we accept as our own. For instance, "I can't possibly teach Black women's writing—their experience is so different from mine," yet how many years have you spent teaching Plato and Shakespeare and Proust? Or another: "She's a white woman and what could she possibly have to say to me?" Or, "She's a lesbian, what would my husband say, or my chairman?" Or again, "This woman writes of her sons and I have no children." And all the other endless ways in which we rob ourselves of ourselves and each other.

We can learn to work and speak when we are afraid in the same way we have learned to work and speak when we are tired. For we have been socialized to respect fear more than our own needs for language and definition, and while we wait in silence for that final luxury of fearlessness, the weight of that silence will choke us.

The fact that we are here and that I speak these words is an attempt to break

that silence and bridge some of those differences between us, for it is not difference which immobilizes us, but silence. And there are so many silences to be
broken.

FOR FURTHER READING

"An Interview: Audre Lorde and Adrienne Rich." In *Sister Outsider: Essays and Speeches,* by
    Audre Lorde, 81–90. Freedom, Calif.: The Crossing Press, 1984.
Keating, AnaLouise. *Women Reading/Women Writing: Self-Invention in Paula Gunn Allen,
    Gloria Anzaldúa, and Audre Lorde.* Philadelphia: Temple University Press, 1996.
Lorde, Audre. *The Cancer Journals.* San Francisco: Spinsters/Aunt Lute, 1980.
———. *Sister Outsider. Essays and Speeches.* Freedom, Calif.: The Crossing Press, 1984.
———. *Zami: A New Spelling of My Name.* Freedom, Calif.: The Crossing Press, 1982.

Merle Woo

1941–

Describing herself as an Asian American queer activist, Merle Woo has worked for social justice during thirty years as a poet, writer, and teacher. She has been a lecturer in Ethnic/Asian Studies at the University of California at Berkeley and subsequently in Women's Studies at San Francisco State University. A member of Radical Women and the Socialist Freedom Party, she brought two landmark free-speech lawsuits against the University of California in the 1980s for race, gender, sexual orientation, and political bias. Woo became widely known when her writing appeared in the groundbreaking 1981 collection, *This Bridge Called My Back: Writings by Radical Women of Color.*

In "Letter to Ma," Woo writes to her mother describing the difficult silences in their relationship and recreates the painful realities of her mother's history and struggle as an immigrant. She creates a sense of intimacy with her readers and deflects the defensive response that her message might evoke from white and Asian readers. But this letter also functions as a public argument articulating the important connections among economic exploitation, racism, sexism, and homophobia. Women on the margin, like Woo, have consistently sought coalition building among oppressed groups in order to address interlocking and systemic oppression that perpetuates the internalized self-loathing and isolation that Woo sees in her mother's life. While this letter contains poignant anecdotes from her own family, these stories also resonate with the experiences of many Asian immigrants to the United States. In this letter to her mother, Woo claims pride in her mother's Chinese-Korean-American heritage and in the identity she finds in the traditions of daily life, the backbreaking work and the resilience her mother provided.

"Letter to Ma"

1980

January, 1980

Dear Ma,

I was depressed over Christmas, and when New Year's rolled around, do you know what one of my resolves was? Not to come by and see you as much anymore. I had to ask myself why I get so down when I'm with you, my mother, who has focused so much of her life on me, who has endured so much; one who I am proud of and respect so deeply for simply surviving.

I suppose that one of the main reasons is that when I leave your house, your pretty little round white table in the dinette where we sit while you drink tea (with only three specks of Jasmine) and I smoke and drink coffee, I am down because I believe there are chasms between us. When you say, "I support you, honey, in everything you do except . . . except. . . ." I know you mean except my speaking out and writing of my anger at all those things that have caused those chasms. When you say I shouldn't be so ashamed of Daddy, former gambler, retired clerk of a "gook suey" store, because of the time when I was six and saw him humiliated on Grant Avenue by two white cops, I know you haven't even been listening to me when I have repeatedly said that I am not ashamed of him, not you, not who we are. When you ask, "Are you so angry because you are unhappy?" I know that we are not talking to each other. Not with understanding, although many words have passed between us, many hours, many afternoons at that round table with Daddy out in the front room watching television, and drifting out every once in a while to say "Still talking?" and getting more peanuts that are so bad for his health.

We talk and we talk and I feel frustrated by your censorship. I know it is unintentional and unconscious. But whatever I have told you about the classes I was teaching, or the stories I was working on, you've always forgotten within a month. Maybe you can't listen—because maybe when you look in my eyes, you will, as you've always done, sense more than what we're actually saying, and that makes you fearful. Do you see your repressed anger manifested in me? What doors would groan wide open if you heard my words with complete understanding? Are you afraid that your daughter is breaking out of our shackles, and into total anarchy? That your daughter has turned into a crazy woman who advocates not only equality for Third World people, for women, but for gays as well? Please don't shudder, Ma, when I speak of homosexuality. Until we can

Reprinted from Woo, Merle. "Letter to Ma." In *This Bridge Called My Back: Writings by Radical Women of Color*, edited by Cherríe Moraga and Gloria Anzaldúa, 140–47. New York: Kitchen Table Women of Color Press, 1983.

all present ourselves to the world in our completeness, as fully and beautifully as we see ourselves naked in our bedrooms, we are not free.

After what seems like hours of talking, I realize it is not talking at all, but the filling up of time with sounds that say, "I am your daughter, you are my mother, and we are keeping each other company, and that is enough." But it is not enough because my life has been formed by your life. Together we have lived 111 years in this country as yellow women, and it is not enough to enunciate words and words and words and then to have them only mean that we have been keeping each other company. I desperately want you to understand me and my work, Ma, to know what I am doing! When you distort what I say, like thinking I am against all "caucasians" or that I am ashamed of Dad, then I feel anger and more frustration and want to slash out, not at you, but at those external forces which keep us apart. What deepens the chasms between us are our different re-actions to those forces. Yours has been one of silence, self-denial, self-efface-ment; you believing it is your fault that you never fully experienced self-pride and freedom of choice. But listen, Ma, only with a deliberate consciousness is my reaction different from yours.

When I look at you, there are images: images of you as a little 10-year-old Korean girl, being sent alone from Shanghai to the United States, in steerage with only one skimpy little dress, being sick and lonely on Angel Island for three months; then growing up in a "Home" run by white missionary women. Scrubbing floors on your hands and knees, hauling coal in heavy metal buckets up three flights of stairs, tending to the younger children, putting hot bricks on your cheeks to deaden the pain from the terrible toothaches you always had. Working all your life as maid, waitress, salesclerk, office worker, mother. But throughout there is an image of you as strong and courageous, and persevering: climbing out of windows to escape from the Home, then later, from an abusive first husband. There is so much more to these images than I can say, but I think you know what I mean. Escaping out of windows offered only temporary res-pites; surviving is an everyday chore. You gave me, physically, what you never had, but there was a spiritual, emotional legacy you passed down which was re-inforced by society: self-contempt because of our race, our sex, our sexuality. For deeply ingrained in me, Ma, there has been that strong, compulsive force to sink into self-contempt, passivity, and despair. I am sure that my 15 years of al-cohol abuse have not been forgotten by either of us, nor my suicidal depres-sions.

Now, I know you are going to think I hate and despise you for your self-ha-tred, for your isolation. But I don't. Because in spite of your withdrawal, in spite of your loneliness, you have not only survived, but been beside me in the worst of times when your company meant everything in the world to me. I just need more than that now, Ma. I have taken and taken from you in terms of needing you to mother me, to be by my side, and I need, now, to take from you two more things: understanding and support for who I am now and my work.

We are Asian American women and the reaction to our identity is what causes the chasms instead of connections. But do you realize, Ma, that I could never have reacted the way I have if you had not provided for me the opportunity to be free of the binds that have held you down, and to be in the process of self-affirmation? Because of your life, because of the physical security you have given me: my education, my full stomach, my clothed and starched back, my piano and dancing lessons—all those gifts you never received—I saw myself as having worth; now I begin to love myself more, see our potential, and fight for just that kind of social change that will affirm me, my race, my sex, my heritage. And while I affirm myself, Ma, I affirm you.

Today, I am satisfied to call myself either an Asian American Feminist or Yellow Feminist. The two terms are inseparable because race and sex are an integral part of me. This means that I am working with others to realize pride in culture and women and heritage (the heritage that is the exploited yellow immigrant: Daddy and you). Being a Yellow Feminist means being a community activist and a humanist. It does not mean "separatism," either by cutting myself off from non-Asians or men. It does not mean retaining the same power structure and substituting women in positions of control held by men. It does mean fighting the whites and the men who abuse us, straightjacket us and tape our mouths; it means changing the economic class system and psychological forces (sexism, racism, and homophobia) that really hurt all of us. And I do this, not in isolation, but in the community.

We no longer can afford to stand back and watch while an insatiable elite ravages and devours resources which are enough for all of us. The obstacles are so huge and overwhelming that often I do become cynical and want to give up. And if I were struggling alone, I know I would never even attempt to put into action what I believe in my heart, that (and this is primarily because of you, Ma) Yellow Women are strong and have the potential to be powerful and effective leaders.

I can hear you asking now, "Well, what do you mean by 'social change and leadership'? And how are you going to go about it?" To begin with we must wipe out the circumstances that keep us down in silence and self-effacement. Right now, my techniques are education and writing. Yellow Feminist means being a core for change, and that core means having the belief in our potential as human beings. I will work with anyone, support anyone, who shares my sensibility, my objectives. But there are barriers to unity: white women who are racist, and Asian American men who are sexist. My very being declares that those two groups do not share my complete sensibility. I would be fragmented, mutilated, if I did not fight against racism and sexism together.

And this is when the pain of the struggle hits home. How many white women have taken on the responsibility to educate themselves about Third World people, their history, their culture? How many white women really think about the stereotypes they retain as truth about women of color? But the perpetuation of dehumanizing stereotypes is really very helpful for whites; they use them to justify their giving us the lowest wages and all the work they don't want to perform. Ma, how can we believe things are changing when as a nurse's aide during World War II, you were given only the tasks of changing the bed linen, removing bed pans, taking urine samples, and then only three years ago as a retired volunteer worker in a local hospital, white women gave themselves desk jobs and gave you, at 69, the same work you did in 1943? Today you speak more fondly of being a nurse's aide during World War II and how proud you are of the fact that the Red Cross showed its appreciation for your service by giving you a diploma. Still in 1980, the injustices continue. I can give you so many examples of groups which are "feminist" in which women of color were given the usual least important tasks, the shitwork, and given no say in how that group is to be run. Needless to say, those Third World women, like you, dropped out, quit.

Working in writing and teaching, I have seen how white women condescend to Third World women because they reason that because of our oppression, which they know nothing about, we are behind them and their "progressive ideas" in the struggle for freedom. They don't even look at history! At the facts! How we as Asian American women have always been fighting for more than mere survival, but were never acknowledged because we were in our communities, invisible, but not inaccessible.

And I get so tired of being the instant resource for information on Asian American women. Being the token representative, going from class to class, group to group, bleeding for white women so they can have an easy answer— and then, and this is what really gets to me—they usually leave to never continue their education about us on their own.

To the racist white female professor who says, "If I have to watch everything I say I wouldn't say anything," I want to say, "Then get out of teaching." To the white female poet who says, "Well, frankly, I believe that politics and poetry don't necessarily have to go together," I say, "Your little taste of white privilege has deluded you into thinking that you don't have to fight against sexism in this society. You are talking to me from your own isolation and your own racism. If you feel that you don't have to fight for me, that you don't have to speak out against capitalism, the exploitation of human and natural resources, then you in your silence, your inability to make connections, are siding with a system that will eventually get you, after it has gotten me. And if you think that's not a political stance, you're more than simply deluded, you're crazy!"

This is the same white voice that says, "I am writing about and looking for themes that are 'universal.'" Well, most of the time when "universal" is used, it is just a euphemism for "white:" white themes, white significance, white culture. And denying minority groups their rightful place and time in U.S. history is simply racist.

Yes, Ma, I am mad. I carry the anger from my own experience and the anger you couldn't afford to express, and even that is often misinterpreted no matter how hard I try to be clear about my position. A white woman in my class said to me a couple of months ago, "I feel that Third World women hate me and that *they* are being racist; I'm being stereotyped, and I've never been part of the ruling class." I replied, "Please try to understand. Know our history. Know the racism of whites, how deep it goes. Know that we are becoming ever more intolerant of those people who let their ignorance be their excuse for their complacency, their liberalism, when this country (this world!) is going to hell in a handbasket. Try to understand that our distrust is from experience, and that our distrust is power*less*. Racism is an essential part of the status quo, power*ful*, and continues to keep us down. It is a rule taught to all of us from birth. Is it no wonder that we fear there are no exceptions?"

And as if the grief we go through working with white women weren't enough; so close to home, in our community, and so very painful, is the lack of support we get from some of our Asian American brothers. Here is a quote from a rather prominent male writer ranting on about a Yellow "sister":

> . . . I can only believe that such blatant sucking off of the identity is the work of a Chinese American woman, another Jade Snow Wong Pochahontas yellow. Pussywhipped again. Oh, damn, pussywhipped again.

Chinese American woman: "another Jade Snow Wong Pochahontas yellow." According to him, Chinese American women sold out—are contemptuous of their culture, pathetically strain all their lives to be white, hate Asian American men, and so marry white men (the John Smiths)—or just like Pochahontas: we rescue white men while betraying our fathers; then marry white men, get baptized, and go to dear old England to become curiosities of the civilized world. Whew! Now that's an indictment! (Of all women of color.) Some of the male writers in the Asian American community seem never to support us. They always expect us to support them, and you know what? We almost always do. Anti-Yellow men? Are they kidding? We go to their readings, buy and read and comment on their books, and try to keep up a dialogue. And they accuse us of betrayal, are resentful because we do readings together as Women, and so often do not come to our performances. And all the while we hurt because we are rejected by our brothers. The Pochahontas image used by a Chinese American man points out a tragic truth: the white man and his ideology are still over us and between us. These men of color, with clear vision, fight the racism in white society, but have bought the white male definition of "masculinity:" men only should take on the leadership in the community because the qualities of "originality, daring, physical courage, and creativity" are "traditionally masculine."

Some Asian men don't seem to understand that by supporting Third World women and fighting sexism, they are helping themselves as well. I understand all too clearly how dehumanized Dad was in this country. To be a Chinese man in America is to be a victim of both racism and sexism. He was made to feel he was without strength, identity, and purpose. He was made to feel soft and weak, whose only job was to serve whites. Yes, Ma, at one time I was ashamed of him because I thought he was "womanly." When those two white cops said, "Hey, fat boy, where's our meat?" he left me standing there on Grant Avenue while he hurried over to his store to get it; they kept complaining, never satisfied, "That piece isn't good enough. What's the matter with you, fat boy? Don't you have respect? Don't wrap that meat in newspapers either; use the good stuff over there." I didn't know that he spent a year and a half on Angel Island; that we could never have our right names; that he lived in constant fear of being deported; that, like you, he worked two full-time jobs most of his life; that he was mocked and ridiculed because he speaks "broken English." And Ma, I was so ashamed after that experience when I was only six years old that I never held his hand again.

Today, as I write to you of all these memories, I feel even more deeply hurt when I realize how many people, how so many people, because of racism and sexism, fail to see what power we sacrifice by not joining hands.

But not all white women are racist, and not all Asian American Men are sexist. And we choose to trust them, love and work with them. And there are visible changes. Real tangible, positive changes. The changes I love to see are those changes within ourselves.

Your grandchildren, my children, Emily and Paul. That makes three generations. Emily loves herself. Always has. There are shades of self-doubt but much less than in you or me. She says exactly what she thinks, most of the time, either in praise or in criticism of herself or others. And at 16 she goes after whatever she wants, usually center stage. She trusts and loves people, regardless of race or sex (but, of course, she's cautious), loves her community and works in it, speaks up against racism and sexism at school. Did you know that she got Zora Neale Hurston and Alice Walker on her reading list for a Southern Writers class when there were only white authors? That she insisted on changing a script done by an Asian American man when she saw that the depiction of the character she was playing was sexist? That she went to a California State House Conference to speak out for Third World students' needs?

And what about her little brother, Paul? Twelve years old. And remember, Ma? At one of our Saturday Night Family Dinners, how he lectured Ronnie (his uncle, yet!) about how he was a male chauvinist? Paul told me once how he knew he had to fight to be Asian American, and later he added that if it weren't for Emily and me, he wouldn't have to think about feminist stuff too. He says he can hardly enjoy a movie or TV program anymore because of the sexism. Or comic books. And he is very much aware of the different treatment he gets from adults: "You have to do everything right," he said to Emily, "and I can get away with almost anything."

Emily and Paul give us hope, Ma. Because they are proud of who they are, and they care so much about our culture and history. Emily was the first to write your biography because she knows how crucial it is to get our stories in writing.

Ma, I wish I knew the histories of the women in our family before you. I bet that would be quite a story. But that may be just as well, because I can say that *you* started something. Maybe you feel ambivalent or doubtful about it, but you did. Actually, you should be proud of what you've begun. I am. If my reaction to being a Yellow Woman is different than yours was, please know that that is not a judgment on you, a criticism or a denial of you, your worth. I have always supported you, and as the years pass, I think I begin to understand you more and more.

In the last few years, I have realized the value of Homework: I have studied the history of our people in this country. I cannot tell you how proud I am to be a Chinese/Korean American Woman. We have such a proud heritage, such a courageous tradition. I want to tell everyone about that, all the particulars that are left out in the schools. And the full awareness of being a woman makes me want to sing. And I do sing with other Asian Americans and women, Ma, anyone who will sing with me.

I feel now that I can begin to put our lives in a larger framework. Ma, a larger framework! The outlines for us are time and blood, but today there is breadth possible through making connections with others involved in community struggle. In loving ourselves for who we are—American women of color—we can make a vision for the future where we are free to fulfill our human potential. This new framework will not support repression, hatred, exploitation and isolation, but will be a human and beautiful framework, created in a community, bonded not by color, sex or class, but by love and the common goal for the liberation of mind, heart, and spirit.

Ma, today, you are as beautiful and pure to me as the picture I have of you, as a little girl, under my dresser-glass.

I love you,
Merle

FOR FURTHER READING

Lim-Hing, Sharon, ed. *The Very Inside: An Anthology of Writing by Asian and Pacific Island Lesbian and Bisexual Women.* Toronto: Sister Vision Press, 1994.

Alice Walker

1944–

Best known for her popular novel *The Color Purple*, Alice Walker was the first African American woman to receive the Pulitzer Prize for fiction. Born in 1944 in Eatonton, Georgia, to sharecropping parents, Walker worked in the Civil Rights Movement in the South during the 1960s. In 1972, at Wellesley College, Walker taught the first class in the United States on African American women writers. She is also responsible for having placed a tombstone on Zora Neale Hurston's unmarked Florida grave in 1973. Always refusing the boundaries between the political and the personal, Walker has published five novels, two books of poetry, and four collections of nonfiction. She currently lives in California.

"In Search of Our Mothers' Gardens" is the title essay in a collection of prose that Walker terms "womanist." A blend of historical narrative, autobiography, poetry, literary criticism, and lyrical language, "In Search of Our Mothers' Gardens" serves as a classic example of "womanist" writing, which Walker describes as "courageous or *willful* behavior. Wanting to know more and in greater depth than is considered 'good' for one" (*In Search of Our Mothers' Gardens* xi). As it turns out, her search for her own artistic heritage brings both pain and joy to this child of poverty who uses her writing to learn about and to honor her influences, those she knows and those she can only imagine. The term "womanist" also refers to a "black feminist" or "feminist of color" who "appreciates and prefers women's culture, women's emotional flexibility . . . and women's strength" (*In Search of Our Mothers' Gardens* xi). Walker finds these characteristics in her own past as she pays homage to her mother.

Walker's essay also offers a revisionist history of women's writing—inserting historical women of color into Virginia Woolf's descriptions of what a woman writer needs; forcing a rereading of Woolf's rhetorical theory; sharpening that theory with class, race, and material contexts. At the same time, Walker challenges her readers to reflect on the art and talent of all the slave foremothers in history and supports them in this pursuit. Within this challenge, she also asserts that knowledge and authority can emerge from the everyday—from the private sphere of home and garden, from women's work—and insists that caretaking and the creation of everyday beauty have equal value with "high art" or public discourse. We chose this essay for this collection because it embodies our belief that each of the women writers here serves as part of the heritage of women's rhetoric, upon which we all stand and write.

"In Search of Our Mothers' Gardens"

1983

> I described her own nature and temperament. Told how they needed a larger
> life for their expression . . . I pointed out that in lieu of proper channels, her
> emotions had over-flowed into paths that dissipated them. I talked, beautifully
> I thought, about an art that would be born, an art that would open the way for
> women the likes of her. I asked her to hope, and build up an inner life against
> the coming of that day. . . I sang, with a strange quiver in my voice, a promise
> song.   —*Jean Toomer, "Avey," CANE*

The poet speaking to a prostitute who falls asleep while he's talking—

When the poet Jean Toomer walked through the South in the early twenties, he discovered a curious thing: black women whose spirituality was so intense, so deep, so *unconscious,* that they were themselves unaware of the richness they held. They stumbled blindly through their lives: creatures so abused and mutilated in body, so dimmed and confused by pain, that they considered themselves unworthy even of hope. In the selfless abstractions their bodies became to the men who used them, they became more than "sexual objects," more even than mere women: they became "Saints." Instead of being perceived as whole persons, their bodies became shrines: what was thought to be their minds became temples suitable for worship. These crazy Saints stared out at the world, wildly, like lunatics—or quietly, like suicides; and the "God" that was in their gaze was as mute as a great stone.

Who were these Saints? These crazy, loony, pitiful women?

Some of them, without a doubt, were our mothers and grandmothers.

In the still heat of the post-Reconstruction South, this is how they seemed to Jean Toomer: exquisite butterflies trapped in an evil honey, toiling away their lives in an era, a century, that did not acknowledge them except as "the *mule* of the world." They dreamed dreams that no one knew—not even themselves, in any coherent fashion—and saw visions no one could understand. They wandered or sat about the countryside crooning lullabies to ghosts, and drawing the mother of Christ in charcoal on courthouse walls.

They forced their minds to desert their bodies and their striving spirits sought to rise, like frail whirlwinds from the hard red clay. And when those frail whirlwinds fell, in scattered particles, upon the ground, no one mourned. Instead, men lit candles to celebrate the emptiness that remained, as people do who enter a beautiful but vacant space to resurrect a God.

Our mothers and grandmothers, some of them: moving to music not yet written. And they waited.

They waited for a day when the unknown thing that was in them would be made known; but guessed, somehow in their darkness, that on the day of their revelation they would be long dead. Therefore to Toomer they walked, and even ran, in slow motion. For they were going nowhere immediate, and the future was not yet within their grasp. And men took our mothers and grandmothers, "but got no pleasure from it." So complex was their passion and their calm.

To Toomer, they lay vacant and fallow as autumn fields, with harvest time never in sight: and he saw them enter loveless marriages, without joy; and become prostitutes, without resistance; and become mothers of children, without fulfillment.

For these grandmothers and mothers of ours were not Saints, but Artists; driven to a numb and bleeding madness by the springs of creativity in them for which there was no release. They were Creators, who lived lives of spiritual waste, because they were so rich in spirituality—which is the basis of Art—that the strain of enduring their unused and unwanted talent drove them insane. Throwing away this spirituality was their pathetic attempt to lighten the soul to a weight their work-worn, sexually abused bodies could bear.

What did it mean for a black woman to be an artist in our grandmothers' time? In our great-grandmothers' day? It is a question with an answer cruel enough to stop the blood.

Did you have a genius of a great-great-grandmother who died under some ignorant and depraved white overseer's lash? Or was she required to bake biscuits for a lazy backwater tramp, when she cried out in her soul to paint watercolors of sunsets, or the rain falling on the green and peaceful pasturelands? Or was her body broken and forced to bear children (who were more often than not sold away from her)—eight, ten, fifteen, twenty children—when her one joy was the thought of modeling heroic figures of rebellion, in stone or clay?

How was the creativity of the black woman kept alive, year after year and century after century, when for most of the years black people have been in America, it was a punishable crime for a black person to read or write? And the freedom to paint, to sculpt, to expand the mind with action did not exist. Consider, if you can bear to imagine it, what might have been the result if singing, too, had been forbidden by law. Listen to the voices of Bessie Smith, Billie Holiday, Nina Simone, Roberta Flack, and Aretha Franklin, among others, and imagine those voices muzzled for life. Then you may begin to comprehend the lives of our "crazy," "Sainted" mothers and grandmothers. The agony of the lives of women who might have been Poets, Novelists, Essayists, and Short-Story Writers (over a period of centuries), who died with their real gifts stifled within them.

And, if this were the end of the story, we would have cause to cry out in my paraphrase of Okot p'Bitek's great poem:

O, my clanswomen
Let us all cry together!
Come,
Let us mourn the death of our mother,
The death of a Queen
The ash that was produced
By a great fire!
O, this homestead is utterly dead
Close the gates
With *lacari* thorns,
For our mother
The creator of the Stool is lost!
And all the young women
Have perished in the wilderness!

But this is not the end of the story, for all the young women—our mothers and grandmothers, our*selves*—have not perished in the wilderness. And if we ask ourselves why, and search for and find the answer, we will know beyond all efforts to erase it from our minds, just exactly who, and of what, we black American women are.

One example, perhaps the most pathetic, most misunderstood one, can provide a backdrop for our mothers' work: Phillis Wheatley, a slave in the 1700s.

Virginia Woolf, in her book *A Room of One's Own*, wrote that in order for a woman to write fiction she must have two things, certainly: a room of her own (with key and lock) and enough money to support herself.

What then are we to make of Phillis Wheatley, a slave, who owned not even herself? This sickly, frail black girl who required a servant of her own at times—her health was so precarious—and who, had she been white, would have been easily considered the intellectual superior of all the women and most of the men in the society of her day.

Virginia Woolf wrote further, speaking of course not of our Phillis, that "any woman born with a great gift in the sixteenth century [insert "eighteenth century," insert "black woman," insert "born or made a slave"] would certainly have gone crazed, shot herself, or ended her days in some lonely cottage outside the village, half witch, half wizard [insert "Saint"], feared and mocked at. For it needs little skill and psychology to be sure that a highly gifted girl who had tried to use her gift for poetry would have been so thwarted and hindered by contrary instincts [add "chains, guns, the lash, the ownership of one's body by someone else, submission to an alien religion"], that she must have lost her health and sanity to a certainty."

The key words, as they relate to Phillis, are "contrary instincts." For when we read the poetry of Phillis Wheatley—as when we read the novels of Nella Larsen or the oddly false-sounding autobiography of that freest of all black women writers, Zora Hurston—evidence of "contrary instincts" is everywhere. Her loyalties were completely divided, as was, without question, her mind.

But how could this be otherwise? Captured at seven, a slave of wealthy, doting whites who instilled in her the "savagery" of the Africa they "rescued" her from . . . one wonders if she was even able to remember her homeland as she had known it, or as it really was.

Yet, because she did try to use her gift for poetry in a world that made her a slave, she was "so thwarted and hindered by . . . contrary instincts, that she . . . lost her health. . . ." In the last years of her brief life, burdened not only with the need to express her gift but also with a penniless, friendless "freedom" and several small children for whom she was forced to do strenuous work to feed, she lost her health, certainly. Suffering from malnutrition and neglect and who knows what mental agonies, Phillis Wheatley died.

So torn by "contrary instincts" was black, kidnapped, enslaved Phillis that her description of "the Goddess"—as she poetically called the Liberty she did not have—is ironically, cruelly humorous. And, in fact, has held Phillis up to ridicule for more than a century. It is usually read prior to hanging Phillis's memory as that of a fool. She wrote:

> The Goddess comes, she moves divinely fair,
> Olive and laurel binds her *golden* hair.
> Wherever shines this native of the skies,
> Unnumber'd charms and recent graces rise. [My italics]

It is obvious that Phillis, the slave, combed the "Goddess's" hair every morning; prior, perhaps, to bringing in the milk, or fixing her mistress's lunch. She took her imagery from the one thing she saw elevated above all others.

With the benefit of hindsight we ask, "How could she?"

But at last, Phillis, we understand. No more snickering when your stiff, struggling, ambivalent lines are forced on us. We know now that you were not an idiot or a traitor; only a sickly little black girl, snatched from your home and country and made a slave; a woman who still struggled to sing the song that was your gift, although in a land of barbarians who praised you for your bewildered tongue. It is not so much what you sang, as that you kept alive, in so many of our ancestors, *the notion of song.*

Black women are called, in the folklore that so aptly identifies one's status in society, "the *mule* of the world," because we have been handed the burdens that everyone else—*everyone* else refused to carry. We have also been called "Matriarchs," "Superwomen," and "Mean and Evil Bitches." Not to mention "Castraters" and "Sapphire's Mama." When we have pleaded for understanding, our character has been distorted; when we have asked for simple caring, we have been handed empty inspirational appellations, then stuck in the farthest corner. When we have asked for love, we have been given children. In short, even our plainer gifts, our labors of fidelity and love, have been knocked down our throats. To be an artist and a black woman, even today, lowers our status in many respects, rather than raises it: and yet, artists we will be.

Therefore we must fearlessly pull out of ourselves and look at and identify with our lives the living creativity some of our great-grandmothers were not allowed to know. I stress *some* of them because it is well known that the majority of our great-grandmothers knew, even without "knowing" it, the reality of their spirituality, even if they didn't recognize it beyond what happened in the singing at church—and they never had any intention of giving it up.

How they did it—those millions of black women who were not Phillis Wheatley, or Lucy Terry or Frances Harper or Zora Hurston or Nella Larsen or Bessie Smith; or Elizabeth Catlett, or Katherine Dunham, either—brings me to the title of this essay, "In Search of Our Mothers' Gardens," which is a personal account that is yet shared, in its theme and its meaning, by all of us. I found, while thinking about the far-reaching world of the creative black woman, that often the truest answer to a question that really matters can be found very close.

In the late 1920s my mother ran away from home to marry my father. Marriage, if not running away, was expected of seventeen-year-old girls. By the time she was twenty, she had two children and was pregnant with a third. Five children later, I was born. And this is how I came to know my mother: she seemed a large, soft, loving-eyed woman who was rarely impatient in our home. Her quick, violent temper was on view only a few times a year, when she battled with the white landlord who had the misfortune to suggest to her that her children did not need to go to school.

She made all the clothes we wore, even my brothers' overalls. She made all the towels and sheets we used. She spent the summers canning vegetables and fruits. She spent the winter evenings making quilts enough to cover all our beds.

During the "working" day, she labored beside—not behind—my father in the fields. Her day began before sunup, and did not end until late at night. There was never a moment for her to sit down, undisturbed, to unravel her own private thoughts; never a time free from interruption—by work or the noisy inquiries of her many children. And yet, it is to my mother—and all our mothers who were not famous—that I went in search of the secret of what has fed that muzzled and often mutilated, but vibrant, creative spirit that the black woman has inherited, and that pops out in wild and unlikely places to this day.

But when, you will ask, did my overworked mother have time to know or care about feeding the creative spirit?

The answer is so simple that many of us have spent years discovering it. We have constantly looked high, when we should have looked high—and low.

For example: in the Smithsonian Institution in Washington, D.C., there hangs a quilt unlike any other in the world. In fanciful, inspired, and yet simple and identifiable figures, it portrays the story of the Crucifixion. It is considered rare, beyond price. Though it follows no known pattern of quilt-making, and though it is made of bits and pieces of worthless rags, it is obviously the work of a person of powerful imagination and deep spiritual feeling. Below this quilt I saw a note that says it was made by "an anonymous Black woman in Alabama, a hundred years ago."

If we could locate this "anonymous" black woman from Alabama, she would turn out to be one of our grandmothers—an artist who left her mark in the only materials she could afford, and in the only medium her position in society allowed her to use.

As Virginia Woolf wrote further, in *A Room of One's Own:*

Yet genius of a sort must have existed among women as it must have existed among the working class. [Change this to "slaves" and "the wives and daughters of sharecroppers."] Now and again an Emily Brontë or a Robert Burns [change this to "a Zora Hurston or a Richard Wright"] blazes out and proves its presence. But certainly it never got itself on to paper. When, however, one reads of a witch being ducked, of a woman possessed by devils [or "Sainthood"], of a wise woman selling herbs [our root workers], or even a very remarkable man who had a mother, then I think we are on the track of a lost novelist, a suppressed poet, of some mute and inglorious Jane Austen. . . . Indeed, I would venture to guess that Anon, who wrote so many poems without signing them, was often a woman. . . .

And so our mothers and grandmothers have, more often than not anonymously, handed on the creative spark, the seed of the flower they themselves never hoped to see: or like a sealed letter they could not plainly read.

And so it is, certainly, with my own mother. Unlike "Ma" Rainey's songs, which retained their creator's name even while blasting forth from Bessie Smith's mouth, no song or poem will bear my mother's name. Yet so many of the stories that I write, that we all write, are my mother's stories. Only recently did I fully realize this: that through years of listening to my mother's stories of her life, I have absorbed not only the stories themselves, but something of the manner in which she spoke, something of the urgency that involves the knowledge that her stories—like her life—must be recorded. It is probably for this reason that so much of what I have written is about characters whose counterparts in real life are so much older than I am.

But the telling of these stories, which came from my mother's lips as naturally as breathing, was not the only way my mother showed herself as an artist. For stories, too, were subject to being distracted, to dying without conclusion. Dinners must be started, and cotton must be gathered before the big rains. The artist that was and is my mother showed itself to me only after many years. This is what I finally noticed:

Like Mem, a character in *The Third Life of Grange Copeland*, my mother adorned with flowers whatever shabby house we were forced to live in. And not just your typical straggly country stand of zinnias, either. She planted ambitious gardens—and still does—with over fifty different varieties of plants that bloom profusely from early March until late November. Before she left home for the fields, she watered her flowers, chopped up the grass, and laid out new beds. When she returned from the fields she might divide clumps of bulbs, dig a cold pit, uproot and replant roses, or prune branches from her taller bushes or trees—until night came and it was too dark to see.

Whatever she planted grew as if by magic, and her fame as a grower of flowers spread over three counties. Because of her creativity with her flowers, even my memories of poverty are seen through a screen of blooms—sunflowers, petunias, roses, dahlias, forsythia, spirea, delphiniums, verbena . . . and on and on.

And I remember people coming to my mother's yard to be given cuttings from her flowers; I hear again the praise showered on her because whatever rocky soil she landed on, she turned into a garden. A garden so brilliant with colors, so original in its design, so magnificent with life and creativity, that to this day people drive by our house in Georgia—perfect strangers and imperfect strangers—and ask to stand or walk among my mother's art.

I notice that it is only when my mother is working in her flowers that she is radiant, almost to the point of being invisible—except as Creator: hand and eye. She is involved in work her soul must have. Ordering the universe in the image of her personal conception of Beauty.

Her face, as she prepares the Art that is her gift, is a legacy of respect she leaves to me, for all that illuminates and cherishes life. She has handed down respect for the possibilities—and the will to grasp them.

For her, so hindered and intruded upon in so many ways, being an artist has still been a daily part of her life. This ability to hold on, even in very simple ways, is work black women have done for a very long time.

This poem is not enough, but it is something, for the woman who literally covered the holes in our walls with sunflowers:

> They were women then
> My mama's generation
> Husky of voice—Stout of
> Step
> With fists as well as
> Hands
> How they battered down
> Doors
> And ironed

Starched white
Shirts
How they led
Armies
Headragged Generals
Across mined
Fields
Booby-trapped
Kitchens
To discover books
Desks
A place for us
How they knew what we
Must know
Without knowing a page
Of it
Themselves.

Guided by my heritage of a love of beauty and a respect for strength—in search of my mother's garden, I found my own.

And perhaps in Africa over two hundred years ago, there was just such a mother; perhaps she painted vivid and daring decorations in oranges and yellows and greens on the walls of her hut; perhaps she sang—in a voice like Roberta Flack's—*sweetly* over the compounds of her village; perhaps she wove the most stunning mats or told the most ingenious stories of all the village storytellers. Perhaps she was herself a poet—though only her daughter's name is signed to the poems that we know.

Perhaps Phillis Wheatley's mother was also an artist.

Perhaps in more than Phillis Wheatley's biological life is her mother's signature made clear.

FOR FURTHER READING

Walker, Alice. *Anything We Love Can Be Saved: A Writer's Activism.* New York: Random House, 1997.
———. *In Search of Our Mothers' Gardens: Womanist Prose.* New York: Harcourt Brace Jovanovich, 1974.
———. *Living by the Word: Collected Writings, 1973–1988.* New York: Harcourt Brace Jovanovich, 1988.
———. *The Same River Twice: Honoring the Difficult: A Meditation on Life, Spirit, Art, and the Making of the Film,* The Color Purple, *Ten Years Later.* New York: Scribner, 1996.
Walker, Alice, with Pratibha Parmar. *Warrior Marks: Female Genital Mutilation and the Sexual Blinding of Women.* New York: Harcourt Brace Jovanovich, 1993.

Evelyn Fox Keller

1936–

Evelyn Fox Keller, physicist and Professor of History and Philosophy of Science at M.I.T., has also taught rhetoric and women's studies at the University of California at Berkeley. Much of her current work analyzes scientific discourse and the way language shapes the nature of scientific research. Keller began studying Barbara McClintock's work as a part of her exploration of the relationship between gender and science. She did not find a simplistic connection in McClintock's work. McClintock rejects notions of "feminine science" and says that in science, "gender drops away" (Keller, *A Feeling* xxv). Keller's biography of McClintock, *A Feeling for the Organism,* draws on her extensive conversations with McClintock and, using McClintock's own voice, documents McClintock's life and her basic assumption that scientific research requires a special "sympathetic understanding" of nature. Keller's biography of McClintock affirms the importance of alternative epistemologies and rhetorics for their potential to advance human understanding of the natural world and our place in it.

In 1983, at the age of eighty-two, Barbara McClintock was awarded the Nobel Prize after decades during which the scientific community either ignored or was bewildered by her work. Later, when the groundbreaking nature of her work on field corn genetics became apparent, some scientists acknowledged that they were simply unable to grasp the importance of her research because McClintock's fundamental methodologies were so far beyond the narrow methodologies of standard science, with its adherence to a dualistic belief in objectivity and subjectivity and to rigid, linear methodologies that at most only render "nature-in-pieces." McClintock says, "Much of the work done, is done, because one wants to impose an answer. They have the answer ready and they know what they want the material to tell them. So anything it doesn't tell them, they don't really recognize as there or they feel it is a mistake and throw it out" (Keller, *A Feeling* 179). There is nothing mystical or sentimental about her complex methods; they embrace holistic and diverse sources of knowledge often stereotypically considered "feminine": creative insight; intuition; induction; emotional investment; connectedness; and, above all, rigorous, attentive observation and the capacity to delight and learn from surprising outcomes—to listen to the organism.

From *A Feeling for the Organism*

1983

> There are two equally dangerous extremes—to shut reason out, and to let
> nothing else in.   –Pascal

If Barbara McClintock's story illustrates the fallibility of science, it also bears
witness to the underlying health of the scientific enterprise. Her eventual vindication demonstrates the capacity of science to overcome its own characteristic kinds of myopia, reminding us that its limitations do not reinforce themselves indefinitely. Their own methodology allows, even obliges, scientists to
continually reencounter phenomena even their best theories cannot accommodate. Or—to look at it from the other side—however severely communication
between science and nature may be impeded by the preconceptions of a particular time, some channels always remain open; and, through them, nature finds
ways of reasserting itself.

But the story of McClintock's contributions to biology has another, less accessible, aspect. What is it in an individual scientist's relation to nature that fa-
cilitates the kind of seeing that eventually leads to productive discourse? What
enabled McClintock to see further and deeper into the mysteries of genetics
than her colleagues?

Her answer is simple. Over and over again, she tells us one must have the
time to look, the patience to "hear what the material has to say to you," the
openness to "let it come to you." Above all, one must have "a feeling for the organism."

One must understand "how it grows, understand its parts, understand when
something is going wrong with it. [An organism] isn't just a piece of plastic, it's
something that is constantly being affected by the environment, constantly
showing attributes or disabilities in its growth. You have to be aware of all of
that. . . . You need to know those plants well enough so that if anything changes,
. . . you [can] look at the plant and right away you know what this damage you
see is from—something that scraped across it or something that bit it or something that the wind did." You need to have a feeling for every individual plant.

"No two plants are exactly alike. They're all different, and as a consequence,
you have to know that difference," she explains. "I start with the seedling, and I
don't want to leave it. I don't feel I really know the story if I don't watch the
plant all the way along. So I know every plant in the field. I know them intimately, and I find it a great pleasure to know them."

This intimate knowledge, made possible by years of close association with the organism she studies, is a prerequisite for her extraordinary perspicacity. "I have learned so much about the corn plant that when I see things, I can interpret [them] right away." Both literally and figuratively, her "feeling for the organism" has extended her vision. At the same time, it has sustained her through a lifetime of lonely endeavor, unrelieved by the solace of human intimacy or even by the embrace of her profession.

Good science cannot proceed without a deep emotional investment on the part of the scientist. It is that emotional investment that provides the motivating force for the endless hours of intense, often grueling, labor. Einstein wrote: ". . . what deep longing to understand even a faint reflexion of the reason revealed in this world had to be alive in Kepler and Newton so that they could in lonely work for many years disentangle the mechanism of celestial mechanics?" But McClintock's feeling for the organism is not simply a longing to behold the "reason revealed in this world." It is a longing to embrace the world in its very being, through reason and beyond.

For McClintock, reason—at least in the conventional sense of the word—is not by itself adequate to describe the vast complexity—even mystery—of living forms. Organisms have a life and order of their own that scientists can only partially fathom. No models we invent can begin to do full justice to the prodigious capacity of organisms to devise means for guaranteeing their own survival. On the contrary, "anything you can think of you will find." In comparison with the ingenuity of nature, our scientific intelligence seems pallid.

For her, the discovery of transposition was above all a key to the complexity of genetic organization—an indicator of the subtlety with which cytoplasm, membranes, and DNA are integrated into a single structure. It is the overall organization, or orchestration, that enables the organism to meet its needs, whatever they might be, in ways that never cease to surprise us. That capacity for surprise gives McClintock immense pleasure. She recalls, for example, the early post–World War II studies of the effect of radiation on *Drosophila:* "It turned out that the flies that had been under constant radiation were more vigorous than those that were standard. Well, it was hilarious; it was absolutely against everything that had been thought about earlier. I thought it was terribly funny; I was utterly delighted. Our experience with DDT has been similar. It was thought that insects could be readily killed off with the spraying of DDT. But the insects began to thumb their noses at anything you tried to do to them."

Our surprise is a measure of our tendency to underestimate the flexibility of living organisms. The adaptability of plants tends to be especially unappreciated. "Animals can walk around, but plants have to stay still to do the same things, with ingenious mechanisms. . . . Plants are extraordinary. For instance, . . . if you pinch a leaf of a plant you set off electric pulses. You can't touch a plant without setting off an electric pulse. . . . There is no question that plants have [all] kinds of sensitivities. They do a lot of responding to their environment. They can do almost anything you can think of. But just because they sit there, anybody walking down the road considers them just a plastic area to look at, [as if] they're not really alive."

An attentive observer knows better. At any time, for any plant, one who has sufficient patience and interest can see the myriad signs of life that a casual eye misses: "In the summertime, when you walk down the road, you'll see that the tulip leaves, if it's a little warm, turn themselves around so their backs are toward the sun. You can just see where the sun hits them and where the sun doesn't hit. . . . [Actually], within the restricted areas in which they live, they move around a great deal." These organisms "are fantastically beyond our wildest expectations."

For all of us, it is need and interest above all that induce the growth of our abilities; a motivated observer develops faculties that a casual spectator may never be aware of. Over the years, a special kind of sympathetic understanding grew in McClintock, heightening her powers of discernment, until finally, the objects of her study have become subjects in their own right; they claim from her a kind of attention that most of us experience only in relation to other persons. "Organism" is for her a code word—not simply a plant or animal ("Every component of the organism is as much of an organism as every other part")—but the name of a living form, of object-as-subject. With an uncharacteristic lapse into hyperbole, she adds: "Every time I walk on grass I feel sorry because I know the grass is screaming at me."

A bit of poetic license, perhaps, but McClintock is not a poet; she is a scientist. What marks her as such is her unwavering confidence in the underlying order of living forms, her use of the apparatus of science to gain access to that order, and her commitment to bringing back her insights into the shared language of science—even if doing so might require that language to change. The irregularities or surprises molecular biologists are now uncovering in the organization and behavior of DNA are not indications of a breakdown of order, but only of the inadequacies of our models in the face of the complexity of nature's actual order. Cells, and organisms, have an organization of their own in which nothing is random.

In short, McClintock shares with all other natural scientists the credo that nature is lawful, and the dedication to the task of articulating those laws. And she shares, with at least some, the additional awareness that reason and experiment, generally claimed to be the principal means of this pursuit, do not suffice. To quote Einstein again, " . . . only intuition, resting on sympathetic understanding, can lead to [these laws]; . . . the daily effort comes from no deliberate intention or program, but straight from the heart."

A deep reverence for nature, a capacity for union with that which is to be known—these reflect a different image of science from that of a purely rational enterprise. Yet the two images have coexisted throughout history. We are familiar with the idea that a form of mysticism—a commitment to the unity of experience, the oneness of nature, the fundamental mystery underlying the laws of nature—plays an essential role in the process of scientific discovery. Einstein called it "cosmic religiosity." In turn, the experience of creative insight reinforces these commitments, fostering a sense of the limitations of the scientific method, and an appreciation of other ways of knowing. In all of this, McClintock is no exception. What is exceptional is her forthrightness of expression—the pride she takes in holding, and voicing, attitudes that run counter to our more customary ideas about science. In her mind, what we call the scientific method cannot by itself give us "real understanding." "It gives us relationships which are useful, valid, and technically marvelous; however, they are not the truth." And it is by no means the only way of acquiring knowledge.

That there are valid ways of knowing other than those conventionally espoused by science is a conviction of long standing for McClintock. It derives from a lifetime of experiences that science tells us little about, experiences that she herself could no more set aside than she could discard the anomalous pattern on a single kernel of corn. Perhaps it is this fidelity to her own experience that allows her to be more open than most other scientists about her unconventional beliefs. Correspondingly, she is open to unorthodox views in others, whether she agrees with them or not. . . .

For years, she has maintained an interest in ways of learning other than those used in the West, and she made a particular effort to inform herself about the Tibetan Buddhists: "I was so startled by their method of training and by its results that I figured we were limiting ourselves by using what we call the scientific method. . . ."

She was equally impressed by the ability that some Tibetans had developed to regulate body temperature: "We are scientists, and we know nothing basically about controlling our body temperature. [But] the Tibetans learn to live with nothing but a tiny cotton jacket. They're out there cold winters and hot summers, and when they have been through the learning process, they have to take certain tests. One of the tests is to take a wet blanket, put it over them, and dry that blanket in the coldest weather. And they dry it."

How were they able to do these things? What would one need to do to acquire this sort of "knowledge"? She began to look at related phenomena that were closer to home: "Hypnosis also had potentials that were quite extraordinary." She began to believe that not only one's temperature, but one's circulation, and many other bodily processes generally thought to be autonomous, could be brought under the influence of mind. She was convinced that the potential for mental control revealed in hypnosis experiments, and practiced by the Tibetans, was something that could be learned. "You can do it, it can be taught." And she set out to teach herself. Long before the word "biofeedback" was invented, McClintock experimented with ways to control her own temperature and blood flow, until, in time, she began to feel a sense of what it took. But these interests were not popular. "I couldn't tell other people at the time because it was against the 'scientific method.'. . . . We just hadn't touched on this kind of knowledge in our medical physiology, [and it is] very, very different from the knowledge we call the only way." What we label scientific knowledge is "lots of fun. You get lots of correlations, but you don't get the truth Things are much more marvelous than the scientific method allows us to conceive."

Our own method could tell us about some things, but not about others—for instance, she reflects, not about "the kinds of things that made it possible for me to be creative in an unknown way. *Why* do you know? Why were you so sure of something when you couldn't tell anyone else? You weren't sure in a boastful way; you were sure in what I call a completely internal way. . . . What you had to do was put it into their frame. Wherever it came in your frame, you had to work to put it into their frame. So you work with so-called scientific methods to put it into their frame *after* you know. Well, [the question is] *how* you know it. I had the idea that the Tibetans understood this *how* you know."

McClintock is not the only scientist who has looked to the East for correctives to the limitations of Western science. Her remarks on her relation to the phenomena she studies are especially reminiscent of the lessons many physicists have drawn from the discoveries of atomic physics. . . . Indeed, as a result of a number of popular accounts published in the last decade, the correspondences between modern physics and Eastern thought have come to seem commonplace. But among biologists, these interests are not common. McClintock is right to see them, and herself, as oddities. And here, as elsewhere, she takes pride in being different. She is proud to call herself a "mystic."

Above all, she is proud of her ability to draw on these other ways of knowing in her work as a scientist. It is that which, to her, makes the life of science such a deeply satisfying one—even, at times, ecstatic. "What is ecstasy? I don't understand ecstasy, but I enjoy it. When I have it. Rare ecstasy."

Somehow, she doesn't know how, she has always had an "exceedingly strong feeling" for the oneness of things: "Basically, everything is one. There is no way in which you draw a line between things: What we [normally] do is to make these subdivisions, but they're not real. Our educational system is full of *subdivisions* that are artificial, that shouldn't be there. I think maybe poets—although I don't read poetry—have some understanding of this." The ultimate descriptive task, for both artists and scientists, is to "ensoul" what one sees, to attribute to it the life one shares with it; one learns by identification. . . .

McClintock reaps the kind of understanding and fulfillment that others acquire from personal intimacy. In short, her "feeling for the organism" is the mainspring of her creativity. It both promotes and is promoted by her access to the profound connectivity of all biological forms—of the cell, of the organism, of the ecosystem.

FOR FURTHER READING

Harding, Sandra. *Whose Science? Whose Knowledge? Thinking from Women's Lives.* Ithaca: Cornell University Press, 1991.

Keller, Evelyn Fox. *Reflections on Gender and Science.* New Haven: Yale University Press, 1985.

————. *Secrets of Life, Secrets of Death: Essays on Language, Gender and Science.* New York: Routledge, 1992.

Keller, Evelyn Fox, and Helen Longino, eds. *Feminism and Science.* New York: Oxford University Press, 1996.

Andrea Dworkin

1946–

Andrea Dworkin, one of the most forceful, articulate radical lesbian feminists of the past twenty years, is best known for her analysis of rape and pornography as by-products of patriarchal social structures and for her documentation of their effects on the lives of women. Dworkin asserts the primary relationship between pornography, prostitution, and rape; between the objectification and the humiliation of women; and between the political/economic systems that produce aggression and militarism and the exercise of power over others' lives.

Dworkin grew up poor in the 1940s and 1950s and became a political and social activist before she found her way to feminism in the late 1960s. She knows the personal atrocities of sexism: she was repeatedly raped as a resident of a women's detention center; she survived a brutal marriage in which she was battered and tortured; and she worked as a prostitute while trying to survive on the streets of New York City.

Dworkin has often single-handedly taken on the pornography industry. But in the 1980s, she worked with feminist legal scholar Catharine MacKinnon to redefine pornography as any depiction of women that objectifies, dehumanizes, and subordinates them through portrayals of rape, violence, or pain in contexts that are presented as sexual. Their model antipornography law sets forth a legal definition of pornography as a systematic cultural practice of sexual exploitation that violates women's civil rights under the Constitution. Because her attacks on pornography and sexism are uncompromising, graphically descriptive, and angry, Dworkin's writing has been widely attacked and misrepresented as man-hating and opposed to free speech.

One only has to read Dworkin's work to see that her ideas and rhetoric are much more complex and subtle than they are often depicted as being. Dworkin begins this speech by self-reflectively describing to her male audience the rhetorical difficulties of speaking to them. In doing so, she acknowledges the barriers that exist between them, but she also engages them with her ethical appeal—directing them to see their own complicity in violence against women; addressing head-on the strategies men use to deny their responsibility for sexual violence; and even directly attacking the men's movement, calling it "a recreational break" in its emphasis on developing more sensitivity and intimacy in men. She exhorts men to stop saying, "But I'm not like that," and to get busy—to move out onto the street; to talk to the pornographers, the "warmongers," the media; to take up the strategic work men ought to be doing to mobilize against the systemic subordination of women. Equality, she says, can never exist while rape and the dehumanization of women still occur.

Like much of Dworkin's work, "I Want a Twenty-Four-Hour Truce" has a sense of urgency and pathos. Her sentences are often clipped and short, with dramatic and shocking imagery. She does not have time, her audience comes to believe, to sugarcoat the truth. Women's lives are at stake, and men must end the violence: "We are very close to death"; "No more. No more rape"; "You've got to stop." Despite her urgent imperatives and bold accusations, Dworkin acknowledges that the social values that support aggression against women also damage men. At the end of this speech, in anger, sadness, and fatigue, she dares her male audience to give her and all women one day of respite, when not a single woman is raped. In making this dramatic plea, she reaffirms, "against all the evidence," her belief in men's humanity and addresses them with what might even be described as tenderness and compassion, perhaps the most significant mark of her rhetorical skill.

"I Want A Twenty-Four-Hour Truce During Which There Is No Rape"

1983

This was a speech given at the Midwest Regional Conference of the National Organization for Changing Men in the fall of 1983 in St. Paul, Minnesota. One of the organizers kindly sent me a tape and a transcript of my speech. The magazine of the men's movement, M., published it. I was teaching in Minneapolis. This was before Catharine MacKinnon and I had proposed or developed the civil rights approach to pornography as a legislative strategy. Lots of people were in the audience who later became key players in the fight for the civil rights bill. I didn't know them then. It was an audience of about 500 men, with scattered women. I spoke from notes and was actually on my way to Idaho—an eight-hour trip each way (because of bad air connections) to give a one hour speech on Art—fly out Saturday, come back Sunday, can't talk more than one hour or you'll miss the only plane leaving that day, you have to run from the podium to the car for the two-hour drive to the plane. Why would a militant feminist under this kind of pressure stop off on her way to the airport to say hi to 500 men? In a sense, this

was a feminist dream-come-true. What would you say to 500 men if you could? This is
what I said, how I used my chance. The men reacted with considerable love and sup-
port and also with considerable anger. Both. I hurried out to get my plane, the first hur-
dle for getting to Idaho. Only one man in the 500 threatened me physically. He was
stopped by a woman bodyguard (and friend) who had accompanied me.

I have thought a great deal about how a feminist, like myself, addresses an audience primarily of political men who say that they are antisexist. And I
thought a lot about whether there should be a qualitative difference in the kind
of speech I address to you. And then I found myself incapable of pretending
that I really believe that that qualitative difference exists. I have watched the
men's movement for many years. I am close with some of the people who participate in it. I can't come here as a friend even though I might very much want
to. What I would like to do is to scream: and in that scream I would have the
screams of the raped, and the sobs of the battered; and even worse, in the
center of that scream I would have the deafening sound of women's silence,
that silence into which we are born because we are women and in which most
of us die.

And if there would be a plea or a question or a human address in that
scream, it would be this: why are you so slow? Why are you so slow to understand the simplest things; not the complicated ideological things. You understand those. *The simple things.* The clichés. Simply that women are human to
precisely the degree and quality that you are.

And also: that we do not have time. We women. We don't have forever.
Some of us don't have another week or another day to take time for you to discuss whatever it is that will enable you to go out into those streets and do something. We are very close to death. All women are. And we are very close to rape
and we are very close to beating. And we are inside a system of humiliation
from which there is no escape for us. We use statistics not to try to quantify the
injuries, but to convince the world that those injuries even exist. Those statistics are not abstractions. It is easy to say, "Ah, the statistics, somebody writes
them up one way and somebody writes them up another way." That's true. But
I hear about the rapes one by one by one by one by one, which is also how they
happen. Those statistics are not abstract to me. Every three minutes a woman is
being raped. Every eighteen seconds a woman is being beaten. There is nothing
abstract about it. It is happening right now as I am speaking.

And it is happening for a simple reason. There is nothing complex and difficult about the reason. Men are doing it, because of the kind of power that men
have over women. That power is real, concrete, exercised from one body to
another body, exercised by someone who feels he has a right to exercise it, exercised in public and exercised in private. It is the sum and substance of
women's oppression.

It is not done 5000 miles away or 3000 miles away. It is done here and it is done now and it is done by the people in this room as well as by other contemporaries: our friends, our neighbors, people that we know. Women don't have to go to school to learn about power. We just have to be women, walking down the street or trying to get the housework done after having given one's body in marriage and then having no rights over it.

The power exercised by men day to day in life is power that is institutionalized. It is protected by law. It is protected by religion and religious practice. It is protected by universities, which are strongholds of male supremacy. It is protected by a police force. It is protected by those whom Shelley called "the unacknowledged legislators of the world:" the poets, the artists. Against that power, we have silence.

It is an extraordinary thing to try to understand and confront why it is that men believe—and men do believe—that they have the right to rape. Men may not believe it when asked. Everybody raise your hand who believes you have the right to rape. Not too many hands will go up. It's in life that men believe they have the right to force sex, which they don't call rape. And it is an extraordinary thing to try to understand that men really believe that they have the right to hit and to hurt. And it is an equally extraordinary thing to try to understand that men really believe that they have the right to buy a woman's body for the purpose of having sex: that that is a right. And it is very amazing to try to understand that men believe that the seven-billion-dollar-a-year industry that provides men with cunts is something that men have a right to.

That is the way the power of men is manifest in real life. That is what theory about male supremacy means. It means you can rape. It means you can hit. It means you can hurt. It means you can buy and sell women. It means that there is a class of people there to provide you with what you need. You stay richer than they are, so that they have to sell you sex. Not just on street corners, but in the workplace. That's another right that you can presume to have: sexual access to any woman in your environment, when you want.

Now, the men's movement suggests that men don't want the kind of power I have just described. I've actually heard explicit whole sentences to that effect. And yet, everything is a reason not to do something about changing the fact that you do have that power.

Hiding behind guilt, that's my favorite. I love that one. Oh, it's horrible, yes, and I'm so sorry. You have the time to feel guilty. We don't have the time for you to feel guilty. Your guilt is a form of acquiescence in what continues to occur. Your guilt helps keep things the way they are.

I have heard in the last several years a great deal about the suffering of men over sexism. Of course, I have heard a great deal about the suffering of men all my life. Needless to say, I have read *Hamlet*. I have read *King Lear*. I am an educated woman. I know that men suffer. This is a new wrinkle. Implicit in the idea that this is a different kind of suffering is the claim, I think, that in part you are actually suffering because of something that you know happens to someone else. That would indeed be new.

But mostly your guilt, your suffering, reduces to: gee, we really feel so bad. Everything makes men feel so bad: what you do, what you don't do, what you want to do, what you don't want to want to do but are going to do anyway. I think most of your distress is: gee, we really feel so bad. And I'm sorry that you feel so bad—so uselessly and stupidly bad—because there is a way in which this really is your tragedy. And I don't mean because you can't cry. And I don't mean because there is no real intimacy in your lives. And I don't mean because the armor that you have to live with as men is stultifying: and I don't doubt that it is. But I don't mean any of that.

I mean that there is a relationship between the way that women are raped and your socialization to rape and the war machine that grinds you up and spits you out: the war machine that you go through just like that woman went through Larry Flynt's meat grinder on the cover of *Hustler*. You damn well better believe that you're involved in this tragedy and that it's your tragedy too. Because you're turned into little soldier boys from the day that you are born and everything that you learn about how to avoid the humanity of women becomes part of the militarism of the country in which you live and the world in which you live. It is also part of the economy that you frequently claim to protest.

And the problem is that you think it's out there: and it's not out there. It's in you. The pimps and the warmongers speak for you. Rape and war are not so different. And what the pimps and the warmongers do is that they make you so proud of being men who can get it up and give it hard. And they take that acculturated sexuality and they put you in little uniforms and they send you out to kill and to die. Now, I am not going to suggest to you that I think that's more important than what you do to women, because I don't.

But I think that if you want to look at what this system does to you, then that is where you should start looking: the sexual politics of aggression; the sexual politics of militarism. I think that men are very afraid of other men. That is something that you sometimes try to address in your small groups, as if you changed your attitudes towards each other, you wouldn't be afraid of each other.

But as long as your sexuality has to do with aggression and your sense of entitlement to humanity has to do with being superior to other people, and there is so much contempt and hostility in your attitudes towards women and children, how could you not be afraid of each other? I think that you rightly perceive—without being willing to face it politically—that men are very dangerous: because you are.

The solution of the men's movement to make men less dangerous to each other by changing the way you touch and feel each other is not a solution. It's a recreational break.

These conferences are also concerned with homophobia. Homophobia is very important: it is very important to the way male supremacy works. In my opinion, the prohibitions against male homosexuality exist in order to protect male power. *Do it to her.* That is to say: as long as men rape, it is very important that men be directed to rape women. As long as sex is full of hostility and expresses both power over and contempt for the other person, it is very important that men not be declassed, stigmatized as female, used similarly. The power of men as a class depends on keeping men sexually inviolate and women sexually used by men. Homophobia helps maintain that class power: it also helps keep you as individuals safe from each other, safe from rape. If you want to do something about homophobia, you are going to have to do something about the fact that men rape, and that forced sex is not incidental to male sexuality but is in practice paradigmatic.

Some of you are very concerned about the rise of the Right in this country, as if that is something separate from the issues of feminism or the men's movement. There is a cartoon I saw that brought it all together nicely. It was a big picture of Ronald Reagan as a cowboy with a big hat and a gun. And it said: "A gun in every holster; a pregnant woman in every home. Make America a man again." Those are the politics of the Right.

If you are afraid of the ascendancy of fascism in this country—and you would be very foolish not to be right now—then you had better understand that the root issue here has to do with male supremacy and the control of women; sexual access to women; women as reproductive slaves; private ownership of women. That is the program of the Right. That is the morality they talk about. That is what they mean. That is what they want. And the only opposition to them that matters is an opposition to men owning women.

What's involved in doing something about all of this? The men's movement seems to stay stuck on two points. The first is that men don't really feel very good about themselves. How could you? The second is that men come to me or to other feminists and say: "What you're saying about men isn't true. It isn't true of me. I don't feel that way. I'm opposed to all of this."

And I say: don't tell me. Tell the pornographers. Tell the pimps. Tell the warmakers. Tell the rape apologists and the rape celebrationists and the pro-rape ideologues. Tell the novelists who think that rape is wonderful. Tell Larry Flynt. Tell Hugh Hefner. There's no point in telling me. I'm only a woman. There's nothing I can do about it. These men presume to speak for you. They are in the public arena saying that they represent you. If they don't, then you had better let them know.

Then there is the private world of misogyny: what you know about each other; what you say in private life; the exploitation that you see in the private sphere; the relationships called love, based on exploitation. It's not enough to find some traveling feminist on the road and go up to her and say: "Gee, I hate it."

Say it to your friends who are doing it. And there are streets out there on which you can say these things loud and clear, so as to affect the actual institutions that maintain these abuses. You don't like pornography? I wish I could believe it's true. I will believe it when I see you on the streets. I will believe it when I see an organized political opposition. I will believe it when pimps go out of business because there are no more male consumers.

You want to organize men. You don't have to search for issues. The issues are part of the fabric of your everyday lives.

I want to talk to you about equality, what equality is and what it means. It isn't just an idea. It's not some insipid word that ends up being bullshit. It doesn't have anything at all to do with all those statements like: "Oh, that happens to men too." I name an abuse and I hear: "Oh, it happens to men too." That is not the equality we are struggling for. We could change our strategy and say: well, okay, we want equality; we'll stick something up the ass of a man every three minutes.

You've never heard that from the feminist movement, because for us equality has real dignity and importance—it's not some dumb word that can be twisted and made to look stupid as if it had no real meaning.

As a way of practicing equality, some vague idea about giving up power is useless. Some men have vague thoughts about a future in which men are going to give up power or an individual man is going to give up some kind of privilege that he has. That is not what equality means either.

Equality is a practice. It is an action. It is a way of life. It is a social practice. It is an economic practice. It is a sexual practice. It can't exist in a vacuum. You can't have it in your home if, when the people leave the home, he is in a world of his supremacy based on the existence of his cock and she is in a world of humiliation and degradation because she is perceived to be inferior and because her sexuality is a curse.

This is not to say that the attempt to practice equality in the home doesn't matter. It matters, but it is not enough. If you love equality, if you believe in it, if it is the way you want to live—not just men and women together in a home, but men and men together in a home and women and women together in a home—if equality is what you want and what you care about, then you have to fight for the institutions that will make it socially real.

It is not just a matter of your attitude. You can't think it and make it exist. You can't try sometimes, when it works to your advantage, and throw it out the rest of the time. Equality is a discipline. It is a way of life. It is a political necessity to create equality in institutions. And another thing about equality is that it cannot coexist with rape. It cannot. And it cannot coexist with pornography or with prostitution or with the economic degradation of women on any level, in any way. It cannot coexist, because implicit in all those things is the inferiority of women.

I want to see this men's movement make a commitment to ending rape because that is the only meaningful commitment to equality. It is astonishing that in all our worlds of feminism and antisexism we never talk seriously about ending rape. Ending it. Stopping it. No more. No more rape. In the back of our minds, are we holding on to its inevitability as the last preserve of the biological? Do we think that it is always going to exist no matter what we do? All of our political actions are lies if we don't make a commitment to ending the practice of rape. This commitment has to be political. It has to be serious. It has to be systematic. It has to be public. It can't be self-indulgent.

The things the men's movement has wanted are things worth having. Intimacy is worth having. Tenderness is worth having. Cooperation is worth having. A real emotional life is worth having. But you can't have them in a world with rape. Ending homophobia is worth doing. But you can't do it in a world with rape. Rape stands in the way of each and every one of those things you say you want. And by rape you know what I mean. A judge does not have to walk into this room and say that according to statute such and such these are the elements of proof. We're talking about any kind of coerced sex, including sex coerced by poverty.

You can't have equality or tenderness or intimacy as long as there is rape, because rape means terror. It means that part of the population lives in a state of terror and pretends—to please and pacify you—that it doesn't. So there is no honesty. How can there be? Can you imagine what it is like to live as a woman day in and day out with the threat of rape? Or what it is like to live with the reality? I want to see you use those legendary bodies and that legendary strength and that legendary courage and the tenderness that you say you have in behalf of women; and that means against the rapists, against the pimps, and against the pornographers. It means something more than a personal renunciation. It means a systematic, political, active, public attack. And there has been very little of that.

I came here today because I don't believe that rape is inevitable or natural. If I did, I would have no reason to be here. If I did, my political practice would be different than it is. Have you ever wondered why we are not just in armed combat against you? It's not because there's a shortage of kitchen knives in this country. It is because we believe in your humanity, against all the evidence.

We do not want to do the work of helping you to believe in your humanity. We cannot do it anymore. We have always tried. We have been repaid with systematic exploitation and systematic abuse. You are going to have to do this yourselves from now on and you know it.

The shame of men in front of women is, I think, an appropriate response both to what men do do and to what men do not do. I think you should be ashamed. But what you do with that shame is to use it as an excuse to keep doing what you want and to keep not doing anything else; and you've got to stop. You've got to stop. Your psychology doesn't matter. How much you hurt doesn't matter in the end any more than how much we hurt matters. If we sat around and only talked about how much rape hurt us, do you think there would have been one of the changes that you have seen in this country in the last fifteen years? There wouldn't have been.

It is true that we had to talk to each other. How else, after all, were we supposed to find out that each of us was not the only woman in the world not asking for it to whom rape or battery had ever happened? We couldn't read it in the newspapers, not then. We couldn't find a book about it. But you do know and now the question is what you are going to do; and so your shame and your guilt are very much beside the point. They don't matter to us at all, in any way. They're not good enough. They don't do anything.

As a feminist, I carry the rape of all the women I've talked to over the past ten years personally with me. As a woman, I carry my own rape with me. Do you remember pictures that you've seen of European cities during the plague, when there were wheelbarrows that would go along and people would just pick up corpses and throw them in? Well, that is what it is like knowing about rape. Piles and piles and piles of bodies that have whole lives and human names and human faces.

I speak for many feminists, not only myself, when I tell you that I am tired of what I know and sad beyond any words I have about what has already been done to women up to this point, now, up to 2:24 p.m. on this day, here in this place.

And I want one day of respite, one day off, one day in which no new bodies are piled up, one day in which no new agony is added to the old, and I am asking you to give it to me. And how could I ask you for less—it is so little. And how could you offer me less: it is so little. Even in wars, there are days of truce. Go and organize a truce. Stop your side for one day. I want a twenty-four-hour truce during which there is no rape.

I dare you to try it. I demand that you try it. I don't mind begging you to try it. What else could you possibly be here to do? What else could this movement possibly mean? What else could matter so much?

And on that day, that day of truce, that day when not one woman is raped, we will begin the real practice of equality, because we can't begin it before that day. Before that day it means nothing because it is nothing: it is not real; it is not true. But on that day it becomes real. And then, instead of rape we will for the first time in our lives—both men and women—begin to experience freedom.

If you have a conception of freedom that includes the existence of rape, you are wrong. You cannot change what you say you want to change. For myself, I want to experience just one day of real freedom before I die. I leave you here to do that for me and for the women whom you say you love.

FOR FURTHER READING

Dworkin, Andrea. *Life and Death: The Unapologetic Writings on the Continuing War Against Women.* New York: Free Press, 1997.

———. *Our Blood: Prophecies and Discourse on Sexual Politics.* New York: Harper and Row, 1976.

———. *Pornography: Men Possessing Women.* New York: E. P. Dutton, 1989.

———. *Woman Hating.* New York: E. P Dutton, 1974.

Dworkin, Andrea, and Catharine MacKinnon, eds. *In Harm's Way: The Pornography Civil Rights Hearings.* Cambridge: Harvard University Press, 1997.

Paula Gunn Allen

1939–

Paula Gunn Allen, raised in a multicultural family that included Laguna, Sioux, Lebanese, and Scottish heritage, is a clan mother of the Laguna Pueblo Oak clan. Allen's book of essays, *The Sacred Hoop: Recovering the Feminine in American Indian Tradition*, provides "a picture of American Indian life and literature un-filtered through the minds of western patriarchal colonizers" (6). Allen recovers the female elements of Native American epistemology and rhetoric. She outlines beliefs about the nature of truth, reason, memory, language, and authority that were erased by European representations of Native culture, in which women's ceremonies, customs, values, and histories were either ignored, trivialized, or degraded. In her essay "Who Is Your Mother? Red Roots of White Feminism," she points to the influence that Native women's cultures had on early white women activists, a connection that white women have not acknowledged. Elizabeth Cady Stanton and others organized the Seneca Falls Convention on the very ground where Native American women led a rebellion in 1600, and early suffragists like Matilda Gage claimed inspiration from Native cultures, including the example of the Iroquois matrilineal and matrilocal system. Paula Gunn Allen asserts that women can little afford to forget their strong connections to each other if they are to accomplish their goals, for "the roots of oppression are to be found in the loss of tradition and memory because that loss is always accompanied by a loss of a positive sense of self" ("Who Is Your Mother?" 210).

The Keres Pueblo tradition provides the basis for Allen's essay "Grand-mother of the Sun." In this tradition, reality is female, and it is the source and generator of meaning: "We understand that woman is the sun and the earth: she is grandmother; she is mother; she is Thought, Wisdom, Dream, Reason, Tradition, Memory, Deity, and Life itself" ("Stealing the Thunder" 268). Allen documents the place of the female gods in Native American traditions and uses the Keres Pueblo tradition to celebrate the power of gynocratic culture. In the preface to this essay, she says: "In the beginning was thought, and her name was Woman. . . . She is the Old Woman who tends the fires of life" (11). Central to this epistemological/rhetorical framework is Thought Woman, a dynamic energy that connects humans to the material world and provides language, spirituality, memory, harmony, understanding, and strength. She cannot be reduced or trivialized as a "fertility goddess," and she transcends Western male binaries: reason/emotion, mind/body, sacred/secular. She is varied, pervasive, and multiple. Thought Woman embodies a concept of reverence, power, and authority arising from the spiritual relationships that link human and non-human worlds in kinship and cooperation and harmony. Unique to tribal cultures, this conception of the feminine as the central force in making knowledge and in shaping the physical and spiritual worlds provides a rich alternative to European conceptual and rhetorical traditions.

"Grandmother of the Sun: Ritual Gynocracy in Native America"

1986

I

There is a spirit that pervades everything, that is capable of powerful song and radiant movement, and that moves in and out of the mind. The colors of this spirit are multitudinous, a glowing, pulsing rainbow. Old Spider Woman is one name for this quintessential spirit, and Serpent Woman is another. Corn Woman is one aspect of her, and Earth Woman is another, and what they together have made is called Creation, Earth, creatures, plants, and light.

At the center of all is Woman, and no thing is sacred (cooked, ripe, as the Keres Indians of Laguna Pueblo say it) without her blessing, her thinking.

> . . . In the beginning Tse che nako, Thought Woman finished everything, thoughts, and the names of all things. She finished also all the languages. And then our mothers, Uretsete and Naotsete said they would make names and they would make thoughts. Thus they said. Thus they did.

This spirit, this power of intelligence, has many names and many emblems. She appears on the plains, in the forests, in the great canyons, on the mesas, beneath the seas. To her we owe our very breath, and to her our prayers are sent blown on pollen, on corn meal, planted into the earth on feather-sticks, spit onto the water, burned and sent to her on the wind. Her variety and multiplicity testify to her complexity: she is the true creatrix for she is thought itself, from which all else is born. She is the necessary precondition for material creation, and she, like all of her creation, is fundamentally female—potential and primary.

She is also the spirit that informs right balance, right harmony, and these in turn order all relationships in conformity with her law.

To assign to this great being the position of "fertility goddess" is exceedingly demeaning: it trivializes the tribes and it trivializes the power of woman. Woman bears, that is true. She also destroys. That is true. She also wars and hexes and mends and breaks. She creates the power of the seeds, and she plants them. As Anthony Purley, a Laguna writer, has translated a Keres ceremonial prayer, "She is mother of us all, after Her, mother earth follows, in fertility, in holding, and taking again us back to her breast."

The Hopi account of their genatrix, Hard Beings Woman, gives the most articulate rendering of the difference between simple fertility cultism and the creative prowess of the Creatrix. Hard Beings Woman (Huruing Wuhti) is of the earth. But she lives in the worlds above where she "owns" (empowers) the moon and stars. Hard Beings Woman has solidity and hardness as her major aspects. She, like Thought Woman, does not give birth to creation or to human beings but breathes life into male and female effigies that become the parents of the Hopi—in this way she "creates" them. The male is Muingwu, the god of crops, and his sister-consort is Sand Altar Woman who is also known as Childbirth Water Woman. In Sand Altar Woman the mystical relationship between water, worship, and woman is established; she is also said to be the mother of the katsinas, those powerful messengers who relate the spirit world to the world of humankind and vice versa.

Like Thought Woman, Hard Beings Woman lived in the beginning on an island which was the only land there was. In this regard she resembles a number of Spirit Woman Beings; the Spirit genatrix of the Iroquois, Sky Woman, also lived on an island in the void which only later became the earth. On this island, Hard Beings Woman is identified with or, as they say, "owns" all hard substances—moon, stars, beads, coral, shell, and so forth. She is a sea goddess as well, the single inhabitant of the earth, that island that floats alone in the waters of space. From this meeting of woman and water, earth and her creatures were born.

The waters of space are also crucial in the Sky Woman story of the Seneca. Sky Woman is catapulted into the void by her angry, jealous, and fearful husband, who tricks her into peering into the abyss he has revealed by uprooting the tree of light (which embodies the power of woman) that grows near his lodge. Her terrible fall is broken by the Water Fowl who live in that watery void, and they safely deposit Sky Woman on the back of Grandmother Turtle, who also inhabits the void. On the body of Grandmother Turtle earth-island is formed. Interestingly, the shell of the turtle is one of the Hard Substances connected to Hard Beings Woman.

Contemporary Indian tales suggest that the creatures are born from the mating of sky father and earth mother, but that seems to be a recent interpolation of the original sacred texts. The revision may have occurred since the Christianizing influence on even the arcane traditions, or it may have predated Christianity. But the older, more secret texts suggest that it is a revision. It may be that the revision appears only in popular versions of the old mythic cycles on which ceremony and ritual are based; this would accord with the penchant in the old oral tradition for shaping tales to reflect present social realities, making the rearing and education of children possible even within the divergent worlds of the United States of America and the tribes.

According to the older texts (which are sacred, that is, power-engendering), Thought Woman is not a passive personage: her potentiality is dynamic and unimaginably powerful. She brought corn and agriculture, potting, weaving, social systems, religion, ceremony, ritual, building, memory, intuition, and their expressions in language, creativity, dance, human-to-animal relations, and she gave these offerings power and authority and blessed the people with the ability to provide for themselves and their progeny.

Thought Woman is not limited to a female role in the total theology of the Keres people. Since she is the supreme Spirit, she is both Mother and Father to all people and to all creatures. She is the only creator of thought, and thought precedes creation.

Central to Keres theology is the basic idea of the Creatrix as She Who Thinks rather than She Who Bears, of woman as creation thinker and female thought as origin of material and nonmaterial reality. In this epistemology, the perception of female power as confined to maternity is a limit on the power inherent in femininity. But "she is the supreme Spirit . . . both Mother and Father to all people and to all creatures."

In the nineteenth century, Fr. Noël Dumarest reported from another Keres Pueblo, Cochiti, on Spider Woman (Thought Woman, although he does not mention her by this name). In his account, when the "Indian sister" made stars, she could not get them to shine, so "she consulted Spider, the creator." He characterized the goddess-sisters as living "with Spider Woman, their mother, at *shipapu*, under the waters of the lake, in the second world." It should be mentioned that while she is here characterized as the sisters' mother, the Cochiti, like the other Keres, are not so much referring to biological birth as to sacred or ritual birth. To address a person as "mother" is to pay the highest ritual respect.

In Keres theology the creation does not take place through copulation. In the beginning existed Thought Woman and her dormant sisters, and Thought Woman thinks creation and sings her two sisters into life. After they are vital she instructs them to sing over the items in their baskets (medicine bundles) in such a way that those items will have life. After that crucial task is accomplished, the creatures thus vitalized take on the power to regenerate themselves—that is, they can reproduce others of their kind. But they are not in and of themselves self-sufficient; they depend for their being on the medicine power of the three great Witch creatrixes, Thought Woman, Uretsete, and Naotsete. The sisters are not related by virtue of having parents in common; that is, they are not alive because anyone bore them. Thought Woman turns up, so to speak, first as Creatrix and then as a personage who is acting out someone else's "dream." But there is no time when she did not exist. She has two bundles in her power, and these bundles contain Uretsete and Naotsete, who are not viewed as her daughters but as her sisters, her coequals who possess the medicine power to vitalize the creatures that will inhabit the earth. They also have the power to create the firmament, the skies, the galaxies, and the seas, which they do through the use of ritual magic.

The idea that Woman is possessed of great medicine power is elaborated in the Lakota myth of White Buffalo Woman. She brought the Sacred Pipe to the Lakota, and it is through the agency of this pipe that the ceremonies and rituals of the Lakota are empowered. Without the pipe, no ritual magic can occur. According to one story about White Buffalo Woman, she lives in a cave where she presides over the Four Winds. In Lakota ceremonies, the four wind directions are always acknowledged, usually by offering a pipe to them. The pipe is ceremonial, modeled after the Sacred Pipe given the people by the Sacred Woman. The Four Winds are very powerful beings themselves, but they can function only at the bidding of White Buffalo Woman. The Lakota are connected to her still, partly because some still keep to the ways she taught them and partly because her pipe still resides with them.

The pipe of the Sacred Woman is analogous in function to the ear of corn left with the people by Iyatiku, Corn Woman, the mother goddess of the Keres. Iyatiku, who is called the mother of the people, is in a ceremonial sense another aspect of Thought Woman. She presently resides in Shipap from whence she sends counsel to the people and greets them when they enter the spirit world of the dead. Her representative, Irriaku (Corn Mother), maintains the connection between individuals in the tribe as well as the connection between the non-human supernaturals and the tribe. It is through the agency of the Irriaku that the religious leaders of the tribe, called Yaya and Hotchin, or hochin in some spellings of the word, (Mother and leader or chief), are empowered to govern.

The Irriaku, like the Sacred Pipe, is the heart of the people as it is the heart of Iyatiku. In the form of the perfect ear of corn, Naiya Iyatiku (Mother, Chief) is present at every ceremony. Without the presence of her power, no ceremony can produce the power it is designed to create or release. These uses of the feminine testify that primary power—the power to make and to relate—belongs to the preponderantly feminine powers of the universe.

According to one story my great-grandmother told me, in time immemorial when the people lived in the White Village or Kush Katret, Iyatiku lived with them. There came a drought, and since many normal activities had to be suspended and since the people were hungry and worried because of the scarcity of food from the drought, Iyatiku gave them a gambling game to while away the time. It was meant to distract them from their troubles. But the men became obsessed and began to gamble everything away. When the women scolded them and demanded that they stop gambling and act responsibly toward their families, the men got mad and went into the kivas.

Now, since the kivas were the men's space, the women didn't go there except for ritual reasons. The men continued to gamble, neglecting their ritual duties and losing all their possessions of value. Because they didn't do the dances or make the offerings as they were supposed to, the drought continued and serious famine ensued. Finally one old man who was also a priest, or cheani, became very concerned. He sought the advice of a shaman nearby, but it was too late. Iyatiku had left Kush Katret in anger at her foolish people. She went back to Shipap where she lives now and keeps an eye on the people. The people were forced to abandon the village, which was inundated by floods brought on by the angry lake spirits. So the beautiful village was destroyed and the people were forced to build a new one elsewhere and to live without the Mother of Corn. But she left with them her power, Irriaku, and told them that it was her heart she left in their keeping. She charged them always to share the fruits of her body with one another, for they were all related, and she told them that they must ever remain at peace in their hearts and their relationships.

The rains come only to peaceful people, or so the Keres say. As a result of this belief, the Keres abhor violence or hostility. They are very careful to contain their emotions and to put a smooth face on things, for rain is essential to the very life of their villages. Without it the crops can't grow, the livestock will starve, there will be no water for drinking or bathing—in short, all life, physical and ceremonial, will come to a halt. For ceremonies depend on corn and corn pollen and birds and water; without these they are not likely to be efficacious, if they can be held at all.

II

There is an old tradition among numerous tribes of a two-sided, complementary social structure. In the American Southeast this tradition was worked out in terms of the red chief and the white chief, positions held by women and by men and corresponding to internal affairs and external affairs. They were both spiritual and ritualistic, but the white chief or internal chief functioned in harmony-effective ways. This chief maintained peace and harmony among the people of the band, village, or tribe and administered domestic affairs. The red chief, also known as the war chief, presided over relations with other tribes and officiated over events that took people away from the village. Among the Pueblo of the American Southwest are two notable traditional offices: that of the cacique (a Spanish term for the Tiamuni Hotchin or traditional leader), who was charged with maintaining internal harmony, and that of the hotchin or "war captain," whose office was concerned with mediating between the tribe and outsiders, implementing foreign policy, and, if necessary, calling for defensive or retaliatory forays. This hotchin, whose title is usually translated "country chief" or "outside chief," was first authorized by Iyatiku when she still lived among the people. At that time there was no "inside" chief other than the Mother herself and the clan mothers whom she instructed in the proper ritual ways as each clan came into being. Since Iyatiku was in residence, an inside chief or cacique was unnecessary. The present-day caciques continue even now to act as her representatives and gain their power directly from her.

Thus the Pueblos are organized—as are most gynocratic tribes—into a moiety system (as anthropologists dub it) that reflects their understanding of ritual empowerment as dialogic. This dyadic structure, which emphasizes complementarity rather than opposition, is analogous to the external fire/internal fire relationship of sun and earth. That is, the core/womb of the earth is inward fire as the heart of heaven, the sun, is external fire. The Cherokee and their northern cousins the Iroquois acknowledge the femaleness of both fires: the sun is female to them both, as is the earth. Among the Keres, Shipap, which is in the earth, is white, as was the isolated house Iyatiku dwelt in before she left the mortal plane entirely for Shipap. The color of Shipap is white. The Hopi see Spider Woman as Grandmother of the sun and as the great Medicine Power who sang the people into this fourth world we live in now.

The understanding of universal functioning as relationship between the inner and the outer is reflected in the social systems of those tribal groups that are based on clan systems. It is reflected in ritual systems, as seen in the widespread incidence of legends about the Little War Twins among the Pueblos or the Sacred Twins among other tribes and Nations. The Sacred Twins embody the power of dual creative forces. The potency of their relationship is as strong as that of the negative and positive charges on magnetic fields. It is on their complementariness and their relationship that both destructive and creative ritual power rests.

Among the western Keres, the war captains are the analogues of the Little War Twins, Ma'sewe and O'yo'yo'we. Their prototype appears to be those puzzling twin sisters of the Keres pantheon, Uretsete and Naotsete, who were sung into life by Thought Woman before the creation of the world. These sisters appear and reappear in Pueblo stories in various guises and various names. One of them, Uretsete, becomes male at some point in the creation story of the Keres. Transformation of this kind is common in American Indian lore, and the transformation processes embedded in the tales about the spirit beings and their alternative aspects point to the regenerative powers embodied in their diversity.

When the whites came, the tribe, who were organized matrifocally resorted to their accustomed modes of dealing with outsiders; they relied on the red chief (or whatever that personage might be called) and on their tribal groups whose responsibility was external affairs. The Iroquois of the northern regions, the Five "Civilized" Tribes of the southern regions, and the Pueblo of the American Southwest—all among those earliest contacted by Anglo-European invaders—had some dual structure enabling them to maintain internal harmony while engaging in hostilities with invading or adversary groups. The Aztecs also had such complementary deities: the internal or domestic god was a goddess, Cihuacoati, Coatlique, or some similar supernatural woman-being; their external god was Quetzalcoatl, the winged serpent, who was a god of amalgamation or expansion.

Indian stories indicate that a dialogic construct based on complementary powers (an interpretation of polarity that focuses on the ritual uses of magnetism) was current among the Pueblos, particularly the Keres. To the Keres Naotsete was the figure associated with internal affairs, and Uretsete was concerned with maintaining tribal psychic and political boundaries.

Essentially, the Keres story goes something like this (allowing for variations created by the informant, the collector-translator, or differences in clan-based variations): Naotsete and Uretsete were sung into life by Ts'its'tsi'nako Thought Woman. They carried bundles from which all the creatures came. The goddess Uretsete gave birth to twin boys, and one of these boys was raised by the other sister, who later married him. Of this union the Pueblo race was born. Some tales (probably of fairly recent origin) make Uretsete the alien sister and Naotsete the Indian sister. Other stories, as noted earlier, make Uretsete male at some undetermined point (but "he" always starts as female). The Indian sister Uretsete is later known as Iyatiku, or Ic'city, and is seen as essentially the same as her. But it is reasonable to conjecture that Uretsete is the prototype for the hotchin, while the cacique (town chief) is derived from the figure Naotsete. Certainly the office of hotchin is authorized by Iyatiku, who counsels the Tiamuni hotchin, Chief Remembering Prayer Sticks, to keep the people ever in peace and harmony and to remember that they are all her children and thus are all entitled to the harvest of her body/thought. She in turn is empowered by Thought Woman, who sits on her shoulder and advises her.

While the tribal heads are known as cacique and hotchin—or town chief and country chief, respectively—the Keres do not like fighting. War is so distasteful to them that they long ago devised ritual institutions to deal with antagonism between persons and groups such as medicine societies. They also developed rituals that would purify those who had participated in warfare. If a person had actually killed someone, the ritual purification was doubly imperative, for without it a sickness would come among the people and would infect the land and the animals and prevent the rainfall. The Warrior Priest was and is responsible for seeing to the orderly running of Pueblo life, and to some extent he mediates between strangers and the people. In this sense he functions as the outside chief. The inside chief maintains an internal conscious awareness of Shipap and the Mother, and he advises, counsels, and exhorts the people to the ways of peace.

Traditional war was not practiced as a matter of conquest or opposition to enemies in the same way it has been practiced by western peoples; it is not a matter of battling enemies into a defeat in which they surrender and come to terms dictated by the conqueror. Warfare among most traditional American Indian tribes who practiced it (went on the war path) was a ritual, an exercise in the practice of shamanism, and it is still practiced that way by the few "long-

hairs" left. Its outcome was the seizure of a certain sacred power, and that outcome could be as the result of defeat as well as of victory. The point was to gain
the attention of supernatural powers, who would then be prevailed upon to
give certain powers to the hero.

The Navajo have a ceremonial and an accompanying myth that commemorate the gain of such a gift as the result of a battle with some Pueblos. The hero
in that tale is a woman who journeys to the spirit world with Snake Man, where
she is initiated by Snake Man's mother. After she has passed the tests provided
for her learning, she is given particular rites to take back to her people. Along
with this ceremonial, which is called Beautyway, is a companion ceremonial,
Mountainway. Its hero is a woman who accompanies Bear Man into the spirit
world and is also taught and tested. Like the Beautyway hero, she returns with
a chantway or healing ceremony to give her people. In a more contemporary
version of these tales, the battle is World War II, and an even later tale might be
about Vietnam. The exact war is not important. What is important is that from
warfare comes certain powers that benefit the people and that are gained by a
hero who encounters and transcends mortal danger.

So the hotchin is a medium for the regulation of external ritual events, and
the cacique is the medium through whom Iyatiku guides, guards, and empowers her people and keeps them whole. Each is responsible for maintaining the
harmonious working of the energies on which the entire existence of the
people depends, and they are necessarily men who must be careful how they
use the energies at their disposal.

III

As the power of woman is the center of the universe and is both heart (womb)
and thought (creativity), the power of the Keres people is the corn that holds
the thought of the All Power (deity) and connects the people to that power
through the heart of Earth Woman, Iyatiku. She is the breath of life to the Keres
because for them corn holds the essence of earth and conveys the power of
earth to the people. Corn connects us to the heart of power, and that heart is
Iyatiku, who under the guidance of Thought Woman directs the people in their
affairs.

It is likely that the power embodied in the Irriaku (Corn Mother) is the
power of dream, for dream connections play an important part in the ritual of
life of the Pueblos as of other tribes of the Americas. As the frightening katsina,
K'oo'ko, can haunt the dreams of uncleansed warriors and thus endanger everything, the power that moves between the material and nonmaterial worlds
often does so in dreams. The place when certain dreams or ceremonies occur is
said to be in "time immemorial." And the point where the two meet is Shipap,
where Earth Woman lives. Corn, like many of its power counterparts is responsible for maintaining linkage between the worlds, and Corn Mother, Irriaku, is
the most powerful element in that link. John Gunn describes the Irriaku as "an

ear of corn perfect in every grain, the plume is a feather from every known bird."

This representative of Iyatiku is an individual's link and the ceremonial link to medicine power. Of similar power is the Sacred Pipe that White Buffalo Woman brought to the Lakota. This pipe is called waka*n*, which means "sacred" or possessing power.

The concept of power among tribal people is related to their understanding of the relationships that occur between the human and nonhuman worlds. They believe that all are linked within one vast, living sphere, that the linkage is not material but spiritual, and that its essence is the power that enables magical things to happen. Among these magical things are transformation of objects from one form to another, the movement of objects from one place to another by teleportation, the curing of the sick (and conversely creating sickness in people, animals, or plants), communication with animals, plants, and nonphysical beings (spirits, katsinas, goddesses, and gods) the compelling of the will of another, and the stealing or storing of souls. Mythical accounts from a number of sources illustrate the variety of forms the uses of ritual power can take.

According to the Abanaki, First Woman, who came to live with a spirit being named Kloskurbeh and his disciple, offered to share her strength and comfort with them. Her offer was accepted and she and the disciple of Kloskurbeh had many children. All was well until a famine came. Then the children were starving and First Woman was very sad. She went to her husband and asked him to kill her so she could be happy again. When he agreed, she instructed him to let two men lay hold of her corpse after she was dead and drag her body through a nearby field until all the flesh was worn away. Then, she said, they should bury her bones in the middle of the field and leave the field alone for seven months. After that time, they should return to the field and gather the food they would find there and eat all of it except for a portion that they should plant. The bones, she said, would not be edible; they should burn them, and the smoke would bring peace to them and their descendants.

As the tale is recorded in one source, the narrator continues.

> Now have the first words of the first mother come to pass, for she said she was born of the leaf of the beautiful plant and that her power should be felt over the whole world, and that all should love her. And now that she is gone into this substance, take care that this, the second seed of the first mother, be always with you, for it is her flesh. Her bones also have been given for your good; burn them, and the smoke will bring freshness to the mind, and since these things came from the goodness of a woman's heart, see that you hold her always in memory; remember her when you eat, remember her when the smoke of her bones rises before you. And because you are all [related], divide among you her flesh and her bones—let all shares be alike—for so will the love of the first mother have been fulfilled.

Worth noting in this passage are the ideas of kinship that requires peaceful-ness and cooperation among people and of the centrality of the woman's power, which is her gift to the disciple. Because she is sacred, her flesh and bones are capable of generating life; because she is embued with power, she can share it with human beings. When she came among them the first time, First Woman told Kloskurbeh and his disciple that she was "born of the beautiful plant of the earth; for the dew fell on the leaf, and the sun warmed the dew, and the warmth was life," and she was that life.

Another important point is that the love of the first mother carries several significances. The love of a mother is not, as is presently supposed, a reference to a sentimental attachment. Rather, it is a way of saying that a mother is bonded to her offspring through her womb. *Heart* often means "womb," except when it means "vulva." In its aspect of vulva, it signifies sexual connection or bonding. But this cannot be understood to mean sex as sex; rather, sexual con-nection with woman means connection with the womb, which is the container of power that women carry within their bodies. So when the teacher Kloskur-beh says that "these things come from the goodness of a woman's heart," he is saying that the seeds of her power are good—that is, they are alive, bearing, nourishing, and cooperative with the well-being of the people.

The tobacco that she leaves to them is connected also with her power, for it is the "beautiful plant" that was her own mother, and its property is clear thought. She was born of clear (harmonious) thought (for beauty and harmony are synonymous among Indians) that was empowered by water (dew) and heat (sun). (Dew is a reference to vaginal secretions during tumescence.) Tobacco smoke is connected to water, for it imitates clouds in appearance and behavior. It is used to evoke spirits as well as a sense of well-being and clearheadedness and is often a feature of religious ceremonies. That First Woman is connected to water is made clear in another passage of the same account: First Woman (who had referred to both Kloskurbeh the teacher and his nephew the disciple as "my children") had said that she was born of the beautiful plant. The famine had made her very sad, and every day she left home and was gone for long pe-riods. One day the disciple followed her and saw her wade into the river, sing-ing. "And as long as her feet were in the water, she seemed glad, and the man saw something that trailed behind her right foot, like a long green blade."

Among medicine people it is well known that immersing oneself in water will enable one to ward off dissolution. Bodies of apprentices, sorcerers, and witches are subject to changes, including transformation from corporeal to spirit. Immersion also helps one resist the pull of supernatural forces unleashed by another sorcerer, though this does not seem to be what occurs in this story. But the connection of First Woman with water is clear: in the water she is happy, centered, powerful, for she is deeply connected to water, as is implied by her birth story. If she was born of the beautiful plant, then she is in some basic sense a vegetation spirit who has taken a human body (or something like it) to further the story of creation. Her "sacrifice" is the culmination of her earthly sojourn: by transferring the power she possesses to the corn and tobacco (her flesh and her bones), she makes certain that the life forms she has vitalized will remain vital. Thus, one aspect of her power is embodied in the children, while another aspect is embodied in the corn and tobacco. In their mutuality of energy transfer, all will live.

In Zia Pueblo version of the Supernatural Woman, Anazia Pueblo, Utset wanted to make certain that the people would have food when they came up from the lower world (previous world and underworld). As their mother (chief), Utset was responsible for their well-being, so she made fields north, west, south, and east of the village and planted in it bits of her heart (power). She made words over the seeds she had planted: "This corn is my heart and it shall be to my people as milk from my breasts." In a Cherokee version of how food was given to the people to guarantee their provision and their connection to the goddess, Selu (Corn Woman) similarly made the first food from her own body-seed, as does Grandmother Spider in a Kiowa version.

According to Goetz and Morley's rendering of the *Popul Vuh*, the sacred myth of the Quiché Mayans, the heart is related to the power of creation. In the beginning the makers (grandparents) were in the water (void) hidden under green and blue feathers. They were by nature great thinkers or sages. "In this manner the sky existed and also the Heart of Heaven, which is the name of God (the All Power)." The grandparents, called feathered beings (Gucumatz), meditated, and it became clear that creation of the earth that human beings inhabit was imminent. "Thus it was arranged in the darkness and in the night by the Heart of Heaven who is called Huracán." The Gucumatz or Bird Grandparents were so called because the flashes of light around their thinking-place resembled the bright wings of the bird now known as quetzal but known to the ancient Mayans as gucumatz. In their appearance they resemble the Irriaku, and in their characterization as Water Winged Beings they resemble the Water Fowl who saved the Iroquois Sky Woman from her fall through the void (designated as water in some versions of that myth). They also resemble representations of Iyatiku as a bird being, as she appears on a Fire Society altar. In a drawing an informant made of her, Iyatiku appears as a bird woman, with the body of a bird and the head of a woman. Her body is spotted yellow "to represent the earth," and centered on her breast is "a red, arrow-shaped heart" which "is the center of herself and the world. Around her is a blue circle to represent the sky, while an inner arc represents the milky way; above it are symbols for sun, moon and the stars."

One of the interesting features of this depiction of Earth Woman is her resemblance of Tinotzin, the goddess who appeared to the Indian Juan Diego in 1659 and who is known as Our Lady of Guadalupe today. The Virgin Morena (the dark virgin), as she is also called, wears a salmon-colored gown that is spotted yellow to represent the stars. She wears a cloak of blue, and her image is surrounded by fiery tongues—lightning or flames, presumably.

Certainly the Keres Fire Society's goddess was made to represent, that is, to produce, medicine power, and the arrow-shaped heart she exhibited spoke to the relationship between the ideas of "heart" and "strength," or power.

A Mayan prayer connected with Huracán, or the Heart of Heaven, that refers to her as "grandmother of the sun, grandmother of the light":

> Look at us, hear us! . . . Heart of Heaven, Heart of Earth! Give us our descen-
> dants, our succession, as long as the sun shall move . . . Let it dawn, let the day
> come! May the people have peace . . . may they be happy . . . give us good life
> . . . grandmother of the sun, grandmother of the light, let there be dawn . . . let
> the light come!

Certainly, there is reason to believe that many American Indian tribes thought that the primary potency in the universe was female, and that under-standing authorizes all tribal activities, religious or social. That power inevita-bly carries with it the requirement that the people live in cooperative harmony with each other and with the beings and powers that surround them. For with-out peacefulness and harmony, which are the powers of a woman's heart, the power of the light and of the corn, of generativity and of ritual magic, cannot function. Thus, when Corn Woman, Iyatiku, was about to leave the people and return to Shipap, she told the cacique how to guide and counsel the people:

> I will soon leave you. I will return to the home whence I came. You will be to my
> people as myself; you will pass with them over the straight road; I will remain
> in my house below and will hear all that you say to me. I give you all my wis-
> dom, my thoughts, my heart, and all. I fill your head with my mind.

The goddess Ixchel whose shrine was in the Yucatán on Cozumel Island, twenty miles offshore, was a goddess of the moon, water childbirth, weaving, and love. The combination of attributes signifies the importance of childbirth, and women go to Ixchel's shrine to gain or increase their share of these powers as well as to reinforce their sense of them.

Ixchel possesses the power of fruitfulness, a power associated with both water and weaving and concerned with bringing to life or vitalization. Also connected with Ixchel is the power to end life or to take life away, an aspect of female ritual power that is not as often discussed as birth and nurturing powers are. These twin powers of primacy, life and death, are aspects of Ixchel as moon-woman in which she waxes and wanes, sometimes visible and some-times invisible. Similarly, her power to weave includes the power to unravel, so the weaver, like the moon, signifies the power of patterning and its converse, the power of disruption. It is no small matter to venerate Iyatiku, Thought Woman, or White Buffalo Woman. Their connection with death and with life makes them the preponderant powers of the universe, and this connection is made through the agency of water.

Pre-Conquest American Indian women valued their role as vitalizers. Through their own bodies they could bring vital beings into the world—a miraculous power whose potency does not diminish with industrial sophistication or time. They were mothers, and that word did not imply slaves, drudges, drones who are required to live only for others rather than for themselves as it does so tragically for many modern women. The ancient ones were empowered by their certain knowledge that the power to make life is the source of all power and that no other power can gainsay it. Nor is that power simply of biology, as modernists tendentiously believe. When Thought Woman brought to life the twin sisters, she did not give birth to them in the biological sense. She sang over the medicine bundles that contained their potentials. With her singing and shaking she infused them with vitality. She gathered the power that she controlled and focused it on those bundles, and thus they were "born." Similarly, when the sister goddesses Naotsete and Uretsete wished to bring forth some plant or creature they reached into the basket (bundle) that The Thought Woman had given them, took out the effigy of the creature, and thought it into life. Usually they then instructed it in its proper role. They also meted out consequences to creatures (this included plants, spirits, and katsinas) who disobeyed them.

The water of life, menstrual or postpartum blood, was held sacred. Sacred often means taboo; that is, what is empowered in a ritual sense is not to be touched or approached by any who are weaker than the power itself, lest they suffer negative consequences from contact. The blood of woman was in and of itself infused with the power of Supreme Mind, and so women were held in awe and respect. The term *sacred*, which is connected with power, is similar in meaning to the term *sacrifice*, which means "to make sacred." What is made sacred is empowered. Thus, in the old way, sacrificing meant empowering, which is exactly what it still means to American Indians who adhere to traditional practice. Blood was and is used in sacrifice because it possesses the power to make something else powerful or, conversely, to weaken or kill it.

Pre-contact American Indian women valued their role as vitalizers because they understood that bearing, like bleeding, was a transformative ritual act. Through their own bodies they could bring vital beings into the world—a miraculous power unrivaled by mere shamanic displays. They were mothers, and that word implied the highest degree of status in ritual cultures. The status of mother was so high, in fact, that in some cultures Mother or its analogue, Matron, was the highest office to which a man or woman could aspire.

The old ones were empowered by their certain knowledge that the power to make life is the source and model for all ritual magic and that no other power can gainsay it. Nor is that power really biological at base; it is the power of ritual magic, the power of Thought, of Mind, that gives rise to biological organisms as it gives rise to social organizations, material culture, and transformations of all kinds—including hunting, war, healing, spirit communication, rain-making, and all the rest.

At Laguna, all entities, human or supernatural, who are functioning in a ritual manner at a high level are called Mother. The story "Arrow Youth, the Witches and the K'a`ts'ina" is filled with addresses of this sort.

The cacique is addressed as mother by the war captain as well as by Arrow Youth. The Turkey-Buzzard Spirit is greeted as mother by the shaman who goes to consult him. When the cacique goes to consult with the k'apina shamans, he greets them saying, "How are things, mothers of everyone, chiefs of everyone." After he has made his ritual offering of corn pollen to them, he says, "Enough . . . mothers, chiefs." He greets them this way to acknowledge their power, a power that includes everything: long life, growth, old age, and life during the daytime. Not all the entities involved in the story are addressed in this fashion. Only those who command great respect are so titled. Yellow Woman herself is acknowledged "the mother of all of us" by the katsina chief or spokesman when he pledges the katsina's aid in her rescue. Many more examples of the practice exist among tribes, and all underscore that motherness is a highly valued characteristic.

But its value signifies something other than the kind of sentimental respect for motherhood that is reflected in Americans' Mother's Day observances. It is ritually powerful, a condition of being that confers the highest adeptship on whoever bears the title. So central to ritual activities is it in Indian cultures that men are honored by the name mother, recognizing and paying respect to their spiritual and occult competence. That competence derives entirely from Mother Iyatiku, and, through her, from Thought Woman herself.

A strong attitude integrally connects the power of Original Thinking or Creation Thinking to the power of mothering. That power is not so much the power to give birth, as we have noted, but the power to make, to create, to transform. Ritual, as noted elsewhere, means transforming something from one state or condition to another, and that ability is inherent in the action of mothering. It is the ability that is sought and treasured by adepts, and it is the ability that male seekers devote years of study and discipline to acquire. Without it, no practice of the sacred is possible, at least not within the Great Mother societies.

And as the cultures that are woman-centered and Mother-ritual based are also cultures that value peacefulness, harmony, cooperation, health, and general prosperity, they are systems of thought and practice that would bear deeper study in our troubled, conflict-ridden time.

FOR FURTHER READING

Allen, Paula Gunn. *Spider Woman's Granddaughters: Traditional Tales and Contemporary Writing by Native American Women.* Boston: Beacon Press, 1989.

————. "Stealing the Thunder: Future Visions for American Indian Women, Tribes, and Literary Studies. In *The Sacred Hoop: Recovering the Feminine in American Indian Traditions,* 262–68. Boston: Beacon Press, 1992.

————. "Who Is Your Mother? Red Roots of White Feminism." In *The Sacred Hoop: Recovering the Feminine in American Indian Traditions,* 209–21. Boston: Beacon Press, 1992.

Keating, AnaLouise. *Women Reading/Women Writing: Self-Invention in Paula Gunn Allen, Gloria Anzaldúa, and Audre Lorde.* Philadelphia: Temple University Press, 1996.

Purley, Anthony. "Keres Pueblo Concepts of Deity." *American Indian Culture and Research Journal* 1.1 (Fall 1974): 25–31.

Tyler, Hamilton A. *Pueblo Gods and Myths.* Norman: University of Oklahoma Press, 1964.

Gloria Anzaldúa

1942–

Gloria Anzaldúa calls herself a "border woman" who has been "straddling" dividing lines all her life. Born on the physical borderland of the Texas–U.S. Southwest/Mexican border, a site that informs all of her writing, Anzaldúa explores in her work what she calls the "psychological borderlands, the sexual borderlands, and the spiritual borderlands" that exist wherever "two or more" cultures, races, or classes "touch." In her preface to *Borderlands/La Frontera*, Anzaldúa describes these borderlands as places of "contradiction," places where "hatred, anger, and exploitation" are part of the landscape, but also sites where she finds a "certain joy," especially at the "unique positionings consciousness takes at these confluent streams."

Anzaldúa was one of the first writers to confront the realities of being a Chicana in North American culture. She named the political, social, and personal struggle of being a woman negotiating the rules of the dominant culture as "border crossing." Anzaldúa, through her self-identification as a "Chicana tejana lesbian-feminist poet and fiction writer," subverts as well as reinforces multifaceted borders in her writing and work: Chicana/American, Chicana/Mexican, lesbian/Chicana, lesbian/feminist, feminist/Chicana. Her work is committed to describing how these borders divide (and conquer) and to confronting the alienation of always being on one side or the other.

Borderlands/La Frontera offers a rhetorical theory of "border crossing" and "borderlands" that has flourished and has shaped discussions of women's writing and rhetoric since its publication. Ana Louise Keating defines Anzaldúa's writing as *"mestizaje ecriture"* (125), writing that disrupts dualistic thinking and refuses monolithic categories. Anzaldúa continually challenges dichotomies, showing in her own writing how interconnected are culture and individual, language and identity, body and intellect. In "How to Tame a Wild Tongue," Anzaldúa blends autobiography, linguistic and colonial history, poetry, and myth into a rhetorical theory that both exposes and overcomes "linguistic terrorism."

Weaving Spanish and English together in this essay, Anzaldúa recreates in her text the reality of bilingual Chicana/Chicano life in North American culture. At the same time, she confronts her English-only-speaking readers with their own limitations; in effect, she puts them on the border she has negotiated all her life. This rhetorical strategy creates two very different effects on her multiple audiences. First, she turns the tables on the dominant culture, forcing English-only speakers to occupy the position of the "other," to read on the "border" of Anzaldúa's text. Simultaneously, the blending and blurring of

Spanish and English celebrates readers who are bilingual, who can, indeed, cross borders fluidly. Keating says that Anzaldúa "uses the differences between herself and her readers to generate new forms of commonality" (13). By highlighting boundaries in this way, and by her careful attention to linguistic differences that shape individual material and psychological lives, Anzaldúa enacts a theory of language as generative: because she is a "shape-changer" herself, she shows her readers the performative power of language to generate selves, cultures, and communities, for good or ill.

"How to Tame a Wild Tongue"

1987

"We're going to have to control your tongue," the dentist says, pulling out all the metal from my mouth. Silver bits plop and tinkle into the basin. My mouth is a motherlode.

The dentist is cleaning out my roots. I get a whiff of the stench when I gasp. "I can't cap that tooth yet, you're still draining," he says.

"We're going to have to do something about your tongue," I hear the anger rising in his voice. My tongue keeps pushing out the wads of cotton, pushing back the drills, the long thin needles. "I've never seen anything as strong or as stubborn," he says. And I think, how do you tame a wild tongue, train it to be quiet, how do you bridle and saddle it? How do you make it lie down?

> "Who is to say that robbing a people of
> its language is less violent than war?"
> —Ray Gwyn Smith

I remember being caught speaking Spanish at recess—that was good for three licks on the knuckles with a sharp ruler. I remember being sent to the corner of the classroom for "talking back" to the Anglo teacher when all I was trying to do was tell her how to pronounce my name. If you want to be American, speak 'American.' If you don't like it, go back to Mexico where you belong."

"I want you to speak English. *Pa' hallar buen trabajo tienes que saber hablar el inglés bien. Qué vale toda tu educación si todavía hablas inglés con un* 'accent,'" my mother would say, mortified that I spoke English like a Mexican. At Pan American University, I, and all Chicano students, were required to take two speech classes. Their purpose: to get rid of our accents.

Attacks on one's form of expression with the intent to censor are a violation

Reprinted with permission from *Borderlands/La Frontera: The New Mestiza.* © 1987 by Gloria Anzaldúa. Published by Aunt Lute Books, San Francisco, 1987.

of the First Amendment. *El Anglo con cara de inocente nos arrancó la lengua.* Wild tongues can't be tamed, they can only be cut out.

Overcoming the Tradition of Silence

Ahogadas, escupimos el oscuro.
Peleando con nuestra propia sombra
el silencio nos sepulta.

En boca cerrada no entran moscas. "Flies don't enter a closed mouth" is a saying I kept hearing when I was a child. *Ser habladora* was to be a gossip and a liar, to talk too much. *Muchachitas bien criadas,* well-bred girls don't answer back. *Es una falta de respeto* to talk back to one's mother or father. I remember one of the sins I'd recited to the priest in the confession box the few times I went to confession: talking back to my mother, *hablar pa' 'tras, repelar. Hocicona, repelona, chismosa,* having a big mouth, questioning, carrying tales are all signs of being *mal criada.* In my culture they are all words that are derogatory if applied to women—I've never heard them applied to men.

The first time I heard two women, a Puerto Rican and a Cuban, say the word *"nosotras,"* I was shocked. I had not known the word existed. Chicanas use *nosotros* whether we're male or female. We are robbed of our female being by the masculine plural. Language is a male discourse.

And our tongues have become
dry the wilderness has
dried out our tongues and
we have forgotten speech.
              —Irena Klepfisz

Even our own people, other Spanish speakers *nos quieren poner candados en la boca.* They would hold us back with their bag of *reglas de academia.*

Oyé como ladra: el lenguaje de la frontera
Quien tiene boca se equivoca.
              —Mexican saying

"*Pocho,* cultural traitor, you're speaking the oppressor's language by speaking English, you're ruining the Spanish language," I have been accused by various Latinos and Latinas. Chicano Spanish is considered by the purist and by most Latinos deficient, a mutilation of Spanish.

But Chicano Spanish is a border tongue which developed naturally. Change, *evolución, enriquecimiento de palabras nuevas por invención o adopción* have created variants of Chicano Spanish, *un nuevo lenguaje. Un lenguaje que corresponde a un modo de vivir.* Chicano Spanish is not incorrect, it is a living language.

For a people who are neither Spanish nor live in a country in which Spanish is the first language; for a people who live in a country in which English is the

reigning tongue but who are not Anglo; for a people who cannot entirely identify with either standard (formal, Castillian) Spanish nor standard English, what
recourse is left to them but to create their own language? A language which they
can connect their identity to, one capable of communicating the realities and
values true to themselves—a language with terms that are neither *español ni inglés,* but both. We speak a patois, a forked tongue, a variation of two languages.

Chicano Spanish sprang out of the Chicanos' need to identify ourselves as a
distinct people. We needed a language with which we could communicate with
ourselves, a secret language. For some of us, language is a homeland closer than
the Southwest—for many Chicanos today live in the Midwest and the East. And
because we are a complex, heterogeneous people, we speak many languages.
Some of the languages we speak are:

1. Standard English
2. Working class and slang English
3. Standard Spanish
4. Standard Mexican Spanish
5. North Mexican Spanish dialect
6. Chicano Spanish (Texas, New Mexico, Arizona and California have
    regional variations)
7. Tex-Mex
8. *Pachuco* (called *caló*)

My "home" tongues are the languages I speak with my sister and brothers,
with my friends. They are the last five listed, with 6 and 7 being closest to my
heart. From school, the media and job situations, I've picked up standard and
working class English. From Mamagrande Locha and from reading Spanish
and Mexican literature, I've picked up Standard Spanish and Standard Mexican
Spanish. From *los recién llegados,* Mexican immigrants, and *braceros,* I learned
the North Mexican dialect. With Mexicans I'll try to speak either Standard
Mexican Spanish or the North Mexican dialect. From my parents and Chicanos
living in the Valley, I picked up Chicano Texas Spanish, and I speak it with my
mom, younger brother (who married a Mexican and who rarely mixes Spanish
with English), aunts and other relatives.

With Chicanas from *Nuevo México* or *Arizona* I will speak Chicano Spanish a
little, but often they don't understand what I'm saying. With most California
Chicanas I speak entirely in English (unless I forget). When I first moved to San
Francisco, I'd rattle off something in Spanish, unintentionally embarrassing
them. Often it is only with another Chicana *tejana* that I can talk freely.

Words distorted by English are known as anglicisms or *pochismos.* The *pocho* is
an anglicized Mexican or American of Mexican origin who speaks Spanish with
an accent characteristic of North Americans and who distorts and reconstructs
the language according to the influence of English. Tex-Mex, or Spanglish,

comes most naturally to me. I may switch back and forth from English to Spanish in the same sentence or in the same word. With my sister and my brother Nune and with Chicano *tejano* contemporaries I speak in Tex-Mex.

From kids and people my own age I picked up *Pachuco*. *Pachuco* (the language of the zoot suiters) is a language of rebellion, both against Standard Spanish and Standard English. It is a secret language. Adults of the culture and outsiders cannot understand it. It is made up of slang words from both English and Spanish. *Ruca* means girl or woman, *vato* means guy or dude, *chale* means no, *simón* means yes, *churro* is sure, talk is *periquiar, pigionear* means petting, *que gacho* means how nerdy, *ponte águila* means watch out, death is called *la pelona*. Through lack of practice and not having others who can speak it, I've lost most of the *Pachuco* tongue.

Chicano Spanish

Chicanos, after 250 years of Spanish/Anglo colonization have developed significant differences in the Spanish we speak. We collapse two adjacent vowels into a single syllable and sometimes shift the stress in certain words such as *maíz/maiz, cohete/cuete*. We leave out certain consonants when they appear between vowels: *lado/lao, majado/majao*. Chicanos from South Texas pronounced *f* as *j* as in *jue (fue)*. Chicanos use "archaisms," words that are no longer in the Spanish language, words that have been evolved out. We say *semos, truje, haiga, ansina,* and *naiden*. We retain the "archaic" *j*, as in *jalar*, that derives from an earlier *h*, (the French *halar* or the Germanic *halon* which is lost to standard Spanish in the 16th century), but which is still found in several regional dialects such as the one spoken in South Texas. (Due to geography, Chicanos from the Valley of South Texas were cut off linguistically from other Spanish speakers. We tend to use words that the Spaniards brought over from Medieval Spain. The majority of the Spanish colonizers in Mexico and the Southwest came from Extremadura—Hernán Cortés was one of them—and Andalucía. Andalucians pronounce *ll* like a *y*, and their *d*'s tend to be absorbed by adjacent vowels: *tirado* becomes *tirao*. They brought *el lenguaje popular, dialectos y regionalismos*.)

Chicanos and other Spanish speakers also shift *ll* to *y* and *z* to *s*. We leave out initial syllables, saying *tar* for *estar, toy* for *estoy, hora* for *ahora (cubanos* and *puertorriqueños* also leave out initial letters of some words.) We also leave out the final syllable such as *pa'* for *para*. The intervocalic *y*, the *ll* as in *tortilla, ella, botella*, gets replaced by *tortia* or *tortiya, ea, botea*. We add an additional syllable at the beginning of certain words: *atocar* for *tocar, agastar* for *gastar*. Sometimes we'll say *lavaste las vacijas*, other times *lavates* (substituting the *ates* verb ending for the *aste*).

We use anglicisms, words borrowed from English: *bola* from ball, *carpeta* from carpet, *máchina de lavar* (instead of *lavadora*) from washing machine. Tex-Mex argot, created by adding a Spanish sound at the beginning or end of an English word such as *cookiar* for cook, *watchar* for watch, *parkiar* for park, and *rapiar* for rape, is the result of the pressures on Spanish speakers to adapt to English.

We don't use the word *vosotros/as* or its accompanying verb form. We don't say *claro* (to mean yes), *imagínate*, or *me emociona*, unless we picked up Spanish from Latinas, out of a book, or in a classroom. Other Spanish-speaking groups are going through the same, or similar, development in their Spanish.

Linguistic Terrorism

Deslenguadas. Somos los del español deficiente. We are your linguistic nightmare, your linguistic aberration, your linguistic *mestisaje*, the subject of your *burla*. Because we speak with tongues of fire we are culturally crucified. Racially, culturally and linguistically *somos huérfanos*—we speak an orphan tongue.

Chicanas who grew up speaking Chicano Spanish have internalized the belief that we speak poor Spanish. It is illegitimate, a bastard language. And because we internalize how our language has been used against us by the dominant culture, we use our language differences against each other.

Chicana feminists often skirt around each other with suspicion and hesitation. For the longest time I couldn't figure it out. Then it dawned on me. To be close to another Chicana is like looking into the mirror. We are afraid of what we'll see there. *Pena.* Shame. Low estimation of self. In childhood we are told that our language is wrong. Repeated attacks on our native tongue diminish our sense of self. The attacks continue throughout our lives.

Chicanas feel uncomfortable talking in Spanish to Latinas, afraid of their censure. Their language was not outlawed in their countries. They had a whole lifetime of being immersed in their native tongue; generations, centuries in which Spanish was a first language, taught in school, heard on radio and TV, and read in the newspaper.

If a person, Chicana or Latina, has a low estimation of my native tongue, she also has a low estimation of me. Often with *mexicanas y latinas* we'll speak English as a neutral language. Even among Chicanas we tend to speak English at parties or conferences. Yet, at the same time, we're afraid the other will think we're *agringadas* because we don't speak Chicano Spanish. We oppress each other trying to out-Chicano each other, vying to be the "real" Chicanas, to speak like Chicanos. There is no one Chicano language just as there is no one Chicano experience. A monolingual Chicana whose first language is English or Spanish is just as much a Chicana as one who speaks several variants of Spanish. A Chicana from Michigan or Chicago or Detroit is just as much a Chicana as one from the Southwest. Chicano Spanish is as diverse linguistically as it is regionally.

By the end of this century, Spanish speakers will comprise the biggest minority group in the U.S., a country where students in high schools and colleges are encouraged to take French classes because French is considered more "cultured." But for a language to remain alive it must be used. By the end of this century, English, and not Spanish, will be the mother tongue of most Chicanos and Latinos.

So, if you want to really hurt me, talk badly about my language. Ethnic identity is twin skin to linguistic identity—I am my language. Until I can take pride in my language, I cannot take pride in myself. Until I can accept as legitimate Chicano Texas Spanish, Tex-Mex and all the other languages I speak, I cannot accept the legitimacy of myself. Until I am free to write bilingually and to switch codes without having always to translate, while I still have to speak English or Spanish when I would rather speak Spanglish, and as long as I have to accommodate the English speakers rather than having them accommodate me, my tongue will be illegitimate.

I will no longer be made to feel ashamed of existing. I will have my voice: Indian, Spanish, white. I will have my serpent's tongue—my woman's voice, my sexual voice, my poet's voice. I will overcome the tradition of silence.

> My fingers
> Move sly against your palm
> Like women everywhere, we speak in code. . . .
>   —Melanie Kaye/Kantrowitz

"Vistas," corridos, y comida: My Native Tongue

In the 1960s, I read my first Chicano novel. It was *City of Night* by John Rechy, a gay Texan, son of a Scottish father and a Mexican mother. For days I walked around in stunned amazement that a Chicano could write and could get published. When I read *I Am Joaquín* I was surprised to see a bilingual book by a Chicano in print. When I saw poetry written in Tex-Mex for the first time, a feeling of pure joy flashed through me. I felt like we really existed as a people. In 1971, when I started teaching High School English to Chicano students, I tried to supplement the required texts with works by Chicanos, only to be reprimanded and forbidden to do so by the principal. He claimed that I was supposed to teach "American" and English literature. At the risk of being fired, I swore my students to secrecy and slipped in Chicano short stories, poems, a play. In graduate school, while working toward a Ph.D., I had to "argue" with one advisor after the other, semester after semester, before I was allowed to make Chicano literature an area of focus.

Even before I read books by Chicanos or Mexicans, it was the Mexican movies I saw at the drive-in—the Thursday night special of $1.00 a carload— that gave me a sense of belonging. *"Vámonos a las vistas,"* my mother would call out and we'd all—grandmother, brothers, sister and cousins—squeeze into the car. We'd wolf down cheese and bologna white bread sandwiches while watching Pedro Infante in melodramatic tearjerkers like *Nosotros los pobres,* the first "real" Mexican movie (that was not an imitation of European movies). I remember seeing *Cuando los hijos se van* and surmising that all Mexican movies played up the love a mother has for her children and what ungrateful sons and daughters suffer when they are not devoted to their mothers. I remember the singing-type "westerns" of Jorge Negrete and Miquel Aceves Mejía. When watching Mexican movies, I felt a sense of homecoming as well as alienation. People who were to amount to something didn't go to Mexican movies, or *bailes* or tune their radios to *bolero, rancherita,* and *corrido* music.

The whole time I was growing up, there was *norteño* music sometimes called North Mexican border music, or Tex-Mex music, or Chicano music, or *cantina* (bar) music. I grew up listening to *conjuntos,* three-or four-piece bands made up of folk musicians playing guitar, *bajo sexto,* drums and button accordion, which Chicanos had borrowed from the German immigrants who had come to Central Texas and Mexico to farm and build breweries. In the Rio Grande Valley, Steve Jordan and Little Joe Hernández were popular, and Flaco Jiménez was the accordion king. The rhythms of Tex-Mex music are those of the polka, also adapted from the Germans, who in turn had borrowed the polka from the Czechs and Bohemians.

I remember the hot, sultry evenings when *corridos*—songs of love and death on the Texas-Mexican borderlands—reverberated out of cheap amplifiers from the local *cantinas* and wafted in through my bedroom window.

Corridos first became widely used along the South Texas/Mexican border during the early conflict between Chicanos and Anglos. The *corridos* are usually about Mexican heroes who do valiant deeds against the Anglo oppressors. Pancho Villa's song, *"La cucaracha,"* is the most famous one. *Corridos* of John F. Kennedy and his death are still very popular in the Valley. Older Chicanos remember Lydia Mendoza, one of the great border *corrido* singers who was called *la Gloria de Tejas.* Her *"El tango negro,"* sung during the Great Depression, made her a singer of the people. The everpresent *corridos* narrated one hundred years of border history, bringing news of events as well as entertaining. These folk musicians and folk songs are our chief cultural mythmakers, and they made our hard lives seem bearable.

I grew up feeling ambivalent about our music. Country-western and rock-and-roll had more status. In the 50s and 60s, for the slightly educated and *agringado* Chicanos, there existed a sense of shame at being caught listening to our music. Yet I couldn't stop my feet from thumping to the music, could not stop humming the words, nor hide from myself the exhilaration I felt when I heard it.

There are more subtle ways that we internalize identification, especially in the forms of images and emotions. For me food and certain smells are tied to my identity, to my homeland. Woodsmoke curling up to an immense blue sky; woodsmoke perfuming my grandmother's clothes, her skin. The stench of cow manure and the yellow patches on the ground; the crack of a .22 rifle and the reek of cordite. Homemade white cheese sizzling in a pan, melting inside a folded *tortilla*. My sister Hilda's hot, spicy *menudo, chile colorado* making it deep red, pieces of *panza* and hominy floating on top. My brother Carito barbequing *fajitas* in the backyard. Even now and 3,000 miles away, I can see my mother spicing the ground beef, pork and venison with *chile*. My mouth salivates at the thought of the hot steaming *tamales* I would be eating if I were home.

Si le preguntas a mi mamá, "¿Qué eres?"

"Identity is the essential core of who
we are as individuals, the conscious
experience of the self inside."
                                   —Kaufman

Nosotros los Chicanos straddle the borderlands. On one side of us, we are constantly exposed to the Spanish of the Mexicans, on the other side we hear the Anglos' incessant clamoring so that we forget our language. Among ourselves we don't say *nosotros los americanos, o nosotros los españoles, o nosotros los hispanos*. We say *nosotros los mexicanos* (by *mexicanos* we do not mean citizens of Mexico; we do not mean a national identity, but a racial one). We distinguish between *mexicanos del otro lado* and *mexicanos de este lado*. Deep in our hearts we believe that being Mexican has nothing to do with which country one lives in. Being Mexican is a state of soul—not one of mind, not one of citizenship. Neither eagle nor serpent, but both. And like the ocean, neither animal respects borders.

Dime con quien andas y te diré quien eres.
(Tell me who your friends are and I'll tell you who you are.)
                                   —Mexican saying

Si le preguntas a mi mamá, "¿Qué eres?" te dirá, "Soy mexicana." My brothers and sister say the same. I sometimes will answer *"soy mexicana"* and at others will say *"soy Chicana" o "soy tejana."* But I identified as "Raza" before I ever identified as *"mexicana"* or "Chicana."

As a culture, we call ourselves Spanish when referring to ourselves a linguistic group and when copping out. It is then that we forget our predominant Indian genes. We are 70–80% Indian. We call ourselves Hispanic or Spanish-American or Latin American or Latin when linking ourselves to other Spanish-speaking peoples of the Western hemisphere and when copping out. We call ourselves Mexican-American to signify we are neither Mexican nor American, but more the noun "American" than the adjective "Mexican" (and when copping out).

Chicanos and other people of color suffer economically for not acculturating. This voluntary (yet forced) alienation makes for psychological conflict, a kind of dual identity—we don't identify with the Anglo-American cultural values and we don't totally identify with the Mexican cultural values. We are a synergy of two cultures with various degrees of Mexicanness or Angloness. I have so internalized the borderland conflict that sometimes I feel like one cancels out the other and we are zero, nothing, no one. *A veces no soy nada ni nadie. Pero hasta cuando no lo soy, lo soy.*

When not copping out, when we know we are more than nothing, we call ourselves Mexican, referring to race and ancestry; *mestizo* when affirming both our Indian and Spanish (but we hardly ever own our Black ancestry); Chicano when referring to a politically aware people born and/or raised in the U.S.; Raza when referring to Chicanos; *tejanos* when we are Chicanos from Texas.

Chicanos did not know we were a people until 1965 when Ceasar Chavez and the farmworkers united and *I Am Joaquín* was published and *la Raza Unida* party was formed in Texas. With that recognition, we became a distinct people. Something momentous happened to the Chicano soul—we became aware of our reality and acquired a name and a language (Chicano Spanish) that reflected that reality. Now that we had a name, some of the fragmented pieces began to fall together—who we were, what we were, how we had evolved. We began to get glimpses of what we might eventually become.

Yet the struggle of identities continues, the struggle of borders is our reality still. One day the inner struggle will cease and a true integration take place. In the meantime, *tenémos que hacer la lucha. ¿Quién está protegiendo los ranchos de mi gente? ¿Quién está tratando de cerrar la fisura entre la india y el blanco en nuestra sangre? El Chicano, si, el Chicano que anda como un ladrón en su propia casa.*

Los Chicanos, how patient we seem, how very patient. There is the quiet of the Indian about us. We know how to survive. When other races have given up their tongue, we've kept ours. We know what it is to live under the hammer blow of the dominant *norteamericano* culture. But more than we count the blows, we count the days the weeks the years the centuries the eons until the white laws and commerce and customs will rot in deserts they've created, lie bleached. *Humildes* yet proud, *quietos* yet wild, *nosotros los mexicanos-Chicanos* will walk by the crumbling ashes as we go about our business. Stubborn, persevering, impenetrable as stone, yet possessing a malleability that renders us unbreakable, we, the *mestizas* and *mestizos,* will remain.

FOR FURTHER READING

Anzaldúa , Gloria. *Friends from the Other Side/Amigos Del Otro Lado.* San Francisco: Children's Book Press, 1985.

———. *Making Face, Making Soul/ Hacienda Caras: Creative and Critical Perspectives by Women of Color.* San Francisco: Aunt Lute Books, 1990.

Keating, AnaLouise. *Women Reading/Women Writing: Self-Invention in Paula Gunn Allen, Gloria Anzaldúa, and Audre Lorde.* Philadelphia: Temple University Press, 1996.

Moraga, Cherrie, and Gloria Anzaldúa, eds. *This Bridge Called My Back: Writings by Radical Women of Color.* New York: Kitchen Table Press, 1984.

June Jordan

1936–

Whether addressing the fate of Nicaragua or the legacy of poverty constructed for black Americans by the U.S. government, June Jordan applies the full force of her conscience and rhetoric to effect social change. She relentlessly challenges cultural scripts such as "the crisis of the black family," demanding that the dangerous evidence used to create these myths be reexamined and recast by the people they oppress. In her internationally acclaimed poetry and prose, Jordan links her lived experiences as a child growing up in a black ghetto, as a woman dealing with rape and poverty, as a mother, writer, teacher, and daughter, with social and political problems throughout the world.

"Don't You Talk About My Momma," delivered to the Williams College Conference on the Black Family in 1987, traces black survival in America and characterizes it as an exceptional feat rather than as the failure that politicians and researchers describe. Jordan, like Fannie Barrier Williams almost one hundred years before her, challenges the rhetorical construction of black women by politicians and the media. She provides her readers—black and white—with a model for critical rhetorical analysis, prompting them to continually ask "Compared to what?" when confronted by official narratives that seek to assign meaning to their lives. Jordan exposes language such as "the collapse of the black family" and "female-headed" as politically motivated, designed to perpetuate white domination, to construct "blackness" as the problem rather than addressing social and economic inequalities. She says that black families are considered substandard in America simply because they have not remade themselves in the likeness of white patriarchal families. Here Jordan not only takes to task those who benefit from these false cultural narratives but also challenges the black Americans who buy into them. Using the childhood insult "Your Momma!" as a metaphor, Jordan illustrates the importance of trusting your experience. She cautions, "when you lose touch with your momma, when you take the word of an absolute, hostile stranger over and above the unarguable truth of your own miraculous, hard-won history, . . . [y]ou better just worry for yourself."

Jordan makes a bold move near the end of this speech: she proposes thirteen "universal entitlements" for all Americans. Ranging from equal pay and opportunities for national health insurance to nuclear disarmament, Jordan's entitlements are still actively fought for today. Jordan's language in this essay, using sarcasm, repetition, and the cadences of the black pulpit and informal speech, affirms the importance of her racial heritage and marks a vivid contrast to the bureaucratic language she critiques. Always privileging truth over order, resistance over complacency, and experience over objectivity, June Jordan's words challenge us to come to a social consciousness rooted in personal history and reflection.

"Don't You Talk About My Momma!"

1987

When I was growing up, the one sure trigger to a down-and-out fight was to say something—anything—about somebody's mother. As a matter of fact, we refined things, eventually, to the point where you didn't have to get specific. All you had to do was push into the face of another girl or boy and, close as you could, almost nose to nose, just spit out the two words: "Your mother!" This item of our code of honor was not negotiable and, clearly, we took it pretty seriously: even daring to refer to someone's mother put you off-limits. From the time you learned how to talk, everybody's momma remained the holiest of the holies. Yes, we were young. And a lot of people probably thought we were hoodlums, or something like that. But we knew we were smart: we made and kept ourselves ready to deal on those dangerous streets. Many of us, there, in Bedford-Stuyvesant, were poor. But very few of us were stupid. You couldn't be. In those days, as now, Black kids enjoyed damned little margin for error.

So we never lost track. We could feel it. We could see it. We could hear it. We could not deny it. And we did not ever forget it, this fact, that the first the last and the most, that the number one persevering, resourceful, resilient, and devoted person in our lives was, and would always be, your mother and my mother.

But sometimes, you know, we grow up without growing wise. Sometimes we become so sophisticated we have to read the *New York Times* in order to figure out whether it's a hot or a rainy day. We read the fine print in order to find out the names of our so-called leaders. We defer to erstwhile experts on the subject of sex. And we watch so much television that we can no longer tell the difference between a president who loves his—which is to say, *this*—country and a president who freely violates the Constitution. But what truly surprises me is Blackfolks listening to a whole lot of white blasphemy against Black feats of survival, Blackfolks paying attention to people who never even notice us except to describe us as "female-headed" or something equally weird. (I would like to know, for a fact, has anybody ever seen a female-headed anything at all? What

Reprinted from Jordan, June. "Don't You Talk About My Momma!" In *Technical Difficulties: African-American Notes on the State of the Union*, 60–85. New York: Pantheon Books, 1992. Reprinted by permission of the author.

did it look like? What did it do? Could you buy or marry one of them?) On the subject of language, let me briefly register my further unhappiness with the phrase "the feminization of poverty." The millions of human beings that lamentable phrase hopes to describe will never agree that poverty is feminine or that they, themselves, participate in the invention of the tortures of poor women in America. Nor will impoverished Black women of America willingly submit to the flagrantly popular, illogical, and misogynist response suggesting that the solution to the impoverishment of Black women/Black mothers is the enablement of everybody else. We know that most Black children now live in Black families headed by Black women. And we know that the most punishing poverty fastens itself to women, per se, and to Black women, always. I submit, therefore, that we also know, in our right minds, that Black women and Black mothers require specific, immediate, programmatic rescue! I mean, if somebody is suffering hunger, then it is she who needs the food.

Now, I am not opposed to sophistication, per se, but when you lose touch with your momma, when you take the word of an absolute, hostile stranger over and above the unarguable truth of your own miraculous, hard-won history, and when you don't remember to ask, again and again, "Compared to what?" I think you don't need to worry about enemies anymore. You better just worry for yourself.

Back in 1965, Daniel P. Moynihan issued a broadside insult to the National Black Community. With the full support of a Democratic administration that was tired of Negroes carrying on about citizenship rights, and integration, and white racist violence, Moynihan came through with the theory that we, Blackfolks, and that we, Black women, in particular, constituted "the problem." It was not the failure of the United States federal and local governments to equally entitle and equally protect all of its citizens, but it was the failure of Black families to resemble the patriarchal setup of White America that explained our unequal, segregated, discriminated-against, and violently hated Black experience of nondemocracy, here. We were, he said, a problem. We were, he said, a pathological culture. Moynihan said these things while white patriarchal America was proving itself to the world in a needless savagery of resistance to our nationwide movement for justice, that's all: just justice.

And I wrote and published this little poem, for Mr. Moynihan, back then:

Memo to Daniel Pretty Moynihan

You done what you done
I do what I can

Don't you liberate me
from my female black pathology

I been working off my knees
I been drinking what I please

And when I vine
I know I'm fine
I mean
All right for each and every
Friday night

But you been screwing me so long
I got a idea something's wrong
with you

I got a simple proposition
You take over my position

Clean your own house, babyface.

That's all he deserved, as I saw it. I couldn't take him seriously, and certainly not to my heart! Plus, I didn't have the time for Mr. Moynihan or any other Mr Man's theories about me. I was busy. I was going to meetings. I was demonstrating outside Chock Full O'Nuts. I was going to work. I was raising my son. (Did that make me or my child or both of us a female-headed whatchamacallit?) I had no time to waste.

And, besides, back then, you didn't bring your enemies into your house: you confronted them on the sidewalks, or in court, or on the floor of Congress. But when you went home, you went home to family. Of course, that meant that you had a family. It might not look like Dick and Jane or Ronald and Nancy but it surely did for you what the White House has never done for Black people: our family took care of us, and helped us to keep on keeping on. Our families might have adult women and children, and no adult men, or our families might have one white parent and one Black parent, and their children, or our families might have three generations living in two rooms, or our families might have, and, back then, as now, the majority did have, a Black father and a Black mother and their children, but regardless, we were all there, for each other when we came home. And we, the people of this allegedly "pathological ghetto culture," we were waging the most principled, unassailably moral revolution of the 20th century: we, the pathological community of Blackfolks were forcing these United States to finally honor the democratic promises responsible for the First American Revolution.

And, in the meantime, how was the dominant, the intact patriarchal white culture of America, how was the allegedly nonpathogenic but, nevertheless, racist and sexist culture of white America responding to this, the Civil Rights Revolution? By blowing up the 16th Street Baptist Church in Birmingham, September 15, 1963. By murdering four Black girls who had gone there for Sunday school. Or, in 1965, by murdering the unarmed white minister, Reverend James Reeb, in Selma. And, as well, in 1965, by publishing The Moynihan Report.

So, no, I didn't take him, or any of my enemies, to heart. But now there are

Black voices joining the choruses of the absurd. There are national Black organizations and purported Black theoreticians who have become indistinguishable from verified enemies of Blackfolks in this country. These sophisticated Black voices jump to page one of the delighted, ultra-reliable *New York Times* because they are willing to be misinterpreted and to lament and defame the incredible triumph of Black women, the victory of Black mothers that is the victory of our continuation as a people in America. Archly delivering jargon phrases about "the collapse of Black family structure" and "the destructive culture of poverty in the ghetto" and, of course, "the crisis of female-headedness," with an additional screaming reference to "the shame of teenage pregnancy," these Black voices come to us as the disembodied blatherings of peculiar offspring: Black men and women who wish to deny the Black mother of their origins and who wish to adopt white Daniel P. Moynihan as their father. I happen to lack the imagination necessary to forgive, or understand, this phenomenon. But the possible consequences of this oddball public outcry demand our calm examination.

According to these new Black voices fathered by Mr. Moynihan, it would seem that the Black family subsists in a terrible, deteriorating state. That's the problem. The source for the problem is the Black Family (i.e., it's not White; it suffers from female-headedness). The solution to the Black Family Problem is, you guessed it, the Black Family. It must, itself, become more white—more patriarchal, less female-headed, more employed more steadily at better and better-paying jobs. Okay?

Not okay. My own assessment of that analysis proceeds as follows:

Number One: The Black Family persists despite a terrible deteriorating state of affairs prevailing in these United States. This is a nation unwilling and progressively unable to provide for the well-being of most of its citizens: our economic system increasingly concentrates our national wealth in the hands of fewer and fewer interest groups. Our economic system increasingly augments the wealth of the richest sector of the citizenry while it diminishes the real wages and the available livelihood of the poor. Our economic system refuses responsibility for the equitable sharing of national services and monies among its various peoples. Our economic system maintains an unmistakable commitment to a Darwinian pseudophilosophy of laissez-faire. Our economic system remains insensitive to the political demands of a democracy and, therefore, our economic system does not yield to the requirements of equal entitlement vis-à-vis women, children, Black men, Hispanic Americans, Native Americans, the elderly, and the disabled. If you total those American people you have an obvious majority of Americans squeezed outside the putative benefits of "free enterprise." Our economic system continues its building, trillion-dollar commitment *not* to the betterment of the lives of its citizens but, rather, to the development and lunatic replication of a military-industrial complex. In this context, then, the Black Family persists, yes, in a terrible deteriorating state. But we did not create this state. Nor do we control it. And we are not suffering "collapse." Change does not signify collapse. The nuclear, patriarchal family structure of White America was never our own; it was not *African*. And, when we arrived to slavery, here, why or how should we emulate the overseer and the master, we who amounted to three-fifths of a human being, we who could, by law, neither marry nor retain our children against the predation of the slave economy? Nonetheless, from under the whip through underpaid underemployment, and worse, Black folks have formulated our own family, our own home base for nurture and for pride. We have done this from extended kinship methods of taking care to teenagers thrilled, not appalled, by the prospect of a child: a Black child. We have loved our own inside a greater environment of systematized contempt.

And when America turned away from our Black men, when America chose to characterize our men as animals or rapists or shiftless or simpletons or, anyhow, and this was always the point, anyway, *unemployable*, when America rejected our fathers and brothers and sweethearts and sons when they came looking for work, and when America allowed big corporations like Chrysler and General Motors to skip town because they'd discovered a labor force even cheaper than Black men, we, Black women, kept things together, you know, not perfectly, but we did it/somebody had to keep things together and we didn't never skip town. We didn't never say, "I'll be back. I'm going to the store," and then just disappear. And thank God, or else, who among us, Black, male or female, would be here today? And is this what all those sophisticated types mean when they gargle out the gobbledygook about "female-headedness"?

Number Two: To continue my assessment, I would agree that the Black family is not white. I do not agree that the problem is "female-headedness." I would rather suggest that the problem is that women, in general, and that Black women, in particular, cannot raise our children and secure an adequately paying job because this is a society that hates women and that thinks we are replaceable/we are dispensable, ridiculous, irksome facts of life aptly described as "female-headed," for example. American social and economic hatred of women means that any work primarily identified as women's work will be poorly paid, if at all. Any work open to women will be poorly paid, at best, in comparison to work open to men. Any work done by women will receive a maximum of 64 cents on the dollar compared to the same work done by men. Prenatal, well-baby care, day care for children, children's allowances, housing allowances for parents of children, paid maternity leave—all of the elemental provisions for the equally entitled citizenship of women, and of children, are ordinary attributes of industrialized nations, except for one: the United States.

The problem, clearly, does not originate with women, in general, or Black women, specifically, who, whether it's hard or whether it's virtually impossible, nevertheless keep things together. Our hardships follow from the uncivilized political and economic status enjoined upon women and children in our country, which has the highest infant mortality rate among its industrial peers.

And, evidently, feels fine, thank you, about that. Not incidentally, Black infant mortality rates hold at levels twice that of whites.

Number Three: The bizarre tautological analysis of the Black family that blames the Black family for being not white/not patriarchal not endowed with steadily employed Black husbands and fathers who enjoy access to middle-income occupations is just that: a heartless and bizarre tautology, a heartless joke. Supposing Black men and Black women *wanted* Black men to become patriarchs of their families, supposing Black men wanted to function as head of the house: shouldn't they probably have some kind of a job? And quite apart from quasi-patriarchal virtues or ambitions, shall anyone truly dare to suggest that the catastrophic 45 percent unemployment rate now crippling adult Black men is something that either Black men or Black women view as positive or desirable? Forty-five percent! What is the meaning of a man in the house if he cannot hold out his hand to help his family make it through the month, and if he cannot hold up his head with the pride and authority that regular, satisfying work for good pay provides? How or whom shall he marry and on what basis? Is it honestly puzzling to anyone that the 45 percent Depression rate of unemployment that imprisons Black men almost exactly mirrors the 47 percent of Black households now headed up by Black women? Our Black families persist despite a racist arrangement of rewards such that a fully employed Black man or Black woman can hope to earn only 56 cents on the dollar as compared to the remuneration received by whites for equal work. And a Black college graduate, male or female, still cannot realistically expect to earn more than a white high school graduate.

We, children and parents of Black families, neither created nor do we control the terrible, deteriorating state of our unjust and meanly discriminating national affairs. In its structure, the traditional Black family has always reflected our particular jeopardy within these unwelcome circumstances. We have never been "standard" or predictable or stabilized in any normative sense even as our Black lives have never been standard or predictable or stabilized inside a benign, nationwide environment. We have been flexible, ingenious, and innovative or we have perished. And we have not perished. We remain and we remain different, and we have become necessarily deft at distinguishing between the negative differences—those imposed upon us—and the positive differences—those that joyously attest to our distinctive, survivalist attributes as a people.

Today, we must distinguish between responsibility and consequence. We are not responsible for the systematic under- and unemployment of Black men or women. We are not responsible for the drastically unequal rewards of employment available to women and to Black adults and teenagers. We are not responsible for racist hatred of us, and we are not responsible for American contempt for women, per se. We are not responsible for a dominant value system that quibbles over welfare benefits for children and squanders deficit billions of dollars on American pie in the sky. But we must outlive the consequences of an inhumane, disposable-life ideology. We have no choice. And because our economic system and because our political system of support for that economy really do subscribe to a disposable-life ideology whenever the conflict appears to pit profit or dominant power against the freedoms of human beings, we no longer constitute a minority inside America. Perforce we have been joined in our precarious quandary, here, by women, and children, Hispanic Americans, and Native Americans and the quickly expanding population of the aged, as well as the temporarily or permanently disabled.

At issue now is the "universal entitlement" as Ruth Sidel terms it in her important book *Women and Children Last*, of American citizens: What should American citizenship confer; what are the duties of the state in relation to the citizens it presumes to tax and to govern?

It is not the Black family in crisis but American democracy in crisis when the majority of our people oppose U.S. intervention in Central America and, nevertheless, the president proceeds to intervene, albeit in circuitous and loony-tune fashion. And the bullets and the bombs falling out from such executive overriding of democratic representation will neither amuse nor merely make believe their unconscionable destruction inside Nicaragua. It is not the Black family in crisis but American democracy at stake when the majority of our people abhor South African apartheid and, nonetheless, the president proceeds to collaborate with the leadership of that evil up to the utmost of his ability to stay awake. It is not the Black family in crisis but American democracy at risk when a majority of American citizens may no longer assume the preservation and/or the development of social programs to let them stay alive and well.

But if we, Black children and parents, have been joined in our precarious quandary, here, may we not also now actively join with these other jeopardized Americans to redefine and to finally secure universal entitlement of citizenship that will at last conclude the shameful American history of our oppression? What should these universal entitlements include?

1. Guaranteed jobs and/or guaranteed income to assure each and every American in each and every one of the fifty states an existence *above* the poverty line.

2. Higher domestic minimum wages and, for the sake of our narrow and broadest self-interests, both, a coordinated, international minimum wage so that exhausted economic exploitation in Detroit can no longer be replaced by economic exploitation in Taiwan, or Soweto, or Manila.

3. Child allowances from the state as well as state guarantees of child support.

4. Equal pay for equal work.

5. Affirmative action to assure broadly democratic access to higher-paying occupations.

6. Compensation for "women's work" equal to compensation for "men's work."

7. Housing allowances and/or state commitments to build and/or to subsidize acceptable, safe, and affordable housing for every citizen.

8. Comprehensive, national health insurance from prenatal through geriatric care.

9. State education, and perpetual reeducation, available through graduate levels of study on the basis of student interest and aptitude rather than financial capacity.

10. A national budget that will invariably commit the main portion of our collective monies to our collective domestic needs for a good life.

11. Comprehensive provision for the well-being of all of our children commensurate with the kind of future we are hoping to help to construct. These provisions must include paid maternity/paternity leave and universal, state-controlled child-care public programs for working parents.

12. Nationalization of vital industries to protect citizen consumers and citizen workers, alike, from the greed-driven vagaries of a "free market."

13. Aggressive nuclear disarmament polices and, concurrently, aggressive state protection of what's left of the life-supportive elements of our global environment.

I do not believe that a just, a civilized nation can properly regard any one of these 13 entitlements as optional. And yet, not one of them is legally in place. And, as these rudimentary aspects of democratic entitlement exist nowhere on our American landscape today, and as Black women and Black men have been historically targeted for the worst social and economic forms of American rejection, is there any reason—any *reason*—for surprise that we may in our Black American daily attempts to keep going evince so many signs of enormous, arduous strain? Who is surprised? And why do we tolerate these expert yammerings/these insufferable accusations of Black family breakdown/Black *moral* breakdown? Black breakdown compared to what?

In the current American context that produces such stunning overall statistics as these—two out of every three officially poor Americans are women and one out of every two marriages ends in divorce—it seems to me that we, Blackfolks, are holding up rather well!

And in the current American atmosphere of moral leadership provided by Ronald Reagan, our American president who grievously breaks international and national law and then regularly lies about those crimes or, better yet, just *forgets* about them—in this atmosphere, who shall presume to say *what* to the domestic victims of this, our executive criminal? We need rescue from his crimes! We do not need the cruel absurdity of patronizing criticism precisely because our beleaguered lives expose the inhumane consequences of Ronald

Reagan's complete code of national dishonor! Since his accession to the presidency, is there *any* federal program for domestic life-support that has not come under his personal, his unpardonable, attack?

And what about teenage pregnancy which, like divorce, has moved forward into critical, destabilizing areas of contemporary dynamics? I say there is nothing inherently bad about young people wanting to become mothers or fathers. There is nothing specifically Black about it, either, or white. It's happening, now, with greater frequency than the teenagers themselves, or the rest of us, can readily accommodate in a civilized, supportive, nondestructive manner. And that's because extremely few Americans apparently know how to successfully mother or father, anyway, and, also, our government is not in the habit of trying to be helpful to new parents, whether they are 35 years old or 17. As a matter of fact, American adults stutter so hypocritically about teenage pregnancies that we on the one hand claim to be upset but then we still can't get it together to guarantee appropriate, universal sex education in our public schools, and universal teenage access to contraceptive means, including abortion, if necessary. I note that, actually, teenage pregnancy rates have declined by 10 percent during the decade from 1973 to 1983. And I note that, notwithstanding that fact, the alarm continues, hysterical and, again, misbegotten in its aim. Before anybody presumes to condemn or to take away the children of our children, we need to confront these questions. Who will instinctively respect a Black boy or a young Black girl? Who needs them? Who cannot live without them? Who else will welcome, without ambivalence, the advent of another Black child besides a Black child, herself, or himself? Who among us is prepared to answer any of those questions with a dedicated programmatic evidence of sincerity? First, it seems to me, we would need to eliminate the reality of 50 percent *plus* unemployment that has taunted young Black men and women for more than ten years in America. And, second, we would need to eliminate the institutionalized educational failure that a 40 to 75 percent high school dropout rate among Black teenagers reveals. Are we ready to do that? Listen to this silence!

Compared to the uncertain, but essential, top-to-bottom, male and female, White and Black, childhood-to-elderly tough coalitional work ahead of us, the revolutionary work that will establish those 13 universal entitlements as our new American Bill of Rights, compared to that stupendous but unavoidable, that emergency undertaking, wouldn't it be fun, instead, to duck into an old movie? You know, that old flick about the Negro Problem or is it the Crisis of the Black Family, or will it be that favorite midnight horror show about "female-headed" monstrosities that catapult an entire people into a cauldron of low-income misery and sloth? Well, go ahead, and good luck inside the movies, and even more good luck to you when you come out again!

In *The State of Black America*, 1986, published by the National Urban League, you will discover these rather tasty morsels of new information:

In most discussions of the recent growth in female-headed families, one fact is invariably omitted—that the largest increases occurred among "middle class" and not "underclass" families. Nine out of every 10 (88%) black female-headed families formed between 1970 and 1981 were headed by women with at least a high school diploma while 1 out of 3 were college educated. Contrary to popular belief, only 12% of the increase in one-parent black families over this period was due to families headed by women who were high school dropouts.

Similarly, 95% of the one-parent black families formed between 1970 and 1981 were headed by women who had been formerly married . . . only 5% of the rise in black one-parent families during the 1970's occurred among women who had *never* married. Similar findings result for female-headed families among whites as well. In short, the largest increases in one-parent families . . . occurred among the black and white middle class—primarily because of spiraling divorce rates over the past two decades. Thus, there is less and less empirical support for the popular view that female-headed families are an intrinsic characteristic of a "culture of poverty."

A couple of pages later we read,

. . . Black youth from one-parent families are about as likely to attend college as are youth from two-parent families. While 13% of children in two-parent families were in college in 1979, so were 10% of the children in one-parent black families. Similarly, among black families with incomes of $20,000 and over, youth in two-parent families were about as likely to attend college (20%) as youth in one-parent black families (23%).

But all of these numbers and percentile comparisons don't do too much for ghetto culture products like myself. I mean all that's useful. And I'm mighty glad to find out that the—what do they call that stuff? empirical data?—move right along in synch with my own head and my own heart. But I personally do not need any of these supersophisticated charts and magical graphs to tell me my own momma done better than she could and my momma's momma, *she* done better than I could. And *everybody's momma* done better than anybody had any right to expect she would. And that's the truth!

And I hope you've been able to follow my meaning. And a word to the wise, they say, should be sufficient. So, I'm asking you real nice: Don't you talk about my momma.

FOR FURTHER READING

Jordan, June. *Affirmative Acts: Political Essays.* New York: Anchor Books/Doubleday, 1998.
———. *Civil Wars.* Boston: Beacon Press, 1981.
———. *Moving Towards Home: Political Essays.* London: Virago Press, 1989.
———. *On Call: Political Essays.* Boston: South End Press, 1985.

Trinh T. Minh-ha

1953–

As filmmaker, composer, writer, and poet, Trinh T. Minh-ha asserts the inter-relationship of rhetoric and identity; she seeks to disrupt Western cultural be-liefs about monolithic selfhood, ethnicity, and gender by rendering the world multidimensional in her visual and written art. She also challenges the modes of representation Western filmmakers and writers use in their depictions of the "other." Her complex perspective arises from the shifting and shattered world she experienced during the Vietnam War. She saw some members of her family following the ideology of the North and others turning to the South. Trinh grew up in Hanoi but also attended the National Conservatory of Music and Theatre in Saigon for one year before she left to study in the United States. Trinh now holds degrees in French and Francophone literatures and teaches film studies and women's studies at the University of California at Berkeley.

Trinh T. Minh-ha's writing and film draw on the available means of feminist discourse to explore the identities and struggles of nonwhite women. She echoes and refigures Virginia Woolf and Hélène Cixous from the perspective of a Third World woman writer, but she shifts perspectives to ask: What does it mean to write as a woman—as a "language stealer"? And what does it mean to write as a woman of color? Following Woolf's claim to a "room of her own" and Cixous's challenge to women that they "write themselves," Trinh seeks to define the rhetorical difficulties Third World women encounter in attempting to represent themselves in writing and visual art: "How do you inscribe differ-ence without bursting into a series of euphoric narcissistic accounts of yourself and your own kind? Without indulging in a marketable romanticism or a naïve whining about your condition? . . . Between the twin chasms of navel-gazing and navel-erasing, the ground is narrow and slippery. None of us can pride our-selves on being sure-footed there"(*Woman, Native, Other* 28). She also highlights the problems of essentialism for women writers: "A woman's room, despite its new seductive paneling, can become a prison as soon as it takes on the appear-ance of a lady's room. . . . The danger in going 'the woman's way' is precisely that we may stop midway and limit ourselves to a series of reactions: instead of walking on. . ." (*Woman, Native, Other* 29).

In her films as well as in her writing, Trinh demonstrates strategies that dis-rupt the official language of rhetorical and aesthetic conventions: breaking up pictures into multiple parts; superimposing images and various written genres together; shifting and repeating viewpoints and providing multiple versions of a single scene; and twisting syntax into unfamiliar patterns to produce the paradoxes valued in Taoism and Zen (Foss, Foss, and Griffin). But she does not advocate discarding or opposing traditional form and conventions. Instead she acknowledges their importance and seeks to call them to our attention. In this excerpt from *Woman, Native, Other*, Trinh challenges traditional norms of clarity, linearity, and single focus, but she also acknowledges that the rhetorician never abandons particular conventions but always writes in the presence of them.

From *Woman, Native, Other*

1989

"The triple bind"

Neither black/red/yellow nor woman but poet or writer. For many of us, the question of priorities remains a crucial issue. Being merely "a writer" without doubt ensures one a status of far greater weight than being "a woman of color who writes" ever does. Imputing race or sex to the creative act has long been a means by which the literary establishment cheapens and discredits the achievements of non-mainstream women writers. She who "happens to be" a (non-white) Third World member, a woman, and a writer is bound to go through the ordeal of exposing her work to the abuse of praises and criticisms that either ignore, dispense with, or overemphasize her racial and sexual attributes. Yet the time has passed when she can confidently identify herself with a profession or artistic vocation without questioning and relating it to her color-woman condition. Today, the growing ethnic-feminist consciousness has made it increasingly difficult for her to turn a blind eye not only to the specification of the writer as historical subject (who writes? and in what context?), but also to writing itself as a practice located at the intersection of subject and history—a literary practice that involves the possible knowledge (linguistical and ideological) of itself as such. On the one hand, no matter what position she decides to take, she will sooner or later find herself driven into situations where she is made to feel she must choose from among three conflicting identities. Writer of color? Woman writer? Or woman of color? Which comes first? Where does she place her loyalties? On the other hand, she often finds herself at odds with language, which partakes in the white-male-is-norm ideology and is used predominantly as a vehicle to circulate established power relations. This is further intensified by her finding herself also at odds with her relation to writing, which when carried out uncritically often proves to be one of domination: as

Reprinted from Minh-ha, Trinh T. *Woman, Native, Other: Writing Postcoloniality and Feminism*, 6, 16–17, 19–20. Bloomington: Indiana University Press, 1989. Used by permission.

holder of speech, she usually writes from a position of power, creating as an "author," situating herself *above* her work and existing *before* it, rarely simultaneously *with* it. Thus, it has become almost impossible for her to take up her pen without at the same time questioning her relation to the material that defines her and her creative work. As focal point of cultural consciousness and social change, writing weaves into language the complex relations of a subject caught between the problems of race and gender and the practice of literature as the very place where social alienation is thwarted differently according to each specific context.

"Vertically imposed language: on clarity, craftsmanship, and She who steals language"

When commitment remains limited to the sociopolitical sphere, the claim of a "functional" writing that advocates the cause of the oppressed and instructs its audience indicates, in Mphahlele's terms, "a dangerous tendency." It tends "to draw a line of distinction between a function in which an author vindicates or asserts black pride or takes a sociopolitical stand and a function in which he seeks to stir humanity as a whole. . . ." What emerges here are the questions that relate to the nature of literature and writing. On the one hand, can literature be a "freedom that has taken freedom as its end" (Sartre) and still concern itself with elements like structure, form, and style—whose totality precisely allows literature to take on its meaning? On the other hand, can a writing that claims to break down rules and myths submit itself to the exclusive rules of a sociopolitical stand? Nothing could be more normative, more logical, and more authoritarian than, for example, the (politically) revolutionary poetry or prose that speaks of revolution in the form of commands or in the well-behaved, steeped-in-convention-language of "clarity." . . . *Clear* expression, often equated with *correct* expression, has long been the criterion set forth in treatises on *rhetoric*, whose aim was to order discourse so as to *persuade*. The language of Taoism and Zen, for example, which is perfectly accessible but rife with paradox does not qualify as "clear" (paradox is "illogical" and "nonsensical" to many Westerners), for its intent lies outside the realm of persuasion. The same holds true for vernacular speech, which is not acquired through institutions— schools, churches, professions, etc.—and therefore not repressed by either grammatical rules, technical terms, or key words. Clarity as a purely rhetorical attribute serves the purpose of a classical feature in language, namely, its instrumentality. To write is to communicate, express, witness, impose, instruct, redeem, or save—at any rate to *mean* and to send out *an unambiguous message*. Writing thus reduced to a mere vehicle of thought may be *used* to orient toward a goal or to sustain an act, but it does not constitute an act in itself. This is how the division between the writer/the intellectual and the activists/the masses becomes possible. To use the language well, says the voice of literacy, cherish its classic form. Do not choose the offbeat at the cost of clarity. Obscurity is an imposition on the reader. True, but beware when you cross railroad tracks for one train may hide another train. Clarity is a means of subjection, a quality both of official, taught language and of correct writing, two old mates of power; together they flow, together they flower, vertically, to impose an order. Let us not forget that writers who advocate the instrumentality of language are often those who cannot or choose not to see the suchness of things—a language as language—and therefore, continue to preach conformity to the norms of well-behaved writing: principles of composition, style, genre, correction, and improvement. To write "clearly," one must incessantly prune, eliminate, forbid, purge, purify; in other words, practice what may be called an "ablution of language" (Roland Barthes).

"Writing for me," says Toni Cade Bambara, "is still an act of language first and foremost." Before being the noble messenger and the loyal message of her/his people, the writer is a wo/man "whose most absorbed and passionate hours are spent arranging words on pieces of paper" (Joan Didion). S/He does not expresses her/his thoughts, passion, or imagination in sentences but *thinks sentences:* she is a sentence-thinker . . . who radically questions the world through the questioning of a how-to write. . . .

"A lady of letters, what a funny expression . . . ," says Simone de Beauvoir in an interview with Jean-Paul Sartre, who wonders what it feels like in life to be such a lady (creature). To write is to become. Not to become a writer (or a poet), but to become, intransitively. Not when writing adopts established keynotes or policy, but when it traces for itself lines of evasion. Can any one of us write *like* a man, *like* a woman, *like* a white? Surely, someone would quickly answer, and this leads us straight back to the old master-servant's Guilt. A sentence-thinker, yes, but one who so very often does not know how a sentence will end, I say. And as there is no need to rush, just leave it open, so that it may later on find, or not find, its closure. Words, fragments, and lines that I love for no sound reason; blanks, lapses, and silences that settle in like gaps of fresh air as soon as the inked space smells stuffy. Learned women have often been described in terms one might use in describing a thief. . . .

Women writers are both prompt to hide in (their) writing(s) and feel prompted to do so. As language-stealers, they must yet learn to steal without being seen, and with no pretense of being a stealer, for fear of "exposing the father." Such a reluctance to say aloud that the emperor has no clothes and therefore to betray or admit of an evidence comes perhaps less from a subjection to man than from an acute awareness of emptiness—emptiness through (his) power, through (his) language, through (his) disguises. Hence the compassion and the desire to protect. By countering a (masculine) disguise with another (feminine) disguise, however, Nin felt she had crippled herself. Double mischief: unspoken and unable to speak, woman in exile with herself. Stolen language will always remain that other's language. Say it obliquely, use trickery, cheat, or fake, for if I tell you now what I would like to hear myself tell you, I will miss it. Words thoroughly invested with realities that turn out to be not-quite-not-yet-mines are radically deceptive. Whenever I *try my best* to say, I never fail to utter the wrong words; I weasel, telling you "hen" when I mean something close to "duck." "It is useless," Virginia Woolf wrote, "to go to the great men writers for help, however much one may go to them for pleasure . . . The ape is too distant to be sedulous. Perhaps the first thing she would find, setting pen to paper, was that there was no common sentence ready for her use." A man's sentence is bound to be unsuited for a woman's use; and no matter how splendid her gift for prose proves to be, she will stumble and fall with such a "clumsy weapon in her hands." "Moreover, a book is not made of sentences laid end to end, but of sentences built, if an image helps, into arcades or domes. And this shape too has been made by men out of their own needs for their own uses." *Literally,* she blabs and cackles and is well known as Ms. Tittle-tattle, always willing to sell off for a song what she has stolen (overheard) from man. *Figuratively,* she goes unheard (even when she yells and especially when she "shrills," as they put it) and remains as dumb as a fish. So where do you go from here? where do I go? and where does a committed woman writer go? Finding a voice, searching for words and sentences: say some thing, one thing, or no thing; tie/untie, read/unread, discard their forms; scrutinize the grammatical habits of your writing and decide for yourself whether they free or repress. Again, order(s). Shake syntax, smash the myths, and if you lose, slide on, *unearth* some new linguistic paths. Do you surprise? Do you shock? Do you have a choice?

FOR FURTHER READING AND VIEWING

Foss, Karen A., Sonja K. Foss, and Cindy Griffin. *Feminist Rhetorical Theories.* Thousand Oaks, Calif.: Sage Publications, 1999.

Minh-ha, Trinh T. *Framer Framed.* New York: Routledge, 1992.

———. *Reassemblage.* Women Make Movies. Third World Newsreel. Museum of Modern Art. Idera, Cinenova, Lightcone, Image Forum, 1982.

———. *Surname Viet Given Name Nam.* Women Make Movies. Museum of Modern Art. Cinenova, Idera, Image Forum, National Library of Australia Film and Video Lending Collection, 1989.

———. *A Tale of Love.* Women Make Movies, 1995.

———. *When the Moon Waxes Red: Representation, Gender and Cultural Politics.* New York: Routledge, 1991.

bell hooks

1952–

Much of women's writing has been viewed as "domestic," concerned with matters of home and hearth, organized into narratives of family life and relationships. In fact, for much of the history of women's writing, such domestic narratives and advice constituted the only acceptable form of public discourse allowed to women. In this essay, bell hooks takes the concept of private domesticity and rereads it as a theoretical stance and as a public act of resistance.

bell hooks is a widely acclaimed author of political and social commentary, of critical race and feminist theory, of memoir, and of pedagogy. Currently a Professor of English at City College, City University of New York, she is the author of over sixteen books since 1981, one of the most prolific women rhetors in this collection. As she does in "Homeplace (a site of resistance)," hooks often combines story with theory, history with contemporary contexts, concrete experience with academic citations. In doing so, she claims what she says her foremothers intuited but did not possess: the ability to "self-consciously articulate in written discourse the theoretical principles of decolonization."

This essay both describes and theorizes the value of "homeplace" for black families living in the colonized world of white supremacy. By describing her grandmother's and mother's struggles to maintain a place of refuge from white hatred, to "transcend their tiredness" in order to create private havens free from racism, hooks first pays homage to what she sees as a conscious and heroic choice on the part of black women. hooks also rereads her mother's and grandmother's ability to create and sustain a refuge from racism as theory and philosophy; thus, this essay echoes one of the larger themes of this whole anthology: that women's rhetorical theory, by necessity, arises not only from public, academic, or philosophical spaces but also from the material reality of women's lives. Rereading women's "natural" caretaker roles as a "radically subversive political gesture," hooks offers a complex theoretical reading of a common theme in women's history, a moving tribute to her own foremothers, and a new lens through which to look at women's place(s) in general. In combining personal narrative, memoir, theory, and scholarship from psychology, philosophy, and history, hooks not only invites her reader to see the domestic sphere in a much fuller way, but she also redefines each genre she uses.

"Homeplace (a site of resistance)"

1990

When I was a young girl the journey across town to my grandmother's house was one of the most intriguing experiences. Mama did not like to stay there long. She did not care for all that loud talk, the talk that was usually about the old days, the way life happened then—who married whom, how and when somebody died, but also how we lived and survived as black people, how the white folks treated us. I remember this journey not just because of the stories I would hear. It was a movement away from the segregated blackness of our community into a poor white neighborhood. I remember the fear, being scared to walk to Baba's (our grandmother's house) because we would have to pass that terrifying whiteness—those white faces on the porches staring us down with hate. Even when empty or vacant, those porches seemed to say "danger," "you do not belong here," "you are not safe."

Oh! that feeling of safety, of arrival, of homecoming when we finally reached the edges of her yard, when we could see the soot black face of our grandfather, Daddy Gus, sitting in his chair on the porch, smell his cigar, and rest on his lap. Such a contrast, that feeling of arrival, of homecoming, this sweetness and the bitterness of that journey, that constant reminder of white power and control.

I speak of this journey as leading to my grandmother's house, even though our grandfather lived there too. In our young minds houses belonged to women, were their special domain, not as property, but as places where all that truly mattered in life took place—the warmth and comfort of shelter, the feeding of our bodies, the nurturing of our souls. There we learned dignity, integrity of being; there we learned to have faith. The folks who made this life possible, who were our primary guides and teachers, were black women.

Their lives were not easy. Their lives were hard. They were black women who for the most part worked outside the home serving white folks, cleaning their houses, washing their clothes, tending their children—black women who worked in the fields or in the streets, whatever they could do to make ends meet, whatever was necessary. Then they returned to their homes to make life happen there. This tension between service outside one's home, family, and kin network, service provided to white folks which took time and energy, and the effort of black women to conserve enough of themselves to provide service (care and nurturance) within their own families and communities is one of the

Reprinted from hooks, bell. "Homeplace (a site of resistance)." In *Yearning: Race, Gender, and Cultural Politics*, 41–49. Boston: South End Press, 1990. Reprinted by permission of South End Press.

many factors that has historically distinguished the lot of black women in patriarchal white supremacist society from that of black men. Contemporary
black struggle must honor this history of service just as it must critique the sexist definition of service as women's "natural" role.

Since sexism delegates to females the task of creating and sustaining a home
environment, it has been primarily the responsibility of black women to construct domestic households as spaces of care and nurturance in the face of the
brutal harsh reality of racist oppression, of sexist domination. Historically, African-American people believed that the construction of a homeplace, however
fragile and tenuous (the slave hut, the wooden shack), had a radical political dimension. Despite the brutal reality of racial apartheid, of domination, one's
homeplace was the one site where one could freely confront the issue of hu-
manization, where one could resist. Black women resisted by making homes
where all black people could strive to be subjects, not objects, where we could
be affirmed in our minds and hearts despite poverty, hardship, and depriva-
tion, where we could restore to ourselves the dignity denied us on the outside
in the public world.

This task of making homeplace was not simply a matter of black women
providing service; it was about the construction of a safe place where black
people could affirm one another and by so doing heal many of the wounds inflicted by racist domination. We could not learn to love or respect ourselves in
the culture of white supremacy, on the outside; it was there on the inside, in
that "homeplace," most often created and kept by black women, that we had
the opportunity to grow and develop, to nurture our spirits. This task of making a homeplace, of making home a community of resistance, has been shared
by black women globally, especially black women in white supremacist societies.

I shall never forget the sense of shared history, of common anguish, I felt
when first reading about the plight of black women domestic servants in South
Africa, black women laboring in white homes. Their stories evoked vivid memories of our African-American past. I remember that one of the black women
giving testimony complained that after traveling in the wee hours of the morning to the white folks' house, after working there all day, giving her time and
energy, she had "none left for her own." I knew this story. I had read it in the
slave narratives of African-American women who, like Sojourner Truth, could
say, "When I cried out with a mother's grief none but Jesus heard." I knew this
story. I had grown to womanhood hearing about black women who nurtured
and cared for white families when they longed to have time and energy to give
to their own.

I want to remember these black women today. The act of remembrance is a
conscious gesture honoring their struggle, their effort to keep something for
their own. I want us to respect and understand that this effort has been and
continues to be a radically subversive political gesture. For those who dominate

and oppress us benefit most when we have nothing to give our own, when they have so taken from us our dignity, our humanness that we have nothing left, no "homeplace" where we can recover ourselves. I want us to remember these black women today, both past and present. Even as I speak there are black women in the midst of racial apartheid in South Africa, struggling to provide something for their own. "We . . . know how our sisters suffer" (Quoted in the petition for the repeal of the pass laws, August 9, 1956). I want us to honor them, not because they suffer but because they continue to struggle in the midst of suffering, because they continue to resist. I want to speak about the importance of homeplace in the midst of oppression and domination, of homeplace as a site of resistance and liberation struggle. Writing about "resistance," particularly resistance to the Vietnam war, Vietnamese Buddhist monk Thich Nhat Hahn says:

> . . . resistance, at root, must mean more than resistance against war. It is a resistance against all kinds of things that are like war . . . So perhaps, resistance means opposition to being invaded, occupied, assaulted and destroyed by the system. The purpose of resistance, here, is to seek the healing of yourself in order to be able to see clearly . . . I think that communities of resistance should be places where people can return to themselves more easily, where the conditions are such that they can heal themselves and recover their wholeness.

Historically, black women have resisted white supremacist domination by working to establish homeplace. It does not matter that sexism assigned them this role. It is more important that they took this conventional role and expanded it to include caring for one another, for children, for black men, in ways that elevated our spirits, that kept us from despair, that taught some of us to be revolutionaries able to struggle for freedom. In his famous 1845 slave narrative, Frederick Douglass tells the story of his birth, of his enslaved black mother who was hired out a considerable distance from his place of residence. Describing their relationship, he writes:

> I never saw my mother, to know her as such more than four or five times in my life; and each of these times was very short in duration, and at night. She was hired by Mr. Stewart, who lived about twelve miles from my house. She made her journeys to see me in the night, traveling the whole distance on foot, after the performance of her day's work. She was a field hand, and a whipping is the penalty of not being in the field at sunrise . . . I do not recollect of ever seeing my mother by the light of day. She was with me in the night. She would lie down with me and get me to sleep, but long before I waked she was gone.

After sharing this information, Douglass later says that he never enjoyed a mother's "soothing presence, her tender and watchful care" so that he received the "tidings of her death with much the same emotions I should have probably felt at the death of a stranger." Douglass surely intended to impress upon the consciousness of white readers the cruelty of that system of racial domination which separated black families, black mothers from their children. Yet he does so by devaluing black womanhood, by not even registering the quality of care that made his black mother travel those twelve miles to hold him in her arms. In the midst of a brutal racist system, which did not value black life, she valued the life of her child enough to resist that system, to come to him in the night, just to hold him.

Now I cannot agree with Douglass that he never knew a mother's care. I want to suggest that this mother, who dared to hold him in the night, gave him at birth a sense of value that provided a groundwork, however fragile, for the person he later became. If anyone doubts the power and significance of this maternal gesture, they would do well to read psychoanalyst Alice Miller's book, *The Untouched Key: Tracing Childhood Trauma in Creativity and Destructiveness.* Holding him in her arms, Douglass's mother provided, if only for a short time, a space where this black child was not the subject of dehumanizing scorn and devaluation but was the recipient of a quality of care that should have enabled the adult Douglass to look back and reflect on the political choices of this black mother who resisted slave codes, risking her life, to care for her son. I want to suggest that devaluation of the role his mother played in his life is a dangerous oversight. Though Douglass is only one example, we are currently in danger of forgetting the powerful role black women have played in constructing for us homeplaces that are the site for resistance. This forgetfulness undermines our solidarity and the future of black liberation struggle.

Douglass's work is important, for he is historically identified as sympathetic to the struggle for women's rights. All too often his critique of male domination, such as it was, did not include recognition of the particular circumstances of black women in relation to black men and families. To me one of the most important chapters in my first book, *Ain't I A Woman: Black Women and Feminism,* is one that calls attention to "Continued Devaluation of Black Womanhood." Overall devaluation of the role black women have played in constructing for us homeplaces that are the site for resistance undermines our efforts to resist racism and the colonizing mentality which promotes internalized self-hatred. Sexist thinking about the nature of domesticity has determined the way black women's experience in the home is perceived. In African-American culture there is a long tradition of "mother worship." Black autobiographies, fiction, and poetry praise the virtues of the self-sacrificing black mother. Unfortunately, though positively motivated, black mother worship extols the virtues of self-sacrifice while simultaneously implying that such a gesture is not reflective of choice and will, rather the perfect embodiment of a woman's "natural" role. The assumption then is that the black woman who works hard to be a responsible caretaker is only doing what she should be doing. Failure to recognize the realm of choice, and the remarkable re-visioning of both woman's role and the idea of "home" that black women consciously exercised in practice, obscures the political commitment to racial uplift, to eradicating racism, which was the philosophical core of dedication to community and home.

Though black women did not self-consciously articulate in written discourse the theoretical principles of decolonization, this does not detract from the importance of their actions. They understood intellectually and intuitively the meaning of homeplace in the midst of an oppressive and dominating social reality, of homeplace as site of resistance and liberation struggle. I know of what I speak. I would not be writing this essay if my mother, Rosa Bell, daughter to Sarah Oldham, granddaughter to Bell Hooks, had not created homeplace in just this liberatory way, despite the contradictions of poverty and sexism.

In our family, I remember the immense anxiety we felt as children when mama would leave our house, our segregated community, to work as a maid in the homes of white folks. I believe that she sensed our fear, our concern that she might not return to us safe, that we could not find her (even though she always left phone numbers, they did not ease our worry). When she returned home after working long hours, she did not complain. She made an effort to rejoice with us that her work was done, that she was home, making it seem as though there was nothing about the experience of working as a maid in a white household, in that space of Otherness, which stripped her of dignity and personal power.

Looking back as an adult woman, I think of the effort it must have taken for her to transcend her own tiredness (and who knows what assaults or wounds to her spirit had to be put aside so that she could give something to her own). Given the contemporary notions of "good parenting" this may seem like a small gesture, yet in many post-slavery black families, it was a gesture parents were often too weary, too beaten down to make. Those of us who were fortunate enough to receive such care understood its value. Politically, our young mother, Rosa Bell, did not allow the white supremacist culture of domination to completely shape and control her psyche and her familial relationships. Working to create a homeplace that affirmed our beings, our blackness, our love for one another was necessary resistance. We learned degrees of critical consciousness from her. Our lives were not without contradictions, so it is not my intent to create a romanticized portrait. Yet any attempts to critically assess the role of black women in liberation struggle must examine the way political concern about the impact of racism shaped black women's thinking, their sense of home, and their modes of parenting.

An effective means of white subjugation of black people globally has been the perpetual construction of economic and social structures that deprive many folks of the means to make homeplace. Remembering this should enable us to understand the political value of black women's resistance in the home. It should provide a framework where we can discuss the development of black female political consciousness, acknowledging the political importance of resistance effort that took place in homes. It is no accident that the South African apartheid regime systematically attacks and destroys black efforts to construct homeplace, however tenuous, that small private reality where black women and men can renew their spirits and recover themselves. It is no accident that this homeplace, as fragile and as transitional as it may be, a makeshift shed, a small bit of earth where one rests, is always subject to violation and destruction. For when a people no longer have the space to construct homeplace, we cannot build a meaningful community of resistance.

Throughout our history, African-Americans have recognized the subversive value of homeplace, of having access to private space where we do not directly encounter white racist aggression. Whatever the shape and direction of black liberation struggle (civil rights reform or black power movement), domestic space has been a crucial site for organizing, for forming political solidarity. Homeplace has been a site of resistance. Its structure was defined less by whether or not black women and men were conforming to sexist behavior norms and more by our struggle to uplift ourselves as a people, our struggle to resist racist domination and oppression.

That liberatory struggle has been seriously undermined by contemporary efforts to change that subversive homeplace into a site of patriarchal domination of black women by black men, where we abuse one another for not conforming to sexist norms. This shift in perspective, where homeplace is not viewed as a political site, has had negative impact on the construction of black female identity and political consciousness. Masses of black women, many of whom were not formally educated, had in the past been able to play a vital role in black liberation struggle. In the contemporary situation, as the paradigms for domesticity in black life mirrored white bourgeois norms (where home is conceptualized as politically neutral space), black people began to overlook and devalue the importance of black female labor in teaching critical consciousness in domestic space. Many black women, irrespective of class status, have responded to this crisis of meaning by imitating leisure-class sexist notions of women's role, focusing their lives on meaningless compulsive consumerism.

Identifying this syndrome as "the crisis of black womanhood" in her essay, "Considering Feminism as a Model for Social Change," Sheila Radford-Hill points to the mid-sixties as that historical moment when the primacy of black woman's role in liberation struggle began to be questioned as a threat to black manhood and was deemed unimportant. Radford-Hill asserts:

> Without the power to influence the purpose and the direction of our collective experience, without the power to influence our culture from within, we are increasingly immobilized, unable to integrate self and role identities, unable to resist the cultural imperialism of the dominant culture which assures our continued oppression by destroying us from within. Thus, the crisis manifests itself as social dysfunction in the black community—as genocide, fratricide, homicide, and suicide. It is also manifested by the abdication of personal responsibility by black women for themselves and for each other . . . The crisis of black

womanhood is a form of cultural aggression: a form of exploitation so vicious, so insidious that it is currently destroying an entire generation of black women and their families.

This contemporary crisis of black womanhood might have been avoided had black women collectively sustained attempts to develop the latent feminism expressed by their willingness to work equally alongside black men in black liberation struggle. Contemporary equation of black liberation struggle with the subordination of black women has damaged collective black solidarity. It has served the interests of white supremacy to promote the assumption that the wounds of racist domination would be less severe were black women conforming to sexist role patterns.

We are daily witnessing the disintegration of African-American family life that is grounded in a recognition of the political value of constructing homeplace as a site of resistance; black people daily perpetuate sexist norms that threaten our survival as a people. We can no longer act as though sexism in black communities does not threaten our solidarity; any force which estranges and alienates us from one another serves the interests of racist domination.

Black women and men must create a revolutionary vision of black liberation that has a feminist dimension, one which is formed in consideration of our specific needs and concerns. Drawing on past legacies, contemporary black women can begin to reconceptualize ideas of homeplace, once again considering the primacy of domesticity as a site for subversion and resistance. When we renew our concern with homeplace, we can address political issues that most affect our daily lives. Calling attention to the skills and resources of black women who may have begun to feel that they have no meaningful contribution to make, women who may or may not be formally educated but who have essential wisdom to share, who have practical experience that is the breeding ground for all useful theory, we may begin to bond with one another in ways that renew our solidarity.

When black women renew our political commitment to homeplace, we can address the needs and concerns of young black women who are groping for structures of meaning that will further their growth, young women who are struggling for self-definition. Together, black women can renew our commitment to black liberation struggle, sharing insights and awareness, sharing feminist thinking and feminist vision, building solidarity.

With this foundation, we can regain lost perspective, give life new meaning. We can make homeplace that space where we return for renewal and self-recovery, where we can heal our wounds and become whole.

FOR FURTHER READING

hooks, bell. *Ain't I a Woman: Black Women and Feminism.* Boston: South End Press, 1981.
———. *All About Love: New Visions.* New York: William Morrow, 2000.

―――. *Black Looks: Race and Representation.* Boston: South End Press, 1992.

―――. *Bone Black: Memories of Girlhood.* New York: Henry Holt, 1996.

―――. *Feminist Theory: From Margin to Center.* Boston: South End Press, 1984.

―――. *Happy to be Nappy.* Illustrated by Christopher Raschka. New York: Hyperion, 1999.

―――. *Killing Rage: Ending Racism.* New York: Henry Holt, 1995.

―――. *Outlaw Culture: Resisting Representations.* New York: Routledge, 1994.

―――. *Remembered Rapture: The Writer at Work.* New York: Henry Holt, 1999.

―――. *Sisters of the Yam: Black Women and Self-Recovery.* Boston: South End Press, 1993.

―――. *Talking Back: Thinking Feminist, Thinking Black.* Boston: South End Press, 1989.

―――. *Teaching to Transgress: Education as the Practice of Freedom.* New York: Routledge, 1994.

―――. *Wounds of Passion: A Writing Life.* New York: Henry Holt, 1997.

hooks, bell, with Cornel West. *Breaking Bread: Insurgent Black Intellectual Life.* Boston: South End Press, 1991.

Nancy Mairs

1943–

Nancy Mairs's rhetoric embodies her survival in a society that shames women, dismisses "cripples," and separates sexuality from daily life. In her five collections of autobiographical essays, her writing and the subjects she addresses challenge received conceptions of what it means to be alive, characterizing human existence as messy and difficult. Jeanne Braham describes Mairs's rhetoric as a "direct assault initially to shock, then to intrigue, and finally to bond her reader to her text" (159). Mairs achieves this bonding by speaking the unspeakable in her work and by bringing common experiences to the fore: experiences of suicide attempts, chronic illness, rape, childbirth, infidelity, disability, and bodily functions.

In this essay, the namesake of her third collection of prose essays, Mairs confronts the shame she feels for her body, like the humiliation that many women feel when comparing their bodies with societal standards. However, Mairs's shame is coupled with her multiple sclerosis and the technologies of her disease: the wheelchair, the cane, the brace. Mairs draws upon Hélène Cixous's essay "Sorties" to challenge the mind/body dichotomy of Western thoughts. In "Carnal Acts," as in much of her work, Mairs reclaims the voice that she views as being artificially disconnected from her body by the unspoken regulations of "proper" talk. In this reclaiming, she exposes her processes of reflection and writing to her readers; she juxtaposes humor with shame and the carnal with the spiritual. In so doing, she reconnects her body, mind, and spirit to one another through her voice, which she sees as newly fused with her body. Mairs's bold prose exposes the realities of living with MS and the importance of speaking about it, reminding us that, "Speaking out loud is an antidote to shame."

"Carnal Acts"

1990

Inviting me to speak at her small liberal-arts college during Women's Week, a young woman set me a task: "We would be pleased," she wrote, "if you could talk on how you cope with your M.S. disability, and also how you discovered your voice as a writer." Oh, Lord, I thought in dismay, how am I going to pull this one off? How can I yoke two such disparate subjects into a coherent presentation, without doing violence to one, or the other, or both, or myself? This is going to take some fancy footwork, and my feet scarcely carry out the basic steps, let alone anything elaborate.

To make matters worse, the assumption underlying each of her questions struck me as suspect. To ask *how* I cope with multiple sclerosis suggests that I *do* cope. Now, "to cope," *Webster's Third* tells me, is "to face or encounter and to find necessary expedients to overcome problems and difficulties." In these terms, I have to confess, I don't feel like much of a coper. I'm likely to deal with my problems and difficulties by squawking and flapping around like that hysterical chicken who was convinced the sky was falling. Never mind that in my case the sky really *is* falling. In response to a clonk on the head, regardless of its origin, one might comport oneself with a grace and courtesy I generally lack.

As for "finding" my voice, the implication is that it was at one time lost or missing. But I don't think it ever was. Ask my mother, who will tell you a little wearily that I was speaking full sentences by the time I was a year old and could never be silenced again. As for its being a writer's voice, it seems to have become one early on. Ask Mother again. At the age of eight I rewrote the Trojan War, she will say, and what Nestor was about to do to Helen at the end doesn't bear discussion in polite company.

Faced with these uncertainties, I took my own teacherly advice, something, I must confess, I don't always do. "If an idea is giving you trouble," I tell my writing students, "put it on the back burner and let it simmer while you do something else. Go to the movies. Reread a stack of old love letters. Sit in your history class and take detailed notes on the Teapot Dome scandal. If you've got your idea in mind, it will go on cooking at some level no matter what else you're doing." "I've had an idea for my documented essay on the back burner," one of my students once scribbled in her journal, "and I think it's just boiled over!"

I can't claim to have reached such a flash point. But in the weeks I've had the themes "disability" and "voice" sitting around in my head, they seem to have converged on their own, without my having to wrench them together and bind them with hoops of tough rhetoric. They *are* related, indeed interdependent, with an intimacy that has for some reason remained, until now, submerged below the surface of my attention. Forced to juxtapose them, I yank them out of the depths, a little startled to discover how they were intertwined down there out of sight. This kind of discovery can unnerve you at first. You feel like a giant hand that, pulling two swimmers out of the water, two separate heads bobbling on the iridescent swells, finds the two bodies below, legs coiled around each other, in an ecstasy of copulation. You don't quite know where to turn your eyes.

Perhaps the place to start illuminating this erotic connection between who I am and how I speak lies in history. I have known that I have multiple sclerosis for about seventeen years now, though the disease probably started long before. The hypothesis is that the disease process, in which the protective covering of the nerves in the brain and spinal cord is eaten away and replaced by scar tissue, "hard patches," is caused by an autoimmune reaction to a slow-acting virus. Research suggests that I was infected by this virus, which no one has ever seen and which therefore, technically, doesn't even "exist," between the ages of four and fifteen. In effect, living with this mysterious mechanism feels like having your present self, and the past selves it embodies, haunted by a capricious and meanspirited ghost, unseen except for its footprints, which trips you even when you're watching where you're going, knocks glassware out of your hand, squeezes the urine out of your bladder before you reach the bathroom, and weights your whole body with a weariness no amount of rest can relieve. An alien invader must be at work. But of course it's not. It's your own body. That is, it's you.

This, for me, has been the most difficult aspect of adjusting to a chronic incurable degenerative disease: the fact that it has rammed my "self" straight back into the body I had been trained to believe it could, through highminded acts and aspirations, rise above. The Western tradition of distinguishing the body from the mind and/or the soul is so ancient as to have become part of our collective unconscious, if one is inclined to believe in such a noumenon, or at least to have become an unquestioned element in the social instruction we impose upon infants from birth, in much the same way we inculcate, without reflection, the gender distinctions "female" and "male." I *have* a body, you are likely to say if you talk about embodiment at all; you don't say, I *am* a body. A body is a separate entity possessable by the "I"; the "I" and the body aren't, as the copula would make them, grammatically indistinguishable.

To widen the rift between the self and the body, we treat our bodies as subordinates, inferior in moral status. Open association with them shames us. In fact, we treat our bodies with very much the same distance and ambivalence women have traditionally received from men in our culture. Sometimes this treatment is benevolent, even respectful, but all too often it is tainted by outright sadism. I think of the bodybuilding regimens that have become popular in the last decade or so, with the complicated vacillations they reflect between self-worship and self-degradation: joggers and aerobic dancers and weightlift- ers all beating their bodies into shape. "No pain, no gain," the saying goes. "Feel the burn." Bodies get treated like wayward women who have to be shown who's boss, even if it means slapping them around a little. I'm not for a moment opposing rugged exercise here. I'm simply questioning the spirit in which it is often undertaken.

Since, as Hélène Cixous points out in her essay on women and writing, "Sor- ties," thought has always worked "through dual, hierarchical oppositions" (p. 64), the mind/body split cannot possibly be innocent. The utterance of an "I" immediately calls into being its opposite, the "not-I," Western discourse being unequipped to conceive "that which is neither 'I' nor 'not-I,'" "that which is both 'I' and 'not-I,'" or some other permutation which language doesn't permit me to speak. The "not-I" is, by definition, other. And we've never been too fond of the other. We prefer the same. We tend to ascribe to the other those qualities we prefer not to associate with our selves: it is the hidden, the dark, the secret, the shameful. Thus, when the "I" takes possession of the body, it makes the body into an other, direct object of a transitive verb, with all the other's repudi- ated and potentially dangerous qualities.

At the least, then, the body had best be viewed with suspicion. And a woman's body is particularly suspect, since so much of it is in fact hidden, dark, secret, carried about on the inside where, even with the aid of a speculum, one can never perceive all of it in the plain light of day, a graspable whole. I, for one, have never understood why anyone would want to carry all that delicate stuff around on the outside. It would make you awfully anxious, I should think, put you constantly on the defensive, create a kind of siege mentality that viewed all other beings, even your own kind, as threats to be warded off with spears and guns and atomic missiles. And you'd never get to experience that inward dreaming that comes when your flesh surrounds all your treasures, holding them close, like a sturdy shuttered house. Be my personal skepticism as it may, however, as a cultural woman I bear just as much shame as any woman for my dark, enfolded secrets. Let the word for my external genitals tell the tale: my pudendum, from the Latin infinitive meaning "to be ashamed."

It's bad enough to carry your genitals like a sealed envelope bearing the cipher that, once unlocked, might loose the chaotic flood of female pleasure— *jouissance*, the French call it—upon the world-of-the-same. But I have an addi- tional reason to feel shame for my body, less explicitly connected with its sexu- ality: it is a crippled body. Thus it is doubly other, not merely by the homo-sexual standards of patriarchal culture but by the standards of physical desirability erected for every body in our world. Men, who are by definition ex- onerated from shame in sexual terms (this doesn't mean that an individual man might not experience sexual shame, of course; remember that I'm talking in general about discourse, not folks), may—more likely must—experience bodily shame if they are crippled. I won't presume to speak about the details of their experience, however. I don't know enough. I'll just go on telling what it's like to be a crippled woman, trusting that, since we're fellow creatures who've been living together for some thousands of years now, much of my experience will resonate with theirs.

I was never a beautiful woman, and for that reason I've spent most of my life (together with probably at least 95 percent of the female population of the United States) suffering from the shame of falling short of an unattainable standard. The ideal woman of my generation was . . . perky, I think you'd say, rather than gorgeous. Blond hair pulled into a bouncing ponytail. Wide blue eyes, a turned-up nose with maybe a scattering of golden freckles across it, a small mouth with full lips over straight white teeth. Her breasts were large but well harnessed high on her chest; her tiny waist flared to hips just wide enough to give the crinolines under her circle skirt a starting outward push. In terms of personality, she was outgoing, even bubbly, not pensive or mysterious. Her milieu was the front fender of a white Corvette convertible, surrounded by teasing crewcuts, dressed in black flats, a sissy blouse, and the letter sweater of the Corvette owner. Needless to say, she never missed a prom.

Ten years or so later, when I first noticed the symptoms that would be diagnosed as MS, I was probably looking my best. Not beautiful still, but the ideal had shifted enough so that my flat chest and narrow hips gave me an elegantly attenuated shape, set off by a thick mass of long, straight, shining hair. I had terrific legs, long and shapely, revealed nearly to the pudendum by the fashionable miniskirts and hot pants I adopted with more enthusiasm than delicacy of taste. Not surprisingly, I suppose, during this time I involved myself in several pretty torrid love affairs.

The beginning of MS wasn't too bad. The first symptom, besides the pernicious fatigue that had begun to devour me, was "foot drop," the inability to raise my left foot at the ankle. As a consequence, I'd started to limp, but I could still wear high heels, and a bit of a limp might seem more intriguing than repulsive. After a few months, when the doctor suggested a cane, a crippled friend gave me quite an elegant wood-and-silver one, which I carried with a fair amount of panache. The real blow to my self-image came when I had to get a brace. As braces go, it's not bad: lightweight plastic molded to my foot and leg, fitting down into an ordinary shoe and secured around my calf by a Velcro strap. It reduces my limp and, more important, the danger of tripping and falling. But it meant the end of high heels. And it's ugly. Not as ugly as I think it is, I gather, but still pretty ugly. It signified for me, and perhaps still does, the permanence and irreversibility of my condition. The brace makes my MS concrete and forces me to wear it on the outside. As soon as I strapped the brace on, I climbed into trousers and stayed there (though not in the same trousers, of course). The idea of going around with my bare brace hanging out seemed almost as indecent as exposing my breasts. Not until 1984, soon after I won the

Western States Book Award for poetry, did I put on a skirt short enough to reveal my plasticized leg. The connection between winning a writing award and baring my brace is not merely fortuitous; being affirmed as a writer really did embolden me. Since then, I've grown so accustomed to wearing skirts that I don't think about my brace any more than I think about my cane. I've incorporated them, I suppose: made them, in their necessity, insensate but fundamental parts of my body.

Meanwhile, I had to adjust to the most outward and visible sign of all, a three-wheeled electric scooter called an Amigo. This lessens my fatigue and increases my range terrifically, but it also shouts out to the world, "Here is a woman who can't stand on her own two feet." At the same time, paradoxically, it renders me invisible, reducing me to the height of a seven-year-old, with a child's attendant low status. "Would she like smoking or nonsmoking?" the gate agent assigning me a seat asks the friend traveling with me. In crowds I see nothing but buttocks. I can tell you the name of every type of designer jeans ever sold. The wearers, eyes front, trip over me and fall across my handlebars into my lap. "Hey!" I want to shout to the lofty world. "Down here! There's a person down here!" But I'm not, by their standards, quite a person anymore.

My self-esteem diminishes further as age and illness strip from me the features that made me, for a brief while anyway, a good-looking, even sexy, young woman. No more long, bounding strides: I shuffle along with the timid gait I remember observing, with pity and impatience, in the little old ladies at Boston's Symphony Hall on Friday afternoons. No more lithe, girlish figure: my belly sags from the loss of muscle tone, which also creates all kinds of intestinal disruptions, hopelessly humiliating in a society in which excretory functions remain strictly unspeakable. No more sex, either, if society had its way. The sexuality of the disabled so repulses most people that you can hardly get a doctor, let alone a member of the general population, to consider the issues it raises. Cripples simply aren't supposed to Want It, much less Do It. Fortunately, I've got a husband with a strong libido and a weak sense of social propriety, or else I'd find myself perforce practicing a vow of chastity I never cared to take.

Afflicted by the general shame of having a body at all, and the specific shame of having one weakened and misshapen by disease, I ought not to be able to hold my head up in public. And yet I've gotten into the habit of holding my head up in public, sometimes under excruciating circumstances. Recently, for instance, I had to give a reading at the University of Arizona. Having smashed three of my front teeth in a fall onto the concrete floor of my screened porch, I was in the process of getting them crowned, and the temporary crowns flew out during dinner right before the reading. What to do? I wanted, of course, to rush home and hide till the dental office opened the next morning. But I couldn't very well break my word at this last moment. So, looking like Hansel and Gretel's witch, and lisping worse than the Wife of Bath, I got up on stage and read. Somehow, over the years, I've learned how to set shame aside and do what I have to do.

Here, I think, is where my "voice" comes in. Because, in spite of my demurral at the beginning, I do in fact cope with my disability at least some of the time. And I do so, I think, by speaking about it, and about the whole experience of being a body, specifically a female body, out loud, in a clear, level tone that drowns out the frantic whispers of my mother, my grandmothers, all the other trainers of wayward childish tongues: "Sssh! Sssh! Nice girls don't talk like that. Don't mention sweat. Don't mention menstrual blood. Don't ask what your grandfather does on his business trips. Don't laugh so loud. You sound like a loon. Keep your voice down. Don't tell. Don't tell. Don't tell." Speaking out loud is an antidote to shame. I want to distinguish clearly here between "shame," as I'm using the word, and "guilt" and "embarrassment," which, though equally painful, are not similarly poisonous. Guilt arises from performing a forbidden act or failing to perform a required one. In either case, the guilty person can, through reparation, erase the offense and start fresh. Embarrassment, less opprobrious though not necessarily less distressing, is generally caused by acting in a socially stupid or awkward way. When I trip and sprawl in public, when I wet myself, when my front teeth fly out, I feel horribly embarrassed, but, like the pain of childbirth, the sensation blurs and dissolves in time. If it didn't, every child would be an only child, and no one would set foot in public after the onset of puberty, when embarrassment erupts like a geyser and bathes one's whole life in its bitter stream. Shame may attach itself to guilt or embarrassment, complicating their resolution, but it is not the same emotion. I feel guilt or embarrassment for something I've done; shame, for who I am. I may stop doing bad or stupid things, but I can't stop being. How then can I help but be ashamed? Of the three conditions, this is the one that cracks and stifles my voice.

I can subvert its power, I've found, by acknowledging who I am, shame and all, and, in doing so, raising what was hidden, dark, secret about my life into the plain light of shared human experience. What we aren't permitted to utter holds us, each isolated from every other, in a kind of solipsistic thrall. Without any way to check our reality against anyone else's, we assume that our fears and shortcomings are ours alone. One of the strangest consequences of publishing a collection of personal essays called *Plaintext* has been the steady trickle of letters and telephone calls saying essentially, in a tone of unmistakable relief, "Oh, me too! Me too!" It's as though the part I thought was solo has turned out to be a chorus. But none of us was singing loud enough for the others to hear.

Singing loud enough demands a particular kind of voice, I think. And I was wrong to suggest, at the beginning, that I've always had my voice. I have indeed always had *a* voice, but it wasn't *this* voice, the one with which I could call up and transform my hidden self from a naughty girl into a woman talking directly to others like herself. Recently, in the process of writing a new book, a memoir entitled *Remembering the Bone House*, I've had occasion to read some of my early writing, from college, high school, even junior high. It's not an experience I recommend to anyone susceptible to shame. Not that the writing was all that bad. I was surprised at how competent a lot of it was. Here was a writer who already knew precisely how the language worked. But the voice . . . oh, the voice was all wrong: maudlin, rhapsodic, breaking here and there into little shrieks, almost, you might say, hysterical. It was a voice that had shucked off its own body, its own homely life of Cheerios for breakfast and seventy pages of Chaucer to read before the exam on Tuesday and a planter's wart growing painfully on the ball of its foot, and reeled now wraithlike through the air, seeking incarnation only as the heroine who enacts her doomed love for the tall, dark, mysterious stranger. If it didn't get that part, it wouldn't play at all.

Among all these overheated and vaporous imaginings, I must have retained some shred of sense, because I stopped writing prose entirely, except for scholarly papers, for nearly 20 years. I even forgot, not exactly that I had written prose, but at least what kind of prose it was. So when I needed to take up the process again, I could start almost fresh, using the vocal range I'd gotten used to in years of asking the waiter in the Greek restaurant for an extra anchovy on my salad, congratulating the puppy on making a puddle outside rather than inside the patio door, pondering with my daughter the vagaries of female orgasm, saying goodbye to my husband, and hello, and goodbye, and hello. This new voice—thoughtful, affectionate, often amused—was essential because what I needed to write about when I returned to prose was an attempt I'd made not long before to kill myself, and suicide simply refuses to be spoken of authentically in highflown romantic language. It's too ugly. Too shameful. Too strictly a bodily event. And, yes, too funny as well, though people are sometimes shocked to find humor shoved up against suicide. They don't like the incongruity. But let's face it, life (real life, I mean, not the edited-for-television version) is a cacophonous affair from start to finish. I might have wanted to portray my suicidal self as a languishing maiden, too exquisitely sensitive to sustain life's wounding pressures on her soul. (I didn't want to, as a matter of fact, but I might have.) The truth remained, regardless of my desires, that when my husband lugged me into the emergency room, my hair matted, my face swollen and gray, my nightgown streaked with blood and urine, I was no frail and tender spirit. I was a body, and one in a hell of a mess.

I "should" have kept quiet about that experience. I know the rules of polite discourse. I should have kept my shame, and the nearly lethal sense of isolation and alienation it brought, to myself. And I might have, except for something the psychiatrist in the emergency room had told my husband. "You might as well take her home," he said. "If she wants to kill herself, she'll do it no matter how many precautions we take. They always do." *They* always do. I was one of "them," whoever they were. I was, in this context anyway, not singular, not aberrant, but typical. I think it was this sense of commonality with others I didn't even know, a sense of being returned somehow, in spite of my appalling act, to the human family, that urged me to write that first essay, not merely speaking out but calling out, perhaps. "Here's the way I am," it said. "How about you?" And the answer came, as I've said: "Me too! Me too!"

This has been the kind of work I've continued to do: to scrutinize the details of my own experience and to report what I see, and what I think about what I see, as lucidly and accurately as possible. But because feminine experience has been immemorially devalued and repressed, I continue to find this task terrifying. "Every woman has known the torture of beginning to speak aloud," Cixous writes, "heart beating as if to break, occasionally falling into loss of language, ground and language slipping out from under her, because for woman speaking—even just opening her mouth—in public is something rash, a transgression" (p. 92).

The voice I summon up wants to crack, to whisper, to trail back into silence. "I'm sorry to have nothing more than this to say," it wants to apologize. "I shouldn't be taking up your time. I've never fought in a war, or even in a schoolyard free-for-all. I've never tried to see who could piss farthest up the barn wall. I've never even been to a whorehouse. All the important formative experiences have passed me by. I was raped once. I've borne two children. Milk trickling out of my breasts, blood trickling from between my legs. You don't want to hear about it. Sometimes I'm too scared to leave my house. Not scared *of* anything, just scared: mouth dry, bowels writhing. When the fear got really bad, they locked me up for six months, but that was years ago. I'm getting old now. Misshapen, too. I don't blame you if you can't get it up. No one could possibly desire a body like this. It's not your fault. It's mine. Forgive me. I didn't mean to start crying. I'm sorry . . . sorry . . . sorry. . . ."

An easy solace to the anxiety of speaking aloud: this slow subsidence beneath the waves of shame, back into what Cixous calls "this body that has been worse than confiscated, a body replaced with a disturbing stranger, sick or dead, who so often is a bad influence, the cause and place of inhibitions. By censuring the body," she goes on, "breath and speech are censored at the same time" (p. 97). But I am not going back, not going under one more time. To do so would demonstrate a failure of nerve far worse than the depredations of MS have caused. Paradoxically, losing one sort of nerve has given me another. No one is going to take my breath away. No one is going to leave me speechless. To be silent is to comply with the standard of feminine grace. But my crippled body already violates all notions of feminine grace. What more have I got to lose? I've gone beyond shame. I'm shameless, you might say. You know, as in "shameless hussy"? A woman with her bare brace and her tongue hanging out.

I've "found" my voice, then, just where it ought to have been, in the body-warmed breath escaping my lungs and throat. Forced by the exigencies of physical disease to embrace my self in the flesh, I couldn't write bodiless prose. The voice is the creature of the body that produces it. I speak as a crippled woman.

At the same time, in the utterance I redeem both "cripple" and "woman" from the shameful silences by which I have often felt surrounded, contained, set apart; I give myself permission to live openly among others, to reach out for them, stroke them with fingers and sighs. No body, no voice; no voice, no body. That's what I know in my bones.

FOR FURTHER READING

Braham, Jeanne. *Crucial Conversations: Interpreting Contemporary American Literary Auto-biographies by Women.* New York: Teachers College Press, 1995.

Mairs, Nancy. *Ordinary Time: Cycles in Marriage, Faith, and Renewal.* Boston: Beacon Press, 1993.

———. *Plaintext: Deciphering a Woman's Life.* Tucson: University of Arizona Press, 1986.

———. *Remembering the Bone House.* New York: Harper and Row, 1989.

———. *Voice Lessons.* Boston: Beacon Press, 1994.

———. *Waist-High in the World: A Life among the Nondisabled.* Boston: Beacon Press, 1996.

Terry Tempest Williams

1955–

We are profoundly connected to the land. This seemingly simple idea infuses all of Terry Tempest Williams's work. A white Mormon woman, she is grounded in the landscape, the geographic place, of the Great Salt Lake in Utah. From this location she writes of the connections among herself, Native peoples, the land, her family, the lake, the birds and wildlife. In Williams's most noted book, *Refuge: An Unnatural History of Family and Place,* she laces moving reflections on the land and geography, family stories, political history, environmental science, and southwestern myth and song. Through her weavings Williams urges us to experience the deep intertwining relationship among place, the personal, and the political.

In her prologue to *Refuge,* Williams writes, "I sit on the floor of my study with journals all around me. I open them and feathers fall from their pages, sand cracks their spines, and sprigs of sage pressed between passages of pain heighten my sense of smell—and I remember the country I come from and how it informs my life. . . . Most of the women in my family are dead. Cancer. At thirty-four, I became the matriarch of my family" (3). In analyzing the effect of nuclear testing on the country she comes from and on the women in her family, in realizing that her dreams of nuclear terror are all too real, Williams, in her rhetoric, could be described as giving a different and powerful twist to the "politics of location." Always setting her environmental arguments not only in political and historical contexts but also in very real, geographical, natural contexts—as well as in personal, local ones—Williams, in her juxtaposition of all the elements that make up "history" and "geography," gives her writing at once both local immediacy and global impact.

Terry Tempest Williams raises her voice in social activism as well. She has testified before local and national governing bodies to advocate for healthy wildernesses, wildernesses free of nuclear waste and other toxic substances created as by-products of modern human existence. In testifying before a Senate Subcommittee on Forest and Public Lands Management on July 13, 1995, Williams said, "What do we wish? To be whole. To be complete. Wildness reminds us what it means to be human, what we are connected to rather than what we are separate from." Williams has committed her life to raising her pen and voice in solidarity with the wildlands; her writing illustrates, as well as argues for, that connection.

"The Clan of One-Breasted Women"

1991

I belong to a Clan of One-Breasted Women. My mother, my grandmothers, and six aunts have all had mastectomies. Seven are dead. The two who survive have just completed rounds of chemotherapy and radiation.

I've had my own problems: two biopsies for breast cancer and a small tumor between my ribs diagnosed as a "borderline malignancy."

This is my family history.

Most statistics tell us breast cancer is genetic, hereditary, with rising percentages attached to fatty diets, childlessness, or becoming pregnant after thirty. What they don't say is living in Utah may be the greatest hazard of all.

We are a Mormon family with roots in Utah since 1847. The "word of wisdom" in my family aligned us with good foods—no coffee, no tea, tobacco, or alcohol. For the most part, our women were finished having their babies by the time they were thirty. And only one faced breast cancer prior to 1960. Traditionally, as a group of people, Mormons have a low rate of cancer.

Is our family a cultural anomaly? The truth is, we didn't think about it. Those who did, usually the men, simply said, "bad genes." The women's attitude was stoic. Cancer was part of life. On February 16, 1971, the eve of my mother's surgery, I accidentally picked up the telephone and overheard her ask my grandmother what she could expect.

"Diane, it is one of the most spiritual experiences you will ever encounter."

I quietly put down the receiver.

Two days later, my father took my brothers and me to the hospital to visit her. She met us in the lobby in a wheelchair. No bandages were visible. I'll never forget her radiance, the way she held herself in a purple velvet robe, and how she gathered us around her.

"Children, I am fine. I want you to know I felt the arms of God around me."

We believed her. My father cried. Our mother, his wife, was thirty-eight years old.

A little over a year after Mother's death, Dad and I were having dinner together. He had just returned from St. George, where the Tempest Company was completing the gas lines that would service southern Utah. He spoke of his love for the country, the sandstoned landscape, bare-boned and beautiful. He had just finished hiking the Kolob trail in Zion National Park. We got caught up in reminiscing, recalling with fondness our walk up Angel's Landing on his fiftieth birthday and the years our family had vacationed there.

Over dessert, I shared a recurring dream of mine. I told my father that for years, as long as I could remember, I saw this flash of light in the night in the desert—that this image had so permeated my being that I could not venture south without seeing it again, on the horizon, illuminating buttes and mesas.

"You did see it," he said.

"Saw what?"

"The bomb. The cloud. We were driving home from Riverside, California. You were sitting on Diane's lap. She was pregnant. In fact, I remember the day, September 7, 1957. We had just gotten out of the Service. We were driving north, past Las Vegas. It was an hour or so before dawn, when this explosion went off. We not only heard it, but felt it. I thought the oil tanker in front of us had blown up. We pulled over and suddenly, rising from the desert floor, we saw it, clearly, this golden-stemmed cloud, the mushroom. The sky seemed to vibrate with an eerie pink glow. Within a few minutes, a light ash was raining on the car."

I stared at my father.

"I thought you knew that," he said. "It was a common occurrence in the fifties."

It was at this moment that I realized the deceit I had been living under. Children growing up in the American Southwest, drinking contaminated milk from contaminated cows, even from the contaminated breasts of their mothers, my mother—members, years later, of the Clan of One-Breasted Women.

It is a well-known story in the Desert West, "The Day We Bombed Utah," or more accurately, the years we bombed Utah: above ground atomic testing in Nevada took place from January 27, 1951 through July 11, 1962. Not only were the winds blowing north covering "low-use segments of the population" with fallout and leaving sheep dead in their tracks, but the climate was right. The United States of the 1950s was red, white, and blue. The Korean War was raging. McCarthyism was rampant. Ike was it, and the cold war was hot. If you were against nuclear testing, you were for a communist regime.

Much has been written about this "American nuclear tragedy." Public health was secondary to national security. The Atomic Energy Commissioner, Thomas Murray, said, "Gentlemen, we must not let anything interfere with this series of tests, nothing."

Again and again, the American public was told by its government, in spite of burns, blisters, and nausea, "It has been found that the tests may be conducted with adequate assurance of safety under conditions prevailing at the bombing reservations." Assuaging public fears was simply a matter of public relations. "Your best action," an Atomic Energy Commission booklet read, "is not to be worried about fallout." A news release typical of the times stated, "We find no basis for concluding that harm to any individual has resulted from radioactive fallout."

On August 30, 1979, during Jimmy Carter's presidency, a suit was filed, *Irene*

Allen v. The United States of America. Mrs. Allen's case was the first on an alphabetical list of twenty-four test cases, representative of nearly twelve hundred plaintiffs seeking compensation from the United States government for cancers caused by nuclear testing in Nevada.

Irene Allen lived in Hurricane, Utah. She was the mother of five children and had been widowed twice. Her first husband, with their two oldest boys, had watched the tests from the roof of the local high school. He died of leukemia in 1956. Her second husband died of pancreatic cancer in 1978.

In a town meeting conducted by Utah Senator Orrin Hatch, shortly before the suit was filed, Mrs. Allen said, "I am not blaming the government, I want you to know that, Senator Hatch. But I thought if my testimony could help in any way so this wouldn't happen again to any of the generations coming up after us . . . I am happy to be here this day to bear testimony of this."

God-fearing people. This is just one story in an anthology of thousands.

On May 10, 1984, Judge Bruce S. Jenkins handed down his opinion. Ten of the plaintiffs were awarded damages. It was the first time a federal court had determined that nuclear tests had been the cause of cancers. For the remaining fourteen test cases, the proof of causation was not sufficient. In spite of the split decision, it was considered a landmark ruling. It was not to remain so for long.

In April 1987, the Tenth Circuit Court of Appeals over-turned Judge Jenkins's ruling on the ground that the United States was protected from suit by the legal doctrine of sovereign immunity, a centuries-old idea from England in the days of absolute monarchs.

In January 1988, the Supreme Court refused to review the Appeals Court decision. To our court system it does not matter whether the United States government was irresponsible, whether it lied to its citizens, or even that citizens died from the fallout of nuclear testing. What matters is that our government is immune: "The King can do no wrong."

In Mormon culture, authority is respected, obedience is revered, and independent thinking is not. I was taught as a young girl not to "make waves" or "rock the boat."

"Just let it go," Mother would say. "You know how you feel, that's what counts."

For many years, I have done just that—listened, observed, and quietly formed my own opinions, in a culture that rarely asks questions because it has all the answers. But one by one, I have watched the women in my family die common, heroic deaths. We sat in waiting rooms hoping for good news, but always receiving the bad. I cared for them, bathed their scarred bodies, and kept their secrets. I watched beautiful women become bald as Cytoxan, cisplatin, and Adriamycin were injected into their veins. I held their foreheads as they vomited green-black bile, and I shot them with morphine when the pain became inhuman. In the end, I witnessed their last peaceful breaths, becoming a midwife to the rebirth of their souls.

The price of obedience has become too high.

The fear and inability to question authority that ultimately killed rural communities in Utah during atmospheric testing of atomic weapons is the same fear I saw in my mother's body. Sheep. Dead sheep. The evidence is buried.

I cannot prove that my mother, Diane Dixon Tempest, or my grandmothers, Lettie Romney Dixon and Kathryn Blackett Tempest, along with my aunts developed cancer from nuclear fallout in Utah. But I can't prove they didn't.

My father's memory was correct. The September blast we drove through in 1957 was part of Operation Plumbbob, one of the most intensive series of bomb tests to be initiated. The flash of light in the night in the desert, which I had always thought was a dream, developed into a family nightmare. It took fourteen years, from 1957 to 1971, for cancer to manifest in my mother—the same time, Howard L. Andrews, an authority in radioactive fallout at the National Institutes of Health, says radiation cancer requires to become evident. The more I learn about what it means to be a "downwinder," the more questions I drown in.

What I do know, however, is that as a Mormon woman of the fifth generation of Latter-day Saints, I must question everything, even if it means losing my faith, even if it means becoming a member of a border tribe among my own people. Tolerating blind obedience in the name of patriotism or religion ultimately takes our lives.

When the Atomic Energy Commission described the country north of the Nevada Test Site as "virtually uninhabited desert terrain," my family and the birds at Great Salt Lake were some of the "virtual uninhabitants."

One night, I dreamed women from all over the world circled a blazing fire in the desert. They spoke of change, how they hold the moon in their bellies and wax and wane with its phases. They mocked the presumption of even-tempered beings and made promises that they would never fear the witch inside themselves. The women danced wildly as sparks broke away from the flames and entered the night sky as stars.

And they sang a song given to them by Shoshone grandmothers:

Ah ne nah, nah	Consider the rabbits
nin nah nah—	How gently they walk on the earth—
ah ne nah, nah	Consider the rabbits
nin nah nah—	How gently they walk on the earth—
Nyaga mutzi	We remember them
oh ne nay—	We can walk gently also—
Nyaga mutzi	We remember them
oh ne nay—	We can walk gently also—

The women danced and drummed and sang for weeks, preparing themselves for what was to come. They would reclaim the desert for the sake of their children, for the sake of the land.

A few miles downwind from the fire circle, bombs were being tested. Rabbits felt the tremors. Their soft leather pads on paws and feet recognized the shaking sands, while the roots of mesquite and sage were smoldering. Rocks were hot from the inside out and dust devils hummed unnaturally. And each time there was another nuclear test, ravens watched the desert heave. Stretch marks appeared. The land was losing its muscle.

The women couldn't bear it any longer. They were mothers. They had suffered labor pains but always under the promise of birth. The red hot pains beneath the desert promised death only, as each bomb became a stillborn. A contract had been made and broken between human beings and the land. A new contract was being drawn by the women, who understood the fate of the earth as their own.

Under the cover of darkness, ten women slipped under a barbed-wire fence and entered the contaminated country. They were trespassing. They walked toward the town of Mercury, in moonlight, taking their cues from coyote, kit fox, antelope squirrel, and quail. They moved quietly and deliberately through the maze of Joshua trees. When a hint of daylight appeared they rested, drinking tea and sharing their rations of food. The women closed their eyes. The time had come to protest with the heart, that to deny one's genealogy with the earth was to commit treason against one's soul.

At dawn, the women draped themselves in mylar, wrapping long streamers of silver plastic around their arms to blow in the breeze. They wore clear masks, that became the faces of humanity. And when they arrived at the edge of Mercury, they carried all the butterflies of a summer day in their wombs. They paused to allow their courage to settle.

The town that forbids pregnant women and children to enter because of radiation risks was asleep. The women moved through the streets as winged messengers, twirling around each other in slow motion, peeking inside homes and watching the easy sleep of men and women. They were astonished by such stillness and periodically would utter a shrill note or low cry just to verify life.

The residents finally awoke to these strange apparitions. Some simply stared. Others called authorities, and in time, the women were apprehended by wary soldiers dressed in desert fatigues. They were taken to a white, square building on the other edge of Mercury. When asked who they were and why they were there, the women replied, "We are mothers and we have come to reclaim the desert for our children."

The soldiers arrested them. As the ten women were blindfolded and handcuffed, they began singing:

You can't forbid us everything
You can't forbid us to think—
You can't forbid our tears to flow
And you can't stop the songs that we sing.

The women continued to sing louder and louder, until they heard the voices of their sisters moving across the mesa:

Ah ne nah, nah
nin nah nah—
Ah ne nah, nah
nin nah nah—
Nyaga mutzi
oh ne nay—
Nyaga mutzi
oh ne nay—

"Call for reinforcements," one soldier said.

"We have," interrupted one woman, "we have—and you have no idea of our numbers."

I crossed the line at the Nevada Test Site and was arrested with nine other Utahns for trespassing on military lands. They are still conducting nuclear tests in the desert. Ours was an act of civil disobedience, but as I walked toward the town of Mercury, it was more than a gesture of peace. It was a gesture on behalf of the Clan of One-Breasted Women.

As one officer cinched the handcuffs around my wrists, another frisked my body. She found a pen and a pad of paper tucked inside my left boot.

"And these?" she asked sternly.

"Weapons," I replied.

Our eyes met. I smiled. She pulled the leg of my trousers back over my boot.

"Step forward, please," she said as she took my arm.

We were booked under an afternoon sun and bused to Tonopah, Nevada. It was a two-hour ride. This was familiar country. The Joshua trees standing their ground had been named by my ancestors, who believed they looked like prophets pointing west to the Promised Land. These were the same trees that bloomed each spring, flowers appearing like white flames in the Mojave. And I recalled a full moon in May, when Mother and I had walked among them, flushing out mourning doves and owls.

The bus stopped short of town. We were released.

The officials thought it was a cruel joke to leave us stranded in the desert with no way to get home. What they didn't realize was that we were home, soul-centered and strong, women who recognized the sweet smell of sage as fuel for our spirits.

FOR FURTHER READING

Trimble, Stephen, and Terry Tempest Williams, comps. *Testimony: Writers of the West Speak Out on Behalf of Utah Wilderness.* Minneapolis: Milkweed, 1996.

Williams, Terry Tempest. *Coyote's Canyon*. Salt Lake City: Peregrine Smith Publisher, 1989.

———. *Leap*. New York: Pantheon Books, 2000.

———. *Pieces of White Shell: A Journey to Navajoland*. Albuquerque: University of New Mexico Press, 1987.

———. Testimony before Senate Subcommittee on Forest and Public Lands Management, 13 July 1995. Available at <http://pantheon.cis.yale.edu/_thomast/texts/tempest.html>.

———. *An Unspoken Hunger: Stories from the Field*. New York: Vintage Books, 1994.

Williams, Terry Tempest, and H. Jackson Clark. *The Owl in Monument Canyon and Other Stories from Indian Country*. Salt Lake City: University of Utah Press, 1993.

Williams, Terry Tempest, Terry Frank, and Mary Frank. *Desert Quartet*. New York: Pantheon, 1995.

Williams, Terry Tempest, William B. Smart, and Gibbs M. Smith, eds. *New Genesis: A Mormon Reader on Land and Community*. Salt Lake City: Gibbs-Smith, 1998.

Patricia Williams

1951–

The great-great-granddaughter of a white southern lawyer and a slave, Patricia Williams is a legal scholar and activist. She writes in order to bridge the gap between theory and practice and to expand the framework within which legal ideas are tested to include philosophy, sociology, history, critical theory, and feminism. Her writing continually examines the power relations underlying legal rhetoric and the law, insistently posing the questions: Who is visible under the law? And whose experience counts in determining issues of truth and justice? Williams is professor of commercial and contract law at Columbia University; a contributing editor and columnist for the *Nation;* and a frequent contributor to the *New York Times,* the *New Yorker,* the *Village Voice,* and television news shows on public issues. In reflecting on her status, she says that to be "black, female, and a commercial lawyer has rendered me simultaneously universal, trendy, and marginal" ("Brass Ring" 7).

Williams's writing and public speaking articulate the connection between life and the law, the inseparability of the personal and the public, and the necessity of grounding and testing claims of truth against the lived experiences of ordinary people. She challenges legal concepts and attempts to "fill the gaps of traditional legal scholarship" by exposing its racial, gender, and class blindness ("Brass Ring" 7). Williams specifically analyzes the rhetoric of the law and posits a new rhetoric of legal discourse. Describing legal rhetoric and scholarship as "static, stable, formal—rationalism walled against chaos," she brings to the rigid official language of legal statutes the narratives that emerge from historically situated lives—her own and others' ("Brass Ring" 7). In doing so she demonstrates that the private is already political and that the public must be personalized with the particular circumstances of race, gender, and class. In her book *The Alchemy of Race and Rights,* Williams emphasizes this principle most dramatically in examining property and contract law, which she grounds in a specific personal and public legal artifact: the contract of sale for her great-great-grandmother—a slave.

In "The Death of the Profane " Williams highlights the way in which so-called objective truth is actually steeped in subjectivity, how legal discourse attempts to erase race in an attempt to conform to conventions of objectivity and neutrality, and in turn, how this erasure produces continued disenfranchisement for African Americans and the poor. Thus, "The Death of the Profane" offers a critique of the way in which legal discourse distorts the truth of experience, as specific people, events, and circumstances are stripped away in order to render experience more "objective." Like much of Williams's writing, this piece begins with a narrative of her own personal experience, in this case Christmas shopping. In addition to creating a sense of immediacy and engagement by using this form, she also increases her proximity to her readers by showing them her journal writing about the event and then juxtaposing it with her academic legal writing about the same event. Then she shows the mutations that occur in her representation of this experience at the hands of legal editors and journalists. This essay demonstrates how Williams uses writing as an analytical tool to investigate experience and its connections to the law, but it also exposes the multilayered contexts and rhetorics that construct public values about race, gender, and rights. In so doing, Williams draws the reader consciously into this interpretive and analytical process, an enactment of her continuing attempt to write in the "active personal" rather than the "passive impersonal."

"The Death of the Profane"

1991

Buzzers are big in New York City. Favored particularly by smaller stores and boutiques, merchants throughout the city have installed them as screening devices to reduce the incidence of robbery: if the face at the door looks desirable, the buzzer is pressed and the door is unlocked. If the face is that of an undesirable, the door stays locked. Predictably, the issue of undesirability has revealed itself to be a racial determination. While controversial enough at first, even civil-rights organizations backed down eventually in the face of arguments that the buzzer system is a "necessary evil," that it is a "mere inconvenience" in comparison to the risks of being murdered, that suffering discrimination is not as bad as being assaulted, and that in any event it is not all blacks who are barred, just "17-year-old black males wearing running shoes and hooded sweatshirts."

The installation of these buzzers happened swiftly in New York; stores that had always had their doors wide open suddenly became exclusive or received people by appointment only. I discovered them and their meaning one Saturday in 1986. I was shopping in Soho and saw in a store window a sweater that I wanted to buy for my mother. I pressed my round brown face to the window and my finger to the buzzer, seeking admittance. A narrow-eyed, white teenager wearing running shoes and feasting on bubble gum glared out, evaluating me for signs that would pit me against the limits of his social understanding.

After about five seconds, he mouthed "We're closed," and blew pink rubber at me. It was two Saturdays before Christmas, at one o'clock in the afternoon; there were several white people in the store who appeared to be shopping for things for *their* mothers.

I was enraged. At that moment I literally wanted to break all the windows of the store and *take* lots of sweaters for my mother. In the flicker of his judgmental gray eyes, that saleschild had transformed my brightly sentimental, joy-to-the-world, pre-Christmas spree to a shambles. He snuffed my sense of humanitarian catholicity, and there was nothing I could do to snuff his, without making a spectacle of myself.

I am still struck by the structure of power that drove me into such a blizzard of rage. There was almost nothing I could do, short of physically intruding upon him, that would humiliate him the way he humiliated me. No words, no gestures, no prejudices of my own would make a bit of difference to him; his refusal to let me into the store—it was Benetton's, whose colorfully punnish ad campaign is premised on wrapping every one of the world's peoples in its cottons and woolens—was an outward manifestation of his never having let someone like me into the realm of his reality. He had no compassion, no remorse, no reference to me; and no desire to acknowledge me even at the estranged level of arm's-length transactor. He saw me only as one who would take his money and therefore could not conceive that I was there to give him money.

In this weird ontological imbalance, I realized that buying something in that store was like bestowing a gift, the gift of my commerce, the lucre of my patronage. In the wake of my outrage, I wanted to take back the gift of apprecia tion that my peering in the window must have appeared to be. I wanted to take it back in the form of unappreciation, disrespect, defilement. I wanted to work so hard at wishing he could feel what I felt that he would never again mistake my hatred for some sort of plaintive wish to be included. I was quite willing to disenfranchise myself, in the heat of my need to revoke the flattery of my purchasing power. I was willing to boycott Benetton's, random white-owned businesses, and anyone who ever blew bubble gum in my face again.

My rage was admittedly diffuse, even self-destructive, but it was symmetrical. The perhaps loose-ended but utter propriety of that rage is no doubt lost not just to the young man who actually barred me, but to those who would appreciate my being barred only as an abstract precaution, who approve of those who would bar even as they deny that they would bar *me*.

The violence of my desire to burst into Benetton's is probably quite apparent. I often wonder if the violence, the exclusionary hatred, is equally apparent in the repeated public urgings that blacks understand the buzzer system by putting themselves in the shoes of white storeowners—that, in effect, blacks look into the mirror of frightened white faces for the reality of their undesirability; and that then blacks would "just as surely conclude that [they] would not let [themselves] in under similar circumstances." (That some blacks might agree merely shows that some of us have learned too well the lessons of privatized intimacies of self-hatred and rationalized away the fullness of our public, participatory selves.)

On the same day I was barred from Benetton's, I went home and wrote the above impassioned account in my journal. On the day after that, I found I was still brooding, so I turned to a form of catharsis I have always found healing. I typed up as much of the story as I have just told, made a big poster of it, put a nice colorful border around it, and, after Benetton's was truly closed, stuck it to their big sweater-filled window. I exercised my first amendment right to place my business with them right out in the street.

So that was the first telling of this story. The second telling came a few months later, for a symposium on Excluded Voice sponsored by a law review. I wrote an essay summing up my feelings about being excluded from Benetton's and analyzing "how the rhetoric of increased privatization, in response to racial issues, functions as the rationalizing agent of public unaccountability and, ultimately, irresponsibility." Weeks later, I received the first edit. From the first page to the last, my fury had been carefully cut out. My rushing, run-on-rage had been reduced to simple declarative sentences. The active personal had been inverted in favor of the passive impersonal. My words were different; they spoke to me upsidedown. I was afraid to read too much of it at a time—meanings rose up at me oddly, stolen and strange.

A week and a half later, I received the second edit. All reference to Benetton's had been deleted because, according to the editors and the faculty adviser, it was defamatory; they feared harassment and liability; they said printing it would be irresponsible. I called them and offered to supply a footnote attesting to this as my personal experience at one particular location and of a buzzer system not limited to Benetton's; the editors told me that they were not in the habit of publishing things that were unverifiable. I could not but wonder, in this refusal even to let me file an affadavit, what it would take to make my experience verifiable. The testimony of an independent white bystander? (a requirement in fact imposed in U.S. Supreme Court holdings through the first part of the century).

Two days *after* the piece was sent to press, I received copies of the final page proofs. All reference to my race had been eliminated because it was against "editorial policy" to permit descriptions of physiognomy. "I realize," wrote one editor, "that this was a very personal experience, but any reader will know what you must have looked like when standing at that window." In a telephone conversation to them, I ranted wildly about the significance of such an omission. "It's irrelevant," another editor explained in a voice gummy with soothing and patience; "It's nice and poetic" but it doesn't "advance the discussion of any principle . . . This is a law review, after all." Frustrated, I accused him of censorship; calmly he assured me it was not. "This is just a matter of style," he said with firmness and finality.

Ultimately I did convince the editors that mention of my race was central to the whole sense of the subsequent text; that my story became one of extreme paranoia without the information that I am black; or that it became one in which the reader had to fill in the gap by assumption, presumption, prejudgment, or prejudice. What was most interesting to me in this experience was how the blind application of principles of neutrality, through the device of omission, acted either to make me look crazy or to make the reader participate in old habits of cultural bias.

That was the second telling of my story. The third telling came last April, when I was invited to participate in a law-school conference on Equality and Difference. I retold my sad tale of exclusion from Soho's most glitzy boutique, focusing in this version on the law-review editing process as a consequence of an ideology of style rooted in a social text of neutrality. I opined:

Law and legal writing aspire to formalized, color-blind, liberal ideals. Neutrality is the standard for assuring these ideals; yet the adherence to it is often determined by reference to an aesthetic of uniformity, in which difference is simply omitted. For example, when segregation was eradicated from the American lexicon, its omission led many to actually believe that racism therefore no longer existed. Race-neutrality in law has become the presumed antidote for race bias in real life. With the entrenchment of the notion of race-neutrality came attacks on the concept of affirmative action and the rise of reverse discrimination suits. Blacks, for so many generations deprived of jobs based on the color of our skin, are now told that we ought to find it demeaning to be hired, based on the color of our skin. Such is the silliness of simplistic either-or inversions as remedies to complex problems.

What is truly demeaning in this era of double-speak-no-evil is going on interviews and not getting hired because someone doesn't think we'll be comfortable. It is demeaning not to get promoted because we're judged "too weak," then putting in a lot of energy the next time and getting fired because we're "too strong." It is demeaning to be told what we find demeaning. It is very demeaning to stand on street corners unemployed and begging. It is downright demeaning to have to explain why we haven't been employed for months and then watch the job go to someone who is "more experienced." It is outrageously demeaning that none of this can be called racism, even if it happens only to, or to large numbers of, black people; as long as it's done with a smile, a handshake and a shrug; as long as the phantom-word "race" is never used.

The image of race as a phantom-word came to me after I moved into my late godmother's home. In an attempt to make it my own, I cleared the bedroom for painting. The following morning the room asserted itself, came rushing and raging at me through the emptiness, exactly as it had been for twenty-five years. One day filled with profuse and overwhelming complexity, the next day filled with persistently recurring memories. The shape of the past came to haunt me, the shape of the emptiness confronted me each time I was about to enter the room. The force of its spirit still drifts like an odor throughout the house.

The power of that room, I have thought since, is very like the power of racism as status quo: it is deep, angry, eradicated from view, but strong enough to make everyone who enters the room walk around the bed that isn't there, avoiding the phantom as they did the substance, for fear of bodily harm. They do not even know they are avoiding; they defer to the unseen shapes of things with subtle responsiveness, guided by an impulsive awareness of nothingness, and the deep knowledge and denial of witchcraft at work.

The phantom room is to me symbolic of the emptiness of formal equal opportunity, particularly as propounded by President Reagan, the Reagan Civil Rights Commission and the Reagan Supreme Court. Blindly formalized constructions of equal opportunity are the creation of a space that is filled in by a meandering stream of unguided hopes, dreams, fantasies, fears, recollections. They are the presence of the past in imaginary, imagistic form—the phantom-roomed exile of our longing.

It is thus that I strongly believe in the efficacy of programs and paradigms like affirmative action. Blacks are the objects of a constitutional omission which has been incorporated into a theory of neutrality. It is thus that omission is really a form of expression, as oxymoronic as that sounds: racial omission is a literal part of original intent; it is the fixed, reiterated prophecy of the Founding Fathers. It is thus that affirmative action is an affirmation; the affirmative act of hiring—or hearing—blacks is a recognition of individuality that replaces blacks as a social statistic, that is profoundly interconnective to the fate of blacks and whites either as sub-groups or as one group. In this sense, affirmative action is as mystical and beyond-the-self as an initiation ceremony. It is an act of verification and of vision. It is an act of social as well as professional responsibility.

The following morning I opened the local newspaper, to find that the event of my speech had commanded two columns on the front page of the Metro section. I quote only the opening lines: "Affirmative action promotes prejudice by denying the status of women and blacks, instead of affirming them as its name suggests. So said New York City attorney Patricia Williams to an audience Wednesday."

I clipped out the article and put it in my journal. In the margin there is a note to myself. Eventually, it says, I should try to pull all these threads together into yet another law-review article. The problem, of course, will be that in the hierarchy of law-review citation, the article in the newspaper will have more authoritative weight about me, as a so-called "primary resource" than I will have; it will take precedence over my own citation of the unverifiable testimony of my speech.

I have used the Benetton's story a lot, in speaking engagements at various schools. I tell it whenever I am too tired to whip up an original speech from scratch. Here are some of the questions I have been asked in the wake of its telling:

> Am I not privileging a racial perspective, by considering only the black point of view?
>
> Don't I have an obligation to include the "salesman's side" of the story?
>
> Am I not putting the salesman on trial and finding him guilty of racism without giving him a chance to respond to or cross-examine me?
>
> Am I not using the store window as a "metaphorical fence" against the potential of his explanation in order to represent my side as "authentic"?
>
> How can I be sure I'm right?
>
> What makes my experience the real black one anyway?
>
> Isn't it possible that another black person would disagree with my experience? If so, doesn't that render my story too unempirical and subjective to pay any attention to?

Always a major objection is to my having put the poster on Benetton's window. As one law professor put it: "It's one thing to publish this in a law review, where no one can take it personally, but it's another thing altogether to put your own interpretation right out there, just like that, uncontested, I mean, with nothing to counter it."

FOR FURTHER READING

Williams, Patricia. "The Brass Ring." In *The Alchemy of Race and Rights: The Diary of a Law Professor*, 3–14. Cambridge: Harvard University Press, 1991.

———. "A Rare Case Study of Muleheadedness and Men." In *Race-ing Justice, En-gendering Power: Essays on Anita Hill, Clarence Thomas, and the Construction of Social Reality*, edited by Toni Morrison, 159–71. New York: Pantheon Books, 1992.

———. *The Rooster's Egg: On the Persistence of Prejudice*. Cambridge: Harvard University Press, 1995.

———. *Seeing a Color Blind Future: The Paradox of Race*. New York: Farrar, Strauss and Giroux, 1998.

Toni Morrison

1931–

"Had I lived the life that the state planned for me from the beginning," Toni Morrison said in 1986, "I would have lived and died in somebody else's kitchen, on somebody else's land, and never written a word. That knowledge is bone deep, and it informs everything I do" (*Boston Globe*, October 8, 1993). In 1993, Toni Morrison became the first African American woman to receive the Nobel Prize for Literature. Her acceptance speech appears below. Author of seven acclaimed novels, including *Beloved* in 1988 (for which she won the Pulitzer Prize) and, most recently, *Paradise* in 1997, Morrison now teaches at Princeton University.

Born Chloe Anthony Wofford in Lorain, Ohio, in 1931, the daughter of Alabama sharecroppers who had migrated north, Morrison earned a B.A. from Howard University in 1953 and an M.A. from Cornell University in 1955, both in English. After teaching at Texas Southern, Howard, and Yale Universities, she joined Random House in 1964, editing books by Andrew Young, Mohammed Ali, and Angela Davis, among many others. In the late 1960s, Morrison began writing at night after her children were asleep; she first showed her work to a women's writing group, which she says gave her the courage to finish and publish *The Bluest Eye* in 1970. In 1983, Morrison resigned from Random House in order to write full time. Both her fiction and her nonfiction enact Morrison's philosophy of language: "Narrative has never been merely entertainment for me. It is, I believe, one of the principal ways in which we absorb knowledge." So she begins her Nobel acceptance speech.

Imagine Morrison standing before the formally dressed gathering of the Swedish Academy and the other Nobel Laureates from every discipline. Imagine her voice ringing out from the podium as she begins to tell a story from her African American and female heritage—the same story that Fannie Lou Hamer used to address the NAACP in 1971. But then Morrison turns that story over and over, looking closely at it from the vantage points of various narrators, listeners, readers, and writers. The speech becomes a position statement on language, told in the poetic rhythm of one of the world's greatest writers. In this public performance, Morrison lays out a rhetorical theory of language attuned to its responsibility and to its consequences for both speaker and hearer, writer and reader. Defining language as "agency," she indicts the academy, the law, the media, and the church for using "dead" and "narcissistic" language. Morrison starkly describes the consequences of "official" language—and of its mimickers—used to "police" and to maintain its own "exclusivity and dominance." In the place of such language, Morrison puts forward for her audience a theory of language as salvation, as a "nuanced," communal, generative force. Her own writing illustrates such language, which "surges toward" rather than limits knowledge, here used by a writer who pays a "mid-wife's" attention to her every syntactic and semantic choice, to her audience, and to the consequences of her work.

"The Nobel Lecture in Literature"

1993

Members of the Swedish Academy, Ladies and Gentlemen:

Narrative has never been merely entertainment for me. It is, I believe, one of the principal ways in which we absorb knowledge. I hope you will understand, then, why I begin these remarks with the opening phrase of what must be the oldest sentence in the world, and the earliest one we remember from childhood: "Once upon a time . . ."

"Once upon a time there was an old woman. Blind but wise." Or was it an old man? A guru, perhaps. Or a *griot* soothing restless children. I have heard this story, or one exactly like it, in the lore of several cultures.

"Once upon a time there was an old woman. Blind. Wise."

In the version I know the woman is the daughter of slaves, black, American, and lives alone in a small house outside of town. Her reputation for wisdom is without peer and without question.

Among her people she is both the law and its transgression. The honor she is paid and the awe in which she is held reach beyond her neighborhood to places far away; to the city where the intelligence of rural prophets is the source of much amusement.

One day the woman is visited by some young people who seem to be bent on disproving her clairvoyance and showing her up for the fraud they believe she is. Their plan is simple: they enter her house and ask the one question the answer to which rides solely on her difference from them, a difference they regard as a profound disability: her blindness. They stand before her, and one of them says,

"Old woman, I hold in my hand a bird. Tell me whether it is living or dead."

She does not answer, and the question is repeated. "Is the bird I am holding living or dead?"

Lecture and Speech of Acceptance, Upon the Award of the Nobel Prize for Literature, Delivered in Stockholm on the Seventh of December, Nineteen Hundred and Ninety-Three. © The Nobel Foundation, 1993.

Still she does not answer. She is blind and cannot see her visitors, let alone what is in their hands. She does not know their color, gender or homeland. She only knows their motive.

The old woman's silence is so long, the young people have trouble holding their laughter.

Finally she speaks, and her voice is soft but stern. "I don't know," she says. "I don't know whether the bird you are holding is dead or alive, but what I do know is that it is in your hands. It is in your hands."

Her answer can be taken to mean: if it is dead, you have either found it that way or you have killed it. If it is alive, you can still kill it. Whether it is to stay alive is your decision. Whatever the case, it is your responsibility.

For parading their power and her helplessness, the young visitors are reprimanded, told they are responsible not only for the act of mockery but also for the small bundle of life sacrificed to achieve its aims. The blind woman shifts attention away from assertions of power to the instrument through which that power is exercised.

Speculation on what (other than its own frail body) that bird in the hand might signify has always been attractive to me, but especially so now, thinking as I have been about the work I do that has brought me to this company. So I choose to read the bird as language and the woman as a practiced writer.

She is worried about how the language she dreams in, given to her at birth, is handled, put into service, even withheld from her for certain nefarious purposes. Being a writer, she thinks of language partly as a system, partly as a living thing over which one has control, but mostly as agency—as an act with consequences. So the question the children put to her, "Is it living or dead?," is not unreal, because she thinks of language as susceptible to death, erasure; certainly imperiled and salvageable only by an effort of the will. She believes that if the bird in the hands of her visitors is dead, the custodians are responsible for the corpse. For her a dead language is not only one no longer spoken or written, it is unyielding language content to admire its own paralysis. Like statist language, censored and censoring. Ruthless in its policing duties, it has no desire or purpose other than to maintain the free range of its own narcotic narcissism, its own exclusivity and dominance. However, moribund, it is not without effect, for it actively thwarts the intellect, stalls conscience, suppresses human potential. Unreceptive to interrogation, it cannot form or tolerate new ideas, shape other thoughts, tell another story, fill baffling silences. Official language smitheried to sanction ignorance and preserve privilege is a suit of armor, polished to shocking glitter, a husk from which the knight departed long ago. Yet there it is; dumb, predatory, sentimental. Exciting reverence in schoolchildren, providing shelter for despots, summoning false memories of stability, harmony among the public.

She is convinced that when language dies, out of carelessness, disuse, indifference, and absence of esteem, or killed by fiat, not only she herself but all users and makers are accountable for its demise. In her country children have bitten their tongues off and use bullets instead to iterate the void of speechlessness, of disabled and disabling language, of language adults have abandoned altogether as a device for grappling with meaning, providing guidance, or expressing love. But she knows tongue-suicide is not only the choice of children. It is common among the infantile heads of state and power merchants whose evacuated language leaves them with no access to what is left of their human instincts, for they speak only to those who obey, or in order to force obedience.

The systematic looting of language can be recognized by the tendency of its users to forgo its nuanced, complex, mid-wifery properties, replacing them with menace and subjugation. Oppressive language does more than represent violence; it is violence; does more than represent the limits of knowledge; it limits knowledge. Whether it is obscuring state language or the faux language of mindless media; whether it is the proud but calcified language of the academy or the commodity-driven language of science; whether it is the malign language of law-without-ethics, or language designed for the estrangement of minorities, hiding its racist plunder in its literary cheek—it must be rejected, altered and exposed. It is the language that drinks blood, laps vulnerabilities, tucks its fascist boots under crinolines of respectability and patriotism as it moves relentlessly toward the bottom line and the bottomed-out mind. Sexist language, racist language, theistic language—all are typical of the policing languages of mastery, and cannot, do not, permit new knowledge or encourage the mutual exchange of ideas.

The old woman is keenly aware that no intellectual mercenary or insatiable dictator, no paid-for politician or demagogue, no counterfeit journalist would be persuaded by her thoughts. There is and will be rousing language to keep citizens armed and arming; slaughtered and slaughtering in the malls, courthouses, post offices, playgrounds, bedrooms and boulevards; stirring, memorializing language to mask the pity and waste of needless death. There will be more diplomatic language to countenance rape, torture, assassination. There is and will be more seductive, mutant language designed to throttle women, to pack their throats like pâté-producing geese with their own unsayable, transgressive words; there will be more of the language of surveillance disguised as research; of politics and history calculated to render the suffering of millions mute; language glamorized to thrill the dissatisfied and bereft into assaulting their neighbors; arrogant pseudo-empirical language crafted to lock creative people into cages of inferiority and hopelessness.

Underneath the eloquence, the glamour, the scholarly associations, however stirring or seductive, the heart of such language is languishing, or perhaps not beating at all—if the bird is already dead.

She has thought about what could have been the intellectual history of any discipline if it had not insisted upon, or been forced into, the waste of time and life that rationalizations for and representations of dominance required—lethal discourses of exclusion blocking access to cognition for both the excluder and the excluded.

The conventional wisdom of the Tower of Babel story is that the collapse was a misfortune. That it was the distraction or the weight of many languages that precipitated the tower's failed architecture. That one monolithic language would have expedited the building, and heaven would have been reached. Whose heaven, she wonders? And what kind? Perhaps the achievement of Paradise was premature, a little hasty if no one could take the time to understand other languages, other views, other narratives. Had they, the heaven they imagined might have been found at their feet. Complicated, demanding, yes, but a view of heaven as life; not heaven as post-life.

She would not want to leave her young visitors with the impression that language should be forced to stay alive merely to be. The vitality of language lies in its ability to limn the actual, imagined and possible lives of its speakers, readers, writers. Although its poise is sometimes in displacing experience, it is not a substitute for it. It arcs toward the place where meaning may lie. When a President of the United States thought about the graveyard his country had become, and said, "The world will little note nor long remember what we say here. But it will never forget what they did here," his simple words were exhilarating in their life-sustaining properties because they refused to encapsulate the reality of 600,000 dead men in a cataclysmic race war. Refusing to monumentalize, disdaining the "final word," the precise "summing up," acknowledging their "poor power to add or detract," his words signal deference to the uncapturability of the life it mourns. It is the deference that moves her, that recognition that language can never live up to life once and for all. Nor should it. Language can never "pin down" slavery, genocide, war. Nor should it yearn for the arrogance to be able to do so. Its force, its felicity, is in its reach toward the ineffable.

Be it grand or slender, burrowing, blasting or refusing to sanctify; whether it laughs out loud or is a cry without an alphabet, the choice word or the chosen silence, unmolested language surges toward knowledge, not its destruction. But who does not know of literature banned because it is interrogative; discredited because it is critical; erased because alternate? And how many are outraged by the thought of a self-ravaged tongue?

Word-work is sublime, she thinks, because it is generative; it makes meaning that secures our difference, our human difference—the way in which we are like no other life.

We die. That may be the meaning of life. But we *do* language. That may be the measure of our lives.

"Once upon a time. . ." Visitors ask an old woman a question. Who are they, these children? What did they make of that encounter? What did they hear in those final words: "The bird is in your hands"? A sentence that gestures toward possibility, or one that drops a latch? Perhaps what the children heard was, "It is not my problem. I am old, female, black, blind. What wisdom I have now is in knowing I cannot help you. The future of language is yours."

They stand there. Suppose nothing was in their hands. Suppose the visit was only a ruse, a trick to get to be spoken to, taken seriously as they have not been before. A chance to interrupt, to violate the adult world, its miasma of discourse about them. Urgent questions are at stake, including the one they have asked: "Is the bird we hold living or dead?" Perhaps the question meant: "Could someone tell us what is life? What is death?" No trick at all; no silliness. A straightforward question worthy of the attention of a wise one. An old one. And if the old and wise who have lived life and faced death cannot describe either, who can?

But she does not; she keeps her secret, her good opinion of herself, her gnomic pronouncements, her art without commitment. She keeps her distance, enforces it and retreats into the singularity of isolation, in sophisticated, privileged space.

Nothing, no word follows her declaration of transfer. That silence is deep, deeper than the meaning available in the words she has spoken. It shivers, this silence, and the children, annoyed, fill it with language invented on the spot.

"Is there no speech," they ask her, "no words you can give us that help us break through your dossier of failures? through the education you have just given us that is no education at all because we are paying close attention to what you have done as well as to what you have said? to the barrier you have erected between generosity and wisdom?

"We have no bird in our hands, living or dead. We have only you and our important question. Is the nothing in our hands something you could not bear to contemplate, to even guess? Don't you remember being young, when language was magic without meaning? When what you could say, could not mean? When the invisible was what imagination strove to see? When questions and demands for answers burned so brightly you trembled with fury at not knowing?

"Do we have to begin consciousness with a battle heroes and heroines like you have already fought and lost, leaving us with nothing in our hands except what you have imagined is there? Your answer is artful, but its artfulness embarrasses us and ought to embarrass you. Your answer is indecent in its self-congratulation. A made-for-television script that makes no sense if there is nothing in our hands.

"Why didn't you reach out, touch us with your soft fingers, delay the sound bite, the lesson, until you knew who we were? Did you so despise our trick, our modus operandi, that you could not see that we were baffled about how to get your attention? We are young. Unripe. We have heard all our short lives that we have to be responsible. What could that possibly mean in the catastrophe this world has become; where, as a poet said, "nothing needs to be exposed since it is already barefaced"? Our inheritance is an affront. You want us to have your old, blank eyes and see only cruelty and mediocrity. Do you think we are stupid enough to perjure ourselves again and again with the fiction of nationhood? How dare you talk to us of duty when we stand waist deep in the toxin of your past?

"You trivialize us and trivialize the bird that is not in our hands. Is there no context for our lives? No song, no literature, no poem full of vitamins, no history connected to experience that you can pass along to help us start strong? You are an adult. The old one, the wise one. Stop thinking about saving your face. Think of our lives and tell us your particularized world. Make up a story. Narrative is radical, creating us at the very moment it is being created. We will not blame you if your reach exceeds your grasp; if love so ignites your words that they go down in flames and nothing is left but their scald. Or if, with the reticence of a surgeon's hands, your words suture only the places where blood might flow. We know you can never do it properly—once and for all. Passion is never enough; neither is skill. But try. For our sake and yours forget your name in the street; tell us what the world has been to you in the dark places and in the light. Don't tell us what to believe, what to fear. Show us belief's wide skirt and the stitch that unravels fear's caul. You, old woman, blessed with blindness, can speak the language that tells us what only language can: how to see without pictures. Language alone protects us from the scariness of things with no names. Language alone is meditation.

"Tell us what it is to be a woman so that we may know what it is to be a man. What moves at the margin. What it is to have no home in this place. To be set adrift from the one you knew. What it is to live at the edge of towns that cannot bear your company.

"Tell us about ships turned away from shorelines at Easter, placenta in a field. Tell us about a wagonload of slaves, how they sang so softly their breath was indistinguishable from the falling snow. How they knew from the hunch of the nearest shoulder that the next stop would be their last. How, with hands prayered in their sex, they thought of heat, then sun. Lifting their faces as though it was there for the taking. Turning as though there for the taking. They stop at an inn. The driver and his mate go in with the lamp, leaving them humming in the dark. The horse's void steams into the snow beneath its hooves and the hiss and melt are the envy of the freezing slaves.

"The inn door opens: a girl and a boy step away from its light. They climb into the wagon bed. The boy will have a gun in three years, but now he carries a lamp and a jug of warm cider. They pass it from mouth to mouth. The girl offers bread, pieces of meat and something more: a glance into the eyes of the one she serves. One helping for each man, two for each woman. And a look. They look back. The next stop will be their last. But not this one. This one is warmed."

It's quiet again when the children finish speaking, until the woman breaks into the silence.

"Finally," she says. "I trust you now. I trust you with the bird that is not in your hands because you have truly caught it. Look. How lovely it is, this thing we have done—together."

"The Acceptance Speech"

Your Majesties, Your Highnesses, Ladies and Gentlemen:

I entered this hall pleasantly haunted by those who have entered it before me. That company of laureates is both daunting and welcoming, for among its lists are names of persons whose work has made whole worlds available to me. The sweep and specificity of their art have sometimes broken my heart with the courage and clarity of its vision. The astonishing brilliance with which they practiced their craft has challenged and nurtured my own. My debt to them rivals the profound one I owe to the Swedish Academy for having selected me to join that distinguished alumni.

Early in October an artist friend left a message which I kept on the answering service for weeks and played back every once in a while just to hear the trembling pleasure in her voice and the faith in her words. "My dear sister," she said, "the prize that is yours is also ours and could not have been placed in better hands." The spirit of her message with its earned optimism and sublime trust marks this day for me.

I will leave this hall, however, with a new and much more delightful haunting than the one I felt upon entering: that is the company of the laureates yet to come. Those who, even as I speak, are mining, sifting and polishing languages for illuminations none of us has dreamed of. But whether or not any one of them secures a place in this pantheon, the gathering of these writers is unmistakable and mounting. Their voices bespeak civilizations gone and yet to be; the precipice from which their imaginations gaze will rivet us; they do not blink or turn away.

It is, therefore, mindful of the gifts of my predecessors, the blessing of my sisters, in joyful anticipation of writers to come that I accept the honor the Swedish Academy has done me, and ask you to share what is for me a moment of grace.

FOR FURTHER READING

Morrison, Toni. *The Dancing Mind: Speech Upon Acceptance of the National Book Foundation Medal for Distinguished Contribution to American Letters on the Sixth of November, Nineteen Hundred and Ninety-Six.* New York: Alfred A. Knopf, 1996.

———. *Playing in The Dark: Whiteness and the Literary Imagination.* Cambridge: Harvard University Press, 1992.

———, ed. *Race-Ing Justice, En-Gendering Power: Essays on Anita Hill, Clarence Thomas, and the Construction Of Social Reality.* New York: Pantheon Books, 1992.

Morrison, Toni, and Claudia Brodsky Lacour, eds. *Birth of a Nation'hood: Gaze, Script, and Spectacle in the O. J. Simpson Case.* New York: Pantheon Books, 1997.

Minnie Bruce Pratt

1946–

"Central to my work is a tracing of the process by which we attempt to transform ourselves, the culture around us, and social institutions into more humane, egalitarian and loving entities," writes Minnie Bruce Pratt, poet, essayist, teacher ("Union Institute"). Pratt's writing challenges the boundaries of categories such as heterosexual, homosexual, bisexual, feminine, masculine. Pratt discovered the realities of how categories manifest themselves in real social oppression when, as an out lesbian mother, she was denied custody rights and access to her two sons. She writes about that experience in her book *Crimes Against Nature*, which received the American Library Association Gay and Lesbian Book Award for Literature in 1991 and was also nominated for a Pulitzer Prize in Poetry.

Pratt's "Gender Quiz" opens her book *S/He*, which is dedicated to her life partner, Leslie Feinberg, an activist, writer, and lecturer on issues of transgendered people. Pratt calls Feinberg "my beloved lesbian husband" and writes that "I fell in love with Leslie because of hir voice, hir vision, and hir revolutionary optimism." The reality of negotiating in real and material ways the identity of being transgendered and of partnering with a transgendered person provides the context for the essays in *S/He*. At the beginning of "Gender Quiz," Pratt relies on rhetorical questions to articulate the struggles and realities of people who are outside the heterosexual male/female "norm." Throughout the essay, Pratt uses a series of questions, often whole paragraphs of questions, in order to highlight the "fluidity" of gender categories and gender expression, which, she argues, is masked by our culture's obsession with right/wrong and true/false answers. This rhetorical strategy of piling question upon question becomes an ironic commentary on the "femme" identity that Pratt claims as a lesbian and as a woman writer, since, of course, women are so often accused of tentativeness, hesitation, and insecurity. Yet in her questions, Pratt suggests a method for finding answers.

Like so many other women rhetors in this collection, Pratt questions boundaries and combines personal story with political commentary and history. She uses flashbacks of nostalgic childhood moments and friends to articulate the seemingly innocent construction of gender roles and responsibilities in dominant culture, but then she transforms this nostalgia into an astute juxtaposition of the heterosexual (visible) world and the gay/lesbian (hidden) world that co-existed in Pratt's early years. She also provides revealing commentary on how the concepts of either/or and insider/outsider are at work within the gay and lesbian community. Tracing her own growth as a femme lesbian and feminist activist alongside her personal life—because theory needs "flesh and breath"—Pratt's rhetoric of questioning is never completely tentative, but always fluid and always tied to "daily life," which is of course never as neat or sure as traditional categories lead us to believe.

"Gender Quiz"

1995

quiz, n. [? suggested by L. quis, who, which, what, quid, how, why, wherefore]. I. [Rare], a queer or eccentric person. 2. a practical joke; hoax. 3. a questioning, especially an informal oral or written examination to test one's knowledge.
Webster's New World Dictionary of the American Language

In 1975, when I first fell in love with another woman, and knew that was what I was doing, I was married to a man, had been for almost ten years, and I had two small sons. Everyone was shocked at the turn I was taking in my life, including me. Everyone—from the male lawyer who handled the divorce to my handful of lesbian friends—wanted to know: Had I ever had these feelings before? When had I realized I was "different"? When had I started to "change"? And the state of North Carolina, where I was living, certainly wanted to know: Did I understand that I could not be both a mother—a good woman—and also a lesbian—a perverted woman?

To answer their questions and my own, I did what perhaps every person who identifies as lesbian or gay does when we come out to ourselves. I looked back at my own life for the clues of memory to use as I struggled through a maze of questions: I didn't feel "different," but was I? (From who?) Had I changed? (From what?) Was I heterosexual in adolescence only to become lesbian in my late twenties? Was I lesbian always but coerced into heterosexuality? Was I a less authentic lesbian than my friends who had "always known" that they were sexually and affectionately attracted to other women? What kind of woman was a lesbian woman? Was I a "real" woman?

What I found at the center of my exploration was my first friendship, when I was five and she was five, with a white girl who had lived next door to me, a tomboy. I had not talked to her since our high school graduation in our small Alabama town, but I knew from my mother that she had never married. I wondered at how intensely I remembered her. Then one evening, as I read my poetry in a Birmingham bookstore, she walked in, looking grown and fine in her cowboy boots, white shirt open at the collar, tailored slacks—looking like the butch dyke she had turned out to be. She was someone who had known me since I was small, but she was as shocked as everyone else that I had grown up to be a lesbian too.

When I found her, I found other questions that required me to turn back and look yet again: How was it possible that coming from the woman-hating, race-baiting, church town of our childhood, we had both grown up to live as lesbians? Why was she the first person I felt passionately about outside my family— someone who was not only a lesbian, but a butch lesbian? How had we recognized each other then, with no language for who we were? What mark had we each left on the other? And who *were* we to each other, at five years old? Were we "butch" and "femme"? Were we "boy" and "girl"? Why was I invisible in her memories, a "girl" but not a "lesbian"?

I turned and looked back again at the two of us, those two girls. I saw the kite string slack in my hand, the kite falling and crumpling, and how she reached out and pulled me forward into the wind with it. I said to her, "But after we were little, I never saw you. You were always playing with the boys. I was afraid of the boys." And she said, "But what you didn't know was that I was afraid of the girls." All through high school she fell miserably in love with straight girls who were aggressively femme, but at the senior prom she dated the captain of the football team. I sat sedate, awkward, and alone, in a strapless pink prom dress, full of anticipated power but unable to sail into a room of dancers who, like me, desired and despised the power of women.

Twenty years later these questions unwound before me: Was my femme style—the tilt of my head, my way of asking questions, the tone of my voice— related to my sexual desire? To my notion of myself as a woman? What did maleness and femaleness have to do with the identities of butch and femme we had grown up into? What did the gestures of masculinity and femininity have to do with us as women?

The next time I came home she arranged another reunion, a dinner with queer folks from our high school years. That night there were five, all of us white, a friendship network as segregated as our education, our never even getting to meet the Black students in the school on the other side of town. We hadn't known much about many of the lives hidden in our town, and now we gathered, ready to find out: Me and the woman who was my first friend, almost my first memory. And my best girlfriend from high school, who'd also grown up to be a lesbian and a mother. My first boyfriend, who'd turned out to be a gay man so sweet I remembered why I wanted to be his girl. And another gay man who still lived in our hometown. We gossiped about who we'd had crushes on, who we held hands with on the sly, who flirted back.

The list of people became staggeringly long, far beyond my idea of who might have been "lesbian" or "gay" in my tiny town of about two thousand. There was the girl classmate, long since married, who'd graduated and then had an affair with a woman gym teacher. And the girl classmate who had gone from one woman lover to another until her front door got broken down in the middle of the night. And the married Sunday School teacher whose daughter, later married, had had an affair with a girlfriend, who years later had had an affair with the teacher-mother. There were the boys who either did it with each other or watched the fucking that went on between them in a church, in a parsonage, with the preacher's son. There was the gay man who opened his door one night to find an envelope on his doorstep stuffed with photographs of a married male acquaintance, and a pleading invitation.

We told stories about taking the compulsory heterosexual quiz in high school, with its two ways to answer, its two ways to turn: straight or gay, heterosexual or queer. One choice would lead us out of the maze into adulthood, the other directly to hell. But it seemed that the public tally of our choices had almost no relation to our hidden lives, to whose hand was on whose ass, to the dream we buried, dead center, in our heart. The institution of heterosexuality certainly existed, but its daily practice—at least in my hometown in the deep South—suddenly seemed no more sturdy than the wedding pictures of man and wife printed on flimsy yellow paper in the local weekly.

Yet law and custom had usually been strong enough to make our public lives match the picture. The boundaries of heterosexuality strengthened other institutions—including those of race and class—whose limits were also unacknowledged. In the town newspaper I saw photographs of the sheriff and his deputies by the courthouse, pouring confiscated whiskey into the street gutters until the town reeked of moonshine. But there were no pictures of my girlfriend inside her house, on her hands and knees in the kitchen with a mother almost broken by poverty. No picture of her father jailed for trying to buy their way out by selling bootleg liquor. When my white father died in the county nursing home, the paper printed one version of his life, from semi-pro baseball to the lumber mill. No mention of him drinking the bootleg whiskey, no mention of his racist theories on who was taking over the world. The Black woman who raised me died across the hall from him in the home. There was nothing in the paper to say she had lived or died, or how many children she had mothered, nothing of her daughters or her grandchildren.

When I was engaged to be married to a man, the local paper published an announcement and a picture of me, groomed and womanly, ready to be a wife. Of those of us gathered at our queer reunion, there was no public record in our town—no note in the weekly chat column from Greenpond or Six Mile—of those we had loved faithfully for five years, ten years, the children we had familied. But in our bodies we knew that our way had not led to a dead end, a blank wall, a blank piece of paper. We had walked through into our own lives.

The last time I went home, I introduced my new love to my first girlfriend, and watched them greet each other warmly. After years of loving butch lesbians, I had taken as my mate a woman so stone in her masculinity that she could, and did, sometimes pass as a queer man. I had no language to talk about her or us together. I had to learn to say that I had fallen in love with a woman so *transgendered,* with such perceived contradictions between her birth sex and her gender expression, that someone at one end of a city block could call her "Ma'am" and someone at the other end would call her "Sir." I was learning that I was more complicated than I'd had any idea. I was beginning to pull the thread of who *I* was out of the tangle of words: *woman* and *lesbian, femme* and *female.*

That night I looked back at my first friend, a girl scalded by her mother's shame. The threats of walk-like-a-lady, of don't-be-so-loud-and-angry. (And hate yourself enough to almost go crazy.) I looked back at myself, the child flirting in photographs with angled head, sidelong glance. The child given an impossible choice by her teachers: Be smart or be a girl, be a girl or be strong. (And hate yourself enough to almost leave your body.) The two of us had sat at playtime in the dirt, barefoot, battling furiously hand-to-hand in the desire to defeat the other. How had we survived to meet again? Survived to grow up to be women for whom the word *woman* did not adequately describe the twists and turns our bodies, our lives, took through sex and gender?

No one had turned to us and held out a handful of questions: How many ways are there to have the *sex* of girl, boy, man, woman? How many ways are there to have *gender*—from masculine to androgynous to feminine? Is there a connection between the *sexualities* of lesbian, bisexual, heterosexual, between desire and liberation? No one told us: The path divides, and divides again, in many directions. No one asked: How many ways can the *body's sex* vary by chromosomes, hormones, genitals? How many ways can *gender expression* multiply— between home and work, at the computer and when you kiss someone, in your dreams and when you walk down the street? No one asked us: What is your dream of who you want to be?

In 1975, when I first fell in love with another woman, and knew that was what I wanted, I had just begun to call myself a feminist. I was learning how many traps the female body could be caught in—sexual assault and rape, beatings in the home, our thoughts turned back in shame on our bodies. I learned how women's bodies could be used to reproduce children without our consent, to produce someone else's "pleasure" at our expense. Most importantly, I began to be able to explain many of the events of my own life that had been unintelligible to me.

I was able to recall and find a pattern in certain acts that had made no sense—like a sexually suggestive comment from a male coworker—and acts that I hadn't understood as significant—such as the fact that a male job interviewer questioned me on my childcare arrangements. For the first time in my

life, I understood myself as *woman*, the "opposite sex," a group of people subject to discrimination and oppression—and capable of resistance. I was able to
locate my body and my life in the maze of history and power.

The oppression of women was a revelation to me; the liberation of women
was my freedom. There was tremendous exhilaration in being part of a liberation movement, in gathering together with other women to explore how to get
to freedom. In consciousness-raising circles, political action groups, cultural
events, literary collectives—in all kinds of women's groups and spaces, we
identified the ways oppression had fenced in our lives.

And we read the theories of women who had ideas about how to end the oppression of women as a sex. I found a few writers who examined the relation of
capitalist economic development to women's oppression. But most of the theory available to me was ahistorical and monocultural. It emphasized that the
solution was to eliminate differences between *women* and *men*. Some proposed
abolishing distinctions in biological functioning—as in Shulamith Firestone's
suggestion for artificial wombs to erase female biological functions that she believed were the basis of male and female, and of inequality. Others felt that the
answer was to end modes of gender expression, patterns of femininity and
masculinity. Carolyn Heilbrun advocated androgyny, the elimination of the po-
larities of "gender roles" that she considered the cause of power differences between men and women. Andrea Dworkin campaigned to alter the practice of
sexual intercourse, to get rid of sexual images and acts she believed would perpetuate maleness and femaleness, and therefore domination and submission.

I found these theories persuasive. Maybe eliminating sex differences or tran-
scending gender expression would end *woman* as a place of oppression. But, in
fact, the theories didn't explain some important aspects of oppression against
me as a woman in my daily life. I'd been pregnant with two children and given
birth to them. The way the doctors treated me only made me ask, "If there were
artificial wombs, whose hands would administer the technology, and for whose
profits?" And those two children had been two boys, each of whom had possessed, by the time he was two or three, his own unique blend of masculine and
feminine. Was it possible to train them into androgyny? Was this the skill they
needed to take action against unjust power in the world? As for intercourse,
this was where I had experienced the most pleasure in my relationship with a
man; my husband had tried carefully to please me. I would have had more
pleasure if my sexual play had not been damaged by fear about pregnancy—and
by shame about what I could want as a woman. But my husband's penis was not
dominating my life. Instead, I was concerned about the power of white men
who interviewed me for possible jobs at large institutions, and then protected
their economic position by never hiring me.

And, when I stood up to face the public opponents of my liberation as a woman,
I got little help from the theories I was reading. When I debated right-wing

women in my community in North Carolina, as they lambasted the Equal
Rights Amendment, their tactics were based on baiting the women's movement precisely on the issue of elimination of sex and gender differences. They
accused: Equal rights means unisex bathrooms. Equal rights means homosexual marriages. They meant: If you challenge gender boundaries, you will
make women more vulnerable to abuse by eliminating gender protection. They
meant: If you challenge gender boundaries, you will have men and women
adopting the behavior of the opposite sex and getting pleasure from it.

I didn't know how to answer their raging remarks, accusations which were
echoed throughout the United States as part of a concerted antifeminist campaign. Some of the first slogans I'd learned in the women's movement were "Biology is not destiny" and "Women are made, not born." I'd read feminist theory
that analyzed how jobs and household chores and emotions were divided up
between men and women according to sex. But I—and the primarily white
middle-to-upper-class reform women's movement that backed the E.R.A.—did
not have an analysis of sex, gender expression, and sexuality that was complex
enough to respond to these right-wing attacks.

We could have said, in these debates, that the answer to violence against
women was not the illusion of protection by limiting women's activity, but a
movement in which women learned to fight back, with allies, to protect ourselves, and to move through the whole world safely. We could have answered
that the split between *man* and *woman* was designed to keep one sex up and one
sex down in an economic system where profiteers make money off a war between the sexes. We could have answered that *woman* was not the opposite of
man, and that liberation meant crossing all arbitrary gender boundaries, to
place ourselves anywhere we chose on the continuum of maleness and femaleness, in any aspect of our lives.

In some more private spaces within women's liberation, we did advance
these arguments. But in hostile public space it was controversial to propose
even the slightest changes in "normal" male and female behaviors. *That* was to
question the foundation of "civilization." The reform wing of the women's
movement was profoundly ambivalent about taking on lesbian and transgender
issues publicly. It dealt with issues of race and class reluctantly and inconsis-
tently, when at all. A victory for these reformers meant only a fractional expansion of the old public boundaries on what was acceptable behavior for "womanhood," on who was a "respectable" woman.

Some of these reformists accepted limits on what constituted womanhood
because of uncritical allegiances to their own class and race positions. For
others, this was a strategic decision; they believed a political definition of
woman that deemphasized difference would secure more territory for more
women in a hostile world. They hoped to establish a bulwark, and then a place
that could be built on for greater liberation. In fact, the exclusion of women
who blurred the edges of what was considered legitimate as *woman*—because of

race or class or sexuality or gender presentation—made women's space smaller and more dangerous, made this aspect of the women's movement weaker and more limited in foundation.

In the end, I moved away from reform politics into cultural and political actions that embraced the complexities of *woman*. The group of women I began to work with was, at first, predominantly white, both working class and middle class, and lesbian. But we had been deeply influenced by the Black civil rights and liberation movements. We saw the freedom of all women as linked inextricably to the elimination of racism. In addition, we learned from the political and theoretical work of feminists and lesbians of color who showed us how to question—and place in an economic and historical context—the many categories of "difference," including those of race, sex, class, and sexuality.

But even as we traced how women's liberation could be extended through these connections, these untanglings and re-braidings, we still had not fully explored sex and gender. There were unanswered questions, and questions that were never raised, about "manhood" and "womanhood." We carried with us many of the negative assumptions and values that the larger culture had assigned to *woman, feminine, man, masculine*—ideas that served to limit women's behaviors and to prevent examination of how "masculinity" and "femininity" are not the basis of sex, race, and class oppression.

Often a lesbian considered "too butch" was assumed to be, at least in part, a male chauvinist. She might get thrown out of her lesbian collective for this, or refused admittance to a lesbian bar. Frequently a lesbian who was "too femme" was perceived as a woman who had not liberated her mind or her body. In ordinary arguments with a lesbian friend or lover, she could be dismissed—as I sometimes was—with, "You act just like a heterosexual woman." Yet during this same time, lesbians who were butch, femme, and all gender expressions in between were trying to decipher which of our behaviors still did reflect oppressive patterns learned in a woman-hating culture. These struggles were present in 1982, in New York City, when an alliance of women with a range of sexualities had planned "The Scholar and the Feminist" annual conference as a way to examine the complex intersections of pleasure and danger in women's sexuality and gender expression. They were condemned as "sexual deviants" and "sluts" by a group of women organizing against pornography, who identified themselves as "real feminists."

At about this time, I was teaching women's studies at a state university near Washington, D.C. One day in the classroom, we were discussing lesbian life in general, and butch/femme in particular. I was dressed casually, but in femme style. The white woman to my left was a muscular, big woman, with short hair and a black leather jacket; she drove a Harley to school every day. She said forcefully, "Butch and femme don't exist anymore." It was a moment typical, in many ways, of the lesbian-feminist space I lived inside during the 1980s. As women and as lesbians we wanted to step outside traps set for us as people sexed as *woman*, to evade negative values gendered to us. We didn't want to be women as defined by the larger culture, so we had to get rid of femininity. We didn't want to be oppressed by men, so we had to get rid of masculinity. And we wanted to end enforced desire, so we had to get rid of heterosexuality.

For some lesbians, one way out of these traps was to choose androgyny, or to practice a sexuality of "mutuality and equality"—an attempt to eliminate the variations of "man" and "woman" we saw in each other every day. Another way was to explain hostility toward "masculine" lesbians and "feminine" lesbians as arising from homophobia, rather than from prejudices about what kind of gender expression was appropriate for "respectable" women and "liberated" women. One answer for many was to deny the deep fear in the larger culture, and therefore within ourselves, about sex and gender fluidity.

The fear can take different forms. The classified sections of gay and lesbian newspapers still run personal ads that say "No butches, no drugs"—a statement equating gender defiance in a woman with self-destruction, a lesbian version of a gay man's "straight-appearing, no femmes" ad. Discussions of sexuality may exclude butch/butch and femme/femme pairings as too homoerotically queer. Some of us who talk of ourselves as butch or femme may reject identification with people like us who live at the extremes of gender. A coolly sophisticated lesbian at a dance may say, "I'm a femme, but I'm not like *her*,"—dismissing the woman she sees as "going too far" in her femininity.

We know, from being alive in the United States in the twentieth century, that there are severe punishments dealt to those who cross sex and gender boundaries, and terrible penalties visited on women who claim their womanhood independently. This is really no surprise, though, since the institutions of power are based, at least in part, on controlling difference—by sex, gender, and sexuality. No wonder we may feel there is safety in moderation, in assimilation, in a "normal" expression of sex and gender. But *moderation* means "to keep within bounds." Inside whose boundaries are we living?

And despite the punishments for boundary crossing, we continue to live, daily, with all our contradictory differences. Here I still stand, unmistakably "feminine" in style, and "womanly" in personal experience—and unacceptably "masculine" in political interests and in my dedication to writing a poetry that stretches beyond the woman's domain of home. Here I am, assigned a "female" sex on my birth certificate, but not considered womanly enough—because I am a lesbian—to retain custody of the children I delivered from my woman's body. As a white girl raised in a segregated culture, I was expected to be "ladylike"— sexually repressed but acquiescent to white men of my class—while other, darker women were damned as "promiscuous" so their bodies could be seized and exploited. I've worked outside the home for at least part of my living since I was a teenager—a fact deemed masculine by some. But my occupation now is that of teacher, work suitably feminine for a woman as long as I don't tell my students I'm a lesbian—a sexuality thought too aggressive and "masculine" to fit with my "femininity."

I am definitely lesbian to myself, but not in a way recognizable to a heterosexual world that assumes lesbians to be "mannish." Unless I announce myself to be lesbian, which I do often—in my classroom, at poetry readings, to curious taxi drivers—I am usually assumed to be straight. But unless I "butch up" my style, sometimes I am suspect inside my lesbian world as too feminine to be lesbian. And both inside and outside lesbian space, there is another assumption held by some: No "real" lesbian would be attracted to as much masculinity as I prefer in my lesbian lover.

How can I reconcile the contradictions of sex and gender, in my experience and my politics, in my body? We are all offered a chance to escape this puzzle at one time or another. We are offered the True or False correct answer. We are handed the questionnaire to fill out. But the boxes that we check, *M* or *F*, the categories *male* and *female*, do not contain the complexity of sex and gender for any of us.

The stories that follow are part of a new theory about that complexity which is appearing at the intersections: between the feminism of U.S. women's liberation; the writings of women of color nationally and internationally; the queer ideas of lesbian, gay, and bisexual liberation; and the emerging thought of transgender liberation—a movement that embraces drag queens and kings, transsexuals, cross-dressers, he-shes and she-males, intersexed people, transgenderists, and people of ambiguous, androgynous, or contradictory sex and gender. These intersections make clear that every aspect of a person's gender expression and sex will not be consistently either masculine or feminine, man or woman. I find many layers of my own experience in this theory, and I find an exhilaration at the connections between myself and others as I see, with increasing clarity, how gender oppression and liberation affect everyone, how my struggle as a woman and a lesbian overlaps and joins with the struggles of other gender and sexually oppressed people. A friend of mine has said of this exhilaration: "It's like being released from a cage I didn't know I was in."

This is a theory that explores the infinities, the fluidities of sex and gender. The African-American woman eating sushi at the next table may be a woman lovely in her bones, gestures, tone of voice, but this does not mean that her genitals are female. If the handsome Filipino man in the upstairs apartment is straight-appearing, this does not mean his erotic preference is the "opposite sex." The white woman next to you at the doctor's office may have been born male, and have a complex history of hormones and surgery. Or she may have been born female and have a different but equally complex history of hormones and surgery. The person on the subway who you perceive as a white man in a business suit may have been born female, may consider herself a butch lesbian, or may identify himself as a gay man. The *M* and the *F* on the questionnaire are useless.

Now here I stand, far from where I was born, from the small segregated hospital in Alabama where a nurse checked *F* and *W* on my birth certificate. Far from my first tomboy girlfriend and the ways we played together, splashing barefoot in rainwater. Far from who I was as a wife and mother, almost twenty years ago, when I began to question the destiny I had been assigned as a woman. I have lived my life at the intersection of great waves of social change in the United States in the twentieth century: the Black civil rights and liberation movements, the women's liberation movement, the lesbian/gay/bisexual liberation movement, the transgender liberation movement. The theory developed by each has complicated our questions about the categories of race, sex, gender, sexuality, and class. And these theories have advanced our ability to struggle against oppressions that are imposed and justified using these categories. But we can not move theory into action unless we can find it in the eccentric and wandering ways of our daily life. I have written the stories that follow to give theory flesh and breath.

FOR FURTHER READING

Pratt, Minnie Bruce. *Crimes Against Nature*. Ithaca: Firebrand Books, 1990.
———. *Rebellion: Essays 1980–1991*. Ithaca: Firebrand Books, 1991.
———. "The Union Institute: Teaching." Available at <http://mbpratt.or/teach.html>.
———. *We Say We Love Each Other*. Ithaca: Firebrand Books, 1991.
Pratt, Minnie Bruce, Elly Bulkin, and Barbara Smith. *Yours In Struggle: Three Feminist Perspectives on Anti-Semitism and Racism*. New York: Long Haul Press, 1984.

Dorothy Allison

1946–

Dorothy Allison's *Two or Three Things I Know for Sure* is, overtly, a memoir about coming to terms with a history of abuse, incest, and hopelessness among women in Allison's family, the topic of much of her fiction, poetry, and theory. But this memoir also functions as rhetorical theory that asserts the right to speak and that offers expanded, alternative strategies for reconceptualizing and changing women's lives. The book begins, "Let me tell you a story," and Allison does; she tells stories about being raped by her stepfather when she was five years old, about being "horrified" by the women she loved most in her life—working-class poor white women in South Carolina—who ran away from abuse and who sometimes stayed. Allison ran. Sprinkled throughout the book, after the stories, are the "two or three things" she has learned "for sure."

Allison was born in 1949 in Greenville, South Carolina, the daughter of a fourteen-year-old girl. Allison's only "father" was a violent, abusive man, and although her mother did not save her from this abuse, Allison credits her mother (and the women in her family) as inspirations—for their perseverance, survival, sense of humor, and their belief that Allison had a right to an education. The first of her family to graduate from high school, Allison went on to earn a B.A. from Florida Presbyterian College and an M.A. from New York's School of Social Research. Today, she is a nationally acclaimed writer and speaker. *Two or Three Things I Know for Sure* began as a piece she performed for audiences, and the intimate, oral quality of that performance remains in the written text. The accompanying photographs of Allison's family members also add a sense of immediacy to her stories.

We chose this excerpt for a collection of women's rhetoric because here Allison is speculating about epistemology—always a foundation for rhetorical theory. She explores how truth is constructed in language, how language is invented and arranged not in order to create something artistic or beautiful, or even primarily to communicate some information, but in order to keep from dying, to make a version of life that she can live. In these stories and her comments Allison is talking about—and giving direction for—what one can do with language. She is asserting that she can and must control reality through her stories/language, but at the same time she is making sure that we realize her powerlessness, her struggle not only through her abusive history but through the veil of language that made it so hard for her to find ways to think, much less speak, about what happened to her. This is not consciousness-raising wallowing, but a strategic method, first, for learning how to speak at all, and then a theory for using language to survive and to change one's reality.

From *Two or Three Things I Know for Sure*

1995

"Let me tell you a story," I used to whisper to my sisters, hiding with them behind the red-dirt bean hills and row on row of strawberries. My sisters' faces were thin and sharp, with high cheekbones and restless eyes, like my mama's face, my aunt Dot's, my own. Peasants, that's what we are and always have been. Call us the lower orders, the great unwashed, the working class, the poor, proletariat, trash, lowlife and scum. I can make a story out of it, out of us. Make it pretty or sad, laughable or haunting. Dress it up with legend and aura and romance.

"Let me tell you a story," I'd begin, and start another one. When we were small, I could catch my sisters the way they caught butterflies, capture their attention and almost make them believe that all I said was true. "Let me tell you about the women who ran away. All those legendary women who ran away." I'd tell about the witch queens who cooked their enemies in great open pots, the jewels that grow behind the tongues of water moccasins. After a while the deepest satisfaction was in the story itself, greater even than the terror in my sisters' faces, the laughter, and, God help us, the hope.

The constant query of my childhood was "Where you been?" The answer, "Nowhere." Neither my stepfather nor my mother believed me. But no punishment could discover another answer. The truth was that I did go nowhere—nowhere in particular and everywhere imaginable. I walked and told myself stories, walked out of our subdivision and into another, walked all the way to the shopping center and then back. The flush my mama suspected hid an afternoon of shoplifting or vandalism was simple embarrassment, because when I walked, I talked—story-talked, out loud—assuming identities I made up. Sometimes I was myself, arguing loudly as I could never do at home. Sometimes I became people I had seen on television or read about in books, went places I'd barely heard of, did things that no one I knew had ever done, particularly things that girls were not supposed to do. In the world as I remade it, nothing was forbidden; everything was possible.

I'll tell you a story and maybe you'll believe me.

There's a laboratory in the basement of the Greenville County General Hospital, I told my sisters. They take the babies down there. If you're poor—from the wrong family, the wrong color, the wrong side of town—they mess with you, alter your brain. That was what happened. That was it.

You believe me?

I'm a storyteller. I'll work to make you believe me. Throw in some real stuff, change a few details, add the certainty of outrage. I know the use of fiction in a world of hard truth, the way fiction can be a harder piece of truth. The story of what happened, or what did not happen but should have—that story can become a curtain drawn shut, a piece of insulation, a disguise, a razor, a tool that changes every time it is used and sometimes becomes something other than we intended.

The story becomes the thing needed.

Two or three things I know for sure, and one of them is what it means to have no loved version of your life but the one you make.

Let me tell you a story. If I could convince myself, I can convince you. But you were not there when I began. You were not the one I was convincing. When I began there were just nightmares and need and stubborn determination.

When I began there was only the suspicion that making up the story as you went along was the way to survive. And if I know anything, I know how to survive, how to remake the world in story.

But where am I in the stories I tell? Not the storyteller but the woman in the story, the woman who believes in story. What is the truth about her? She was one of them, one of those legendary women who ran away. A witch queen, a warrior maiden, a mother with a canvas suitcase, a daughter with broken bones. Women run away because they must. I ran because if I had not, I would have died. No one told me that you take your world with you, that running becomes a habit, that the secret to running is to know why you run and where you are going—and to leave behind the reason you run.

My mama did not run away. My aunt Dot and aunt Grace and cousin Billie with her near dozen children—they did not run. They learned resilience and determination and the cost of hard compromises. None of them ever intended to lose their lives or their children's lives, to be trapped by those hard compromises and ground down until they no longer knew who they were, what they had first intended. But it happened. It happened over and over again.

Aunt Dot was the one who said it. She said, "Lord, girl, there's only two or three things I know for sure." She put her head back, grinned, and made a small impatient noise. Her eyes glittered as bright as sun reflecting off the scales of a cottonmouth's back. She spat once and shrugged. "Only two or three things.

That's right," she said. "Of course it's never the same things, and I'm never as sure as I'd like to be. . . ."

Let me tell you about what I have never been allowed to be. Beautiful and female. Sexed and sexual. I was born trash in a land where the people all believe themselves natural aristocrats. Ask any white Southerner. They'll take you back two generations, say, "Yeah, we had a plantation." The hell we did.

I have no memories that can be bent so easily. I know where I come from, and it is not that part of the world. My family has a history of death and murder, grief and denial, rage and ugliness—the women of my family most of all.

The women of my family were measured, manlike, sexless, bearers of babies, burdens, and contempt. My family? The women of my family? We are the ones in all those photos taken at mining disasters, floods, fires. We are the ones in the background with our mouths open, in print dresses or drawstring pants and collarless smocks, ugly and old and exhausted. Solid, stolid, wide-hipped baby machines. We were all wide-hipped and predestined. Wide-faced meant stupid. Wide hands marked workhorses with dull hair and tired eyes, thumbing through magazines full of women so different from us they could have been another species.

I remember standing on the porch with my aunt Mandy brushing out my hair; I was feeling loved and safe and happy. My aunt turned me around and smoothed my hair down, looked me in the eye, smiled, and shook her head. "Lucky you're smart," she said.

Brown-toothed, then toothless, my aunt Dot showed me what I could expect.

"You're like me," she announced when she saw my third-grade school picture. "Got that nothing-gonna-stop-you look about you, girl."

I studied the picture. All I saw was another grinning girl in dark-framed glasses, missing a tooth.

"No, look." She produced a picture I would find later among Mama's treasures. In this one Aunt Dot was a smooth-skinned teenager with a wide jaw and a straightforward glare, sturdy and fearless at fifteen as she would be three decades later.

"I see," I assured her, keeping my head down and away from her demanding eyes.

What I saw was a woman who had never been beautiful and never allowed herself to care. When she found me once, red-faced and tearful, brooding over rude boys who shouted insults and ran away, she told me to wipe my face and pay no attention.

"It never changes," she said in her gravelly voice. "Men and boys, they all the same. Talk about us like we dogs, bitches sprung full-grown on the world, like we were never girls, never little babies in our daddy's arms. Turn us into jokes 'cause we get worn down and ugly. Never look at themselves. Never think about what they're doing to girls they've loved, girls they wore out. Their girls."

"You ugly old woman," my grandfather called my grandmother.

"You ugly old woman," all my uncles called all my aunts.

"You ugly bitch," my cousins called their sisters, and my sisters called me.

"You ugly thing!" I screamed back.

The pretty girls in my high school had good hair, curled or straightened to fit the fashion, had slender hips in tailored skirts, wore virgin pins on the right side or knew enough not to wear such tacky things at all. My cousins and I were never virgins, even when we were. Like the stories told about Janis Joplin in Port Arthur, Texas, there were stories about us in Greenville, South Carolina. The football players behind the bleachers, boys who went on to marry and do well.

"Hell, it wasn't rape. She never said no. Maybe she said stop, but in that little bitty voice, so you know she wants you to love her, hell, love her for ten minutes or half an hour. Shit, who could love a girl like her?"

Who?

Beauty is a hard thing. Beauty is a mean story. Beauty is slender girls who die young, fine-featured delicate creatures about whom men write poems. Beauty, my first girlfriend said to me, is that inner quality often associated with great amounts of leisure time. And I loved her for that.

We were not beautiful. We were hard and ugly and trying to be proud of it. The poor are plain, virtuous if humble and hardworking, but mostly ugly. Almost always ugly.

"You know Dot's husband left her," Cousin Billie told me once. "Came back after a while, then left again. Way she talked you'd think she never noticed. Some days I don't know whether to be proud of her or ashamed."

I thought about stories I'd been told, about women whose men left them or stayed to laugh out the sides of their mouths when other men mentioned other women's names. Behind my aunt Dot was a legion of female cousins and great-aunts, unknown and nameless—snuff-sucking, empty-faced creatures changing spindles at the textile plant, chewing gum while frying potatoes at the truck stop, exhausted, angry, and never loved enough.

The women I loved most in the world horrified me. I did not want to grow up to be them. I made myself proud of their pride, their determination, their stubbornness, but every night I prayed a man's prayer: Lord, save me from them.

Do not let me become them.

Let me tell you the mean story.

For years and years, I convinced myself that I was unbreakable, an animal with an animal strength or something not human at all. Me, I told people, I take damage like a wall, a brick wall that never falls down, never feels anything, never flinches or remembers. I am one woman but I carry in my body all the stories I have ever been told, women I have known, women who have taken damage until they tell themselves they can feel no pain at all.

That's the mean story. That's the lie I told myself for years, and not until I began to fashion stories on the page did I sort it all out, see where the lie ended and a broken life remained. But that is not how I am supposed to tell it. I'm only supposed to tell one story at a time, one story. Every writing course I ever heard of said the same thing. Take one story, follow it through, beginning, middle, end. I don't do that. I never do.

Behind the story I tell is the one I don't.

Behind the story you hear is the one I wish I could make you hear.

Behind my carefully buttoned collar is my nakedness, the struggle to find clean clothes, food, meaning, and money. Behind sex is rage, behind anger is love, behind this moment is silence, years of silence.

The man raped me. It's the truth. It's a fact.

I was five, and he was eight months married to my mother. That's how I always began to talk about it—when I finally did begin to talk about it. I'd say, "It was rape, the rape of a child." Then I'd march the words out—all the old tearing awful words.

For years, every time I said it, said "rape" and "child" in the same terrible sentence, I would feel the muscles of my back and neck pull as taut as the string of a kite straining against the wind. That wind would blow and I would resist, then suddenly feel myself loosed to fall or flee. I started saying those words to get to that release, that feeling of letting go, of setting loose both the hatred and the fear. The need to tell my story was terrible and persistent, and I needed to say it bluntly and cruelly, to use all those words, those old awful tearing words.

I need to be a woman who can talk about rape plainly, without being hesitant or self-conscious, or vulnerable to what people might be saying this year.

I need to say that my mama didn't know what was going on, that I didn't tell her, that when I finally did tell someone it was not her. I need to say that when I told, only my mama believed me, only my mama did anything at all, that thirty years later one of my aunts could still say to me that she didn't really believe it, that he had been such a hardworking, good-looking man. Something else must have happened. Maybe it had been different.

How? I wanted to ask. How could it have been different for a five-year-old and a grown man? Instead I just looked at her, feeling finally strong enough to know she had chosen to believe what she needed more than what she knew.

Two or three things I know for sure, but none of them is why a man would rape a child, why a man would beat a child.

Why? I am asked. Why do you bring that up? Must you talk about that? I asked myself the same questions until finally I began to understand. This was a wall in my life, I say, a wall I had to climb over every day. It was always there for me, deflecting my rage toward people who knew nothing about what had happened to me or why I should be angry at them.

It took me years to get past that rage, to say the words with grief and insistence but to let go of the anger, to refuse to use the anger against people who knew nothing of the rape. I had to learn how to say it, to say "rape," say "child," say "unending," "awful," and "relentless," and say it the way I do—adamant, unafraid, unashamed, every time, all over again—to speak my words as a sacrament, a blessing, a prayer. Not a curse. Getting past the anger, getting to the release, I become someone else, and the story changes. I am no longer a grown-up outraged child but a woman letting go of her outrage, showing what I know: that evil is a man who imagines the damage he does is not damage, that evil is the act of pretending that some things do not happen or leave no mark if they do, that evil is not what remains when healing becomes possible.

All the things I can say about sexual abuse—about rape—none of them are reasons. The words do not explain. Explanations almost drove me crazy, other people's explanations and my own. Explanations, justifications, and theories. I've got my own theory. My theory is that rape goes on happening all the time. My theory is that everything said about that act is assumed to say something about me, as if that thing I never wanted to happen and did not know how to stop is the only thing that can be said about my life. My theory is that talking about it makes a difference—being a woman who can stand up anywhere and say, I was five and the man was big.

So let me say it.

He beat us, my stepfather, that short, mean-eyed truck driver with his tight-muscled shoulders and uneasy smile. He was a man who wasn't sure he liked women but was sure he didn't like smart, smart-mouthed tomboys, stubborn little girls who tried to pretend they were not afraid of him. Two or three things I know, but this is one I am not supposed to talk about, how it comes together—sex and violence, love and hatred. I'm not ever supposed to put together the two halves of my life—the man who walked across my childhood and the life I have made for myself. I am not supposed to talk about hating that man when I grew up to be a lesbian, a dyke, stubborn, competitive, and perversely lustful.

"People might get confused," a woman once told me. She was a therapist and a socialist, but she worried about what people thought. "People might imagine that sexual abuse makes lesbians."

"Oh, I doubt it." I was too angry to be careful. "If it did, there would be so many more."

Her cheeks flushed pink and hot. She had told me once that she thought I didn't respect her—her oddly traditional life and commonplace desires, her

Ruth Gibson, 1950.

Ruth Gibson Allison and her sister Dorothy "Dot" Yearwood, 1981

Aunt Dot as a young wife, 1952

Aunt Dot at 63, a year before her death

Dorothy, 1954

Dorothy and Anne, 1954

Dorothy and Anne, 1956

Dorothy in Easter outfit, 1957

Dorothy Allison, 1958

Dorothy and Anne, 1960

Dorothy, Wanda, and Anne, 1963

Dorothy, New York City Gay Pride March, 1972

Dorothy, 1974 (Photo credit: Morgan Gwenwald)

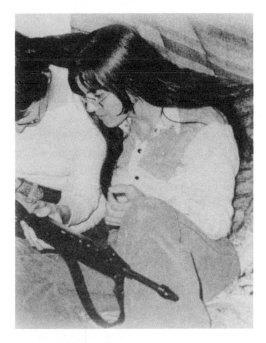

Dorothy with friend, 1974

husband of twelve years and female companion of five. Looking into her stern, uncompromising face brought back my aunts and their rueful certainty that nothing they did was ever quite right. Two or three things and none of them sure, that old voice whispered in my head while this woman looked at me out of eyes that had never squinted in regret.

"Tell me, though," I added, and shifted my shoulders like Aunt Dot leaning into a joke, "if people really believed that rape made lesbians, and brutal fathers made dykes, wouldn't they be more eager to do something about it? What's that old Marxist strategy—sharpen the contradiction until even the proletariat sees where the future lies? We could whack them with contradictions, use their bad instincts against their worse. Scare them into changing what they haven't even thought about before."

She opened her mouth like a fish caught on a razor-sharp line. For the first time in all the time I had known her I saw her genuinely enraged. She didn't think my suggestion was funny. But then, neither did I.

How *does* it come together, the sweaty power of violence, the sweet taste of desire held close? It rises in the simplest way, naturally and easily, when you're so young you don't know what's coming, before you know why you're not supposed to talk about it.

It came together for me when I was fifteen and that man came after me with a belt for perhaps the thousandth time and my little sister and I did not run. Instead we grabbed up butcher knives and backed him into a corner. And oh, the way that felt! For once we made him sweat with the threat of what we'd do if he touched us. And oh! the joy of it, the power to say, "No, you son of a bitch, this time, no!" His fear was sexual and marvelous—hateful and scary, but wonderful, like orgasm, like waiting a whole lifetime and finally coming.

I know. I'm not supposed to talk about sex like that, not about weapons or hatred or violence, and never to put them in the context of sexual desire. Is it male? Is it mean? Did you get off on it? I'm not supposed to talk about how good anger can feel—righteous, justified, and completely satisfying. Even at seventeen, when I learned to shoot a rifle, I knew not to tell anyone what I saw and felt as I aimed that weapon. Every time I centered on the target it was his heart I saw, his squint-eyed, mean-hearted image.

I knew that the things I was not supposed to say were also the things I did not want to think about. I knew the first time I made love with a woman that I could cry but I must not say why. I cried because she smelled like him, the memory of him, sweaty and urgent, and she must not know it was not her touch that made me cry. Breathing her in prompted in me both desire and hatred, and of the two feelings what I dared not think about was the desire. Sex with her became a part of throwing him off me, making peace with the violence of my own desire.

I know. I'm not supposed to talk about how long it took me to wash him out of my body—how many targets I shot, how many women I slept with, how many times I sat up till dawn wondering if it would ever change, if I would ever change. If there would come a time in my life when desire did not resonate with fury.

Two or three things I know for sure, and one of them is that change when it comes cracks everything open.

Let me tell you a story. Let me tell you the story that is in no part fiction, the story of the female body taught to hate itself.

It is so hard to be a girl and want what you have never had. To be a child and want what you cannot imagine. To look at women and think, Nobody else, nobody else has ever wanted to do what I want to do. Hard to be innocent, believing yourself evil. Hard to think no one else in the history of the world wants to do this. Hard to find out that they do, but not with you. Or not in quite the way you want them to do it.

Women.

Lord God, I used to follow these girls.

They would come at me, those girls who were not really girls anymore. Grown up, wounded, hurt and terrible. Pained and desperate. Mean and angry. Hungry and unable to say just what they needed. Scared, aching, they came into my bed like I could fix it. And every time I would try. I would do anything a woman wanted as long as she didn't want too much of me. As long as I could hide behind her need, I could make her believe anything. I would tell her stories. I would bury her in them. I have buried more women than I am willing to admit. I have told more lies than I can stand.

I never thought about what I needed, how hurt and desperate I was, how mean and angry and dangerous. When I finally saw it, the grief I had been hiding even from myself, the world seemed to stop while I looked. For a year, then another, I kept myself safe, away from anyone, any feeling that might prompt that rage, that screaming need to hurt somebody back.

When I finally let someone into my narrow bed, the first thing I told her was what I could not do. I said. "I can't fix it, girl. I can't fix anything. If you don't ask me to fix it, you can ask anything else. If you can say what you need, I'll try to give it to you."

I remember the stories I was told as a girl, stories like soap operas, stories that went on for generations—how she loved him and left him and loved him still, how he hurt her and hurt her and never loved her at all, how that child they made told lies to get them to look at her, how no one knows the things done in that home, no one but her and she don't tell.

Women lose their lives not knowing they can do something different. Men eat themselves up believing they have to be the thing they have been made. Children go crazy. Really, even children go crazy, believing the shape of the life they must live is as small and mean and broken as they are told. Oh, I could tell you stories that would darken the sky and stop the blood. The stories I could tell no one would believe. I would have to pour blood on the floor to convince anyone that every word I say is true. And then? Whose blood would speak for me?

Let me tell you a story. I tell stories to prove I was meant to survive, knowing it is not true. My stories are no parables, no *Reader's Digest* Unforgettable Characters, no women's movement polemics, no Queer Nation broadsides. I am not here to make anyone happy. What I am here for is to claim my life, my mama's death, our losses and our triumphs, to name them for myself. I am here to claim everything I know, and there are only two or three things I know for sure. . . .

The last time my stepfather beat me, I was sixteen years old. It was my birthday, and he got away with it because he pretended that what he was doing was giving me a birthday spanking, a tradition in our family as in so many others. But two of my girlfriends were standing there, and even they could see he was hitting me harder than any birthday ritual could justify. I saw their faces go pink with embarrassment. I knew mine was hot with shame, but I could not stop him or pull free of him. The moment stretched out while his hand crashed down, counting off each year of my life. At sixteen, I jumped free and turned to face him.

"You can't break me," I told him. "And you're never going to touch me again."

It was a story to tell myself, a promise. Saying out loud, "You're never going to touch me again"—that was a piece of magic, magic in the belly, the domed kingdom of sex, the terror place inside where rage and power live. Whiskey rush without whiskey, bravado and determination, this place where for the first time I knew no confusion, only outrage and pride. In the worst moments of my life, I have told myself that story, the story about a girl who stood up to a monster. Doing that, I make a piece of magic inside myself, magic to use against the meanness in the world.

I know. I am supposed to have shrunk down and died. I know. I am supposed to be deeply broken, incapable of love or trust or passion. But I am not, and part of why that is so is the nature of the stories I told myself to survive. Like the stories my mama told herself, and my aunt Dot and my cousin Billie, my stories shaped my life. Of all the stories I know, the meanest are the stories the women I loved told themselves in secret—the stories that sustained and broke them.

When I make love I take my whole life in my hands, the damage and the pride, the bad memories and the good, all that I am or might be, and I do indeed love myself, can indeed do any damn thing I please. I know the place where courage and desire come together, where pride and joy push lust through the bloodstream, right to the heart.

I go to bed like I used to go to karate. Want and need come together in a body that is only partly my own. Like my sisters, like my mama, I am and am not this thing the world sees—strong chin, hard eyes, a mouth too soft when it should be firm, a creature of lust who does not know how to feel what I feel. Biblical? Damned? Hopeful. What is lust when you have never known love?

I took my sex back, my body. I claimed myself and remade my life. Only when I knew I belonged to myself completely did I become capable of giving myself to another, of finding joy in desire, pleasure in our love, power in this body no one else owns.

I am the only one who can tell the story of my life and say what it means. I knew that as a child. It was one of the reasons not to tell. When I finally got away, left home and looked back, I thought it was like that story in the Bible, that incest is a coat of many colors, some of them not visible to the human eye, but so vibrant, so powerful, people looking at you wearing it see only the coat. I did not want to wear that coat, to be told what it meant, to be told how it had changed the flesh beneath it, to let myself be made over into my rapist's crea-tion. I will not wear that coat, not even if it is recut to a feminist pattern, a post-modern analysis.

Two or three things I know for sure, and one is that I would rather go naked than wear the coat the world has made for me.

What is the story I will not tell? The story I do not tell is the only one that is a lie. It is the story of the life I do not lead, without complication, mystery, cour-age, or the transfiguration of the flesh. Yes, somewhere inside me there is a child always eleven years old, a girlchild who holds the world responsible for all the things that terrify and call to me. But inside me too is the teenager who armed herself and fought back, the dyke who did what she had to, the woman who learned to love without giving in to fear. The stories other people would tell about my life, my mother's life, my sisters', uncles', cousins', and lost girl-friends'—those are the stories that could destroy me, erase me, mock and deny me. I tell my stories louder all the time: mean and ugly stories; funny, almost bitter stories; passionate, desperate stories—all of them have to be told in order not to tell the one the world wants, the story of us broken, the story of us never laughing out loud, never learning to enjoy sex, never being able to love or trust love again, the story in which all that survives is the flesh. That is not my story. I tell all the others so as not to have to tell that one.

Two or three things I know, two or three things I know for sure, and one of them is that to go on living I have to tell stories, that stories are the one sure way I know to touch the heart and change the world. . . .

Other night I went over to Providence to read in a line, a marathon of poets and fiction writers.

Afterwards, as I was sipping a Coke, a young man came up to me, fierce and tall and skinny, his wrists sticking out of his sleeves.

He said, "Hypertext. I've been wanting to tell you about it."

"Hypertext?"

"Your work. I've read everything you've ever published three or four times— at least. I know your work. I could put you in hypertext."

There was a girl behind him. She reached past his sleeve, put her hand on mine, said, "Oh yes, we could do it. We could put you in hypertext." She spoke the word with conviction, passion, almost love.

"Hypertext?" I spoke it through a blur of bewilderment.

"CD-ROM, computers, disks or files, it doesn't matter," the boy said in a rush of intensity. "It's the latest thing. We take one of your stories, and we put you in. I know just the story. It goes all the way through from beginning to end. But all the way through, people can reach in and touch a word. Mouse or keyboard or a touchable screen. Every time you touch a word, a window opens. Behind that word is another story. You touch the word and the story opens. We put one of your stories behind that story. And then maybe, maybe you could write some more and we could put in other things. Every word the reader touches, it opens again."

The girl tugged my arm urgently. "It's so beautiful," she said. "After a while it's like a skin of oil on the water. If you look at it from above it's just one thing, water and oil in a spreading shape. But if you looked at it from the side, it would go down and down, layers and layers. All the stories you've ever told. All the pictures you've ever seen. We can put in everything. Hypertext."

The boy nodded.

I reached for a glass of wine. I took a long drink, rubbed my aching back, said, "Yeah, right, I'll think about it."

That night I had a dream.

I was walking in a museum, and I was old. I was on that cane I had to use the whole length of 1987. My right eye had finally gone completely blind. My left eye was tearing steadily. I saw everything through a scrim of water, oily water. Way way down three or four corridors, around a turn, I hit a wall.

My story was on this wall.

I stood in front of my wall. I put my hand on it. Words were peeling across the wall, and every word was a brick. I touched one.

"Bastard."

The brick fell away and a window opened. My mother was standing in front of me. She was saying, "I'm not sick. I would tell you if I was sick, girl. I would tell you."

I touched her face and the window opened.

She was behind it, flesh cooling, still warm. Hair gone, shadows under her eyes. I was crying. I touched her hand. It was marble, it was brick. It fell away. She was seventeen and she was standing on the porch. He was sitting on the steps. She was smiling at him. She was saying, "You won't treat me bad, will you? You'll love my girls, won't you?"

I touched the brick. It fell away.

He was standing there. I was holding my arm. The doctor was saying, "What in God's name happened to this child?"

I touched the wall and the brick fell away.

My mama had her hand on my neck. She was handing me pictures. She was saying, "I didn't want to know who they were. I don't know what happened. I never wanted to tell you what happened. You make it up for yourself."

I put my hand on the photograph and the window opened onto a movie. I was eight years old. Cousins and aunts and strangers were moving across the yard. I was clinging to my mother's neck. I was saying "Mama" in that long, low plea a frightened child makes.

She reached for me, put her arms around me. I fell away. She was holding onto her mama's neck saying the same thing, saying "Mama" in that same cry. My hands met the brick of her flesh. She fell away.

My son was climbing up my lap into my arms, putting his arms around my neck.

He said, "Mama."

The last brick fell down. I was standing there looking up through tears. I was standing by myself in the rubble of my life, at the bottom of every story I had ever needed to know. I was gripping my ribs like a climber holding on to rock. I was whispering the word over and over, and it was holding me up like a loved hand.

I can tell you anything. All you have to believe is the truth.

FOR FURTHER READING

Allison, Dorothy. *Bastard out of Carolina*. New York: E. P. Dutton, 1992.

———. *Skin: Talking about Sex, Class, and Literature*. Ithaca: Firebrand Books, 1994.

———. *Trash*. Ithaca: Firebrand Books, 1988.

Nomy Lamm

1975–

Describing herself as a fat, Jewish, disabled, anarchist dyke, Nomy Lamm, with her "riot grrrrl" punk message, confronts cultural constructions of beauty, femininity, and desirability. A freelance writer, Lamm was named one of *Ms.* magazine's 1997 Women of the Year for her essays on fat and body image. Her essays have appeared in *Ms.* and in collections of essays by young feminist writers. She creates and publishes the confrontational zine, *I'm So Fucking Beautiful,* which attempts to go beyond mainstream feminism's "body image" rhetoric with its outspoken and irreverent analysis of fat prejudice. Lamm has also recently become a performance artist, touring with "Sister Spit," an all-girl spoken-word road show.

Writing in a punk style that nevertheless echoes both Virginia Woolf and Hélène Cixous's proclamation that women must "write the body," Lamm claims writing and speaking as the anarchistic and revolutionary strategy that allows her to acknowledge her unruly body, name herself "dyke, queer, Jewish, crippled, and fat," and thus rob the power from those who would name her "deviant." Writing enables her to confront and deconstruct cultural myths and contradictions about "woman's body," starting with her own. Although she claims her own marginal status as queer, fat, and disabled, she also acknowledges the power that resides in her location as an educated, middle-class white woman.

Lamm's self-reflexive rhetoric in "It's a Big Fat Revolution" deliberately places her writing in a complex relationship both within and in opposition to conventional rhetoric. First she claims, "It will be clear, concise and well thought-out, and will be laid out in the basic thesis paper, college essay format. I will deal with these issues in a mature and intellectual manner." But then she immediately eschews these conventions, defining her writing against the tradition of formal patriarchal rhetorical constraints with her casual, irreverent, and profane language and her colloquial tone, while also acknowledging the artificiality of her rebellious rhetoric. Although Lamm is cautious about the power of rhetoric to bring on the "revolution," she nevertheless affirms that through writing and speaking—girls talking to each other, writing to and for each other about oppression, sexuality, abuse, money—the "revolution" is underway.

"It's a Big Fat Revolution"

1995

I am going to write an essay describing my experiences with fat oppression and the ways in which feminism and punk have affected my work. It will be clear, concise and well thought-out, and will be laid out in the basic thesis paper, college essay format. I will deal with these issues in a mature and intellectual manner. I will cash in on as many fifty-cent words as possible.

I lied. (You probably already picked up on that, huh?) I can't do that. This is my life, and my words are the most effective tool I have for challenging White-boyworld (that's my punk-rock cutesy but oh-so-revolutionary way of saying "patriarchy"). If there's one thing that feminism has taught me, it's that the revolution is gonna be on my terms. The revolution will be incited through my voice, my words, not the words of the universe of male intellect that already exists. And I know that a hell of a lot of what I say is totally contradictory. My contradictions can coexist, cuz they exist inside of me, and I'm not gonna simplify them so that they fit into the linear, analytical pattern that I know they're supposed to. I think it's important to recognize that all this stuff does contribute to the revolution, for real. The fact that I write like this cuz it's the way I want to write makes this world just that much safer for me.

I wanna explain what I mean when I say "the revolution," but I'm not sure whether I'll be able to. Cuz at the same time that I'm being totally serious, I also see my use of the term as a mockery of itself. Part of the reason for this is that I'm fully aware that I still fit into dominant culture in many ways. The revolution could very well be enacted against me, instead of for me. I don't want to make myself sound like I think I'm the most oppressed, most punk-rock, most revolutionary person in the world. But at the same time I do think that revolution is a word I should use as often as I can, because it's a concept that we need to be aware of. And I don't just mean it in an abstract, intellectualized way, either. I really do think that the revolution has begun. Maybe that's not apparent to mainstream culture yet, but I see that as a good sign. As soon as mainstream culture picks up on it, they'll try to co-opt it.

For now the revolution takes place when I stay up all night talking with my best friends about feminism and marginalization and privilege and oppression and power and sex and money and real-life rebellion. For now the revolution takes place when I watch a girl stand up in front of a crowd of people and talk about her sexual abuse. For now the revolution takes place when I get a letter from a girl I've never met who says that the zine I wrote changed her life. For now the revolution takes place when the homeless people in my town camp out for a week in the middle of downtown. For now the revolution takes place when I am confronted by a friend about something racist that I have said. For now the revolution takes place in my head when I know how fucking brilliant my girlfriends and I are.

And I'm living the revolution through my memories and through my pain and through my triumphs. When I think about all the marks I have against me in this society, I am amazed that I haven't turned into some worthless lump of shit. Fatkikecripplecuntqueer. In a nutshell. But then I have to take into account the fact that I'm an articulate, white, middle-class college kid, and that provides me with a hell of a lot of privilege and opportunity for dealing with my oppression that may not be available to other oppressed people. And since my personality/being isn't divided up into a privileged part and an oppressed part, I have to deal with the ways that these things interact, counterbalance and sometimes even overshadow each other. For example, I was born with one leg. I guess it's a big deal, but it's never worked into my body image in the same way that being fat has. And what does it mean to be a white woman as opposed to a woman of color? A middle-class fat girl as opposed to a poor fat girl? What does it mean to be fat, physically disabled and bisexual? (Or fat, disabled and *sexual at all?*)

See, of course, I'm still a real person, and I don't always feel up to playing the role of the revolutionary. Sometimes it's hard enough for me to just get out of bed in the morning. Sometimes it's hard enough to just talk to people at all, without having to deal with the political nuances of everything that comes out of their mouths. Despite the fact that I do tons of work that deals with fat oppression, and that I've been working so so hard on my own body image, there are times when I really hate my body and don't want to deal with being strong all the time. Because I am strong and have thought all of this through in so many different ways, and I do have naturally high self-esteem, I've come to a place where I can honestly say that I love my body and I'm happy with being fat. But occasionally, when I look in the mirror and I see this body that is so different from my friends', so different from what I'm told it should be, I just want to hide away and not deal with it anymore. At these times it doesn't seem fair to me that I have to always be fighting to be happy. Would it be easier for me to just give in and go on another diet so that I can stop this perpetual struggle? Then I could still support the fat grrrl revolution without having it affect me personally in every way. And I know I know I know that's not the answer and I could never do that to myself, but I can't say that the thought never crosses my mind.

And it doesn't help much when my friends and family, who all know how I feel about this, continue to make anti-fat statements and bitch about how fat they feel and mention new diets they've heard about and are just dying to try. "I'm shaped like a watermelon." "Wow, I'm so happy, I now wear a size seven instead of a size nine." "I like this mirror because it makes me look thinner."

I can't understand how they could still think these things when I'm constantly talking about these issues, and I can't believe that they would think that these are okay things to talk about in front of me. And it's not like I want them to censor their conversation around me. . . . I just want them to not think it. I know that most of this is just a reflection of how they feel about themselves and isn't intended as an attack on me or an invalidation of my work, but it makes it that much harder for me. It puts all those thoughts inside me. Today I was standing outside of work and I caught a glimpse of myself in the window and thought, "Hey, I don't look that fat!" And I immediately realized how fucked up that was, but that didn't stop me from feeling more attractive because of it.

I want this out of me. This is not a part of me, and theoretically I can separate it all out and throw away the shit, but it's never really gone. When will this finally be over? When can I move on to other issues? It will never be over, and that's really fucking hard to accept.

I am living out this system of oppression through my memories, and even when I'm not thinking about them they are there, affecting everything I do. Five years old, my first diet. Seven years old, being declared officially "overweight" because I weigh ten pounds over what a "normal" seven-year-old should weigh. Ten years old, learning to starve myself and be happy feeling constantly dizzy. Thirteen years old, crossing the border from being bigger than my friends to actually being "fat." Fifteen years old, hearing the boys in the next room talk about how fat (and hence unattractive) I am. Whenever I perform, I remember the time when my dad said he didn't like the dance I choreographed because I looked fat while I was doing it. Every time I dye my hair I remember when my mom wouldn't let me dye my hair in seventh grade because seeing fat people with dyed hair made her think they were just trying to cover up the fact that they're fat, trying to look attractive despite it (when of course it's obvious what they should really do if they want to look attractive, right?). And these are big memorable occurrences that I can put my finger on and say, "This hurt me." But what about the lifetime of media I've been exposed to that tells me that only thin people are lovable, healthy, beautiful, talented, fun? I know that those messages are all packed in there with the rest of my memories, but I just can't label them and their effects on my psyche. They are elusive and don't necessarily feel painful at the time. They are well disguised and often even appear alluring and romantic. (I will never fall in love because I cannot be picked up and swung around in circles. . . .)

All my life the media and everyone around me have told me that fat is ugly. Which of course is just a cultural standard that has many, many medical lies to fall back upon. Studies have shown that fat people are unhealthy and have short life expectancies. Studies have also shown that starving people have these same peculiarities. These health risks to fat people have been proven to be a result of continuous starvation—dieting—and not of fat itself. I am not fat due to lack of willpower. I've been a vegetarian since I was ten years old. Controlling what I eat is easy for me. Starving myself is not (though for most of my life I wished it was). My body is supposed to be like this, and I've been on plenty of diets where I've kept off some weight for a period of several months and then gained it all back. Two years ago I finally ended the cycle. I am not dieting anymore because I know that this is how my body is supposed to be, and this is how I want it to be. Being fat does not make me less healthy or less active. Being fat does not make me less attractive.

On TV I see a thin woman dancing with a fabulously handsome man, and over that I hear, "I was never happy until I went on [fill in the blank] diet program, but now I'm getting attention from men, and I feel so good! I don't have to worry about what people are saying about me behind my back, because I know I look good. You owe it to yourself to give yourself the life you deserve. Call [fill in the blank] diet program today, and start taking off the pounds right away!" TV shows me a close-up of a teary-eyed fat girl who says, "I've tried everything, but nothing works. I lose twenty pounds, and I gain back twenty-five. I feel so ashamed. What can I do?" The first time I saw that commercial I started crying and memorized the number on the screen. I know that feeling of shame. I know that feeling of having nowhere left to turn, of feeling like I'm useless because I can't lose all that "unwanted fat." But I know that the unhappiness is not a result of my fat. It's a result of a society that tells me I'm bad.

Where's the revolution? My body is fucking beautiful, and every time I look in the mirror and acknowledge that, I am contributing to the revolution.

I feel like at this point I'm expected to try to prove to you that fat can be beautiful by going into descriptions of "rippling thighs and full smooth buttocks." I won't. It's not up to me to convince you that fat can be attractive. I refuse to be the self-appointed full-figured porno queen. Figure it out on your own.

It's not good enough for you to tell me that you "don't judge by appearances"—so fat doesn't bother you. Ignoring our bodies and "judging only by what's on the inside" is not the answer. This seems to be along the same line of thinking as that brilliant school of thought called "humanism": "We are all just people, so let's ignore trivialities such as race, class, gender, sexual preference, body type and so on." Bullshit! The more we ignore these aspects of ourselves, the more shameful they become and the more we are expected to be what is generally implied when these qualifiers are not given—white, straight, thin, rich, male. It's unrealistic to try to overlook these exterior (and hence meaningless, right?) differences, because we're still being brainwashed with the same shit as everyone else. This way we're just not talking about it. And I don't want to be told, "Yes you're fat, but you're beautiful on the inside." That's just another way of telling me that I'm ugly, that there's no way that I'm beautiful on the outside. Fat does not equal ugly, don't give me that. My body *is* me. I want you to see my body, acknowledge my body. True revolution comes not when we learn to ignore our fat and pretend we're no different, but when we learn to use it to our advantage, when we learn to deconstruct all the myths that propagate fat-hate.

My thin friends are constantly being validated by mainstream feminism, while I am ignored. The most widespread mentality regarding body image at this point is something along these lines: Women look in the mirror and think, "I'm fat," but really they're not. Really they're thin.

Really they're thin. But really I'm fat. According to mainstream feminist theory, I don't even exist. I know that women do often look in the mirror and think that they are fatter than they are. And yes, this is a problem. But the analysis can't stop there. There are women who *are* fat, and that needs to be dealt with. Rather than just reassuring people, "No, you're not fat, you're just curvy," maybe we should be demystifying fat and dealing with fat politics as a whole. And I don't mean maybe, I mean it's a necessity. Once we realize that fat is not "inherently bad" (and I can't even believe I'm writing that—"inherently bad"— it sounds so ridiculous), then we can work out the problem as a whole instead of dealing only with this very minute part of it. All forms of oppression work together, and so they have to be fought together.

I think that a lot of the mainstream feminist authors who claim to be dealing with this issue are doing it in a very wrong way. Susie Orbach, for example, with *Fat Is a Feminist Issue*. She tells us: Don't diet, don't try to lose weight, don't feed the diet industry. But she then goes on to say: But if you eat right and exercise, you will lose weight! And I feel like, great, nice, it's so very wonderful that that worked for her, but she's totally missing the point. She is trying to help women, but really she is hurting us. She is hurting us because she's saying that there's still only one body that's okay for us (and she's the one to help us get it!). It's almost like that *Stop the Insanity* woman, Susan Powter. One of my friends read her book and said that the first half of it is all about fat oppression and talks about how hard it is to be fat in our society, but then it says: So use my great new diet plan! This kind of thing totally plays on our emotions so that we think, Wow, this person really understands me. They know where I'm coming from, so they must know what's best for me.

And there are so many "liberal" reasons for perpetuating fat-hate. Yes, we're finally figuring out that dieting never works. How, then, shall we explain this horrible monstrosity? And how can we get rid of it? The new "liberal" view on fat is that it is caused by deep psychological disturbances. Her childhood was bad, she was sexually abused, so she eats and gets fat in order to hide herself away. She uses her fat as a security blanket. Or maybe when she was young her parents caused her to associate food with comfort and love, so she eats to console herself. Or maybe, like with me, her parents were always on diets and always nagging her about what she was eating, so food became something shameful that must be hoarded and kept secret. And for a long, long time I really believed that if my parents hadn't instilled in me all these fucked-up attitudes about food, I wouldn't be fat. But then I realized that my brother and sister both grew up in exactly the same environment, and they are both thin. Obviously this is not the reason that I am fat. Therapy won't help, because there's nothing to cure. When will we stop grasping for reasons to hate fat people and start realizing that fat is a totally normal and natural thing that cannot and should not be gotten rid of?

Despite what I said earlier about my friends saying things that are really hurtful to me, I realize that they are actually pretty exceptional. I don't want to make them seem like uncaring, ignorant people. I'm constantly talking about these issues, and I feel like I'm usually able to confront my friends when they're being insensitive, and they'll understand or at least try to. Sometimes when I leave my insular circle of friends I'm shocked at what the "real world" is like. Hearing boys on the bus refer to their girlfriends as their "bitches," seeing fat women being targeted for harassment on the street, watching TV and seeing how every fat person is depicted as a food-obsessed slob, seeing women treated as property by men who see masculinity as a right to power . . . I leave these situations feeling like the punk scene, within which most of my interactions take place, is so sheltered. I cannot imagine living in a community where I had nowhere to go for support. I cannot imagine living in the "real world."

But then I have to remember that it's still there in my community—these same fucked-up attitudes are perpetuated within the punk scene as well; they just take on more subtle forms. I feel like these issues are finally starting to be recognized and dealt with, but fat hating is still pretty standard. Of course everyone agrees that we shouldn't diet and that eating disorders are a result of our oppressive society, but it's not usually taken much further than that. It seems like people have this idea that punk is disconnected from the media. That because we are this cool underground subculture, we are immune to systems of oppression. But the punkest, coolest kids are still the skinny kids. And the same cool kids who are so into defying mainstream capitalist "Amerika" are the ones who say that fat is a symbol of capitalist wealth and greed. Yeah, that's a really new and different way of thinking: Blame the victim. Perpetuate institutionalized oppression. Fat people are not the ones who are oppressing these poor, skinny emo boys.

This essay is supposed to be about fat oppression. I feel like that's all I ever talk about. Sometimes I feel my whole identity is wrapped up in my fat. When I am fully conscious of my fat, it can't be used against me. Outside my secluded group of friends, in hostile situations, I am constantly aware that at any moment I could be harassed. Any slight altercation with another person could lead to a barrage of insults thrown at my body. I am always ready for it. I've found it doesn't happen nearly as often as I expect it, but still I always remain aware of the possibility. I am "the Fat Girl." I am "the Girl Who Talks About Fat Oppression." Within the punk scene, that's my security blanket. People know about me and know about my work, so I assume that they're not gonna be laughing behind my back about my fat. And if they are, then I know I have support from other people around me. The punk scene gives me tons of support that I know I wouldn't get elsewhere. Within the punk scene, I am able to put out zines, play music, do spoken-word performances that are intensely personal to me. I feel really strongly about keeping nothing secret. I can go back to the old cliché about the personal being political, and no matter how trite it may sound, it's true. I went for so long never talking about being fat, never talking about how that affects my self-esteem, never talking about the ways that I'm oppressed by this society. Now I'm talking. Now I'm talking, I'm talking all the time, and people listen to me. I have support.

And at the same time I know that I have to be wary of the support that I receive. Because I think to some people this is just seen as the cool thing, that by supporting me they're somehow receiving a certain amount of validation from the punk scene. Even though I am totally open and don't keep secrets, I have to protect myself.

This is the revolution. I don't understand the revolution. I can't lay it all out in black and white and tell you what is revolutionary and what is not. The punk scene is a revolution, but not in and of itself. Feminism is a revolution; it is solidarity as well as critique and confrontation. This is the fat grrrl revolution. It's mine, but it doesn't belong to me. Fuckin' yeah.

FOR FURTHER READING

Lamm, Nomy. "Fishnets, Feather Boas, and Fat." In *Adios Barbie: Young Women Write About Body Image and Identity,* edited by Ophira Edut, 78–87. Seattle: Seal Press, 1998.

Leslie Marmon Silko

1948–

"You don't have anything if you don't have the stories," Leslie Marmon Silko writes in her award-winning novel *Ceremony*. In all of her writing Silko enacts the integral place of the oral tradition and storytelling in preserving traditional knowledge, sustaining community, and maintaining connection to the natural and spiritual worlds.

Implicit in the Pueblo storytelling tradition is the rhetorical understanding that the narrator's choices are always influenced by her "interior and exterior landscape" and that truth is rarely easily definable. Silko says, "The ancient Pueblo people sought a communal truth, not an absolute truth. For them this truth lived somewhere within the web of differing versions, disputes over minor points, and outright contradictions tangling with old feuds and village rivalries ("Interior and Exterior Landscapes" 32). Silko's essays on Pueblo culture present a rhetorical theory of storytelling and explore the epistemology underlying that tradition in Pueblo culture.

Born in Albuquerque, New Mexico, in 1948, Silko grew up on the Laguna Pueblo reservation and describes herself as Laguna, Pueblo, Mexican, and white. As an activist, she has worked to preserve the oral traditions and ceremonies of the Laguna Pueblo. A former professor of English at the University of Arizona, Tucson, Silko also writes about U.S. immigration policies, violence against women, and the subjugation of Native Americans.

In "Yellow Woman and a Beauty of the Spirit," Silko grapples with differences between "old-time" and "modern" ways of looking at people and the world. She views the racism, sexism, homophobia, and standards of beauty held by white culture from the old-time perspective and demonstrates how the old-time perspective opens up possibilities for equity and justice. Silko makes this argument through stories inhabited by Grandma A'mooh, Thought Woman, and especially Yellow Woman. Yellow Woman, the central figure in a series of oral (and subsequently written) stories, flouts traditional sexuality and gender roles to embrace love and desire and in doing so sustains a life-giving connection with the natural and human worlds. In this essay, Silko explains that the Yellow Woman stories are relevant to her life because they taught her about living with and valuing difference.

Silko's essay, rooted in her lived experiences and in the oral tradition and landscape of the Laguna Pueblo, enacts a rhetoric in which "the words most highly valued are those spoken from the heart, unpremeditated and unrehearsed" ("Language and Literature" 48). In "Language and Literature from a

Pueblo Indian Perspective," she says that writing or a speech that is written down is highly suspect because the writing obscures the true feelings of the speaker and may be too detached from the audience and the occasion. The rhetorical expression the Pueblo people value, Silko says, "resembles something like a spider's web—with many little threads radiating from the center, crisscrossing one another. As with the web, the structure emerges as it is made, and you must simply listen and trust, as the Pueblo people do, that meaning will be made" (48–49). In "Yellow Woman and a Beauty of the Spirit," she asks readers to set aside our conventional views of argument and even of story and to embrace a more fluid, all-encompassing theory of aesthetics and rhetorics.

"Yellow Woman and a Beauty of the Spirit"

1996

From the time I was a small child, I was aware that I was different. I looked different from my playmates. My two sisters looked different too. We didn't look quite like the other Laguna Pueblo children, but we didn't look quite white either. In the 1880s, my great-grandfather had followed his older brother west from Ohio to the New Mexico Territory to survey the land for the U.S. government. The two Marmon brothers came to the Laguna Pueblo reservation because they had an Ohio cousin who already lived there. The Ohio cousin was involved in sending Indian children thousands of miles away from their families to the War Department's big Indian boarding school in Carlisle, Pennsylvania. Both brothers married full-blood Laguna Pueblo women. My great-grandfather had first married my great-grandmother's older sister, but she died in childbirth and left two small children. My great-grandmother was fifteen or twenty years younger than my great-grandfather. She had attended Carlisle Indian School and spoke and wrote English beautifully.

I called her Grandma A'mooh because that's what I heard her say whenever she saw me. A'mooh means "granddaughter" in the Laguna language. I remember this word because her love and her acceptance of me as a small child were so important. I had sensed immediately that something about my appearance was not acceptable to some people, white and Indian. But I did not see any signs of that strain or anxiety in the face of my beloved Grandma A'mooh.

Younger people, people my parents' age, seemed to look at the world in a more modern way. The modern way included racism. My physical appearance seemed not to matter to the old-time people. They looked at the world very differently; a person's appearance and possessions did not matter nearly as much as a person's behavior. For them, a person's value lies in how that person interacts with other people, how that person behaves toward the animals and the earth. That is what matters most to the old-time people. The Pueblo people believed this long before the Puritans arrived with their notions of sin and damnation, and racism. The old-time beliefs persist today; thus I will refer to the old-time people in the present tense as well as the past. Many worlds may coexist here.

I spent a great deal of time with my great-grandmother. Her house was next to our house, and I used to wake up at dawn, hours before my parents or younger sisters, and I'd go wait on the porch swing or on the back steps by her kitchen door. She got up at dawn, but she was more than eighty years old, so she needed a little while to get dressed and to get the fire going in the cookstove. I had been carefully instructed by my parents not to bother her and to behave, and to try to help her any way I could. I always loved the early mornings when the air was so cool with a hint of rain smell in the breeze. In the dry New Mexico air, the least hint of dampness smells sweet.

My great-grandmother's yard was planted with lilac bushes and iris; there were four o'clocks, cosmos, morning glories, and hollyhocks, and old-fashioned rosebushes that I helped her water. If the garden hose got stuck on one of the big rocks that lined the path in the yard, I ran and pulled it free. That's what I came to do early every morning: to help Grandma water the plants before the heat of the day arrived.

Grandma A'mooh would tell about the old days, family stories about relatives who had been killed by Apache raiders who stole the sheep our relatives had been herding near Swahnee. Sometimes she read Bible stories that we kids liked because of the illustrations of Jonah in the mouth of a whale and Daniel surrounded by lions. Grandma A'mooh would send me home when she took her nap, but when the sun got low and the afternoon began to cool off, I would be back on the porch swing, waiting for her to come out to water the plants and to haul in firewood for the evening. When Grandma was eighty-five, she still chopped her own kindling. She used to let me carry in the coal bucket for her, but she would not allow me to use the ax. I carried armloads of kindling too, and I learned to be proud of my strength.

I was allowed to listen quietly when Aunt Susie or Aunt Alice came to visit Grandma. When I got old enough to cross the road alone, I went and visited them almost daily. They were vigorous women who valued books and writing. They were usually busy chopping wood or cooking but never hesitated to take time to answer my questions. Best of all they told me the *hummah-hah* stories, about an earlier time when animals and humans shared a common language. In the old days, the Pueblo people had educated their children in this manner;

adults took time out to talk to and teach young people. Everyone was a teacher, and every activity had the potential to teach the child.

But as soon as I started kindergarten at the Bureau of Indian Affairs day school, I began to learn more about the differences between the Laguna Pueblo world and the outside world. It was at school that I learned just how different I looked from my classmates. Sometimes tourists driving past on Route 66 would stop by Laguna Day School at recess time to take photographs of us kids. One day, when I was in the first grade, we all crowded around the smiling white tourists, who peered at our faces. We all wanted to be in the picture because afterward the tourists sometimes gave us each a penny. Just as we were all posed and ready to have our picture taken, the tourist man looked at me. "Not you," he said and motioned for me to step away from my classmates. I felt so embarrassed that I wanted to disappear. My classmates were puzzled by the tourists' behavior, but I knew the tourists didn't want me in their snapshot because I looked different, because I was part white.

In the view of the old-time people, we are all sisters and brothers because the Mother Creator made all of us—all colors and all sizes. We are sisters and brothers, clanspeople of all the living beings around us. The plants, the birds, fish, clouds, water, even the clay—they all are related to us. The old-time people believe that all things, even rocks and water, have spirit and being. They understood that all things want only to continue being as they are; they need only to be left as they are. Thus the old folks used to tell us kids not to disturb the earth unnecessarily. All things as they were created exist already in harmony with one another as long as we do not disturb them.

As the old story tells us, Tse'itsi'nako, Thought Woman, the Spider, thought of her three sisters, and as she thought of them, they came into being. Together with Thought Woman, they thought of the sun and the stars and the moon. The Mother Creators imagined the earth and the oceans, the animals and the people, and the *ka'tsina* spirits that reside in the mountains. The Mother Creators imagined all the plants that flower and the trees that bear fruit. As Thought Woman and her sisters thought of it, the whole universe came into being. In this universe, there is no absolute good or absolute bad; there are only balances and harmonies that ebb and flow. Some years the desert receives abundant rain, other years there is too little rain, and sometimes there is so much rain that floods cause destruction. But rain itself is neither innocent nor guilty. The rain is simply itself.

My great-grandmother was dark and handsome. Her expression in photographs is one of confidence and strength. I do not know if white people then or now would consider her beautiful. I do not know if the old-time Laguna Pueblo people considered her beautiful or if the old-time people even thought in those terms. To the Pueblo way of thinking, the act of comparing one living being with another was silly, because each being or thing is unique and therefore incomparably valuable because it is the only one of its kind. The old-time people thought it was crazy to attach such importance to a person's appearance. I understood very early that there were two distinct ways of interpreting the world. There was the white people's way and there was the Laguna way. In the Laguna way, it was bad manners to make comparisons that might hurt another person's feelings.

In everyday Pueblo life, not much attention was paid to one's physical appearance or clothing. Ceremonial clothing was quite elaborate but was used only for the sacred dances. The traditional Pueblo societies were communal and strictly egalitarian, which means that no matter how well or how poorly one might have dressed, there was no social ladder to fall from. All food and other resources were strictly shared so that no one person or group had more than another. I mention social status because it seems to me that most of the definitions of beauty in contemporary Western culture are really codes for determining social status. People no longer hide their face-lifts and they discuss their liposuctions because the point of the procedures isn't just cosmetic, it is social. It says to the world, "I have enough spare cash that I can afford surgery for cosmetic purposes."

In the old-time Pueblo world, beauty was manifested in behavior and in one's relationships with other living beings. Beauty was as much a feeling of harmony as it was a visual, aural, or sensual effect. The whole person had to be beautiful, not just the face or the body; faces and bodies could not be separated from hearts and souls. Health was foremost in achieving this sense of well-being and harmony; in the old-time Pueblo world, a person who did not look healthy inspired feelings of worry and anxiety, not feelings of well-being. A healthy person, of course, is in harmony with the world around her; she is at peace with herself too. Thus an unhappy person or spiteful person would not be considered beautiful.

In the old days, strong, sturdy women were most admired. One of my most vivid preschool memories is of the crew of Laguna women, in their forties and fifties, who came to cover our house with adobe plaster. They handled the ladders with great ease, and while two women ground the adobe mud on stones and added straw, another woman loaded the hod with mud and passed it up to the two women on ladders, who were smoothing the plaster on the wall with their hands. Since women owned the houses, they did the plastering. At Laguna, men did the basket making and the weaving of fine textiles; men helped a great deal with the child care too. Because the Creator is female, there is no stigma on being female; gender is not used to control behavior. No job was a man's job or a woman's job; the most able person did the work.

My Grandma Lily had been a Ford Model A mechanic when she was a teenager. I remember when I was young, she was always fixing broken lamps and appliances. She was small and wiry, but she could lift her weight in rolled roofing or boxes of nails. When she was 75, she was still repairing washing machines in my uncle's coin-operated laundry.

The old-time people paid no attention to birthdays. When a person was ready to do something, she did it. When she no longer was able, she stopped. Thus the traditional Pueblo people did not worry about aging or about looking old because there were no social boundaries drawn by the passage of years. It was not remarkable for young men to marry women as old as their mothers. I never heard anyone talk about "women's work" until after I left Laguna for college. Work was there to be done by any able-bodied person who wanted to do it. At the same time, in the old-time Pueblo world, identity was acknowledged to be always in a flux; in the old stories, one minute Spider Woman is a little spider under a yucca plant, and the next instant she is a sprightly grandmother walking down the road.

When I was growing up, there was a young man from a nearby village who wore nail polish and women's blouses and permed his hair. People paid little attention to his appearance; he was always part of a group of other young men from his village. No one ever made fun of him. Pueblo communities were and still are very interdependent, but they also have to be tolerant of individual eccentricities because survival of the group means everyone has to cooperate.

In the old Pueblo world, differences were celebrated as signs of the Mother Creator's grace. Persons born with exceptional physical or sexual differences were highly respected and honored because their physical differences gave them special positions as mediators between this world and the spirit world. The great Navajo medicine man of the 1920s, the Crawler, had a hunchback and could not walk upright, but he was able to heal even the most difficult cases.

Before the arrival of Christian missionaries, a man could dress as a woman and work with the women and even marry a man without any fanfare. Likewise, a woman was free to dress like a man, to hunt and go to war with the men, and to marry a woman. In the old Pueblo worldview, we are all a mixture of male and female, and this sexual identity is changing constantly. Sexual inhibition did not begin until the Christian missionaries arrived. For the old-time people, marriage was about teamwork and social relationships, not about sexual excitement. In the days before the Puritans came, marriage did not mean an end to sex with people other than your spouse. Women were just as likely as men to have a *si'ash,* or lover.

New life was so precious that pregnancy was always appropriate, and pregnancy before marriage was celebrated as a good sign. Since the children belonged to the mother and her clan, and women owned and bequeathed the houses and farmland, the exact determination of paternity wasn't critical. Although fertility was prized, infertility was no problem because mothers with unplanned pregnancies gave their babies to childless couples within the clan in open adoption arrangements. Children called their mother's sisters "mother" as well, and a child became attached to a number of parent figures.

In the sacred kiva ceremonies, men mask and dress as women to pay homage and to be possessed by the female energies of the spirit beings. Because differences in physical appearance were so highly valued, surgery to change one's face and body to resemble a model's face and body would be unimaginable. To be different, to be unique was blessed and was best of all.

The traditional clothing of Pueblo women emphasized a woman's sturdiness. Buckskin leggings wrapped around the legs protected her from scratches and injuries while she worked. The more layers of buckskin, the better. All those layers gave her legs the appearance of strength, like sturdy tree trunks. To demonstrate sisterhood and brotherhood with the plants and animals, the old-time people make masks and costumes that transform the human figures of the dancers into the animal beings they portray. Dancers paint their exposed skin; their postures and motions are adapted from their observations. But the motions are stylized. The observer sees not an actual eagle or actual deer dancing, but witnesses a human being, a dancer, gradually changing into a woman/buffalo or a man/deer. Every impulse is to reaffirm the urgent relationships that human beings have with the plant and animal world.

In the high desert plateau country, all vegetation, even weeds and thorns, becomes special, and all life is precious and beautiful because without the plants, the insects, and the animals, human beings living here cannot survive. Perhaps human beings long ago noticed the devastating impact human activity can have on the plants and animals; maybe this is why tribal cultures devised the stories about humans and animals intermarrying, and the clans that bind humans to animals and plants through a whole complex of duties.

We children were always warned not to harm frogs or toads, the beloved children of the rain clouds, because terrible floods would occur. I remember in the summer the old folks used to stick big bolls of cotton on the outside of their screen doors as bait to keep the flies from going in the house when the door was opened. The old folks staunchly resisted the killing of flies because once, long, long ago, when human beings were in a great deal of trouble, a Green Bottle Fly carried the desperate messages of human beings to the Mother Creator in the Fourth World, below this one. Human beings had outraged the Mother Creator by neglecting the Mother Corn altar while they dabbled with sorcery and magic. The Mother Creator disappeared, and with her disappeared the rain clouds, and the plants and the animals too. The people began to starve, and they had no way of reaching the Mother Creator down below. Green Bottle Fly took the message to the Mother Creator, and the people were saved. To show their gratitude, the old folks refused to kill any flies.

The old stories demonstrate the interrelationships that the Pueblo people have maintained with their plant and animal clanspeople. Kochininako, Yellow Woman, represents all women in the old stories. Her deeds span the spectrum of human behavior and are mostly heroic acts, though in at least one story, she chooses to join the secret Destroyer Clan, which worships destruction and death. Because Laguna Pueblo cosmology features a female Creator, the status of women is equal with the status of men, and women appear as often as men in the old stories as hero figures. Yellow Woman is my favorite because she dares to cross traditional boundaries of ordinary behavior during times of crisis in order to save the Pueblo; her power lies in her courage and in her uninhibited sexuality, which the old-time Pueblo stories celebrate again and again because fertility was so highly valued.

The old stories always say that Yellow Woman was beautiful, but remember that the old-time people were not so much thinking about physical appearances. In each story, the beauty that Yellow Woman possesses is the beauty of her passion, her daring, and her sheer strength to act when catastrophe is imminent.

In one story, the people are suffering during a great drought and accompanying famine. Each day, Kochininako has to walk farther and farther from the village to find fresh water for her husband and children. One day she travels far, far to the east, to the plains, and she finally locates a freshwater spring. But when she reaches the pool, the water is churning violently as if something large had just gotten out of the pool. Kochininako does not want to see what huge creature had been at the pool, but just as she fills her water jar and turns to hurry away, a strong, sexy man in buffalo-skin leggings appears by the pool. Little drops of water glisten on his chest. She cannot help but look at him because he is so strong and so good to look at. Able to transform himself from human to buffalo in the wink of an eye, Buffalo Man gallops away with her on his back. Kochininako falls in love with Buffalo Man, and because of this liaison, the Buffalo People agree to give their bodies to the hunters to feed the starving Pueblo. Thus Kochininako's fearless sensuality results in the salvation of the people of her village, who are saved by the meat the Buffalo People "give" to them.

My father taught me and my sisters to shoot .22 rifles when we were seven; I went hunting with my father when I was eight, and I killed my first mule deer buck when I was thirteen. The Kochininako stories were always my favorite because Yellow Woman had so many adventures. In one story, as she hunts rabbits to feed her family, a giant monster pursues her, but she has the courage and presence of mind to outwit it.

In another story, Kochininako has a fling with Whirlwind Man and returns to her husband ten months later with twin baby boys. The twin boys grow up to be great heroes of the people. Once again, Kochininako's vibrant sexuality benefits her people.

The stories about Kochininako made me aware that sometimes an individual must act despite disapproval, or concern for appearances or what others may say. From Yellow Woman's adventures, I learned to be comfortable with my differences. I even imagined that Yellow Woman had yellow skin, brown hair, and green eyes like mine, although her name does not refer to her color, but rather to the ritual color of the east.

There have been many other moments like the one with the camera-toting tourist in the schoolyard. But the old-time people always say, remember the stories, the stories will help you be strong. So all these years I have depended on Kochininako and the stories of her adventures.

Kochininako is beautiful because she has the courage to act in times of great peril, and her triumph is achieved by her sensuality, not through violence and destruction. For these qualities of the spirit, Yellow Woman and all women are beautiful.

FOR FURTHER READING

Silko, Leslie Marmon. "Landscape, History, and the Pueblo Imagination." *Antaeus* 57 (Autumn 1986): 83–94.

———. "Interior and Exterior Landscapes: The Pueblo Migration Stories." In *Yellow Woman and a Beauty of the Spirit: Essays on Native American Life Today*, 25–47. New York: Simon and Schuster, 1997.

———. "Language and Literature from a Pueblo Indian Perspective." In *Yellow Woman and a Beauty of the Spirit: Essays on Native American Life Today*, 48–59. New York: Simon and Schuster, 1997.

———. *Sacred Water: Narratives and Pictures.* Tucson: Flood Plain Press, 1993.

———. *Storyteller.* New York: Seaver Books, 1981.

———. *Yellow Woman.* Edited by Melody Graulich. New Brunswick: Rutgers University Press, 1993.

Wright, Anne, ed. *The Delicacy and Strength of Lace: Letters Between Leslie Marmon Silko and James Wright.* St. Paul: Graywolf Press, 1986.

Ruth Bader Ginsburg

1933–

Ruth Bader Ginsburg, the second woman Justice of the United States Supreme Court, is criticized by some for her judicial restraint and by others for her judicial activism; she has been praised as a liberal feminist and attacked by feminists for being too conservative. However she is viewed, she is credited with landmark legal decisions involving sex discrimination, an injustice that she herself has experienced. As a student at Harvard, she and the few other women students were asked by the dean why they were taking up spaces reserved for men when law firms would not hire women. Ginsburg's response was to graduate (first in her class) from Columbia College of Law in 1960. Nevertheless, Justice Felix Frankfurter refused to accept her as a law clerk for the Supreme Court, especially when he learned that she was married with a five-year-old daughter. Ginsburg went on to become clerk for a U.S. district judge, after which she was invited back to teach at Columbia College of Law in 1972, the first year Title IX of the Education Amendment was extended to academic institutions. She served as a judge on the U.S. Court of Appeals until her appointment to the U.S. Supreme Court in 1993.

Ginsburg began working on sex-discrimination issues when she founded the ACLU Women's Rights Project in 1971. During the next two decades she successfully challenged laws that bestowed special privileges or disadvantages on men and women based on a belief in certain natural or essential roles or dispositions. Laws affecting employment, social services, civic responsibility, and rights often categorized women and men as either breadwinners or housewives and mothers. In many of her legal opinions, Ginsburg argues that women should be treated as individuals, not as members of the female sex. Despite these landmark opinions, however, Ginsburg is known for her judicial restraint; her judgments often mirror changes that have already occurred in mainstream society rather than breaking new or radical ground.

The argument Ginsburg makes in the VMI decision carefully traces, in her words, "volumes of history" in which gender-based educational discrimination has been justified over and over again. Her argument systematically discredits those claims and reaffirms the arguments for education that women have made for centuries. The selection we include here follows standard legal rhetorical conventions, citing legal precedent (we omitted some citations for reasons of length), but its boldness comes as Ginsburg argues that institutions must open their doors to all women who aspire to the goals those institutions seek to achieve. Like women before her, Ginsburg reaffirms that stereotypes about masculinity or femininity are not legal bases for the allocation of resources, rights, or privileges. Phyllis Schlafly criticized Ginsburg's VMI decision, saying it represented Ginsburg's "activist determination to write her radical feminist goals into the Constitution." Ginsburg replied, "The judgment was 7–1, for goodness' sake!" (Rosen 65).

From *United States v. Virginia et al.*
Certiori to the United States Court of Appeals for the Fourth Circuit

NO. 94-1941. Argued January 17, 1996—Decided June 26, 1996
Cite as: 518 U.S. 515 (1996)
Opinion of the Court

JUSTICE GINSBURG delivered the opinion of the Court.

I. Virginia's public institutions of higher learning include an incomparable military college, Virginia Military Institute (VMI). The United States maintains that the Constitution's equal protection guarantee precludes Virginia from reserving exclusively to men the unique educational opportunities VMI affords. We agree.

Founded in 1839, VMI is today the sole single-sex school among Virginia's 15 public institutions of higher learning. VMI's distinctive mission is to produce "citizen-soldiers," men prepared for leadership in civilian life and in military service. VMI pursues this mission through pervasive training of a kind not available anywhere else in Virginia. Assigning prime place to character development, VMI uses an "adversative method" modeled on English public schools and once characteristic of military instruction. VMI constantly endeavors to instill physical and mental discipline in its cadets and impart to them a strong moral code. The school's graduates leave VMI with heightened comprehension of their capacity to deal with duress and stress, and a large sense of accomplishment for completing the hazardous course.

VMI has notably succeeded in its mission to produce leaders; among its alumni are military generals, Members of Congress, and business executives. The school's alumni overwhelmingly perceive that their VMI training helped them to realize their personal goals. VMI's endowment reflects the loyalty of its graduates; VMI has the largest per-student endowment of all public undergraduate institutions in the Nation.

United States v. Virginia et al., United States Supreme Court, Certiorari to the United States Court of Appeals for the Fourth Circuit. No. 94-1941. Argued January 17, 1996—Decided June 26, 1996. (Opinion of Justice Ruth Bader Ginsburg for the majority.)

Neither the goal of producing citizen-soldiers nor VMI's implementing methodology is inherently unsuitable to women. And the school's impressive record in producing leaders has made admission desirable to some women. Nevertheless, Virginia has elected to preserve exclusively for men the advantages and opportunities a VMI education affords. . . .

IV. We note, once again, the core instruction of this Court's pathmarking decisions in *J.E.B. v. Alabama ex rel. T.B.*, 511 U.S. 127, 136–137, and n. 6 (1994), and *Mississippi Univ. for Women*, 458 U.S., at 724: Parties who seek to defend gender-based government action must demonstrate an "exceedingly persuasive justification" for that action.

Today's skeptical scrutiny of official action denying rights or opportunities based on sex responds to volumes of history. As a plurality of this Court acknowledged a generation ago, "our nation has had a long and unfortunate history of sex discrimination." *Frontiero v. Richardson*, 411 U.S. 677, 684 (1973). Through a century plus three decades and more of that history, women did not count among voters composing "We the People;" not until 1920 did women gain a constitutional right to the franchise. And for a half century thereafter, it remained the prevailing doctrine that government, both federal and state, could withhold from women opportunities accorded men so long as any "basis in reason" could be conceived for the discrimination. . . .

In 1971, for the first time in our nation's history, this Court ruled in favor of a woman who complained that her state had denied her the equal protection of its laws. *Reed v. Reed*, 404 U.S. 71, 73. . . . Since Reed, the Court has repeatedly recognized that neither federal nor state government acts compatibly with the equal protection principle when a law or official policy denies to women, simply because they are women, full citizenship stature—equal opportunity to aspire, achieve, participate in and contribute to society based on their individual talents and capacities. . . .

To summarize the Court's current directions for cases of official classification based on gender: Focusing on the differential treatment or denial of opportunity for which relief is sought, the reviewing court must determine whether the proffered justification is "exceedingly persuasive." The burden of justification is demanding and it rests entirely on the State. See *Mississippi Univ. for Women*, 458 U.S., at 724. The State must show "at least that the [challenged] classification serves 'important governmental objectives and that the discriminatory means employed' are 'substantially related to the achievement of those objectives.'" (quoting *Wengler v. Druggists Mut. Ins. Co.*, 446 U.S. 142, 150 (1980). The justification must be genuine, not hypothesized or invented *post hoc* in response to litigation. And it must not rely on overbroad generalizations about the different talents, capacities, or preferences of males and females. See *Weinberger v. Wiesenfeld*, 420 U.S. 636, 643, 648 (1975); *Califano v. Goldfarb*, 430 U.S. 199, 223–224 (1977) (STEVENS, J., concurring in judgment).

The heightened review standard our precedent establishes does not make sex a proscribed classification. Supposed "inherent differences" are no longer accepted as a ground for race or national origin classifications. See *Loving v. Virginia*, 388 U.S. 1 (1967). Physical differences between men and women, however, are enduring: "[T]he two sexes are not fungible; a community made up exclusively of one [sex] is different from a community composed of both." *Ballard v. United States*, 329 U.S. 187, 193 (1946).

"Inherent differences" between men and women, we have come to appreciate, remain cause for celebration, but not for denigration of the members of either sex or for artificial constraints on an individual's opportunity. Sex classifications may be used to compensate women "for particular economic disabilities [they have] suffered," *Califano v. Webster*, 430 U.S. 313, 320 (1977) (per curiam), to "promot[e] equal employment opportunity . . ." to advance full development of the talent and capacities of our nation's people. But such classifications may not be used, as they once were . . . to create or perpetuate the legal, social, and economic inferiority of women.

Measuring the record in this case against the review standard just described, we conclude that Virginia has shown no "exceedingly persuasive justification" for excluding all women from the citizen-soldier training afforded by VMI. We therefore affirm the Fourth Circuit's initial judgment, which held that Virginia had violated the Fourteenth Amendment's Equal Protection Clause. Because the remedy proffered by Virginia—the Mary Baldwin VWIL program—does not cure the constitutional violation, *i.e.*, it does not provide equal opportunity, we reverse the Fourth Circuit's final judgment in this case. . . .

V. . . . Neither recent nor distant history bears out Virginia's alleged pursuit of diversity through single sex options. In 1839, when the Commonwealth established VMI, a range of educational opportunities for men and women was scarcely contemplated. Higher education at the time was considered dangerous for women; reflecting widely held views about women's proper place, the nation's first universities and colleges—for example, Harvard in Massachusetts, William and Mary in Virginia—admitted only men. . . . In 1879, the State Senate resolved to look into the possibility of higher education for women, recognizing that Virginia "'has never, at any period of her history,'" provided for the higher education of her daughters, though she "'has liberally provided for the higher education of her sons.'" . . . Despite this recognition, no new opportunities were instantly open to women. . . .

Debate concerning women's admission as undergraduates at the main university continued well past the century's midpoint. Familiar arguments were rehearsed. If women were admitted, it was feared, they "would encroach on the rights of men; there would be new problems of government, perhaps scandals; the old honor system would have to be changed; standards would be lowered to those of other coeducational schools; and the glorious reputation of the university, as a school for men, would be trailed in the dust."

Ultimately, in 1970, "the most prestigious institution of higher education in

Virginia," the University of Virginia, introduced coeducation and, in 1972, began to admit women on an equal basis with men. . . .

In sum, we find no persuasive evidence in this record that VMI's male-only admission policy "is in furtherance of a state policy of 'diversity.'" No such policy, the Fourth Circuit observed, can be discerned from the movement of all other public colleges and universities in Virginia away from single-sex education. That court also questioned "how one institution with autonomy, but with no authority over any other state institution, can give effect to a state policy of diversity among institutions." A purpose genuinely to advance an array of educational options, as the Court of Appeals recognized, is not served by VMI's historic and constant plan—a plan to "affor[d] a unique educational benefit only to males." However "liberally" this plan serves the Commonwealth's sons, it makes no provision whatever for her daughters. That is not *equal* protection.

Virginia next argues that VMI's adversative method of training provides educational benefits that cannot be made available, unmodified, to women. Alterations to accommodate women would necessarily be "radical," so "drastic," Virginia asserts, as to transform, indeed "destroy," VMI's program. . . .

The United States does not challenge any expert witness estimation on average capacities or preferences of men and women. Instead, the United States emphasizes that time and again since this Court's turning point decision in *Reed v. Reed*, 404 U.S. 71 (1971), we have cautioned reviewing courts to take a "hard look" at generalizations or "tendencies" of the kind pressed by Virginia, and relied upon by the District Court. State actors controlling gates to opportunity, we have instructed, may not exclude qualified individuals based on "fixed notions concerning the roles and abilities of males and females." *Mississippi Univ. for Women*, 458 U.S., at 725; (equal protection principles, as applied to gender classifications, mean state actors may not rely on "overbroad" generalizations to make "judgments about people that are likely to . . . perpetuate historical patterns of discrimination").

It may be assumed, for purposes of this decision, that most women would not choose VMI's adversative method. As Fourth Circuit Judge Motz observed, however, in her dissent from the Court of Appeals' denial of rehearing *en banc*, it is also probable that "many men would not want to be educated in such an environment." (On that point, even our dissenting colleague might agree.) Education, to be sure, is not a "one size fits all" business. The issue, however, is not whether "women—or men—should be forced to attend VMI"; rather, the question is whether the Commonwealth can constitutionally deny to women who have the will and capacity, the training and attendant opportunities that VMI uniquely affords.

The notion that admission of women would downgrade VMI's stature, destroy the adversative system and, with it, even the school, is a judgment hardly proved, a prediction hardly different from other "self-fulfilling prophec[ies]," once routinely used to deny rights or opportunities. When women first sought admission to the bar and access to legal education, concerns of the same order were expressed. For example, in 1876, the Court of Common Pleas of Hennepin County, Minnesota, explained why women were thought ineligible for the practice of law. Women train and educate the young, the court said, which "forbids that they shall bestow that time (early and late) and labor, so essential in attaining to the eminence to which the true lawyer should ever aspire. It cannot therefore be said that the opposition of courts to the admission of females to practice . . . is to any extent the outgrowth of . . . 'old fogyism[.]' . . . [I]t arises rather from a comprehension of the magnitude of the responsibilities connected with the successful practice of law, and a desire to *grade* up the profession." A like fear, according to a 1925 report, accounted for Columbia Law School's resistance to women's admission, although "[t]he faculty . . . never maintained that women could not master legal learning. . . . No, its argument has been . . . more practical. If women were admitted to the Columbia Law School, [the faculty] said, then the choicer, more manly and red-blooded graduates of our great universities would go to the Harvard Law School!" *The Nation*, Feb. 18, 1925, p. 173. . . .

Women's successful entry into the federal military academies, and their participation in the nation's military forces, indicate that Virginia's fears for the future of VMI may not be solidly grounded. . . .

The Commonwealth's misunderstanding and, in turn, the District Court's, is apparent from VMI's mission: to produce "citizen-soldiers," individuals "'imbued with love of learning, confident in the functions and attitudes of leadership, possessing a high sense of public service, advocates of the American democracy and free enterprise system, and ready . . . to defend their country in time of national peril.'" 766 F. Supp., at 1425 (quoting Mission Study Committee of the VMI Board of Visitors, Report, May 16, 1986).

Surely that goal is great enough to accommodate women, who today count as citizens in our American democracy equal in stature to men. Just as surely, the Commonwealth's great goal is not substantially advanced by women's categorical exclusion, in total disregard of their individual merit, from the Commonwealth's premier "citizen-soldier" corps. Virginia, in sum, has fallen far short of establishing the "exceedingly persuasive justification," *Mississippi Univ. for Women*, 458 U.S., at 731, that must be the solid base for any gender-defined classification. . . .

VII. . . . VMI, too, offers an educational opportunity no other Virginia institution provides, and the school's "prestige"—associated with its success in developing "citizen-soldiers"—is unequaled. Virginia has closed this facility to its daughters and, instead, has devised for them a "parallel program," with a faculty less impressively credentialed and less well paid, more limited course offerings, fewer opportunities for military training and for scientific specialization. VMI, beyond question, "possesses to a far greater degree" than the VWIL program "those qualities which are incapable of objective measurement but which make for greatness in a . . . school," including "position and influence of the alumni, standing in the community, traditions and prestige." Women seeking and fit for a VMI-quality education cannot be offered anything less, under the Commonwealth's obligation to afford them genuinely equal protection.

A prime part of the history of our Constitution, historian Richard Morris recounted, is the story of the extension of constitutional rights and protections to people once ignored or excluded. VMI's story continued as our comprehension of "We the People" expanded. There is no reason to believe that the admission of women capable of all the activities required of VMI cadets would destroy the Institute rather than enhance its capacity to serve the "more perfect Union."

FOR FURTHER READING

Rosen, Jeffrey. "The New Look of Liberalism on the Court." *The New York Times Magazine* (5 October 1977): 60–65, 86, 90, 96.

Ruth Behar

1956–

Ruth Behar, through her work as a feminist anthropologist, is creating a new methodology and a new rhetoric for writing research. Within a field where "objective" empirical research is often seen as the most legitimate form of data gathering, analysis, and theorizing, Behar bravely and unapologetically subverts that model and defends anthropology that does not uphold the pretense of detachment but that instead, in Dorothy Allison's words, takes "the reader by the throat [and] break[s] her heart."

Behar's mestiza heritage provided her with a clear understanding that some things cannot be represented with generalizations, numbers, and data collection. She is a Cuban-born Jew who is often seen as a "white woman," but whom institutions often count/tally/empirically represent as a "woman of color." Like the work of Patricia Williams in law and of Evelyn Fox Keller in science, Behar's feminist anthropological methodology demands that the researcher carefully and completely articulate his or her social, political, and economic locations in relation to the individual(s) and cultures being researched. In her book *Translated Woman*, a study in which Behar chronicles the life and culture of Esperanza, a rural Mexican woman, Behar carefully examines the power relationships and assumptions associated with researcher/subject and the inherent object/subject dichotomies and connections that exist between her and Esperanza. In her narrative about her research Behar creates a form of cultural interpretation that identifies the assumptions and power relationships that are often hidden in more traditional empirical research. In *The Vulnerable Observer*, she creates a more careful model for acknowledging the connections between researcher and researched, a model of a self-to-self relationship rather than a self-to-other relationship, one that is rigorous but not disinterested.

In the essay "Anthropology That Breaks Your Heart," Behar presents an anthropological and rhetorical analysis of a particular rhetorical moment in her career as an academic anthropologist, the culmination of a personal and professional journey she had undertaken over several years. The essay explores the most fundamental questions concerning knowledge, truth, and academic research, the role of subjectivity, and the personal lives of scholars involved in research. She brings readers with her into the "culture" of an academic conference, at which emotion and subjective feeling are the contested subjects. We are present with her as she shows us the room in which she speaks, describes what she is wearing ("I have put on a red knit top"), and then, within the essay, presents her speech with reflective commentary that brings us into the drama and tension of the moment. The persuasive argument within her narrative demonstrates how emotion—in this instance grief over a terrible loss—came to produce a critical interpretation that an "objective" analysis would not have made possible. Her research, documented in *Translated Woman* and *The Vulnerable Observer*, creates a new method of interpreting culture, rigorously but not disinterestedly, a method that acknowledges and even welcomes intersubjectivity in research and demands a new rhetorical form, one that embraces the roles of pathos and catharsis in the making of knowledge.

"Anthropology That Breaks Your Heart"

1996

When I sit down to make my stories I know very well that I want to take the reader by the throat, break her heart, and heal it again. With that intention I cannot sort out myself, say this part is for the theorist, this for the poet, this for the editor, and this for the wayward ethnographer who only wants to document my experience.
—Dorothy Allison, *Skin: Talking About Sex, Class, and Literature*

But, you may say, if I don't want to be in Texas, why am I here before a lectern in a hotel where the chandelier dangles by a thread? I don't know if it's the immigrant in me or the neurotic in me, but I am like that. Although I am here, I imagine there is somewhere else I ought to be instead. And so I don't stop tormenting myself: Is this where the voyage through the long tunnel leads? Is this why my parents left Cuba?

I should try, as the Vietnamese Buddhist monk Thich Nhat Hanh urges, to dwell in the present moment. As he says, we ought not "to sacrifice the journey for the sake of the arrival." So I remind myself that I am here, at the meeting of the American Ethnological Society, for a very good reason: to defend the kind of anthropology that matters to me. It is important to me that the meeting, this year, is organized by a Chicano anthropologist, José Limón; that the incoming president of the American Ethnological Society, Renato Rosaldo, is also a Chicano anthropologist; that Latina/Latino anthropologists are (maybe for the first and last time) highly visible in the program; and that the theme of all our discussions is the border.

I am here because I am a woman of the border: between places, between identities, between languages, between cultures, between longings and illusions, one foot in the academy and one foot out. But I am also here because I have an intellectual debt to the Chicano critique of anthropology and the crea-

From *The Vulnerable Observer: Anthropology that Breaks Your Heart,* by Ruth Behar ©1996 by Ruth Behar. Reprinted by permission of Beacon Press, Boston.

tive writing of Chicana authors. Beginning with Américo Paredes, it was Chicano and Chicana critics—not the Nuer—who turned around the anthropological mirror, questioning the way they had been represented by outsiders and offering their own, more complex and more lacerating representations, which made salient the question of who has the authority to speak for whom. It was the Chicano critique that wryly brought home the brutal role of subjectivity in cultural interpretation by pointing to the unreality and, even worse, the humorlessness of accounts written by Anglo anthropologists, who failed to understand when the natives were joking and when they were speaking seriously, and so produced parodies of the societies they intended to describe. In turn, it was Chicana poets and writers who created new self-representations that not only included feminism but put the border on the map for all Latinas.

I say I am here to "defend" the kind of anthropology that matters to me, which suggests that it is under attack. That may be too strong a way to put it, but lately there is tremendous anxiety that anthropology is becoming "activist art" overrun by "interpretive virtuosos." And it is no exaggeration to say that anthropology is going through another terrible identity crisis. There have been crises before, about anthropology's complicity with conquest, with colonialism, with functionalism, with realist forms of representation, with racism, with male domination. But the discipline has always managed to weather the storms and come out stronger, more inclusive, at once more vexed and more sure of itself.

This time, however, it may not recover so easily. There are serious problems. Many of them. For one thing, anthropology has lost exclusive rights over the culture concept, which was its birthright. The culture concept is now invoked not only across the disciplines, but far beyond the academy in an increasingly global society that is at pains to understand its various multiculturalisms. Even anthropology's second-fiddle genre, the ethnography, has become the newly beloved form of a vast range of scholars, writers, artists, dancers, filmmakers, and talk show hosts. In our time, in this special period, this *periodo especial,* where bearing testimony and witnessing offer the only, and still slippery, hold on truth, every form of representation must pay homage to its roots in the ethnographic experience of talking, listening, transcribing, translating, and interpreting.

All this, you would think, should make anthropologists proud of themselves. How amazing—our vision of the world is actually *wanted* by the world. What incredible foresight we had, right? But the problem with such "appropriations" is that they threaten to leave anthropology without a place to hang its hat in the academy. The role that anthropology departments used to play as melting pots of vagabonds doing research in out-of-the-way places, where no one else wanted to go, is lately being filled by international institutes and area studies programs. And now that anthropologists have largely abandoned their old role as experts on the "origins" of our modern discontents, and too many of us are doing research at home, is there anything left that makes us unique? Has anthropology finally become dispensable?

The critics of the kind of anthropology that matters to me claim that the price anthropology must pay to survive into the next century is to become science, or risk becoming nothing. Anthropology has always stood uneasily on the border between the humanities and the sciences. But in recent years there are more anthropologists—and interested outsiders—who want to place the discipline squarely within the territory of science. It is not too late, they say. Anthropology can be "reconquered" if its "grotesque tendencies"—postmodernist, feminist, relativist, multiculturalist—are reined in and anthropologists are enjoined "to abandon the pleasures of subjective narrativity for the fuddy-duddy rigors of empirical and statistical research."

Clearly, there are important strategic reasons to induce anthropologists to re-fashion the discipline in ways that would allow it to pass better as science. Consider, as the 1994 Survey of Departments puts it, that "academic anthropology is a small discipline spread thinly across the land," with "only 16% of the nation's 2,157 colleges and universities presently offer[ing] an anthropology degree." Add to that the fact that, "in the academy, anthropology's size means that its programs are more vulnerable to changes than those of large disciplines, such as biology, psychology and history."

Anthropology, what a vulnerable observer you are! You may well have to jump into the arms of the scientists if you are going to try to keep your grass hut in the academy.

But, you remind me, I am not in Texas to address anthropology's seduction by the scientists. No, I am here on a different mission—to defend the kind of anthropology that matters to me from the surprisingly ruthless criticism of the humanists.

The four panelists have spoken and now I must take the stage. I am to play the role of discussant. This means I must come up with something brilliant to say about some ordinary academic papers. Something dramatic. In only 15 minutes. To help my cause, I have put on a red knit top, a long tight black skirt, and high-heeled sandals that tie at the ankles. I feel daring, ready for a bullfight, and just a little dizzy. I stayed up almost the entire night worrying and writing, re-writing and worrying, a woman in a hotel room in Texas, listening to the graceful waltz of my husband and son breathing in their sleep. I begin, in that academic voice I have learned to turn on and off, like a faucet:

> "The essays you have heard today are grappling, in different ways, with the fundamental shift that has taken place in anthropology in the last decade—the shift toward viewing identification, rather than difference, as the key defining image of our theory and practice. Our classical dichotomies of Self and Other, Subject and Object, the West and the Rest have become hopelessly inadequate in the face of feminist and minority cultural critiques, the growing strength of

various forms of 'native' anthropology, and the increasing borderization of our world. Yet the shift toward an intersubjective, Self-Self relation challenges the boundaries of anthropological discourse and raises some crucial questions: Is the turn toward identification going to lead us to ever more insular forms of anthropology? Even to anthropology's demise? On the other hand, on a less apocalyptic note, couldn't we say that the new focus on the possibilities and limits of identification is making anthropology finally and truly possible by leading us toward greater depth of understanding, greater depth of feeling about those whom we write about? Of course, 'feeling' is one of the subjects being contested in the presentations by literary critics Scott Michaelson and David Johnson, which urge us—not without feeling, I would add—to reconsider the role of the emotions not only in contemporary anthropology but in the academy and in cultural politics. This question of feeling, in turn, is related to the issues raised by the two anthropologists on the panel. To Jane Adams's question—to whom do we speak? And to Glen Perice's concern about the anxieties embedded in the relationships we form with our co-conspirators in the field. How might we speak so that we won't sell out to the dominant powers? Can we speak in a way that matters, in a way that will drive a wedge into the thick mud of business as usual?

I look around the room. It is still quite early in the morning but there isn't a seat available. People are even standing in the back. The silence in the room is thick and heavy. Here and there, tucked among strangers, I see the familiar faces of colleagues, students, friends. I try to meet their gaze, to somehow show in a quick glance that I am grateful they have come, that I will do my best not to disappoint them. In those milliseconds when I am catching my breath, my eyes are scouring the entire room, trying to find him. The person I hope will hear these words . . . No, he's not here . . . It must be too painful . . . But still I wish . . . I turn to the far right corner and see Jose Limón, who looks more than a little apprehensive. But I look firmly in his direction and continue:

"When José Limón asked me to be the discussant for this panel, he warned me that the critique of Renato Rosaldo's work, from what he could gather of the abstracts, promised to be quite severe, even discomforting. Did I want to take it on? I didn't hesitate for a minute. If there was a strong challenge out there to Renato Rosaldo's work, and especially to his 'Grief and a Headhunter's Rage,' I needed to know about it. For me, 'Grief and a Headhunter's Rage' is a classical work of vulnerable writing carried out in the service of attaining the most profound ethnographic empathy possible. In that essay, Rosaldo asserts that he only came to fully understand the meaning of the rage in grief, which characterizes Ilongot headhunting in the Philippines, after the sudden tragic death of his wife, the anthropologist Michelle Zimbalist Rosaldo, while they were in the field. By courageously writing from his own grief, Renato Rosaldo returned to anthropology at a time when no return seemed possible."

I glance up and see Gabriel waving to me from the back of the room. What a wonderfully bright-eyed boy, a wonderfully long-legged boy. I wink at him and smile. He waves again, and as he leaves the room with David, I want to throw an invisible net around him, to protect him from all wounds, all hurts, all fears, all sadnesses. I think of Michelle Rosaldo, falling from the cliff to her death. Michelle was on her way to look over a new fieldwork site. She had good strong legs. She wasn't afraid. She expected to be back before nightfall. Renato had stayed in the old site with their two young sons. She told him to get the kids ready for bed. She'd be back to read them a story. But on the cliff, she lost her footing. And they came to tell Renato. And it was Renato who had to go find her at the bottom of the cliff. And yell at her for dying and not saying good-bye. And take her broken body to her Jewish grave in New York. And leave the Philippines. Leave and not return. And mourn. Mourn. By himself. For a long time. And then mourn with the Ilongots. In memory. With hindsight. And then mourn with other anthropologists, by writing an essay, unheard of until then in the history of anthropology, that is nothing less than an act of *shivah*—"to dwell with loss, to recover one's poverty, to be linked together in the presence of those absent and to give them . . . an everlasting name."

"This is, obviously, a timely moment to discuss Renato Rosaldo's work in all its complexity and contradictions. As Renato now becomes president of the American Ethnological Society, his essay 'Grief and a Headhunter's Rage' marks its 12th anniversary. Indeed, that essay was first delivered at a meeting of the American Ethnological Society. It is an essay that marked a turning point, not only for Rosaldo himself, but for anthropology, and certainly it deserves a most careful and engaged reading. I am grateful to Scott Michaelson and David Johnson for beginning that reading in their papers, and more generally for seeking to expand the boundaries of literary discourse by turning their analytical lens to an anthropological text. I welcome them to this meeting and hope their presence signals the beginning of more exchanges between anthropologists and literary critics."

I immediately feel foolish, like a hostess at the garden party of anthropology welcoming the foreign guests from the land of literary criticism and trying to put them at their ease. I try to smile in the direction of Michaelson and Johnson who glance back at me indifferently.

"Yet I disagree with many, indeed most, of the ways in which Michaelson and Johnson read Rosaldo's work. They accuse Rosaldo of ushering in a 'new sentimentalism' that is actually an old sentimentalism, says Michaelson, based in 19th-century Victorian women's culture, and anachronistic 'in the late twentieth century . . . after decades of Freudianisms, structuralisms, and post-structuralisms.' He feels—or rather thinks—that scholars in literature and anthropology are returning to questions that absorbed Nathaniel Hawthorne and

Harriet Beecher Stowe, returning to universal humanist thinking. Johnson, in turn, finds suspect the recent turn toward viewing 'the former "objects" of ethnographical inquiry, cultural others, as being like us, subjects.' He feels—or rather thinks—that this trend toward doing away with the ideology of the transcendental observer is giving personal experience too much weight in ethnography. The difficulty is that personal experience, in his view, 'is what no one would be obliged to believe, to trust, perhaps not even to concede.'

"Although both Michaelson and Johnson read Rosaldo attentively, they have curiously chosen to disregard one of his central points—namely, the key role that the position of the observer in social analysis, including, I would think, literary analysis. Let me put it more colloquially: I want to know where Michaelson and Johnson are coming from. What is at stake for them in their critiques? I can only begin to guess at an answer to that question, since neither of them are reflexive about their own intellectual process and criticism. But reading them with feminist eyes, I am struck by the obvious—that here we have two men criticizing the work of another man who has made himself extremely vulnerable while refusing to make themselves vulnerable in how they read him. It is difficult not to invoke Harold Bloom and the anxiety of influence. It is difficult not to see the Michaelson/Johnson critique in terms of the quintessential drama of the male writer's Oedipal slaying of powerful male literary precursors. It is difficult not to see in these critiques the desire of two young scholars to get 'a head' by decapitating a father—it would not, alas, be the first case of headhunting in the academy."

I know I'm being clever, even obnoxiously clever. Michaelson and Johnson look straight ahead, past me, past the audience.

"My interpretation is further complicated by the fact that Renato is a literary father who is self-consciously taking on feminist, even 'feminine' positions. He is cross-dressing as it were. In *Culture and Truth*, he is explicit in his critique of Max Weber's 'manly' ethic, which, as he puts it, 'underestimates the analytical possibilities of "womanly weaknesses" and "unmanly states," such as rage, feebleness, frustration, depression, embarrassment, and passion.' Daring to speak of his sorrow, of his loss, his rage, daring, yes, to privilege sentiments, he dares to be 'feminine'—that is, feminine in the terms of our cultural logic and the way we ascribe genders to our writing. And immediately the sons come along to chastise him for not being macho enough."

Here I pause. I think I can drink something now, at this moment. But then I remember that I left my glass of ice water at the far end of the podium where I was sitting. I must keep going with a dry throat.

"The chastising is carried out in the name of Michelle Zimbalist Rosaldo. Michaelson writes that Renato views mourning as something that cannot be collapsed within ritual 'because emotions are primary, real, and fundamentally human.' Yet, with an almost wicked sense of righteousness, he points out that, in contrast, 'Michelle argues that emotions are produced in the first place through the mechanisms of routine and ritual.' He concludes, cruelly, I think, that Michelle's death 'finally permits' Renato 'to critique her.' And to wound just a little more, he adds that Michelle's death gives Renato a newfound sense of ethnographic authority, a sense that he is 'capable of feeling everything the Ilongot do. He recognizes their emotions, including their anger, within himself . . . The experience of "rage" in grief is the same for both the Ilongot and Renato Rosaldo.' Johnson follows the same harsh path in his criticism. He insists that, regardless of the new turn toward subjectivity, 'anthropology needs an object' and that 'object' is Michelle Rosaldo's dead body. Her 'inert body guarantees the immediate repositioning of the subject, of the I of ethnography . . . Over her dead body anthropology finds itself.' Listening to these crude words—especially for many here in the audience who knew Michelle Rosaldo—is terribly painful. One wants to mourn the use of such language, which resuscitates Michelle Rosaldo only to kill her for a second time. Yet both Michaelson and Johnson, I want to believe, have to believe, are trying desperately to imagine 'Grief and a Headhunter's Rage' from Michelle Rosaldo's perspective. I think they are sincere in feeling compelled to try to hear her voice, in defending the anthropology for which she stood, in seeking to keep the memory of her work alive."

My pulse is starting to race. I'm going to say what I've been holding back, what I think I've now earned the right to say after speaking intelligently and cleverly.

"Michelle Rosaldo's death had a huge impact on me. I was a graduate student, just back from a year of fieldwork in northern Spain, when news of her death reached us at Princeton. It terrified me. Gave me nightmares. I'd heard Michelle Rosaldo speak at Princeton just a year before—"

What I remember is this: she sat in the front of the long seminar table, patiently peeling an orange and eating it, segment by segment, as she spoke, and she caught my glance once and held it, hard, and I thought, she's not tender, she's of that generation of women that didn't get anything easy, and afterward I didn't try talking to her, I felt too weak, too uncertain about everything.

"And I thought—how could such a strong woman, such an important feminist anthropologist, die? And die like that, in the field, in that place charged with so much symbolism, that place where we, as women, become 'honorary males' and thus *macha* enough to gain acceptance into the anthropology club, which is so profoundly rooted in male quests and male musings about foreign lands?"

Yes, that was what had scared me most: that you could die doing fieldwork, that the danger of dying was real, because fieldwork is about nothing more primitive than confronting, with our contemporaries, our own mortality.

"We can only begin to imagine what direction feminist anthropology might have taken if Michelle Rosaldo were still alive today. And yet I don't think that Michaelson and Johnson do any service to Michelle Rosaldo in their efforts to resurrect her and pit her work on the emotions against the work of her grieving husband. The agency they grant her is patronizing, at best. And, at worst, Michaelson and Johnson are disrespectful and insensitive in the way they speak about her as merely a body. Renato, it seems to me, never, never does that— rather, in the process of mourning and healing he incorporates aspects of Michelle's life and work into his own life and work, including her feminism, her attention to the language of emotion, her concern to bridge the border between the private and the public. We must honor the dead, never walk on their tombs if we can help it."

Once, at Michigan, on my way to my office, on an especially gloomy day, I'd stopped and stared at the skulls in the paleoanthropology lab. Like a medieval ascetic, I brought my face close to a skull and pondered my own dissolution and thought of the legacy of the intellectual discipline to which I'd attached myself, this discipline which is so wrapped up with graves, with tombstones, with burial practices, with scraping away at layers upon layers of dead civilizations, with offerings left to those who are no longer with us, this discipline which, as Claude Levi-Strauss put it in *Tristes Tropiques,* that most melancholy of ethnographies, is "so tormented by remorse." Too often, when people find out I'm an anthropologist, they ask: "Have you dug up any interesting bones lately?"

"'Grief and a Headhunter's Rage' is itself a kind of tomb, a memorial to Michelle Zimbalist Rosaldo, and we must tread on it lightly. That essay, it seems to me, clearly marks the end of Rosaldo's sojourn as an anthropologist in the Philippines. Forced to part with Michelle, he also parts ways with the Ilongot, though he holds on to them both emotionally and intellectually. But that ending also marks a new beginning, a threshold for Renato, a return home. It is only after 'Grief and a Headhunter's Rage' that Renato comes out actively as a Chicano intellectual and develops his position as a theorist of the meaning of citizenship in the United States. He didn't do his research in the Philippines from a Chicano borderlands perspective, but rather from the perspective of a Harvard trained anthropologist, very much influenced by a classical concept of culture which could only speak of natives in native lands, a concept of culture which was still inarticulate about borders. Anthropologists would only become articulate about borders thanks to the writing of Chicanas like Gloria Anzaldúa and Sandra Cisneros—who had to invent their own borderland anthropology in poetry, myths, and fictions because it didn't exist in the academy."

No, he hasn't come . . . There's too much pain. I think I understand, but I don't. I still wish . . . Later, they will tell me he sat in the lobby, alone, while I spoke.

"In my view, it isn't an accident that the effort to engage with the emotions in current anthropological and feminist writing follows upon Freudianisms, structuralisms, and poststructuralisms. I think what we are seeing are efforts to map an intermediate space we can't quite define yet, a borderland between passion and intellect, analysis and subjectivity, ethnography and autobiography, art and life. Consider, for example, the debate around Bill T. Jones's dance work 'Still/Here,' which was sparked by Arlene Croce's *New Yorker* essay where she announced she had refused to see the work on the grounds that his use of dancing inspired by the movements of HIV positive dancers and video testimony by AIDS patients turned the art of dance into 'victim art,' a 'traveling medicine show.' As Homi Bhabha notes, what disturbs Croce about so-called 'victim art' is that its effect is 'to solicit sympathy and collusion, rather than disinterested critical reading.' The anxiety around such work is that it will prove to be beyond criticism, that it will be undiscussable. But the real problem is that we need other forms of criticism, which are rigorous yet not disinterested; forms of criticism which are not immune to catharsis, forms of criticism which can respond vulnerably, in ways we must begin to try to imagine."

On an airplane, a few months later—coming back from a conference in San Francisco about women's health, where I think I made myself extremely vulnerable by talking about my panic episode—I will sit next to a woman from Detroit whose mother was murdered. "Your mother murdered!" I will say, in a voice cracking with astonishment rather than with compassion. Yes, by the newspaper boy. Shot her. He was on drugs. I will look at the woman's face and ask: "But aren't you enraged? How do you live with the loss of your mother? How do you live with the fact that her murderer is still alive?" And she will say to me: "I belong to a group called Murder Victims Families for Reconciliation. I am against the death penalty. I have traveled up and down the California coast, talking to legislators, talking to victims, talking to teachers, teaching that you can't solve violence with more violence. You must forgive." This woman, I will think, is another angel in my path. Mourning, she reminds me, "is not replacing the dead but making a place for something else to be in relation to the past . . . We bring the past to the present, we allow ourselves to experience what we have lost, and also what we are—that we are—despite this loss." The Ilongot, as I have learned from Renato Rosaldo, don't forgive. What they don't forgive is death. No, death cannot be forgiven. Can I be horribly honest? I am afraid. Too afraid to even imagine a headhunt.

"Michaelson asks: 'Of what value are sorrow and tears? How can one put them to use for purposes of a life politics?' Let me try to answer what is perhaps intended to be nothing more than a rhetorical question, a question for which no answer is really desired. I think of the film *Shoah*, which is a working through of sorrow, because all the tears have already been cried. Claude Lanzmann's aim is not to present gruesome images from the past, but to grapple with the impossibility of telling the story of the Holocaust. His effort is to 'screen loss.' He wants to make 'present in the film the absence of the dead.' Lanzmann returns with his camera to the prosaic sites where Jews passed from the normal world to the world of the camp. He goes back to the station building, the rails, the platforms, which are just as they were in 1942, not changed at all. 'I needed that,' Lanzmann says, 'a permanence of iron, of steel. I needed to attach myself to it.' He films survivors crossing the line between the world of the camp and the rest of the world. He films the distance, between present and past, the living and the dead. 'They can cross over, but neither they nor we are anywhere but in the present.'"

No, we are nowhere but in the present. And I am here, in Texas, where I didn't think I wanted to be, but since I am here, I take a deep breath, and smile, and take joy that I am alive, and like a melodramatic soap opera star or maybe a country-western singer with a taut guitar, I look my audience in the eye and get ready to belt out those words I wrote very late at night when I was very tired and just wanted to get to sleep and forget everything. And I say:

"Call it sentimental, call it Victorian and 19th century, but I say that anthropology that doesn't break your heart just isn't worth doing anymore."

And I mean it. Really mean it. Because my heart is broken. Because the one person I wish had heard me sing this lament for him isn't here. Can't be here.

FOR FURTHER READING

Behar, Ruth. *Santa Maria Del Monte: The Presence of the Past in a Spanish Village.* Princeton: Princeton University Press, 1986.

——. *Translated Woman.* Boston: Beacon Press, 1993.

——, ed. *Bridges to Cuba.* Ann Arbor: University of Michigan Press, 1995.

Behar, Ruth, and Deborah A. Gordon, eds. *Women Writing Culture.* Thousand Oaks, Calif.: Sage Publications, 1994.

Gloria Steinem

1934–

In 1971 *Newsweek* placed Gloria Steinem on its cover, proclaiming her "the un-likely guru" of the then-fledgling women's movement. However unfair or un-deserved the other leaders of the movement believed this title to be, *Newsweek*'s proclamation gave the American public a face and a name with which to associ-ate the mainstream and largely white women's movement for the next thirty years. Steinem is the founder of the Ms. Foundation for Women, the National Women's Political Caucus, and the Coalition of Labor Union Women. In 1993 she was inducted into the National Women's Hall of Fame in Seneca Falls, New York. Because of her celebrity and her untiring work writing, speaking, and act-ing against sexism and racism, historian Miriam Schneir has said, "Gloria Stei-nem has been to the second wave of American feminism what Susan B. An-thony was to the first" (408).

Steinem's parents divorced when she was ten, and she moved with her mother to Toledo, while her older sister, Susan, began college at Smith. Because her mother suffered from severe depression, Steinem found herself struggling in poverty while trying to take care of her mother and their household. With the help of her sister, Steinem left Toledo after high-school graduation to at-tend Smith College. Upon her graduation with honors in 1956, Steinem went to India for two years, where she worked with a group of Ghandi's followers who traveled the country trying to end caste violence, an experience that she de-scribes as one of those "few events that divide our lives into 'before' and 'after'" (Heilbrun 76). She returned to the United States only to realize that few, if any, jobs existed for women journalists interested in covering the serious news of the Vietnam War or the Civil Rights Movement. Instead, as a "girl reporter" she was assigned stories about fashion or the wives of political figures. Unsatisfied with this work, Steinem freelanced on the side and eventually was able to sup-port herself as a contributor to magazines like *Esquire* and *Glamour*. Perhaps the best-known piece from this stage of her career is the 1963 article, "I Was a Play-boy Bunny," which describes her undercover experience in "an underpaid wait-ressing job in a torturing costume." Steinem's career flourished as she became a contributing editor and guest columnist for *New York Magazine*, which not only gave her license to choose her stories but also provided her a forum in which to write about the developing women's movement.

In 1972 Steinem cofounded *Ms.* magazine, which was welcomed by many feminists as the first mass-market magazine addressing feminist issues. It was also criticized by some feminists for pandering to audiences and appealing to sentimental notions of sisterhood. Regardless of these criticisms, the publication of *Ms.* revolutionized industry conceptions of advertising and gender. But the magazine always struggled financially, largely because *Ms.* refused to accommodate advertisers by tailoring its content to their products. From 1978–87, *Ms.* was published as the organ of the Ms. Foundation for Education and Communication, until it was sold and publication suspended. In 1990, Steinem relaunched *Ms.*, this time without advertising. It remains one of only a few magazines to survive on reader support alone. Also in 1972, Steinem organized the Ms. Foundation for Women to support women's causes and provide funds for women's self-help programs. Since its founding, the Ms. Foundation has supported women's shelters, women workers, and women's entrepreneurship, as well as launching the Take Our Daughters to Work Day program in 1993. Steinem considers this foundation to be as important a legacy as the magazine and hopes that its endowment will grow until it becomes the nation's "permanent feminist institution" (Heilbrun 412). The author of three books and many articles, as well as a speaker in great demand, she confronts contemporary issues with a rhetorical strategy that relies on changing readers' perspectives, most recently in her work on aging and against pornography.

Steinem turns her critical gaze to the issue of school shootings in "Supremacy Crimes." Steinem's rhetorical method here relies, first, on the naming of a fact that she says is "buried deep in the culture": most violent crimes are committed by white, non-poor, heterosexual males, a fact obscured and made "invisible" by the culture and by the media's depiction of the Columbine shooters, for example, as "our" children. Then, Steinem begins to ask a series of questions that push readers toward deeper, more specific, and more pointed questions—not, for example, "What's wrong with our society?" but "What's wrong with these boys?" Steinem's answer is "supremacy," which she names as a drug that is "pushed by a male-dominant culture that presents dominance as a natural right" and that results in racism, sexism, and homophobia, which seem to be the catalyst for the shootings. Finally, Steinem uses the rhetorical strategy of stating opposite cases, challenging her readers to examine their own generalities and assumptions about gender, violence, economics, and status. As she does in her other work, here Steinem pushes the media and the U.S. culture to question what they often take as fact. Her admonition to raise both male and female children in more holistic ways, offering to both genders the value of empathy and social consciousness, is a theme that runs throughout Steinem's interviews and books.

"Supremacy Crimes"

1999

You've seen the ocean of television coverage, you've read the headlines: "How to Spot a Troubled Kid," "Twisted Teens," "When Teens Fall Apart."

After the slaughter in Colorado that inspired those phrases, dozens of copycat threats were reported in the same generalized way: "Junior high students charged with conspiracy to kill students and teachers" (in Texas); "Five honor students overheard planning a June graduation bombing" (in New York); "More than 100 minor threats reported statewide" (in Pennsylvania). In response, the White House held an emergency strategy session titled "Children, Violence, and Responsibility." Nonetheless, another attack was soon reported: "Youth With 2 Guns Shoots 6 at Georgia School."

I don't know about you, but I've been talking back to the television set, waiting for someone to tell us the obvious: it's not "youth," "our children," or "our teens." It's our sons—and "our" can usually be read as "white," "middle class," and "heterosexual."

We know that hate crimes, violent and otherwise, are overwhelmingly committed by white men who are apparently straight. The same is true for an even higher percentage of impersonal, resentment-driven, mass killings like those in Colorado; the sort committed for no economic or rational gain except the need to say, "I'm superior because I can kill." Think of Charles Starkweather, who reported feeling powerful and serene after murdering ten women and men in the 1950s; or the shooter who climbed the University of Texas Tower in 1966, raining down death to gain celebrity. Think of the engineering student at the University of Montreal who resented females' ability to study that subject, and so shot to death 14 women students in 1989, while saying, "I'm against feminism." Think of nearly all those who have killed impersonally in the workplace, the post office, McDonald's.

White males—usually intelligent, middle class, and heterosexual, or trying desperately to appear so—also account for virtually all the serial, sexually motivated, sadistic killings, those characterized by stalking, imprisoning, torturing, and "owning" victims in death. Think of Edmund Kemper, who began by killing animals, then murdered his grandparents, yet was released to sexually torture and dismember college students and other young women until he himself decided he "didn't want to kill *all* the coeds in the world." Or David Berkowitz, the Son of Sam, who murdered *some* women in order to feel in control of *all* women. Or consider Ted Bundy, the charming, snobbish young would-be law-

Reprinted with permission from Steinem, Gloria. "Supremacy Crimes." First printed in *Ms. Magazine* (August/September 1999): 45–47.

yer who tortured and murdered as many as 40 women, usually beautiful students who were symbols of the economic class he longed to join. As for John Wayne Gacy, he was obsessed with maintaining the public mask of masculinity, and so hid his homosexuality by killing and burying men and boys with whom he had had sex.

These "senseless" killings begin to seem less mysterious when you consider that they were committed disproportionately by white, non-poor males, the group most likely to become hooked on the drug of superiority. It's a drug pushed by a male-dominant culture that presents dominance as a natural right; a racist hierarchy that falsely elevates whiteness; a materialist society that equates superiority with possessions, and a homophobic one that empowers only one form of sexuality.

As Elliott Leyton reports in *Hunting Humans: The Rise of the Modern Multiple Murderer*, these killers see their behavior as "an appropriate—even 'manly'—response to the frustrations and disappointments that are a normal part of life." In other words, it's not their life experiences that are the problem, it's the impossible expectation of dominance to which they've become addicted.

This is not about blame. This is about causation. If anything, ending the massive cultural cover-up of supremacy crimes should make heroes out of boys and men who reject violence, especially those who reject the notion of superiority altogether. Even if one believes in a biogenetic component of male aggression, the very existence of gentle men proves that socialization can override it.

Nor is this about attributing such crimes to a single cause. Addiction to the drug of supremacy is not their only root, just the deepest and most ignored one. Additional reasons why this country has such a high rate of violence include the plentiful guns that make killing seem as unreal as a video game; male violence in the media that desensitizes viewers in much the same way that combat killers are desensitized in training; affluence that allows maximum access to violence-as-entertainment; a national history of genocide and slavery; the romanticizing of frontier violence and organized crime; not to mention extremes of wealth and poverty and the illusion that both are deserved.

But it is truly remarkable, given the relative reasons for anger at injustice in this country, that white, non-poor men have a near-monopoly on multiple killings of strangers, whether serial and sadistic or mass and random. How can we ignore this obvious fact? Others may kill to improve their own condition—in self-defense, or for money or drugs; to eliminate enemies; to declare turf in drive-by shootings; even for a jacket or a pair of sneakers—but white males addicted to supremacy kill even when it worsens their condition or ends in suicide.

Men of color and females are capable of serial and mass killing, and commit just enough to prove it. Think of Colin Ferguson, the crazed black man on the Long Island Railroad, or Wayne Williams, the young black man in Atlanta who kidnapped and killed black boys, apparently to conceal his homosexuality. Think of Aileen Carol Wuornos, the white prostitute in Florida who killed abusive johns "in self-defense," or Waneta Hoyt, the upstate New York woman who strangled her five infant children between 1965 and 1971, disguising their cause of death as sudden infant death syndrome. Such crimes are rare enough to leave a haunting refrain of disbelief as evoked in Pat Parker's poem "jonestown": "Black folks do not/Black folks do not/Black folks do not commit suicide." And yet they did.

Nonetheless, the proportion of serial killings that are not committed by white males is about the same as the proportion of anorexics who are not female. Yet we discuss the gender, race, and class components of anorexia, but not the role of the same factors in producing epidemics among the powerful.

The reasons are buried deep in the culture, so invisible that only by reversing our assumptions can we reveal them.

Suppose, for instance, that young black males—or any other men of color—had carried out the slaughter in Colorado. Would the media reports be so willing to describe the murderers as "our children"? Would there be so little discussion about the boys' race? Would experts be calling the motive a mystery, or condemning the high school cliques for making those young men feel like "outsiders"? Would there be the same empathy for parents who gave the murderers luxurious homes, expensive cars, even rescued them from brushes with the law? Would there be as much attention to generalized causes, such as the dangers of violent video games and recipes for bombs on the Internet?

As for the victims, if racial identities had been reversed, would racism remain so little discussed? In fact, the killers themselves said they were targeting blacks and athletes. They used a racial epithet, shot a black male student in the head, and then laughed over the fact that they could see his brain. What if *that* had been reversed?

What if these two young murderers, who were called "fags" by some of the jocks at Columbine High School, actually had been gay? Would they have got the same sympathy for being gay-baited? What if they had been lovers? Would we hear as little about their sexuality as we now do, even though only their own homophobia could have given the word "fag" such power to humiliate them?

Take one more leap of the imagination: suppose these killings had been planned and executed by young women—of any race, sexuality, or class. Would the media still be so disinterested in the role played by gender-conditioning? Would journalists assume that female murderers had suffered from being shut out of access to power in high school, so much so that they were pushed beyond their limits? What if dozens, even hundreds of young women around the country had made imitative threats—as young men have done—expressing admiration for a well-planned massacre and promising to do the same? Would we be discussing their youth more than their gender, as is the case so far with these male killers?

I think we begin to see that our national self-examination is ignoring something fundamental, precisely because it's like the air we breathe: the white male factor, the middle-class and heterosexual one, and the promise of superiority it carries. Yet this denial is self-defeating—to say the least. We will never reduce the number of violent Americans, from bullies to killers, without challenging the assumptions on which masculinity is based: that males are superior to females, that they must find a place in a male hierarchy, and that the ability to dominate *someone* is so important that even a mere insult can justify lethal revenge. There are plenty of studies to support this view. As Dr. James Gilligan concluded in *Violence: Reflections on a National Epidemic*, "If humanity is to evolve beyond the propensity toward violence . . . then it can only do so by recognizing the extent to which the patriarchal code of honor and shame generates and obligates male violence."

I think the way out can only be found through a deeper reversal: just as we as a society have begun to raise our daughters more like our sons—more like whole people—we must begin to raise our sons more like our daughters—that is, to value empathy as well as hierarchy; to measure success by other people's welfare as well as their own.

But first, we have to admit and name the truth about supremacy crimes.

FOR FURTHER READING

Heilbrun, Carolyn G. *The Education of a Woman: The Life of Gloria Steinem*. New York: The Dial Press, 1995.

Schneir, Miriam, ed. *Feminism in Our Time*. New York: Vintage Books, 1994.

Steinem, Gloria. "Coming Up: The Unprecedented Woman." *Ms.* (July 1985): 85–86, 106–8.

———. *Moving Beyond Words*. New York: Simon and Schuster, 1994.

———. *Outrageous Acts and Everyday Rebellions*. New York: Holt, Rinehart, and Winston, 1983.

———. "Race and Gender: Charlie Rose Interviews." In *Postmortem: The O. J. Simpson Case: Justice Confronts Race, Domestic Violence, Lawyers, Money, and the Media*, edited by Jeffrey Abramson, 91–104. New York: Basic Books, 1996.

———. *Revolution From Within: A Book of Self-Esteem*. Boston: Little, Brown and Co., 1992.

———. "The Way We Were—And Will Be." *Ms.* (December 1979): 60–94.

Steinem, Gloria, and Patricia Williams. "Hollywood Cleans Up Hustler." *New York Times* (7 January 1997).

We offer this alternative table of contents in order to highlight some of the rhetorical features we believe are most important in studying this emerging body of rhetoric. This table of contents is arranged by rhetorical themes—the occasions on which women speak and write, their claiming of the right to literacy and public voice, their use of traditional forms of evidence and their subversion of traditional means of persuasion, the diverse identities and epistemologies underlying women's rhetorics, as well as women writers on writing itself and the process of achieving literacy. We hope this alternative table of contents will generate other groupings and will assist readers in expanding their reading of women's rhetorics and in inventing their own means of persuasion.

I. Claiming the Right to Speak and Write

Hortensia   16
"Speech to the Triumvirs" (42 B.C.E)   17

Christine de Pizan   32
From *The Book of the City of Ladies* (1404)   33

Margery Kempe   43
From *The Book of Margery Kempe* (1436)   44

Jane Anger   50
From *Jane Anger Her Protection for Women . . .* (1589)   51

Rachel Speght   61
From *A Mouzzel for Melastomus* (1617)   62

Margaret Fell   66
From *Womens Speaking Justified, Proved and Allowed by the Scriptures* (1666)   67

Belinda   89
"Petition of an African Slave" (1782)   90

Sarah Grimké   114
"Letter to Theodore Weld" (1837)   115

Seneca Falls Convention   138
"Declaration of Sentiments and Resolutions" (1848)   139

Sojourner Truth   143
"Speech at the Woman's Rights Convention, Akron, Ohio" (1851)   144

Susan B. Anthony   151
From *The United States of America v. Susan B. Anthony* (1873)   152

Audre Lorde   301
"The Transformation of Silence into Language and Action" (1977)   302

Gloria Anzaldúa   356
"How to Tame a Wild Tongue" (1987)   357

Dorothy Allison   435
From *Two or Three Things I Know for Sure* (1995)   436

II. Claiming the Right to Education

Catherine of Siena   29
"Letter 83: To Mona Lapa, her mother, in Siena" (1376)   30

Christine de Pizan   32
From *The Book of the City of Ladies* (1404)   33

Sor Juana Inés de la Cruz   71
From "La Respuesta" (1691)   72

Mary Astell   79
From *A Serious Proposal to the Ladies* (1694)   80

Lady Mary Wortley Montagu   84
"Letter to Lady Bute" (1753)   85

Mary Wollstonecraft   92
From *A Vindication of the Rights of Woman* (1792)   93

Margaret Fuller   125
From *Woman in the Nineteenth Century* (1845)   126

Anna Julia Cooper   163
"The Higher Education of Women" (1892)   164

Fannie Barrier Williams   179
From "The Intellectual Progress of the Colored Women of the United States
since the Emancipation Proclamation" (1893)   180

Alice Dunbar Nelson   233
"Facing Life Squarely" (1927)   234

Ruth Bader Ginsburg   471
From *United States v. Virginia et al.* (1996)   472

III. Rhetoric as Civic Participation

Hortensia   16
"Speech to the Triumvirs" (42 B.C.E.)   17

Margaret Fell   66
From *Womens Speaking Justified, Proved and Allowed by the Scriptures* (1666)   67

Belinda   89
"Petition of an African Slave" (1782)   90

Mary Wollstonecraft   92
From *A Vindication of the Rights of Woman* (1792)   93

Cherokee Women   106
"Cherokee Women Address Their Nation" (1817)   107

Maria W. Stewart   109
"Lecture Delivered at the Franklin Hall" (1832)   110

Angelina Grimké Weld   119
"Address at Pennsylvania Hall" (1838)   120

Margaret Fuller   125
From *Woman in the Nineteenth Century* (1845)   126

Seneca Falls Convention   138
"Declaration of Sentiments and Resolutions" (1848)   139

Sojourner Truth   143
"Speech at the Woman's Rights Convention, Akron, Ohio" (1851)   144

Susan B. Anthony   151
From *The United States of America v. Susan B. Anthony* (1873)   152

Sarah Winnemucca   157
From *Life Among the Piutes* (1883)   158

Fannie Barrier Williams   179
From "The Intellectual Progress of the Colored Women of the United States since the Emancipation Proclamation" (1893)   180

Ida B. Wells   188
"Lynch Law in All its Phases" (1893)   189

Charlotte Perkins Gilman   204
From *Women and Economics* (1898)   205

Margaret Sanger   223
"Letter to the Readers of *The Woman Rebel*" (1914)   224

Emma Goldman   226
From "Marriage and Love" (1914)   227

Alice Dunbar Nelson   233
"Facing Life Squarely" (1927)   234

Dorothy Day   237
"Memorial Day in Chicago" (1937)   238

Zora Neale Hurston   247
"Crazy for This Democracy" (1945)   248

Rachel Carson   259
"A Fable for Tomorrow" (1962)   260

Fannie Lou Hamer   262
"The Special Plight and the Role of the Black Woman" (1971)   263

Andrea Dworkin   330
"I Want A Twenty-Four Hour Truce During Which There Is No Rape" (1983)
331

June Jordan   366
"Don't You Talk About My Momma!" (1987)   367

Terry Tempest Williams   401
"The Clan of One-Breasted Women" (1991)   402

Patricia Williams   409
"The Death of the Profane" (1991)   410

Ruth Bader Ginsburg   471
From *United States v. Virginia et al.* (1996)   472

Gloria Steinem   489
"Supremacy Crimes" (1999)   491

IV. Rhetorics of Identity

Heloise   20
From "Letter I. Heloise to Abelard" (1132)   21

Christine de Pizan   32
From *The Book of the City of Ladies* (1404)   33

Margery Kempe   43
From *The Book of Margery Kempe* (1436)   44

Queen Elizabeth I   48
"To the Troops at Tilbury" (1588)   49

Jane Anger   50
From *Jane Anger Her Protection for Women* . . . (1589)   51

Rachel Speght   61
From *A Mouzzel for Melastomus* (1617)   62

Mary Astell   79
From *A Serious Proposal to the Ladies* (1694)   80

Lady Mary Wortley Montagu   84
"Letter to Lady Bute" (1753)   85

Mary Wollstonecraft   92
From *A Vindication of the Rights of Woman* (1792)   93

Cherokee Women   106
"Cherokee Women Address Their Nation" (1817)   107

Maria W. Stewart   109
"Lecture Delivered at the Franklin Hall" (1832)   110

Sarah Grimké   114
"Letter to Theodore Weld" (1837)   115

Margaret Fuller   125
From *Woman in the Nineteenth Century* (1845)   126

Sojourner Truth   143
"Speech at the Woman's Rights Convention, Akron, Ohio" (1851)   144

Sarah Winnemucca   157
From *Life Among the Piutes* (1883)   158

Anna Julia Cooper   163
"The Higher Education of Women" (1892)   164

Elizabeth Cady Stanton   171
From "The Solitude of Self" (1892)   172

Fannie Barrier Williams   179
From "The Intellectual Progress of the Colored Women of the United States
since the Emancipation Proclamation" (1893)   180

Charlotte Perkins Gilman   204
From *Women and Economics* (1898)   205

Emma Goldman   226
From "Marriage and Love" (1914)   227

Virginia Woolf   241
"Professions for Women" (1942)   242

Simone de Beauvoir   252
From the Introduction to *The Second Sex* (1952)   253

Fannie Lou Hamer   262
"The Special Plight and the Role of the Black Woman" (1971)   263

Adrienne Rich   267
"When We Dead Awaken: Writing as Re-Vision" (1971)   268

Combahee River Collective   291
"The Combahee River Collective Statement" (1977)   292

Merle Woo   306
"Letter to Ma" (1980)   307

Gloria Anzaldúa   356
"How to Tame a Wild Tongue" (1987)   357

Nancy Mairs   391
"Carnal Acts" (1990)   392

Minnie Bruce Pratt   424
"Gender Quiz" (1995)   425

Dorothy Allison   435
From *Two or Three Things I Know for Sure* (1995)   436

Nomy Lamm   454
"It's a Big Fat Revolution" (1995)   455

V. Rhetorics of Difference

Belinda   89
"Petition of an African Slave" (1782)   90

Cherokee Women   106
"Cherokee Women Address Their Nation" (1817)   107

Maria W. Stewart   109
"Lecture Delivered at the Franklin Hall" (1832)   110

Sojourner Truth   143
"Speech at the Woman's Rights Convention, Akron, Ohio" (1851)   144

Frances Ellen Watkins Harper   147
"We Are All Bound Up Together" (1866)   148

Sarah Winnemucca   157
From *Life Among the Piutes* (1883)   158

Fannie Barrier Williams   179
From "The Intellectual Progress of the Colored Women of the United States
since the Emancipation Proclamation" (1893)   183

Alice Dunbar Nelson   233
"Facing Life Squarely" (1927)   234

Fannie Lou Hamer   268
"The Special Plight and the Role of the Black Woman" (1971)   269

Combahee River Collective   291
"The Combahee River Collective Statement" (1977)   292

Audre Lorde   301
"The Transformation of Silence into Language and Action" (1977)   302

Merle Woo   306
"Letter to Ma" (1980)   307

Gloria Anzaldúa   356
"How to Tame a Wild Tongue" (1987)   357

Nancy Mairs   391
"Carnal Acts" (1990)   392

Minnie Bruce Pratt   424
"Gender Quiz" (1995)   425

Dorothy Allison   435
From *Two or Three Things I Know for Sure* (1995)   436

Nomy Lamm   454
"It's a Big Fat Revolution" (1995)   455

VI. Rhetorics of the Body

Julian of Norwich   25
From *Revelations of Divine Love* (c. 1390s)   26

Queen Elizabeth I   48
"To the Troops at Tilbury" (1588)   49

Sojourner Truth   143
"Speech at the Woman's Rights Convention, Akron, Ohio" (1851)   144

Virginia Woolf   241
"Professions for Women" (1942)   242

Audre Lorde   301
"The Transformation of Silence into Language and Action" (1977)   302

Nancy Mairs   391
"Carnal Acts" (1990)   392

Terry Tempest Williams   401
"The Clan of One-Breasted Women" (1991)   402

Minnie Bruce Pratt   424
"Gender Quiz" (1995)   425

Nomy Lamm   454
"It's a Big Fat Revolution" (1995)   455

Leslie Marmon Silko   462
"Yellow Woman and a Beauty of the Spirit" (1996)   463

VII. Rhetorics of Spirituality

Julian of Norwich   25
From *Revelations of Divine Love* (c. 1390s)   26

Catherine of Siena   29
"Letter 83: To Mona Lapa, her mother, in Siena" (1376)   30

Margery Kempe   43
From *The Book of Margery Kempe* (1436)   44

Sor Juana Inés de la Cruz   71
From "La Respuesta" (1691)   72

Margaret Fell   66
From *Womens Speaking Justified, Proved and Allowed by the Scriptures* (1666)   67

Dorothy Day   237
"Memorial Day in Chicago" (1937)   238

Paula Gunn Allen   340
"Grandmother of the Sun: Ritual Gynocracy in Native America" (1986)   341

Leslie Marmon Silko   462
"Yellow Woman and a Beauty of the Spirit" (1996)   463

VIII. Women's Writing and Language

Margaret Fell   66
From *Womens Speaking Justified, Proved and Allowed by the Scriptures* (1666)   67

Virginia Woolf   241
"Professions for Women" (1942)   242

Adrienne Rich   267
"When We Dead Awaken: Writing as Re-Vision" (1971)   268

Hélène Cixous   283
From "Sorties" (1975)   284

Audre Lorde   301
"The Transformation of Silence into Language and Action" (1977)   302

Alice Walker   314
"In Search of Our Mothers' Gardens" (1983)   315

Gloria Anzaldúa   356
"How to Tame a Wild Tongue" (1987)   357

Trinh T. Minh-ha   377
From *Woman, Native, Other* (1989)   378

Nancy Mairs   391
"Carnal Acts" (1990)   392

Patricia Williams   409
"The Death of the Profane" (1991)   410

Minnie Bruce Pratt   424
"Gender Quiz" (1995)   425

Dorothy Allison 435
From *Two or Three Things I Know for Sure* (1995) 436

Nomy Lamm 454
"It's a Big Fat Revolution" (1995) 455

Leslie Marmon Silko 462
"Yellow Woman and a Beauty of the Spirit" (1996) 463

Ruth Behar 478
"Anthropology That Breaks Your Heart" (1996) 479

IX. Rhetorical Theory

Diotima 9
"On Love" from Plato's *Symposium* (c. 360 B.C.E.) 10

Sor Juana Inés de la Cruz 71
From "La Respuesta" (1691) 72

Margaret Fuller 125
From *Woman in the Nineteenth Century* (1845) 126

Gertrude Buck 211
"The Present Status of Rhetorical Theory" (1900) 212

Mary Augusta Jordan 218
From *Correct Writing and Speaking* (1904) 219

Virginia Woolf 241
"Professions for Women" (1942) 242

Adrienne Rich 267
"When We Dead Awaken: Writing as Re-Vision" (1971) 268

Hélène Cixous 283
From "Sorties" (1975) 284

Audre Lorde 301
"The Transformation of Silence into Language and Action" (1977) 302

Alice Walker 314
"In Search of Our Mothers' Gardens" (1983) 315

Paula Gunn Allen 340
"Grandmother of the Sun: Ritual Gynocracy in Native America" (1986) 341

Gloria Anzaldúa   356
"How to Tame a Wild Tongue" (1987)   357

Trinh T. Minh-ha   377
From *Woman, Native, Other* (1989)   378

bell hooks   382
"Homeplace (a site of resistance)" (1990)   383

Patricia Williams   409
"The Death of the Profane" (1991)   410

Toni Morrison   416
"The Nobel Lecture in Literature" and "The Acceptance Speech" (1993)   417

Minnie Bruce Pratt   424
"Gender Quiz" (1995)   425

Dorothy Allison   435
From *Two or Three Things I Know for Sure* (1995)   436

Leslie Marmon Silko   462
"Yellow Woman and a Beauty of the Spirit" (1996)   463

Ruth Behar   478
"Anthropology That Breaks Your Heart" (1996)   479

X. Discovering New Means of Persuasion

Christine de Pizan   32
From *The Book of the City of Ladies* (1404)   33

Sor Juana Inés de la Cruz   71
From "La Respuesta" (1691)   72

Margaret Fuller   125
From *Woman in the Nineteenth Century* (1845)   126

Ida B. Wells   188
"Lynch Law in All its Phases" (1893)   189

Charlotte Perkins Gilman   204
From *Women and Economics* (1898)   205

Simone de Beauvoir   252
From the Introduction to *The Second Sex* (1952)   253

Rachel Carson   259
"A Fable for Tomorrow" (1962)   260

Hélène Cixous   283
From "Sorties" (1975)   284

Alice Walker   314
"In Search of Our Mothers' Gardens" (1983)   315

Evelyn Fox Keller   323
From *A Feeling for the Organism* (1983)   324

Paula Gunn Allen   340
"Grandmother of the Sun: Ritual Gynocracy in Native America" (1986)   341

Gloria Anzaldúa   356
"How to Tame a Wild Tongue" (1987)   357

bell hooks   382
"Homeplace (a site of resistance)" (1990)   383

Nancy Mairs   391
"Carnal Acts" (1990)   392

Terry Tempest Williams   401
"The Clan of One-Breasted Women" (1991)   402

Patricia Williams   409
"The Death of the Profane" (1991)   410

Toni Morrison   416
"The Nobel Lecture in Literature" and "The Acceptance Speech" (1993)   417

Minnie Bruce Pratt   424
"Gender Quiz" (1995)   425

Dorothy Allison   435
From *Two or Three Things I Know for Sure* (1995)   436

Ruth Behar   478
"Anthropology That Breaks Your Heart" (1996)   479

XI. Creating New Forms of Disciplinary Argument

Diotima   9
"On Love" from Plato's *Symposium* (c. 360 B.C.E.)   10

Margaret Fell 66
From *Womens Speaking Justified, Proved and Allowed by the Scriptures* (1666) 67

Margaret Fuller 125
From *Woman in the Nineteenth Century* (1845) 126

Charlotte Perkins Gilman 204
From *Women and Economics* (1898) 205

Gertrude Buck 211
"The Present Status of Rhetorical Theory" (1900) 212

Mary Augusta Jordan 218
From *Correct Writing and Speaking* (1904) 219

Rachel Carson 259
"A Fable for Tomorrow" (1962) 260

Hélène Cixous 283
From "Sorties" (1975) 284

Audre Lorde 301
"The Transformation of Silence into Language and Action" (1977) 302

Evelyn Fox Keller 323
From *A Feeling for the Organism* (1983) 324

Patricia Williams 409
"The Death of the Profane" (1991) 410

Ruth Behar 478
"Anthropology That Breaks Your Heart" (1996) 479

XII. Public Speeches

Aspasia 1
"Pericles' Funeral Oration" from Plato's *Menexenus* (c. 387–367 B.C.E.) 2

Hortensia 16
"Speech to the Triumvirs" (42 B.C.E.) 17

Queen Elizabeth I 48
"To the Troops at Tilbury" (1588) 49

Cherokee Women 106
"Cherokee Women Address Their Nation" (1817) 107

Maria W. Stewart   109
"Lecture Delivered at the Franklin Hall" (1832)   110

Angelina Grimké Weld   119
"Address at Pennsylvania Hall" (1838)   120

Sojourner Truth   143
"Speech at the Woman's Rights Convention, Akron, Ohio" (1851)   144

Frances Ellen Watkins Harper   147
"We Are All Bound Up Together" (1866)   148

Susan B. Anthony   151
From *The United States of America v. Susan B. Anthony* (1873)   152

Elizabeth Cady Stanton   171
From "The Solitude of Self" (1892)   172

Fannie Barrier Williams   179
From "The Intellectual Progress of the Colored Women of the United States since the Emancipation Proclamation" (1893)   180

Virginia Woolf   241
"Professions for Women" (1942)   242

Fannie Lou Hamer   262
"The Special Plight and the Role of the Black Woman" (1971)   263

Adrienne Rich   267
"When We Dead Awaken: Writing as Re-Vision" (1971)   268

Audre Lorde   301
"The Transformation of Silence into Language and Action" (1977)   302

Andrea Dworkin   330
"I Want A Twenty-Four Hour Truce During Which There Is No Rape" (1983)   331

June Jordan   366
"Don't You Talk About My Momma!" (1987)   367

Toni Morrison   416
"The Nobel Lecture in Literature" and "The Acceptance Speech" (1993)   417

Dorothy Allison   435
From *Two or Three Things I Know for Sure* (1995)   436

XIII. Letters

Heloise 20
From "Letter I. Heloise to Abelard" (1132) 21

Catherine of Siena 29
"Letter 83: To Mona Lapa, her mother, in Siena" (1376) 30

Sor Juana Inés de la Cruz 71
From "La Respuesta" (1691) 72

Lady Mary Wortley Montagu 84
"Letter to Lady Bute" (1753) 85

Sarah Grimké 114
"Letter to Theodore Weld" (1837) 115

Margaret Sanger 223
"Letter to the Readers of *The Woman Rebel*" (1914) 224

Merle Woo 306
"Letter to Ma" (1980) 307

Note: We offer this bibliography as a resource to readers and teachers, a beginning point in the study of women's rhetorics. We have tried to limit entries to those works that directly address women's rhetorical theory/performance and to those that either collect women's rhetorics or collect works by a significant figure in women's rhetorics not included in *Available Means*. Except for a few central works, we have not repeated entries included under "For Further Reading" in the text of the anthology.

Anderson, Bonnie S., and Judith Zinnser. *A History of Their Own: Women in Europe from Prehistory to the Present*. 2 vols. New York: Harper and Row, 1988.

Andrews, William, ed. *Journeys in New Worlds: Early American Women's Narratives*. Madison: University of Wisconsin Press, 1990.

Annas, Pamela. "Style as Politics: A Feminist Approach to the Teaching of Writing." *College English* 47.4 (1985): 360–71.

Belenky, Mary F., Blythe M. Clinchy, Nancy R. Goldberger, and Jill M. Tarule. *Women's Ways of Knowing*. New York: Basic Books, 1986.

Bell-Scott, Patricia, ed. *Life Notes: Personal Writings by Contemporary Black Women*. New York: W. W. Norton and Company, 1994.

Benstock, Shari. *Textualizing the Feminine: On the Limits of Genre*. Norman: University of Oklahoma Press, 1991.

Biesecker, Barbara. "Coming to Terms with Recent Attempts to Write Women into the History of Rhetoric." *Philosophy and Rhetoric* 25 (1992): 140–61.

Bizzell, Patricia. "Opportunities for Feminist Research in the History of Rhetoric." *Rhetoric Review* 11.1 (1992): 50–58.

———. "Praising Folly: Constructing a Postmodern Rhetorical Authority as a Woman." In *Feminine Principles and Women's Experience in American Composition and Rhetoric*, edited by Louise Wetherbee Phelps and Janet Emig, 27–42. Pittsburgh: University of Pittsburgh Press, 1995.

Bizzell, Patricia, and Bruce Herzberg, eds. *The Rhetorical Tradition: Readings from Classical Times to the Present*. Boston: Bedford Books of St. Martin's Press, 1990.

Bleich, David. "Genders of Writing." *Journal of Advanced Composition* 9 (1989): 10–25.

Brody, Miriam. *Manly Writing: Gender, Rhetoric and the Rise of Composition*. Carbondale: Southern Illinois University Press, 1993.

Butler, Judith P. *Gender Trouble: Feminism and the Subversion of Identity*. New York: Routledge, 1999.

Cameron, Deborah. *Verbal Hygiene*. New York: Routledge, 1995.

———, ed. *The Feminist Critique of Language: A Reader*. New York: Routledge, 1990.

Campbell, Karlyn Kohrs, ed. *A Critical Study of Early Feminist Rhetoric*. Vol. 1 of *Man Cannot Speak for Her*. New York: Praeger, 1989.

———, ed. *Key Texts of the Early Feminists*. Vol. 2 of *Man Cannot Speak for Her*. New York: Praeger, 1989.

———, ed. *Women Public Speakers in the United States, 1800–1925: A Biocritical Sourcebook*. Westport, Conn.: Greenwood, 1993.

———, ed. *Women Public Speakers in the United States, 1925–1993: A Bio-Critical Sourcebook*. Westport, Conn.: Greenwood, 1994.

Cixous, Hélène. "The Laugh of the Medusa." In *New French Feminisms*, edited by Elaine Marks and Isabelle de Courtivron, 245–64. New York: Schocken Books, 1981.

Clark, Gregory, and S. Michael Halloran, eds. *Oratorical Culture in Nineteenth-Century America: Transformations in the Theory and Practice of Rhetoric*. Carbondale: Southern Illinois University Press, 1993.

Code, Lorraine. *What Can She Know? Feminist Theory and the Construction of Knowledge*. Ithaca: Cornell University Press, 1991.

Cole, Susan Guettel. "Could Greek Women Read and Write?" In *Reflections of Women in Antiquity*, edited by Helene P. Foley, 219–45. New York: Gordon, 1981.

Collins, Patricia Hill. *Black Feminist Thought*. New York: Routledge, 1990.

Connors, Robert. "Gender Influences: Composition-Rhetoric as an Irenic Rhetoric." In *Composition-Rhetoric: Backgrounds, Theory, Pedagogy*, 23–68. Pittsburgh: University of Pittsburgh Press, 1997.

Culley, Margaret, ed. *A Day at a Time: The Diary Literature of American Women from 1764 to the Present*. New York: The Feminist Press, 1985.

Davis, Angela Y. *Women, Race, and Class*. New York: Vintage Books, 1983.

Delamotte, Eugenia, Natania Meeker, and Jean O'Barr, eds. *Women Imagine Change: A Global Anthology of Women's Resistance from 600 BCE to Present*. New York: Routledge, 1997.

de Lauretis, Teresa. *Technologies of Gender*. Bloomington: Indiana University Press, 1987.

Enos, Theresa. *Gender Roles and Faculty Lives in Rhetoric and Composition*. Carbondale: Southern Illinois University Press, 1996.

Farrell, Thomas J. "The Female and Male Modes of Rhetoric." *College English* 40.8 (1979): 909–21.

Finke, Laurie A. *Feminist Theory, Women's Writing*. Ithaca: Cornell University Press, 1992.

Flynn, Elizabeth. "Composing as a Woman." *College Composition and Communication* 39.4 (1988): 423–35.

Foss, Karen A., and Sonya K. Foss. *Women Speak: The Eloquence of Women's Lives*. Prospect Heights, Ill.: Waveland Press, 1991.

Foss, Karen A., Sonja K. Foss, and Cindy Griffin. *Feminist Rhetorical Theories*. Thousand Oaks, Calif.: Sage Publications, 1999.

Garcia, Alma M. *Chicana Feminist Thought: The Basic Historical Writings*. New York: Routledge, 1997.

Gere, Anne Ruggles. *Intimate Practices: Literacy and Cultural Work in U.S. Women's Clubs, 1880–1920*. Urbana: University of Illinois Press, 1997.

Giddings, Paula. *When and Where I Enter: The Impact of Black Women on Race and Sex*. New York: William Morrow, 1984.

Gilbert, Sandra, and Susan Gubar. *No Man's Land: The Place of the Woman Writer in the 20th Century*. 3 vols. New Haven: Yale University Press, 1988.

———, eds. *The Norton Anthology of Women's Literature*. 2nd ed. New York: W. W. Norton and Company, 1996.

Gilligan, Carol. *In a Different Voice: Psychological Theory and Women's Development*. Cambridge: Harvard University Press, 1982.

Glenn, Cheryl. "Author, Audience, and Autobiography: Rhetorical Technique in *The Book of Margery Kempe*." *College English* 54.5 (1992): 540–53.

———. "Remapping Rhetorical Territory." *Rhetoric Review* 13.2 (1995): 287–303.

———. *Rhetoric Retold: Regendering the Tradition from Antiquity through the Renaissance*. Carbondale: Southern Illinois University Press, 1997.

———. "Sex, Lies, and Manuscript: Refiguring Aspasia in the History of Rhetoric. *College Composition and Communication* 45.2 (1994): 180–99.

———. "Women's Empowerment/Women's Enslavement: Stories from the History of Literacy." *Freshman English News* 17 (1989): 29–31.

Goldman, Anne E. *Autobiographical Innovations of Ethnic American Women*. Berkeley: University of California Press, 1996.

Haraway, Donna. *Simians, Cyborgs, and Women: The Reinvention of Nature*. New York: Routledge, 1991.

Harding, Sandra. *Whose Science? Whose Knowledge? Thinking from Women's Lives*. Ithaca: Cornell University Press, 1990.

Harjo, Joy, and Gloria Bird, eds. *Reinventing the Enemy's Language: Contemporary Native Women's Writings of North America*. New York: W. W. Norton and Company, 1997.

Harris, Sharon, ed. *American Women Writers to 1800*. New York: Oxford University Press, 1996.

Hull, Gloria, Patricia Scott, and Barbara Smith, eds. *All the Women Are White, All the Blacks Are Men, But Some of Us Are Brave: Black Women's Studies*. New York: The Feminist Press, 1982.

Iragaray, Luce. *This Sex Which Is Not One*. Translated by Catherine Porter. Ithaca: Cornell University Press, 1985.

Jarratt, Susan C. "Beside Ourselves: Rhetoric and Representation in Postcolonial Feminist Writing." *JAC: A Journal of Composition Theory* 18.1 (1998): 57–76.

———. "Feminism and Composition: The Case for Conflict." In *Contending with Words: Composition and Rhetoric in a Postmodern Age*, edited by Patricia Harkin, Patricia Schilb, and John Schilb, 105–23. New York: Modern Language Association, 1991.

———. *Rereading the Sophists*. Carbondale: Southern Illinois University Press, 1991.

———. "Speaking to the Past: Feminist Historiography in Rhetoric." *Pre/Text: A Journal of Rhetorical Theory* 11 (1990): 189–209.

———, ed. "Feminist Rereadings in the History of Rhetoric." Introduction by Susan C. Jarratt. *Rhetoric Society Quarterly* 22 (1992). Special issue.

Jarratt, Susan C., and Nedra Reynolds. "The Splitting Image: Contemporary Feminisms and the Ethics of Ethos." In *Ethos: New Essays in Rhetorical and Critical Theory*, edited by James S. Baumlin and Tita French Baulin, 37–63. Dallas: Southern Methodist University Press. 1994.

Jarratt, Susan C., and Lynn Worsham, eds. *Feminism and Composition Studies: In Other Words*. New York: Modern Language Association, 1998.

Joeres, Ruth, Ellen Boetcher, and Elizabeth Mittman, eds. *The Politics of the Essay: Feminist Perspectives*. Bloomington: Indiana University Press, 1993.

Johnson, Nan. *Nineteenth-Century Rhetoric in North America*. Carbondale: Southern Illinois University Press, 1991.

Jones, Ann Rosalind. "Writing the Body: Toward an Understanding of *L'Ecriture Féminine*." In *The New Feminist Criticism*, edited by Elaine Showalter, 361–78. New York: Pantheon Books, 1985.

Keating, AnaLouise. *Women Reading/Women Writing: Self-Invention in Paula Gunn Allen, Gloria Anzaldúa, and Audre Lorde*. Philadelphia: Temple University Press, 1996.

Keller, Evelyn Fox. *A Feeling for the Organism: The Life and Work of Barbara McClintock*. New York: W. H. Freeman, 1983.

———. *Secrets of Life, Secrets of Death: Essays on Language, Gender and Science*. New York: Routledge, 1992.

Kerber, Linda K. *Toward an Intellectual History of Women*. Chapel Hill: University of North Carolina Press, 1997.

Kim, Elaine H., L. Villanueva, and Asian Women United of California, eds. *Making Waves: More New Writing by Asian American Women*. Boston: Beacon Press, 1997.

Kirsch, Gesa. *Women Writing the Academy: Audience, Authority, and Transformation*. Carbondale: Southern Illinois University Press, 1993.

Kramarae, Cheris, and Pamela Treicher. *A Feminist Dictionary*. Boston: Pandora Press, 1985.

Kristeva, Julia. *The Kristeva Reader*. Edited by Toril Moi. New York: Columbia University Press, 1986.

Lakoff, Robin. *Language and Women's Place*. New York: Harper and Row, 1975.

———. *Talking Power: The Politics of Language in Our Lives*. New York: Basic Books, 1990.

Lamb, Catherine. "Beyond Argument in Feminist Composition." *College Composition and Communication* 42.1 (1991): 11–24.

Langer, Susanne K. *Mind: An Essay on Human Feeling*. 3 vols. Baltimore: Johns Hopkins University Press, 1982.

Lerner, Gerda. *The Creation of Feminist Consciousness: From the Middle Ages to Eighteen-Seventy*. New York: Oxford University Press, 1993.

———. *The Creation of Patriarchy*. New York: Oxford University Press, 1986.

———, ed. *Black Women in White America: A Documentary History*. New York: Vintage Books, 1972.

Logan, Shirley Wilson. *"We Are Coming": The Persuasive Discourse of Nineteenth-Century Black Women*. Carbondale: Southern Illinois University Press, 1999.

———, ed. *With Pen and Voice: A Critical Anthology of Nineteenth-Century African-American Women*. Carbondale: Southern Illinois University Press, 1995.

Lorde, Audre. *The Cancer Journals*. San Francisco: Spinsters/Aunt Lute, 1980.

Lunsford, Andrea, ed. *Reclaiming Rhetorica: Women in the Rhetorical Tradition*. Pittsburgh: University of Pittsburgh Press, 1995.

MacKinnon, Catharine A. *Only Words*. Cambridge: Harvard University Press, 1993.

Marks, Elaine, and Isabelle de Courtivron, eds. *New French Feminisms*. New York: Schocken Books, 1981.

McAlister, Linda Lopez, ed. *Hypatia's Daughters: Fifteen Hundred Years of Women Philosophers*. Bloomington: Indiana University Press, 1996.

Miedzian, Myriam, and Alisa Malinovich, eds. *Generations: A Century of Women Speak about Their Lives*. New York: Atlantic Monthly Press, 1997.

Miller, Susan. "The Feminization of Composition." In *The Politics of Writing Instruction: Postsecondary*, edited by Richard H. Bullock and John Trimbur, 39–53. Portsmouth, N.H.: Boynton, 1991.

Millett, Kate. *Sexual Politics*. Garden City: Doubleday, 1970.

Moraga, Cherrie, and Gloria Anzaldúa, eds. *This Bridge Called My Back: Writings by Radical Women of Culture*. New York: Kitchen Table Press, 1983.

Moynihan, Ruth, Cynthia Russett, and Laurie Crumpacker, eds. *From 1865 to the Present*. Vol. 2 of *Second to None: A Documentary History of American Women*. Lincoln: University of Nebraska Press, 1993.

O'Connor, Lillian. *Pioneer Women Orators: Rhetoric in the Ante-Bellum Reform Movement*. New York: Columbia University Press, 1954.

Olsen, Tillie. *Silences*. New York: Bantam Doubleday, 1978.

Peaden, Catherine Hobbs, ed. *Nineteenth-Century Women Learn to Write: Past Cultures and Practices of Literacy*. Charlottesville: University of Virginia Press, 1994.

Pearlman, Mickey, and Katherine Usher Henderson, eds. *A Voice of One's Own: Conversations with America's Writing Women*. New York: Houghton Mifflin Company, 1992.

Peck, Elizabeth G., and JoAnna S. Mink, eds. *Common Ground: Feminist Collaboration in the Academy*. Albany: State University of New York Press, 1998.

Penelope, Julia. *Speaking Freely: Unlearning the Lies of the Father's Tongue*. New York: Teachers College Press, 1990.

Penelope, Julia, and Susan J Wolfe. "Consciousness as Style; Style as Consciousness." In *Language, Gender, and Society*, edited by Barrie Thorne, Cheris Kramarae, aand Nancy Henley, 25–36. Rowley, Mass.: Newbury House, 1983.

Perry, Linda A. M., Lynn H. Turner, and Helen M. Sterk, eds. *Constructing and Reconstructing Gender*. Albany: State University of New York Press, 1992.

Phelps, Louise Wetherbee, and Janet Emig, eds. *Feminine Principles and Women's Experience in American Composition and Rhetoric*. Pittsburgh: University of Pittsburgh Press, 1995.

Philip, Marlene Nourbese. "The Absence of Writing or How I Almost Became a Spy." In *She Tries Her Tongue Her Silence Softly Breaks*, 10–25. Charlottetown, PEI, Canada: Ragweed Press, 1989.

Ratcliffe, Krista. *Anglo-American Feminist Challenges to the Rhetorical Traditions: Virginia Woolf, Mary Daly, Adrienne Rich*. Carbondale: Southern Illinois University Press, 1995.

Ritchie, Joy and Kate Ronald. "Riding Long Coattails, Subverting Tradition: Why and How Feminists Should Teach Rhetoric(s)." In *Feminism and Composition Studies: In Other Words*, edited by Susan C. Jarratt and Lynn Worsham, 217–238. New York: Modern Language Assocation, 1998.

Rossi, Alice S., ed. *The Feminist Papers: From Adams to de Beauvoir*. New York: Columbia University Press, 1973.

Royster, Jacqueline Jones. *Traces of a Stream: Literacy and Social Change Among African American Women*. Pittsburgh: University of Pittsburgh Press, 2000.

Russ, Joanna. *How to Suppress Women's Writing*. Austin: University of Texas Press, 1983.

Schmidt, Jan Z., ed. *Women/Writing/Teaching*. Albany: State University of New York Press, 1998.

Schneir, Miriam, ed. *Feminism: The Essential Historical Writings*. New York: Random House, 1972.

———, ed. *Feminism in Our Time: The Essential Writings, World War II to the Present*. New York: Random House, 1994.

Shelnutt, Eve, ed. *The Confidence Woman: 26 Women Writers at Work*. Atlanta: Longstreet, 1991.

Smith, Barbara, ed. *Home Girls: A Black Feminist Anthology.* New Brunswick: Rutgers University Press, 2000.

Snyder, Jane McIntosh. *The Woman and the Lyre: Women Writers in Classical Greece and Rome.* Carbondale: Southern Illinois University Press, 1989.

Spender, Dale. *Man Made Language.* London: Pandora, 1990.

Spivak, Gayatri. "Can the Subaltern Speak?" In *Marxism and the Interpretation of Culture,* edited by Cary Nelson and Lawrence Grossberg, 271–311. Urbana: University of Illinois Press, 1988.

Sternberg, Janet. *The Writer on Her Work.* Vol. 1. W. W. Norton and Company, 1980.

———. *The Writer on Her Work.* Vol. 2. W. W. Norton and Company, 1991.

Tannen, Deborah. *The Argument Culture: Moving from Debate to Dialogue.* New York: Random House, 1988.

———. *Gender and Discourse.* New York: Oxford University Press, 1994.

Welch, Kathleen E. *Electric Rhetoric: Classical Rhetoric, Oralism, and a New Literacy.* Cambridge: MIT Press, 1999.

Wertheimer, Molly, ed. *Listening to Their Voices: The Rhetorical Activities of Historical Women.* Columbia: University of South Carolina Press, 1997.

Worsham, Lynn. "Writing against Writing: The Predicament of *Ecriture Féminine* in Composition Studies." In *Contending with Words: Composition Studies in a Postmodern Age,* edited by Patricia Harkin and John Schilb, 82–104. New York: Modern Language Association, 1991.

Abelard, Peter, 20
Abolitionist rhetoric, 93, 109–13, 119–24, 143–46
African American rhetors: Belinda, 89–91, 495, 497, 500; Combahee River Collective, 148, 291–300, 500, 501; Cooper, xxii, xxiii, 163–70, 179, 233, 496, 499; Dunbar Nelson, 233–36, 496, 498, 501; Hamer, 262–66, 416, 498, 500, 501, 508; Harper, xxvi, 147–50, 158, 179–80, 291, 501, 508; hooks, xxvi, xxix, 247, 382–90, 505, 506; Hurston, xviii, 247–51, 314, 498; J. Jordan, 366–76, 498, 508; Lorde, xxi, xxv, 267, 301–5, 496, 501, 502, 503, 504, 507, 508; Morrison, xxii, xxix, 416–23, 505, 506, 508; Stewart, 109–13, 497, 499, 501, 508; Truth, xxii, xxv, 143–46, 148, 291, 496, 497, 499, 501, 502, 508; Walker, 242, 247, 267, 314–22, 503, 504, 506; Wells, 179, 188–203, 223, 233, 291, 497, 505; F. B. Williams, xxiv, xxv, 179–87, 366, 496, 497, 500, 501, 508; P. Williams, xxii, 409–15, 478, 498, 503, 505, 506, 507
Allegory, 32
Allen, Paula Gunn, xix, xxv, 340–55; rhetorical themes of, 503, 504, 506
Allison, Dorothy, xviii, xxviii–xxix, 435–53, 478; rhetorical themes of, 496, 500, 501, 504, 505, 506, 508
Analogies, 204
Anger, Jane, xxv, 32, 50–60, 79; rhetorical themes of, 495, 499
Anthony, Susan B., 67, 147, 151–56, 171, 489; rhetorical themes of, 496, 497, 508
Antislavery rhetoric. See Abolitionist rhetoric
Antistrephon, 61, 66
Anzaldúa, Gloria, xxvii, xxix, 356–65; rhetorical themes of, 496, 500, 501, 503, 505, 506

Appian, 16
Argument, new forms of, 66–67, 506–7
Aristotle, xvii, xxiv
Asian American rhetors: Trinh, 377–81; Woo, 306–13
Aspasia, xix, xxiii, 1–8, 20, 126; rhetorical themes of, 507
Astell, Mary, xxiii, 79–83; rhetorical themes of, 496, 499
Audience awareness, 48, 79, 110, 171, 218, 248, 330–31, 356–57
Authority: classical rhetors as, 20–21, 61; context as, 314; legal precedent as, 471; notable women as, 71; scripture as, xvii–xviii, xxii, 61, 66, 109, 114, 158; self as, 32, 157. See also Ethos
Autobiographical writing: Allison, 435–53; Anzaldúa, 356–65; Belinda, 89–91; Kempe, 43–47; Mairs, 391–400; Pratt, 414–34; Sor Juana, 71–78; Walker, 314–22; P. Williams, 409–15; T. T. Williams, 401–8; Winnemucca, 157–62; Woo, 306–13
Awiakta, Marilou, 106

Beauvoir, Simone de, xxvi, 205, 252–58, 283; rhetorical themes of, 500, 505
Behar, Ruth, 247, 478–88; rhetorical themes of, 504, 505, 506, 507
Belinda, 89–91; rhetorical themes of, 495, 497, 500
Berkman, Alexander, 226
Birth Control Review, 224
Bitzer, Lloyd, xxiv
Bizzell, Patricia, xix, 66
Body, rhetorics of the, xxiii, xxvi, xxvii, 223–25, 283–84, 502
Braham, Jeanne, 391
Buck, Gertrude, 211–17, 218; rhetorical themes of, 504, 507

Campbell, JoAnn, 212
Campbell, Karlyn Kohrs, xv, xxii, 143
Candid language, 67, 227, 262–63, 331, 454
Canon, rhetorical, xvi, xx, xxix
Carby, Hazel, 179
Carson, Rachel, 259–61; rhetorical themes of, 498, 506, 507
Catharsis, 479
Catherine of Siena, Saint, 29–31; rhetorical themes of, 496, 502, 509
Catholic Worker, 237
Character. *See* Ethos
Cherokee women, 106–8, 138; rhetorical themes of, 497, 499, 501, 507
Chicago Record-Herald, 179
Chicana rhetors: Anzaldúa, xxvii, xxix, 356–65, 496, 500, 501, 503, 505, 506
Christine de Pizan, 32–42, 79; rhetorical themes of, 495, 499, 505
Cicero, 1, 16
Civic participation, rhetoric as, 497–98
Cixous, Hélène, xxiii, xxvii, 283–90, 377, 391, 454; rhetorical themes of, 503, 504, 506, 507
Collaborative voice, 79, 126, 138, 211–12
Combahee River Collective, 148, 291–300; rhetorical themes of, 500, 501
Contexts, xvii, xxi, xxvii, 9, 71–72, 283–84, 314, 382. *See also* Public-private discourse
Cooper, Anna Julia, xxii, xxiii, 163–70, 179, 233; rhetorical themes of, 496, 499

Darwinian theory, 204
Davis, Angela, 205
Day, Dorothy, 237–40; rhetorical themes of, 498, 503
Dial, The, 125
Difference, rhetorics of, xxv, xxvi, 500–501. *See also* Gender
Diotima, 9–15; rhetorical themes of, 504, 506
Douglass, Frederick, 138, 172
Dunbar Nelson, Alice, 233–36; rhetorical themes of, 496, 498, 501
Dworkin, Andrea, 330–39; rhetorical themes of, 498, 508

Education, claiming rights to, xvii, xxiii, 496–97
Eisenstein, Zillah, 291
Elizabeth I (England), 48–49; rhetorical themes of, 499, 502, 507
Ellsberg, Robert, 237
Emerson, Ralph Waldo, 125
Emig, Janet, xxix
Environmental rhetorics, 259–61, 401–8
Ethics, xxii
Ethos, xviii, xxii, xxiv, 43, 110, 119, 144, 171, 218, 248
Evening Star, 188
Experience, xxii

Fables, 259
Feinberg, Leslie, 424
Fell, Margaret, xvii–xix, 66–70; rhetorical themes of, 495, 497, 503, 507
Feminism, xxii, xxviii, 211
Feminist manifestos, xx, 92–105, 138–42, 252–58
Forerunner, The, 204
Form, xx–xxi
Fox, George, 66
Frankfurter, Felix, 471
Frazier, Demita, 291
Free Speech and Headlight, 188
Frick, Henry Clay, 226
Friedan, Betty, 205
Fuller, Margaret, xxii, 125–37, 227; rhetorical themes of, 496, 497, 499, 504, 505, 507
Funeral orations, 1–2

Gage, Frances, 143–44
Gage, Matilda, 138, 340
Gender, xxvi, xxviii, 50–51, 92, 424–34. *See also* Difference, rhetorics of
Gere, Anne Ruggles, xviii
Giddings, Paula, 180
Gilman, Charlotte Perkins, xxvi, 204–10; rhetorical themes of, 498, 500, 505, 507
Ginsburg, Ruth Bader, xxiii, 471–77; rhetorical themes of, 497, 498
Glenn, Cheryl, xv–xvii, 1, 9, 16, 25, 43
Goldman, Emma, xxv, 226–32; rhetorical themes of, 498, 500

Greeley, Horace, 125
Grimké, Sarah, 109, 114–18; rhetorical
    themes of, 495, 499, 509

Hamer, Fannie Lou, 262–66, 416; rhetori-
    cal themes of, 498, 500, 501, 508
Harper, Frances Ellen Watkins, xxvi,
    147–50, 158, 179–80, 291; rhetorical
    themes of, 501, 508
Harris, Sharon, 89
Heloise, xviii, 20–24; rhetorical themes
    of, 498, 509
Heroic rhetors, xix
Herzberg, Bruce, xix, 66
hooks, bell, xxvi, xxix, 247, 382–90; rhe-
    torical themes of, 505, 506
Hortensia, xxiii, 16–19; rhetorical themes
    of, 495, 497, 507
Hull, Gloria T., 233
Humor, 263
Hurston, Zora Neale, xviii, 247–51, 314;
    rhetorical themes of, 498

Identity, xviii–xx, xxiv–xxv, 498–500. See
    also Querelle des femmes
Invisibility of women, xviii–xix
Irony, xxii, 248

Jarratt, Susan, xxiii–xxv
Jim Crow laws, rhetorics against, xviii,
    247–51
Jordan, June, 366–76; rhetorical themes
    of, 498, 508
Jordan, Mary Augusta, 218–22; rhetorical
    themes of, 504, 507
Juana Inés de la Cruz, Sor, xvii, 32, 71–78;
    rhetorical themes of, 496, 502, 504,
    505, 509
Julian of Norwich, xix, 25–28, 29, 43; rhe-
    torical themes of, 502

Keating, Ana Louise, 356–57
Keller, Evelyn Fox, 323–29, 478; rhetorical
    themes of, 506, 507
Kempe, Margery, xix, xxiii, xxvi, 43–47;
    rhetorical themes of, 495, 499, 502
Kitzhaber, Albert R., 211
Kolodny, Annette, 126

Lamm, Nomy, xxv, 454–61; rhetorical
    themes of, 500, 501, 502, 504
Language, xxii, 416–17, 435, 503–4
Latin American rhetors: Behar, 247,
    478–88, 504, 505, 506, 507; Sor Juana,
    xvii, 32, 71–78, 496, 502, 504, 505, 509
Legal rhetoric, 409–10, 471–77
Lerner, Gerda, xix
Lesbian rhetors: Anzaldúa, xxvii, xxix,
    356–65, 496, 500, 501, 503, 505, 506;
    Combahee River Collective, 291–300;
    Dworkin, 330–39; Lamm, 454–61;
    Lorde, 301–5; Pratt, 424–34; Rich,
    267–82; Woo, 306–13
Letters, list of, 509
Lewalski, Barbara, 61
Liberator, The, 109
Lincoln, Abraham, 259
Literacy, xvii
Literary writing, xviii, xxi
Logan, Shirley Wilson, xv, xvi, xviii, xxix,
    179
Logic, xviii, xxii, 20, 109, 189, 248
Lorde, Audre, xxi, xxv, 267, 301–5; rhetori-
    cal themes of, 496, 501, 502, 503, 504,
    507, 508
Love and marriage, 9–15, 20–24, 79, 84,
    226–32
Lunsford, Andrea, xv, xvi, xxiii, xxviii,
    xxix
Lynching, rhetorics against, xviii, 188–203

MacKinnon, Catharine, 330
Magnusson, Lynne, 50
Mairs, Nancy, xxi, xxvii, 391–400; rhetor-
    ical themes of, 500, 501, 502, 503, 506
Mankiller, Wilma, 138
Marriage. See Love and marriage
Martin, Randall, 50
McClintock, Barbara, 323–29
McClintock, Mary Ann, 138
Memory, xviii–xix
Men as conveyors of women's rhetoric,
    xxiii, 1, 9, 43
Men's movement, 330
Messenger, The, 233
Metaphors, 366; as tools, 61, 171; used for
    selections anthologized, xvi–xvii

Minh-ha, Trinh T. *See* Trinh T. Minh-ha
Misogyny. *See Querelle des femmes*
Montagu, Lady Mary Wortley, 79, 84–91;
    rhetorical themes of, 496, 499, 509
Morrison, Toni, xxii, xxix, 416–23; rhetor-
    ical themes of, 505, 506, 508
Mother Earth, 226
Mott, Lucretia, 67, 138
Ms., 489–90

Naming, xxv, xxviii, 490
Nanyehi, 106
Native American rhetors: Allen, xix, xxv,
    340–55, 503, 504, 506; Cherokee wom-
    en, 106–8, 138, 497, 499, 501, 507; Silko,
    xxii, xxix, 462–70, 502, 503, 504, 505;
    Winnemucca, xxi, 157–62, 497, 499, 501
New York Age, 179, 189
New York Magazine, 489
Noffke, Suzanne, 29
Nye, Andrea, 21

Opposite cases, stating of, 490
"Other," the, 252, 283, 377

Passion, 20–21
Pathos, 89, 171, 223, 331, 479
Peabody, Elizabeth, 157
Pericles, 1
Personal power. *See* Ethos
Persuasion, xxii–xxiii, xxv, 16, 259, 505–6
Phelps, Louise, xxix
Physicality. *See* Body, rhetorics of the
Plato, 1–2, 9, xxiii
Plays on words, 50
Plutarch, xxiii, 1
Powell, Malea, 157
Pratt, Minnie Bruce, xxii, xxvi–xxviii,
    424–34; rhetorical themes of, 500, 501,
    502, 503, 505, 506
Praxis in women's rhetoric, xxvii–xxviii
Preaching cadences, 29–30, 366
Public-private discourse, xx–xxi, 43, 157,
    171, 237, 267, 301, 409. *See also* Contexts

Quaker religion, 66
Querelle des femmes, 25, 32, 50, 61, 79. *See
    also* Identity

Questions, 109, 223, 227, 424, 490
Quilligan, Maureen, 32
Quintillian, 16

Rape, rhetorics against, 330–39
Ratcliffe, Krista, xv, xxviii, xxix
Rhetorical theory, xxvii–xxix, 211–12, 218,
    283–84, 356, 416–17, 504–5
Rhetoric(s): definition of, xvii, xxi; ed-
    ucation in, xvii, 61, 211; selections an-
    thologized, criteria for, xx–xxii;
    themes of, xxii, 495–509
Ribicoff, Abraham, 259
Rich, Adrienne, 242, 267–82; rhetorical
    themes of, 500, 503, 504, 508
Rinehart, William V., 157
Royster, Jacqueline Jones, xv, xvi, xviii,
    xxix, 188

Sanger, Margaret, 223–25, 237; rhetorical
    themes of, 498, 509
Sappho, xv, xxi
Sarcasm, 233, 248, 284, 366
Sartre, Jean-Paul, 252–53
Schlafly, Phyllis, 472
Schneir, Miriam, xv, 489
Scripture, xvii–xviii, xxii, 61, 66, 109, 114,
    158
Seneca Falls convention, 125, 138–42, 171;
    rhetorical themes of, 495, 497
Silko, Leslie Marmon, xxii, xxix, 462–70;
    rhetorical themes of, 502, 503, 504, 505
Similes, 61
Smith, Barbara, 291–92
Smith, Beverly, 291
Socrates, 1–2, 9
Speaker as rhetorical tool. *See* Ethos
Speaking and writing, claiming rights to,
    xvii, xxii–xxiv, 71–78, 241, 301, 495–96
Spectator, The, 84
Speeches, 188–203, 507–8
Speght, Rachel, xxv, 32, 61–65, 66, 79; rhe-
    torical themes of, 495, 499
Spirituality, rhetorics of, 502–3
Spivak, Gayatri, xxv
Stanton, Elizabeth Cady, 138, 147–48, 151,
    171–78, 340; rhetorical themes of, 499,
    508

Statistical evidence, xviii, 223
Steinem, Gloria, 489–94; rhetorical themes of, 498
Stewart, Maria W., 109–13; rhetorical themes of, 497, 499, 501, 508
Stowe, Harriet Beecher, 204, 259
Straightforwardness of language. *See* Candid language
Swearingen, C. Jan, 9
Swetnam, Joseph, 61
Synecdoche, 50

Teresa of Ávila, Saint, 29
Thoreau, Henry David, 125
Thought woman concept, 340–41
Timberlake, Henry, 106
Topoi, xxiii–xxvi. *See also* Contexts
Transcribers of women's rhetoric, xxiii, 1, 9, 43, 143–44
Transgendered. *See* Gender
Transgressions, xviii, xx–xxi, xxiv, 25
Trinh T. Minh-ha, 377–81; rhetorical themes of, 503, 505
Truth, Sojourner, xxii, xxv, 143–46, 148, 291; rhetorical themes of, 496, 497, 499, 501, 502, 508
Tubman, Harriet, 291

Virginia Military Institute (VMI), 471–77

Walker, Alice, 242, 247, 267, 314–22; rhetorical themes of, 503, 504, 506
Ward, Nancy, 106
Washington, Mary Helen, 163
Weld, Angelina Grimké, xxii, 67, 109, 114, 119–24; rhetorical themes of, 497, 508
Weld, Theodore, 114, 119

Wells, Ida B., 179, 188–203, 223, 233, 291; rhetorical themes of, 497, 505
White, privileged women. *See* Women
Whittier, John Greenleaf, 119
Williams, Fannie Barrier, xxiv, xxv, 179–87, 366; rhetorical themes of, 496, 497, 500, 501, 508
Williams, Patricia, xxii, 409–15, 478; rhetorical themes of, 498, 503, 505, 506, 507
Williams, Terry Tempest, 401–8; rhetorical themes of, 498, 502, 506
Winnemucca, Sarah, xxi, 157–62; rhetorical themes of, 497, 499, 501
Wollstonecraft, Mary, xxii, 92–105; rhetorical themes of, 496, 497, 499
Womanhood, cult of true, 164, 241
Woman Rebel, The, 223
Women: of color, xxii, xxiv–xxvi, xxix, 301; cult of true womanhood and, 164, 241; *querelle des femmes* and, 25, 32, 50, 61, 79; white, privileged, xxii, xxiv–xxvi, xxix, 147–48, 180, 262–63, 291, 301, 340
Women's Era, 179
Woo, Merle, 306–13; rhetorical themes of, 500, 501, 509
Woolf, Virginia, xxii–xxiv, xxvi, 92, 241–46, 283, 314, 377, 454; rhetorical themes of, 500, 502, 503, 504, 508
Wright, Martha Coffin, 138

Yellin, Jean, 109